After a Fashion

After a Fashion

HOW TO REPRODUCE, RESTORE, AND WEAR VINTAGE STYLES

BY

FRANCES GRIMBLE

ILLUSTRATED BY

DEBORAH KUHN

LAVOLTA PRESS
20 MEADOWBROOK DRIVE
SAN FRANCISCO, CA 94132

Published by
Lavolta Press
20 Meadowbrook Drive
San Francisco, CA 94132

Text and cover illustrations by
Deborah Kuhn
11317 Corliss Avenue North
Seattle, WA 98133

Book and cover design, typography, electronic
pagination, and production management by
Arrow Graphics, Inc.
P.O. Box 291
Cambridge, MA 02238

Printed and bound in the United States of America

First edition

Library of Congress Catalog Card Number: 93-80046
Library of Congress Cataloging in Publication data applied for

ISBN 0-9636517-0-6

To Allan, who is always with me

Acknowledgments

I'd like to thank Deborah Kuhn, whose artistic talent, technical knowledge, and enthusiasm turned my rough drawings into polished illustrations. Her contribution to this book was immeasurable.

Thanks are also due to Alvart Badalian and Aramais Andonian of Arrow Graphics. They designed the book, typeset it by desktop publishing, and supervised offset printing. Alvart handled numerous details with warmth and charm. Aramais created the cover design.

My parents, Ralph and Helen Grimble, are responsible for my early interest in collecting vintage clothes. Their encouragement in this project has been important to me. My brother, Bob Grimble, contributed his legal expertise.

Last but not least I'd like to thank my husband, Allan Terry, for his constant support. Commenting on the manuscript, taking photos, maintaining my computer, interpreting government regulations, rushing to the post office—there was nothing he was unwilling or unable to do.

Contents

Introduction

After a Fashion is for everybody who wears historic styles, reproduction or real. It's for reenactors and living history enthusiasts; for vintage clothing collectors and dealers; and for dancers, musicians, and actors who create their own costumes. It's for men and women. And it's for people at all levels of costuming and collecting experience.

The first four chapters focus on reproducing styles from the Middle Ages to the Art Deco period. The last three focus on buying, mending, and altering vintage clothes, especially Victorian through Art Deco. But there's overlap. The style descriptions in the first chapter, and the research how-to in the second, will help collectors identify and date vintage clothes. The instructions for mending and altering vintage clothes also work for reproductions.

I wanted this book to be comprehensive, practical, and easy to use. To make it comprehensive, I included information on each stage of a reproduction project and all aspects of collecting vintage clothes. Some techniques are the fruit of my own experience. Particularly the ones for using vintage and scale patterns, and the ones for altering vintage clothes. I haven't seen these published elsewhere.

To make the book practical, I gave detailed instructions and advice. Most sewing instructions are numbered and illustrated. The advice on other topics—such as planning reproduction projects, writing sewing instructions, evaluating vintage clothes, and comparing prices—should steer you past many pitfalls.

To make the book easy to use, I organized it so you can go directly to information when you need it. If you're an experienced costumer, you can just read about techniques that are new to you. If you want to hem a dress in a hurry, you can do it without first reading the whole book. If you need supplies, you can look up sources in the up-to-date resource appendix. Because some information must be conveyed visually, I had 147 illustrations drawn especially for this book.

On a personal level, *After a Fashion* is an attempt to use my experience to help other costumers and collectors. I hope it succeeds in helping you.

—— Frances Grimble

1 Choosing a Historic Period

Maybe you've just joined a reenactment society. Or you volunteered for a living history museum. Or you're invited to a vintage dance. Everyone will wear costumes. But you don't have a clear picture of that period's styles.

This chapter surveys the styles worn during historic periods that are especially popular with reenactors. Reading it will help you decide what to wear. It will also give you an idea of how styles evolved, before and after your era. And if you plan to buy vintage clothes, it will help you identify and date them.

To describe every style in depth, or give a complete history of costume, is impossible in a single chapter. For more information, refer to the book list in appendix A.

🖎 THE MIDDLE AGES

The Middle Ages lasted from about 500 to 1500 A.D. This time period varies depending on how you define "Middle Ages" and what geographic area you're discussing. Frankly, I'm daunted by the prospect of describing a thousand years of costume in part of one chapter. Especially since information for the earlier centuries is rather scant. So I'm focusing on the 12th through the 14th centuries, and on upper-class English styles.

Many medieval garments are composed of geometric sections. See chapter 4 for instructions on drafting this type of pattern.

THE TWELFTH CENTURY

One characteristic of 12th-century costumes is the layered look. The bottom layer was a shirt (for men) or chemise (for women). Over this was worn a tunic (or gown) and sometimes an overtunic (or overgown). All three layers had much the same cut, with the following exceptions. The overtunic was often shorter than the undertunic. It had wider sleeves and a neck low enough to show the shirt or chemise. The top layer was a mantle, often worn open in front to display the other garments.

The fabrics most often used were silk, wool, linen, and mixtures of these. The grandest silks were interwoven with gold threads to produce a shot effect or brocaded pattern (cloth of gold).

Color contrasts were strong. An outfit worn by Henry II is described as combining crimson, gold, white, blue, and dark brown.

Men's fashions

In the early 12th century garments were long enough to drag on the ground. The tunic was full, with wide or close-fitting sleeves. A waist girdle was optional. Breeches and hose were hidden by the tunic. The mantle was semicircular or rectangular. It was lined with fur or a contrasting color of silk, and decorated with embroidered borders. The mantle was fastened at the neck with cords attached to jeweled ornaments or eyelets; the cords could be left loose or pulled tight.

Around 1130 the tunic shortened to ankle length (see figure 1). It was tight at the chest but long enough to wrinkle above the waist. It had a full skirt, slightly longer in back. The tunic had deep embroidery around the neck, and narrower embroidery around the sleeve and skirt hems.

At the same time the bliaut, a type of overtunic, became fashionable. The bliaut body was cut like the tunic body. It had fairly wide sleeves. The separately cut skirt consisted of two semicircles gathered or pleated to the waist along the straight edges. The curved edges fell in points at the sides, or at center front and back. The bliaut was decorated like the tunic.

The phrygian cap, which had a forward-curved peak, was worn throughout the century.

Shoes were made of leather, silk, or wool, sometimes embroidered with geometric patterns. They were generally a slip-on style, cut away at the top of the foot and higher behind the heel, or an ankle boot with a turned-over top. Jewelry consisted of coronets, circlets, girdles, brooches, and rings.

By mid century the tunic was knee length in front and slightly longer in back. The mantle shortened to just cover the tunic. Hoods became fashionable. A hat was often carried, or left hanging down the back, even when the hood was worn. Most hats were bowl-shaped with a stiff brim and a little knob on top.

At the end of the century, the tunic was full and calf length. The sleeves, cut in one with the body, were wide at the underarm and narrow at the wrist. The tunic was belted with a narrow leather or silk girdle set with jeweled or enameled metal plaques. The girdle had a waist clasp and a long end hanging in front. The mantle, now two-thirds of a circle, was worn with one side drawn over the left shoulder and tucked into the girdle. New footgear included a shoe cut away asymmetrically over the foot and fastened with an ankle strap, and ornamental garters criss-crossed up the hose.

Two forms of decoration, whose popularity peaked in the 14th century, were introduced. One was dagging—cutting a garment edge into scallops or other shapes. The other was particolor. A particolored garment was divided into halves or

Twelfth-century styles are among the easiest to make. They flatter most people except those who are overwhelmed by a layered look.

Figure 1: Men's fashions circa 1130

smaller sections by the use of contrasting colors. Sometimes one fabric was striped or embroidered and the other plain.

Women's fashions

During the first third of the 12th century women's clothes, like men's, were exceedingly long (see figure 2). The gown bodice was fitted by lacing (and worn over a corset). The overgown often had wide sleeves turned up into cuffs. Another sleeve style was more closely fitted with a long pendant at the end. The undergown had tight sleeves cut long and pushed up to wrinkle at the wrists. The gown was embroidered at the neck, wrists, and the upper arm where the sleeve joined the bodice. It was held in with a waist girdle.

Women wore semicircular mantles fastened like men's. Their headdress was a long circular, semicircular, or oblong veil that covered the hair. Women's shoes were probably similar to men's, though they were hidden by the gown. Women's jewelry was also similar.

Around 1130 women adopted the bliaut. Its construction has been interpreted in various ways. A fine, textured fabric—probably pleated or crimped—was used. The fitted bodice and full skirt were probably separate. The sleeves were an "angel" shape, gathered around the upper arm and very wide at the wrist. Most mysterious was a fabric band between the bust and waist. My favorite interpretation is that the bodice was cut very long and the extra fabric gathered, shirred, or smocked. The bliaut was worn with a very long girdle wound around the waist, then the hips to fall in a front pendant.

A loose overgown, later called the peliçon, was introduced during this period. It was calf length, had a front opening clasped by a brooch below the waist, and had wide angel sleeves. This peliçon was made of light, border-embroidered material.

From about 1130 to at least mid century women wore their hair in two long braids. Each braid had either three sections twined in what we consider the usual manner, or two bound with ribbon. Braids had fabric casings at the bottom (often stuffed with false hair) and were weighted with metal ornaments.

The bliaut went out of fashion in the 1160s in favor of a simple, loose, full-skirted gown. Its sleeves were tight around the upper arm and very wide from elbow to wrist. The peliçon, now cut more like the gown, was made of heavier fabric and lined with fur.

Around 1170 the braided hair was crossed behind and brought around the head. The barbette, a narrow, folded linen strip, was passed under the chin and the ends pinned to the

If medieval braided styles require more hair than you have, buy inexpensive matching braids. These look more natural than a wig. Appendix A lists sources.

Figure 2: Women's fashions circa 1100–1150

hair. A circular veil, which hung to mid back, was draped over the hair. The headdress was secured by a metal fillet or narrow fabric band.

Around 1190 the wimple was used as an alternative to the barbette. It was a shaped piece of fabric with the top pinned to the headdress and the bottom tucked into the gown neck.

THE THIRTEENTH CENTURY

Thirteenth-century styles were simpler than those of the 12th century. They featured little decoration, though they were made of rich fabrics and furs. A new fabric was velvet, imported from Italy.

Men's fashions

The most distinctive 13th-century garment was the cyclas or sideless surcote, an overtunic with several variations. At first it was a length of fabric, slightly flared from shoulder to hem, with a head opening and a center skirt slit. (See figure 3.) The sides were unseamed and there were no sleeves. The cyclas might, or might not, be girdled.

By the 1240s the cyclas was sewn or buttoned from below a wide armhole to knee level. The chest was more fitted and the skirt more flared. Fabric with multicolored horizontal stripes was fashionable, as was a hem decorated with silk or gold fringe, or dagging.

Another style had cylindrical sleeves only partly sewn to the armhole. The arm could be passed through the resulting slit or through the sleeve end.

The gardcorp was a hooded cyclas with wide sleeves pleated to the shoulders. These had an arm slit, which, when used, caused the pleated portion to form a short sleeve. The rest hung in folds to about knee level. The gardcorp was worn as an overcoat and was popular for travel.

The ganache, from the last quarter of the century, had an attached hood and wide cape sleeves cut in one with the garment. The sides might or might not be seamed. There were no skirt slits.

Hem lengths varied from floor- to low-calf-level. The overtunic was often longer than the undertunic.

Rich, semicircular, almost floor-length mantles were worn as in the late 12th century.

Headgear included the coif, which looked like a baby's cap and was often worn under a hat or hood; a wool or felt skull cap; and a cap with a knob on top and an upstanding brim. The pointed top of the hood grew a long tail called the liripipe. Shoes and jewelry were much the same as in the late 12th century.

Figure 3: Men's fashions circa 1240

Women's fashions

Women also wore the cyclas, and its cut evolved in the same way as the man's. The early sleeveless overgown had a train. It was made of rich material, such as brocade, and lined with contrasting silk. Around 1250 the cyclas was partly joined at the sides and was slit from knee to hem. Later it was cut closer in the bodice and fuller in the skirt; the skirt back was carried over the arm. (See figure 4.) This cyclas was often shorter than the undergown. A gardcorp like a man's was worn for riding.

In the last quarter of the century the gown had medium-wide sleeves, showing tightly buttoned undergown sleeves, and a lower neckline than the undergown. The skirt was very full, falling in many folds to an embroidered hem.

The mantle worn throughout the 13th century was an oval with a wedge cut out at the front. The back trailed on the ground. The mantle was made of rich materials and the edges decorated with embroidery or braid.

Jewelry and shoes were much the same as in the 12th century.

Till about 1250 hair was braided and wound around the head as in the late 12th century; there was a curled fringe on the forehead. Another style had a center part with tresses bound with ribbon from the forehead to the nape, then falling in a long braid down the back. In the late 13th century hair was dressed in a very thick braid at each side, then wound around the ears in "ram's horns."

Thick, braided hair was the foundation for several elaborate headdresses, all of which gave an impression of width. Before 1250 the barbette was worn directly over the hair. The coif, a shallow pillbox hat that was invariably white, was placed over the barbette. The coif might have an upturned brim. When it was brimless, a metal fillet or coronet was worn around the rim.

After 1250 the hair was enclosed in a crispine, a gold, silver, or silk net that might be jewel set at intervals. The barbette was worn over the crispine. Over the barbette was placed a fillet or coif. The structure was topped with a shoulder-length veil.

For one late-century style, a piece of silk was laid over the head and side braids, which were then wound into ram's horns. The wimple was pinned to the top of the silk-encased ram's horns, then tucked into the dress neck. Optionally, a veil was hung over the head and secured with a fillet.

A crispine can be made from a coarse curtain netting dyed to match the gown. Sew pearl beads at thread intersections.

Figure 4: Women's fashions after 1250

THE FOURTEENTH CENTURY

In the 14th century, and particularly from mid century on, styles became extravagant and fanciful. Garments were either very tight (and for men, short) or very loose. Hems were dagged in elaborate shapes, such as leaves and fern fronds. Sleeve, mantle, and hood hems were dagged as well as the bottoms of main garments. Dags were themselves decorated with small bells. Almost any garment could be particolored. Particolor was often used in combination with large heraldic devices. Smaller devices were embroidered on the fabric in an allover pattern. Men's hoods were creatively draped in "chaperon" styles. And their shoes were made with extremely long, pointed toes—sometimes over twice the length of the foot.

Men's fashions

During the first quarter of the 14th century men's styles differed little from those of the late 13th. Garments became slightly tighter. The overtunic was worn over the girdle and had arm slits for reaching the pouch hung on it.

The circular mantle could be worn with the head through the head opening and the arms through the arm slits. Alternatively, the right arm was slipped through its proper slit, the head was slipped through the left arm slit, and the front opening and (three or four) ornamental fastenings fell on the right side.

The hood was often worn with the face opening over the head, the bulk of the hood draped on one side, and the liripipe (now at least six feet long), on the other. Or the hood was pleated in a fan shape above the forehead. The hood was also worn with the face at the face opening, but with the liripipe wound round the fabric to create a turban.

Around the second quarter of the century men's clothes became tight and short. A jacket called the paltock was worn over the shirt. The paltock had long tight sleeves, buttoned from elbow to wrist, which could be either sewn into the armholes or laced with "points"—laces with metal tags at the end.

Over the paltock was the cotehardie, a thigh-length jacket (see figure 5). It fastened in front with buttons, which could be enameled or jeweled. The sleeves were elbow length with long (up to five feet), narrow tippets (streamers) sewn to the ends. Another style had a skirt hanging in folds from the hips to mid thigh. The skirt was flared by the insertion of gores or cut separately and sewn on.

After about 1350 the paltock was padded in the chest and renamed the pourpoint. Tippets went out of fashion. Around 1370 the cotehardie was made with a standing collar. It could

Figure 5: Men's fashions circa 1327–1377

have long sleeves with cuffs over the hand, wide flared sleeves, or bagpipe sleeves (see below). The most expensive cotehardies were richly embroidered or jeweled.

Slops—short breeches shaped like swim trunks—were worn under the paltock. Hose were better fitted than before. They were made of fine wool or silk, sometimes velvet. They were laced to the paltock.

A massive girdle was worn over the cotehardie at the hips. It was composed of geometrically shaped metal plaques linked together; the plaques were enameled, filigreed, or jeweled. By about 1370 there was a long pendant on one side. Sometimes a waist belt was worn in addition to the girdle. Garters, both men's and women's, were made of embroidered or jeweled silk or velvet. Men wore necklaces and chains, but women didn't till the end of the century.

In the last quarter of the century, a long, loose, full-sleeved robe called the houppelande came into fashion. It eventually supplanted the cotehardie. The houppelande could be extra long and trained, ankle length for street wear, or knee length for riding. It had wide, long flared sleeves with a contrasting lining, or bagpipe sleeves, which were tight at the armhole and wrist but full at the elbow. The houppelande was pulled over the head or buttoned up the front, and held in with a waist girdle. It had a high collar or a wide capelike one.

As well as the hood, a cap with a rolled brim and bag crown was fashionable. The bag part could be stiffened, rather like a Victorian top hat. A large jeweled brooch was pinned in front.

Women's fashions

Before about 1325, women wore either the loose gown popular in the late 13th century, or a style with a closely fitted bodice and trained circular skirt.

The newer gown was worn with a cyclas called the sideless gown (see figure 6). This had a loose bodice with a low neck and armholes cut larger in front than in back, and a full, trained skirt. The hem and armholes were sometimes edged with fur.

One style of overgown was shaped like a gown, except for elbow-length sleeves; the sleeve back fell in a straight piece with curved ends.

Toward mid century the cotehardie came into fashion. This gown had a very tight, low-necked bodice laced in back or buttoned up the front. The sleeves could be long and buttoned from elbow to wrist with knuckle-length cuffs (which could be turned back). Or they could be elbow length to show the undergown sleeves. Both styles had tippets sewn to the elbows.

Fourteenth-century hose were cut from fabric on the bias, using a leg-shaped pattern. They weren't joined at the waist. But if you don't wish to make hose, buy heavy, winter-weight or wrestler's tights.

Figure 6: Women's fashions circa 1350

The skirt was full and trained, with front slits to hold it up while walking. It may have been cut separately.

The cotehardie was worn over an undergown and often under the sideless gown. It could also be worn under a peliçon with the same shape except for flared elbow-length sleeves and a shorter skirt with side slits. Or under a loose, capelike surcote with wide straight sleeves that could be buttoned around the arm or left hanging.

Women wore heavy girdles like men's. The girdle was worn over the cotehardie, but under the sideless gown or loose over-gown. Fillets and bodice ornaments were constructed of linked plaques like the girdle. Brooches secured the shoulders, and sometimes the center front, of low-necked bodices.

For the first half of the century women wore the ram's horn hairstyle, covered by the wimple and veil, or similar arrangements of looped braids, wimple, fillet, and often a crispine. After about 1350 the braids were arranged in columns at the sides of the face and secured by a fillet or coronet. Sometimes they were encased in two crispines, which looked like (and perhaps were) rigid cylinders.

🥀 THE ELIZABETHAN ERA

At the court of Elizabeth I (who ruled 1558–1603), dress was characterized by financial and stylistic extravagance, which increased as the reign went on.

Fabrics were luxurious. They included silk satin, brocade, taffeta, tufted taffeta (with a pile design of stripes or spots), velvet, tufted velvet, cloth of gold or silver, tinsel (which included gold or silver threads), and tissue (which did also). There were several qualities of linen and wool.

Garment decorations were detailed and intricate. They included embroidery (in gold, silver, colors, or blackwork), spangles (sequins), sewn-on pearls or jewels, large jeweled buttons, rows of braid, lace, panes (making a garment from fabric strips to show a contrasting lining), slashing (cutting slits in the fabric), pinking (cutting serrated slits or edges), and tabs or "pickadils" at garment edges. Aglets (ornamental metal tags) were attached to functional ties or purely decorative.

Colors early in the reign were rich and dark, set off by white frills at the neck and wrists. In the 1570s they became lighter and brighter. A typical combination was red, gold, white, and black. Blue was a common lower-class color and therefore unfashionable.

Although glasses were probably invented in the late 13th century, they look out of place at reenactments. If your vision needs correction I recommend contact lenses (unless your optometrist objects).

Choosing a Historic Period

Figure 7: Couple in fashions of 1567–1577 dancing the volta

MEN'S FASHIONS

The first garment an Elizabethan man put on was his shirt. This was a loose, long-sleeved garment, often embroidered at the neck opening, collar, sleeves, and cuffs. Initially the collar was edged with a frill, which developed into a separate ruff by the 1560s.

The ruff was a strip of linen edged with lace or blackwork and pleated in a figure-of-eight design. It could have one, two, or three layers. The ruff increased in size until it was a cartwheel, worn tilted from back to front. A rectangular collar that fell over the doublet became an alternative in the 1580s. It eventually supplanted the ruff.

After donning his shirt and neckwear, the courtier turned his attention to his suit (see figure 7). This consisted of a matching doublet, hose, and often a jerkin.

The doublet was closely fitted with a high standing collar. It had shoulder wings to hide the ties (points) joining the body to the sleeves. The doublet front was padded and stiffened at center front with a busk (a strip of wood, whalebone, or metal). The padding increased till about 1590, when it became less exaggerated. The doublet was shaped to the waist with a point at center front. The point lengthened until, by about 1575, it hung over the sword belt. (See figure 8.) This shape was called the peascod; it declined along with chest padding. An abbreviated skirt concealed the ties that attached the hose.

The jerkin was put on over the doublet. It had the same shape, except that sleeves were optional.

There were many styles of hose. The two basic types of upper hose were trunk hose, a full rounded style made in panes, and breeches, which looked like baggy knickers. Like other garments, upper hose became fuller into the 1580s, then shrank. Trunk hose were worn with tight-knee length extensions called canions, which could match or contrast. Stockings—also called hose—covered the rest of the leg. They could be either made from bias-cut fabric or knitted.

The sword belt was a narrow girdle, often richly embroidered. It was arranged on the waistline, with a loop on the left side for hanging a rapier and dagger.

The cloak, an important item of attire, was worn over the suit. It was either a matching color or black, and ornamented with embroidery or braid. The style could be a short, circular, hooded "spanish" cape; a short "dutch" cloak with shaped hanging sleeves; or a short or (from the 1580s on) a long "french" cloak worn over the left shoulder.

Hats varied from high- to low-crowned and from wide- to narrow-brimmed. They were made from rich fabric,

Finish slashes in fabric by hand overcasting.

Choosing a Historic Period

Figure 8: Men's fashions circa 1588

leather, or (very fashionable) beaver felt. Dyed ostrich plumes were often stuck into a silk hatband, and a jeweled brooch pinned to it.

Long-fingered gloves (with gauntlets after about 1570), were another important accessory. Shoes had bluntly pointed toes, and ranged from low-cut slippers to knee-length boots.

WOMEN'S FASHIONS

An Elizabethan woman began dressing by putting on her chemise. This was cut and decorated almost exactly like a man's shirt. A separate yoke called the partlet was worn over the chemise. This was made of embroidered linen, rich fabric studded with pearls or jewels, or transparent net or fine lawn that showed the chemise edge underneath.

She then put on a corset that flattened and pushed up the bust. A long busk was tied into a front pocket.

Another foundation garment was the farthingale. This was a cone-shaped hoopskirt till about 1590, when the wheel farthingale came into fashion. The wheel farthingale supported the skirt for 8 to 48 inches straight out from the waist, then allowed it to fall. Sometimes a stuffed "bum roll" supplemented or substituted for the wheel farthingale.

A petticoat, which might have an attached bodice, was worn over the farthingale. The petticoat was made of rich fabric because it was sometimes exposed by a reverse-V-shaped opening in the skirt front. Alternatively, a contrasting triangular panel called the forepart was fastened below the opening, or a closed skirt was worn.

The dress itself had a separate bodice and skirt, with the sleeves tied into the bodice. (See figure 7.) In the 1560s, the bodice often had a low neckline that arched upward to the center front and curved gently down in back, wings or padded rolls set just on the shoulder, and a pointed waist. Sleeves fitted the arm fairly closely. They could be slashed to show puffs of a contrasting lining. Or they could be embroidered, with sheer oversleeves to protect the embroidery. The pleated skirt swelled smoothly out from the waist.

From about 1575, the silhouette became fuller and stiffer (see figure 9). The neckline became wider, the shoulder wings less prominent, and the sleeves fuller. Neck and sleeve ruffs became deeper and wider; the neck ruff appeared to separate the head from the body. By the 1580s, the bodice was very narrow with an extremely pointed, stiffened waist and very large sleeves. It was balanced by a wide skirt short enough to show the shoes. In the 1590s, shoulder wings again became distinctive. The ruff was worn so wide and tilted that a wire support was necessary. The skirt was pinned in a tuck around

Figure 9: Women's fashions circa 1593

the edge of the wheel farthingale, giving the appearance of a separate flounce.

Hair was worn pulled back with the front hair showing beyond the headdress. It was more puffed and curled as the reign went on. Headdresses included the french and Mary Stuart hoods, both wired to curve in front, with fabric falling in back; the caul, a close-fitting hairnet made of gold or silk thread; and delicate, wired pearl headdresses. Outdoors, women wore a high-crowned hat with a jeweled band and an ostrich plume.

Strings of pearls or chains were looped across the bodice front. The waistline was covered by a narrow girdle, from which hung a miniature or a pomander to mask bad smells. A feather fan was another fashionable accessory.

An overgown, often fur-lined, was worn for warmth or pregnancy. This was a long, fairly loose, one-piece garment that fell in folds from the waist or the shoulder. It had a high collar, a full-length front opening (which might be worn unfastened), and often short puffed sleeves.

❧ THE AMERICAN REVOLUTION

Before the revolution (1775–1783), most cloth, lace, ready-made clothes, and accessories were imported from England. Colonists in larger cities dressed in fashionable English styles.

In the late 1760s, a movement began to wear homespun wool and linen. When England banned trade with the colonies in 1775, these became the only available new textiles. Quantities were limited, however. Presumably shortages impelled some colonists to wear their old clothes, especially since sympathy for the revolution was not universal. Imports were resumed after the revolution.

MEN'S FASHIONS

An 18th-century suit consisted of a dress coat or frock coat, a waistcoat, and knee breeches. All three could match in fabric and ornamentation. Alternatively, the waistcoat or breeches contrasted with the other two garments.

The dress coat was worn for the most formal assemblies (see figure 10). In the 1770s and 1780s it was made of silk, velvet, or high-quality wool. Silks might have a small pattern. Bright or dark colors—puce, chocolate, blue, and rose—were favored for winter, and pastels for summer. The coat might be sumptuously embroidered down the front and the center back vent, and around the pockets, cuffs, and standing collar. It had large ornamental buttons.

A slender silhouette was achieved by cutting the coat with

Underclothes are seldom depicted in early illustrations. But some women might have worn drawers (a calf- or knee-length nether garment) as early as the late 16th century. Wear drawers with a full back and an open inner seam for all periods until the 1920s. The waistband is trapped under several layers, so you can't take them down.

an unfastened front edge that curved sharply toward the sides. The back and sleeves were very narrow. The skirt was cut in one with the body, with a pleated back vent.

The dress coat was worn with a single-breasted, buttoned waistcoat. It had a short skirt (which became shorter in the 1780s) and a standing collar like the coat's.

The frock coat, worn for most occasions, was a simpler, somewhat looser garment. It had a double-breasted fastening, with the top button left undone to form lapels, and a turned-down collar. The skirt was set in at the waist. The frock coat was made of dark blue, dark green, light or dark brown, or black wool. It was worn with a double-breasted waistcoat that came just below the waist in the 1770s and straight across it in the 1780s. The waistcoat had a small standing collar and lapels.

Breeches were tight over the thigh and knee, but baggy in the seat. They were cut to meet the waistcoat and had a front flap opening. Knee fastenings were buckled or laced. Buff-colored or leather breeches were worn with the frock coat.

A white linen or cotton neckcloth was worn with both formal and informal dress. In the 1770s this was usually a stock—a gathered band of fabric passed around the neck and tied or buckled in back. In the 1780s the cravat became common. This was a square folded into a triangle, then a rectangle and tied in front with a knot or bow.

The voluminous powdered wigs worn for most of the century were going out of fashion. The natural hair was curled; powder was optional. The back hair, whether natural or a wig, was encased in a black silk bag at the neck.

A hat was always worn or carried. The tricorne—a hat cocked on three sides—was the most formal style. The bicorne—cocked on two sides—was less formal. A round uncocked hat, originally a riding hat, gradually replaced both styles.

Footwear consisted of silk stockings and leather shoes or boots. Shoes had rounded toes and low heels. They fastened with large, oblong or oval, silver or faceted steel buckles. Soft knee-length riding boots became fashionable town wear.

The usual overcoat was a greatcoat. This was longer and looser than the coat, with wide sleeves, turned-back cuffs, and a center back vent. It could be single- or double-breasted. In the 1780s it had several overlapping capelike collars.

WOMEN'S FASHIONS

Eighteenth-century dresses were worn over a loose chemise and a rigidly boned corset. The corset had a narrow back and a cone-shaped front that pushed the bust forward. A pair of stiff-

To make a man's cravat, narrow-hem a 30-inch square of fine white linen or cotton. To make a woman's neckerchief, hem a 22- to 36-inch square. Experiment with sizes before cutting. Selvages need not be hemmed.

Figure 10: Couple in 1770s formal dress dancing the minuet

ened hip panniers supported the sack dress. A crescent-shaped pad called a "rump" was worn with most other styles.

The robe à la française or sack was the most formal dress, though it was passing out of fashion in the 1770s. (See figure 10.) In front, the bodice was fitted to the body and seamed to the skirt. In back, the sack hung in two box pleats from the shoulders into a trained skirt. The bodice, like most 18th-century bodices, had a wide square neck rounded at the corners. The center opened in a V shape covered by a detachable stomacher. The elbow-length sleeves had two or three self-fabric ruffles, augmented by two or three lace or embroidered muslin ruffles. The skirt opened in front to display a matching petticoat.

The sack was made of silk brocade or satin. It was profusely trimmed with flounces, ruched fabric, silk flowers, gauze puffs, etc. However, the effect was light and delicate.

The most common style was the robe à l'anglaise or nightgown (see figure 11). The bodice was fitted both front and back. It was seamed to the skirt all around except at the center back in the 1770s, and all around in the 1780s. The bodice front could meet edge-to-edge. Or it met at the top and sloped away to the sides; a contrasting false front filled the gap. Sleeves were elbow or (more fashionable) wrist length. The bodice came to a blunt point below the waist in front and a sharp one in back. The skirt could be closed or open.

A formal nightgown was made of light silk with small, stylized flowers, stripes, or spots. The petticoat was made of matching fabric, unpatterned silk, or the newly fashionable white muslin. Informal or morning nightgowns were made of printed cotton or linen; medium-sized, trailing floral patterns were popular.

The nightgown tended to be accessorized rather than trimmed. A large, sheer kerchief was puffed over the bosom, then tucked into the dress. Or a long scarf (today termed a fichu) was crossed over the front and tied in back. Gauzy aprons were also fashionable.

Either the sack or the nightgown skirt could be looped up in a "polonaise." It was pulled through openings in the side seams (originally intended for reaching hanging pockets) or tied inside with tapes.

An informal style, common in America, was a jacket worn over an ankle-length petticoat. Many jackets looked like shortened sacks or nightgowns. Rural and working women wore a bedgown or shortgown. This was a hip-length T-shaped tunic with sleeves cut in one with the bodice. Back pleats or a drawstring waist provided some shaping.

In the 1780s the chemise à la reine, a Parisian style influenced by Louisiana hot-weather wear, came into fashion.

Figure 11: Woman's nightgown circa 1780s

Eighteenth-century
formal dresses were
trimmed with ruched
strips of dress fabric at
the neck, bodice edges,
skirt front edges, and on
the petticoat. You'll need
two or three widths;
experiment. Cut out
strips with pinking
shears or edge them
with narrow metal lace.
A scalloped or vandyked
edge is especially pretty.
Or cut strips on the bias
and pull out threads to
fray like fringe. Gather
in the middle or near
both edges of each strip.
Hand sew to dress.

This was a loose pullover or wraparound gown with elbow-length sleeves. It was fitted by drawstrings at the neck (which was often ruffled), waist, and sleeves. A wide silk sash gave the appearance of a high waist. The dress fabric was always white muslin.

Powdered wigs were highly fashionable in the 1770s. A foot or more high, they were extravagantly decorated with bows, feathers, garlands, chains, and jewels.

In the 1780s wigs were replaced by a wide hairstyle with loose curls all over the head and ringlets down the back. Although more natural, this required careful arrangement and powdering. It became more feasible to wear a hat. Usually this was a low-crowned straw with a wide brim tilted or turned up at one side. For town wear hats were covered with silk and trimmed with feathers and flowers.

Women's shoes had pointed toes and curved heels about two inches high. They fastened with buckles. They were silk-covered till the 1780s, when leather became stylish.

THE ENGLISH REGENCY

From 1811 to 1820, the Prince of Wales acted as regent during George III's mental illness. The classical/rural/natural trend in clothing styles, which began with the chemise dress and the acceptance of men's riding clothes for town wear, continued. But by the end of the decade the transition to the Romantic period had begun.

MEN'S FASHIONS

The coat, breeches, and waistcoat were seldom made in the same fabric or color. The coat was wool unless it was worn at court. There were three styles, which were supposed to be perfectly fitted and tailored.

The dress or tail coat was worn for all formal occasions, day and evening (see figure 12). It was cut across the waist in a slight upward curve till about 1815, then straight across. The narrow tails hung straight down in back. The tail coat could be single- or double-breasted; it might be too small to fasten in front. It had either a shawl collar or a collar with lapels. Sleeves had a little fullness at the shoulder and, like women's, were cut knuckle length. A range of dark colors was popular—dark blue, green, brown, wine, and black. Gilt buttons were very smart.

The morning coat had front edges that curved smoothly back. Originally a riding coat, it became popular informal wear. The other informal coat, the frock coat, had straight front edges and a full skirt that hung to the knee. (See figure 13.)

There were also three styles of legwear—breeches, pan-

Figure 12: Couple in fashions of 1815–1820 dancing the Regency waltz

taloons, and trousers. Breeches and pantaloons were tight garments that showed off the wearer's legs. Breeches came just below the knee; the front fastened with a flap and the knees buttoned. Pantaloons were calf length till about 1817, then ankle length with a strap to pass under the foot. Breeches and pantaloons were made of elastic material such as wool jersey. They were light colored for day and cream or black for evening.

Trousers were the most casual garment, though they were accepted for informal evening wear after 1817. They were somewhat looser than pantaloons. A wide style gathered at the waist and ankles, known as cossacks, was worn in mid decade. Trousers were calf length around 1807, but full length with a foot strap by 1817.

The waistcoat was the most colorful part of the ensemble. It contrasted with the coat and breeches and had a woven or embroidered pattern. It was cut straight across the waist, could be single- or double-breasted, and often had a high standing collar.

The shirt was made of fine white linen with a double ruffle of finer linen down the front. The collar, which was attached to the shirt, was deep, starched, and worn turned up, the tips overlapping the wearer's cheeks. It was held in place by a starched cravat. This was black or colored for day, patterned white for informal evenings, and plain white for balls.

Ankle-length greatcoats with overlapping cape collars were still worn. Another style was a fitted topcoat cut like a frock coat.

Boots were more fashionable than shoes except for formal evening events, when low slipperlike shoes were worn.

Hairstyles were longish and had a windswept, Byronic look. Long sideburns were common. A black or gray top hat was worn for day. A bicorne or a collapsible, crescent-shaped opera hat was worn for evening.

Nineteenth-century etiquette required gloves for most occasions. Regency men's gloves were plain styles in natural-colored or white kid. Another 19th-century man's accessory was a watch with a chain hung with fobs or seals.

WOMEN'S FASHIONS

Women's undergarments consisted of drawers, a chemise, and a linen or cotton petticoat with an attached bodice. The bust was supported by a high-waisted corset or flaps inside the dress. A small bustle pad kept the skirt away from the hollow of the back.

Dresses were very high waisted (see figure 12). The bodice might or might not have a little gathered front and/or back

Figure 13: Men's day fashions circa 1817

fullness. The neckline was high for day, low for evening. Sleeves were short and puffed, long and plain, or long with a top puff or puffs all down the arm. The skirt was gored with some gathers at center back. It was fairly narrow, but widened as the decade went on. The hem cleared the ground.

The sheer white muslins that were almost universal from 1800 to 1810 were giving way to a range of firmer, more colored and patterned fabrics. Muslin had woven stripes or spots, or embroidered flowers and vines. Sometimes the pattern was colored; gold and silver embroidery were fashionable for evening. Some ball dresses had a colored satin underdress and a gauze or net overdress. Printed cottons were made into morning dresses. Skirts were trimmed with tucks, flounces, and, for evening, gauze caught with narrow silk or satin rouleaux (bias tubes). Bodices had matching trim. A pleated muslin neck ruff was a common accessory.

Long rectangular shawls, wildly popular from 1800 to 1810, were still worn. The most expensive were cashmeres from India, with deep borders at the short ends. Other shawls were made from plain, colored wool and trimmed with fringe. Newly fashionable were fitted spencers and pelisses. Both were cut like the dress, except that they fastened in front. The spencer just reached the dress waist and the pelisse was full length. Satin and velvet were the most popular fabrics; winter pelisses were fur trimmed.

Hair was cut fairly short with a front fringe and parted in the center. A chignon was attached to the crown or back of the head and a comb stuck in front of it. A frilled muslin cap was worn indoors. A hat was the most common outdoor wear early in the decade, but later the bonnet predominated. Turbans were sometimes worn for evening, or the hair was decorated with combs, flowers, and jewels.

Shoes were low-heeled slippers with oval, pointed, or square toes. They tied with ribbons round the ankle. The color matched some part of the ensemble.

Gloves were white (the only proper evening color), natural-colored, or pastel. Short gloves were worn with long-sleeved dresses, long gloves with short-sleeved ones. Because the skirt was too narrow to hide hanging pockets, it was necessary to carry a little bag called a reticule. Jewelry was simple and generally consisted of a short necklace or pendant.

You can transform a low-necked Regency dress into a decorous day dress by wearing a chemisette. It should be fine white cotton, linen, or net and have a high neck with two or three pleated frills. Another trick is to make sleeves in two parts—a puffed upper sleeve and a plain knuckle-length lower sleeve—so the lower sleeves can be removed. To extend your wardrobe of evening dress(es), make sleeveless spencers with different colors and decoration.

Ballet slippers (with flexible toes) are a good substitute for Regency shoes. They're inexpensive and sturdier than they look. Dye white slippers an interesting color and sew on ribbon ties.

𝒲 THE CIVIL WAR

During the American Civil War (1861–1865), the cut of men's uniforms was based on day dress. Civilians continued to adopt Parisian and London styles, with some time lag. Although women's clothes were elaborate and colorful, men's were standardized and somber. Elegance was conveyed by quality fabric and tailoring.

MEN'S FASHIONS

The tail coat was worn for formal evening (but not day) occasions. (See figure 14.) It was made of firm, smooth wool—always black. It had a lower waist, a higher neck, and broader tails than during the Regency. Long lapels, faced with silk or velvet, revealed the waistcoat and shirt.

The frock coat was the predominant day coat (see figure 15). It was somewhat shaped and fastened with a double- or single-breasted closing. The straight-fronted skirt hung to the knees. The usual fabric was a smooth wool in black, dark blue, or dark gray, with a self- or velvet collar.

The morning coat was worn for informal morning occasions. It buttoned on the center of the chest and curved away to the back.

The sack or lounge coat was introduced in the 1850s. Originally country and sports wear, it was becoming accepted for informal day occasions. The sack coat was looser, boxier, shorter, and wider-sleeved than more formal coats. It was made of textured wool such as tweed.

Trousers were often straight and tubular, with a buttoned center front fly. There was neither a foot strap nor a center crease. Another style, called "peg tops," was cut full at the waist and tapered to the ankle; but peg tops were incorrect for evening. Knickerbockers (full knee breeches) were paired with a sack coat for shooting and hiking.

Evening trousers matched the coat and had narrow black braid down the outside seam of the leg. Plain, striped, checked, or plaid trousers were worn with the frock or morning coat. Dark color mixes were popular—for example, gray and blue for summer, brown and black for winter. The sack coat sometimes had a matching waistcoat and trousers, or matching knickerbockers. Trousers were held up with plain linen or embroidered suspenders, adjusted with buckles.

The fancy waistcoat was going out of fashion. Waistcoats sometimes matched the trousers or formed part of a three-piece sack suit. The evening waistcoat was made of lighter material. It was white for the most formal occasions and black for less formal ones.

Figure 14: Couple in fashions of 1861–1865 dancing the polka

The shirt was usually white linen, though striped cotton was worn for the country and sports. The evening shirt had a pleated or tucked front panel. The shirt collar was detachable. It could be single (upright), which was the most formal style, or double (turned-down), which was less formal. Formality was also indicated by the amount of starch; an unstarched turned-down collar was worn with sports outfits. Likewise, cuffs could be single or double (french), but the double cuff was more formal.

Because evening shirts were heavily starched, they fastened with studs and cuff links. These were gold or silver and set with mother-of-pearl, pearls, or jewels.

Neckwear was a bow tie secured with a tie pin or a longer tie knotted "four-in-hand" style. A plain white bow tie was always worn for evening, but day ties were colored and patterned.

There were many overcoat styles. A tweed inverness was favored for traveling. This was a loose, knee-length overcoat with a long shoulder cape and wide sleeves. A number of informal coats were referred to as paletots. They were always loose and had no waist seam. The chesterfield was most fashionable and formal. It was a straight coat with a single-breasted, double-breasted, or concealed button front closing.

Hair was rather long and curly and merged into long sideburns. Beards and curled moustaches were popular.

A high silk top hat was worn with the tail and frock coats. It could be black, white, or beige. More informal coats were worn with a wideawake, bowler (derby), or boater. The wideawake had a low crown and a wide brim; it was made of felt or straw. The bowler was felt; it had a hard, bowl-shaped crown and a narrow, curled brim. The boater was a stiff straw hat with a flat crown and medium-wide brim.

Short, round-toed boots (often black) were worn for day. They could lace or button. Low-heeled pumps were worn with the tail coat. Men habitually sported a watch and chain, gloves (dark for day, white for evening), and a cane with a decorative handle.

WOMEN'S FASHIONS

Women's figures were given an hourglass shape by a corset and a crinoline (hoopskirt). The corset made the bust look rounded and smooth. In the early 1860s the crinoline was evolving from a round bell into an ellipse—flat in front and larger in back. A petticoat was worn under the crinoline and another on top. The overpetticoat could be colored if worn with a looped-up walking dress. Other undergarments included drawers, a chemise, and a corset cover (camisole).

Businesses that rent modern formal wear often sell used tails and morning coats. These can be adapted for Victorian costumes. Buy trousers a bit large and replace the zipper with buttons. Choose a modern formal shirt with a tucked bosom— no frills. Remove collar stays and starch the collar. Iron it upward, bending the tips down slightly. A pretied bow tie and black dress or dance shoes complete the effect.

Figure 15: Men's day fashions circa 1860

The fabric, trimmings, and to some extent the cut of a woman's dress depended on when it was worn. The basic styles were day and evening dress. Day dress was subdivided into morning (home) dress, walking dress, afternoon dress, and other types. Evening dress could be a dinner dress, opera gown, or ball gown (see figure 14). Most style differences appeared in the bodice. Often a day and an evening bodice, or a dinner and a ball gown bodice, were made to match a single skirt.

The day bodice hooked or buttoned in front (see figure 16). It had a high neck with a round lace collar or a low square neck worn over a chemisette. The waist was round and rather high. Day sleeves were long and often featured epaulettes (shoulder wings). The most popular styles were the bishop and the pagoda. The bishop sleeve was full and pleated into the armhole and wristband. The pagoda sleeve was pleated into the armhole, but wide and open at the wrist. It was worn over lace-trimmed or embroidered white undersleeves. An underblouse could be worn instead of a chemisette or undersleeves.

The ball gown bodice had a low, off-the-shoulder neck trimmed with a lace flounce or draped bertha. Sleeves were short and puffed. The waist was often deeply pointed at center front and back, though the round waist was also worn. The bodice was hooked up the center back or laced through embroidered eyelets. Other evening bodices had more modest necklines and large full sleeves.

A new style, the princess dress, was at this date mostly worn in the evening. It had no waist seam and buttoned in front.

A blouse and skirt could be worn for informal day occasions, usually with a jacket, waistcoat, and/or belt. The blouse was often made of white muslin, tucked or pleated, with a high neck and long full sleeves. Another type, the garibaldi shirt, was made of fine scarlet wool with black braid trim and black buttons. Jackets were short and worn open; the bolero, with curved front edges, was popular. The belt could be either a wide tailored style or pointed above and below the waist in front.

Day and evening skirts had the same cut. Skirts worn over the round crinoline were made of unshaped fabric widths pleated into a waistband. Skirts worn over the elliptical crinoline were shaped (gored), with the greatest fullness at center back, which was slightly trained. They were box pleated at the top; pleats were sometimes stacked three deep. Evening dresses frequently had double skirts. The top skirt might be lace.

Day dresses were made of satin, plain taffeta, and moiré (watered) taffeta; cashmere, merino, and other lightweight wools; and, for summer, light- to medium-weight cottons. Cottons often had woven stripes or geometric prints. Fabrics

You can make several Civil War outfits by mixing and matching a few garments. Sew a taffeta or satin skirt without much trim. Make matching day and evening bodices. For another day outfit, make a coordinating bolero jacket and a white batiste blouse. Depending on the day bodice style, the bolero or blouse may be wearable with it. To vary the evening dress, make a fancy fichu or a striking velvet sash. The sash can also be worn with the blouse/skirt outfit.

Figure 16: Women's walking dress circa 1864

printed à disposition—with designs planned for specific garment sections—were very popular in the 1850s and still used in the 1860s. Colors tended to be strong, sometimes harsh. Day dresses were trimmed with contrasting bias bands, braid, or cord applied in bold geometric patterns.

Evening dresses were lighter (or brighter) in color, fabric, and trimming. Fabrics included satin, taffeta, brocade, velvet (favored for opera gowns), gauze, tulle (a gossamer silk), and tarlatan (a fine open-weave muslin). Quantities of lace were used, both cream-colored and black. Other trimmings included silk flowers, ribbons, and pleated gauze.

Hair was parted in the center with fullness around the ears. The rest was massed at the back of the head in a chignon, clusters of curls, or braids. These were augmented with false hair. The chignon might be encased in a snood—a black, white, or colored hairnet.

Indoors, married women wore small, lace- and ribbon-trimmed morning caps. Outdoors, all women wore a bonnet or hat. The bonnet was often a "spoon" style with a high crown. It could be any color and was lavishly trimmed with feathers, ribbons, and flowers. It tied under the chin with broad ribbons. Hats were considered less formal and were preferred by young women. Both wide-brimmed straws, with ribbon ties and long streamers, and medium-brimmed boaters were popular. The evening headdress consisted of a fancy comb or wreath decked with lace, flowers, and/or ribbons.

Ankle boots, with square toes and two-inch curved "louis" heels, were generally worn for day. They could lace or button. Dance shoes were low-cut, low-heeled pumps. White stockings were worn with light-colored dresses, black stockings with dark ones. Colored and patterned stockings could be glimpsed below short walking dresses.

Short gloves or mitts (fingerless lace or net gloves) were available in a wide range of colors. A fan was carried for evening; it hung from the wrist when not in use. Fichus (shaped lace shoulder scarves) accessorized summer and evening dresses.

Outer garments included wool paisley and embroidered Chinese shawls, a variety of loose or semifitted cloaks and mantles, and, for day, tailored coats and jackets.

Fabric woven à disposition can be imitated by sewing a patterned fabric to a plain one. One color in the pattern should match the plain fabric. I saw an original 1850s dress that exhibited this technique. The basic dress fabric was a plain silk. Three deep skirt flounces were constructed by horizontally piecing it to a coordinating plaid.

Paisley and embroidered Chinese shawls, in wearable condition, are available in antique and vintage clothing stores.

In the 1890s men's clothes were similar to those of the 1860s, with minor variations. Women's were notable for the popularity of tailored suits, due to increased participation in office work and sports.

MEN'S FASHIONS

The black tail coat was still correct for formal evening occasions (see figure 17). It was worn with black trousers braided down the outside seam, a white or black silk waistcoat with a deeply cut U neck, a starched dress shirt, a white or black bow tie, and black patent leather shoes.

A new coat, called the dress lounge, dinner jacket, or tuxedo, was acceptable for informal evening wear. It was cut like a sack coat with a shawl collar and continuous lapels. The tuxedo was made of black wool with silk- or satin-faced lapels. The rest of the evening outfit was the same, except that the bow tie was black.

The most fashionable day coat was the single-breasted morning coat, which could be worn for either formal occasions or business. The formal morning coat was black or dark gray. It was worn with a waistcoat and striped gray trousers. The informal version was a three-piece textured or tweed suit.

The frock coat had a well-fitted body and a comparatively long and full skirt. It was often worn open. It was made of black or gray wool.

A sack suit was acceptable for ordinary day wear. The coat was single-breasted with three or four buttons and four outside pockets. The fabric was tweed, worsted, serge, or flannel.

The day waistcoat could be single- or double-breasted, and might or might not have a collar and lapels. Trousers had a center crease. If worn with a sack suit they had turned-up cuffs.

Shirt collars, even turnover collars, were very high—up to three inches. In the late 1890s colored shirts with white collars became acceptable for day. Striped bow ties were the most popular day neckwear. Neckties tied with a four-in-hand knot and ascots (wrapped or folded cravats) were also worn.

Sports coats included the norfolk, the reefer or yachting jacket, and the blazer. The norfolk jacket had two box pleats in front and two in back; the fullness was held in by a belt. It buttoned high at the neck and sometimes around the wrists like a shirt. There was a patch pocket at each hip. The norfolk was worn with knickerbockers and wool stockings.

The reefer was a longer, boxier version of the sack coat. It could be single- or double-breasted. It was used as a sports jacket or light overcoat. The blazer was a short jacket with

Figure 17: Couple in late 1890s fashions dancing the waltz

patch pockets. It was made from flannel, often brightly colored or striped. It was worn with flannel trousers for the seaside and summer sports.

Hair was shorter than in the 1860s. Older and conventional men wore beards, but the clean-shaven look was considered "artistic." As well as the top hat, bowler, and boater, men wore the homburg and trilby. Both hats had a dented crown and curved brim, but the homburg was made of stiffer felt and had a silk-bound brim. Tweed caps were worn in the country and for sports.

Short boots were still more popular than shoes. Black was more formal, but brown or tan could be worn with a sack suit. Some boots had buff or gray cloth tops.

The chesterfield was still the most stylish overcoat; it came to well below the knee. A tweed ulster was popular for traveling. This was a long, single- or double-breasted coat with a half belt in back and a detachable hood. It could have a shoulder cape. Another coat, the raglan, had what is still known as a raglan sleeve, cut to a point at the neck with no shoulder seam. The raglan coat was loose, light, and often had a waterproof finish.

WOMEN'S FASHIONS

In the 1890s the silhouette was a small waist set off by large shoulders and hips. Most dresses were two-piece.

Fabrics, though not necessarily heavy, had body. They included velvet, satin, brocade, taffeta, faille (a ribbed silk), suit wools, and for summer, linen, piqué (a stout ribbed cotton), and crisp light cottons such as organdy.

The skirt was floor length and slightly trained (the evening train could be longer). It fit the hips smoothly, with gathers concentrated at center back, and flared at the hem. Trimmings were simple or absent.

The bodice was mounted on a firm, close-fitting, boned underlining. Its sleeves gradually widened, becoming enormous balloon or leg-of-mutton shapes around 1895, then began to shrink. Short, but wide, sleeves were worn for evening. Day dresses had high, stiffened collars. Evening dresses had very low necks adorned with deep flounces (see figure 17).

In contrast to the skirt, the bodice was highly decorated. Decorations included sleeves, epaulettes, and lapels in a contrasting color and/or fabric; a lace collar and yoke; a draped or gathered front; and jet beading.

Around 1898 the Edwardian pigeon-breasted silhouette took hold. The bodice pouched slightly over the waist in front; the skirt clung more closely; and lighter fabrics were used.

Tailored suits were extremely popular (see figure 18). They

You can buy 1890s suits in sound condition. Often the date was written on a paper slip by the tailor and sewn into an inside breast pocket. Because few dealers carry men's wear, try a specialist or a vintage clothing show. When you find a selection, buy a black coat with the original trousers—it's hard to match shades.

Figure 18: Women's day fashions circa 1894

consisted of a plain wool or linen skirt and a close-fitting long-sleeved jacket in the same material. The jacket buttoned to the chest, then spread into lapels (sometimes prettily curved or asymmetrical) and a collar.

Suits were worn with a shirtwaist (blouse). This was usually white, sometimes black, and occasionally other colors. The fabric was cotton, linen, silk, or taffeta. Shirtwaists were decorated with tucks, hand or machine embroidery, lace insertion, or made entirely of lace or Irish crochet. Some were even plain. A wide leather or fabric belt with an ornate silver, brass, or enameled buckle accented the waist. All American women wore this "gibson girl" outfit for occasions ranging from office work to informal evening events.

The hourglass figure was created by a heavily boned corset that supported and defined the bust. Lingerie included petticoats, chemises, camisoles, drawers, and combinations (a chemise or camisole combined with drawers). White cotton and linen lingerie was flounced, embroidered, pin tucked, and appliqued with fine lace. Dark taffeta petticoats were trimmed with rows of ruffles.

Capes and mantles were made full to accommodate the dress sleeves. The most common style was a flared circular cape that reached to or below the waist. It had a high standing collar or a flared "medici" one that framed the face. It could have a wide shoulder ruffle or lapels. Tailored capes were made of firm wool, with designs carried out in narrow braid or bias bands. Some had fur edging. Dressier (but not necessarily evening) capes were made of satin, faille, or brocade. They were trimmed with beading or lace, and sometimes neck ruffles and a big satin bow at the nape or throat. Judging from surviving examples, wool capes were typically brown or camel and silk ones black.

Hair was fluffed or arranged around a frame, then coiled in a bun on top of the head or at the nape of the neck. Many hairstyles had a curled forehead fringe. Elaborate combs and pins were worn for evening. Hats were small, jaunty, and piled with trimmings. Shirtwaists and sports clothes were worn with a boater. This was trimmed simply with a ribbon band and a bow or loops. Around 1897 the wide-brimmed hats typical of the Edwardian era appeared.

Long gloves were worn for day and evening. They were made in many colors and decorated with beads, lace, or printing. Shoes had pointed toes and high louis heels. They included laced or buttoned ankle boots, oxfords, and pumps with bows or buckles.

Eighteen-nineties belt buckles and reproductions are widely available. When you look at one you'll understand how to attach a belt. If you don't work with leather, use embroidered braid, upholstery brocade, or velvet. Although this should be faced, many surviving belts aren't stiffened.

To make shoes look more antique, lace them with flat cotton tape in the shoe color. Finish the ends with metal tips.

✒ THE RAGTIME ERA

The first ragtime music was written in the late 1890s. However, I'm defining the ragtime era as 1910 to 1920. Most ragtime dances reached the height of popularity in 1914. And most ragtime dancers prefer styles from this decade.

A formal evening dance required formal evening wear. Both formal day (afternoon) clothes and ordinary day clothes were acceptable at an afternoon tea dance.

MEN'S FASHIONS

Nineteen-tens styles were similar to those of the turn of the century. World War 1 (1914–1918) involved a large percentage of the male population (larger in England than America) and discouraged changes in civilian dress.

For formal evening occasions, the impeccably dressed man wore a black wool tail coat and matching trousers. The tail coat had notched lapels faced with silk or satin. It was worn unbuttoned to expose the waistcoat. The trousers were rather narrow, braided down the outside seams, had center creases, and did not have turned-up cuffs. The waistcoat was made of white duck (a tightly woven cotton) or silk. It was cut low in front and could be single- or double-breasted.

This dress suit was worn with a stiffly starched white shirt with a pleated front, a separate wing collar, and a plain white cotton bow tie. For dancing, low-cut black patent-leather pumps with flat silk bows were worn. Proper accessories were white kid gloves and a black opera hat (a collapsible top hat). Acceptable jewelry consisted of pearl studs to fasten the shirt front and a pocket watch.

The tuxedo was looser than the tail coat and was cut straight across the bottom. It could have either notched lapels or a shawl collar. The fabric was black or gray wool. The lapels were faced like the tail coat's.

The tuxedo was worn with the same evening trousers as the tail coat. The waistcoat, which was exposed in front, could be black or gray. The shirt was white, pleated in front, and worn with a turnover or wing collar and a black bow tie. An opera hat, bowler, or soft hat was worn with the tuxedo.

The frock coat had gone out of fashion. The usual formal day coat was the morning coat (see figure 19). As before, this was a single-breasted, cutaway style with the front edges curving back from the waist and tails with a center back pleat. The morning suit could be a black morning coat with striped or check trousers and a contrasting waistcoat, or a matching three-piece suit (checked tweed was popular). The waistcoat was also single-breasted and its bottom button might be left undone.

The least formal day suit was still the three-piece sack suit. Its coat was fairly long and loose and buttoned up high to cover the waistcoat. It could be single- or double-breasted and had short lapels, cuff slits fastened with buttons, and several outside pockets. The trousers had creases and turned-up cuffs.

The day shirt could be white or colored, starched or soft. It was worn with a separate turned-down collar and a necktie. Natty colored shirts had pleated fronts or were made of silk.

The top hat was correct for formal day occasions, a bowler or soft hat for less formal ones. Shoes were preferred to boots. They were long with spade-shaped toes. Buttoned shoes were going out of fashion. Black shoes were correct for the city, brown for the country.

The chesterfield was a suitable overcoat for both day and evening. After the war short, double-breasted wool officer's coats and rain-repellant cotton gabardine trench coats were adapted for civilian use.

Men's hairstyles were short and neatly trimmed. Oil and brilliantine made them look smoother. Chins—ideally cleft, manly, and noble—were clean-shaven.

WOMEN'S FASHIONS

From about 1910 to 1915 the silhouette was high-waisted and tubular. Around 1910 it closely resembled the Regency line, but was soon altered by oriental influences.

The dress bodice was simply and loosely cut (see figure 19). It was slightly pouched in front. The neckline of the day bodice was high (but often collarless) or a modest V. Simple set-in sleeves and kimono sleeves cut in one with the bodice were popular. The evening bodice had a deep V neck filled in to create a broad square, and short sleeves. Bodice and sleeves were covered with transparent drapery.

At the beginning of this period the skirt was narrow and touched the top of the foot. One extremely narrow, confining style was the hobble skirt. It was sometimes slit at the side or draped up in front for easier movement. Another style was an orientally inspired tunic (short overskirt) over a straight skirt. The evening skirt often had a small rectangular or pointed train.

The dress bodice and skirt were joined. Many dresses had a complex fastening arrangement that went down the bodice front, partway around the waist, then down the side of the skirt. The princess cut, or a semiprincess with a waist seam only at the sides, emphasized the narrow line. This type of dress fastened in back.

In the mid 1910s the waistline was lower but still above the natural waist. The skirt became wider and shorter. For day it was well above the ankle. It could have two or three tiers or

You can make some modern men's shirts look like day shirts from 1890 to 1930. Choose a regular-fit dress shirt with single or french cuffs. A good pattern is a narrow, closely spaced stripe in blue, red, or brown on a white background. Take off the collar. Add buttonholes for collar studs to the left front and center back of the neckband. Replace plastic buttons with mother-of-pearl.

Figure 19: Couple in fashions of circa 1913 dancing the one-step

multiple flounces. Bodice styles were similar to those of 1910–1914. The evening bodice was a straight strip of material with shoulder straps, covered with drapery.

By 1919 the waist was back to its natural level or slightly below. The skirt dropped to ankle length and became narrower again. It was sometimes two-tiered. One style was a barrel silhouette that tapered in at the hem. The bodice had a rectangular flat collar tapering to a V neck or framing a center front panel.

The loose chemise dress came into fashion around 1919 and remained popular in the 1920s.

Nineteen-tens evening and afternoon dresses were composed of a light silk, satin, or taffeta foundation and several layers and lengths of drapery in plain net, embroidered net, and/or chiffon. (See figure 20.) Beading and sequins were popular but seldom covered the entire dress. The oriental craze brought in strong colors for evening, such as scarlet, orange, and purple; black was also chic.

Silk afternoon dresses were more subdued. Another type of afternoon dress was the lingerie dress. It was distinguished not by its style, but by the fact that it was made from light, white cottons like those used for lingerie. It was exquisitely decorated with white embroidery and lace.

Tailored suits were still popular for day. Skirts were simple. The most common decorations were cording and large, nonfunctional buttons. Jackets became progressively looser throughout the decade. Blouses were cut and decorated like lingerie dress bodices.

The narrow silhouette required light, unbulky lingerie. This could be cotton, linen, or silk. Lingerie included camisoles, drawers, combinations, chemises, fitted princess slips, and petticoats. Camisoles had V or horizontal necklines. Drawers could be open or closed. Petticoats were fairly narrow, straight, untrained, and featured few flounces. Silk lingerie was sometimes pastel and trimmed with lace and tiny rosebuds.

For support, women wore a long corset that began below the bust and confined the hips. Elastic was replacing whalebone and steel. The brassière was invented to give the bust support no longer supplied by the corset.

Because skirt hemlines had risen, shoes and stockings were important. Shoes were narrow with pointed toes and medium louis heels. "Tango" shoes—pumps laced up the ankle with criss-crossed ribbons—were the rage. Stockings were sometimes embellished with embroidery or lace insertion.

Simple hairstyles were fashionable from about 1911, with the hair drawn into a coil or knot at the back of the head. In the mid 1910s the first bobs appeared. Bandeaux of light metal-embroidered material, spangled net, or even jeweled

One ragtime dance manual recommends adapting the narrow early 1910s line by wearing a split skirt fastened with snaps that can be undone to reveal a pleated silk or chiffon petticoat.

Choosing a Historic Period

Figure 20: Women's evening fashions circa 1911

Figure 21: Women's 1910s evening cape

metal were worn for evening. Upright plumes were often attached to these at the forehead.

Enormous picture hats laden with plumes were worn till about 1911. Smaller, less heavily trimmed hats were worn for the rest of the decade. Some had a high crown and a narrow brim, with the vertical effect enhanced by upright feathers at the front, back, or side. Some had a shallow crown and wide brim. There were also tricornes and a variety of irregular shapes. Colors were strong, for example burnt orange, bright navy, gray, and brown.

Outerwear included tailored day coats and lavish cocoon-shaped evening wraps (see figure 21).

🦅 THE ART DECO PERIOD

In the 1920s people wanted to look modern. They wanted to forget World War I and enjoy the economic boom that followed. Women wanted to exercise the independence and equality gained during the war.

The complex sartorial codes that governed the Victorian and Edwardian eras relaxed. Styles became looser and more informal. A boyish look was the fashionable ideal for women. Modernity was also expressed by awareness of artistic trends— the paintings of artists like Picasso and Matisse, and exhibits at the Paris 1925 Expo Deco. Women's clothes featured clean geometric lines broken up by abstract decoration.

MEN'S FASHIONS

Although the tail coat was still worn for formal evening occasions, the tuxedo was becoming more popular. (See figure 22.) The morning coat was worn for very formal day affairs such as weddings. The sack suit was the usual day wear.

The sports jacket was the most popular casual jacket. This was similar to a single-breasted sack coat, but looser. It was made of tweed, with matching or flannel trousers. Sweaters— fair isle, shawl collared, and turtleneck—were welcomed into a gentleman's wardrobe.

From 1925 to 1930 trousers were cut wider and pleated at the top with no tapering at the ankle. The most extreme, known as "oxford bags," measured 24 inches around the cuffs. To balance the trousers, jackets were cut shorter and fuller. They had broader shoulders, higher, looser waists, and often double-breasted closings. "Collegiate" suits were made in bold checks or stripes, with matching or contrasting waistcoats.

Formal evening dress still required a starched white shirt. It had a pleated bosom or was made of textured fabric. Toward 1930 an unstarched shirt could be worn with a tuxedo. A

Figure 22: Couple in mid 1920s fashions dancing the Charleston

morning coat might be worn with a starched or unstarched dress shirt, or a striped shirt with a white wing collar. A sack suit was worn with a colored shirt with a matching, soft double collar. A wide range of colors was available; for example putty, peach, blue-gray, and cedar. The sports jacket was worn with a colored flannel shirt and a soft collar.

A bow tie was appropriate for most outfits. Shaped silk ties, knotted four-in-hand style and secured with a tie pin, were worn with morning and sack suits. Another type was the macclesfield, a long, unlined scarf with square ends. Tie fabrics had small geometric patterns or diagonal stripes.

Hair was cut short and brilliantined. The top hat was relegated to evening wear; a black bowler was worn for day. Soft felt hats with squarish crowns, and straw panamas, accompanied casual outfits.

Shoes were lace-up styles with round toes. Oxfords, and brogues with fringed tongues, were popular. Two-toned shoes, in white plus tan or black, were worn with sports clothes. Although suede was available, it was considered faddish and caddish. Either black patent leather pumps or oxfords were worn for evening.

Overcoats were familiar chesterfields, raglans, and ulsters.

WOMEN'S FASHIONS

Although a rectangular silhouette remained constant, hems and waistlines fluctuated. In 1920 hems were mid-calf length and waists natural. In 1921 both hems and waists dropped—hems to below the calf and waists to hip level. Hems then began to rise, the most extreme reaching the knee around 1927 (see figure 22). In 1928–1929 dresses had uneven hems that were longer at the sides or back. By this time the waist had risen to almost its normal level.

Man-tailored day suits accentuated the boyish look (see figure 23). They had plain, fairly straight skirts. The jacket was long enough to cover the derrière. It was straight, with a low closure that just met or wrapped over, and worn loosely belted. It had either a shawl collar or one with lapels. A cardigan or pullover sweater, either the same length or hip length, might stand in for the jacket.

Blouses were loose, with drooping collars. They could either tuck into the skirt or hang over it to the hips. An overblouse might or might not be belted.

The chemise dress was worn for day and evening. It was cut straight with a modest round neckline. The sleeves could be any length. For evening the chemise was sleeveless and the neckline lower in back.

Another style had a loose chemise top and a full skirt

Figure 23: Women's day fashions circa 1925

added to the low hip line. The skirt could be pleated all around or in panels; have gathered, shirred, or handkerchief drapery panels; or have inserted godets (gores). A high-fashion version, the robe de style, was inspired by 18th-century styles. It had a full skirt stiffened with panniers.

Day dresses were made of printed silk, voile, or organdy; silk crepe; soft twill flannel; or knitted silk or wool jersey. Heavier knits were used for sweaters and cardigan suits. Evening fabrics included chiffon, soft satin, thin velvet, metallic brocade, and allover silver or gold lace. Chemise dresses were heavily embroidered with beads or sequins, or covered with rows of fringe.

Lingerie was straight and simple. It was made of rayon, silk, or thin satin. Although many colors were available, the most common were peach, pink, and ivory. Lingerie was decorated with ecru lace and pin tucks. The usual wear sequence was chemise, corset and brassière or corselette, knickers, and in the early 1920s a narrow waist petticoat.

The chemise was a short straight slip with narrow shoulder straps. Knickers were shrunken drawers that were well above the knee by 1927. Camiknickers, also called step-ins, might be worn instead of a chemise and knickers. This was a short chemise with a flap to button between the legs; the skirt might be flared or straight.

The corset suppressed the hips and derrière. It had elasticized panels and gussets. Till mid decade the brassière was a bust flattener, a straight band with side darts. It then began to allow for natural curves. The corselette was a combined corset and brassière.

Stockings were usually rayon or silk, though cotton and wool were still used. They were neutral, flesh-colored, or sun-tan-colored. They were held up with suspender belts.

In the early 1920s shoes had pointed toes and slender louis heels. By the end of the decade rounder toes and square cuban heels predominated. Many shoes were pumps with one or two straps across the foot, or T-straps with a strap from toe to ankle, then around the ankle. Court shoes with buckles were worn for evening. In the mid 1920s there was a fad for dance shoes with black lacquer heels set with fake jewels.

Although most women had bobbed their hair by 1924, a minority wore it long. Long hair was drawn back into a loose coil and ornamented with a large "spanish" comb made of real or imitation tortoiseshell. Or the hair was braided, drawn back, and secured with a bandeau. Bandeaux were worn for evening with both long and short hair.

During most of the 1920s the main hat style was the cloche. This had a deep crown that fit closely over bobbed hair and was pulled down to the eyes. The brim was narrow or

Although 1920s clothes are widely available, you may wish to sew reproductions. See chapter 4 for information on using vintage patterns.

nonexistent. Trimmings either created texture or emphasized the downward effect. An alternative for summer and semiformal wear was the straw picture hat. The brim was wide at the sides and narrow in back. The picture hat had soft trimmings such as drooping feathers, hanging flowers and fruit, ribbons, and lace.

In the evening a woman carried a jewel-like beaded or metal mesh purse and a large ostrich feather folding fan. The chemise dress provided a perfect foil for jewelry—dangling earrings, a long rope of beads, and quantities of bangle bracelets. Entrance and exit were dramatized by a very full velvet or brocade wrap.

2 Planning Your Outfit

Historic costuming is creative and fun. It also requires you to spend some time, effort, and money. Everyone wants to use these resources efficiently. The key, as with so many other things, is advance research and planning.

When designing your costume the question of accuracy is bound to come up. Many people think accuracy must be traded off against money or effort. In fact, you don't necessarily have to spend more or work harder to make an accurate outfit. You do need to research enough to know what one looks like. Guidance from a reliable source—which this book tries to be—will help.

🖋 ASSESSING YOUR NEEDS, BUDGET, AND SCHEDULE

Before you start leafing through suppliers' catalogs, make a general assessment of your needs, budget, and schedule. Writing down ideas and alternatives will help you think.

DECIDING WHAT YOU NEED

The first step in designing an ensemble is to figure out how you'll use it. Decide what historic period you'll focus on. If you need several outfits, design your first for the events you most frequently attend. Or give priority to the outfit that's easiest to assemble. Maybe you already own components, or the outfit can be bought from a vintage clothing store or reenactment supplier, or it's simple to sew.

Consider typical event settings. If they're dirty or outdoors, common sense dictates easily cleaned fabrics and dark colors. Keep outdoor dress lengths as short as the period allows. For warm weather use lightweight fabrics and hold garment layers to a minimum. No matter what season it is, you'll want an outer garment for evenings and cool days. You may need an additional, more protective one for bad weather.

Also consider the formality of events. For most periods there is a difference between formal and informal dress. For greatest flexibility, design an outfit that will work for both by changing one or two components.

If you'll engage in physical activity—dancing or even walking around all day—your outfit should be relatively lightweight

The reproduction information in chapters 2 through 4 applies to all periods, not just periods surveyed in chapter 1.

Although this book was written to help you make accurate costumes, I'm disturbed by the trend toward policing other people's. Negative or intrusive comments help no one and create an unpleasant atmosphere for all.

If you need an outfit immediately, ask friends to lend you one. Or sell you one they've grown tired of, or that no longer fits. Theater, opera, and film companies periodically sell old costumes; give local ones a call. Also consider renting from a costume shop.

and allow easy movement. Never wear poorly fitted or impractical shoes. Of course, period combat and some sports require specialized protective gear.

Plan all components of an outfit, including accessories, before making or buying any. Coordinate styles, colors, and trims. If you already own some components, think through how (or whether) to use them.

Circling items on the following list will help you mentally assemble a fashionable outfit for almost any period. If you need a specialized costume—for example a military outfit or occupational dress—you'll have to write in some items.

Undertunic/tunic/robe/overtunic
Undergown/gown/sideless gown/overgown
Dress (one-piece/two-piece/three-piece)
Suit (man's/woman's)
Paltock/pourpoint/cotehardie/doublet/coat/jacket
Sweater
Trunk hose/canions/slops/breeches/pantaloons/trousers
Skirt
Girdle/belt/sash/suspenders
Jerkin/waistcoat
Shirt/blouse
Partlet/stomacher
Neck ruff/collar
Jabot/stock/cravat/necktie
Neckerchief/scarf/boa
Wrist ruffs/elbow ruffles
Corset/brassière
Farthingale/bum roll/panniers/rump/crinoline/bustle
Overpetticoat/underskirt/forepart
Underpetticoat (one/two/three)
Chemise/slip
Combinations/camiknickers
Corset cover/camisole
Drawers
Hose/stockings/socks
Garters/suspender belt
Mantle/cloak/cape/shawl
Overcoat/outer jacket
Shoes/boots/slippers
Spats
Gloves
Apron
Hairpiece/wig
Crispine/caul/snood/hairnet
Wimple/barbette/veil
Hood/cap/hat/bonnet/evening headdress

Always wear a shirt or chemise next to the skin, even if it's unseen. Undergarments protect outer layers from perspiration and are easier to clean.

Fillet/coronet/tiara/bandeau/comb
Necklace/pendant/chain/watch/brooch/bracelet/earrings
Collar pin/stickpin/tie pin/studs/cuff links
Knee buckles/shoe buckles
Chatelaine and fittings
Eyeglasses/monocle/pince-nez/lorgnette
Beauty patches/mask
Bag/pouch/pockets/purse
Sword/dagger/knife
Parasol/umbrella/cane
Fan
Muff

OVERCOMING BUDGET LIMITATIONS

A good costume is an investment. One that's well made from quality materials lasts for years. Unlike your ordinary clothes, it will never go out of style. Until quite recently people wore their clothes as long as possible, with occasional retrimming or size alterations. This philosophy was, and still is, highly economical.

That said, here are some specific money-saving suggestions.

- Allocate a monthly costume budget. Save up for large purchases. Buy smaller ones on a per-month basis.

- Historic clothing isn't equally expensive for all periods. If you can, choose a period that doesn't emphasize opulence or that requires small quantities of fabric and trim. But skimping on materials for an inherently expensive period will just make your costume look cheap (and inauthentic).

- The informal and working-class wear of any period is usually the least expensive.

- Sticking to one historic period enables you to use the same undergarments for all your outfits. If you narrow it down—for example to the Civil War, rather than the Victorian era—you can use the same foundation garments.

- To get the most mileage from outer wear, make it in the period's simplest styles and neutral colors.

- Accessories are useful look changers. For some periods they can even transform an informal outfit into a formal one.

- Get the basics of your outfit first. If shoes or outer wear won't be seen much, get by on less authentic ones for a while. Some undergarments may not be crucial (but using incorrect foundation garments, or omitting them, ruins the look). Plan for authentic components, though, and add them as your budget allows.

- The cost of lace, braid, and other purchased trims can really mount up. Use self-fabric trims such as flounces, or make flowers or appliques from scraps. Or buy a patterned fabric—a brocade, stripe, plaid, or print—and use less trim.

- Shop for fabric and trim at sales or outlets, rather than skimping on quality. Stockpiling purchases for future costumes saves money only if you're realistic about your sewing schedule.

- Buy frequently used supplies—such as hooks and snaps—in bulk from a dressmaking/tailoring supplier. This saves shopping time as well as money.

- A mail-order catalog typically costs several dollars. Before buying every catalog for your era, try borrowing from friends. Some companies refund the catalog price with your first order. When you receive an order, the company may include a free catalog. You may be put on a regular mailing list.

- Compare mail-order prices. Reenactment suppliers are often forced to mark up merchandise bought from pattern companies, theatrical suppliers, and dressmaking suppliers.

- Compare shipping/handling charges. Some companies charge significantly more than others. And when a company sends the wrong merchandise, due to their error, make sure there is no additional charge for shipping a replacement.

- You may be costuming for enjoyment, rather than because you need an outfit right away. Choose a long, complex project that challenges your skills, rather than a quick one that costs the same amount.

SCHEDULING YOUR PROJECT

Assembling a complex costume requires you to make and/or obtain several garments. Sewing may consume your spare time for weeks, even months. I find that planning a project schedule helps me use my time efficiently. It's essential if you're determined to complete a project by a certain date (or have been hired to do so).

As soon as you list the items you need, decide which to make and which to buy. Research where to buy (see the section below); don't leave purchases to chance. You may want to mail order accessories, garments you can't sew (or don't have time to), and supplies not available in local stores. Start the mail-order process right away. There may be unexpected delays or disappointments.

Many people set a deadline of wearing a costume to a specific event. However, if the deadline is tight you may feel pressured or forced to compromise on quality. Because I'm costuming for fun, I only set deadlines I'm sure to meet.

For accurate fit, plan to make (or buy) garments in the order they're put on. First make undergarments that touch the skin, then foundation garments, then any undergarments that cover them. The top of most two-piece outfits overlaps the bottom, so make the bottom first. Make outer garments last. Unfitted accessories can be made during bits of spare time. But changing the basic order is the cause of most poorly fitted costumes you see.

Working backward, divide large tasks—such as the completion of each garment—among the weeks or months available. Does the division seem realistic, given your sewing skills and schedules for any previous projects? If you can't schedule large tasks within your final deadline, set a new one.

Now look at your sewing instructions to see what tasks are required to complete each garment. Distribute them roughly among the days you have time to sew. You don't have to be strict about this. But if it's clear you can't complete most daily tasks in a day, you need to rearrange your schedule.

Schedule a regular sewing time, even if half an hour is all you can manage. Resist being swamped by other activities. But be flexible enough to take advantage of times you feel especially inspired.

You can do handwork during low-energy activities such as listening to the radio or commuting on public transit. If your schedule is temporarily disrupted by travel, take some handwork along so you don't lose touch with the project.

✒ FINDING LOCAL AND MAIL-ORDER SOURCES

Before you decide on styles and colors, scout sources of reproduction supplies. It's smart to look into every source you hear of. You'll get the best idea of what's available, where, in what price range. You'll probably end up buying from several sources.

BUYING LOCALLY

I suggest buying fabric from a local store rather than by mail. In a store you can shop for yourself. Most fabric stores carry a good selection of plain fabrics and a few with designs suitable for reproductions.

Upholstery and drapery fabrics, which often have traditional designs, are sold in many fabric stores. Upholsterers can order a much larger selection, but seldom will for sewers. They may sell remnants and (smaller) discontinued samples, especially when moving or going out of business. Don't pay a pro-rated per-yard price. Remnants are too small for most garments. If you have an upholstery or drapery job done, ask for the remnants to be saved (it isn't done routinely). And casually ask whether the upholsterer wants to discard any others. When I had furniture reupholstered, I was given several large pieces of magnificent brocade that were lying around the shop.

Vintage clothing stores are the best source of clothes from the 1890s and later. They're worth checking out even if you're costuming for an earlier period. Turn-of-the-century chemises, drawers, and stockings can be worn under earlier styles (see figure 24). So can petticoats, though you may have to redistribute the gathering. Basic hat shapes are highly adaptable. You'll also find costume jewelry based on historic models. And some shops sell handmade lace, metallic braid, and other trims.

Some reproduction makers exhibit at reenactments and nostalgic crafts fairs. In my experience they focus more on capes, accessories, and jewelry than fitted clothes. Their merchandise may be painstakingly authentic, vaguely nostalgic, or individualistic wearable art. Much of it is lovely; but if you want an authentic costume, learn to distinguish authentic reproductions.

One good place to find reproductions of pre-Victorian jewelry is a museum store (or its mail-order catalog). Victorian

Chintz meant for home furnishing may have a glaze or waterproof finish that's unsuitable for clothes. You can sometimes get rid of this, especially if dry cleaning is recommended for an otherwise washable fabric. Machine wash the fabric several times with detergent. Rearrange it in the washer each time.

Chapter 5 contains detailed information on buying vintage clothes.

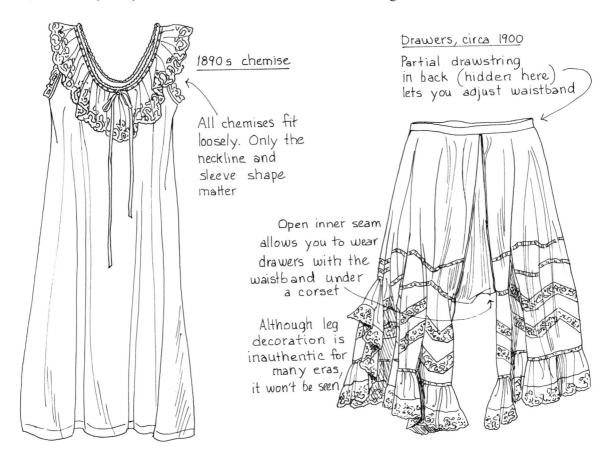

1890s chemise

All chemises fit loosely. Only the neckline and sleeve shape matter

Drawers, circa 1900
Partial drawstring in back (hidden here) lets you adjust waistband

Open inner seam allows you to wear drawers with the waistband under a corset

Although leg decoration is inauthentic for many eras, it won't be seen

Figure 24: Vintage lingerie that can be worn under many reproductions

costume jewelry is currently fashionable, and reproductions are sold in department and other mainstream stores. Be careful to choose pieces that aren't obviously brass-and-glass. Reproductions should always cost less than originals.

During the past few years I've seen many men's and women's shoes based on historic models. These include men's and women's Renaissance flat shoes, women's baroque brocade pumps, men's cavalier shoes, a great many women's Victorian ankle boots, and women's two-strap ragtime pumps. Although not museum copies, they're quite wearable. When a style passes out of mainstream fashion it should crop up in thrift stores.

BUYING BY MAIL

The larger reenactment suppliers carry most items reenactors need, for most eras. Their catalogs list esoteric sewing supplies, clothes, accessories, and "living goods"—things like Civil War style camping gear. Smaller suppliers focus on a range of items for one era. Or on specialized products, for example patterns or weapons. Unless you're lucky enough to have a local store catering to reenactors, you'll order from at least one company.

Send for every catalog that lists appropriate items. Don't hesitate to contact companies with questions about their merchandise or policies. Make sure you can return any item for any reason and get a full refund. The company will expect items to be returned unused (or unphotocopied), within a specified time period. This is only fair.

Because some companies are run on a part-time basis, there may be delays. If you must receive an item by a certain date, explain this when you order. If your merchandise doesn't arrive within six weeks, ask whether it (or your order) was lost in the mail. If the delay isn't the postal service's fault, politely but firmly request that the merchandise be delivered or your money refunded within the next month.

For some reason patterns tend to be listed well before publication. Your money may be tied up for months if publishing problems occur. Verify that patterns exist before you order. Find friends who've received them, see whether they're listed by larger suppliers, and/or call the company.

I don't recommend ordering most clothes ready-made. True, ready-made hoopskirts, capes, and unfitted garments can be worn by a person of average height. Authentic reproductions of shoes and other accessories may be available only by mail. But the main parts of your outfit should be custom-made—by you or someone else. Most historic styles were carefully fitted to the individual, and custom construction is the only way to get that fit. And it's the only way for you to exercise your own taste and quality control.

Adapting a modern garment never looks authentic. No matter what you do to a tuxedo or bridesmaid's dress, it looks like one. Modern nostalgic styles (such as those by Jessica McClintock and Laura Ashley) are instantly recognizable.

Reenactment suppliers seldom offer a large fabric selection, though some carry specially produced handwoven or uniform fabrics. If you must mail order regular fabric, choose a fabric store that has a swatching service. (Fabric clubs seldom offer anything suitable for reproductions.) Send them detailed information on the fiber and weight, color, and pattern. I'd send a short written description, a fabric scrap or paint chip of the color, and a photocopy or sketch of the type of design. Ask the store to send several swatches that match your idea. With luck, one will work.

If you're not sure whether you'll like a mail-order company's goods or service, place a small first order.

COMMISSIONING CUSTOM CLOTHES

Historic clothing should be commissioned from someone with experience in making it. If you go to a regular seamstress or tailor, you'll have to teach them about historic style and techniques. And they'll probably think the oufit is "weird" and wonder why they should spend much trouble on it—an attitude that won't produce good results.

Most living history groups have members who sew for others. Ask around. Or contact companies that sell custom clothing by mail. Be sure to discuss fitting procedures. Have the company send a muslin or lining (which a friend can help fit) before making the garment. They should also be willing to alter the finished garment if necessary.

An alternative is to call the costume department of a professional or university theater. Make it clear you want the costumer to use historic rather than theatrical techniques. Stage costumes are designed to look good from a distance, not close up.

When you find candidates, ask to see examples, or at least color photos, of their work. Get references. Ask these not only whether the work was satisfactory, but whether the costumer was businesslike and cooperative.

If you have little experience you may be relying on the costumer's expertise. But your needs can't be met unless you explain what they are. Before drawing up project specifications, review your assessment of your needs, budget, and schedule. Copy any pictures that strike you. Read the guidelines on choosing a pattern and materials. Dig up any potentially suitable ones on hand. Take all notes, pictures, and materials to your first meeting with the costumer.

A good costumer will listen closely. If the outfit you envision would be inauthentic, unflattering, technically impossible, or prohibitively expensive, the costumer should explain how and offer alternatives. Suggestions should be made without railroading you. Beware of the "artist" who insists on fulfilling his or her vision regardless of your needs, or who refuses to be bound by any schedule.

By the end of your first meeting, you and the costumer should have agreed on—and sketched—a design. Both of you should participate in selecting materials and trims. You may accidentally choose a material that looks authentic but is the wrong weight. The costumer may choose a color shade that they like more than you do. Either shop together or exchange swatches.

Also discuss the project budget and schedule. Expect to pay for materials when purchased. The costumer may charge for labor on either a per-project or an hourly basis. An hourly rate is safest from the costumer's point of view. But since you don't want your bill to be an unpleasant surprise, insist that the costumer provide an upper estimate (ceiling) for the project. Agree that you won't pay more than this estimate even if it's exceeded.

If there are several garments, set a completion date for each. The costumer is entitled to work for other clients. But once your schedule is agreed on, they should stick to it.

Put all terms of your agreement—including sketches—into a written, signed contract or work order. A contract is not a hostile instrument: it prevents, rather than creates, disagreements. Writing it will clarify whether you and the costumer really have agreed on what you've discussed. It may bring up questions you forgot to ask, but which should be resolved before the project begins. And it will induce both parties to take the terms more seriously.

✍ FINDING MORE INFORMATION

If chapter 1 describes the costume for your chosen period, you may want to skip this section. On the other hand, you may want additional information. Here's how to evaluate what you read and see.

- Researchers classify sources as either primary or secondary. Original information—for example a period portrait, fashion plate, or pattern—is primary. A source based on primary sources—for example a book on the history of costume—is secondary.

- Consult and compare as many sources as possible.

- Never accept statements—verbal or visual—without evaluation. Consider whether information is logical and consistent, and how the source might be biased.

- Be careful about older sources. Although the Victorians and Edwardians had a keen interest in costume, some of their research has been superceded.

- Note that repetition of a statement doesn't guarantee its accuracy. Sometimes writers use information from other books without verifying it.

Some fabric stores have bulletin boards where professional sewers pin their cards. You may find a card indicating a costuming specialty.

I'm surprised by the number of costumers who undertake large projects without a contract. And I know some who did what they thought the client wanted, then weren't paid because the client didn't like it.

The research techniques in this chapter are useful for dating vintage clothes as well as planning reproductions.

Most college libraries are open to the public and grant check-out privileges for a modest annual fee. If the college has a theater arts or clothing design program, its library may have a good selection of costume books.

Appendix A includes a bibliography of costume books and addresses for mail-order sources.

- If you can afford it, build your own library. It's convenient to have information on hand. And your public library may have few costume books, or refuse to let you check them out. Many costume books are printed in small quantities. Buy new books as soon as you see them and search dealers' catalogs for out-of-print ones.

- Even if you've read all your books, leaf through one or two at odd moments. You'll gain new insights each time. And you'll refresh your memory of where to find specific information.

- You'll see few original sources from before the Civil War. You can collect later ones. But it's cheaper and easier to buy reprints and pictorial anthologies.

- When looking at primary sources consider how they were used by people of the period. Submerge yourself in their culture, rather than trying to impose your own on it.

GETTING AN OVERVIEW

The best way to get an overview of European/American dress is to read histories of costume. These are entertaining, profusely illustrated books that survey styles and their relationship to cultural trends. A book that covers several centuries will place your chosen period in context. If it's a popular history, it will have lots of color photos but will focus on fashionable upper-class clothes and provide little technical detail. Such books are most useful early in your costuming career.

Histories aimed at theatrical costumers are less lavishly illustrated, but provide somewhat more technical detail. One that describes all the components of an outfit—fabrics, accessories, hairstyles—is most useful. There are also specialized histories that focus on one period, or a topic such as mourning wear or hats. Some are popular, others more academic.

RESEARCHING DETAILS

Before you make a costume, look at pictures of similar ones. This will give you an innate feel for the period that a written summary never will. You'll get ideas for styles and trims, and you'll be able to judge whether a pattern is authentic. And you can return to pictures for information your pattern doesn't provide. For example, it has an abnormally low waist when fitted and you want to make sure this is really correct.

A reasonable number of garments survive from the Elizabethan period on, in increasing quantities. Of course the earliest and most spectacular are in museums; but many have been photographed for exhibit catalogs. Catalogs are definitely worth accumulating because the garments are reliably identified and dated. The photos are high quality and seldom appear in other publications. The only drawback of exhibit catalogs is that most exhibits, like costume histories, focus on upper-class and couture clothes.

You don't need to attend the exhibit (though do if you can). When it's reviewed (usually in a costume society publication; see appendix A), any catalog will be mentioned. Write to the museum and ask to mail order it. Old catalogs are often available from costume book dealers. If the exhibit is very popular, an accompanying book may be published and sold in mainstream bookstores.

Paintings, especially portraits, are the main source of visual information before photography. You'll mostly work with photos of them in costume and art books. Go for size. Small photos obscure details.

When examining a portrait consider not only its date, but the subject's nationality, social status, and age. Most portraits are of the wealthy.

One potential pitfall is that people weren't always painted in the clothes you'd expect. Fifteenth-century religious paintings may show contemporary, ecclesiastical, stylized, and/or theatrical clothes. Some Renaissance and baroque portraits depict masquerade costumes. In the late 17th and early 18th centuries, there was a fashion for being painted in loose draperies. In the 18th and 19th centuries, portraits in fancy dress—classical, historic, foreign, or rustic—were held to be more timeless. Some costumes were painters' studio properties. Others were fancy dresses the subjects wore to balls. Don't rely on the text for information on which clothing is realistic. This is not an art critic's area of expertise.

When fashionable clothing is shown, the painter may have distorted it intentionally for artistic effect. Or unintentionally through an inability to deal with detail or perspective.

In addition to portraits, art sources include genre paintings, manuscript illuminations, drawings, engravings, woodcuts, sculptures, memorial brasses—anything that depicts people. These sources are more likely to show working-class, old-fashioned, and other nonmainstream styles. The artist doesn't have to be considered "great," but if they are you're more likely to see their work. Coffee-table history books, which appear regularly in remainder catalogs, often reproduce more unfamiliar pictures.

Photographic portraits were taken by professionals and enthusiastic amateurs from the 1840s on. Because the process was initially expensive most early photos represent the middle and upper classes. But by the 1860s the working classes could afford studio photography. Pictures of celebrities became available for public sale. And photography was used for reporting during the Civil War.

Naturally photographers and subjects wanted portraits to look attractive. People wore clothes they thought would photograph well and were becomingly posed, often against studio backdrops. Photos were retouched to overcome technical problems or reduce the subject's waistline. Another consideration for researchers is that color photography wasn't developed until the early 20th century.

In general, portrait photos are a reliable source. Unlike fashion plates, they show real clothes as worn by real people, including wrinkles and ridges. The biggest problem with original photos is that few are dated. Fortunately you can buy anthologies of period ones, accurately identified and dated, with descriptive captions.

The first pictures to emphasize clothes, as opposed to their wearers, were the costume plates of national and regional dress that appeared in the late 15th century. They proliferated throughout Europe in the 16th and 17th centuries. Costume plates were designed to satisfy curiosity about what foreigners wore, rather than to inspire imitation.

True fashion plates showing the latest styles were first published in France in the late 18th century. A tremendous number (some colored, some not) appeared in periodicals until the early 1930s. At this time fashion photographs, which were common by the late 19th century, took over. Because France was viewed as the fashion leader French plates circulated in America and Europe. Some were altered to suit national taste.

A customer would show fashion plates to a dressmaker or tailor, or vice versa, in the interactive process of designing an outfit. Plates were occasionally copied line for line. But more often they were used for ideas on colors, trims, or variations on the period's basic cuts. Completed garments tended to be simpler than fashion plates. As now, the fashionable ideal was too expensive, extreme, unflattering, or uncomfortable for many individuals.

Catalogs for ready-made clothes were intended for a mass market, therefore are excellent guides to what average people wore. Some ready-mades were available in city shops as early as the Elizabethan era. By the mid 19th century most components of a man's wardrobe could be bought ready-made. Women clung longer to custom clothes, but by the 1870s undergarments and simple wrappers could be bought by mail. By the 1920s a full range of ready-to-wear was available for both sexes. Most catalogs you'll see will date from the 1870s (when mail order really took off in the United States) or later.

One final source of inspiration is films. These fall into two categories: old films showing contemporary clothes and modern films showing historic costumes. From the 1920s through

Museum catalogs sometimes include photos of garments that have been sketched, or used for patterns, in other books. These are a useful cross-reference.

Pictorial histories, which consist of pictures redrawn from portraits and photos, are less accurate than the originals. Dictionaries of costume—word definitions with occasional drawings—are pretty useless.

When you read period novels, biographies, and diaries, look for comments that throw light on costume.

the 1940s, people were especially inclined to emulate the clothes, cosmetics, and hairstyles worn by Hollywood stars. Of course, they were rarely able to achieve the same glamour.

At their best, films costumed for an earlier period convey the impact of a whole society of living people wearing such clothes. At their worst, films contain jarring or even ridiculous anachronisms. Generally the most recent films—particularly English ones—have the most accurate costumes. However, I recommend using films as a source of inspiration only after you know enough to judge whether the costumes are accurate. The same can be said, by the way, of reproductions seen at reenactments.

You may be wondering why I haven't mentioned period sewing manuals, patterns, and fashion magazines published by pattern companies. That's because they're discussed in chapter 4, along with techniques for using them.

🦢 FINDING A PATTERN

Only a few years ago, if you wanted a pattern in your size you had to buy a fashion pattern vaguely reminiscent of a historic style. Then you had to alter the heck out of it. Or even design the whole thing, using a sloper (basic modern pattern) and flat pattern alteration techniques.

While good costumes can be produced by these methods, they have two major disadvantages. One is that any modern pattern follows modern assumptions about fit and seam placement. These don't hold true for other eras. For example, during the Civil War women's shoulder seams were positioned toward the back, rather than right on the shoulder line as now. Unless you knew a lot about design, you'd overlook this feature in favor of more obvious ones like a spreading skirt. Such small inaccuracies add up to a "not quite right" look.

The other disadvantage is that redesigning a pattern is work. Fortunately there's no need to. A respectable selection of sized reproduction patterns is available from small companies. Because these patterns aren't equally authentic or easy to use, you'll have to evaluate more than the envelope picture.

The catalog may say what original sources were used, in general and sometimes for specific garments. If not, ask. Patterns developed from modern slopers are least accurate, especially if designed to fit without period foundations. A pattern that specifies anachronistic materials or techniques may be OK if equal weight is given to period ones.

Patterns taken from original garments or sewing patterns are most accurate. Any company producing Victorian or later designs should be able to locate such sources. Some patterns for earlier periods resemble drafts in well-known books. If you can

When you date an actual garment, information from the original owner or a descendant may appear unimpeachable. Not so. Peoples' memories get blurred. Information is distorted as it's passed down. And many people need to believe in family legends, or that they own something old and valuable.

Chapter 4 explains how to use one-size patterns, including original sewing patterns, scale drafts, and patterns from vintage garments.

do your own fitting and instructions, you may want to just use the book.

You may notice that a friend made up the pattern, or another from the same company. Look over the garment, accounting for their sewing skills and any changes they made. Ask how they liked using the pattern.

MATCHING PATTERNS TO YOUR SEWING SKILLS

When deciding whether to tackle a pattern there are two things to consider: the complexity of the project and the quality of the pattern instructions.

You can make almost anything if you have patience and a good pattern. It's true that styles with lots of sections or trimmings are more time consuming than styles with few. But they're no harder (see figure 25). Although tight garments require more fitting, adjustments are pretty obvious.

Neat hand sewing requires care and practice. You'll have to do some, particularly on the outside of pre-1860s clothes. But you may want to postpone hand sewing entire garments till later in your career. Extensive surface decoration (such as quilt-

Dress, early 1880s

Bodice fits closely, but adjustments are obvious

Light but not featherweight fabric is easy to sew

Ruffles time consuming but easy to attach

Shape molded with underlining and padding

Heavy wool is harder to sew

Tail coat, circa 1825–1840

Figure 25: Styles that are easier or harder than they look

ing, pin tucks, or applied braid) requires precision whether it's done by hand or machine.

Tailoring is a word that makes many sewers nervous. True tailoring techniques involve molding the garment by padding, interlining, and pressing. To be honest, I don't suggest tailoring unless you have experience, a teacher, or great pattern instructions. However, many styles referred to as "tailored" don't actually require tailoring techniques. These include lightweight fitted jackets, and trousers, skirts, shirts, and blouses worn with tailored jackets.

The more detailed the instructions, the easier the pattern is to use. If possible, examine them (or instructions for another pattern from the same company) before purchase. Borrow from a friend or ask the company to send a sample.

Read the instructions while looking at the envelope picture. The materials list should include all materials mentioned in the instructions. Make sure all pictured sections and features are covered. Check whether cross-references are carried out. For example, if section B tells you to attach a belt, did section A tell you to assemble it? Period techniques should be explained in detail. Although not every step must be illustrated, make sure the most difficult and unusual ones are.

If you can examine the actual pattern, check how well its markings supplement the instructions. A grain line on each pattern piece is essential. Upper garments are much easier to fit if the waist is marked. Length alteration lines are also helpful. Printed seam allowances and notches aren't necessary if the standard seam allowance is explained. But darts, pleats, tucks, and other internal details must be marked.

If you love a pattern that's beyond your skills, consider making the garment in a sewing class (formal or informal). Or have all or part of it made by a professional.

If the instructions seem obscure, look for a similar pattern from another company. Or write your own using the information in chapter 4.

CHOOSING FLATTERING STYLES

Many reenactment periods are long enough to embrace several major style changes. And styles were interpreted differently by different countries, social classes, and age groups. Choose the style that's most flattering to you and practical for your situation.

You've probably read modern style guides explaining how to improve your appearance by following basic rules of line and proportion. For example, because horizontal lines make an area look wider, you're told not to wear horizontal stripes across your behind.

You'll experience a natural urge to beautify or improve on historic styles. But if you yield to it, you'll risk modernizing them.

Line rules hold true for historic styles as well. However, each era has different esthetics—1880s bustles intentionally made women look like they had large behinds. You may find a style that turns figure "flaws" into assets. Or an exaggerated one that completely conceals them (the modern ideal of "naturalness" is inappropriate for most periods).

Modern guides also advise developing the "look"—tailored, frilly, sophisticated, or whatever—that best suits your personality. Each period has its own characteristic look. If it's the same as yours you're in luck. But if not, figure out what features make up your look. You can probably find a style with most of them. Suppose your look is tailored, with simple lines, subdued colors, and tweedy fabrics. While you can't wear a tweed ball gown, you can wear a simple one in a subdued color.

Most pattern companies sell components of two-piece dresses and suits separately. You can mix and match bodices and skirts, jackets and trousers (see figure 26). You can make a day and evening bodice to match a single skirt, or two jackets to match the same trousers. You can even buy two bodice patterns and swap the sleeves, buy two skirt patterns and swap overskirts, or buy two dress patterns and swap trims. However, the patterns should be of about the same date, and the resulting style should correspond to a period one.

BUYING THE RIGHT SIZE

Naturally you have to take some measurements before buying a pattern. (If you haven't sewn for awhile, don't rely on old ones.) At this stage bust or chest, waist, and hip measurements are enough.

Some pattern companies have their own size charts. Buy the size indicated by the measurements on the company's chart, rather than your modern sewing or ready-to-wear size. If your proportions differ from the chart's, buying components separately eliminates some pattern alterations. Extra-large sizes are usually available. Custom sizes may be available on request.

The bust or chest is the hardest pattern area to alter. Therefore one-piece dresses, bodices, blouses, and jackets should be bought by bust/chest size. Men's shirts may be sized by either the chest or neck measurement. Purchase skirts by hip size. Men's trousers should be bought by waist size.

It's quite possible that your critical measurements fall between two sizes. Buy the smaller one if you're small-boned and/or the garment is loose fitting. Buy the larger size if you're large-boned or the garment fits closely.

If the company doesn't sell the pattern in your size, look for a similar style in another company's catalog. Or buy the closest size and fit the pattern using the techniques in chapter 3.

You may be varying the style by transferring garment sections between patterns. Both patterns should be the same size and preferably from the same company. The sections should be

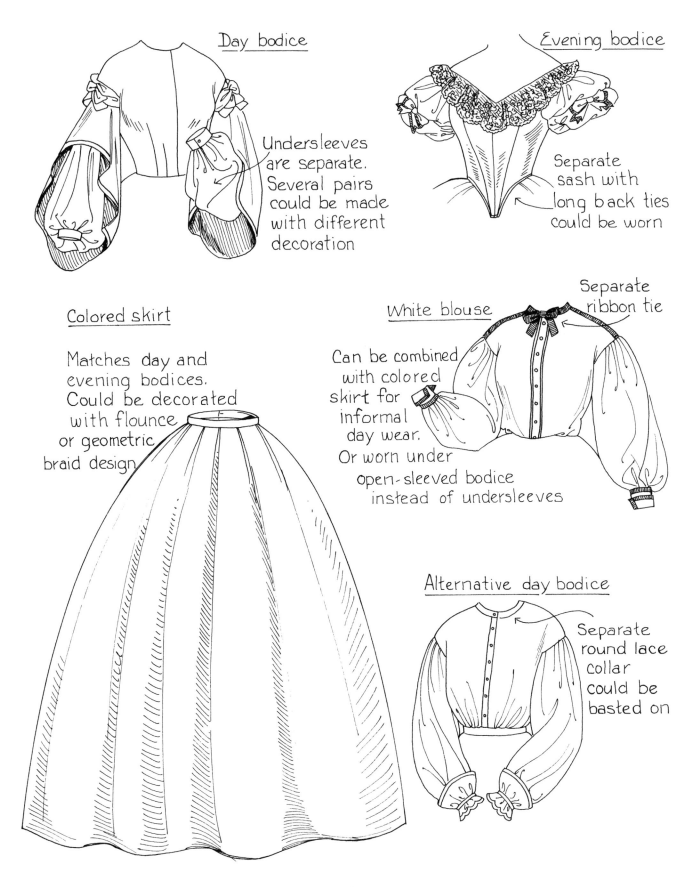

Day bodice

Undersleeves are separate. Several pairs could be made with different decoration

Evening bodice

Separate sash with long back ties could be worn

Colored skirt

Matches day and evening bodices. Could be decorated with flounce or geometric braid design

White blouse

Separate ribbon tie

Can be combined with colored skirt for informal day wear.
Or worn under open-sleeved bodice instead of undersleeves

Alternative day bodice

Separate round lace collar could be basted on

Figure 26: A mix-and-match Civil War outfit

the same shape where they're attached. For example, if a bodice requires a rounded set-in sleeve, substitute another set-in sleeve rather than a kimono one. Even if you follow these guidelines, extra pattern adjustments may be required.

⚛ CHOOSING MATERIALS

Fabric and trim are as important as style in creating an authentic effect. As with modern clothes, the fabric must be the right fiber and weight for the style. The color and design must be correct for the period.

The best way to coordinate your outfit is to buy all fabrics and trims before making the first garment. Or at least the first visible one. It seems reasonable to assume you can buy a basic fabric in an ordinary color at any time. However, materials go in and out of fashion just like clothes. By shopping ahead you'll be sure to get ones that work together.

I always buy extra of everything. I've found that materials lists can be imprecise. Slight pattern enlargements may require you to change the layout, which can use up more fabric than you thought. It's reassuring to know that if you spoil a section you can cut another, and that materials damaged during wear can be patched. And you won't want to replace all the buttons every time one gets lost.

FINDING AUTHENTIC FABRIC

Because so many modern clothes are made from synthetics, you're probably used to their essentially plastic appearance. But synthetics make period clothes look shoddy and inauthentic. Even if the material is partly natural, or used on only one area of one garment. Synthetics also trap heat and moisture. This is an important consideration with period outfits, which are heavier and more layered than modern ones.

In other words, reproduction fabrics and trims should be made entirely of linen, cotton, wool (including cashmere and other animal-hair fabrics), silk, or a blend of these. (There are some other cellulose fibers which are seldom found today.) The only exception is rayon, which is cellulose based. Rayon looks most natural blended with silk or cotton. I'm particularly fond of rayon/silk satins and brocades, and cotton velvet over a rayon base. But all-rayon fabrics (especially velvet) can definitely be too shiny.

Natural fibers come in many weights and finishes. Follow the fabric guidelines in your pattern (and chapter 1). Photos of period garments show what the fabrics look like made up.

Historically, fabric colors and patterns have been as important to fashion as garment cuts. Some periods favor bright col-

Leftover fabric and trim aren't a waste of money. They come in handy for lining or accessorizing future projects.

Embroidered mantle, circa 1130

12th- or 13th-century brocade

14th-century allover
embroidered heraldic pattern

Figure 27: Medieval textile designs

ors, others subdued ones or pastels. Sometimes strong color combinations have been fashionable, and sometimes a monochrome look.

Pay attention to the colors in photos of period clothes. It's tempting to apply your "season's" color chart from a modern guide, but the combinations will be inaccurate for some periods. Instead, choose a predominant (or close-to-your-face) color that appears in both your chart and the photos. If necessary, choose less flattering but historically accurate colors for the rest of the outfit.

Some people assume natural dyes always produce subdued earth tones, and that these are the only authentic colors for pre-Civil-War clothes. Earth tones were typical of home dyeing with local dyestuffs. But even in the Middle Ages, professional dyers could achieve bright, clear colors. By the mid 19th century the use of natural dyes was extremely sophisticated.

Authentic designs are harder to find than appropriate colors (see figures 27–34). First look at clothing and textile photos till you get a feel for the period. Are designs simple or complex? Abstract or pictorial? If pictorial, what do they represent? How large are they? How do they work with garment styles?

From a partlet,
circa 1576

From a sleeve,
circa 1598

From a sleeve,
circa 1573

Figure 28: Elizabethan blackwork embroidery patterns

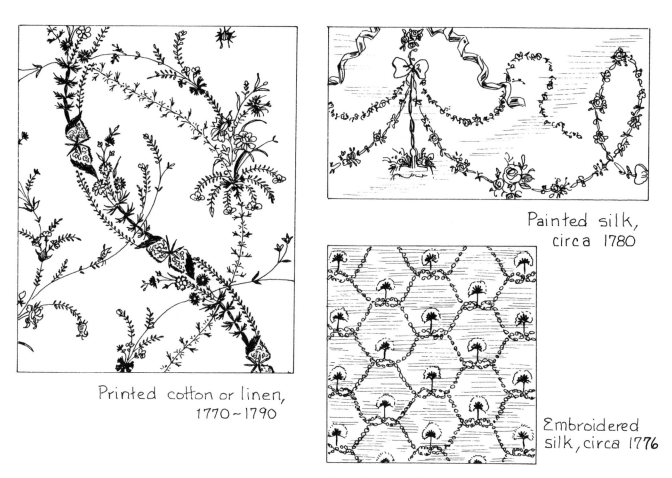

Painted silk, circa 1780

Printed cotton or linen, 1770~1790

Embroidered silk, circa 1776

Figure 29: Colonial era textiles

Designs can be woven, printed, or embroidered. The technique, as well as the design, should be appropriate. Substituting a print for a brocade just doesn't work.

The simplest woven patterns—such as stripes and checks—are easy to find. Many modern dress brocades have oriental (or modified oriental) designs. These are great for eras when oriental fabrics were popular in Europe and America. Some Indian silk saris are usable for the "classical" styles of 1790–1820. Upholstery and drapery brocades often feature historic European designs, sometimes accurate copies. Select a lightweight one that isn't too stiff.

Fabrics were block printed in imitation of brocades as early as the 12th century. But generally speaking prints are inappropriate for periods before the early 17th century, when Indian calicos were first imported into Europe. Eighteenth-century-style prints are available in cotton drapery, and sometimes dress, fabrics. And many fabric stores carry faithful copies of William Morris and Liberty designs.

High-quality machine embroidery can look convincingly like hand embroidery. However, you'll find only regular, repeated designs. There are some excellent imported cotton

Chapter 5 explains how to buy vintage materials.

Leather and furs are authentic for some garments, as are knits for comparatively modern styles. But special techniques for sewing them are outside the scope of this book.

Pine cone is traditional shawl motif

Figure 30: Detail of an 1820 cashmere shawl

eyelets in both fabric and trim widths. These have many uses in 19th- and early 20th-century reproductions.

What about real antique fabric? Although few pre-1930 fabrics can withstand extensive sewing and wearing stress, later ones may. Using them might be the best way to get luxury fibers and handwork at a good price. If you can't find a large piece of fabric, or are worried about its durability, use it for only part of the garment. The fabric may already be made up—say into a wedding dress. Unpick the dress till it lies flat. Mark a grain line on each piece by basting between two vertical threads. Press the pieces, then cut them like new yardage.

You may wonder whether some fabrics are too much for your sewing skills. I've found that ease-of-use depends mostly on weight. The heaviest fabrics, such as outer coat wools, tax the motors of some home sewing machines. Rent an industrial machine—they sew anything. The lightest fabrics, such as silk organza, pucker and get dragged into the feed dog. I prefer to sew such fabrics by hand. Slightly heavier fabrics, such as handkerchief linen, can be given body while stitching by placing tissue paper underneath. Then tear off the paper and pick out any remaining bits with tweezers. Velvet and satin are common bugaboos because they're slippery. Just baste all seams closely before sewing (and press velvet over a needle board). Or buy a walking foot for your sewing machine.

CHOOSING LININGS, UNDERLININGS, AND INTERFACINGS

Many garments require a lining or underlining, and perhaps some interfacing. All should be compatible with the garment fabric. That is, they should be an appropriate weight and color, pressable at the same temperature, and cleanable by the same method.

Technically, a lining is a complete inner garment that is sewn independently, then attached to the outer garment so that no seam allowances show. A lining provides a very attractive inside finish and, if slippery fabric is used, makes the garment easier to put on. Because it's seen when the garment is removed, a lining should be made of garment-quality fabric.

Coats, capes, wraps, and both outer and suit jackets are almost always lined. Silk or rayon, in a plain, taffeta, satin, or brocade weave, are the best fabric choices. Check period pictures to see whether patterned fabrics and strong color con-

Muslin with woven stripes and resist-printed rose pattern, circa 1860–1863

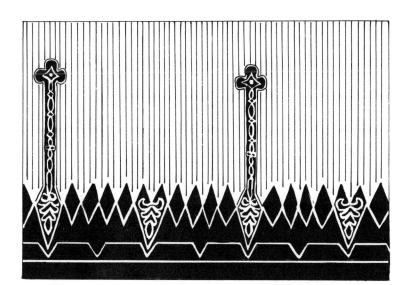

Wool/cotton fabric with woven stripes and appliqued velvet and braid pattern, circa 1870

Figure 31: 1860s textile designs

trasts were used. Skirts, dresses, vests, and other nonouter garments may be lined. The fabric should be lighter weight than for a coat. Lightweight silk linings are best for lace garments.

An underlining is cut from the same pattern as the garment, but each underlining section is handled as a unit with the corresponding garment section. An underlining provides body rather than enhancing appearance. Underlinings have been used for most nonouter garments. Whether you should use one depends on period construction techniques and the garment fabric weight.

Closely woven cottons make good underlinings. The color shouldn't show through the garment fabric. Fancy turn-of-the-century dresses were underlined with taffeta. This is prettier than cotton, but more susceptible to perspiration damage.

Interfacing is an inner layer that provides extra body in specific areas, such as button plackets and waistbands. Self-fabric interfacings, or scraps of closely woven cotton in a similar color, are usually suitable. If more body is needed, buy a stiffened commercial woven interfacing. Never use iron-on interfacing. It spoils the period impression, complicates cleaning, and is no easier to apply.

Linings are a great way to use up leftover fabrics and colors that don't quite go with your complexion. But don't let economy mislead you into using a fabric that doesn't work for the garment.

Theater costumers underline most garments. They refer to underlining as "mounting" or "flatting."

1894 silk
with peacock feather pattern

1901 velvet
with ribbon-and-floral
voided pattern

Figure 32: 1890s textile designs

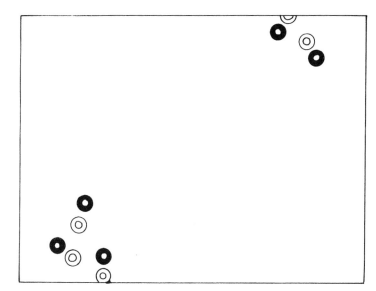

Small, rather widely
spaced patterns

Figure 33: 1910s printed silks

CHOOSING LACE AND OTHER TRIMS

I love lace and use it extensively. But few modern laces are suitable for reproductions. To get the right lace you may have to hunt around and spend more money than you'd like. But the results are worth it.

No matter what your budget, never, never use nylon or polyester lace. It looks totally plastic. Most new natural-fiber laces are cotton.

Also avoid colored lace. During much of history, lace was expensive even for the rich. Because it was reused until it wore out, lace was made in shades that would coordinate with any fabric. These were natural off-white (not yellow), black, metallic gold, and metallic silver. The Victorians sometimes used colored wool lace. Antique lace held tremendous cachet for the Victorians and Edwardians. To make lace look older, they dyed it ecru with tea, coffee, or a mixture. Art Deco lingerie laces are a pinker shade of beige. Some 1910s and 1920s dresses use colored net or lace fabric. And that's about it for permissible lace colors.

Although lace designs have been important to fashion, what people notice in a reproduction is the lace's general effect.

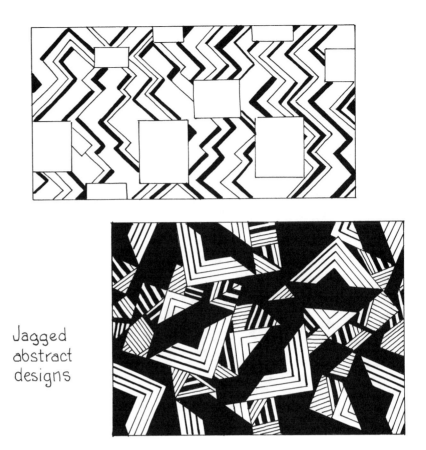

Jagged abstract designs

Figure 34: Art Deco prints

If you can't find an authentic design choose one with a similar scale and density. If you can't find the right width, sew two or more different laces together. Or two lengths of the same lace. Patterns should be aligned in a planned way.

I use vintage laces wherever possible (see figures 35–37). My favorites are the bold handmade laces from the turn of the 20th century, which were designed to give a 17th- or 18th-century effect. These are sold by vintage lace and clothing dealers. I've found that linen and cotton laces are sturdier than fabric of the same age. But most silk ones, and black laces in any fiber, are too weak for use.

Delicate machine laces of the valenciennes type are quite available, especially in narrow widths. Unused ones are sold by heirloom sewing and dollmaking suppliers, as well as vintage dealers. Some are old store stock and some are reproductions. It's hard to tell the difference.

Stockpile laces you like because it's difficult to find them on short notice. The longest lengths are most useful. Small circular pieces such as doily edgings are least useful. Compare the price of the lace for a reproduction to a similar vintage item. Try to pay less, because you must add the cost of the fabric and your labor.

Any hand lace costs more than machine lace. Always verify that the lace really is handmade, because it's not uncommon for an otherwise knowledgeable dealer to mislabel a lace. When in doubt, assume the lace is machine made.

Machine lace is made of cotton, silk, wool, or synthetic thread, but not linen (which is stiffer than cotton). Hand lace is generally linen, cotton, or silk.

The structure of hand laces is clearly visible. (You'll need a magnifier to examine very fine ones.) A fuzzy appearance indicates machine manufacture. Even a well-made hand lace is slightly irregular (check the straight edge). Hand crocheted, knitted, and tatted laces look more three-dimensional than their machine counterparts.

Examine the back of embroidered net, whitework, and other embroidery. In machine embroidery threads are carried across the material with perfect regularity. In hand embroidery you can see where ends were tucked in. Machine embroidery often minimizes the amount of thread in back, giving a sketchy, flattened appearance.

Purchased trims other than lace include braid, fringe, tassels, and ribbon. These too should be appropriate for the era.

I'm defining "lace" as any open, airy trimming or fabric. This includes needle lace, bobbin lace, filet (lacis), crochet, knitting, tatting, battenberg (tape) lace, and net. Lace experts consider handmade needle and bobbin lace to be the only "true" laces. But this distinction is unimportant to sewers.

If you sew pre-1930 lace, trim, or fabric to a reproduction, the entire garment must be hand washed or hand dry cleaned. Small lace pieces, such as collars, can be basted and removed for separate cleaning.

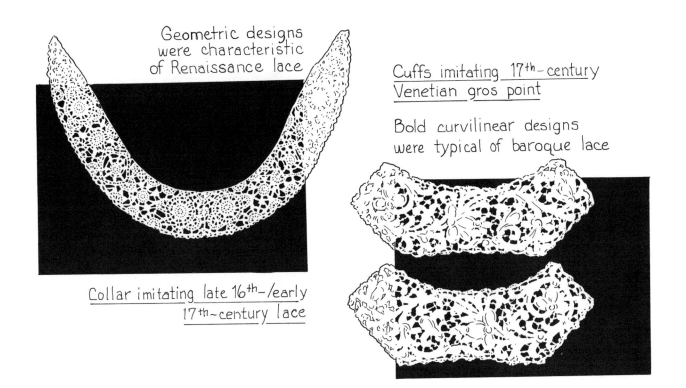

Geometric designs were characteristic of Renaissance lace

Collar imitating late 16th-/early 17th-century lace

Cuffs imitating 17th-century Venetian gros point

Bold curvilinear designs were typical of baroque lace

Figure 35: Handmade turn-of-the century lace copying earlier designs

They must made of natural, or at least natural-looking, fibers. Ribbons should not be wired.

The best trim sources are large fabric stores and specialized trim shops. Vintage trims are rarely found in quantity. Upholstery shops carry heavy fringe, braid, and tassels suitable for some Victorian clothes.

Metallic laces may be stocked in the braid section. Choose shades as close to natural gold and silver as you can get. I have a weakness for a slightly tarnished look. I don't like bright metallics and figure that historic ones didn't look new for long.

Some people use embroidered or woven braid to simulate hand embroidery. This looks authentic only where a straight narrow strip with a regular design would have been used. Much historic embroidery is more free-form. Of course, braid or patterned ribbon was used as such during many periods. You can use striped floral upholstery brocade as an alternative. Cut apart the stripes, turn under the edges, and apply like braid.

Silk ribbon, both patterned and plain, is becoming more available. If you can't find it at a fabric store, try heirloom sewing and dollmaking suppliers.

A sewer's yard sale may feature unused lace in currently unavailable designs. If it's over 10 years old it may have a mellowed vintage look. Vintage-looking hand crochet is another likely find.

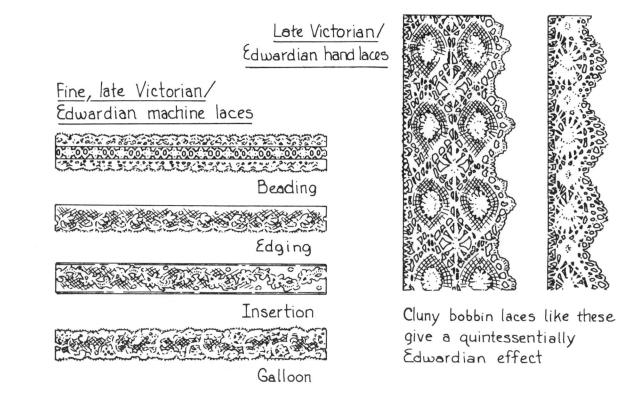

Late Victorian/ Edwardian hand laces

Fine, late Victorian/ Edwardian machine laces

Beading

Edging

Insertion

Galloon

Cluny bobbin laces like these give a quintessentially Edwardian effect

Figure 36: Commonly found turn-of-the-century laces

BUYING NOTIONS

The most obvious notions are closures. Depending on the garment, these may be tapes or other ties, pins or brooches, clasps, hooks and eyes, snaps, or buttons. Closures can be concealed or visible. Some, such as buttons, may be purely ornamental.

Velcro is not only unhistoric, it doesn't hold well under strain. The zipper wasn't widely used till the mid 1930s. Elastic was incorporated into garters, suspenders, corsets, and boots as soon as rubber was vulcanized in the mid 1840s. But I've seen few garments with elastic from before the late 1910s, when it was used to hold in blouse bottoms. Although buttons can be made of many natural substances, most plastic imitations look unnatural.

Reproduction metal clasps, belt buckles, and buttons are available from fabric and museum stores as well as reenactment suppliers. Plain mother-of-pearl, wood, and metal buttons are sold in most fabric stores. Fancy natural buttons can be found at some fabric stores, crafts fairs, and vintage clothing and button shops.

A few specialized notions are required for foundation gar-

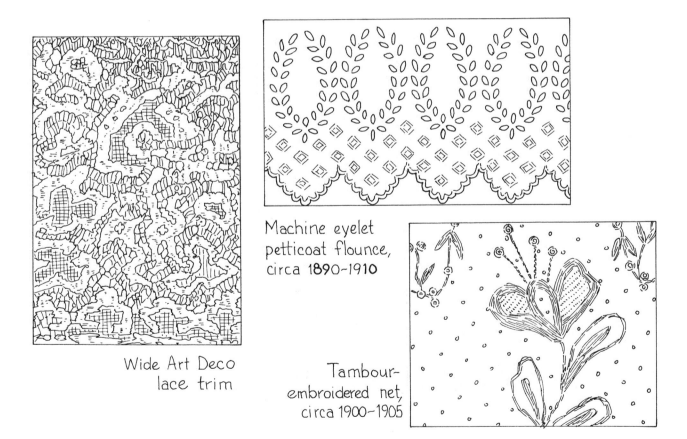

Wide Art Deco
lace trim

Machine eyelet
petticoat flounce,
circa 1890-1910

Tambour-
embroidered net,
circa 1900-1905

Figure 37: Vintage lace fabric and wide trims

ments: corset boning, corset clasps or busks, metal eyelets, and hoop wire. There are few choices. Most reenactment and theatrical suppliers distribute the same items.

Corset boning can be continuous plastic yardage, separate metal bones, or spiral wire boning (see figure 38). I like the plastic. It gives a period shape while being more comfortable than metal, it's easy to work with, and it's available in fabric stores. If you need a lot of support, you may prefer metal. Spiral boning is necessary where bones must curve.

Metal bones and corset clasps come in a limited number of lengths. You may need an in-between length. Buy the bones too long, cut them with a hacksaw, and round the ends with a file. Some suppliers sell a tipping solution for the cut ends.

As far as I know, busks for pre-Victorian corsets are not commercially available. However, a wooden ruler or yardstick can be trimmed to the correct shape and the rough edges sanded. If you need an especially sturdy busk (to dance the volta, for example), you can use a narrow aluminium strip about 1/8 in. thick. Several widths are sold in large hardware stores; look in the screen-door section. Cut the strip with a hacksaw and file the ends smooth.

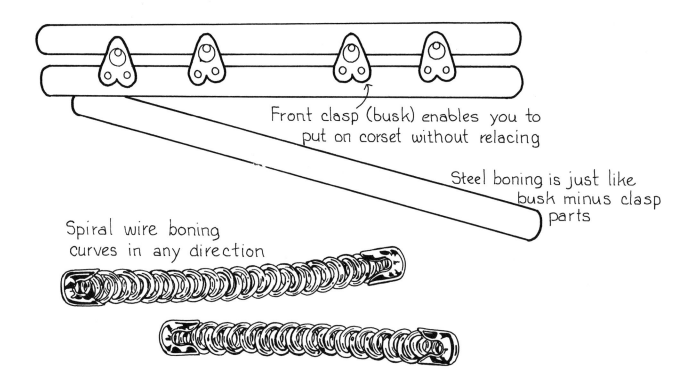

Front clasp (busk) enables you to put on corset without relacing

Steel boning is just like busk minus clasp parts

Spiral wire boning curves in any direction

Figure 38: Corset boning and clasp

Although some people use plastic boning in hoops, I prefer metal hoop wire. It supports heavy materials better and is just as comfortable. You'll need tin snips to cut it. U-tips are sold for covering the sharp ends.

I also like metal corset eyelets (grommets) because they're sturdier than hand-embroidered ones. Fabric stores sell them in gold or silver color, in several sizes. You'll need an application tool; a different size is sold for each size eyelet. However, metal eyelets look too glaring on outer garments. For these I work hand eyelets using a blanket stitch. A wire ring can be placed underneath for strength.

Corset laces aren't really a specialty item. Just buy boot laces at a shoe store. Or buy metal or clear plastic tips from a sewing supplier and add them to any colored cord. The Victorians used two or three shorter corset laces, which gives not only finer control but more options in laces.

Synthetics are acceptable in completely concealed notions like bias tape. In my experience cotton, polyester, and blended sewing threads all serve equally well and look about the same. You'll need buttonhole or strong embroidery thread for hand buttonholes and eyelets, and heavy thread (such as quilting thread) for pulling in cartridge pleats. Thread should be one shade darker than the dominant fabric color or a precise match, but no lighter.

Details are what make a garment look truly authentic. Particularly if they're obscure, or unusual by modern standards.

A detail doesn't look accurate just because it existed during the period. It should have been fairly common. For example, one of my reference books shows a zipper with a patent date of 1905. But in years of collecting, I've never seen a pre-1930 garment with a zipper.

3 Making Your Costume

The clothing of any historic period has distinctive styles and fabrics. It may require a few unusual sewing techniques. But most sewing skills can be transferred from era to era. This means any sewing experience will help in making your costume. And if you're a raw beginner, you'll start building that experience now.

This chapter assumes you're using a modern reproduction pattern. It supplements such patterns with information on historic fit and sewing techniques.

✄ ALTERING A PATTERN

Even if you bought the correct size pattern, you'll probably have to do fitting alterations. Human body shapes aren't standardized. Many period styles require a customized fit. And some historic patterns aren't as polished as those from large companies. You may also want to do style alterations, adding or changing period details.

You'll have to go through at least two fitting stages: altering the paper pattern and fitting a muslin (sample garment). If you've made drastic alterations or the pattern is very rough, repeat the process till the muslin fits well. Be patient. It's worthwhile to spend as much time as necessary perfecting the pattern. Major changes may be impossible after you've cut out the garment.

To alter a pattern and make a muslin you'll need these materials (most are also necessary for sewing the garment):

- *A flexible tape measure.* To measure yourself, curved seams, and sewn garments that aren't amenable to a straight ruler.

- *A pocket calculator.* Optional, but makes it easier to deal with arithmetic and cuts down on errors.

- *Rulers.* I have a 6 in. ruler, a 12 in. one, and a yardstick. A small ruler is easier to handle, so use the smallest one that works.

- *An L-square.* For drawing alteration lines and rectangles.

- *A set of french curves.* For redrawing curved lines.

- *A hip curve.* Optional, but useful. Get one marked off as a ruler. The top often works for redrawing armholes.

- *A double tracing wheel.* Optional; for drawing new cutting lines.

- *Writing tools.* A soft writing pencil and an eraser. Ink is hard to erase and will accidentally stain fabric if you leave the pen lying around.

- *Pattern paper.* This can be commercial pattern paper dotted at 1 in. intervals, scrap paper, or graph paper.

- *Cheap scissors for cutting paper.* Paper blunts garment shears.

- *Adhesive tape.* Of the "scotch" type.

- *Scrap fabric for muslins.* Any firmly woven medium-weight scraps will do; they can be different colors. It's helpful to use a muslin fabric with some similarity to the garment fabric. For example, you can use heavy scraps for an outer garment, or striped ones to test the effect of stripes.

- *A cardboard cutting board.* To protect the cutting table.

- *Straight pins.* Silk pins are best for delicate garment fabrics, so buy them if you only want one type of pin.

- *Sharp garment shears.* A large pair for cutting out and a smaller one for trimming seams, etc.

- *Thread or embroidery scissors.* For cutting thread.

- *Safety pins.* Helpful for fitting tight garments.

- *Tailor's chalk.* For marking fabric.

- *Dressmaker's carbon paper* (ordinary carbon smudges). Convenient but not essential for marking muslin fabric. Don't use it on garment fabric. No matter what the package says you can't be sure marks will wash out.

- *A regular tracing wheel.* For transferring pattern marks to muslin fabric or pattern paper. These can damage delicate fabrics.

- *A sewing machine.* Although muslins can be pinned or hand basted, machine sewn ones are more accurate and easier to fit.

- *Machine and hand basting thread.* Any thread in any color will do. Basting is a great way to use up spool ends and old, fragile thread.

- *A steam iron.* Pressing is important when making muslins, as well as garments.

- *Ironing boards.* You'll need a sleeve board as well as a regular ironing board.

- *A tailor's ham.* For pressing curves.

- *A dress form.* This is optional but useful for fitting muslins. Get one that can be adjusted to your measurements by repositioning sections (most flexible for figure changes) or padding. Men's forms are available.

- *A full-length mirror and a hand mirror.* Necessary if you're fitting on yourself. Use the hand mirror to check the garment back.

ALTERING FIT

Most sewers keep a complete chart of measurements on file. These should be retaken once a year or whenever there's a change in your weight or body shape (which isn't always correlated to your weight). Historic pattern companies, like modern ones, assume measurements are taken over modern underwear. You'll need a friend to help. Use figure 39 or 40 as a guideline and fill in your chart as you go. The tape measure should be pulled taut and close to your body, but not tight.

Cut out the pattern pieces before altering them. Leave wide margins. Otherwise you may have to tape on extensions when widening seams. Although this is easy it makes the pattern harder to pin. If you need to tape on paper, use pattern sheet scraps or other paper of the same weight. If heavy paper and tissue are combined the tissue shreds when you cut out. Press the pattern with a warm, preferably dry iron.

You alter a period pattern using the same techniques as for a modern one. Only the most common alterations are described here. You may use other methods you've learned, or experiment. It's usual to make routine fitting adjustments on paper—you'll find that your figure type requires you to make similar adjustments to most patterns. The rest can be made in the muslin.

When altering a pattern, retain the basic shape of each piece. The grain line should stay in position and the altered piece should lie flat. Altering the center front and center back may cause distortion. Avoid altering darts unless the muslin shows this to be necessary. Be sure to alter all related pieces. For example, if you shorten a skirt above the hips the overskirt must be shortened the same amount in the same place.

Compare your measurements to those of the assumed wearer as described on the company's size chart. This is more accurate than measuring the pattern. The pattern has added fitting ease, so you can move. Its back waist length is shorter than the wearer's if the neckline is lower. The pattern also has style ease, fullness added in certain areas to create the distinctive style.

Determine how much to add or subtract in each area. Do length alterations first because they change where width is positioned. For width alterations, divide the amount among the number of garment sections to be altered. Keep in mind that if a pattern piece is cut twice, it makes two sections. Many

Not all measurements are needed for all patterns. But it's useful to keep a complete chart on hand.

If a pattern is unavailable in your size, buy the closest size and do more alterations. You can also use commercial grading techniques. These are too complex to cover here; see the book list in appendix A.

High bust _____

Bust _____

Diaphragm _____

Waist _____

High hip _____

Full hip _____

Hip depth _____

Back waist length _____

Front waist length _____

Bust point _____

Back width _____

Front width _____

Shoulder _____

Neck _____

Upper arm _____

Wrist _____

Shoulder to elbow _____

Elbow to wrist _____

Total arm length _____

Waist to floor _____

Thigh (pants only) _____

Knee (pants only) _____

Calf (pants only) _____

Ankle (pants only) _____

Crotch depth (pants only) _____

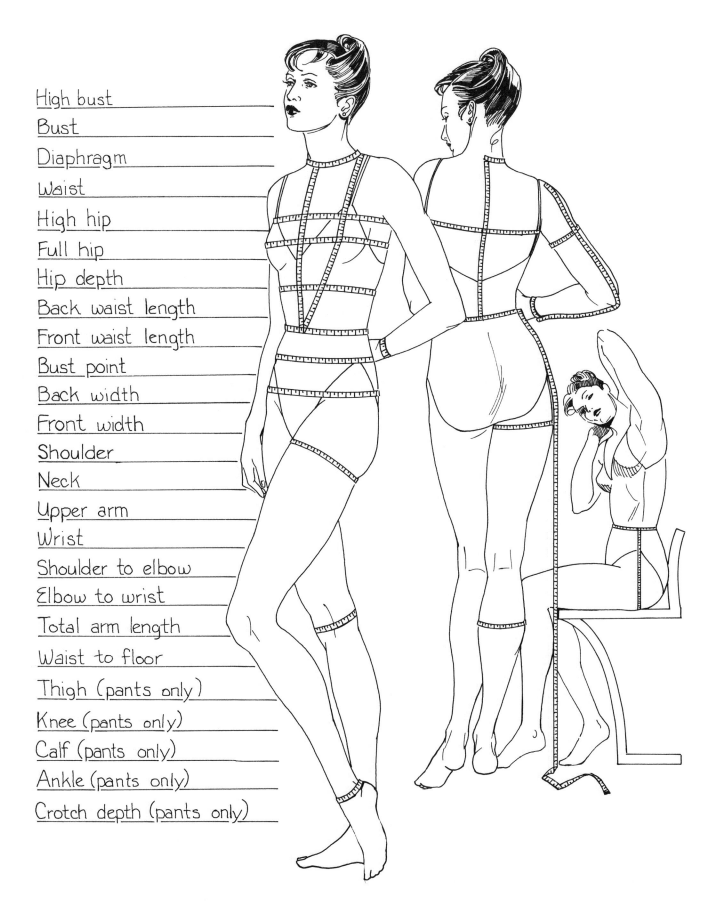

Figure 39: Measurement chart for women

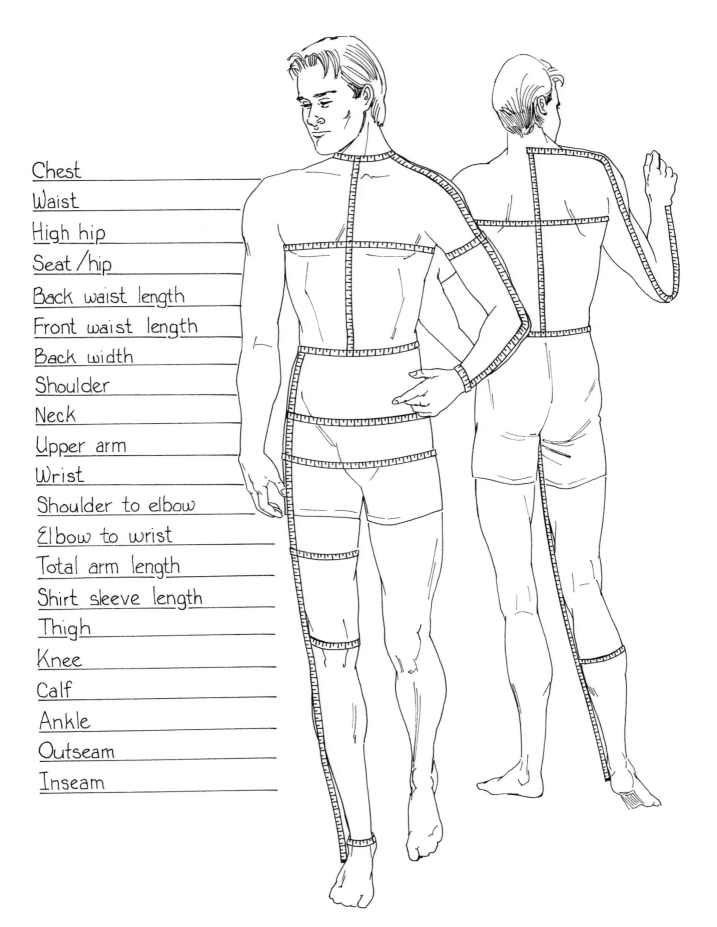

Chest _____

Waist _____

High hip _____

Seat /hip _____

Back waist length _____

Front waist length _____

Back width _____

Shoulder _____

Neck _____

Upper arm _____

Wrist _____

Shoulder to elbow _____

Elbow to wrist _____

Total arm length _____

Shirt sleeve length _____

Thigh _____

Knee _____

Calf _____

Ankle _____

Outseam _____

Inseam _____

Figure 40: Measurement chart for men

women are exactly one size larger on the bottom than the top. In this case you can connect different size lines from a multisize pattern without doing detailed calculations.

Be conservative about reducing pattern size, in either width or length, till you see the muslin. It's good practice to leave 1 (or even 2) in. allowances on the side and center back seams for fitting, and for letting out the garment if you gain weight. Some sewers make all seams 1 in. Never make seams narrower than 1/2 in. on the final pattern. If less bulk is desired, trim them after sewing. Seam lines should stay regular, which means new lines must be tapered into the originals.

If your back waist length is short or long, alter the bodice length. Shortening isn't essential for loose tuck-in upper garments unless you want to save fabric. For an Empire waistline make all length alterations in the skirt.

To alter bodice length:

1. Figure the difference between the size chart's back waist length measurement and yours. (You can usually ignore the front waist length.)

2. All bodice pieces are shortened or lengthened the same amount in the same way (see figure 41). To shorten, mea-

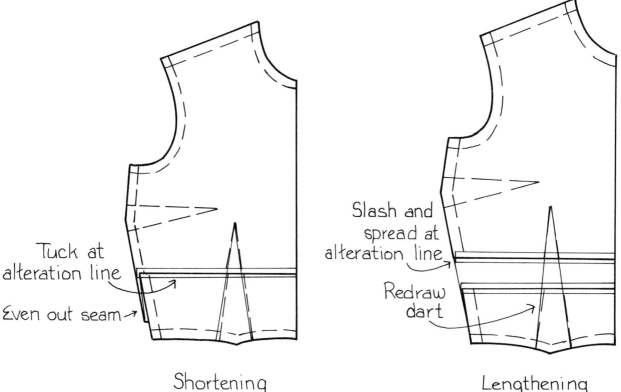

Figure 41: How to shorten or lengthen a bodice

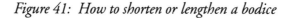

Making Your Costume

sure up the correct amount from the length alteration line. Using a ruler, draw a parallel line there. Crease the pattern between the two lines. Fold the tuck up and tape it down.

To lengthen, slash the pattern at the alteration line. On pattern paper draw an identical line, and another the correct distance above it. Or use graph paper. Lay the original alteration line over your duplicate. Lay the other cut edge over the new line. Tape down.

If there is no alteration line, draw one 1 1/2 in. above the waist. If the alteration line or waistline is marked on only some pieces, lay the adjoining pieces next to the marked ones. Measure both seams from the bottom (you'll need a tape measure for curved seams) to see exactly where the line falls on the unmarked piece. Mark it and draw across the pattern at right angles to the grain. If the waist position is completely unmarked, you can often figure it out by the pattern curves.

3. Smooth each vertical seam line by adding and subtracting an equal amount from the original one. Redraw vertical darts from the wide end to the point, using a french curve if necessary.

4. Trim excess pattern paper.

There are several places skirt length can be altered. If the skirt is fitted to the hips, you may need to alter it above the hip line. If not, or if you're short- or long-legged, you may need to alter the skirt below the hips. Both areas may require alteration.

To alter hip depth:

1. Compare your hip depth measurement to the size chart's. If the size chart doesn't include one, measure the pattern to the hip line—where the pattern curves out most at the sides—with a hip curve or tape measure.

2. If there is an alteration line, tuck or spread the correct amount as for a bodice. If there is none, draw one halfway between the waistline and the hip line.

3. Redraw seams (using a hip curve or large french curve) and darts as for a bodice.

To alter skirt length:

1. Compare your skirt length measurement to the size chart's. Subtract the amount of any hip depth alteration. The remainder is the amount the skirt should be altered at the bottom.

If there's no skirt length measurement, calculate the difference between your height and the "average" person's. Modern pattern companies consider this to be about 5 ft. 6

The best location for alteration lines varies with the style. Draw them where vertical seams are fairly straight; if possible avoid darts unless their length needs changing. Alteration lines should be perpendicular to the grain line. Mark the alteration line at the seam. Align an L-square with one arm along the grain line and another reaching the mark. Then draw the alteration line.

in. for a (barefoot) woman and 5 ft. 10 in. for a man. Then subtract bodice length, as well as hip depth, alterations. Leave the skirt longer rather than shorter and remember that hoops, or even just petticoats, take up skirt length.

2. If there are no alteration lines, on a full-length skirt draw two. One should be about 4 in. below the hip line and the other 4 in. above the skirt bottom. Tuck, or slash and spread, as for a bodice. Remember to leave a hem allowance.

3. Redraw seams.

Trousers and other nether garments may also be altered between the waist and crotch and/or at the bottom, in the same manner as a skirt.

A fitted sleeve is usually altered both above and below the elbow so that the curve, dart, or gathering falls at the elbow when the arm is bent. A loose sleeve may be altered in one place only.

To alter sleeve length:

1. The size chart probably doesn't give separate shoulder-to-elbow and elbow-to-wrist measurements. Although it's useful to compare your total arm length to the chart's, also pin the pattern around your arm to see where the elbow falls.

2. On the alteration line or lines, tuck or spread the pattern as for a bodice. Redraw the vertical seam lines.

   If there are no alteration lines, draw the top one about 4 in. above the elbow. On a full-length sleeve draw the bottom one about 4 in. below it.

If you bought the correct size pattern, you don't need to alter the bodice bustline or the hips of a separate skirt. You also don't need to alter very loose garments such as chemises. Alter full, gathered or pleated skirts at the waistband only.

Other styles may need hip and/or waist adjustment. Methods vary according to the amount of alteration. Most circumference alterations are made only at the sides. For complex styles you may need to alter other seams to keep sections in the right place on the body.

To make a reduction of 1 in. or less to the waist and hips of a bodice, skirt, or one-piece dress:

1. Compare your waist and hip measurements to the size chart and figure out how much to reduce. Divide this by the number of sections to be altered. This is four if you're altering the side seams only.

2. Mark the alterations at the waist and hip.

3. Draw a new seam line that tapers into the old one. End

tapering just below the bust (indicated by a horizontal dart, the point of a vertical dart, or the widest part of the bodice pattern). Taper as far below the hips as is necessary to retain the basic pattern shape.

To reduce the waist but not the hips, taper to above the original hip line.

To make a reduction of more than 1 in. to the waist and hips of a bodice or skirt:

1. Compare your hip measurement to the size chart and figure out how much to reduce. Divide this by the number of sections to be altered.

2. For a bodice, draw a diagonal alteration line from the bottom seam line, between the side seam and any vertical dart, to the side seam line just below the bust. (See figure 42.) For a skirt, draw the line from the top seam, between the side seam and any dart, almost to the hem (or as far as needed for the pattern to lie flat when overlapped). Slash along the line.

3. Overlap the cut edges the correct amount and tape.

The waist and hips of a one-piece dress are reduced over 1

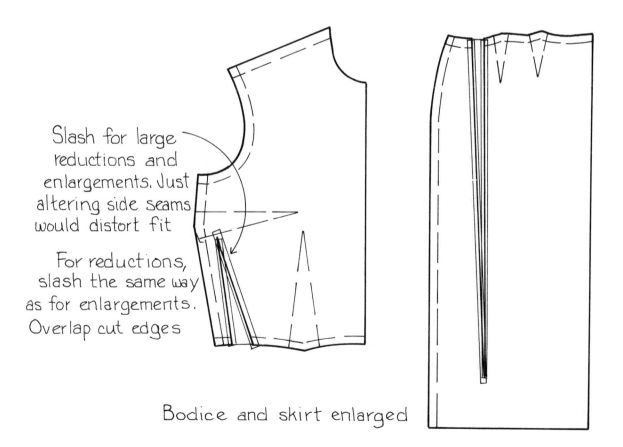

Slash for large reductions and enlargements. Just altering side seams would distort fit

For reductions, slash the same way as for enlargements. Overlap cut edges

Bodice and skirt enlarged

Figure 42: Slashing lines for altering a dress more than an inch

in. by redrawing the side seams—no slashing is required.

To enlarge the waist and hips of a bodice, skirt, or one-piece dress:

1. Compare your waist and hip measurements to the size chart and figure out how much to enlarge. Divide this by the number of sections to be altered.

2. If the alteration is 1 in. or less, tape pattern paper under the seam. Mark the waist and hip alterations. Redraw the seam line from below the bust to below the hips.

3. If the alteration is more than 1 in., slash the pattern in the same places as for reductions. For a one-piece dress you'll also need a horizontal slash at the waist (so the other slashes can be spread). Put paper underneath the slashes. Spread them the correct amount. Tape down.

To enlarge only the hips of a long bodice, skirt, or one-piece dress:

1. Compare your hip measurement to the size chart and figure out how much to enlarge. Divide this by the number of sections to be altered.

2. If the alteration is 2 in. or less, tape pattern paper under the seam. Mark the hip alteration. Taper into the original seam line.

3. If the alteration is more than 2 in., slash parallel to the grain line all the way through the bottom edge (see figure 43). A long bodice or one-piece dress will also need a horizontal slash at the waist. Put paper under the slash(es). Spread the vertical slash evenly and tape.

4. Redraw the skirt top or dress side seam line. Reduce the side seam at the waist if necessary.

Trousers are altered at the waist and hips the same way as a skirt.

Chapter 7 gives step-by-step instructions for altering finished garments.

ALTERING STYLE

The easiest way to alter a pattern is to substitute style elements from other period patterns. These can be garment sections, style lines, or trims. I copy pattern pieces before altering them because I might want to start over or use the originals for some other project. Copying can be done either by photocopying or tracing the pattern.

A fitted garment section to be swapped in must be the same shape as the original where it's attached. Suppose you're swapping jacket lapels. Compare and measure the seam lines (not the pattern edges) of the new lapel and the original. If they're different, fold the original along the seam line. Lay it along the new lapel's seam and use it as a template to redraw the line on the new lapel. Fix the seam allowance where necessary.

If the new garment section is gathered—for example you're adding a fuller sleeve—you may not need to change the seam line.

You can also use another pattern as a template for drawing low-cut necklines, intricately shaped edges, and other style lines. Of course, there's nothing to stop you from drawing style lines yourself, using a ruler and french curves. Just be aware that the more changes you make, the more you'll have to fit the muslin.

Applied trims, such as fabric appliques or flounces, can also be swapped. Although it's convenient to use patterns for straight flounces, these are easy to draft yourself. First test the scale by draping fabric or paper across your body. Unless you're a skilled artist it's best to copy complex designs for surface trims, such as ornately curved braid. As well as sewing patterns, sources include period magazines, embroidery and other textile arts books, collections of historic ornamental motifs, and even historic coloring books. Trim designs can be resized by photocopying. Many trims that change a garment's look require no

Chapter 4 explains how to alter style using the flat pattern method, how to draft simple shapes, and how to resize with a photocopier.

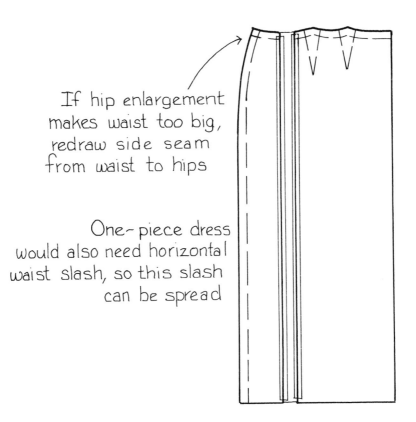

If hip enlargement makes waist too big, redraw side seam from waist to hips

One-piece dress would also need horizontal waist slash, so this slash can be spread

Figure 43: How to enlarge hips more than two inches

pattern; for example border braid, gathered lace, seam piping, and ribbon bows.

FITTING A MUSLIN

It's essential to make a muslin for any fitted period style. The muslin should include all close-fitting sections, any whose fit or proportions you're unsure of, and any sections needed to hold these together. The main bodice sections and the sleeves are always made up. Full skirts seldom are. Skirts and trousers that are fitted at the hips are usually made up to below the hips, or full length if desired. Berthas, overskirts, and other pieces applied to the basic sections are optional. Waistbands, tight cuffs, and suchlike should be tested even if the sections gathered into them aren't.

It's common to make up only one side of the garment. However, I find that fit and appearance are easier to check if I make up both sides, including sleeves.

The muslin should be cut out as accurately as the final garment, so use the instructions for garments below. Transfer sewing marks (such as pleats) by placing dressmaker's carbon under the pinned pattern and scoring the marks with a tracing wheel. In addition, transfer any position marks to the right side of the fabric. These include the center front, center back, and waistline (a marked waistline is crucial for corsets).

I fit a muslin in several stages. For example, when making a dress I assemble the bodice, sleeves, and skirt and fit each separately. Where changes are required I unpick, press, and restitch seams. For drastic changes I recut the section. I then baste in the sleeves and refit the bodice. If I'm testing sections applied to the basic bodice or skirt, I add those next. Finally, I attach the bodice to the skirt and study the overall effect.

You can stay stitch seams that are especially likely to stretch, using the method described below, but remember you'll handle the muslin less than the garment. Then pin and sew the muslin using a large machine stitch. Leave seams likely to be adjusted on the outside. Press during assembly as for the finished garment. Raw edges (such as a neckline to be faced, or a waist seam before the skirt is attached) should be pressed under. First clip curves to the seam line.

The muslin absolutely must be fitted over everything to be worn underneath. You can fit either on yourself or a customized dress form. Both have advantages. Fitting on yourself tells you how the garment feels, as well as how it looks. You'll need a helper, who doesn't have to have sewing experience but must be able to follow directions. You must maintain good posture throughout the fitting.

Fitting on a dress form enables you to work alone. A form

doesn't fidget, can have pins stuck into it, and can be left dressed if fitting is interrupted. It enables you to study the garment from any angle. However, you must try on sleeves and trousers unless you own a dress form with limbs.

Dress forms are often marked at the waist (and other position lines). If yours isn't, or you're fitting on yourself, mark the waist by tying a tape around it. Put the muslin on you or the form. Adjust it till it sits as well as possible. Pin closures, including overlap.

Be very particular when fitting. An error of 1/4 in. is noticeable. Make sure adjustments don't distort the grain or seam positions. Pin seams (or darts or pleats) to be taken in equally on both sides of the muslin. Rip seams to be let out and pin. Fold edges under more or less as needed, clipping curves to make seams lie flat. Mark any other changes with chalk.

Although period styles differ, here are some general fitting rules.

- The muslin should be neither too tight nor too loose, either all over or in one area. Closures and vertical seams shouldn't strain. The neckline and armholes shouldn't gap (but they'll be pulled in somewhat when the collar and sleeves are attached). You should be able to make any movements required when you wear the garment (remembering that many period styles are more restrictive than modern ones). If the garment fabric is much heavier than the muslin, or the garment is boned, fit the muslin loosely.

- The center front and back should be aligned with the body center front and back. Side seams should divide the body front and back equally. They should be perpendicular to circumference lines and the floor. Circumference lines (the neckline, armholes, waistline, wristline, and hemline) should follow natural body curves. Vertical design lines (such as pleats) should be perpendicular to the floor.

- The waistline should be at the correct level for the period (or all garment proportions will look wrong). This is often above or below the natural waist. The sleeve elbow should be exactly at the body elbow when the arm is bent.

- Bust and hip darts should point directly to the fullest part of the curve. They should be neither too long nor too short.

- The fabric grain shouldn't be distorted. The center front and back should be on the lengthwise (warp) grain and perpendicular to the floor. At the hip and bust the crosswise (weft) grain should be horizontal as far as the point of the bulge. In sleeves the lengthwise grain should be straight

Some old sewing manuals recommend using the muslin as a garment lining. However, unless the muslin is a throwaway you'll feel inhibited about changing it.

You can fit a muslin simply by taking in and letting out fabric till a perfect fit is obtained. But for instructions on solving specific problems, refer to one of the modern sewing manuals listed in appendix A.

You can use a plumb line to check whether grain lines and seams are truly vertical or horizontal. Tie a metal weight, such as a large washer, to about 5 ft. of strong string or twill tape.

from the center of the shoulder tip to the elbow. The crosswise grain of the sleeve cap should be perpendicular to it. Where the grain runs on the bias it should be symmetrical on both sides of the body. Adjusting ease often corrects grain distortion.

- Seam lines should be flattering. Curved lines should look graceful. The garment should appear balanced on the body.

Although most alterations should be made in the muslin, it's wise to recheck the garment bodice before inserting the sleeves. And skirt and trouser hems must be marked when the garment is almost complete.

FINISHING THE PATTERN

Once the muslin fits perfectly, transfer the changes to your sewing pattern. In addition, you can add marks to make the pattern easier to use.

1. Even out pin, chalk, or stitching lines on the muslin, using chalk and a ruler or french curve.

2. Measure from the old seam and dart lines to the new ones on the muslin, then on the pattern. Draw the new lines on the pattern.

   If changes are complex you can take the muslin apart and press under the new seams. Trace the outline onto pattern paper. Use a ruler and french curves to trace against, or to clean up the traced lines. Copy marks from the old pattern by measuring as described above. Or trace by laying the old pattern over the new one and scoring lines through with a tracing wheel. Then go over them with a pencil and a ruler or french curve.

3. Alter related pattern pieces to conform to the ones they're sewn to.

4. Adjust seam allowances so that all seams are 1/2 in. (or whatever standard you're using). Side seams can be 1 in. or wider to allow for later alteration. At curved seams, lay a transparent ruler over the seam line and mark at such short intervals that the marks join (see figure 44). Or use a double tracing wheel and go over the marks with a pencil and french curve.

5. Extend short grain lines. Lay a yardstick along the original line and continue to the pattern edges.

6. Add any notches that will help match patterned fabrics or assemble the garment. Carefully measure a seam on both pattern pieces and pencil a mark where they'll join. Or chalk across the sewn muslin seam and transfer the mark.

7. You may want to cut the garment fabric in a single layer (see below). It's convenient to extend pattern pieces designed to be cut on the fold, and to copy marks to the backs of all others. Draw a line on pattern paper to represent the fold line. Turn the pattern over (to the wrong side) and lay its fold line along the paper's. Trace the pattern outline. Copy marks as described above. Cut out the extension. Turn the original pattern back over and tape it to the extension at the fold line.

Most pattern paper is translucent, so printed marks on the other pieces should be visible from the back. Just turn over and pencil trace, using a ruler and french curves where necessary. Or copy the whole pattern piece to speed cutting out.

Save the muslin until the project is complete. You may want to recheck measurements or test a new idea.

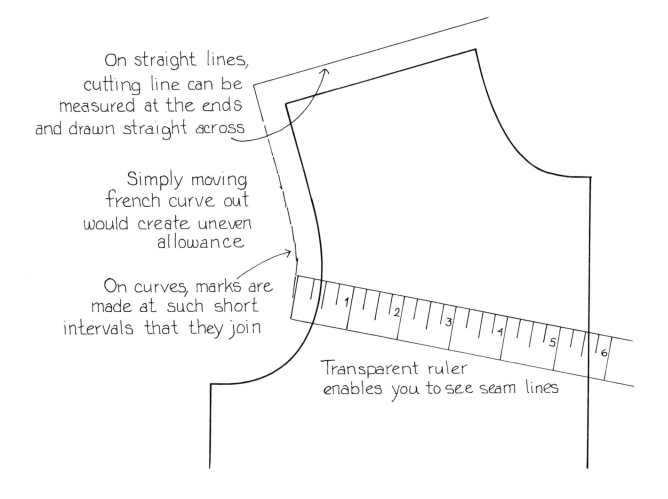

On straight lines, cutting line can be measured at the ends and drawn straight across

Simply moving french curve out would create uneven allowance

On curves, marks are made at such short intervals that they join

Transparent ruler enables you to see seam lines

Figure 44: One way to draw cutting lines

✐ PREPARING TO SEW

Occasionally fabric is off-grain when purchased—the warp and weft threads aren't at right angles. Most sewing manuals recommend yanking or ironing the grain into position. This seldom works, so I advise against buying off-grain fabric.

You can test whether a material will shrink, calculate the amount of shrinkage, and figure out how much extra you'll need. Measure and cut a sample a few inches square. Preshrink, then measure again. To calculate the total shrinkage, divide the original measurement of the sample by the shrunk measurement to obtain the adjustment factor. Multiply this factor by the amount of material recommended. The result will be the amount you really need.

All fabric and trim should be preshrunk before cutting to prevent seam puckers, garment shrinkage, and running dyes. Washable materials can be shrunk by washing and drying like the garment, then pressing. Tie lace or braid into an old pillowcase before machine washing so it won't tangle around the agitator. Alternatively, you can soak washables in the hottest tap water for half an hour to an hour, then press until dry. Because dry cleanables shrink when steam pressed (which is part of both sewing and dry cleaning), I preshrink the yardage by pressing it at least twice.

Straighten both short ends of the fabric by cutting along a visible weft thread or, for finer fabrics, pulling one out and cutting along the run. Never tear off the ends—this stretches or damages most fabrics.

LAYING OUT THE PATTERN

You'll need to do your own cutting layout if the pattern doesn't include one. Or you may want to change the layout for a variety of reasons: you've altered the pattern (even small alterations change a close layout), your fabric width is different from that suggested, or your fabric type is different (for example, it's velvet but there's no "with nap" layout). By measuring this layout you can determine or confirm the amount of fabric needed.

Layout is usually done on the fashion fabric. But if the fabric hasn't been bought, a trial layout can be done on a floor or cutting table marked with the fabric width. Ideally the pattern should be altered first. If not avoid very close layouts and assume some extra fabric will be needed.

Experiment with different pattern piece arrangements till you find the one that uses the least fabric. I arrange the large pieces first and fill in the cracks with the rest. Align grain lines precisely with the selvages (long fabric edges). Otherwise the garment will hang badly. A pattern edge parallel to the grain line can be laid right on the selvage. Selvages provide an excellent finish for the edges of flounces and bulky seams.

Any fabric can be cut in a single layer, and I feel this is always more accurate. Single-layer cutting is imperative for some fabrics: slippery ones like silk, satin, velvet, and brocade, and fabrics with designs that need careful positioning. Other fabrics can be cut folded in half. The most efficient layout may involve cutting some pattern pieces from a double layer and others from a single.

Most fabrics that require single-layer cutting also require a nap layout. That is, one end of the fabric must be designated as the top and the tops of all pattern pieces oriented toward it.

This is because napped and shiny fabrics appear to be different colors when viewed from different angles. Fabrics with directional designs—for example, flowers growing upward—also require a nap layout.

Wash even clean-looking vintage lace. A surprising amount was never preshrunk.

When modern pattern companies suggest fabric widths they assume that if one or two pattern pieces are wide the whole pattern must be cut from fabric wide enough to accommodate them. However, until recent decades sewers were accustomed to a variety of fabric widths and to piecing (seaming) fabric before cutting large garment sections. I piece fabric often. I've found that the seams are invisible if placed in an inconspicuous spot such as the underarm, near a skirt hem, or under a wide tuck. Busy fabrics can be pieced almost anywhere if the design is well matched.

To piece, place the pattern piece so it covers as much fabric as possible (see figure 45). Where it's too wide, sew a scrap (from cutting out other pieces) onto the selvage, matching the design and grain (use another selvage for the best "seam" finish). Then cut out. An alternative is to create a garment seam in some logical place.

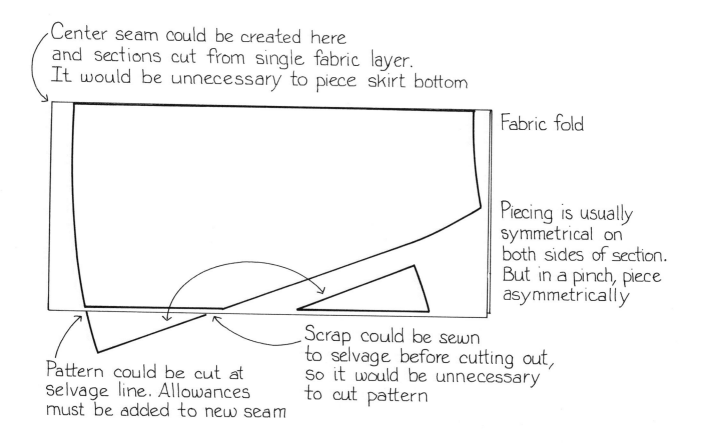

Center seam could be created here and sections cut from single fabric layer. It would be unnecessary to piece skirt bottom

Fabric fold

Piecing is usually symmetrical on both sides of section. But in a pinch, piece asymmetrically

Pattern could be cut at selvage line. Allowances must be added to new seam

Scrap could be sewn to selvage before cutting out, so it would be unnecessary to cut pattern

Figure 45: How to piece a garment section

If the fabric has a border along one or both selvages; has large motifs; or is a stripe, plaid, or check; the layout must be customized to the fabric design. This invariably uses more fabric. Customize layout according to the seams, not the pattern edges. Remember to account for overlapping closures and garment sections.

Border prints, eyelets, and laces are often arranged so that the border falls at the hem and any flounce or overskirt edges. Edwardian whites use eyelet borders to good effect—along V-necks, across bodice tops and cut-in-one kimono sleeves, down set-in sleeves, around sleeve bottoms, along cuffs and waistbands, and down skirt fronts. Border layouts often require reversing the crosswise and lengthwise grain (aligning grain lines with the fabric top/bottom), and piecing.

The positions of large woven or printed motifs should be intentional. Experiment till you find the most attractive placement for each pattern piece. I aim to put the dominant motif in the center of each piece, except at center front and back closures where I put it a slight distance from the closure edge (so it doesn't look crammed). I then adjust pattern pieces so that (if possible) no motif is chopped. If there are both large and small motifs I place small pieces only on small motifs.

When pinning the pattern I carefully measure each motif's vertical and horizontal distance from the seams. Needless to say, this measurement should be identical for two sections cut from one pattern piece. When piecing a motif I seam it in the middle. I thrust pins vertically through both fabric layers till the motif alignment is exact. Then I pin the seam for sewing as usual, remove the vertical pins, and sew.

Fabric stripes can run either vertically or horizontally, on the fabric itself and on the garment. If the suggested layout runs in the wrong direction, reverse the crosswise and lengthwise grain. Stripes should run in one direction throughout most garment sections; vertical stripes are most flattering. However, waistbands, cuffs, men's shirt yokes, and other such small sections are often cut with the stripes horizontal. And one or more large sections can be cut with a reversed—or even diagonal—stripe direction for authenticity or dramatic effect.

If stripes are vertical, the edge of one stripe (the most dominant if there are several) should fall exactly at closure edges and the centers of other garment sections. If stripes are horizontal, the edge of one stripe should fall exactly at straight skirt, flounce, and sleeve hems. The middle of one stripe should fall in the middle of narrow horizontal sections like waistbands and cuffs. Many stripes (and plaids) are easier to arrange using a nap layout.

At slanted seams the stripes will form an angle. Where possible they should meet. If a dart changes the grain direc-

If you don't have quite enough fabric, use scraps of coordinating fabric for facings or contrasting garment sections.

Reversing the crosswise and lengthwise grain, or using the bias, changes the way the garment drapes. Don't change the grain unless the fabric design has more visual impact than the drape.

Some printed and embroidered motifs are, when examined, actually stripes and should be laid out the same way. So should ribbed fabrics like wide-wale corduroy.

tion, match stripes as far along the seam as you can. For a two-piece garment or suit, stripes should be matched to form continuous lines or rows. Some period cuts prohibit matching; for example skirts where bias seams are sewn to straight. If examples show that such a nonmatch was accepted, feel free to use striped fabric.

Plaids, and checks 1/2 in. or larger, should be laid out following the same principles as for stripes. However, plaids are more difficult because their stripes not only cross, but are several widths and colors. The plaid may be even (with a perfectly square repeat), or uneven. Test by folding the fabric diagonally through the center of any repeat, then by folding vertically or horizontally through a repeat center. (See figure 46.)

It's best to use plaids only for simple styles consisting mostly of large garment sections. Small sections, often impossible to match, can be cut on the bias. Draw a bias grain line at a 45-degree angle to the lengthwise grain.

Where designs must match, baste seams with a slip stitch (described in chapter 6) before sewing.

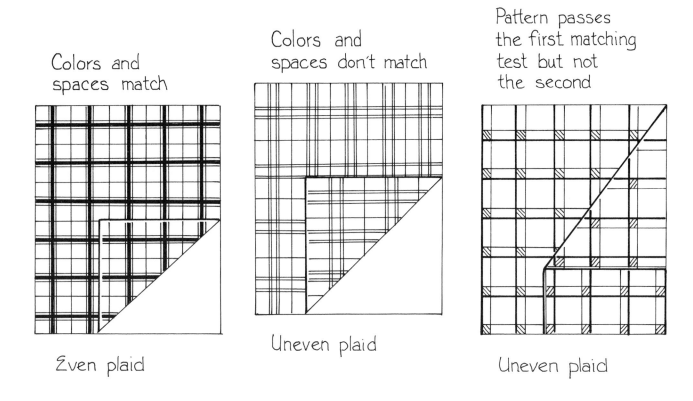

Colors and spaces match

Colors and spaces don't match

Pattern passes the first matching test but not the second

Even plaid

Uneven plaid

Uneven plaid

Figure 46: Even and uneven plaids

CUTTING OUT

Construction is more efficient if you cut out and prepare all fabrics before sewing, including the outer fabric, lining or underlining, and interfacing. Trims can be cut during construction when needed.

Napped and shiny fabrics can be cut with the nap running down for a deeper, richer color, or running up for a lighter shade. Plain fabrics should be cut with a consistent right side. If it's not obvious which side this is, choose the one with the cleanest selvage finish.

Press the fabric right before cutting. Put the cutting board on a large table, or if necessary the floor. Arrange the fabric on it in a precise rectangle, using the printed marks on the board. For ease in marking, lay fabric to be cut in a single layer right side up. Fold fabric to be cut double with the right sides together; pin the layers at the top and selvages. If the selvages buckle, clip them every few inches till flat. Smooth out wrinkles.

Even silk pins may leave permanent marks in satin and other delicate fabrics. Pin these within the seam lines only, while both cutting and sewing. While cutting secure pattern pieces in the middle with commercial pattern weights, or a substitute like heavy (and clean) metal washers. Weights also keep slippery fabrics from migrating off the cutting table.

Press pattern pieces with a warm dry iron. Lay them in their approximate positions. Measure from a selvage to each grain line with a yardstick (if cutting double along a fold, the fold is on the grain). Adjust the piece till the grain line is precisely aligned with the selvage. For stripes and plaids, also make sure that stripes meet; that is, that the notches indicating seam joins fall on the same stripe. (See figure 47.) Secure by pinning or weighting along the grain line.

Smooth the pattern piece. Pin to the fabric, placing pins at right angles to the edges and about 1 in. apart. Don't distort the shape during pinning—I place pins alternately on opposite sides. Or place pattern weights in the middle, at each corner, and wherever else they're needed to secure the piece.

Cut out, holding the pattern down with your free hand. Cut notches outward (cutting inward weakens seams and promotes fraying).

Unless your cutting surface is enormous or your garment small, you'll cut pattern pieces in several batches. Realign the selvages and resmooth the fabric for each batch. If necessary restraighten the cut short end. If cutting in a single layer, first cut each pattern piece printed side up. Transfer marks and remove pins. Then turn the piece over, cut the other side, and mark.

Save all fabric scraps of a reasonable size till you finish the garment. They're useful for small sections not cut from pattern pieces, and for testing sewing and pressing techniques.

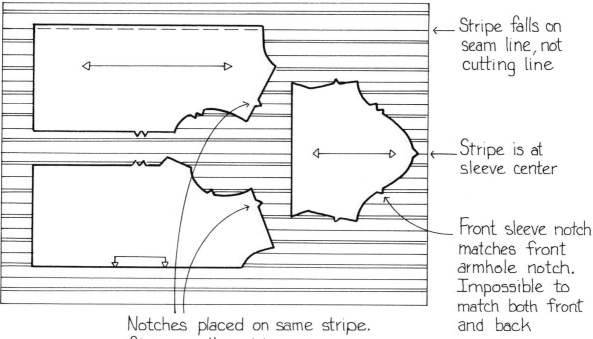

Stripe falls on seam line, not cutting line

Stripe is at sleeve center

Front sleeve notch matches front armhole notch. Impossible to match both front and back

Notches placed on same stripe. Stripes will meet in a chevron on sewn shoulder seam

Figure 47: Pattern arranged on striped fabric

TRANSFERRING PATTERN MARKS

Transfer printed (or your drawn) marks on the pattern to the fabric, before removing pins from the cut pieces. If the garment is lined, both layers should be marked. If it's underlined, just mark the underlining except for any surface decoration on the outer fabric (this should be applied before the underlining is attached). Interfacings need not be marked.

All construction and surface decoration marks should be transferred. The one exception is seam allowances. Except for complicated corners seams can be accurately judged by the lines on your sewing machine plate. Grain lines and position marks shouldn't be transferred to any garment fabric—fitting questions should have been resolved in the muslin.

Unless your fabric is very delicate, transfer marks by the pin-and-chalk method:

1. Place pins through the pattern and fabric at small marks, the beginning and end of long straight lines, and where necessary to define curved lines. (See figure 48.)

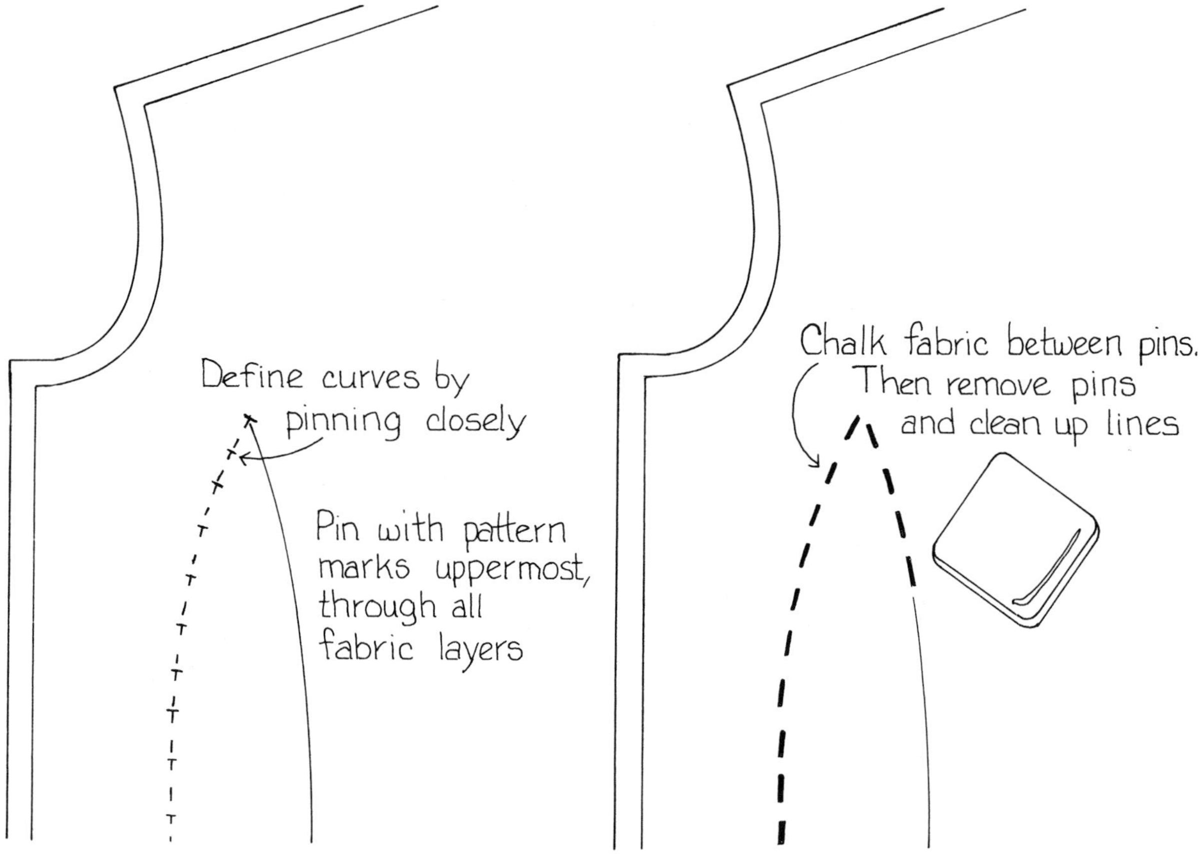

Define curves by
pinning closely

Pin with pattern
marks uppermost,
through all
fabric layers

Chalk fabric between pins.
Then remove pins
and clean up lines

Figure 48: The pin-and-chalk method

2. Turn the pattern over. Get some white tailor's chalk unless the fabric is white, in which case use blue or pink. Rub alongside the pins.

3. Remove pins. Use a ruler or french curve to finish or clean up lines.

4. If you cut double, unpin the pattern and use the pin marks (which show temporarily on most fabrics) to chalk the second piece.

5. Baste along lines that must be visible from the right side, or that seem likely to rub off when the section is handled. Small circles and suchlike can be marked with tailor's tacks.

Mark very delicate and pile fabrics with tailor's tacks:

1. Thread a needle with a long double strand, but don't knot.

2. At each small symbol, take a single stitch through the pattern and all layers of fabric. Then another that crosses over it, leaving a long thread loop (see figure 49).

3. Mark each long line with a series of such tacks.

4. Clip the loops and the long threads between tacks.

5. Carefully pull the pattern paper off the threads.

Modern sewing manuals say to carry out step 4 with the pattern pinned, forcing the pin heads through the paper. This doesn't work with the heavy paper used for most historic patterns.

6. If there are two fabric layers, gently separate the top and bottom and clip between them, leaving thread ends on both layers.

The lines produced by chalk and tailor's tacks aren't clear or durable enough for complex surface decoration designs, such as those for embroidery or curved braid. Such designs are often transferred directly to the right side of the fabric because basting them through blurs details. There are several transfer methods. Some are indelible, so the decoration must completely cover the transfer.

First you need the design to be transferred. If it's not included with the pattern, photocopy it or hand trace it onto regular weight artist's tracing paper.

If the design covers only one pattern piece it may be transferred before or after cutting out. If the design crosses seam lines it must be transferred after they're sewn. You can align the design with cut pieces by adding position marks to both.

One method is to place dressmaker's carbon, carbon side down, between the design and the fabric. Use white for all colors except white, for which blue is best. Anchor with weights.

Chalk and tailor's tacks are impermanent. Handle marked pieces as little as possible. Renew marks that start to come off before use.

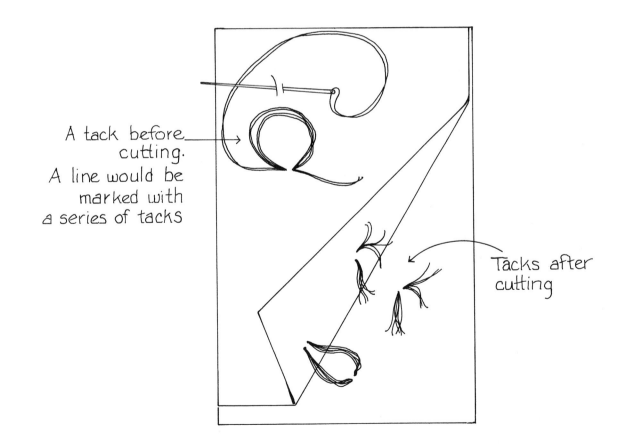

A tack before cutting. A line would be marked with a series of tacks

Tacks after cutting

Figure 49: Tailor's tacks

Trace the outline very heavily with a pencil. Check the transfer's success by periodically lifting the paper layers (without disturbing the alignment).

Another method is called pouncing or pricking. For dark fabrics, get some cornstarch or talcum powder. For light fabrics, mix cinnamon with the cornstarch or buy powdered charcoal.

Prick many holes through the back of the design with a pin or needle. Or sew with an unthreaded machine.

Place the design over the fabric and weight it. Using a wadded felt scrap and a circular motion, rub the powder through the holes. Shake the surplus off the fabric.

You can also buy transfer pencils with which you can draw the design on tracing paper, then iron it onto the fabric like a commercial iron-on embroidery transfer.

STAY STITCHING AND ATTACHING UNDERLINING

All garment sections, from all layers except interfacing, should be stay stitched to prevent distortion during construction and to reinforce clipped curves. Stay stitching also provides a seam guideline (should one be needed).

To stay stitch, machine stitch sections along curved and bias edges in the grain direction. (I stay stitch all edges but this is optional.) To find the grain direction, run your finger against the edge in both directions and see which doesn't cause fraying. You'll notice the grain differs along curves (see figure 50). For example, a round neckline has the grain running toward the center front and back from both shoulders. Rather than stay stitching along an "average" grain, follow the grain as it changes.

Use a regular machine stitch length and stitch 1/8 in. from the seam allowance. Press puckered sections, on the wrong side. If any stay stitching shows after construction, clip the thread and pick it out with tweezers.

Underlining sections must be attached to the corresponding outer ones before any seams are sewn. Lay the sections together wrong side to wrong side. Smooth wrinkles. Pin the sections together. If either fabric is slippery, baste just within the seam line and remove pins. Machine sew using the regular stitch length. Remove pins or basting. Press.

🌿 SEWING THE GARMENT

When sewing the garment you can choose between two levels of authenticity: perfection and the appearance of it. For a perfectly authentic garment only period construction techniques are used. Because perfection requires more research, handwork,

---

Even if you've stay stitched it's best to sew seams along the grain. But for convenience, choose an average grain for complex curves.

For most underlined garments I sew on the underlining, then finish fabric and underlining edges by hand overcasting together. Finishing seams before sewing prevents fraying, and it's easier to handle separate pieces.

Occasionally you can combine underlining and lining techniques. I recently made an underlined 1880s tunic bodice. Before starting construction, I decided I didn't want to hem it. Instead, I sewed the garment and underlining sections together, right side to right side, at the bottom edges. I turned the sections wrong side to wrong side and pressed the enclosed seams. Then I basted the garment and underlining together at the remaining edges.

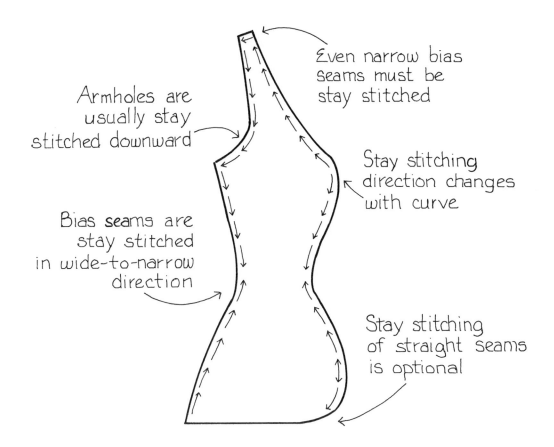

Even narrow bias seams must be stay stitched

Armholes are usually stay stitched downward

Stay stitching direction changes with curve

Bias seams are stay stitched in wide-to-narrow direction

Stay stitching of straight seams is optional

Figure 50: 18th-century sleeveless jacket showing stay-stitching directions

and time, you may not want to strive for it. But you can make an equally authentic-looking garment by using period techniques where they show and modern ones elsewhere. If you enjoy handwork you can concentrate on outside decoration rather than invisible inside stitching.

Outside stitching is the most obvious example of a technique that shows. On pre-Civil-War styles topstitching, buttonholes, hems, and the application of trims and notions should be done by hand. Also hand sew inner areas that will be visible during wear, such as open sleeves. But the main construction can be done with a sewing machine, using specialized stitches where needed. The seams can be finished by any method appropriate for the fabric.

Inner details that affect the garment's shape or drape should also be authentic. These include linings, underlinings, interfacings, padding, boning, staybands, ties, facings, and hems.

This section describes machine sewing and pressing techniques you'll use for all reproductions. It also describes sewing and fitting techniques appropriate only for some eras. Hand sewing is covered in chapter 6.

If your pattern has no instructions, or they're very sketchy or confusing, see chapter 4 for information on writing your own.

The easiest way to make a hand buttonhole is to first make a regular machine buttonhole, then go over it by hand with a blanket or buttonhole stitch. The extra stitching will make the hole slightly smaller.

FINISHING SEAMS

To join a plain seam, lay the fabric edges right sides together. Insert pins at right angles to the seam, at 1 in. intervals. If there's any chance of slippage, baste and remove pins. Machine sew, backstitching at both ends to secure them. Remove pins or basting and trim off thread ends. Press the seam open.

Although this is the basic seaming technique, most seams are a bit more complex. Some seam allowances must be trimmed to eliminate bulk or distortion that would be visible from the outside. And all seams that leave fabric edges raw must be finished to prevent fraying, unless the garment is lined. Seams on the same garment may need different finishes.

Do any trimming before pressing or finishing the seam. Cut away only where, and as much as, necessary. You should seldom trim to less than 1/4 in. Leave a larger allowance if the fabric frays easily.

At some seams you may wish to reduce bulk, for example where a hem will turn up. Trim both allowances evenly to about 1/4 in. (See figure 51.) Cut off any corners, especially if the seam will cross another one.

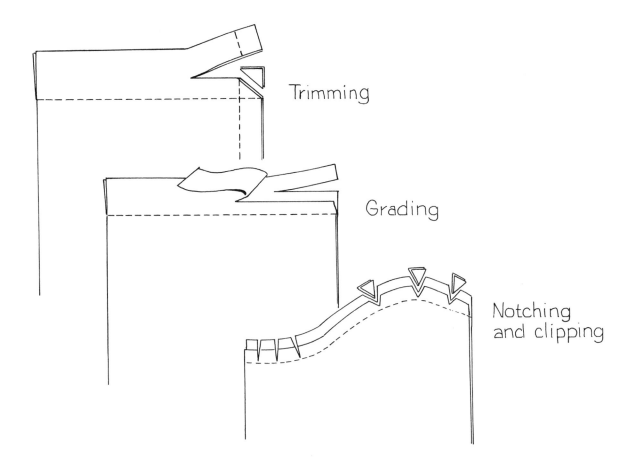

Figure 51: Ways to reduce seam bulk

Some seam allowances will be pressed in the same direction and/or will be enclosed. For example, where a lining joins the garment. Each fabric layer must be trimmed a different amount to avoid a ridge. This is called grading. Leave the widest seam allowance on the garment fabric. Grade corners too.

Curved seams leave more (or less) fabric in the seam allowances than on the outside, and so may pull or buckle. If the fabric molds easily, curved seams may be induced to lie flat by judicious pressing over a tailor's ham. If not clip the seam allowances. First do any grading. At an outward curve cut out small wedges 1/2 to 1 in. apart, depending on the sharpness of that part of the curve. At an inward curve make straight cuts 1/2 to 1 in. apart. Notch or clip almost to the stitches, being careful not to sever them.

My favorite seam finish for medium- to heavy-weight and underlined fabrics is overcasting (see figure 52). I like to do this by hand. Sew the seam and press it open. Unless the fabric is firm stitch about 1/8 in. from each raw edge. Overcast or whipstitch the edges and around any notches. Press again.

A quicker alternative is to zigzag near the edges. Or use a serger to simultaneously sew and finish the seam.

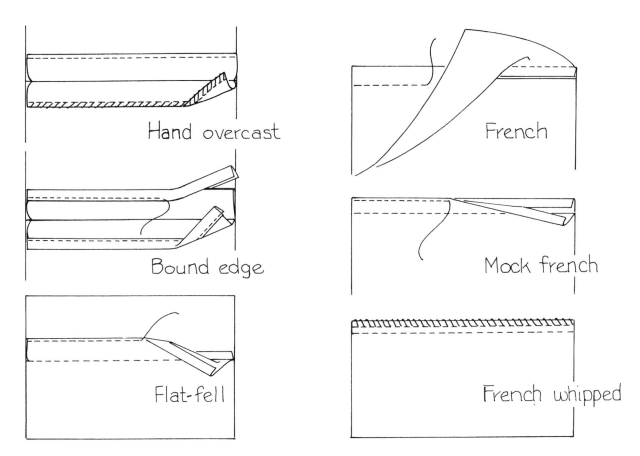

Figure 52: Classic seam finishes

Bias binding is another good seam finish for medium to heavy fabrics. Sew and press open the seam. Get some commercial double-fold binding in a matching or coordinating color (a slight contrast adds an interesting touch). Lay it over the raw edge with the narrow side on top. Pin, baste, and remove pins. Stitch close to the binding edge. Remove basting. Press.

An alternative is to cut 1 in. bias strips from your garment, underlining, or other lightweight fabric. Lay a strip over the seam allowance right side to right side, matching edges. Pin, baste, and remove pins. Sew 1/4 in. from the edges. Remove basting. Turn or press the strip to the seam underside. Baste. Sew next to the bias/seam allowance "seam." Remove basting and press.

The flat-fell seam has long been popular for men's shirts and other medium-weight nonformal garments. Sew a plain seam with either the wrong or the right sides together (the latter is called a mock flat-fell). Press the seam to one side. Trim the lower seam allowance to 1/8 in. Fold or press under the upper seam allowance 1/4 in. Cover the under allowance with it. Pin the folded edge in place, baste, and remove pins. Machine sew it to the garment fabric, or slip stitch if stitches shouldn't show. Remove basting. Press.

The best finish for sheers and laces is some variation of the french seam. To sew a classic french seam, pin the wrong sides together. Sew 1/4 to 3/8 in. from the seam line (depending on whether the allowance is 1/2 or 5/8 in.). Press the seam open. Fold the fabric right sides together along the seam and press again. Pin. Stitch along the seam line. Press to one side. The result will look like a neat tuck on the inside.

Because the french seam doesn't curve easily, you should use the mock french seam or french whipped seam for armholes and other curves. To make a mock french seam, first stitch along the seam line with right sides together. Don't press the seam open; press under 1/4 in. of the seam allowances. Lay the folds together. Pin, baste, and remove pins. Stitch near the fold line. Remove basting. Press to one side.

The french whipped seam is useful where a french seam would be too bulky. Sew a plain seam, stitch 1/8 in. away from it, and trim to 1/8 in. away from this stitching. Overcast or zigzag the raw edges together. Press to one side.

Seam allowances may be held in place by topstitching—stitching through all layers from the right side—near the seam line. This is especially useful for lining/garment seams and thick fabrics. Topstitch after the seam is finished. A seam that's enclosed or pressed to one side will have one line of topstitching. A pressed-open seam can have two lines. Topstitching may be done by machine or hand, depending on the era, but should always look neat and straight.

Sew napped fabric to unnapped with the unnapped fabric on top, to reduce slippage. Sew a delicate fabric to a less delicate one with the delicate fabric on top, to prevent any damage. Sew a bias or curved edge to a straight one with the bias edge on top, to prevent stretching.

SEWING DARTS

Darts can be straight, or have concave or convex curves (see figure 53). Most darts are sewn from the wide end to the point. Pin or baste closely along the marked line and stitch precisely over it. Don't fasten threads at the point by backstitching; this may cause lumps. Instead, pull the upper thread to the wrong side (use a pin for leverage). Tie both threads in a square knot (right over left, then left over right). Or form a loop, bring the end through it, and pull tight.

Press darts over a tailor's ham as described below. Sometimes a dart is so wide, or the fabric so thick, that a ridge shows on the outside. Cut the dart to 1 or 1/2 in. from the point, overcast the edges, and press open. Darts in sheer fabrics are trimmed and finished like a french whipped seam.

A contour or fish dart, which usually occurs at the waist, has a wide middle and two pointed ends. Unless the fabric is firm a contour dart should be begun in the middle and stitched toward each end (that is, sewn in two stages). Slash several times along the fold, to within 1/8 in. of the stitches, until the dart lies flat.

Very wide darts are sometimes replaced by short seams. That is, excess fabric is trimmed when you cut out the garment rather than after you sew the dart. Sew these seams like darts.

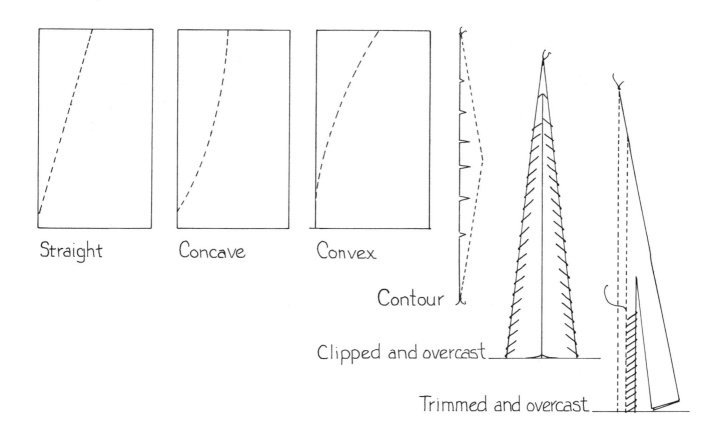

Figure 53: Darts and how to finish them

MAKING BIAS STRIPS

Bias strips are extremely useful because you can mold them to any shape or curve. A straight strip can face a hem, neckline, or other opening; cover a garment/flounce seam; be inserted as piping or cording; be sewn into a tube, then wound into button loops or frogs; or used in many other ways.

Bias strips may be made from the garment fabric, lining fabric, or a same-color or contrasting remnant. Generally a closely woven, rather lightweight fabric is most suitable.

1. Even the fabric into a rectangle by pulling threads (weft and/or warp) and cutting along them.

2. Fold a corner diagonally to find the true bias (see figure 54). Crease or press the fold line.

3. Lay the fabric on the cutting board wrong side up. Draw along the crease with a yardstick and chalk. Measure out from this line (not along the selvage) the desired width of the first strip.

4. Continue measuring from the first line until enough strips have been marked off. If using a napped or directional fabric, chalk the top of each strip.

Some fabrics are too slippery or stretchy to chalk accurately. Make a paper pattern for the strips. Pin the pattern, cut out a strip, and pin again along the cut line.

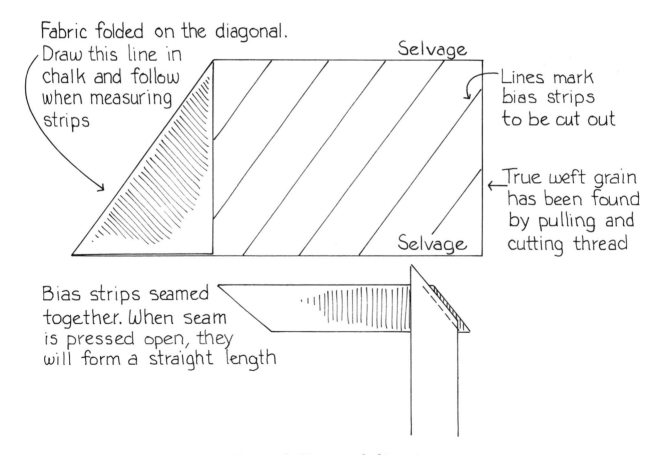

Fabric folded on the diagonal. Draw this line in chalk and follow when measuring strips

Selvage

Lines mark bias strips to be cut out

True weft grain has been found by pulling and cutting thread

Selvage

Bias strips seamed together. When seam is pressed open, they will form a straight length

Figure 54: How to make bias strips

5. Cut out strips.

To join bias strips, lay them right sides together at right angles, matching any nap. Each piece should protrude the width of the seam allowance (usually 1/4 in.) at one end. Pin, baste, and remove pins. Sew and remove basting. Press, then cut off protruding bits.

GATHERING

Gathers are often used to control fullness in light- to medium-weight fabrics and trims.

1. You can gather large areas more evenly if you add joining marks to the garment section to be gathered and the section it will be sewn to. If your pattern doesn't provide joining marks, use a yardstick to divide both sections into halves, quarters, or eighths. Mark with chalk.

2. Run a double row of machine basting stitches at the edge to be gathered (a single row gathers unevenly). One row should be just inside the seam line, the other 1/8 or 1/4 in. closer to the edge. (See figure 55.) Begin new rows at each joining mark. Leave long thread ends instead of backstitching.

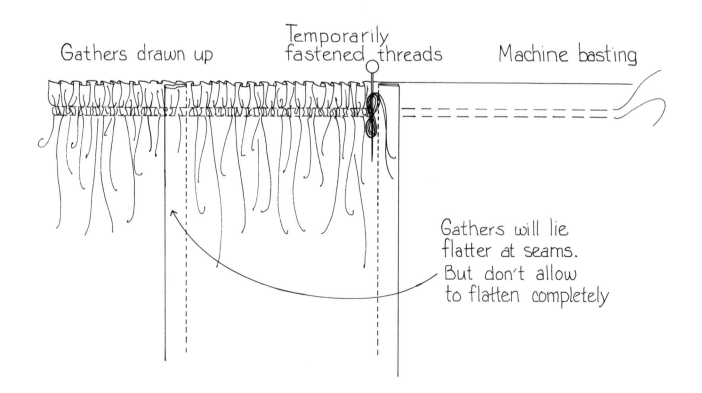

Figure 55: How to gather

Another gathering method is to attach a single heavy-duty thread to the fabric by zigzagging over it. Fasten one end and pull up the other till the section is the desired length.

The quickest way to ruffle large quantities of trim is to use a sewing machine's ruffler or pleater attachment.

3. Pin garment sections together at the joining marks.

4. Draw up gathering threads until the gathered section is the right length. Pull the under threads to the top. Fasten threads temporarily by winding them around the pins in a figure eight.

5. Adjust gathers evenly between pins with your fingers.

6. Pin down, baste closely, and remove pins. Tie threads in square knots and trim off long ends.

7. Sew (using a regular machine stitch) with the gathered section uppermost.

8. Remove basting and press. Finish seam by covering with bias binding, or by some other method.

PLEATING

Pleats are used to control fullness in firm, but not thick fabrics where minimal bulk is desired. They usually take up about three times as much fabric as the finished width.

Three common types are knife pleats, which have all folds turned to one side; box pleats, which consist of two pleats whose edges meet on the wrong side; and inverted box pleats, whose edges meet on the right side. (See figure 56.) Pleats may be unpressed (rolled), pressed, or topstitched (edgestitched) at the pressed edge.

Precision is important at all pleating stages.

1. If the pattern doesn't include pleat marks, use scrap fabric or paper to experiment with pleat types and sizes.

2. Lay the fabric wrong side up on a large table. Measure and chalk the fold lines (where pleats are rolled or folded) and placement lines (where folded edges are brought).

3. Do any construction that must be done before pleating.

4. Fold pleats one at a time, working from the wrong side. Fold along the fold line and bring the fold to the placement line. Fold unpressed pleats to an inch or so beyond the seam line, pressed ones to the garment bottom.

5. Turn pleats in the direction they will be pressed. Pin folds, baste them down, and remove pins.

6. Turn fabric to the right side and lay a press cloth over it. Press pleats (since basting is on the wrong side it won't leave marks).

7. Edgestitch pleats if a crisp, tailored look is desired.

8. Remove basting unless pleats must be secured during subsequent construction stages.

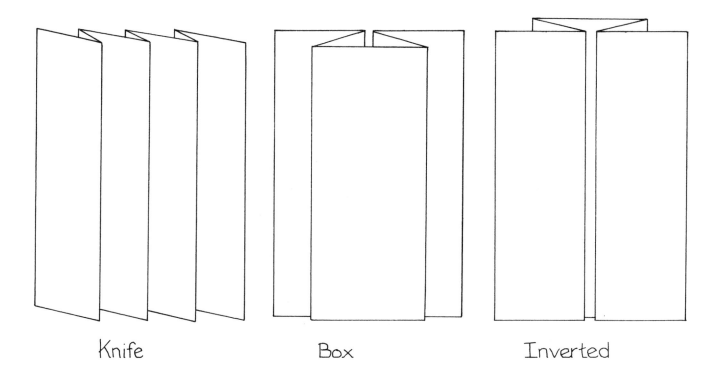

Knife   Box   Inverted

Figure 56: Common types of pleats

Some sewers prefer to have knife and box pleats made by a commercial pleater. Two other types, accordion and sunburst pleats, are usually made commercially. The folds of accordion pleats stand out instead of lying flat. Sunburst pleats are similar, but widen toward the lower edge.

To find a commercial pleater, check your local Yellow Pages or ask fabric store employees. Because some fabrics don't respond well, have a 9 by 9 in. sample pleated first. Check whether the pleats look crisp and whether the fabric's texture changed. Measure shrinkage so you can calculate how much fabric to send. Test pleat permanency by cleaning the sample. If you encounter problems, find another construction technique or another fabric.

Some sewing suppliers sell manual devices for folding knife pleats, in a variety of widths.

CARTRIDGE PLEATING AND GAUGING

Cartridge pleats and gauging are formed by the same method. However, cartridge pleats look like round, unpressed pleats and are usually used on heavy or underlined fabric. (See figure 57.) They're attached at the pleat fold. Gauging looks like even gathering and is done on thinner fabrics suited to gathering. Gauged areas are sewn into seams like gathered ones.

To make cartridge pleats:

1. Finish the raw edge.

2. Determine how long the pleats will be before they fall. The minimum pleat length is 1 in. For long pleats, or where body is needed, it may be 4 to 6 in.

3. Press the amount of pleat length to the wrong side, measuring as you go. Baste the fold if necessary.

4. Calculate the pleat size, using scrap fabric mock-ups. There is no space between cartridge pleats. Their size depends on the fabric thickness, the quantity to be gotten into the finished measurement, and the desired effect. The pleats may be graduated; for example larger on a skirt back than the front.

5. Mark the pleats on the edge turned to the wrong side. Measure with a clear plastic ruler and make dots with tailor's chalk. There should be at least two rows, more for longer pleats, and they should be about 1/2 in. apart. Dots must be accurately marked and aligned with the fabric grain. The rows must be identical.

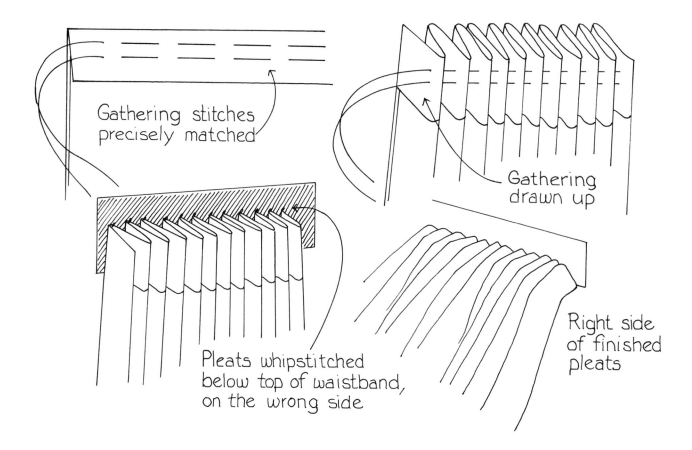

Gathering stitches precisely matched

Gathering drawn up

Pleats whipstitched below top of waistband, on the wrong side

Right side of finished pleats

Figure 57: Cartridge pleats

6. Cut a length of quilting or other strong thread for each row. This should be several inches longer than the area to be pleated. Large garments can be pleated in several sections. Knot one end.

7. Run a gathering thread through each row. Use a running stitch and bring the thread in at one dot, out at the next, and so on.

8. Pull up the threads as tightly as possible to form the pleats. Trim and fasten threads.

9. To attach the pleated section to another section, butt the folds up against it on the inside. Using double thread, secure each fold with about three whipstitches. Cartridge pleats are sewn to a waistband below the top edge.

10. If the seam needs pressing, remove any basting along the fold and press without crushing the pleats.

Gauging is finer than cartridge pleating and requires more closely spaced dots. Many rows may be drawn up to create a decorative effect; this is called shirring. A related technique is smocking, where the pleats are joined with embroidery.

MAKING PLACKETS

Although plackets aren't authentic for some historic garments, invisible ones should be added where possible. The extra fabric layers prevent tears due to strain and fastener weight.

Quite likely patterns and instructions for most types of plackets are scattered throughout your pattern library. It's worth copying these and filing them in their own envelope, for quick retrieval when you use patterns without plackets. But if you lack placket patterns, here are some instructions. All facings should be cut from the garment fabric unless it's too heavy. In this case use the lining or underlining, or color-matched scraps.

The continuous lapped placket can be inserted in either a slash in the fabric or a seam (see figure 58). It's often used for sleeves, but can be used for neckline and other openings.

1. If the opening isn't in a seam, slash the fabric the desired length of the opening. If it is in a seam, leave the opening unstitched.

2. Cut a straight strip of fabric twice the length of the opening and 1 1/4 in. wide, with one long side on the selvage.

3. If the opening is slashed, run a line of reinforcement stitching about 1/8 in. from the edge. If it's in a seam, clip the seam allowances at the bottom of the opening. Trim the opening seam allowances to 1/4 in.

Heirloom sewing suppliers sell smocking aids that are useful for gauging and shirring. These include iron-on transfer dots that can be substituted for chalk marks. And smocking pleaters that run multiple gathering threads through lightweight fabric.

Cartridge pleating is one way to make an Elizabethan ruff. Finish both edges (one with lace, one with a fine hem) before pleating. Sew to the top of a grosgrain ribbon neckband.

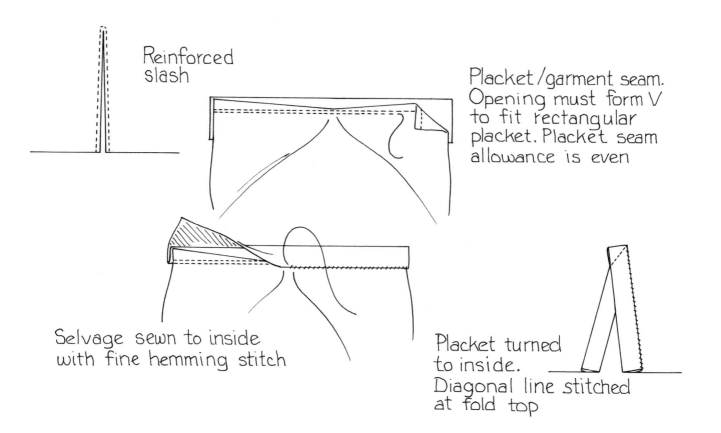

Reinforced slash

Placket/garment seam. Opening must form V to fit rectangular placket. Placket seam allowance is even

Selvage sewn to inside with fine hemming stitch

Placket turned to inside. Diagonal line stitched at fold top

Figure 58: How to insert continuous lapped placket in a slash

4. Spread the opening over the placket, right side to right side, matching raw edges. Allow the opening to form a V shape in the middle, but make sure it can be held by a 1/4 in. seam. Pin, baste, and remove pins.

5. Stitch. Remove basting and press seam toward placket.

6. Turn the selvage side of the placket to the wrong side of the garment. Pin the selvage over the placket seam. Baste and remove pins.

7. Sew with a fine hemming stitch. Remove basting and press.

8. From the wrong side, arrange the sleeve as it will be when worn. The placket should be entirely turned to the wrong side and form a V shape. Stitch a diagonal line across the placket top (without catching the sleeve) so the placket can't roll to the outside.

The extension placket is suitable for most skirt openings (see figure 59). If you plan ahead you can cut it in one with the garment, minimizing seaming.

1. Baste the skirt seam except for the opening. Try on to make sure the opening is long enough. If not, correct.

2. Mark the opening seam line with basting on each side.

3. Sew the seam up to the opening. Clip across the seam allowances.

4. Cut a straight facing for the top part of the placket. It should be the desired placket width plus a 1/4 in. seam allowance. One long side should be a selvage.

5. Overcast the bottom of the facing.

6. Pin the facing to the opening edge right side to right side. Baste and remove pins.

7. Sew with a 1/4 in. seam. Remove basting and press.

8. Turn the facing to the wrong side, so that the seam won't show. Press and baste the fold.

9. Pin the selvage side of the facing to the garment. Baste and remove pins.

10. Hem with a fine hemming stitch.

11. Remove all basting from the top placket. Press.

12. Cut a straight facing for the bottom part of the placket. It should be 1 in. longer than the opening and 1 1/2 times as

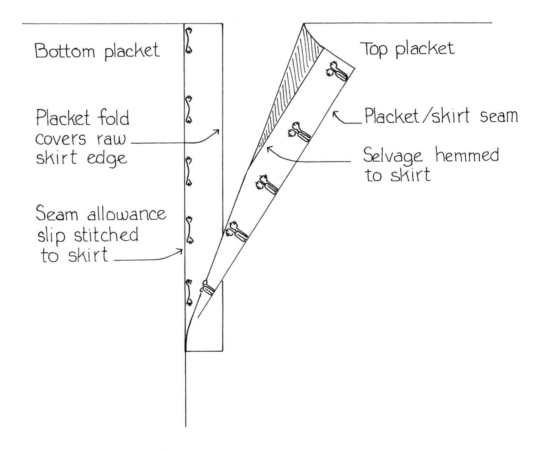

Figure 59: Extension placket inserted in skirt seam

Chapter 6 gives instructions for sewing on fasteners. Chapter 7 explains how to make and attach a waistband.

Before sewing an unseen pocket into a costume, consider whether it can hold anything without bulging. It's often more practical to carry a pouch or purse.

wide as the top placket, plus a 1/4 in. seam allowance. One long side should be a selvage. This facing will be wrapped around the opening edge. The finished bottom placket will be narrower than the top, so it won't show.

13. Overcast the bottom of the facing.

14. Press under the seam allowance. Baste.

15. Slip the facing over the opening edge, making sure it's within the marked seam line. Put the selvage side on the wrong side of the garment. Pin, baste, and remove pins.

16. Slip stitch the folded edge to the garment. Hemstitch the selvage.

17. Remove all basting and press.

BONING CORSETS AND BODICES

Many people are tempted to omit corsets and/or bodice boning because they think boning is inherently uncomfortable. In fact, for any era you can make a practical corset that gives a period look. Here are several tips:

- Some periods allow a variety of corset styles. Choose the style that's shortest and closest to your body shape.

- A period look relies on stiffness as much as compression. Use stiff fabric, such as upholstery brocade, and omit some bones. Underline the bodice.

- Pad the corset bust and/or hips instead of compressing your waist. Even better, wear a dress style that gives the illusion of a small waist.

- Use plastic boning rather than steel.

There are three ways to insert bones. On a corset, you can sandwich them between the outer fabric and lining (tunnel casing). On a corset or heavy garment you can use a single applied casing (see figure 60). On a lighter garment both sides must be cased.

To make a corset with tunnel casings:

1. Mark bone positions on the outer fabric and the lining. (Note that plastic bones are narrower than metal ones; you may have to respace marks if the pattern assumes you're using a different type.) Thread trace to the right side.

2. Assemble the outer fabric and lining sections.

3. Press under the bottom seam allowances and baste.

4. With right sides together, pin the outer fabric and lining together along the top and sides. If using a split clasp, leave loop openings. Baste and remove pins.

5. Stitch the basted seams.

6. Remove basting from them. Turn the corset right side out. Press so the seam doesn't show on the outside. Topstitch if desired.

7. Insert the clasp.

8. As accurately as possible, pin along the boning lines through both layers. Work in a consistent direction, for example top to bottom. Baste in that direction. Remove pins.

9. Measure and cut the bones. They should be about 3/8 in. shorter than the finished corset. Some costumers number them to keep track. (If you wish you can cut plastic boning as you go; insert it then trim at the bottom.)

10. Baste a fabric scrap and a lining scrap together. Sew trial casings (composed of parallel lines) of different widths. Slip bones between them till you find the ideal width. Bones should neither move nor strain the casing.

11. Working from the right side, make a casing for each boning line. The boning line should be in the middle. Stitch in the direction it was basted. Remove basting.

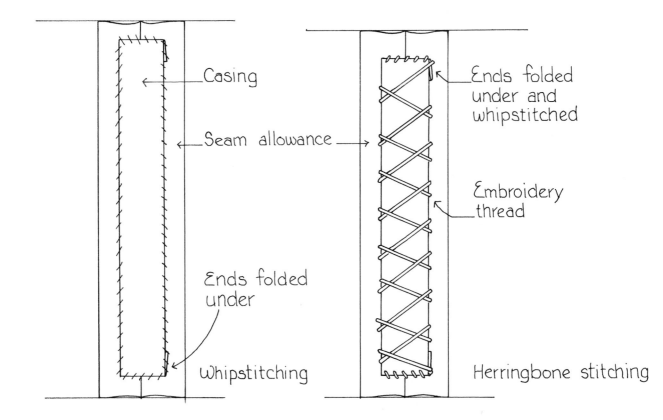

Figure 60: Two ways to attach cased bones

12. Insert each bone in its casing.

13. Baste, then slip stitch the bottom seam.

14. Remove basting and press.

15. Add metal or embroidered eyelets.

Applied casings can be made of twill tape, colored grosgrain ribbon, or lightweight braid. (I discard the flimsy casing sold with plastic boning.) The material should be just wide enough to allow boning and stitching—3/8 or 1/2 in. Although a contrasting color can be used, it shouldn't show on the outside.

To make a corset with applied casings:

1. Mark bone positions on the lining. Thread trace to the right side.

2. Assemble the outer fabric and lining sections.

3. Press under the bottom seam allowances and baste.

4. With right sides together, pin the outer fabric and lining together along the top and sides. If using a split clasp, leave loop openings. Baste and remove pins.

5. Stitch the basted seams.

6. Remove basting from them. Turn the corset right side out. Press so the seam doesn't show on the outside. Topstitch if desired.

7. Insert the clasp.

8. Measure and cut the bones. They should be about 3/8 in. shorter than the finished corset.

9. Cut casings the bone length plus 1/2 in. For a lightweight garment, cut two per bone.

10. If you cut two casings per bone, baste with bones between them. Sew with a whipstitch or machine straight stitch. Remove basting.

11. Turn under casings 1/4 in. at each end. Baste.

12. Baste each casing in position along the long sides.

13. Casings should be sewn to the lining, underlining, or seam allowances—never the outer fabric. Sew with a whipstitch, including one short end. Remove basting.

14. Insert each bone in its casing (if using a single casing).

15. Whipstitch the other end of the casings.

16. Baste, then slip stitch the corset's bottom seam.

17. Remove basting and press.

18. Add metal or embroidered eyelets.

Don't try to splice two short bones—it won't work.

Casings can sometimes be applied with a machine straight stitch when you're making a reproduction. But this is hard when you're reboning a vintage garment.

A herringbone stitch can be substituted for the whipstitch. Find a strong, matching or contrasting embroidery thread. Insert the needle from under the top right corner. Make a diagonal stitch across and down the bone. Then make a smaller stitch up that side. Make another diagonal stitch across (and down) the bone in the opposite direction. Then stitch up that side. Continue till you've reached the bottom, then fasten thread. Whipstitch the ends.

MAKING HOOPS AND BUSTLES

Hoops and bustles can be made in many ways. These include adding hoop wire to a shaped cloth foundation, joining wire with woven tape to create a "cage," and stuffing cloth casings like a pillow. Most shapes can be created by the first method, and many patterns are available. Construction is easy. Nonetheless I've seen many costumes spoiled by badly made hoops. Here's how to make a good one:

- During eras when hoops or bustles were worn, a variety of sizes was acceptable. A conservative size is appropriate and practical for most costumes. If you're short, choose the smallest size.

- A hoop or bustle should be narrower than the skirt covering it (this goes for petticoats too). Otherwise it will be seen straining through the skirt. Always make the hoop or bustle first and fit the skirt over it.

- A hoopskirt should be several inches shorter than the dress skirt. But don't make it too short because the skirt will fall straight (or "break") from the bottom hoop.

- Sew on gathered flounces to soften the ridges the wire creates. This enables you to skip a separate overpetticoat—unless the dress fabric is thin or you want the petticoat to add shaping. On hoopskirts, a short additional ruffle below the bottom hoop hides the skirt break.

I make cloth foundations from sturdy medium-weight cotton. Use bias casings and apply them as for a corset, leaving the ends open at one side seam. Thread the wire through each casing, leaving 1 1/2 or 2 in. overlap, and cut with tin snips. Cover the ends with U-tips, then join them with masking tape. Don't join them permanently because you'll have to pull the wire out when you wash the garment. Whipstitch the casings closed.

For periods when skirts were supported by multiple, heavy petticoats you can substitute one narrow, lightly wired hoop.

SCALLOPING AND DAGGING EDGES

Scalloped and dagged edges are used on many medieval garments.

1. On the pattern, measure the edge(s) to be dagged. Determine how deep and wide the design should be and how many projections each edge will contain. The projections may be the same size or graduated, for example gradually enlarging down a hanging sleeve. Seams should fall between projections.

2. Using french curves and/or a ruler, draw the dagging design onto the garment pattern. Add 1/2 in. seam allowances. Trim the pattern.

3. Cut out the garment.

4. The dagged edges must be lined or faced (see figure 61). If the garment is unlined, make a fitted facing pattern following the directions in chapter 4. The facing should be deep enough to look like a lining during wear. Allow a 1/4 in. turnunder at the top.

5. Cut out the facing, on the same grain as the garment. Press, then baste, the top under 1/4 in.

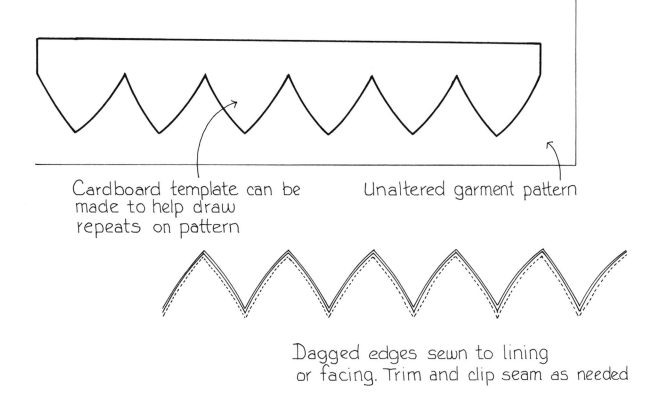

Cardboard template can be made to help draw repeats on pattern

Unaltered garment pattern

Dagged edges sewn to lining or facing. Trim and clip seam as needed

Figure 61: How to dag edges

6. Pin the garment to the lining or facing, right side to right side. Baste and remove pins.

7. Stitch around the edges.

8. Remove basting. Grade seam allowances and clip curves.

9. Turn the garment right side out. Pointed edges will have to be worked out carefully with a narrow, rather blunt tool such as a bodkin.

10. Press, using a press cloth. Press dagged edges over a tailor's ham to prevent wrinkles.

11. If using a facing, hem the basted edge to the garment. Remove basting and press.

Dagging was sometimes cut into a straight strip which was then applied as an edging.

CREATING ATTACHED TABBED EDGES

Elizabethan doublets and corsets are frequently decorated with attached tabs (pickadils). These may be made of either fabric or braid (see figure 62).

To make fabric tabs:

1. Measure the garment edge(s) to see how much tab yardage you need.

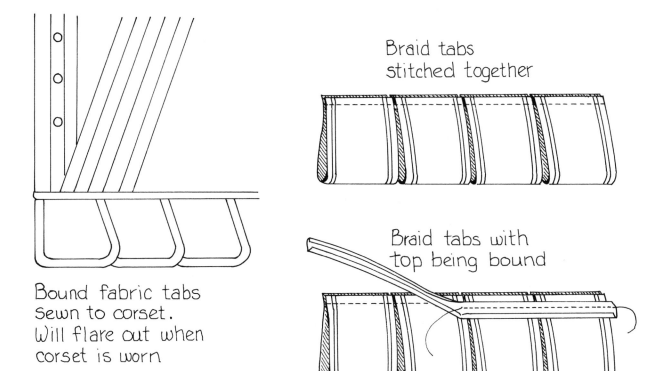

Bound fabric tabs sewn to corset. Will flare out when corset is worn

Braid tabs stitched together

Braid tabs with top being bound

Figure 62: Fabric and braid tabs

2. Draw a paper pattern for one tab.

3. Use it to cut two fabric layers per tab.

4. Pin them wrong sides together, then baste and remove pins.

5. Make some attractive bias binding. Press under one long edge.

6. Working with one tab at a time, pin the unpressed binding edge around the curved tab edge right side to right side. Baste and remove pins. Stitch.

7. Remove basting and press.

8. Pin, then baste the pressed-under binding edge to what is now the wrong side of the tab. (That is, cover the raw fabric edges.) Slip stitch. Remove basting and press.

9. The tabs are still separate and the tops unfinished. Cut another length of binding and press under one long edge.

10. Lay the tab tops over the unpressed edge right side to right side, as close together as possible. Pin, baste, stitch, and press.

11. Pin, then baste the pressed edge of the binding to the wrong side of the tab tops. Slip stitch, remove basting, and press.

12. Attach the tab yardage by butting the top against the finished garment edge and whipstitching.

Tabs on early corsets are not purely decorative; they keep waistbands from slipping under the corset. If the tab fabric isn't stiff enough, use heavier fabric or add interfacing. Wear your petticoat under the corset point in front and over the tabs in back.

If you do not wish to bind the tab bottoms you can sew the tab layers right sides together. Clip curves, turn right side out, and press.

To make braid tabs, cut a double length of braid for each tab. Fold it wrong sides together and baste at the top. Bind the tabs together at the top like fabric tabs. Whipstitch to the finished garment edge.

PIPING EDGES AND SEAMS

Piping (cording) was very popular in the Victorian period. Theatrical costumers use it for many others because piping gives garments definition. Piping also helps fit low necklines (which tend to gap away from the body) because you can pull up the cord.

Piping can be made of the garment fabric, a solid that picks up one color in a multicolor design, or a contrasting color. The cord may be any cotton string or cord of the desired diameter. Remember to preshrink it.

Piping can also be bought ready-made in the braid section of a fabric store. A decorative cord and a single, finished seam allowance are woven in one piece. You must preshrink it. Hand sew the allowance to the wrong side of the garment or enclose it in a seam.

To pipe a garment edge:

1. Measure the garment pattern to see how much piping you need.

2. Cut bias strips about 2 1/2 in. wide. Sew together for a long length.

3. Fold the bias strip off-center, one-third over two-thirds, wrong side to wrong side. Place the cord in the fold (see figure 63). Baste next to the cord.

4. Stitch as close to the cord as possible, using a zipper or piping foot.

5. Remove basting. Press under the edge of the wide seam allowance.

6. Lay the garment seam allowance over the piping seam allowance that was not pressed under, so that the cord extends beyond the garment edge. Pin, baste, and remove pins.

7. Stitch along the previous line. Remove basting. Grade seam allowances.

8. The pressed-under piping seam allowance should be on the wrong side of the garment. Pin, baste, and remove pins.

9. Hem with a slip stitch. Remove basting and press.

To pipe a garment seam, make piping with equal seam

Tubular piping was a fashionable surface decoration in the early 19th century. Cut a bias strip three times the cord width plus 1 in. Cut twice the necessary cord length. Fold the bias strip wrong sides together and stitch next to the cord. Trim the seam closely. Just where the tube ends, sew the cord to it. Turn the tube right side out by pulling the encased cord. The other half will now be encased.

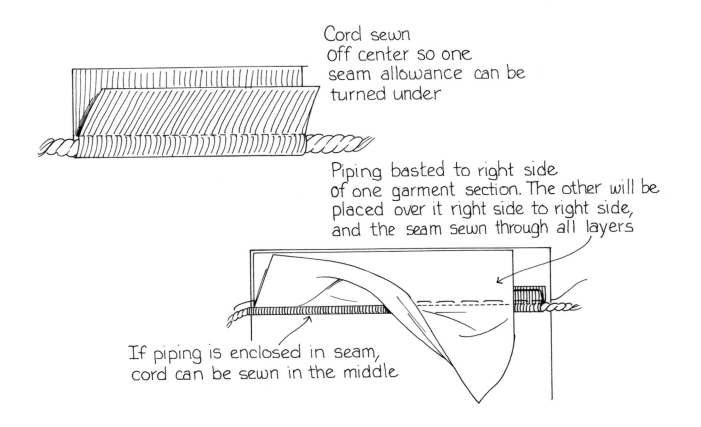

Cord sewn off center so one seam allowance can be turned under

Piping basted to right side of one garment section. The other will be placed over it right side to right side, and the seam sewn through all layers

If piping is enclosed in seam, cord can be sewn in the middle

Figure 63: How to make and attach piping

allowances. Pin, then baste it between the garment seam layers so that the piping will be on the right side after the garment is sewn. Stitch, remove basting, and press the seam.

PRESSING DURING CONSTRUCTION

When you sew, you'll find yourself making regular trips to the ironing board. First, you should always press crumpled fabric before cutting or stitching. Pressing is often required to prepare for stitching or mold curves. Every seam and dart must be pressed before you pin intersecting seams. Surface stitching, such as buttonholes, causes slight wrinkles that should be pressed. And finally, finished garments require a touch-up.

Partially completed garments are apt to stretch. This means you must move the iron by raising and lowering it, rather than gliding across the fabric. You must work with the fabric grain. And you must protect the fabric from excess heat, crushing, and imprinted marks.

Test iron temperatures by pressing a scrap of each fabric, interfacing, and trim. The correct temperature should produce a good crease without harming the texture. Even so, pressing should be confined to the wrong side whenever possible. When you must press the right side, protect it with a press cloth. You can use a scrap of medium-weight white cotton or the garment fabric; it should measure about 12 by 18 in.

Pile fabrics such as velvet will crush permanently unless you press them over a needle board—a flat surface with projecting wire or synthetic "pile." In a pinch you can use a velvet scrap or thick terry towel. Raised surface decoration should also be pressed over a towel.

Remove pins and basting before pressing to avoid imprints. If seam allowances leave imprints, press seams over a seam roll—a hard stuffed sausage. Or slip brown paper strips, at least 2 in. wider than the seam, under the allowances. If enclosed seams leave imprints, press the area over a towel.

Darts and curved seams should be pressed over a tailor's ham—a hard ham-shaped pillow—to maintain the curve. Press darts from the wide end to the point. Vertical darts are pressed toward the garment center; horizontal darts are pressed down.

Press long sleeve seams over a sleeve board—a little two-tiered ironing board. The sleeve board is also useful for hard-to-access areas.

If a hem allowance has excess fullness you can shrink out at least some by steam pressing. First insert a brown paper strip, 2 in. wider than the hem, between the hem and garment.

Curved or softly draped areas, such as a lapel roll, should be set with steam only. Place the garment on a dress form. Hold the iron about 3 in. above the fabric and mold the curve

To avoid scratching your iron, don't press directly over metal fasteners.

with your fingers (unless the fabric is velvet). Leave the garment on the form till completely dry.

FITTING DURING CONSTRUCTION

If you altered the pattern and muslin carefully you won't do much fitting during construction. However, you should recheck tight bodices and jackets before sleeve insertion. And it's impossible to accurately mark skirt and trouser hems till the main seams are sewn.

Try on the garment with everything to be worn underneath. Also any belts, sashes, suspenders, or shoes that affect the fit.

If a bodice is too loose or tight, adjust the side seams. If a low-cut neckline is unsatisfactory, adjust the shoulders. Necklines can also be altered by adding a drawstring or frill.

Hang skirts and trousers for 24 hours before marking to get stretching over with. Marking usually requires assistance.

Plain, straight skirts and trousers are marked from the bottom:

1. Complete everything except the hem.

2. Put on the garment. Pin it up here and there till you find the desired length. Have your helper measure its distance from the floor with a yardstick. Remove pins.

3. Stand in a natural position while your helper crawls round you marking the hem's distance from the floor at 2 in. intervals. Or better, stand on a small stool. Your helper may mark with straight pins, but should not turn up the hem.

4. Take off the garment. Spread the hem flat on a table. Use a ruler and chalk to draw a definitive hemline.

5. Pin up the hem temporarily, look at it in a mirror, and spot-check measurements. Correct if necessary.

6. Hem according to the directions in chapter 7.

If a skirt lining is attached only at the waistband, it must be marked separately. Floor length and slightly trained skirts can be marked from the bottom. But skirts with long trains, extensive bottom decoration, tops shaped to a bodice point, or underlying hoops or bustles—these must be leveled from the top.

To level a skirt:

1. Complete everything except the top, including the bottom hem.

2. Mark the skirt in quarters with chalk. If there is to be extra fullness in back, or a flat front, adjust the side marks.

Chapter 6 describes hemming stitches. Chapter 7 gives step-by-step instructions for hems and a variety of garment alterations.

3. Cut a strong twill tape to the waistband measurement plus 12 in. Allowing 6 in. on each end for tying, mark the tape in quarters.

4. Put on the skirt. Tie the tape over it at your waist, allowing the skirt top to stick above the tape (see figure 64).

5. Adjust the skirt length from the top. The fabric should hang straight rather than pulling diagonally. Pin the skirt to the tape at the quartering marks.

6. Adjust the skirt fullness by finger pleating or finger gathering under the tape (depending on the method to be used).

7. Chalk a line on the skirt at the tape top. Some costumers chalk only half the skirt.

8. Unpin the tape. Take off the skirt and lay it on a table. Use a ruler to even out anomalies in the chalk line. Transfer the line to the other side if necessary.

9. Trim excess top fabric. Gather or pleat the skirt and attach to the waistband.

Fabric stores sell several devices for marking hems from the bottom. Some enable you to do without assistance.

Alter a one-piece garment with dagging or other border decoration by tucking above the decoration (see chapter 7).

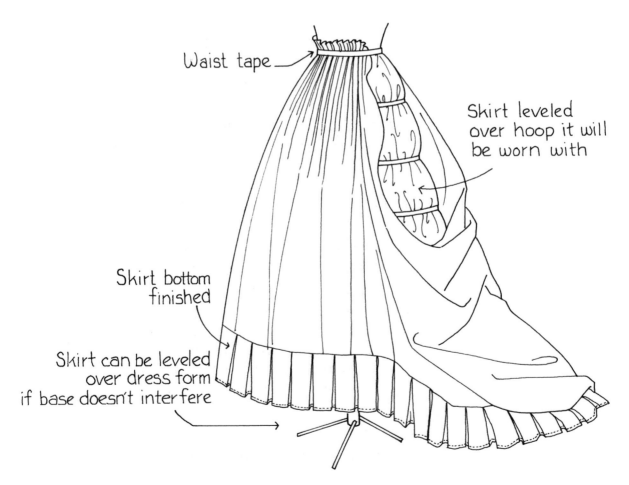

Waist tape

Skirt leveled over hoop it will be worn with

Skirt bottom finished

Skirt can be leveled over dress form if base doesn't interfere

Figure 64: A skirt being leveled

4 Learning More Advanced Reproduction Techniques

Although modern reproduction patterns are convenient, they're not available in every style for every era. But there are several excellent alternatives:

- *Your modifications of reproduction or period patterns.* Style alterations are most successful when the original pattern is for the same period.

- *Sized vintage paper patterns.* These are most available for styles from the 1890s and later.

- *Scale drafts of period garments.* Mostly for styles from the Renaissance through the 1930s.

- *Scale drafts developed from a modern sloper.* Available for many eras (though by no means all styles). Generally intended for theatrical use.

- *Drafting instructions that include scale patterns.* From tailoring manuals, dressmaking manuals, and magazines. Most available for styles from the Victorian period on.

- *Your copies of vintage garments.* Probably the styles available to you will be Victorian or later.

- *Your drafts of period styles.* Although an experienced drafter can draw any style, it's best to start with simple, geometric ones.

Most of my outfits require several types of patterns. First I view all alternatives for each garment and decide on a style. If equivalent styles are available, I choose the pattern that's easiest to use. Altering style is harder than altering fit. Enlarging a draft is simple, but takes some time. Developing a pattern is of course more complex than using an existing one. Most patterns require you to figure out assembly. But any existing directions, notes, or pattern marks help.

A packaged reproduction pattern isn't always easier. I once began to use one for a Regency spencer. I couldn't achieve good results with the sleeves even after six muslins. I gave up and enlarged a scale draft of a period spencer. The draft was more accurate, both technically and stylistically. It turned out to be exactly my size. And it was easy to assemble without directions.

137

✒ Altering Style with Flat Pattern Techniques

In previous chapters I discouraged developing historic patterns from a modern sloper or fashion pattern. Unless you're very familiar with the period's cuts, your design will be subtly modernized. But you can produce accurate results, much more easily, by beginning with a pattern for the era. You can then change details, such as sleeve width. Or transform a basic style into a more specialized one, such as sports clothes or masquerade dress.

First design the garment. You may want to copy one in a museum catalog, period photo, or other picture. Or combine features from several sources. Just make sure the general look is correct for the period and the elements harmonize. Most pictures show the garment from the front. To examine back and side construction, find pictures of similar garments. Read any accompanying descriptions closely.

Choose a pattern with the same basic cut as your design, plus as many other similar style elements as possible. It may be a reproduction pattern or one of the other types discussed in this chapter. Then look for patterns with style elements your basic pattern doesn't have. It's easier to trace a neckline or borrow a sleeve than to experiment.

Before altering the pattern style, make your usual fitting alterations. If necessary make a muslin and transfer the corrections. Then trace or photocopy all pieces to be altered. If you botch one, you can recopy it and start over. Cut off the seam allowances.

Read the directions for the original pattern to make sure you thoroughly understand its construction. Compare pattern pieces to your design. List changes to be made, down to the smallest detail. Then consider how to make them.

There is a small number of flat pattern alteration techniques whose exact application varies with the project. Instructions for most are given below. You'll understand the instructions better—and gain practice—if you work through them using copies of a miniature sloper (see figures 65 and 66). I used the sloper for many examples because it's simpler than any "real" garment and is used in most books on flat pattern alterations.

When you alter a garment pattern, keep experimenting and making muslins till you produce the desired style.

You'll need the following materials:

- *Rulers.* I recommend a 6 in. ruler, a 12 in. one, and a yardstick. Clear plastic is best.

- *A large L-square.* Available in art stores.

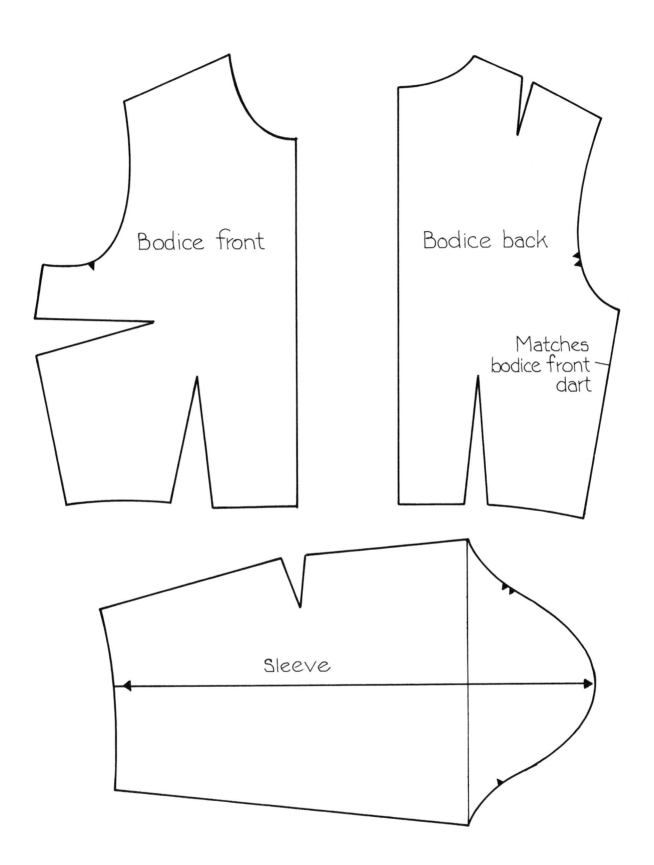

Bodice front

Bodice back

Matches bodice front dart

Sleeve

Figure 65: Woman's miniature bodice sloper

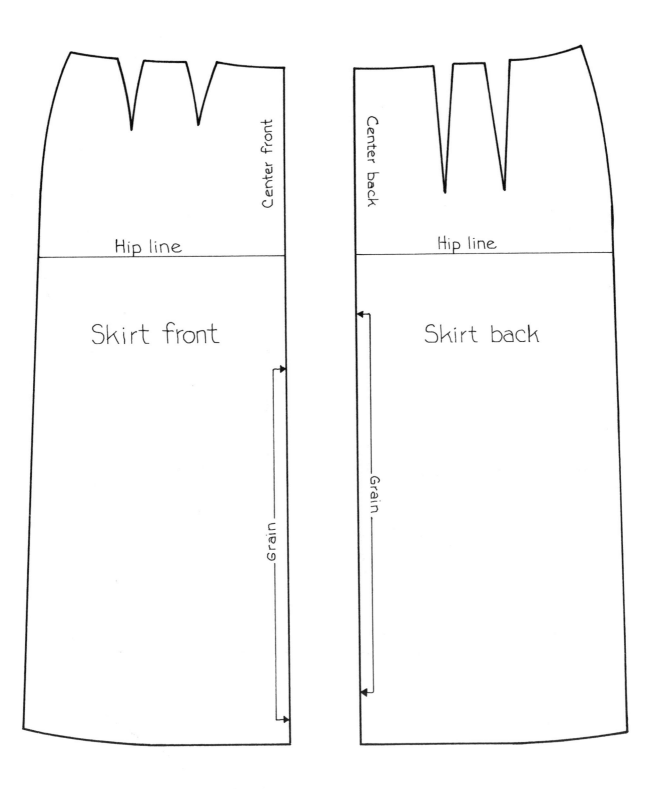

Figure 66: Woman's miniature skirt sloper

- *A right triangle.* Available in art stores. Optional.
- *A set of french curves.* For drawing curved lines.
- *A hip curve.* Get one marked off as a ruler. The top often works for armholes.
- *Writing tools.* A soft writing pencil and an eraser.
- *Pattern paper.* Plain or marked in 1 in. squares.
- *Graph paper.* To keep a slashed pattern aligned and spread slashes evenly.
- *Cheap scissors.* For cutting paper.
- *Adhesive tape.* Of the "scotch" type.
- *Thumbtacks.* For stab pinning the pattern when it must be held down.
- *A cardboard cutting board.* For stab pinning.
- *A double tracing wheel.* For drawing cutting lines. Optional.

Professional designers always sketch their designs. However, a sketch is optional if you can visualize without it and are making for yourself.

MANIPULATING DARTS

Darts are used on fitted garments to mold fabric to body curves: the chest, shoulders, shoulder blades, elbows, abdomen, hips, and seat. The dart point is located at or near the highest part of the bulge. The wide end is at a seam. Darts can be moved, divided, combined, converted to ease, or concealed in seams. If the style is very loose they can be omitted.

To move a dart:

1. The dart shape must usually be changed before you work with it. A curved dart must be redrawn as a triangle. A dart reaching to near the bulge point must be redrawn all the way to the point (see figure 67).

2. Draw a line where you want the center of the new dart. The line must extend from the pattern edge to the bulge point. It can radiate in any direction from that point.

3. Slash along the new dart line to the bulge point.

4. Fold the old dart closed. Tape. The new dart will spread.

5. Smooth the pattern flat. Tape the spread dart over pattern paper.

6. Redraw the dart to its original length. Curve if desired. Fold closed temporarily and redraw the seam line. Then press the pattern flat.

7. Add seam allowances. First trace or tape the pattern onto a larger piece of paper. On straight edges measure out from each end and connect the lines. For curved edges draw short lines at such frequent intervals that they connect. Or

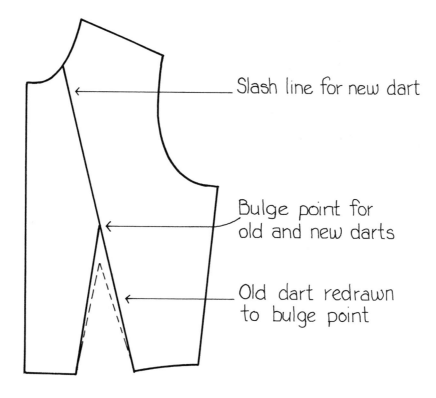

Slash line for new dart

Bulge point for
old and new darts

Old dart redrawn
to bulge point

Figure 67: Bust dart moved from waist to neck

use a double tracing wheel to indent the paper, then pencil over the indents.

A dart to be moved only a small distance can be redrawn rather than radiating from the same point (see figure 68).

Darts can be divided or combined only if they radiate from the same bulge point. This is most common with bust darts. To divide a dart, draw two (or more) new dart lines and divide the amount of spread between them. To combine darts, draw one dart line, close both old darts, and add all the spread to the new dart.

To convert a dart to ease, simply mark the wide end for gathers. If the result looks skimpy, combine darts first or add extra fullness as described below.

The seams in which darts may be hidden include princess seams, bodice yokes, skirt yokes, and skirt gores (sections). Move the dart(s) to where you want the seam. Treat the outer lines as part of the seam lines, omitting folded material (see figure 69).

Paper inserts, tape, and scratched-out marks can make an altered pattern piece confusingly messy. After testing it in muslin, trace the piece and copy relevant marks.

Learning More Advanced Reproduction Techniques

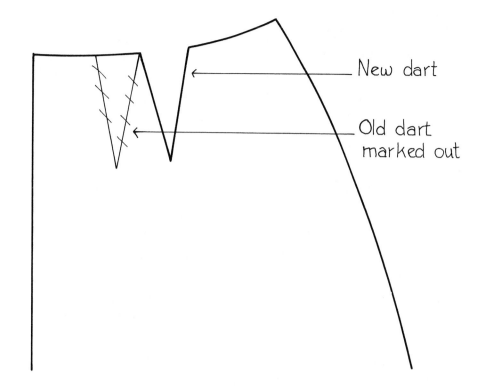

Figure 68: Skirt hip dart moved a slight distance

New dart

Old dart
marked out

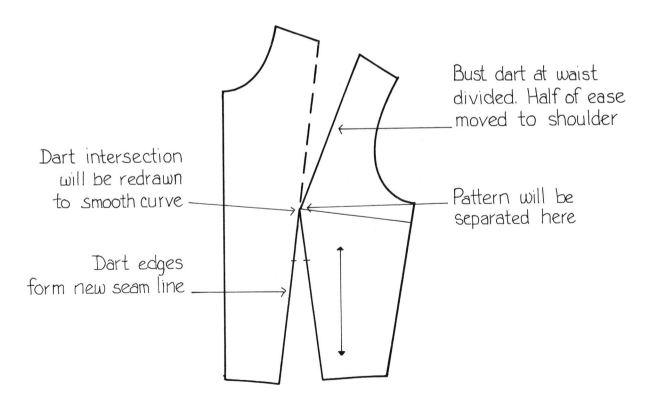

Bust dart at waist
divided. Half of ease
moved to shoulder

Dart intersection
will be redrawn
to smooth curve

Pattern will be
separated here

Dart edges
form new seam line

Figure 69: Bust darts included in princess seam

ADDING FULLNESS

Fullness is added by slashing and spreading the pattern. It can be added evenly by cutting the pattern apart and spreading it with the cut edges parallel (see figure 70). Or unevenly by spreading one pattern edge more than the other (see figure 71); this creates flare. Added fullness can be controlled by gathers, tucks, pleats, or drapery.

To add even fullness for gathering:

1. Draw a horizontal guideline, perpendicular to the grain line, across the pattern.

2. Slash the pattern as shown. If gathers will incorporate a dart, redraw the dart to the bulge point. Draw one slash to that point.

3. Spread the pattern over graph paper. Align the cut edges with vertical lines on the paper. Align the guideline with a horizontal line.

4. The spread seam line(s) will curve. If you want gathers to puff out, add additional length.

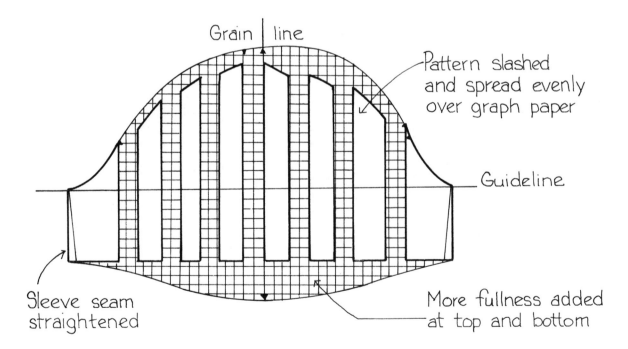

Figure 70: Even fullness added to sleeve

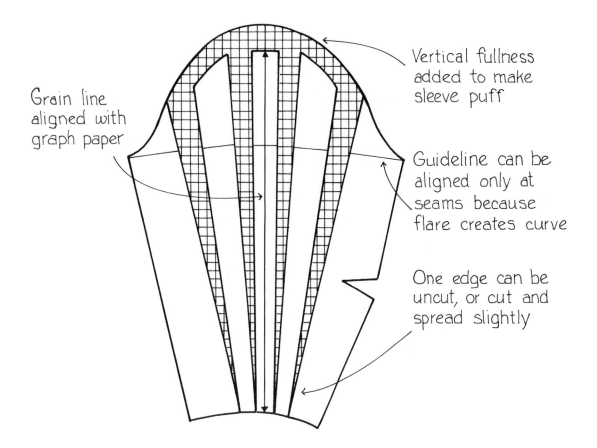

Grain line aligned with graph paper

Vertical fullness added to make sleeve puff

Guideline can be aligned only at seams because flare creates curve

One edge can be uncut, or cut and spread slightly

Figure 71: Flare added to create leg-of-mutton sleeve

5. When satisfied, tape down the pieces. Draw the new seam lines.

6. Mark the edge(s) to be gathered with a dotted line. Add seam allowances.

Tucks can be stitched all the way down and function as surface decoration. Or they can be stitched partway and release fullness into the rest of the pattern piece.

For purely decorative tucks, especially pin tucks, you may not need to alter the pattern. Tuck some fabric, then cut it using the original pattern piece.

Wider or released tucks can be added by slashing and spreading over graph paper. On the pattern each tuck should be twice its sewn width. Tape down the pieces. Draw stitching lines; fold lines are optional. Add arrows showing the fold direction. Then fold the pattern and cut across tucks to true the seam line (see figure 72). This can be done after adding seam allowances. Press the pattern.

Pleats are usually used in skirts or long flowing garments. Three common types are knife, box, and inverted box pleats (see figure 73).

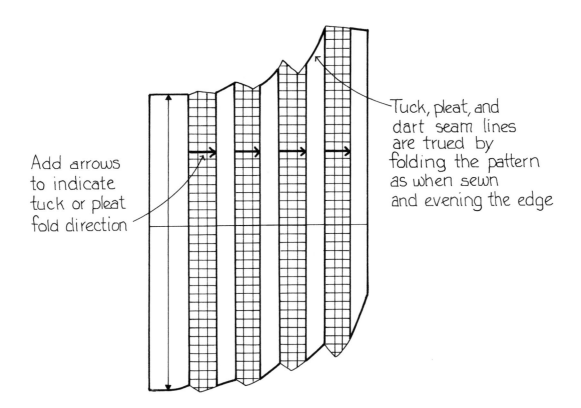

Add arrows
to indicate
tuck or pleat
fold direction

Tuck, pleat, and
dart seam lines
are trued by
folding the pattern
as when sewn
and evening the edge

Figure 72: Tucks added to bodice front

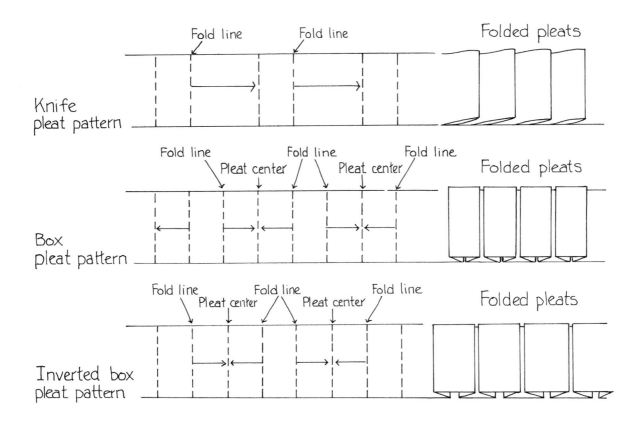

Fold line   Fold line   Folded pleats

Knife
pleat pattern

Fold line   Fold line   Fold line
       Pleat center   Pleat center   Folded pleats

Box
pleat pattern

Fold line   Fold line   Fold line
     Pleat center   Pleat center   Folded pleats

Inverted box
pleat pattern

Figure 73: Pleat patterns

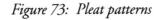

To add pleats:

1. Fold paper into pleats to work out the type and approximate size. If there will be only a few pleats you can also work out their number.

2. Measure the waistband or other section the pleats will be sewn to. Divide this measurement by the pleat size to get the number of pleats. Or by the number of pleats to get the pleat size.

3. Draw a horizontal guideline, perpendicular to the grain line, on the pattern.

4. Alter the pattern by slashing and spreading over graph paper. Most pleats should be three times their finished width. They should follow the lengthwise grain. Garment openings and seams (including any piecing seams) should be hidden by a folded pleat. You can eliminate a hip dart by dividing it into fourths to fall on two pleat edges (see figure 74). When satisfied, tape down.

5. Draw pleat fold and stitching lines. Indicate the fold direction(s) with arrows. Fold pleats in pattern to true the top seam line and bottom hemline. Press the pattern.

6. Add seam allowances.

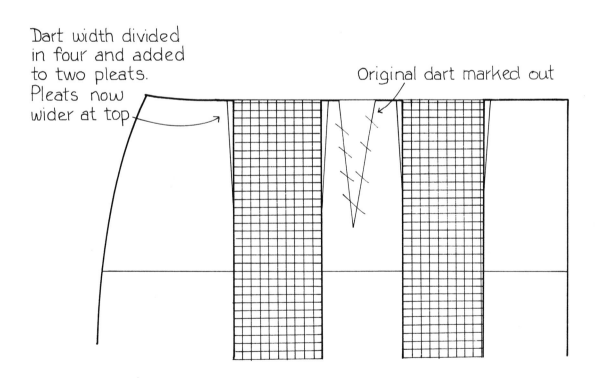

Figure 74: Hip dart incorporated into skirt pleats

A single, graduated, inverted box pleat is often used at a skirt center front. By graduated, I mean wider at the bottom than the top.

Mark, then slash the pattern where you want the pleat. Fold the pleat, full size, in paper. Press flat. Tape the slashed pattern edges over the pleat edges (see figure 75). Draw pleat fold lines; mark the fold direction. True the seam lines. Then press the pattern.

If the pleat doesn't hang well in the muslin, try cutting the skirt and pleat separately and sewing in the pleat.

Flare is a form of fullness that adds little or no bulk at one seam line. Slash the pattern to but not through the edge that won't be spread, or through it if it will be spread a little. (See figure 71 again.) Spread the pattern at the edge(s) where you want flare. Distribute the flare evenly across an edge, carefully preserving the resulting curve.

Drapery folds make sophisticated use of the fabric bias. They can be horizontal, vertical, diagonal, or curved. A cowl neckline is one example.

Draped styles were little used before the 1930s. I don't recommend them for the pattern-making novice. But if you want

To add ease, add less than half the original measurement. To add minimum fullness, add one and a half times the original measure. To add moderate fullness, add twice the original measure. And for maximum fullness, add three times the original measure.

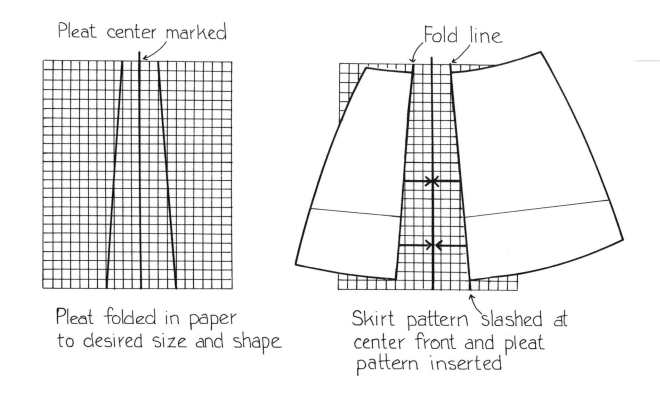

Pleat center marked

Fold line

Pleat folded in paper
to desired size and shape

Skirt pattern slashed at
center front and pleat
pattern inserted

Figure 75: How to design a graduated pleat

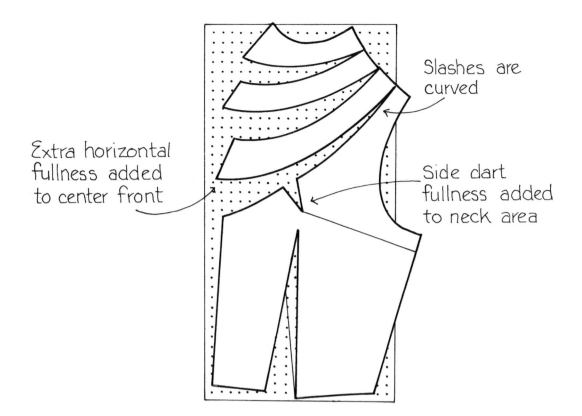

Slashes are
curved

Extra horizontal
fullness added
to center front

Side dart
fullness added
to neck area

Figure 76: Drapery folds added to create a cowl neck

to try adding drapery, make curved slashes, then spread to add
the desired fullness (see figure 76). Test in muslin till you like
the effect.

DIVIDING AND ADDING TO SECTIONS

One way to change pattern design is to cut sections apart, for
example into yokes or skirt gores. Another way is to add them
together.

A yoke can be any shape, even asymmetrical. It may be
purely decorative. But it can also improve fit by incorporating
darts or eliminating bulky gathers. Favorite places for yokes are
bodice shoulders and skirt hips.

To create a plain yoke, cut the section apart (see figure 77).
If you must move a dart to incorporate it do this first. If the
dart forms the seam line into a sharp angle, redraw it to curve
gently. Transfer the grain line from the main pattern piece and
add seam allowances.

A yoke may continue from one pattern piece to another,
for example from a blouse front to the back. You can eliminate
the shoulder seam by taping the yoke pieces together. This
changes the grain of one piece.

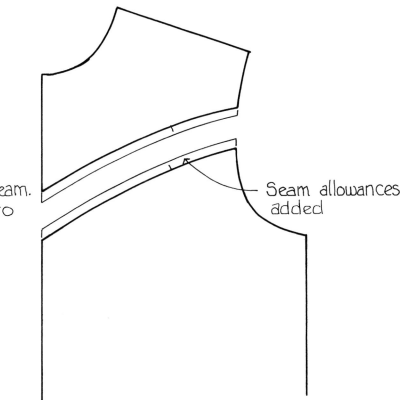

Unless yoke is high, transfer a bust dart to yoke/bodice seam. Redraw seam to smooth curve

Seam allowances added

Figure 77: Bodice divided to create a simple yoke

An intricately shaped yoke has an irregular edge that is best sewn over the other section (see figure 78). Trace the pattern piece to where the yoke bottom will be. Cut the copy into the yoke shape. Cut the original piece into a plain shape that will reach slightly under the yoke. Add seam allowances to both pieces. When you sew the garment, turn under the yoke seam allowance and sew it over the other section. The bottom seam allowance can then be trimmed to the yoke shape.

An alternative is to make a plastron (a section sewn over the bodice) instead of a yoke. Copy the pattern piece and carve the yoke out of it, but leave the original piece untouched. When you make the garment, the plastron will cover part of the original piece.

A gored skirt is created by cutting a fitted skirt pattern into sections and flaring them at the bottom. Goring adds flattering vertical lines. By changing the grain, it changes the way the skirt hangs.

The basic fitted skirt is two-gore; it consists of a front and a back. To create a four-gore skirt:

1. Straighten curves at the sides (see figure 79).

A yoke looks especially decorative if cut from lace (which may be pieced insertion); a napped, embroidered, or pin-tucked fabric; or a contrasting color. You can attach it with a piped, embroidered, or other ornamental seam.

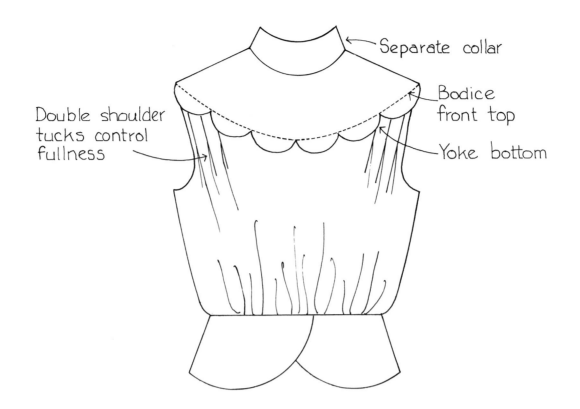

Figure 78: Blouse with yoke sewn over bodice front

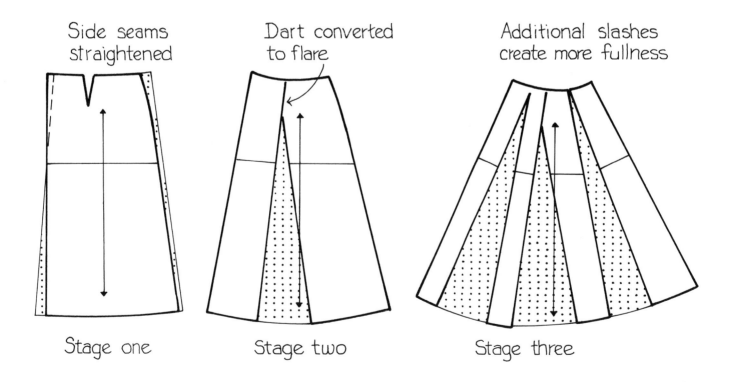

Figure 79: Basic skirt pattern transformed into four-gore skirt

2. Divide the front and back equally.

3. Slash from the hip darts to the bottom. Tape hip darts closed.

4. Make more slashes and spread the skirt evenly till it flares the desired amount. Tape down.

5. Draw grain lines. If the grain is placed in the middle of each gore, seams will be somewhat bias. If the grain is placed to one side of the gore, that side will be straight and the other more bias. Straight edges may be sewn to bias if the style requires it.

6. Redraw the hemline in a smooth curve.

7. Add seam and hem allowances.

A six-gore skirt divides the front and back into three unequally sized sections. The center front panel is narrowest; for the most flattering effect, its width should be planned carefully. The grain line should be centered. The two side front panels absorb the rest of the pattern front. Incorporate the hip dart into the center front/side panel seam. The side panel grain line should be centered or perpendicular to the hip line.

The back may be divided into three equal sections. Or it may have a narrow center back panel, or a wide gathered one. The back panel may also be divided to create a seven-gore skirt.

Flare can be added evenly to a six- or seven-gore skirt. But some period styles require adding it unevenly near the side of each gore (see figure 80).

A skirt can also have five gores, or nine, or as many as your design requires.

Sections are often added together at the waistline to raise or lower it, or to create a peplum. To lower the waist, mark the new waistline on the skirt. Cut it there and tape it to the bodice at the waist (see figure 81). If necessary redraw the skirt dart to align with the bodice dart. Fix seam allowances.

To raise the waistline, cut off the bodice at the waist and tape it to the skirt top.

A peplum is a short overskirt (hip length or above) attached to a bodice or jacket. Its edges may be plain, curved at the center front opening, or intricately shaped at the bottom. The peplum must flare enough to fit smoothly over the skirt; it may flare more for effect. Trace a basic skirt pattern to the peplum length. Add flare and redraw the edges till you achieve the design (see figure 82).

I've found I can sew seams accurately without using notches. But if you want to add them to a pattern, draw them across the seam line before cutting sections apart.

When planning gores, consider the skirt fabric. Soft fabrics collapse on the bias grain; stiff ones stand out. If stripes must meet, add flare evenly to the gores and put grain lines in the middle.

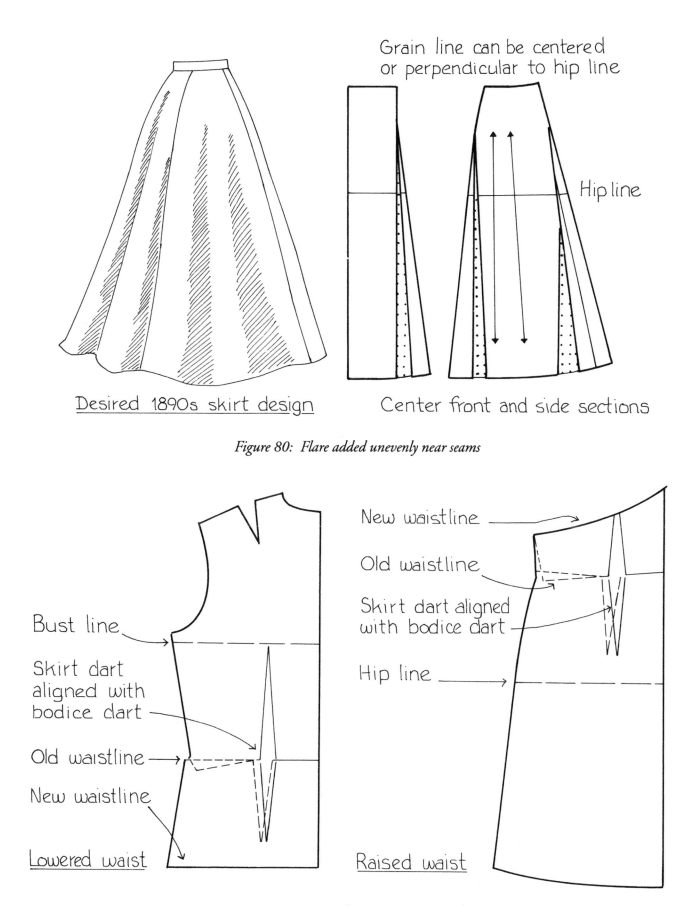

Grain line can be centered
or perpendicular to hip line

Hip line

Desired 1890s skirt design

Center front and side sections

Figure 80: Flare added unevenly near seams

New waistline

Old waistline

Skirt dart aligned
with bodice dart

Hip line

Bust line

Skirt dart
aligned with
bodice dart

Old waistline

New waistline

Lowered waist

Raised waist

Figure 81: How to lower or raise a waistline

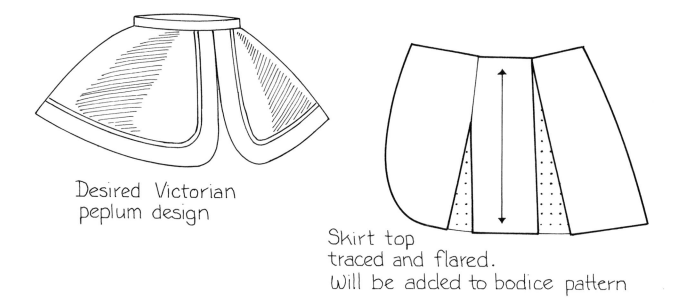

Desired Victorian peplum design

Skirt top traced and flared. Will be added to bodice pattern

Figure 82: A peplum pattern

DRAWING FACINGS

Facings are used to finish and support edges such as necklines, hems, and openings. They may be extensions—cut in one with the garment—or sewn on.

A straight garment opening usually has a simple extension facing. To draw one:

1. Calculate how wide the facing must be to hold the fasteners. Consider what type you'll use; add extra width if they'll be buttons of an as-yet-undetermined size. When closed, the garment must meet on the center front or back line.

2. Draw this amount straight out from the garment edge (see figure 83).

3. Add a seam allowance so you can slip stitch the facing to the wrong side. Or substitute for an interfacing by adding an allowance almost the full facing width.

4. Fold the extension on the fold and seam lines to true the top and bottom seams.

A curved edge can be faced with either a hemmed-down bias strip (which requires no pattern) or a fitted facing. A fitted facing duplicates the shape of the opening to be faced (see figure 84).

Large buttons should be spaced far apart, small ones close together. Spacing in groups, rather than evenly, creates interest and is appropriate for some eras.

Learning More Advanced Reproduction Techniques

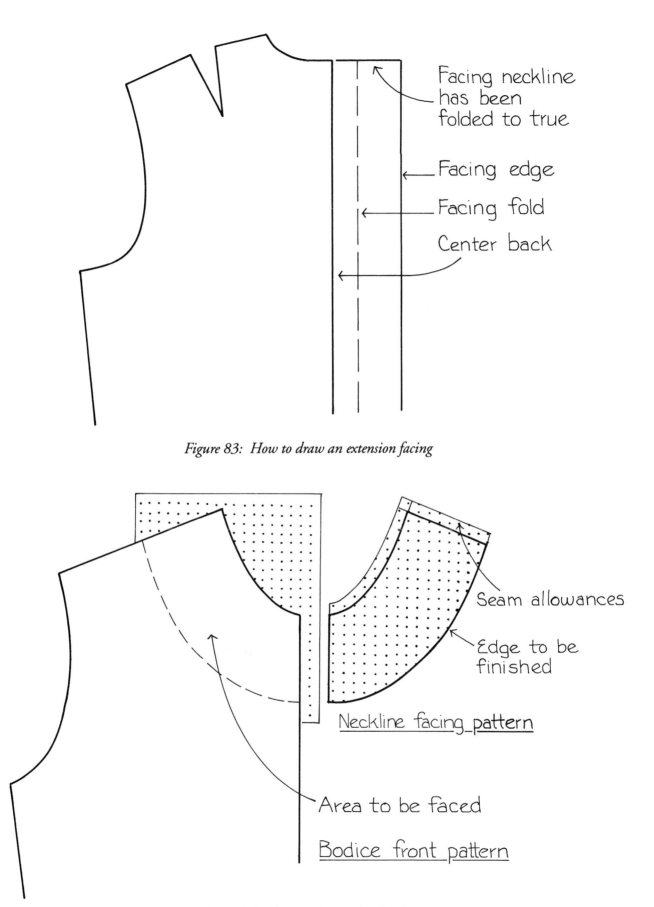

Figure 83: How to draw an extension facing

Facing neckline
has been
folded to true

Facing edge

Facing fold

Center back

Seam allowances

Edge to be
finished

Neckline facing <u>pattern</u>

Area to be faced

<u>Bodice front pattern</u>

Figure 84: How to draw a fitted facing

To make a fitted facing:

1. If the pattern has no seam allowance for attaching a facing, add one to each relevant piece.

2. Trace the opening from each piece onto pattern paper. Trace several inches down shoulder or other intersecting seams. Also trace grain lines.

3. On the facing pieces, draw the other long edge about 3 in. away from the opening edge, or 3 1/4 in. if the facing is to be turned under and hemmed to the garment on the inside (rather than hanging free). Duplicate the opening edge by laying a clear plastic ruler over it and drawing the new lines at short intervals.

To reduce bulk, you can draw a shaped facing that omits seams crossing the opening. Temporarily tape the original pattern together at those seams before tracing. For a neckline, use the grain line of the section where the garment opens. For an armhole, use the front grain.

🖋 SEWING WITH A VINTAGE PATTERN

The most fruitful sources for original vintage patterns are vintage clothing stores and shows, and mail-order dealers in used costume/textile arts books. (See appendix A.) Patterns also turn up at flea markets, yard sales, and suchlike. Because they're often incomplete, examine them (or question the seller) before purchase. Compare the number of pieces to the number shown on the envelope. The envelope has much other vital information, so don't buy a pattern without one. A separate instruction sheet is helpful but not essential. Many companies didn't include one till the 1920s.

You can also mail order copies of old patterns from a company that reissues them. Copies are guaranteed to be complete and sturdy. A good selection is available.

Even though several sizes were originally published, today a vintage pattern is usually available in only one size. Body measurements, rather than size numbers, may be used. Either the most important measurement or a complete size chart is printed on the envelope. Unless the garment is very loose or you're experienced at pattern alterations, it's best to start with a pattern in your bust/chest size. The hip, waist, and especially the length measurements are easier to alter.

Note that many separate 1910s patterns for "waists" (bodices or blouses) and skirts were designed to be assembled as dresses if desired. Choose a style combination that appeals to you and works for your measurements. Patterns can be combined even when the bodice and skirt open in different places.

Instead of making a pattern, you can sew an unshaped piece of facing material to the garment, right side to right side. Trim the facing to size and clip curves. Turn to the inside and finish the edge.

You can date a vintage pattern by comparing it to fashion magazines and mail-order catalogs from what you think is the correct period. Sometimes a patent date on the envelope is too early because it's for the drafting system used to create the pattern, not the pattern itself.

This section focuses on patterns from the late 19th century to about 1930. You'll seldom find earlier ones. And later patterns have more familiar marks and instructions.

Learning More Advanced Reproduction Techniques

BUYING MATERIALS

You'll notice that although vintage pattern envelopes tell you roughly how much fabric you need, they seldom explain what kind. They are especially lacking in yardages, or even ideas, for trim. This is because companies gave detailed fabric and trim information in the fashion magazines they published to help market the patterns. Research these as much as possible if you want an authentic reproduction. Vintage garments are also an extremely helpful source.

The envelope will give a table of fabric widths and quantities. Assume quantities are underestimated because they often don't account for nap, stripes, hems, or facings. And of course they can't account for your alterations. I always end up shortening patterns because I'm even smaller than most turn-of-the-century women. But to be safe I buy about a yard extra if using a directional fabric and half a yard if using a nondirectional one.

Finally, fasteners, seam bindings, and other notions are seldom explicitly mentioned. If you are expected to use buttons the envelope picture shows them; you'll have to figure button size and spacing. Otherwise use hooks or snaps.

Chapter 3 explains how to arrange an efficient pattern layout.

Vintage pattern envelopes seldom warn you that stripes and plaids can't be matched. Test the effect by using a similar muslin fabric.

PRESERVING AN ORIGINAL

Always copy an original pattern before use because the paper is extremely fragile. Photocopy both sides of the envelope and instruction sheet (if any), using the enlarger for greater reading ease. Place each pattern piece flat on a table and smooth it gently to remove creases, or use a very cool dry iron if necessary. Don't try to repair tears with adhesive tape—it causes more damage. Cover the pattern with a sheet of clear plastic film (available in art stores) so you don't score or dent it. Place tissue paper on the plastic.

Using a soft pencil, trace the pattern outline and perforations (holes) onto the tissue. Cut out the copy with plenty of margin to allow for alterations. To preserve the original, store it flat in an inert plastic envelope (which you can buy in stores that sell old comic books) or between sheets of acetate film or acid-free tissue paper.

One vintage pattern format, often used in women's magazines, has overlapping pieces for several patterns printed on a single sheet. Patterns are distinguished by different line styles. Trace the relevant pieces like a packaged tissue pattern. Or make several photocopies, using a large-format copier if necessary, and cut out the pieces.

MARKING THE PATTERN

All pattern pieces will be illustrated on the envelope. Identify each piece and label it with a pencil. If a piece is missing, consider whether you really need it—two alternatives for sleeves or other details are sometimes given. Or you might find a replacement in a similar vintage pattern. Sometimes facings and plackets aren't provided because sewers were expected to create them.

The first printed seam allowances and marks appeared around 1919, but most companies didn't use them till after 1938. Instead, each company used a slightly different system of perforations and notches. Although these may seem mysterious, they're explained on the envelope and provide most of the same information as printed marks.

Seam allowances (which were not always included) vary from 3/8 in. to 1 in. and may be marked by a line of perforations or notches. Choose the most appropriate seam finish for your fabric and alter the allowances if necessary. You may want to add extra for size adjustments. The fabric grain is usually marked by a row of large holes. The waistline is sometimes marked by notches or perforations, perhaps in the underarm area. Other sizes and groupings of holes are used to mark darts (often called "plaits"), areas to gather, and so on. Length alteration lines are often unmarked. Guidelines for drawing them are given in chapter 3.

I translate perforations into modern symbols on the pattern. For example, if the beginning and end of an area to be gathered are indicated by holes, I draw a dotted line in between. But you can add whatever marks or notes you find helpful.

ALTERING THE PATTERN

Until 1930, when pattern sizes were standardized, each company used its own "typical" body measurements. If there's a chart of these on the envelope (or you can find one in the company's catalog or sewing manual), compare them to yours and alter the pattern accordingly. Note that period sizing generally assumes women were shorter, smaller-waisted, and larger-hipped than now. If there isn't a complete set of measurements for your size, alter the pattern as well as you can and do the rest at the muslin stage.

I take period style, as well as sizing, into account. I closely examine the envelope picture and if necessary other sources. I use the taper-the-line and slash-and-spread alteration techniques described in chapter 3. Until I fit the muslin, I'm conservative. I leave more rather than less fabric. I avoid changing darts or seams other than the side seams. If extra fullness is provided by gathers, I fine-tune the fit by gathering more or less.

I've found that 1910s bodice patterns may extend 6 in. or more below the waist—usually not an even amount all around. They may also be larger-waisted than the size chart implies. My theory is that companies were using patent drafting systems or slopers from a few years earlier, when longer, puffier bodices were stylish. It's best to deal with the excess during construction, not pattern alteration. (I'll explain how.)

Late Victorian/Edwardian patterns assume an average woman's height of about 5 ft. 2 or 3 in. Make most length alterations in the skirt. A hem allowance may or may not be included; check the envelope. If not either lengthen the pattern or use a bias hem facing (which I prefer for flared skirts). I always have to alter skirts at the waist and/or hips because period sizing assumes about a 15 in. difference. Although I'm sometimes able to slash-and-spread, I often have to add/subtract width and use a hip curve to redraw the side seams.

If you combine a bodice and skirt into a dress, or the pattern is unclear, you must determine where the garment opens. This problem is most likely with 1910s dresses, which can open at any seam or several. Bodices often open at center front and the skirt at the side or back; an overskirt may not open where the skirt does. This is possible because 1910s garment sections are attached to a "stay belt" made of strong cotton webbing. If there are two openings the belt overlaps around the waist between them (see figure 85). When the garment is put on, the belt's short ends are fastened with hooks. Then the skirt is fastened to the waist with largish snaps. A separate outer belt or sash conceals the join.

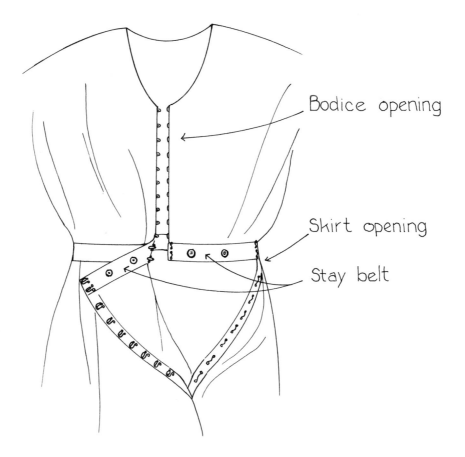

Figure 85: 1910s dress with front bodice opening and side skirt opening

Even if a dress has only one opening, the stay belt is vital for fitting. If little support is needed, you can use a wide grosgrain ribbon. For 1910s skirts, which have a raised waist that hangs from the top of the belt, you can use commercial belting. Or make an inner, interfaced self-fabric waistband. Whatever the material, make the belt the width stated on the pattern—otherwise the garment will fit badly.

Create plackets, neck facings, and armhole facings after fitting the muslin.

CONSTRUCTING THE GARMENT

Most late 19th- and early 20th-century sewing techniques are similar to those used today. An exception is a technique called "hanging" used to arrange the excess fabric of 1910s bodices. I hang mine during construction, but if you wish you can mark the muslin instead. Here is how I hung the bodice of a 1910s dress with a grosgrain stay belt.

First I chalked the stay belt at the center front, back opening, and side seams. I put the belt on my dress form so the bottom was at the waistline (the bodice waist was raised to the belt top). I then pinned the belt to the form at the marked seams. To facilitate removal I placed the pins vertically with the heads down.

Then I put the bodice on the form so the marked seams (plus the shoulders and neck) were correctly positioned, and pinned them to the belt. For stability I also pinned the bodice to the form all the way down the center front, back, and sides and across the shoulders. Working from the center front and back toward the side seams, I pleated the excess width (see figure 86). (I could have marked it for gathering instead.) I had to use different-sized pleats, which I arranged symmetrically, to achieve the best fit. When satisfied I pinned them to the belt. I allowed about 1 in. vertical ease, as in vintage dresses; the rest hung below the belt.

I carefully withdrew only the pins that fastened the belt to the form and lifted off the bodice. Once it was laid on a table I could easily even out the waistline just like a hem. I basted, then machine stitched, the bodice to the belt's top edge. Only then did I cut off the excess length.

Finally, I pinned and basted the skirt, then the tunic (overskirt) to the belt without using the form. The belt provided an inside finish because the dress was sewn on top. I slip stitched a contrasting silk waistband to the outside to cover the raw edges.

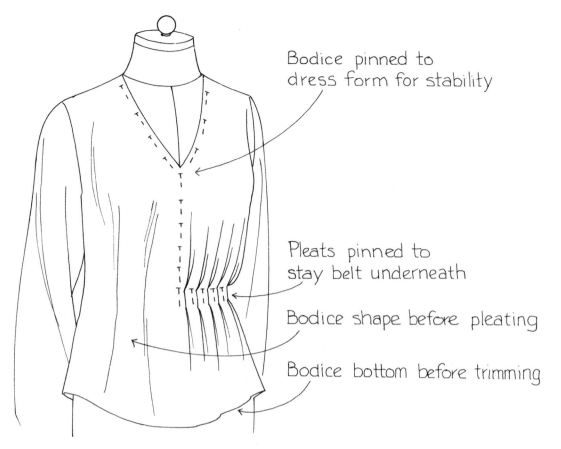

Bodice pinned to dress form for stability

Pleats pinned to stay belt underneath

Bodice shape before pleating

Bodice bottom before trimming

Figure 86: How to hang a 1910s bodice

✈ ENLARGING A SCALE DRAFT

A scale draft is any pattern whose size has been accurately scaled down. It can be a copy of a period garment or a theatrical pattern developed from a modern sloper. It can also be a pattern from a tailoring or dressmaking publication that, though intended for drafting, is drawn to scale.

Designs intended for surface decoration (or that you want to adapt for it) are usually full size. However, you may need to change the size to fit your pattern. This can be done by pattern-scaling methods.

There are two common enlargement methods: projection and the grid method. I've also developed a method for enlargement or reduction with a photocopier. None of these methods requires pattern-drafting expertise.

Projection is the easiest, most flexible method. It can make any scale pattern almost any size, quickly. It can enlarge, but not reduce, full-size surface decoration designs.

The grid method enlarges patterns drawn to a standard scale (1/8, 1/10, 1/4, or 1/5) to full size. However, it doesn't work for some patterns intended for drafting. When printed, these may have become a peculiar scale for which commercial grids are unavailable.

The patterns in this section are for illustrative purposes only. They are not suitable for enlargement.

Photocopying can enlarge or reduce surface decoration designs or clothing patterns a specified percentage. However, it's best for pieces that fit on one sheet of paper both before and after copying.

PROJECTING A PATTERN

Although projection works well for any scale pattern, my example will be a pattern intended for drafting. If yours was intended for enlargement, skip the section on how to determine whether a pattern is drawn to scale.

Throughout the 19th and early 20th centuries, there was a strong movement to make pattern drafting more "scientific"—more dependent on measurement and method, and less dependent on eye and experience. A great many "systems" were developed, some requiring patent tools that had to be bought from the developer. Many developers wrote one or more books that explained how to use their system and provided pattern diagrams with drafting instructions. Some magazines published diagrams, which might not require a particular system.

A number of these pattern books have been reprinted (see appendix A). Original books and magazines are often sold by dealers in used costume books. If the patterns are drawn to scale (and most reprinted ones are) they can be projected instead of drafted.

To project a pattern you'll need:

- *A pocket calculator.* For drafts for which no scale is given.

- *An overhead projector.* Some people recommend an opaque projector. However, transparency projectors are brighter and more readily available. Some are portable. You may be able to borrow a projector from work.

- *A wall.* Or some other large, smooth, flat, perfectly vertical surface.

- *Pattern paper.* This should be marked in 1 in. squares.

- *Masking tape.* To tape pattern paper to the wall.

- *A clear plastic ruler.* 6 in., 12 in., or both.

- *A clear plastic yardstick.* Transparent tools don't block projection.

- *A set of small french curves.* Optional. Freehand drawing is easy with this method.

- *A hip curve.* Or other long shallow curve; optional.

- *A flexible spline.* This is a length of plastic-covered lead that can be bent into any curve. Optional, but very useful if you often scale up patterns.

You can draft pattern diagrams by following the original instructions if you have drafting experience and no patent tools are necessary. Original books have usually parted company with their tools. But most reprints don't require any.

Learning More Advanced Reproduction Techniques

Determining whether the pattern is accurately scaled

Most pattern drafts consist of a diagram with lettered or numbered points plus instructions on how to draw from point to point. Key measurements are given for the final size. A few others are given in the instructions or on the diagram.

Pick two lines for which measurements are given. One should be vertical and the other horizontal, to test scaling in both dimensions. Long lines are easier to measure accurately.

On the draft in figure 87, the vertical line I picked was the back waist length, A to C. The size chart says this is 17 in. On the original diagram, it measures 4 3/16 in.

The horizontal line was the "half breast measure," B to S. The size chart says the full breast (chest) measure is 36 in. But because the vest will have four pieces when cut out, this measurement is 9 in. On the original diagram, it's 2 5/16 in.

Now compare the ratio of the full-scale measurements to the ratio of the diagram's. You can divide the horizontal measurement by the vertical one or vice versa. Just be consistent.

I divided the full-scale measurements, 9 by 17, to get a ratio of 0.529. Before I could use the calculator to get a ratio

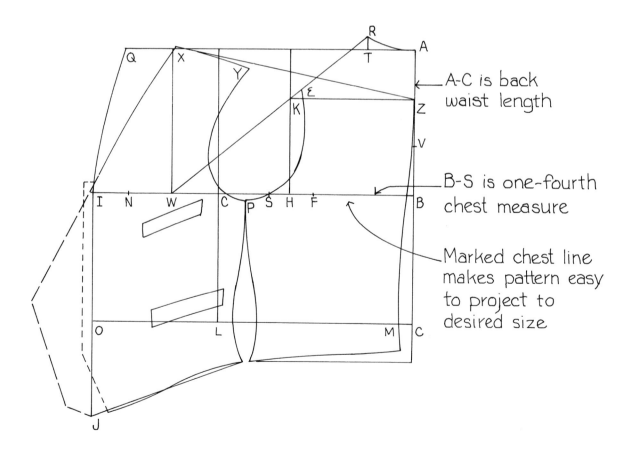

A-C is back
waist length

B-S is one-fourth
chest measure

Marked chest line
makes pattern easy
to project to
desired size

Figure 87: Drafting diagram suitable for projection

for the diagram's measurements, 2 5/16 and 4 3/16, I had to convert the fractions to decimals. I divided 5 by 16 to get .3125, and 3 by 16 to get .1875. I then divided 2.3125 by 4.1875 to get a ratio of 0.552.

Theoretically, if the diagram is accurately scaled the ratio of its measurements is identical to the ratio of the full-scale ones. In practice this seldom happens. You may have made minor measurement errors, or the diagram may have been slightly distorted by printing. However, if there's a small percentage of difference between the two ratios, you can consider the diagram accurately scaled.

To see what the percentage of difference is, subtract the full-scale ratio from the diagram's, then divide the result by the full-scale ratio. When I subtracted 0.529 from 0.522, I got -0.023. (The minus sign can be omitted from subsequent calculations; what matters is the distance from zero.) When I divided that by 0.529, I got 0.044. I multiplied this figure by 100 to convert it to a percentage, 4.4%.

What percentage of difference is acceptable? As a rule of thumb, a percentage under 5% indicates very accurate scaling. A percentage over 10% indicates enough distortion to make the diagram unsuitable for projection. If you get a percentage between 5% and 10%, check your measurements and math. Ideally you should start over with two more lines. If the percentage is still between 5% and 10%, you can project the pattern. But expect to make more fitting adjustments.

Drawing the pattern

Unless you're using an opaque projector, photocopy the diagram onto transparency film. This won't cause noticeable distortion.

Although you can project a pattern alone, an assistant is very useful. He or she can help adjust the projector, tape up large pieces of paper, and hold one end of the yardstick while you draw. Two people can even trace different pattern pieces simultaneously.

A pattern can be projected to either full scale or the desired size. For example, the vest in figure 87 can be projected to a chest measurement of 38 in., rather than 36 in. However, only the key measurement—the bust/chest for upper garments, the hips for lower ones—can be adjusted correctly. If you've ever gained or lost weight you've noticed that it doesn't distribute evenly around the body. The more you change the size, the more you'll have to fit the pattern.

Set up the projector facing the wall. Then adjust the projector till it's exactly the right distance from the wall and facing the wall straight on.

To adjust distance for a pattern, project the diagram onto the bare wall. Use the plastic yardstick to measure its size on the wall. To enlarge to full scale, measure the scale or graph provided, or the key measurement. To enlarge to another size, adjust till the key measurement is correct. This is especially easy with diagrams because key measurements are marked by lines and adjoining pieces are often laid together.

The distance for a surface decoration design should be adjusted by projecting directly onto the pattern piece it will be applied to, rather than the wall.

Now you need to adjust the straightness of the projector to the wall. Unless the diagram was printed on a graph, take it off the projector. Lay the plastic ruler horizontally on the projector. On the wall, measure one division (1/8 in. is good) at each end of the ruler. Wiggle the projector from side to side till both divisions measure the same. Then lay the ruler vertically on the projector. Adjust the projector by raising and lowering the front end.

If the diagram was printed on a graph, any angling of the projector is obvious. If you often project patterns, it's handy to copy graph paper onto a transparency and use it to check straightness.

Put the diagram back on the projector in the desired position. The pieces you'll trace first should be reachable on the wall. Cut a sufficiently large piece of pattern paper, remembering to allow for seams and pattern adjustments. Hold up the paper and align a row of dots with the scale ruler or another vertical line. Tape down that side. Then finish taping, smoothing the paper and adjusting dots to vertical and horizontal lines as you go.

Now for the easy part—drawing the pattern. Projected lines look thick. You'll have to decide whether to trace the outsides or the insides; be consistent. I trace the middles of interior lines. Draw long straight lines against a yardstick, short ones against the more easily held ruler. Curves can be drawn freehand or against appropriate french curves or a spline. Trace all pattern marks. Try to keep the pencil perpendicular to the wall.

Finishing the pattern

Take the pattern off the wall and roughly cut apart the pieces. Measure edges that will be seamed together. If they're different lengths, check the original measurements and redraw as necessary. True seam lines where fabric will be folded into darts, pleats, or facings. Fold the pattern like the fabric and redraw nonmatching lines.

Add seam allowances by measuring out from the pattern edge with the plastic ruler. For straight edges measure each end

Occasionally pattern pieces on the same page are drawn to different scales (this is visible in the drawing). Move the projector to the correct position for each piece.

A diagram can also be projected onto another pattern to aid in style alterations.

Art stores sell templates for small shapes. These enable you to draw perfect circular button marks, triangular notches, etc.

Another way to add allowances to curved seams is to use a felt-tip pen to draw seam and cutting lines on a small, smooth piece of cardboard. Align the card seam line with the pattern's. Move the card along while transferring its cutting line to the pattern with a pencil. Some pattern makers find this faster than using a ruler.

and connect the lines. For curved edges draw short lines at such frequent intervals that they connect. Or use a double tracing wheel to indent the paper, then pencil over the indents.

Draw a grain line following a long vertical row of pattern-paper dots. Label the pieces with the pattern source, garment type, and style date. Indicate how many times each piece will be cut from fashion fabric, lining, underlining, and/or interfacing. Where necessary mark the front, back, top, and/or bottom. If the design is asymmetrical indicate whether this is the right or left side.

EXPANDING FROM A GRID

If your draft was printed over a grid you'll need:

- *Pattern paper.* This should be marked in 1 in. squares.
- *A clear plastic ruler.* 6 in., 12 in., or both.
- *A yardstick.*
- *A ruled L- or T-square.* Optional.
- *A set of small french curves.*
- *A hip curve.* Or other long shallow curve.
- *A flexible spline.* Optional.

If your draft isn't gridded, you'll also need:

- *A pocket calculator.*
- *Access to a photocopier.* It must have enlargement capabilities.
- *Transparent graph paper.* Stock both 8 squares to the inch and 10. A gridded polyester mylar is sold at art stores. Although you can copy graph paper onto a transparency, the graph will be reduced about 1%.

Measuring the scale

Your draft was probably drawn at an 8-to-1 or 10-to-1 scale. The publisher may have reduced the draft further to fit the book page. An ungridded draft should show the scale with a little ruler or some measurements. Measure this to figure out the reduction—as accurately as possible because errors will be magnified by enlargement. Figure 88 shows a piece of cloth, labeled "35 in." The ruler laid beside it shows 1 3/4 in. A calculator can't handle fractions, so I translated this to 1.75 in. I then divided the desired size, 35 in., by the actual size, 1.75 in. The result, 20, shows the draft is 1/20 scale, or 20 squares to the inch.

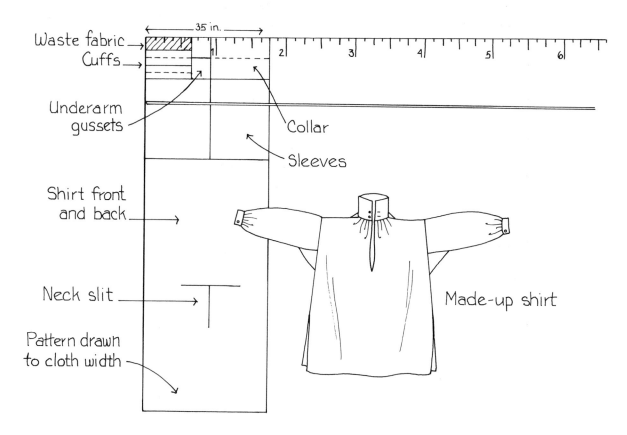

Labels in figure:
Waste fabric
Cuffs
Underarm gussets
Shirt front and back
Neck slit
Pattern drawn to cloth width
35 in.
Collar
Sleeves
Made-up shirt

Figure 88: Diagram of Regency shirt with scale being measured

Adding a grid

Although this simple draft could be drawn without a grid, I prefer one for most drafts. First I use the photocopier to enlarge the draft to fit a 1/8 or 1/10 scale grid, whichever is most convenient—in this case 1/10 scale. To scale 20 squares to the inch to 10 I divided the current number of squares per inch by the desired number to come up with 2. In other words, the draft must be enlarged 200%.

Most office photocopiers can enlarge up to 150% or 175%. You can enlarge a draft further by passing it through two or more times; see table 1. If you're enlarging by a percentage not shown in the table, use your calculator to figure out how much each enlargement should be. The quickest way to find two numbers that multiply to equal a given magnification is to use the square root button and adjust the result. For example, the square root of 2 is 1.41 plus some decimal points. But 1.41 multiplied by itself equals approximately 1.98, not 2; you get a more accurate result by multiplying 1.41 by 1.42.

To enlarge this many times	Use this sequence of percentage enlargements
1.75x	132, 132
2x	141, 142
2.25x	150, 150
2.5x	158, 158
2.75x	166, 166 or 140, 140, 140
3x	173, 173 or 144, 144, 145
3.25x	148, 148, 148
3.5x	141, 142, 175 or 136, 137, 137, 137
3.75x	155, 155, 155 or 139, 139, 139, 140
4x	158, 159, 159 or 141, 141, 142, 142
4.25x	162, 162, 162 or 143, 143, 144, 144
4.5x	145, 146, 146, 146
4.75x	147, 148, 148, 148
5x	171, 171, 171 or 149, 149, 150, 150

Table 1: Percentages for photocopy enlargements

This means your first enlargement should be 141%; your second, 142%.

Check the final enlarged copy with your ruler to make sure it's correct. Then position the mylar over it, aligning vertical pattern lines with the grid, and photocopy with no enlargement. You now have a gridded pattern at a scale that's easy to work with (see figure 89).

When enlarged for gridding, a pattern may no longer fit on one sheet of paper.

Enlarging the pattern

Photocopy the gridded pattern if you want to preserve it from marks and overhandling. Lay an ample piece of dotted pattern paper on your work table. Put the gridded pattern beside it.

The first step in enlarging a gridded pattern piece is to plot points from the grid onto the pattern paper, which is simply a larger grid. (See figure 90.) Start at the center front, center back, or a straight line of the pattern piece. On the pattern

Pattern enlarged in two sections

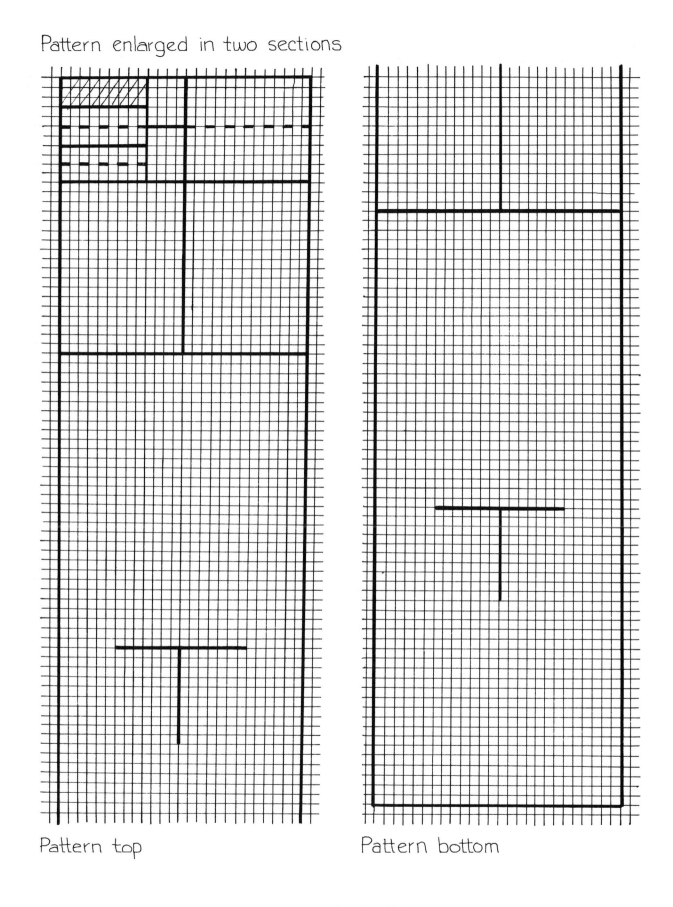

Pattern top   Pattern bottom

Figure 89: Enlarged and gridded pattern

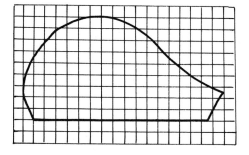 Gridded pattern

For curves plot near
each grid intersection

Cut pattern paper large enough
to add seams, plus some extra

For straight lines
plot end points only

Draw an initial straight line
before plotting the rest if this
makes measurement easier

Figure 90: How to scale up a gridded pattern

paper, pencil a mark that represents one end of this line. If the line is perfectly straight, count the squares to the other end on the grid. Count the same number of squares on your pattern paper and pencil another mark.

If the line is curved count the squares, or portions thereof, up (or down) and across to the next point. Mark that point on your pattern paper. Continue counting and marking till you finish the section.

You'll note that you have some choice as to how many points to plot and where. Plot as many as are needed to accurately represent the line. It's best to plot points at grid lines or intersections, but sometimes you'll have to estimate where a point falls in the middle of a square.

The next step is connecting the points to draw the pattern. Use a yardstick or L-square for straight lines. Fit french curves against a curved area till you find the best match. Sometimes you'll need to use more than one curve for an area or draw it freehand. This is where a flexible spline comes in handy.

Eyeball the full-size pattern to make sure it looks correct. Measure adjoining pattern pieces at the seams. Redraw lines where necessary. I usually find I drew some curves too shallow or sharp, or that some measurements are off because I counted squares wrong.

Copy the author's marks for joining, gathering, and so on. Draw grain lines. Add labels and seam allowances as described for a projected pattern.

Compare the full-size pattern measurements to yours. Alter the pattern using the instructions in chapter 3, taking period fitting standards into account.

ENLARGING WITH A PHOTOCOPIER

The method for enlarging a draft for gridding can also be used to enlarge pattern pieces to full size. Ideally this is smaller than the copy paper. Small pieces can be enlarged with an office copier. Larger ones can be enlarged at a copy shop with a large-format machine. If you can't find one, enlarge the pieces in sections. The sections should overlap slightly, and the overlap area should include one or two distinctive pattern marks. Align two sections at the marks and tape. Draw new seam allowances after copying.

The photocopier method allows you to freely experiment with different sizes. I wanted an unusually shaped Victorian bag to carry ballet slippers to dances, but my full-size pattern was too small. I photocopied it without a grid at 150%, 175%, and 200%. When I laid the slippers over each copy it was clear the largest one should be the pattern.

A surface decoration design can be made either larger or

smaller. Photocopy at different percentages till you like the size. To transfer the design to the pattern piece (rather than directly to the fabric), photocopy it onto a transparency. Then lay the design over the pattern and copy both together.

◈ COPYING A VINTAGE GARMENT

Copying vintage garments enables you to get authentic patterns that haven't been published. If you're an unusual size and the garment fits well, you may prefer copying to pattern alterations. And copying enables you to reline a garment whose lining is missing or too damaged to trace.

Choose a simple garment for your first project. It shouldn't have lots of sections, gathers, or bias cutting. The fabric shouldn't be delicate or slippery. And the grain should be clearly visible—woven stripes are ideal.

There are two copying methods. One duplicates the garment in cloth and the other relies on measurements. Try both. You may wish to use the cloth method for shaped sections and the measurement method for rectangular ones.

To take a pattern you'll need:

- *A flat surface.* A large table protected with a cutting board is essential. Some sections may be copied more efficiently if slipped over an ironing board, sleeve board, or tailor's ham.

- *Pattern-tracing cloth.* A translucent cloth, similar to light nonwoven interfacing, printed with 1 in. squares or dots at 1 in. intervals. For the cloth method.

- *Pattern paper marked in 1 in. squares.* For the measurement method.

- *Large sheets of graph paper.* For taking a scale pattern by the measurement method. The most common scale is 1/8 in. to 1 in.

- *Cheap scissors.* For cutting paper.

- *A large magnifying glass.* Depending on the fabric and your eyesight, you may need this to find the grain.

- *Extra-fine silk or butterfly pins.* Regular sewing pins may leave permanent holes.

- *A tape measure.* For the measurement method you may need two.

- *A soft, sharp lead pencil.* And an eraser.

- *Drawing tools.* A yardstick, clear plastic rulers, french curves, a hip curve, and a spline.

- *A double tracing wheel.* If you use one to add seam allowances.

If a garment is in poor condition and not very old or unusual, you can take it apart and trace around the pieces. This is recommended only for expendable garments.

Learning More Advanced Reproduction Techniques

TAKING A CLOTH PATTERN

Start by copying a simple, small, fairly unshaped section. Copy from the right side.

Find the grain line by following a vertical thread in (approximately) the middle. Mark it by inserting a line of pins or basting between this thread and the next. If you wish, you may also mark the horizontal grain.

Cut a piece of pattern cloth a few inches larger than the section. Draw a grain line on it using a soft pencil and ruler.

Smooth the section flat. Lay the cloth over the section, matching grain lines. Pin them together. Then pin the cloth to the garment at the seams (see figure 91). Work out from the grain line, continually smoothing and forming the cloth to the garment. Insert pins alternately on each side of the section. Do your best to insert pins between threads; this prevents damage.

If there are darts, gathers, or pleats, pin the flat parts of the section while working toward the fuller ones. For a dart, pinch the cloth into the dart shape. Test the size by feeling the garment dart underneath with your fingers. Then pin the pattern dart as if sewn.

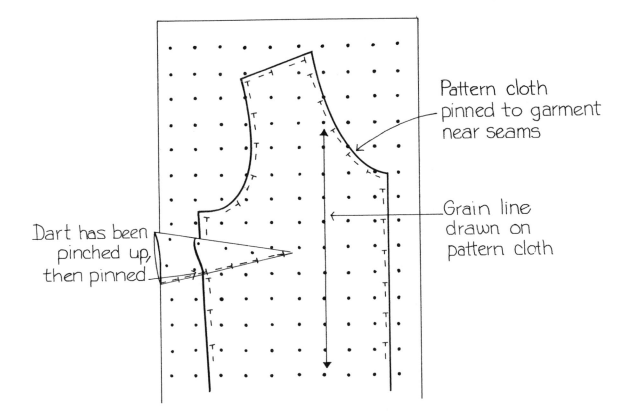

Figure 91: How to trace by the cloth method

Pleats and tucks are also copied by folding and pinning the pattern cloth. Simulate garment gathers by pushing up the cloth. Secure pattern gathers with closely spaced pins.

With your pencil, mark all construction lines: seam lines, garment edges, dart lines and points, pleat folds, and where gathers begin and end. Also mark where trims are attached.

Unpin the cloth and lift it off the garment. Immediately label it on the right side with the section name. If the section is oddly shaped mark the top/bottom and right/left. It's easy to scramble pattern pieces. Then press.

Finish the copy by taking a separate pattern of each unique section. If a section was used twice, copy the one that's least damaged or stretched.

Clean up the lines with a ruler and french curves. You can add joining marks by leaving pins inserted across garment seams and marking their locations on adjoining sections.

MEASURING THE GARMENT

Copying by the measurement method is similar to enlarging a gridded draft. In fact, points can be plotted on graph paper to create a scale pattern. For a full-size one, use dotted pattern paper.

First mark off base lines on the pattern or graph paper. Label a bottom corner 0. Then number a vertical and a horizontal row of dots or lines (see figure 92). If using pattern paper, assign a number to each dot (1, 2, 3, and so on). You'll have to draw base lines for each large section or group of small ones. If using 1/8 in. graph paper, you can number rows at intervals (8, 16, 24, and so on). You'll be able to copy the whole garment onto one or two large sheets, but may still need several sets of base lines.

Sections should have the same orientation on the pattern or graph paper as on the garment (the section top pointing up, etc.). On graph paper, where sections won't be cut apart, they should be arranged as they're sewn together.

Start with a simple section. Mark a vertical grain line unless the section is a perfect rectangle (check whether threads angle at the seams) or one edge is obviously cut on the straight of grain. Insert a line of pins or basting between the threads. You can also mark the horizontal grain. Draw the grain line(s) on the pattern paper.

Now figure out where plotting points should be (see figure 93). A straight line needs plotting points at the beginning and end, which means a rectangle can just be measured and drafted. A curved line needs as many points as required to draw the curve, whether it's pronounced or subtle. All details that inter-

You may need new base lines
for each group of pattern pieces

Some pattern
paper has
numbered dots.
Renumber
rather than
accommodating
base lines
to printed numbers

Leave margin
in case you
position pattern
incorrectly
or need to add
seam allowances ⟶

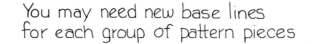

Figure 92: Base lines marked on pattern paper

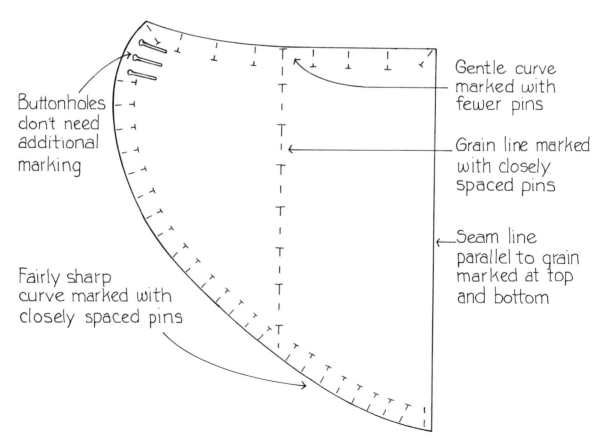

Buttonholes
don't need
additional
marking

Gentle curve
marked with
fewer pins

Grain line marked
with closely
spaced pins

Seam line
parallel to grain
marked at top
and bottom

Fairly sharp
curve marked with
closely spaced pins

Figure 93: Plotting points marked on jacket skirt front

Some published pattern drafts provide only the main garment sections. Facings, trims, and so on are indicated by lines drawn on the main sections, or even omitted. You'll find your pattern easier to use if, instead of following this practice, you copy all sections. Work from the inside where necessary.

rupt a line must be marked—intersecting seams, darts, gathers, pockets, etc.

Mark each plotting point by inserting a pin between the threads. Lay a tape measure along the grain line and weight the ends. Use another tape to measure from the grain line, at right angles, to the first plotting point. (The two tape measures act like an L square, but are flexible.) Plot it on the paper with a pencil dot. Remember to account for the tape measure's width. Continue measuring and plotting till you have a good outline of the section. Then plot trim placement lines. Leave a few pins across garment seams so you can add joining marks.

Now draw the paper pattern by connecting the points. Use the size of ruler, or shape of curve, that best suits the line. Don't alter any line to fit a convenient curve. Use the spline or draw freehand. Eyeball the pattern to make sure it looks correct. Then move on to the next section.

FINISHING A COPIED PATTERN

Compare the seam lengths of adjoining sections. If there's a discrepancy, measure the garment and correct the pattern. True seam lines where fabric will be folded.

For a full-size pattern, add seam and hem allowances. Label each section with the garment type, date, and section name. Indicate how many times each piece should be cut and what material(s) to cut it from. Mark darts, gathers, pleats, pockets, and trim placement like a commercial pattern.

For a scale draft, omit seam and hem allowances. Do indicate the hem depth. Label the pattern sheet, rather than individual sections, with the garment type and date. Mark everything else like a full-scale pattern.

Make a muslin. Compare its shape and drape to the garment's. For complex sections you may have to experiment with flat pattern alterations till you get a muslin that looks right. Transfer all corrections to the pattern.

Make detailed notes on the garment materials and construction. You can work on these as you take the copy and polish them afterward. Be especially meticulous if you don't own the garment or need a scholarly record. Published scale drafts often have the notes written directly on the pattern. But this limits available information and makes the notes harder to use, so I recommend keeping them separate.

⚜ DESIGNING GARMENTS COMPOSED OF GEOMETRIC SHAPES

Cloth production is a labor-intensive process involving many stages. Consequently many historic styles utilize cloth with as little waste as possible. Widths are sewn together much as they come off the loom. Wealth is displayed not by a more elaborate cut, but by adding fullness to the basic one. (Wealth is also expressed by more expensive cloth and more decoration.) Such styles are easy to draft because they consist entirely of geometric shapes: the rectangle, square, triangle, and circle.

UNDERSTANDING GEOMETRIC DESIGN PRINCIPLES

There several basic types of geometric garment. One is an unseamed rectangle or square that is draped on the body. Examples are the great plaid of Scotland (worn from the late 16th to the late 17th century) and most kerchiefs, cravats, shawls, stoles, and veils.

A second type might be described as "rectangles gathered into a band." It includes skirts and petticoats from the late 16th through the 17th century, and again from the 1830s through the 1850s, plus 18th-century petticoats. Most aprons belong to this type. So do many 1910s and 1920s chemises, nightgowns, and camisoles. (These have shoulder straps as well as a yoke band.)

A third type is the T-tunic, of which there are many variations. The basic concept is to use one cloth width for the front, another for the back, and two widths or half-widths for the sleeves (see figures 94 and 88). The neckline is cut into the cloth. Flare is created by cutting off long triangles in one place (such as the shoulders) and sewing them to another (such as the hem). T-tunics often have dropped shoulders and underarm gussets. Neck and sleeve shapes, and the presence of a collar, cuffs, and/or frills, vary with the era and garment.

From the 6th through the 13th centuries, most styles for both sexes were based on the T-tunic. The cut survived in undergarments—men's shirts, women's chemises, and nightgowns—into the Victorian period. And in some widely worn but unfashionable garments, such as the 18th-century shortgown and the 19th-century smock frock.

The fourth type of geometric garment I'll discuss is the circular cape. Long capes made from a full, half, three-quarter, or other large segment of a circle were worn by both sexes from the 6th century through the 15th. Short men's capes were fashionable from the mid 15th century well into the 17th.

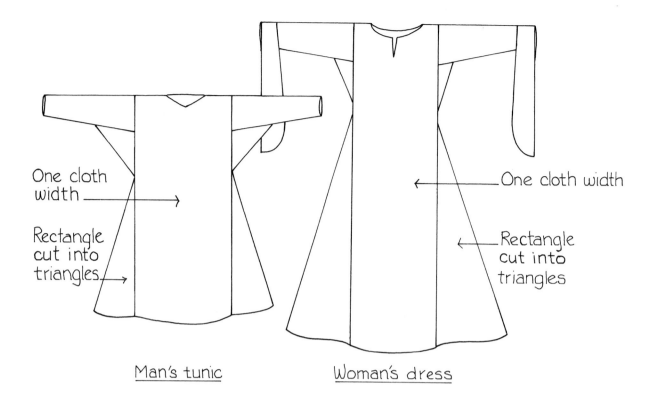

One cloth width

Rectangle cut into triangles

One cloth width

Rectangle cut into triangles

Man's tunic

Woman's dress

Figure 94: Thirteenth-century T-tunics

DRAFTING A PATTERN

Once you understand the principles behind geometric styles it's easy to detect a pattern shape from a picture. Unseamed garments can be measured and cut without a pattern. A garment gathered into a band can be designed by cutting the band to your measurements and seaming cloth widths to the desired fullness.

To draft a T-tunic, first cut pattern paper to an authentic cloth width. If your sources don't deal with this topic, 30 to 35 in. is usually suitable and convenient. Handwoven fabric is seldom wider than 45 in. and may well be about 20 in. You can cut the garment from an inauthentically wide fabric, as long as it was designed for the correct width.

Although geometric garments fit loosely, consider your height, arm length (for sleeved garments), and whether you are small, medium, or large. Also decide whether you want the most basic cut or a fuller luxury version. Figure out approximate measurements for the largest pattern pieces.

Then draw the pattern shapes on the paper. Start with the large pieces, which are most important in terms of both cloth usage and your size. Draw the other pieces beside or at the end

Geometric styles were worn as soon as the loom was invented. They were retained in folk costumes and church vestments after largely disappearing from fashionable dress. However, their full history is outside the scope of this book.

If you often draft circles it may be worth buying a large compass at a drafting supply store.

Even complex garments have geometric pattern pieces—waistbands, cuffs, shoulder straps—that can be drafted.

Learning More Advanced Reproduction Techniques

of the large ones. Aim for little or no wastage. If an inch or so seems left over, include it in a pattern piece rather than cutting it away. Draw the cut-out neckline last. It's uneccessary to add seam allowances to this type of pattern.

A circular cape should also be designed with pattern paper cut to an authentic width. Figure out where piecing seams will be. Then temporarily tape the paper together there, overlapping seam allowances.

A circle must be drafted with a compass. You can make one by cutting a piece of nonstretch string some inches longer than the radius (half-width). Fasten one end to where the middle of the circle will be. Shove a thumbtack through the string (knotted if necessary) and pattern paper, right into your cutting board. Then measure out the width of the radius. Tie a pencil there, using the string end beyond the radius. Then draw the circle by holding the pencil vertically with the string taut and moving it around the circle. Although you can easily draw a half or full circle, for an in-between size it's best to draw a full circle and chop out a wedge. Draw the neckline and opening, then untape the paper.

✍ WRITING YOUR OWN SEWING INSTRUCTIONS

All pattern types discussed in this chapter have one thing in common: they don't have complete, step-by-step sewing instructions. And some sized reproduction patterns lack instructions, or have rough or confusing ones. Here's how to write your own.

Start writing instructions at the beginning of the project, before you cut out. You'll have to research and/or figure out missing information anyway. By doing it early, you'll save time and prevent mistakes.

COLLECTING INFORMATION

Assemble all information provided with the pattern. A reproduction pattern may well have a printed envelope and instruction sheet. A vintage pattern may or may not include instructions. Drafts intended for enlargement often have construction pointers written on the pattern or in accompanying text. Period drafting instructions sometimes include a paragraph on making up. You may have made notes while taking or drafting a pattern.

Write down the information in what you think is the correct order. Even if it's already printed. (If a reproduction pattern has complete instructions, copy only sections that must be changed for your alterations.) This will induce you to analyze it, as well as providing the basis for polished instructions. A word-processing program will enable you to freely add, rewrite, reorganize, and reprint.

Proofread your instructions against the original information. Correct any errors. Now study any pictures (or an original copied garment) more closely. Add the construction information these provide.

Pattern in hand, mentally work through your instructions to check for missing information. Here are some questions to ask. Some answers require you to write information on the pattern, as well as in the instructions.

- Can you identify all pattern pieces?

- Which is the back, front, top, and bottom of each piece?

- Do you know which other pieces each pattern piece is sewn to?

- Are enough marks provided for assembly? Do you understand them all?

- If one side of a seam is longer than the other, do you know what to do with the extra fabric (easing, gathering, pleating, tucking, overlapping)?

- Are any pattern pieces missing? These are likely to be small or interior sections—facings, plackets, interfacings.

- How will you obtain missing pieces? By adapting existing ones? Borrowing from other patterns? Drafting?

- Are all pattern pieces mentioned in the instructions?

- Is the garment lined? Underlined?

- Do the instructions cover seam finishes, special seams, hems, and closures?

- What trims will be used?

- How will trims be attached? Before or after assembling the garment section(s)?

Chapter 2 contains additional information on evaluating existing instructions and researching sources.

It's OK to use copyrighted instructions for personal projects. But it's illegal to publish or distribute them. Vintage materials may or may not have a current copyright; check. Modern ones certainly do. Note that copyright applies to small sections as well as the entire document. And to unpublished materials as well as published.

Many answers will be provided by your common sense and sewing experience. Add them to your instructions. But you may have to research other information, particularly on authentic period techniques. There are many options for constructing any garment. But for authenticity, look for information specific to your historic period and if possible your garment style. The most useful sources focus on clothing construction.

Large chunks of step-by-step instructions are easiest to adapt. You'll most likely find them in reproduction patterns for other garments. (Also see chapters 3 and 7.) Next look in theatrical costuming guides. They've probably solved problems you face (and which may not be clarified by period sources because they weren't problems to period readers). Also read

Learning More Advanced Reproduction Techniques

period sewing manuals; these are most available from the Victorian era on.

Suppose your research indicates that a technique is authentic, but you can't find clear instructions. Look in a modern, but traditionally oriented, sewing manual (see appendix A). Books on ornamentation and trimming, couture sewing, and heirloom sewing may also be useful.

If these sources don't answer all your questions, check less technical ones. Visual information provided by portraits, period photos, fashion plates, and photos of originals is very valuable. Academic books and articles contain nuggets of information unavailable elsewhere. And take advantage of any opportunities to examine actual garments.

ORGANIZING THE INSTRUCTIONS

Once you've done all the research, translate it into instruction steps. Make your decisions on assembly order as final as possible before testing. Assembly order varies with the garment; it can be changed somewhat for convenience. But here are some general rules for a fairly complex garment, a sleeved dress with a waist seam.

- Follow chapter 3's instructions on preparing fabric, determining layout, cutting, marking, stay stitching, and underlining. In that order. But these steps are the same for all garments, so don't bother adding them to your instructions.

- For ease of handling, work with the smallest possible portion of the garment. Add small pieces like pockets to a section before sewing it to another section.

- Any piece that crosses seams, such as a neckline facing or bottom flounce, must be attached after those seams are sewn.

- Assemble the bodice front and back.

- Sew them together at the sides and shoulders.

- Add the collar or neckline facing.

- Stitch the long sleeve seams; attach any cuffs.

- Sew sleeves to the bodice.

- Assemble the skirt front and back.

- Sew the skirt side seams.

- Sew the bodice and skirt together.

- If the dress is lined, assemble the lining separately in the same order as the dress. Then sew the dress and lining together.

- Hems and fasteners are generally sewn last.

Vintage pattern envelopes, drafting diagrams, and modern scale drafts sometimes show pattern pieces in assembly order.

POLISHING THE INSTRUCTIONS

Even if your instructions are just for you, I recommend being as specific and thorough as possible. When you sew the garment you'll want to concentrate on that, not puzzling out incomplete instructions. Your project may be interrupted; it's amazing how fast information stored in memory can be forgotten. Or you may reuse the pattern, or make up a similar one, several years from now.

Here are some tips on polishing instructions:

- Make a complete materials list, including fabric, lining or underlining, trims, seam binding, boning, fasteners, and thread. Your research may have revealed several alternatives. Include the ones you won't use now for future reference.

- Break down the instructions into short, discrete steps.

- If it's unclear why something should (or shouldn't) be done, explain.

- Add special techniques or tips you've discovered.

- Draw a sketch where it's impossible to give a purely verbal explanation.

- Actively test the instructions while making the muslin, and again while sewing the garment. Edit and reprint as necessary.

- Proofread.

- File the instructions with the pattern, plus other related information such as the transparency of a scale draft. Put everything in a large, sturdy, clearly labeled envelope. If you have a drawing of the complete garment, tape a photocopy to the outside.

I store my patterns—of all types—in lidded copy-paper boxes. They're organized first by date, then by garment type. Each box is labeled with the categories it contains.

5 Buying Vintage Clothes

The central question when you buy a vintage garment is: what do you plan to do with it? The answer affects how much you'll pay for the garment, how you'll care for it, and even whether you should buy it in the first place.

Most people classify vintage clothes as either collectible or wearable. Collectibles are items the owner wants to preserve as long as possible. Ideally they're cleaned, mended, and stored using museum conservation techniques. They are never worn and are displayed only occasionally, in a carefully controlled manner.

Wearables are clothes the owner actively uses. They may be worn to reenactments or to work. They may be displayed in relatively uncontrolled settings—for example by live models at a vintage fashion show. They may be altered to fit. The owner's goal is to preserve the clothes long enough to get full value out of them. Cleaning, mending, and storage techniques are more radical—and more practical—than those used by museums. But they're gentler than those used on new clothes.

No one has come up with a generally accepted definition of which clothes are collectibles and which wearables. You are the only person who can decide how to use the ones in your possession. You may choose to preserve them all, wear them all, or preserve some and wear others. Common decision criteria include age, rarity, fragility, association with a famous historic person or event, creation by a famous designer, and artistic merit.

My policy is to regard clothes from before 1890 as collectibles because most are too fragile to wear. I do wear them occasionally for photography. I wear clothes from after 1890 freely and without guilt, usually for vintage dance. I've found that if you buy an item in good condition and care for it properly, you can wear it many times. This book assumes your philosophy is similar to mine, and that most items you buy are wearables.

🌿 FINDING SOURCES

The vintage clothing business works like a food chain. Often a garment first sold at an estate sale is purchased by a series of dealers until it reaches an individual buyer. It may travel

Appendix A lists books that tell you how to preserve collectibles.

Even museums are unable to preserve every vintage garment that comes their way. Some routinely sell deaccessions and unwanted donations to dealers. I've bought gorgeous clothes that were deaccessioned.

around the country as dealers buy from each other at shows or by mail. Each time the garment is sold, its price rises.

Your buying strategy will depend on how much time and money you have, where you live, and how much market research you do. You'll save money buying at the first links in the chain—estate sales, yard sales, and country auctions. However, you'll spend a good deal of time shopping, cleaning, and mending. And in some parts of the country truly vintage clothes are seldom found at these sources.

You'll save time buying clean, mended clothes from a dealer who consistently sells what you like. You'll also spend more money. But you don't have to pay maximum prices, even if you live in a pricey area. Mail order and vintage clothing shows offer a wide range of options. And it pays to check out sources wherever you travel.

SCOURING YARD, GARAGE, AND ESTATE SALES

Yard, garage, and estate sales are all basically the same type of sale. The merchandise may or may not include vintage clothes. The most likely sales are those held in older neighborhoods or neighborhoods where older people live, and sales of the estates of older people.

Sales are advertised in small neighborhood papers, trade sheets, and larger dailies, and by street signs. Read the ads before the weekend. Use a map to plan an efficient route. Get cash from the bank in case you run into a seller who won't take checks.

Because you'll be competing with dealers, the best items will be sold very early. Your only strategy is to arrive even earlier. If a sale offers nothing of interest, go on to the next immediately.

SEARCHING FLEA MARKETS AND ANTIQUE SHOWS

Flea markets are advertised in antiques publications as well as dailies. They feature a wide variety of merchandise in variable condition. Many dealers are regulars and may also have stores. Sometimes individuals rent a booth for the day instead of holding a yard sale. Prices are higher than at estate sales but lower than in vintage clothing stores.

With flea markets the strategy is to arrive early—as the booths are set up—and shop fast. You may have to dig through unrelated items to find vintage clothes and accessories. But do your best to ignore them, and skip unlikely booths on your first round. You can always come back. If you're still around at the end of the day, see if dealers will reduce prices to avoid hauling the items home.

An obvious source of vintage clothes is older relatives and friends. Be open, but tactful, about the intended use of the clothes and the question of payment.

Don't bother asking dealers what their sources are. They'll never tell you.

When a dealer tells you an item can't be found anywhere, it often just means they don't carry it. Keep looking.

The most aggressive buyers arrive before the sale begins. They may even call a few days ahead and talk their way into getting the first pick.

There will probably be no place to try clothes on. Wear a light, unbulky outfit so you can slip things on over it at the booth. Carry a small mirror if you're buying hats or jewelry. Take a tape measure. With practice, you'll be able to discern your size by eye. Remember that you can seldom return items at a flea market.

An antique show is just an upscale flea market. The merchandise is usually high quality and priced accordingly. You won't find any bargains by arriving early. However, you may find vintage clothes at an average price, maybe a good price if the dealer has another specialty.

You'll also find "secondary" vintage jewelry—"real" jewelry that's within the reach of the average person. Typical examples are cameos with gold-filled settings, stickpins with small semi-precious stones, and silver brooches.

BIDDING AT AUCTIONS

There are two types of auctions where you're likely to find vintage clothes. Large auction houses regularly hold antique auctions that may include clothes. Sometimes there are specialty clothing auctions.

These auctions are advertised in antiques publications, local newspapers, and mailers from the auction houses. Auction houses are listed in the Yellow Pages. Call them to find out whether they sell clothes and to get their mailers.

Often an auction catalog is available that describes the items and estimated prices (which may have little relation to the selling prices). Some houses allow absentee bidding by dropping off or mailing a form, or by phone. Contact them for procedures.

Country auctions usually sell off the entire contents of an estate, which may include several decades' worth of clothes. They are commonly held in the seller's yard. Attendees are expected to bring their own folding chairs, lunches, and foul-weather gear. These auctions are advertised in local newspapers and regional antiques publications. The ads briefly list the most interesting items.

At all auctions items are sold strictly as-is, so it's important to attend the preview. Large auction houses hold one for several days before the sale. Country auctioneers hold one an hour or two before the sale, or even during the sale. Also do a cursory inspection during bidding. Other potential buyers may have handled items roughly or swapped box contents.

During the preview, decide which items you want and how much each is worth to you. Clothes are often sold in lots, which will include some items you don't want. Don't pay more for a lot than you would for just the desirable items. Write down each item number along with your spending limit for it. Don't bid over this limit, no matter what. Because bidding is competitive it's easy to get carried away, but you'll regret it when you get home.

Ask about bidding and payment procedures. In most cases you'll register and get a numbered paddle or card. For efficiency bidding increments will be specified. They may increase as the item is bid up. You must pay for items right after you buy them, when you leave the auction, or, in the case of absentee bids, within a specified time period. Acceptable forms of payment vary. You may be able to use credit cards but not checks or vice versa. Auction houses charge sales tax.

The auctioneer will begin by suggesting a bid, usually more than he or she expects the item to sell for. If no one accepts the bid, the auctioneer will lower it until someone does—or suggests a different amount. The bidding goes up from there. To accept a bid, raise your paddle or card, or your hand. To bid a different amount, yell it out. When the bidding has reached its limit, the auctioneer announces the winning number.

Take your purchases home when you leave (frequent auction-goers buy trucks). Mix-ups, or even thefts, of items left for collection are not unknown.

BUYING AT VINTAGE CLOTHING SHOWS

Vintage clothing shows are my favorite source because a tremendous variety of garments and accessories is sold at a wide range of prices. Usually at least 50 dealers exhibit. Some have local stores, but many are from out of state or sell only at shows. Shows run for one to three days.

Because most merchandise will interest you, you'll have to figure out how to allocate your budget effectively. My strategy is to walk through the show twice. On the first round I look through the larger items—clothes and hats—as quickly as possible. I buy what I really want without worrying that there is something better at the next booth. On the second round I look at small items that take more time—lace, jewelry, and buttons. And I reexamine clothes I liked but couldn't decide on immediately—if they're still there.

Age is one of my most important buying criteria, so I skip booths that only display recent items. I seldom try on or use a tape, but I don't recommend this unless you're very good at judging by eye. Most shows do have mirrored dressing areas.

Pick up business cards from dealers whose merchandise you like. Ask for advance notification of items they bring to the next show. If they're local, ask whether they have a shop or sell from their home.

Don't worry about bidding on an expensive item by accident. It just doesn't happen.

You may be able to split a lot with another bidder. Decide ahead who will bid and how to share the lot. Or you can try to sell items to, or buy them from, another bidder. But don't count on it.

I think it's unfair to ask dealers to hold items while you make up your mind. This reduces the chance of selling them to someone else. Many dealers refuse to hold, or break their promises when a more decisive customer comes along. If you must have a hold, limit the time period to an hour or less.

If you want to return on the second day of a show to look at an item you're considering, ask the dealer for a free pass.

SHOPPING AT VINTAGE CLOTHING STORES

Vintage clothing stores are the best place to find vintage clothes on a frequent, regular basis. They're also the most expensive, because owners must not only find and restore the clothes but pay for store overhead.

Store prices vary with the geographic area and whether the store is in a high-rent district. Prices also vary with the store's emphasis and the shop owner's tastes. A store that specializes in Edwardian whites charges more for them than a store that carries a range of clothes from 1900 to 1940. A shop owner who dislikes brown will unconsciously price brown garments lower.

So shop around. Get the Yellow Pages for all areas within driving distance. Most stores are listed under a heading like "Clothing, Used." Call ahead if you have to drive any distance or are visiting a strange city. Verify the address and hours. Also check whether the store is worth visiting. Many stores carry only merchandise from a specific date range. Or they specialize in either men's or women's clothes. Sometimes the same ad is printed (in the Yellow Pages and elsewhere) for years after the store's emphasis has changed.

Most stores are well organized, but the items on display may not correspond to those on sale. Always tell the owner what you're looking for—it may be hidden in a drawer, basket, or the back room. Conversely, some owners confusingly (and in my opinion amateurishly) mingle their personal collections with the merchandise. You'll have to ask about each item that interests you. Often an item without a price, or with an exceptionally high one, isn't really for sale.

Charitable outlets, thrift stores, and rummage sales are no longer reliable, inexpensive sources of vintage clothes. Most are sold directly to dealers. Or they appear in a special area of the shop, at higher prices than other merchandise. Antique stores occasionally carry a few vintage clothes, at variable prices.

Dates on store tags aren't necessarily reliable. Use the research techniques in chapter 2 to date styles that aren't described in chapter 1.

ORDERING BY MAIL

Mail order is a great source of items that aren't readily available in your area. It's also a way to get around the prevailing local prices. Clothes are usually clean and restored (if not you should get a price break). And mail order poses no risks as long as the dealer has a full, unconditional return policy.

Mail-order dealers advertise in antiques and specialty vintage clothing publications. When you find dealers whose merchandise you like at shows or out-of-town stores, ask whether they sell by mail.

When searching through ads I choose dealers who say explicitly that they sell by mail, on a retail basis (some sell only wholesale). Then I focus on those who give details on what they carry. For example, I am more likely to contact "Jane Doe, women's evening wear 1900–1930" than "Jane Doe, vintage clothing." In my experience when a dealer gives a wide date range, such as "1850–1950," most items are from the more recent years.

Mail-order procedures vary from dealer to dealer. A few supply a price list or illustrated catalog for a minimal fee. Usually you must send full payment in advance, but can return unwanted merchandise for a refund within a stipulated number of days.

Many dealers, however, sell "on approval." You describe your needs, the dealer sends an approval box, you choose some items and return payment along with the unwanted ones.

When I'm eager to order, I contact several dealers at once. I've found that many do not respond for several months. If you need an item by a specific date, contact dealers at least three months ahead and mention your deadline.

I contact dealers by letter so they have a clear description of my needs that can be filed. It includes a date range, types of garments, desired condition, and my favorite (and least favorite) colors. I give both ready-to-wear sizes and key measurements. I also say I'm buying retail.

In my opinion it isn't useful to state a price range in your contact letter. One dealer's "medium" range is another dealer's "high." You may think a dealer "overprices" some items but "underprices" others. You have to see the actual item to determine whether its price is appropriate.

I conclude my letter by asking the dealer to contact me before sending a box; I provide a phone number and a self-addressed stamped envelope. This enables me to clear up details about the dealer's policies, to preselect items, and to make sure no boxes are sent when I am away on a trip.

Because dealers incur a substantial financial risk by shipping on approval, some ask for security. This may be a check for a flat amount—say $50—or a proportion of the box's value—say half. If the goods you choose amount to less than the deposit, the dealer sends a refund. The only problem I have found with large deposits is that my money is tied up for three to four weeks even when I merit a refund, due to shipping and check-processing delays. Some dealers accept a credit card number as security without making a charge.

Ask if you pay for initial, as well as return, shipping. Usually you do. Most dealers use United Parcel because it's cheaper than the post office. If a dealer insists on UPS's more expensive second-day air service, ask them to pay shipping costs. Dealers seldom care whether a box is returned via UPS or the post office, as long as it's fully insured.

Finally, find out how much time is allowed for evaluating the box. Three to five days is usual. Some dealers expect you to call them within the approval period.

From both your viewpoint and the dealer's, a successful

transaction is one in which you want many of the items offered. Ask dealers to describe what they plan to send even if you buy from them regularly. Occasionally snapshots or sketches are available; these should be returned when you are through with them. Because no description or picture is equivalent to the actual item, I ask to see any I'm unsure about.

The dealer can further refine knowledge of your tastes if you enclose an explanatory note with returned items. Be constructive and tactful.

Building mail-order relationships also requires that you avoid damaging approval items. Pack and unpack carefully. If a garment looks too fragile to try on, don't. It is unethical to use a garment in any way—by wearing it, taking a pattern from it, or displaying it for resale—until you have paid for it.

There are minor variations in the way dealers do business. For example, whether they send boxes regularly or only on request and how much merchandise they like to send. If everyone's expectations are communicated you can work with many dealers.

Appendix A includes a list of mail-order dealers.

Occasionally I encounter a dealer who seems to customize prices. Watch out for large price increases in second and third approval boxes. Especially if you bought a lot from the first box and/or the others are sent just a few weeks later. Suggest alternative prices based on those for similar items in the first box. Or return the box with a note saying the prices are too high.

⌘ JUDGING CONDITION

The most important indicator of a garment's condition is its age. As I mentioned earlier, I think the cut-off date for wearable vintage is around 1890. The newer a garment is, the stronger it is likely to be. However, many other factors affect condition and you should evaluate any garment carefully before buying.

The clothes from before 1890 that are most likely to be wearable are heavy coats, loose wraps of any weight, and sturdy nonsilk dresses.

EXAMINING FABRICS

First look through the fabric at a strong light. Especially check stress areas such as a high collar, shoulders, underarms, sleeve cuffs, the waistband, the seat, and the hem. Look for tears, holes, and thin spots. A multiplicity of these, in several areas, indicates overall fabric deterioration (and a bad buy).

Many Victorian and Edwardian silks were weighted with metal salts to improve the luster. Over time the silk becomes brittle, develops splits, then rapidly disintegrates. This condition is known as shattered silk and there is nothing you can do to stop it (see figure 95).

Some dark fabric dyes used in this period also cause deterioration. Look for tiny round holes.

Check woolens, silks, furs, and feathers for moth damage. One or two holes may be acceptable, but the garment should be immediately quarantined in moth repellant and dry cleaned as soon as possible to kill the larvae. More holes may appear after cleaning.

Never suspend your judgement when evaluating condition. When someone tells you a silk with a just a few splits is repairable, don't believe them. When a dealer in restored merchandise claims a stain is removable, ask yourself why they couldn't remove it.

Cotton and linen are suprisingly strong even when sheer. In Edwardian whites overall deterioration may be a result not of age, but of improper cleaning by the seller. Ask about his or her washing methods, and check the garment very carefully if it was machine washed or chlorine bleached. Don't be misled by a clean, starched appearance.

A common problem with silk and rayon is underarm perspiration damage, heralded by discoloring or fading. This doesn't wash out, and the fabric is weakened as well as stained. Consider whether you are willing to replace the underarms and can find matching fabric.

Check fabrics for even color by comparing the inside seam allowances to the outside and garment sections to each other. Some fading may be acceptable as long as the outside color is even. Colors that have streaked during washing can't be evened out.

Although fold lines may be softened by cleaning and pressing, they can seldom be entirely removed.

Seam splits aren't serious, though there should be enough ease to take in a frayed seam. Tears and holes in cottons can usually be mended. Even filthy cottons can be cleaned well.

Buying a cleaned garment not only saves you work, but is a guarantee of condition. It shows the garment is strong enough to clean, and whether stains and dirt are removable.

First split was mended and area reinforced with applique. But fabric continues to shred

Fabric cracks along warp threads

Figure 95: Split silk

But don't bank on removing old stains, particularly if the seller has already tried to. The worst ones are scorch marks and the reddish rust stains caused by old steel fasteners.

Damage in lace is shown by tears, old mends, a stripped appearance, and unraveling threads. Brittleness indicates weakness. Black laces are fragile because corrosive (and not very fast) dye was used. So are silk laces because silk is the least durable natural fiber. Pull on an inconspicuous corner. If the lace breaks easily, don't buy it.

If only one or two highly stressed garment sections, such as a collar, are damaged they can be replaced. Sections or garments pieced from lace yardage may show seam splits—easily mended.

Be cautious about bead embroidery (see figure 96). Old beading thread can be so weak the beads are falling off—a condition you hear as well as see if the floor is uncarpeted. Missing beads are hard to match and tedious to replace. And in some 1910s and 1920s dresses the beading is OK, but the thin silk underneath is becoming too deteriorated to support it.

You can often tell how (or whether) a dealer cleaned a garment by checking whether it smells like soap, chlorine bleach, dry-cleaning fluid, perspiration, or dust.

Sometimes usable lace is sewn to badly deteriorated fabric. Buy the item if the lace can be unpicked without damage and you pay no more than you would for the lace alone. Unpicking is most successful with heavy or loosely sewn lace.

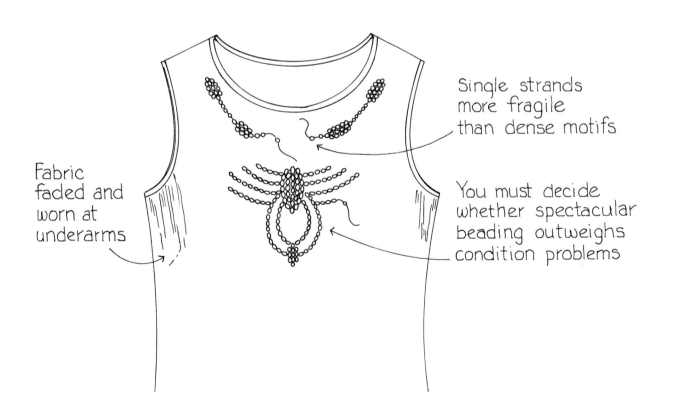

Single strands more fragile than dense motifs

Fabric faded and worn at underarms

You must decide whether spectacular beading outweighs condition problems

Figure 96: Typical problems of a 1920s beaded dress

TESTING ACCESSORIES

Beaded bags in excellent condition are available and I recommend buying them that way. Repairs are exceptionally hard for the nonexpert. The most common problem is that the beading is coming apart. Examine the fringe, the bottom, and where the bag joins the frame. Steel beads shouldn't be rusty or faded. The silk lining, which protects the beads, should be sound.

If you plan to wear a fur coat daily, buy one made in the 1940s or later. Some earlier furs are wearable on an occasional basis. Worn fur collars and cuffs on cloth coats can be replaced.

On the outside look for bald spots, especially at the front closing, sleeve ends, and seat. Falling hairs indicate irreparable moth damage (moths attack fur at the roots). Feel the fur's skin through the lining to make sure it's supple. A dry, stiff, or brittle fur is never worth buying. Check for skin splits at stress points such as the shoulders, upper back, elbows, and pockets. Lumpy areas indicate where splits were mended. One or two splits or mends are OK, but a large number means the fur won't last long.

Leather goods should be flexible. Brittle, flaking, or cracked leather can't be restored. A leather purse should be examined at the seams, bottom, and lining. Make sure a purse intended for practical use is large enough, and that the clasp holds. Shoes can apparently be resoled and reheeled an infinite number of times. But pass up shoes with damaged uppers.

A hat should hold its shape when it's not on your head. Minor dents can be steamed out at home. Felt hats and fabric coverings should pass the same tests as garment fabrics. Straws shouldn't be split or crushed. A few dyed straws are so brittle they crumble; bend gently to test.

Never pay much for vintage silk stockings. Even if they're in good condition, they last through only one or two wearings.

✎ EVALUATING FIT

Vintage clothes rarely fit perfectly because typical body types change. And period fitting standards (a closer or looser fit all over or in certain areas) change too. You'll need your clothes to be a wearable size. But you'll look more authentic, and do fewer alterations, if you get used to the fitting standards of the styles you collect. It also pays to be more flexible about fit than you'd be with modern clothes.

Size labels in a vintage clothing store are only the owner's interpretations. Even measurements may be inaccurate. So try on any garment that interests you if it isn't obviously too small or too fragile. If you'll wear period undergarments that affect fit, try on over the best approximations the store has.

Here are some general guidelines to what can and can't be altered (also see figure 97). Evaluate the following areas:

Lace used for alterations would blend into lace decoration

Elbow-length sleeves fit any arm, but could be made full length by sewing a fitted lace tube to the bottom

Bodice gathers could be let out or taken in at waist

Waistband could be taken in, extended, or replaced

Skirt pleats could be let out or taken in at waist

Skirt could be taken up at waist, tucked above one or both flounces, or tucked underneath top flounce

Skirt could be lengthened with more lace

Figure 97: Back of Edwardian dress showing alteration areas

- *The overall size.* If a garment is too small all over or enormously large, pass it up. But it's easier to take in a bit than to let out.

- *The shoulders and back.* If these are too narrow in a front-closing garment, they usually can't be altered. In some back-closing dresses and blouses you can add an inch or so to each edge of the center back. Too-wide shoulders in a lightweight garment can be pulled in with pleats.

- *The waist.* If extra fabric is provided in seams, gathering, or pleats, the waist can be let out. Men's trousers can be taken in, or let out, up to three inches. Sometimes a dress's waist level can be changed.

- *The sleeves.* Even if there are cuffs or lots of trim, sleeves can be shortened one to four inches. If there's no fabric to let down, they can be lengthened with a lace frill or added cuff.

- *The hem.* A skirt hem can be raised one to eight inches even when there is a flounce or lace overskirt. And it can be lengthened with a flounce or trim. Trousers can be shortened, or lengthened an inch or two.

Chapter 1 contains more information on period fitting standards. Chapter 7 gives detailed alterations instructions.

Needless to say, you should avoid damaging garments when you shop. Don't wear make-up. Remove high-heeled shoes. And ask for help with difficult fastenings.

🐚 PAYING THE RIGHT PRICE

Once you've found a vintage garment you like, that's in good condition, and that fits, you must decide whether its price is acceptable to you. There's no such thing as a standard price. Weigh your budget and your desire for the item against your knowledge of the market.

KNOWING THE MARKET

Get into the habit of researching, remembering, and comparing prices. Although there are always exceptions, you'll find that prices are affected by the following factors:

- *Age.* Older wearables cost more than newer ones. Even older, but nonwearable garments are in less demand.

- *Condition.* Items in poor condition cost less. Clean, mended items cost more than basically sound but unrestored ones.

- *Size.* Very small sizes are sometimes priced lower.

- *Attractiveness.* Elaborate styles and/or handwork bring higher prices. Inexpert design and construction bring lower ones.

- *Fashionableness.* Styles are priced higher if they're currently popular with collectors, are being reproduced in mainstream fashion, or are locally in demand. Styles are priced

If you're skilled at restoration, dealers may target you as a customer for damaged garments. Insist on viewing quality merchandise too. If you do buy an unrestored item, pay significantly less than for a restored one.

lower if there are few public occasions for wearing them. Nightwear, occupational uniforms, and specialized sports outfits fall into this category.

- *Source.* Sources with low overhead—estate sales, auctions, and dealers who don't have stores—charge less than sources with high overhead.

- *Geographic area.* Prices are lower in the Midwest and higher on the two coasts, especially the West Coast. They're higher in big cities than small ones.

- *The national economy.* The vintage clothing market, like others, is affected by recessions.

Frankly, I've never gotten any use out of a price guide. But if you want to try one, choose a guide that gathers data from a variety of sources and explains how it was interpreted. Avoid guides that only say what the author/dealer would charge. These bear little relation to the overall market. Also avoid guides that don't say where they got the data. Finally, make sure the guide was published within the past two years.

BARGAINING

Most vintage clothing dealers bargain in most selling situations. Some give a standard discount for the asking. Others give discounts that depend on their estimated chances of selling an item, on how much you're spending, or on whether this has been a slow month or show.

The first bargaining step is to simply ask for a discount. Common openers are "Is that your best price?" and "Would you consider a reduction?" If I'm considering several items I ask, "Could you give a group price on these?"

Stop right there if the dealer says he or she never bargains (or if "Firm" is written on all the price tags). If there is a standard discount you'll be told something like "Yes, I'll take off ten percent." That's probably all you'll get.

A dealer who expects a longer bargaining process will say something vague, like "I might be able to come down on that" or a doubtful "Well, I don't know if I can come down on that." It doesn't much matter what arguments you advance, as long as you're pleasant. Dealers bargain because they enjoy the game and the interaction with customers.

Point out flaws—which the dealer already knows about—without insulting the dealer or the merchandise. Keep acting as if your mind is almost but not quite made up. Knowing a show is almost over or that sales aren't good gives you an edge, but it's tactless to say so. Never claim you can get similar items cheaper from another source. The dealer will tell you to go there instead, and stop bargaining.

An unpicked or partially unpicked garment should be bought only at a low price. You won't know whether all the pieces are there till you start restoration. If alterations were abandoned it's because they weren't working out. You may be unable to either complete them or restore the original style.

After you point out a flaw or two you'll be offered a discount. You may be able to lower the price once more (unless you named the figure) but that's about all. The dealer will tell you when the lowest figure has been reached. The usual closing argument is "That's as low as I can go because I paid a lot for it."

☙ KNOWING WHEN TO SAY NO

Some people have a highly structured approach to accumulating vintage clothes; for example, buying only metal mesh bags in every design ever manufactured. I'm not one of them. But I've found I need some guidelines in addition to the ones for judging condition, size, and price.

- My main guideline is: buy only things you really love. If you buy a lot of so-so ones you'll run out of resources for the others. By resources, I mean care time and storage space as well as money.

- You may be drawn to things that don't flatter you. Buy wearable vintage clothes using the same line and color rules as for modern ones. If you've always looked best in tailored outfits, an Edwardian walking suit is a better buy than a ruffled lingerie dress.

- It is useful to own a few so-so or well-worn clothes for wear under dirty or stressful circumstances. But you don't have to seek these out; you'll find you've acquired them somehow.

- If you're buying for living history events, focus on appropriate styles for the period(s). Try to build up one outfit before buying components of the next.

- Buy only clothes that fit, or can be made to fit, your current figure. If you lose weight you can take them in. But the world is full of people who have meant to lose ten pounds for ten years.

- Don't feel compelled to buy something because you drove a long way to the shop, or because it's cheap, or it's what your friends are buying.

- Your tastes will change over time. That's fine. But if you frequently make mistakes, reassess your buying habits.

Sometimes people get hung up worrying about missed opportunities, or envying someone else's possessions. Don't. You'll never see, let alone buy, most of the vintage clothes in the world. Just focus on selecting from what's available to you, now.

☙ CLEANING A GARMENT

I clean a garment as soon as I buy it (if it hasn't been cleaned by the seller), whenever it's absorbed perspiration (or any liquid other than water), and whenever it starts to look dirty (even if it's been hanging in a closet).

Your first decision is whether to dry clean or wash. Fabrics that should be dry cleaned include pile fabrics (such as velvet); brocade; fabrics with multicolored embroidery; beaded fabrics; metallics; most woolens, silks, and rayons; and garments composed of a dry-cleanable plus a washable fabric (such as a satin dress with a cotton lining). Although some wool sweaters can be hand washed, dry cleaning is safer. Cottons, linens, silk and rayon lingerie, and laces should be hand washed.

Before cleaning a garment by any method, remove rusty fasteners, collar stays, and anything else that may poke holes in it. Don't do mending or alterations yet because the fabric color will be different when the dirt is gone. Large tears can be temporarily basted to prevent further damage during cleaning.

WASHING

Most vintage cottons, linens, lingerie silks and rayons, ribbons, and small lace pieces can be safely hand washed in a clean sink or plastic tub. Silks and rayons should be washed in cool to lukewarm water. Cottons and linens should be washed in warm water. Rinse water should be the same temperature. I use Woolite (a mild detergent) for all fabrics, because I can no longer find a pure soap on the grocery store shelves. However, some people claim silk retains its luster better if washed in soap. Conservators use soap for all washables; the preferred brand is a concentrate called Orvus WA Paste, available from conservation suppliers. Silks, rayons, and colored fabrics definitely shouldn't be exposed to strong detergents, bleaches, or other harsh chemicals.

Wash vintage garments one at a time to prevent dirt and old dyes from circulating. Colored washables may run a little the first time, but washing is still more successful than dry cleaning.

If the soap-and-water mixture goes gray immediately, change it. Always think in terms of supporting the garment; squeeze rather than lift. Cotton and linen are stronger when wet, silk and rayon weaker. Rinse till the water is clear (otherwise soap and bleach continue to work). This can take a long time if the garment retains old soap or starch.

All-lace and other delicate garments require flat washing. Clean your bathtub well, run just enough lukewarm water to cover the garment, and mix in a mild soap. Lower the garment into the water. After a little soaking, press the suds through it with a new plastic sponge. Rinse in repeated changes of water without wringing or twisting.

BLEACHING AND STAIN REMOVAL

If white cottons are really filthy you can presoak them in hot water and an oxygen bleach such as Biz. For a blouse add

Never machine wash, machine dry, or machine dry clean a pre-1930 garment.

I've twice bought whites at auction that had been weakened by the Victorian method of bleaching with sulfuric or hydrochloric acid. Although they showed only tiny holes, gentle washing turned them into soup. If this ever happens to you, it's not your fault.

Single feathers can be cleaned in mildly soapy lukewarm water. Gently wave the feather back and forth in the wash water, then the rinse water. A dry feather can be curled by carefully running a blunt knife or scissors against each frond.

about two tablespoons of Biz to a sinkful of water, and for a dress about four to a plastic tubful of water. Thoroughly dissolve the Biz before adding the garment—otherwise it may deposit blue specks. Soak the garment for two to eight hours. Then hand wash.

If the garment still looks dirty I recommend repeating the Biz treatment. I'm not an advocate of chlorine bleach because it weakens the fabric.

Stain removal is a branch of chemistry. There's a different method for each stain. It must be applied before the stain has set (chemically changed), preferably the minute you take off the garment. For a new stain on a vintage garment, use the appropriate method from a modern stain-removal guide.

Biz bleaches at least some color out of most stains. However, it doesn't affect rust stains. Many books recommend oxalic acid or lemon juice, but are vague about their application and effectiveness. My experiments with both have been unsuccessful. But I've had good luck with the old remedy of boiling rust-stained cotton whites in water and cream of tartar. This makes the stains much fainter without harming the fabric.

To be on the safe side, don't use your regular cooking tools. Get a large old soup pot, a long-handled wooden spoon, and an old aluminum colander or strainer. You'll need four teaspoons of cream of tartar to each pint of water. I called around till I found a health food store that sold it in bulk.

Dissolve the cream of tartar in the water as it comes to a boil. Then immerse the garment. Turn down the heat but make sure the mixture stays boiling. Periodically rotate the garment with the wooden spoon and check its progress. Boil until the stain is faint enough—I've boiled garments for as long as three hours. Put the colander in the sink and cautiously pour the contents of the pot into it. Then rinse the garment in the hottest tap water, gradually lowering the temperature till you can touch it.

Finally, hand wash to remove the cream of tartar crystals.

Period cleaning methods are fascinating to read about. But most will probably destroy vintage clothes. Fibers weaken over time.

DRYING AND IRONING

Dry small garments such as blouses on tubular plastic hangers. Lay large or delicate ones flat on a big folding sweater dryer. You can buy these at places that sell closet accessories. It's OK if the ends or sleeves hang off the edges, as long as most of the garment is supported. Colored garments, silks, and rayons should be dried inside because sunlight damages them. But white cottons and linens can be sun bleached.

Although the terms "pressing" and "ironing" are sometimes used interchangeably, there's a distinction. When you press, you lower and raise the iron without moving it along the fabric. Pressing is less likely to cause distortion and is necessary when you're sewing. It's also useful for bias-cut and very delicate garments; velvets; and fabrics with raised surfaces, beading, or long threads that catch in the iron tip.

However, pressing is slower than ordinary ironing. I prefer to iron sturdy vintage garments and have found it's quite safe. Whichever method you use, work with the fabric grain, use the lowest effective heat setting, and make sure the iron soleplate is clean.

I use a steam iron on all fabrics except those that water spot (most irons have unpredictable leaks). But it's still necessary to spray cottons and many washable silks with water before ironing. I iron cottons on the right side to cut down on rewrinkling. But silks, rayons, and linens that shouldn't turn shiny must be ironed on the wrong side. If the right side needs touching up, protect it with a press cloth.

Complex garments tend to rewrinkle during ironing. You can minimize this by ironing them in the right order. If there is lace beading or a drawstring casing, I iron that first, thread the ribbon through, then iron the rest. I iron any flounces or free-hanging trims on a section before the flat parts. I move the iron tip toward gathers and avoid ironing them flat. If there are multiple flounces, I iron them in bottom-to-top order.

On skirts and sleeves I work from the bottom up. I iron sleeves over a sleeve board. On bodices I iron the collar and shoulders, then work down. If the bodice is tight fitting, I press curves over a tailor's ham. Lined jackets must sometimes be pressed on both sides; I do the inside first. If a heavy or slippery garment wants to slide off the ironing board, I support the part I'm not working on with a chair.

I don't starch cottons because starch not only messes up the ironing board cover and the iron soleplate, it attracts bugs and mold. My only exception is men's detachable shirt collars, which look terrible unstarched. First I soak the collar with commercial spray starch. Then I iron it between two clean rags until almost dry. Finally, I arrange it in a circle and close it with a large rustproof safety pin passed through the front stud holes.

I let garments dry for at least an hour after ironing—if you put them away damp they'll mildew.

DRY CLEANING

The usual mechanical dry-cleaning process can damage vintage garments. Have the garment placed in a mesh bag. You may want to ask about hand pressing or have the garment returned unpressed and do it yourself. Lastly, ask your cleaner to use fresh, not filtered (recycled) cleaning fluid.

If the garment was made before 1930, find someone who

If your iron has an unreliable thermostat, start with a setting slightly below the one it recommends. Test press an inconspicuous place. If necessary, turn up the heat slowly till wrinkles start disappearing.

Lace, embroidery, and beading can be pressed over a towel to protect raised surfaces.

Never iron a dirty or stained garment—you'll seal in the dirt.

You can freshen up vel-
vet between dry clean-
ings by steaming with a
hand-held garment
steamer such as
Wrinkles Away. To
prevent crush marks,
don't touch the velvet
till it's dry.

does hand cleaning. This will probably be a small, independent establishment—preferably one that often cleans vintage clothes. Get a reference from a vintage clothing store owner or museum textile curator. Don't entrust your clothes to a cleaner who seems uneasy about the job.

Victorian silk clothing often has lace collars and trim basted on, rather than sewn, so that they can be removed and cleaned separately. Carefully unpick the lace, hand wash it, and baste it on again after the garment is cleaned.

Fur trims should also be unpicked for separate cleaning.

CLEANING FURS

If a fur smells musty, first try a thorough airing. If it continues to smell or looks dirty, you'll have to clean it. Never have furs dry cleaned—it ruins them. Instead, have them cleaned and glazed by a furrier. Ideally you should do so every spring before storage.

You can also periodically do an inexpensive home touch-up. Heat cornmeal in the oven until warm (but not hot). Rub it into the fur to absorb dirt and grease. When through, remove as much cornmeal as you can by shaking the coat outdoors. Then vacuum with a hand-held vacuum cleaner, holding the nozzle above the fur.

If you and your fur
get caught in the rain,
hang it in an open area,
away from direct heat.
Shake well when it's
completely dry.

Now glaze the fur. You can either buy a spray glaze and glazing brush from a fur-supply source (see appendix A) or use lukewarm water. Brush on the water without wetting the skin. Allow to dry naturally. Then brush gently along the fur grain.

❧ WEARING VINTAGE CLOTHES

You'll enjoy yourself more if you can focus on what you're doing rather than on what you're wearing. Here are some strategies I've developed for wearing vintage clothes for both everyday and living history activities. And for allowing others to wear them, which you may be asked to do.

ADDING VINTAGE STYLES TO YOUR EVERYDAY WARDROBE

Designers have relied on vintage styles for inspiration throughout the 20th century. So it's likely that in any year, some vintage clothes will blend into your everyday wardrobe. But just which ones varies. The "Out of Africa" styles that looked mainstream one year looked costumey the next. For this reason I'm giving general guidelines rather than suggestions for specific outfits.

Read fashion magazines to see what vintage styles are being

copied. Designers may copy entire outfits from a given era or use only one or two ideas. Or they may combine styles from different decades (not all of which are described in this book).

See what vintage clothes you have, or can buy, that work with the current look. Generally it's best to combine them with modern clothes or accessories, rather than wearing a complete vintage outfit. Consider whether a garment's uniqueness, handwork, natural materials, or low price makes it preferable to a more durable modern copy.

Some vintage clothes and accessories can be incorporated into your wardrobe in practically any year. Here are some examples.

- *Lingerie.* Silk slips, teddies, camisoles, and tap pants from the 1920s and 1930s work under most modern outfits. So do the less full Edwardian cotton camisoles. (See figure 98.)

- *Nightwear.* Many contemporary nightgowns and robes are similar to Victorian/Edwardian, 1920s, or 1930s styles.

- *Sweaters.* One-of-a-kind sweaters are often fashionable. Look for hand knits, sophisticated hand crochet, and hand decoration such as embroidery. Also for machine knits in

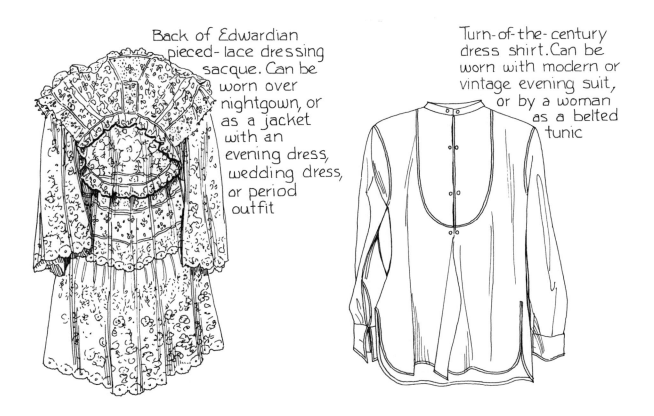

Back of Edwardian pieced-lace dressing sacque. Can be worn over nightgown, or as a jacket with an evening dress, wedding dress, or period outfit

Turn-of-the-century dress shirt. Can be worn with modern or vintage evening suit, or by a woman as a belted tunic

Figure 98: Vintage clothes suitable for modern wear

classic styles (such as cardigans and V-neck pullovers) and luxury materials (such as cashmere and angora).

- *Tuxedos, tail coats, and dress shirts.* Because men's formal outfits are survivals of vintage styles, vintage ones blend right in.

- *Wedding dresses.* Many Victorian and Edwardian dresses—not just white ones—are wonderful for a formal wedding. (See figure 99.) So are actual wedding dresses from almost any decade. And if you want a handmade lace veil, it will have to be vintage.

- *Jewelry.* It's always acceptable to wear heirloom jewelry. Or to express your individuality with offbeat costume jewelry.

- *Scarves, purses, and other accessories.* Because accessories are accent pieces they're easy to work into a contemporary wardrobe.

- *Buttons.* Plastic buttons downgrade even the most expensive new garments. Replace them with vintage ones made of natural materials—mother-of-pearl, metal, porcelain, or wood.

Vintage clothes need frequent pressing. When packing them for travel, include a light dry iron and a collapsible sleeve board.

Mid-1900s velvet afternoon dress would make a lovely wedding dress even though it's not white

Late 1910s embroidered net dress would be perfect for a wedding or vintage dance

Figure 99: Vintage dresses suitable for weddings or period events

AVOIDING DAMAGE

Advance planning is the key to wearing vintage clothes safely and without headaches. For a special occasion put together your outfit, including undergarments and accessories, at least a day ahead. Consider what you'll do while wearing it. For example, you may be able to safely wear an 1880s bustle dress for a fashion show, but not dancing.

If you're not used to wearing the style, practice moving around. If a garment has tight sleeves or a narrow back, can you move your arms? If it has a train, can you manage it without tripping? Is the skirt wide enough for your movements? Can the fabric be cleaned easily (especially if you're going to eat)? If you find that either you or your outfit are under strain, you may want to wear something else.

Vintage dance outfits should be lightweight and allow easy movement. To prevent perspiration damage to a silk dress, wear period cotton lingerie and clean the dress after each wearing. If you must wear a corset, it should be a custom-fitted reproduction and not tight laced. Sew a loop onto a train so you can hang it from your arm. Or better, find a Victorian skirt lifter—a metal grip through which you can thread a colored cord—that can be used with any dress. (See figure 100.) Period shoes are fragile and hard to dance in. I substitute modern dance shoes even if they look less authentic.

Try on even newer vintage outfits to make sure they really do work. Few things are more irritating than a last-minute discovery that the slip you planned to wear is too long, the dress has a missing button, and the jacket, while a coordinating color, is the wrong style for the dress.

Do any necessary mending now to avoid further damage. Then iron or steam out wrinkles and hang everything up again.

It's a good idea to carry several sizes of safety pins and a little mending kit. Another safety feature is to wear several layers of clothes and/or carry a jacket so that, if a garment does tear badly, you won't be subject to embarrassment.

At this point I can't resist including some etiquette tips on wearing vintage clothing that I feel would be useful to enthusiasts.

- The most attractive way to wear vintage clothing is to be unconscious of it, neither trying to attract notice nor constantly checking for possible damage.

- Sometimes vintage clothing lovers allow their enthusiasm, desire for authenticity, or—let's face it—competitiveness to overcome politeness. Inappropriate comments I've heard include "Do you know you're wearing a petticoat as a skirt?" "The date of your outfit is four years too late for

Never wear high heels with a full-length vintage skirt. I've seen countless punctured hems at shows.

A fur is easily damaged by pinning jewelry to it or wearing a shoulder bag.

this event" "Oh, a *pretied* bow tie" "I have a cape just like that at home, but mine has lots more beading" "and "I think you're so *brave* to wear that!"

- If someone else's clothes become unbuttoned or torn, offer practical, discreet aid. It's impolite to tell them their outfit is too fragile or valuable to be worn—even if it's true.

LENDING

When word gets around that you own hard-to-find vintage items, you may be asked to lend them for various purposes. These include friends' wear, pictures in publications, fashion shows, theatrical performances, exhibits, and copying. My policy is never to lend anything I wouldn't give away—which means I almost never lend.

You may be more generous. But be aware that performances and modeling are much harder on a garment than normal use. Inept copying can be destructive. And promises to care for your possessions, however sincere, don't legally bind the promiser or reimburse you for damage.

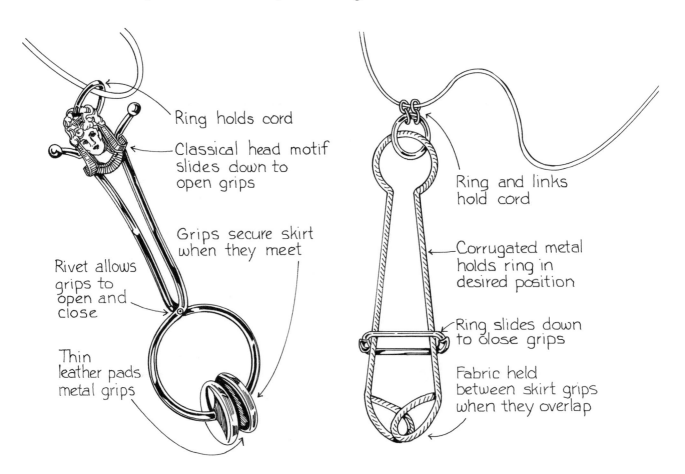

Figure 100: Two Victorian skirt lifters

When lending to any organization I suggest drawing up a written contract. This should specify how the garment is to be used, the date it's to be returned, that it should be returned undamaged, its value (which doesn't require an appraisal), the amount you'll be paid in case of damage or nonreturn, and the deadline for paying it. It's a good idea to include photos of the garment when lent.

Think twice before lending to a money-making business, however small. If you want free advertising for your vintage clothing or reproduction business, make sure the credits say how to contact you. If a publication runs ads, ask for free or discounted ad space in addition to credits. If you have no business you may derive no real benefit from lending. Charge a rental fee. A business is used to paying for such services and can deduct them from taxes. At the very least you should get a generous number of free tickets to the show or free copies of the publication.

A friend borrowing for personal use would be upset if you asked for a contract. Ask yourself whether the friendship will be damaged if the garment is, and proceed accordingly. But if the friend has a business, ask them to cooperate with your "routine business procedures."

Even if a garment is wearable, you have much more control when you wear it than when someone else does.

An acquaintance who runs a vintage clothing rental business recommends stating an outrageously high reimbursement value on the contract to ensure extra care.

✈ STORING CLOTHES

Clean a garment before long-term storage, preferably right after you wear it. Even if it looks clean, it may have absorbed perspiration or invisible liquid spills that set and discolor over time.

Choose a storage area (or areas) that's clean, dark, dry, has an even temperature, and is closed to rodent and insect invasions. This will probably be in the main part of your house rather than an attic or basement.

CHOOSING A SAFE STORAGE METHOD

Most lightweight blouses and dresses, sturdy coats and suits, and men's clothes are strong enough to hang in a closet. Never use wire hangers—they cause shoulder strain and leave rust marks. Instead, use tubular plastic hangers for lightweight sleeved garments. Use padded or shaped, varnished wooden hangers for heavy ones. Make sure hangers aren't too wide for the shoulders. Use plain slotted hangers—not suit hangers with sharp extra grips—for sleeveless garments. Extra wide hangers are available for off-the-shoulder dresses. Hang lightweight cotton skirts from skirt hangers with metal grips—they'll work free from plastic or plastic-coated ones. Insert tissue paper between the garment and the grips. Trousers can be hung from varnished wooden trouser hangers or folded over plastic ones.

Do up all the fasteners to keep them from catching on other garments. Cotton garment bags provide extra protection against dust and light. You can make them from white or well-faded sheets; wash them when they get dusty. Plastic cleaner's bags just provide an ideal environment for mildew. Leaving some space around garments helps prevent mildew, as well as damage when you take them in and out.

Many vintage clothes should be stored flat. These include heavy dresses and skirts, beaded and bias-cut garments, some silks, knits, anything that shows shoulder strain, and most pre-1890 garments.

The best storage area is a drawer or chest big enough so you don't have to fold things much. It should be sealed against dust and light (even interior light fades dyes) and lined with old cotton sheets. Put the heaviest garments on the bottom, and don't pack things too tightly.

Ideally you should use tissue paper to pad the garment shape, prevent creases at fold lines, and separate garments. Acid-free tissue is recommended because most paper and wood (including furniture and wooden hangers) contain acids that damage cloth. Flat garments, such as shawls and lace veils, can be rolled between two layers of tissue. I roll 1920s beaded dresses to protect the beading.

Hats should be stored in sturdy hat boxes with lids. I think vintage hat boxes are overpriced and too fragile for real use. Instead, I use new hat boxes from closet accessory or conservation suppliers. Lidded copy-paper boxes are an acceptable substitute. If you have enough boxes, store each hat in its own box after the crown has been padded with acid-free tissue. If not put several hats of the same shape in one box. Stuff the bottom crown and stack the others.

Shoes can be stuffed with tissue, or placed on shoe trees, to maintain their shape. Most purses can also be stuffed with tissue. Beaded and metal mesh bags should be wrapped in tissue and stored flat. Store fans and parasols folded, or just slightly open, so they're not under strain.

PROTECTING STORED ITEMS

Moths are the bane of vintage clothing enthusiasts. They eat wool, silk, fur, trims made from these substances, and feathers. They like rugs and upholstery as well as clothes. They'll chew through synthetics to get at the woolens.

The usual preventive is to store all susceptible items in well-sealed containers and include a moth repellant in each container or garment bag. Paradichlorobenzene is clearly effective, which isn't true of some herbal repellants. However, you shouldn't breathe the fumes or get it on your skin or in your

The techniques for storing vintage clothes will also preserve your reproductions longer.

Padded hangers provide the best support, but are expensive. You can make your own by winding cotton batting around a wooden hanger, then covering it with clean white cotton fabric.

eyes. The repellant should be placed at the top of the container, wrapped in a clean rag so it doesn't touch the clothes.

Other helpful measures are regular renewal of repellants and vacuuming the storage area. Dry cleaning kills moth eggs and makes the fabric unappetizing for several months. If you notice moth damage on any clothes or home furnishings, immediately inspect all susceptible items and dry clean the affected ones.

Having said all this I should add that I've never had moths. I've collected for over 20 years and I don't store clothes with repellant. It's true my containers are well sealed and I have no wool home furnishings. But I think the real secret is to not bring in clothes that harbor moth eggs.

When I buy woolens I ask whether they've been dry cleaned. Although I ask about silks, I don't worry as much about them because I've never seen holes that were clearly caused by moths. I don't buy from dealers who have a lot of infested stock. Occasionally I buy something with small holes if a dealer I trust assures me it was recently cleaned.

The moment I get home, I quarantine all susceptible items that weren't cleaned. I stow each separately in a tightly closed suitcase with moth repellant, in my garage. I go to the cleaners at the next opportunity, usually the following weekend.

Woolens bought at estate sales are most likely to cause an infestation. If badly moth-eaten ones are included in a lot, I immediately seal them in plastic bags and throw them away. All others are quarantined, then cleaned.

Silverfish eat anything. They often come into your house via vintage paper rather than clothes. Store paper collectibles separately, if possible outside the main part of your house. If you see silverfish, spray insecticide all around your baseboards (including closets) as many times as necessary.

Mildew and mold spores are always present in the air. However, they require moisture (especially warm moisture) and nourishment to grow. Usually storing clothes clean, dry, and with some airflow around them prevents mildew. Periodically air stored clothes. Keep leather purses and shoes on shelves rather than the floor. If you live in a damp climate, add packages of silica gel to your storage containers.

If you see or smell mildew, seek out all affected items. Brush off the spores—outside, where they won't get on your other clothes. Then immediately wash washables and dry clean cleanables. Wipe leathers with a solution of 50 percent alcohol and 50 percent water. Air dry, then rub with leather conditioner to prevent overdrying.

Flea bombs also work for silverfish and moths. If your insect problems really get out of hand, call an exterminator.

STORING CLOTHES EFFICIENTLY

If you accumulate many vintage clothes you're likely to run out of storage space. You'll also forget where you stored specific items. These problems may have no permanent solution other than to quit buying, which few people are willing to do. But here are some suggestions that should stave off crises for a while.

- Measure your closets and figure out how to get maximum use from the space. A rectangular closet can have a pole on the long side and another on at least one short side. Support long poles in the middle with braces. Put in two poles, arranged vertically, for short garments like blouses. Add as many shelves as possible above the poles.

- Buy antique wardrobes and replace the original hooks with poles.

- Use high chests of drawers rather than the low kind with mirrors.

- Turn a small, inconvenient room or nook into a huge walk-in closet. Add wardrobes, chests of drawers, even poles across the room. Or build storage cabinets along the walls.

- Store items of the same type together (for example coats and wraps) and organize them by date.

- List your clothes using a word-processing or database program and update the list regularly. Sections can be printed out to label storage containers and to create catalogs when you weed out your collection. Keep a copy outside your home—preferably in a safe-deposit box—so you can collect homeowner's insurance in case of disaster.

- Weed out your collection regularly.

❧ SELLING WHAT YOU DON'T WANT

You're bound to acquire clothes you don't want—mistakes, auction lot leftovers, things that no longer fit your body or lifestyle. If you accumulate many, they'll take up storage space and make it hard to get at the wearables.

You can certainly sell at least some of your mistakes. Whether you'll make a profit is more questionable. The sad fact is that vintage clothes are a poor investment. Some basically aren't very desirable, which may be why you're getting rid of them. All clothes deteriorate over time. Some styles may have gone down in price since you bought them. And an individual can't charge as much as a dealer even for the most desirable items.

Of course, if you're selling rare collectibles bought decades ago for low prices, you can make real money. But if you're just clearing out the closets, you'll be happiest if you consider money as a side benefit.

So where do you sell vintage clothes? The same places you buy them. Options include selling to friends; selling through a vintage clothing store; mail order; selling from your home; a booth at a vintage clothing show, flea market, or swap meet; even an auction.

SELLING SMALL QUANTITIES

If there are just a few pieces, your best choices are selling to friends, through a store, or by mail. I like dealing with friends because I feel I've done them a favor, even if I don't make much money. If the friend has something you want you can trade.

Some stores will sell for you on consignment. You receive 50 percent of the price if the item sells. Others buy outright, paying about 25 or 30 percent of their selling price. If you'll accept exchange (trade) credit, they'll buy more willingly and give you 30 or 35 percent. Set your sale price yourself; don't let the dealer do it. Figure out the dealer's probable price, ask for a little more than you expect, and bargain down.

No matter what the arrangement is, stores expect all items to be clean, in good condition, and generally desirable. Even so they'll reject part of a batch unless you set a group price.

Mail order is an easy way to sell in either small or large quantities. Place an inexpensive ad in a vintage clothing or living history newsletter, or an antiques trade sheet. A few items can be described in the ad.

If you have more, draw up a list and have people send for it. They should pay enough to cover your costs—maybe a dollar for the list and/or a self-addressed stamped envelope. The list should briefly describe each item, including the style, approximate date, fabric, color, size or key measurements, condition, and price. You can offer snapshots or good-quality sketches for an extra charge. Also mention your shipping charges, which should include packing materials. If you're willing to trade you can list desired items.

Neither you nor your customers will want to take risks. They won't buy unless you offer a return policy. Give them three to seven days to consider the items. You should insist on certified checks or delay shipping until personal checks clear.

When I first sold to stores I let dealers suggest prices. They'd tell me they couldn't possibly sell an item for more than a certain amount. In every instance, I later saw it in the store priced several times higher.

SELLING LARGE QUANTITIES

Selling at a vintage clothing show, flea market, or swap meet exposes your merchandise to many potential customers. You should have a respectable amount of it because you'll have to rent a booth. Unless it's a clothing show you can include items other than apparel. Another option is sharing the booth with friends.

Contact the organizers to find out booth charges. They may provide display tables or racks. If not you'll have to haul these to the show. Tag items before show day. Begin setting up as early as possible. Take at least one person to help manage the booth and spell you during breaks.

Holding a sale at your home is cheaper but more work. Advertise by all free or inexpensive methods. These include posters, notices on community bulletin boards, flyers left at related events, ads in newsletters and trade sheets, and word of mouth.

A vintage clothing sale (as opposed to a yard sale with some clothes) should be held inside. You'll have to clean your house; tag items; set up hanging racks, tables, and mirrors; and provide a place to try on. You can share the work load, and probably attract more customers, by holding a group sale with friends.

When you work with friends at a show or home sale, get organized. Each person should be clear about, and make a firm commitment to, their responsibilities. These include expenses, advertising efforts, and minding the sale. It should also be clear how profits are shared.

One easy accounting system is to have distinctive tags, and a separate large envelope, for each person. As soon as an item sells, mark any price reductions on the tag and put it in the correct envelope. At the end of the day, add up the sales total. Agree to split the difference evenly if it's more (or less) than the tag total.

One way to dispose of a whole collection is to hold an auction. You can either consign it to an auction house or hire an auctioneer. In either case you'll pay a percentage for the service. If you're holding your own auction, advertise in regional antiques publications as well as vintage clothing and living history newsletters. Send flyers to local stores and all the vintage clothing lovers you know.

At both shows and home sales, customers are attracted by sheer quantity of merchandise. Quality helps too, of course.

Few people will buy a large collection intact. If they do, they'll pay less than the value of the individual pieces.

6 Mending Garments

I find mending one of the more satisfying vintage clothing care tasks. It makes a garment wearable quickly and extends its life. And mending involves a lot of individual attention to the garment, including hand sewing, which I really enjoy. (I'll give alternative machine methods for those who enjoy it less.)

A garment should be frequently checked for flaws and mended as soon as possible to prevent further damage. I give each one a checkup when I buy it, before each wearing, after each wearing, and once again after cleaning.

If you've bought an uncleaned garment, clean it first. Otherwise your mending thread and patches won't match. Even white comes in several shades. Also press the area to be mended—wrinkles distort measurements and stitches.

Many techniques in this chapter are useful for both mending and construction. And they can be applied to modern, as well as vintage, clothes.

Separate clothes that need work from the wearable ones. It's frustrating to be ready to put on a garment, only to discover you can't wear it after all.

✒ ASSEMBLING MATERIALS

You'll find yourself needing the same tools and materials for most mending and alteration tasks, so it helps to keep them on hand.

BUYING EQUIPMENT

Here's a list of the mending tools I find most useful.

- *Hand sewing needles*—crewels, sharps, and beading needles—in a range of sizes. Use the thinnest needle that works. I use crewel 8s for fine fabrics. Short needles are best for thick fabrics because they don't bend; long ones are best for basting.

- *Machine sewing needles* in a range of sizes. Use the smallest size that works.

- *A bodkin* (heavy, large-eyed needle). For threading ribbons through casings.

- *Pins.* Silk pins are excellent for most tasks, but keep a few glass-headed ones for heavy fabrics.

- *Sharp embroidery scissors.* Useful for trimming threads and unpicking seams. A seam ripper is redundant and more likely to cause damage.

- *Sharp medium-sized sewing shears.* Useful for trimming seams and cutting out small pieces.

- *Tweezers.* These help in removing bits of thread from basted and unpicked seams.

Several commonly used supplies work no better than the ones listed and can actually damage vintage garments. These include iron-on patches and fabric pens. All glues—including products designed to prevent fraying—are unsuitable for vintage garments, though they can sometimes be used on shoes and hats.

- *A clear plastic ruler.* I have two, a 6 in. ruler and a 12 in. one that doubles as a T-square.
- *A yardstick.* Preferably clear plastic.
- *A flexible tape measure.* Use this only for measuring curved areas, such as the waistband of a garment on a dress form. Rulers are best for most tasks.
- *A sleeve board.* Slip sleeves over this for measuring and pinning as well as pressing.
- *A press cloth.* For protecting fabrics when you press them on the right side. Any medium-weight white cotton scrap about 12 by 18 in. will do.
- *Tailor's chalk.* White chalk is best for all colors except white, for which you need blue or pink. Don't be tempted by a handy pen or pencil—the marks probably won't come off.

COLLECTING FABRICS, TRIMS, AND CLOSURES

If you go to estate sales you've noticed that previous generations cultivated a "bit box." This included trim remnants, odd buttons, etc., left over from sewing projects or removed from discarded garments. A bit box was, and still is, immensely useful for mending.

My bit box includes vintage materials that are in fairly good condition but somehow unsuitable for reproductions. The lengths of trim are short (less than 1/2 yd.), the lace collars are a bit worn, the buttons are in ones or twos. However, I've found that it's useless to mend with damaged or inferior materials.

Vintage fabrics are so fragile that I save only a few hard-to-match ones, mostly from altered garments that might need patching later. Because thread deteriorates faster than fabric I use vintage thread only for basting. I don't save vintage hooks or snaps because they're seldom rustproof.

Several types of vintage buttons are worth accumulating in sets. These include any size mother-of-pearl buttons, crochet-covered buttons, patterned black silk buttons for men's suits, and any buttons you find especially attractive.

My bit box also includes modern materials. Anything left over from a reproduction comes in handy someday. Materials retrieved from modern mass-produced garments are seldom suitable for vintage repairs. However, a good-quality, nostalgically styled garment may yield an all-cotton lace collar or fabric-covered buttons.

No matter how large your bit box grows, you'll need to buy some materials. Because color difference is the most obvious

The bit box can be a concept rather than an actual box. I keep all materials of the same type together—lace with lace, buttons with buttons, etc. But I know which items belong to the bit box.

For the best color match, choose mending materials by natural light.

Shell and bone buttons can be washed in mild soap and rubbed with a soft rag, or a soft toothbrush if necessary. You can restore the sheen to mother-of-pearl by rubbing on a bit of jeweler's rouge with a soft rag, or by rubbing on a baking soda-and-water paste with your fingers. Then buff with a clean rag. Crocheted buttons without a hard core can be washed like fabric. Unpainted metal buttons can be washed in soap and water, then air dried. If you must use a metal cleaner or polish, first test a hidden area.

Mending Garments

indication of mending, don't hesitate to buy thread, a fabric remnant, or bias binding if you don't have a good match.

New supplies worth stocking include appliques (lace and embroidered); narrow and wide bias binding in white, cream, and black; 1/2 in. white twill tape; pliable silk or rayon ribbon for lingerie drawstrings, in widths ranging from 1/8 to 1 in.; and several sizes of hooks and snaps.

🖋 KNOWING THE BASIC HAND STITCHES

An important part of hand stitching is supporting the garment areas you're not working on. They should be neither crammed into your lap nor hanging off it so as to drag on your work. The ideal solution is to sit at a table and spread the garment on it. The table must be a comfortable height. Because mine isn't, I sit cross-legged on a clean floor and let it support the garment. (This is a traditional tailor's position.)

PREPARING TO SEW WITH BASTING

Basting secures seams, hems, and anything else that needs securing until the area is permanently sewn. (Figure 101 shows the basting stitch and all others described in this section.) It's especially useful for slippery fabrics, thick layers, hard-to-reach areas, pattern matching, and other tricky situations. And it prevents wobbly stitching over pins.

Use a contrasting color thread. Insert the needle on a side that won't be enclosed after stitching (otherwise you can't remove the knot). Take even stitches 1/4 to 1 in. long, depending on the control needed. For example, if you were setting in a gathered silk sleeve, you'd use 1/4 in. stitches. If you were basting the hem of a cotton dress, you'd use 1 in. stitches.

Basting should be removed before pressing to avoid marks. Clip the thread here and there and pull out the short pieces.

You may need to stab stitch very thick layers; that is, insert the needle only once before pulling the thread through. To precisely match a stripe or plaid, baste with a slip stitch (see below).

USING THE RUNNING STITCH AND BACK STITCH

The running stitch is useful for mending seams that are hard to reach with a sewing machine, and for repairing gathers. Take even stitches 1/16 to 1/8 in. long (for seams) or 1/8 to 1/4 in. long (for gathers). Pick up several stitches before pushing the needle through the fabric.

The back stitch is suitable only for seams; it's more secure

When I buy a jar of old buttons, I sort them by material. Mother-of-pearl, china, and bone can look almost identical to plastic imitations. But natural materials are colder and heavier.

I often prick my fingers while hand sewing. To prevent blood spots from setting, moisten a fabric scrap or paper towel with saliva or cold water. Press it against the spot until absorbed. Wear an adhesive bandage till you quit bleeding (which is usually in a few minutes).

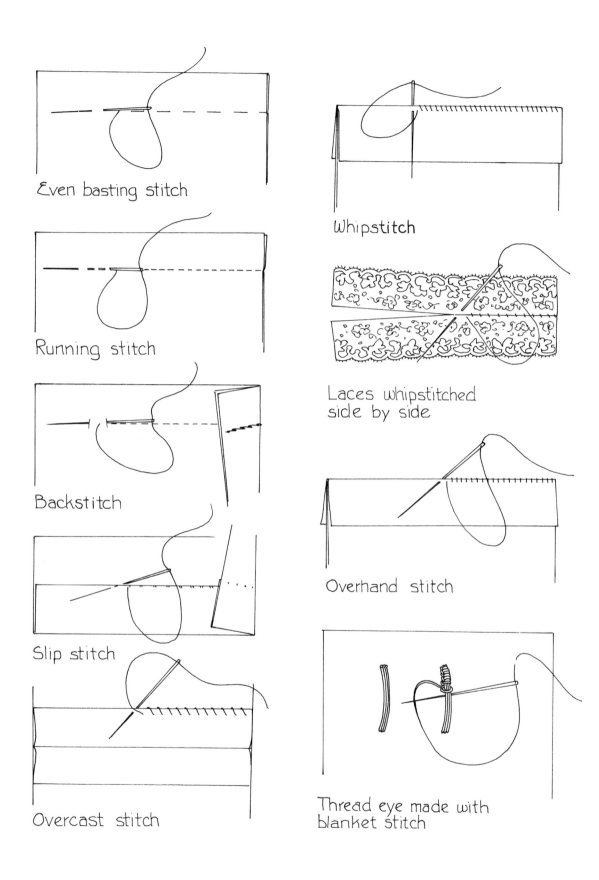

Even basting stitch

Running stitch

Backstitch

Slip stitch

Overcast stitch

Whipstitch

Laces whipstitched side by side

Overhand stitch

Thread eye made with blanket stitch

Figure 101: Basic hand stitches

than the running stitch. Bring the needle up through the fabric and take a stitch backward 1/16 to 1/8 in., then bring the needle up 1/16 to 1/8 in. ahead of the first stitch. Repeat. The stitches on the wrong side will overlap.

Instead of constantly back stitching, you can take one back stitch after several running or basting stitches.

SEWING INVISIBLY WITH THE SLIP STITCH

The slip stitch is used to sew a folded edge (such as a lining, hem, or patch) to an unfolded one. It's one of my favorite stitches because it's invisible and protects the thread from abrasion.

Slide the needle under the folded edge of the top fabric and take a stitch about 1/8 in. long. Then take a stitch in the under fabric. This should be the same length unless you're hemming, in which case you should pick up only a thread or two.

OVERCASTING, WHIPSTITCHING, AND OVERHANDING

I use overcasting to finish most raw edges. It can be done on one or more fabric layers. You can work from right to left or vice versa. To prevent fraying, work in the grain direction.

Insert the needle straight into the fabric to take a diagonal stitch. Make one stitch before drawing up the thread. Stitch length and spacing depend on the fabric's thickness and tendency to fray. For medium-weight fabric, make stitches about 1/4 in. deep and 1/8 to 1/4 in. apart.

If you don't like overcasting, the seam finishes provided by your sewing machine won't harm authenticity if they don't show on the outside.

The whipstitch is a variant of the overcast stitch; I use it to seam laces. Lay the straight lace edges together and insert the needle at a right angle to them, making a diagonal stitch. Stitches should be 1/16 to 1/8 in. deep and the same distance apart.

Alternatively, you can lay the edges side by side and whipstitch across them. If one edge is scalloped, lap it over the other enough to close any gaps.

Another stitch, called the overhand stitch, is just like the whipstitch except that you insert the needle diagonally to make a straight stitch.

USING THE BLANKET STITCH

In mending, the blanket stitch is useful for reinforcing buttonholes and making thread loops. Because these should be strong, use a double thread.

Most sewing books recommend wearing a thimble on the middle finger of the sewing hand to help push the needle through the fabric. Try a thimble and see how it feels. I've never been comfortable with one, but I do have calloused—and sometimes sore—fingers.

The blanket stitch looks like an overhand stitch with a ridge on one side. Both sides of the stitch are secure, but for appearance you must decide where the ridge should lie. I work blanket stitches vertically, but it's traditional to work them right to left.

Insert the needle from the wrong side of the fabric. Place and hold the thread on the ridge side of the stitch. For closely spaced stitches, reinsert the needle very slightly below and to the right of the first insertion point, to form a loop. Now put the needle through the loop and pull the thread as tight as you can without distorting the fabric.

Continue making stitches till the buttonhole edge or thread loop is completely covered.

✒ REPLACING AND REINFORCING CLOSURES

Vintage garments have lots of fasteners, which by this time are usually coming off. It's a good idea to reinforce them all. In fact, if the garment is washable it's best to replace metal fasteners with new, rustproof ones.

ATTACHING HOOKS AND EYES

Hooks and eyes are used on closely fitted garments where concealed fasteners are desired. They are more secure under strain than snaps, but may come undone if no strain is present.

There are two types of eyes, loops and bars. Loops are used for edges that don't overlap at all. The bars used for overlapping edges are not always packaged with hooks as they used to be, but can be ordered from sewing suppliers (see appendix A). Or you can make thread eyes, which show less anyway. A single flat, heavy-duty metal hook with a long bar is excellent for the waistband of a heavy skirt.

Hooks and eyes are usually sewn to a waistband or placket (a double fabric layer is needed for reinforcement). The hook is sewn to the wrong side of the overlapping edge, and no stitches should show on the right side. The eye is sewn to the underlap. If the edges just meet, position the hook 1/16 in. in from one edge and the loop 1/16 in. out from the other.

To attach a hook, stitch around the circular holes, each time taking up a garment thread or two (see figure 102). Slide the needle under the fabric to the hook end and fasten it with a few stitches.

Attach an eye by sewing around the holes as for a hook. For a loop, slide the needle under the fabric to the closure end and fasten each side with a few stitches.

For a thread eye to hold well it should be carefully positioned and only as long as needed to hold the hook. Use a good length of double matching thread—you don't want to run out while making the eye.

To make a thread eye:

1. Make three or four foundation stitches, depending on how thick the eye will be. Insert the needle, from the wrong side, where the eye should begin. Then reinsert it where the eye should end. Pulling the foundation taut with a pin held in the nonsewing hand, make the other foundation stitches. Secure them by taking a few short stitches on the wrong side, then push the needle through to the right side.

2. Without cutting the thread, work blanket stitches from the top to the bottom of the foundation. I put the ridge of the stitch next to the garment edge. I continue to hold the foundation taut for the first few stitches.

3. Continue making blanket stitches, as closely as possible, till you cover the foundation. Then fasten the thread on the wrong side.

When you make a Victorian outfit with a separate bodice and skirt, add hidden hooks and eyes to keep the garments together when worn.

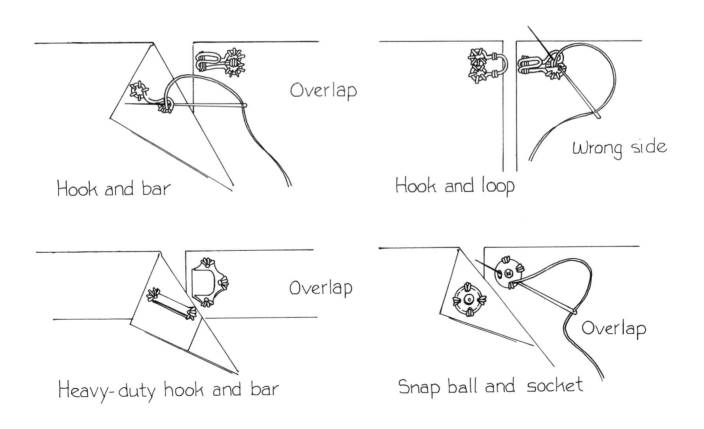

Figure 102: Metal closures and attachment methods

ATTACHING SNAPS

Snaps are used only on overlapping edges. The ball part is sewn to the under side of the overlap, and the socket to the upper side of the underlap.

Stick a pin through the fabric at the ball location and slide the ball over the pin. Take several small stitches through each hole, passing the thread under the fabric between holes. (On original snaps the thread is often carried over the snap between holes, but this looks messy and is less durable.) Remove the pin.

Position the garment as when closed and mark the socket location with another pin. Attach the socket the same way.

DEALING WITH BUTTON CLOSURES

Vintage buttons are usually closed with buttonholes, but may be closed with loops or be purely decorative. Because button closures wear a little more than other types my techniques for reinforcing plackets are described here.

To attach a button:

1. Choose a replacement button that fits easily through the buttonhole. Position it over the traces of the old button, with two holes parallel to the buttonhole. (If the fabric is weak, first reinforce the placket as described below.)

2. Sew across the holes over and over. If the button has four holes, sew across two at a time parallel to the buttonhole. Or in an X, though this puts more strain on the button center. If the button has a shank, rather than holes, sew it parallel to the buttonhole.

3. When sewing a holed button onto thick fabric you must create a shank. Place a toothpick between the holes and sew over it (see figure 103). Then remove the toothpick, which leaves a thread loop. Pull the button to the top of the loop and wind the thread tightly around it several times.

4. Fasten the thread on the wrong side.

If a garment has vintage fabric or crochet-covered buttons you'll need to reattach them every time the garment has been washed. These buttons are usually shankless, but are sewn flat to the fabric regardless of its thickness. The stitches should be invisible. Here's the technique:

1. Hold the button in place with one hand. Insert the needle from the wrong side of the garment. Slide it through the under side of the button fabric (you'll feel a hard form inside) to a point directly opposite, but a little within the button edge. Reinsert the needle in the garment.

2. Take another stitch on the garment's wrong side, across the circle, to a point about 1/8 in. away from where you inserted the thread. Push the needle to the right side a little within the button edge.

3. Stitch through the button fabric again. Continue around the circle to create a pattern like wheel spokes.

4. Tug gently on the button to check for loose areas. Reinforce them with a couple of stitches along the edge.

5. Fasten the thread on the wrong side.

Torn buttonholes can be mended with overcast or blanket stitches about 1/16 in. wider than the originals. Putting the blanket stitch ridge along the cut edge adds a little strength, but slightly reduces the buttonhole size. The ridge looks prettiest against the fabric.

If many buttonholes are torn you can whipstitch them closed, cover them with ornamental buttons, and use snaps as the actual fasteners.

Make replacement thread button loops like thread eyes, only longer. In fact, it's safest to make them a little too long, to

If a garment shows a gap when buttoned, add a hook or snap rather than another button (which would be unevenly spaced from the others).

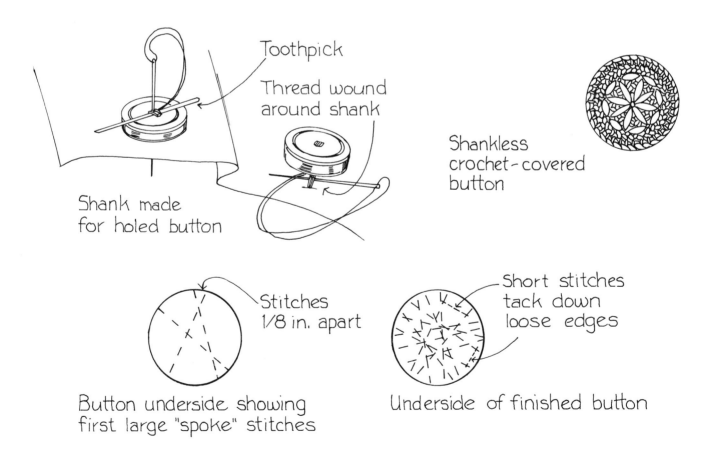

Toothpick

Thread wound around shank

Shank made for holed button

Shankless crochet-covered button

Stitches 1/8 in. apart

Button underside showing first large "spoke" stitches

Short stitches tack down loose edges

Underside of finished button

Figure 103: Flat buttons sewn with and without a shank

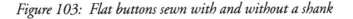

You can imitate vintage embroidered and crocheted buttons by covering purchased button forms with a double fabric/lace layer. Use fine lace for small buttons or an embroidered look. Use coarser lace for large ones or a crocheted look. Make sure the lace motif(s) is in the same position on all buttons. Fabric may be the same color or a contrast.

reduce strain, rather than too short. If you crochet you can make loops from crochet cotton, using the chain stitch.

I don't use thread loops on heavy outer garments. Instead, I sew on short lengths of soutache or some other very narrow braid. Purchased frogs (fancy button-and-loop closures made from narrow braid) often work for outer garments that already have braid decoration.

If the placket is torn at one or two button locations, patch them on the wrong side (with the button(s) removed). If there are many tears, patch the placket all along the wrong side. Slip stitch on a length of matching bias binding. Or whipstitch a length of seam binding, twill tape, or, for sheer fabrics, lace. You can use machine stitching if it won't show.

✎ Reinforcing a Hem

If a hem is coming apart here and there, a few inches at a stretch, it needs reinforcement.

1. The hem top should have been finished with a fold, stitching, or attached seam binding. Repair the finish if necessary, using the original method. Fasten any loose threads.

2. Press undone and weak areas along the original crease. If the crease doesn't hold well, baste 1/4 in. above it.

3. Pin the hem top. Baste 1/4 in. down from the top in the undone area, plus 1 to 1 1/2 in. on either side of it. Remove pins.

4. Sew with the original stitch or one that resembles it on the right side. Begin where you basted; that is, stitch over 1 to 1 1/2 in. of secure hem. Work from right to left.

   The basic hemming stitch is suitable for most hems (see figure 104). Insert the needle under, and about 1/8 in. below, the hem top and bring it through. Take a diagonal stitch across the top to a point about 1/4 in. away, and pick up one or two garment threads. Bring the thread back under the top, 1/4 in. away. Continue like this.

   Don't pick up too many garment threads or pull the sewing thread tight. Check the right side periodically for bulges and visible hemming threads.

5. Remove basting. Press the entire hem.

An alternative stitch is the blind stitch, which is looser and invisible on both sides. I use it for chiffon velvets because they're strongly inclined to form lumpy hems, and to tack down facings.

Roll back the finished and basted hem top about 1/4 in. Alternately pick up one or two garment threads and one or two

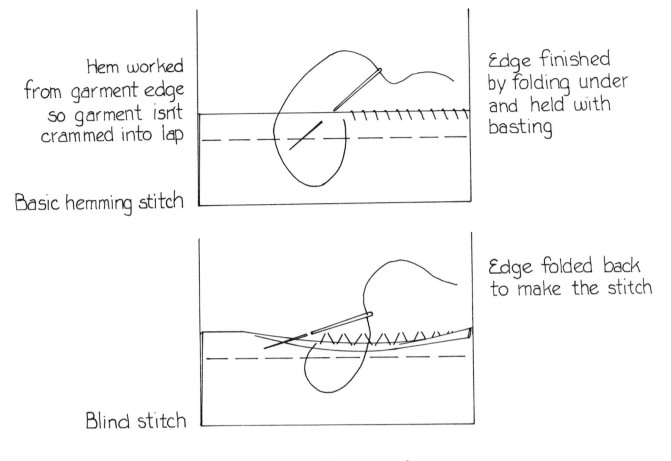

Hem worked from garment edge so garment isn't crammed into lap

Edge finished by folding under and held with basting

Basic hemming stitch

Blind stitch

Edge folded back to make the stitch

Figure 104: Hemming stitches

hem threads. Make stitches 1/4 in. apart. Leave the thread rather loose.

If the hem is loose all over, the fabric is fraying, or the garment is the wrong length, you'll need to rehem the garment. See chapter 7 for directions.

Also consider rehemming if you're unsatisfied with the appearance or durability of the current method. Turn-of-the century garments sometimes have machine-stitched hems that are quite visible on the right side. I rehem these using a slip stitch for fine fabrics and a hemming stitch for most others. And I sometimes have to redo nonoriginal hems botched by previous owners.

✍ REPAIRING SPLIT SEAMS

Repair a split seam by stitching along the original seam line, or a little within it if the fabric is frayed.

1. If you're changing the seam line, draw the new one with chalk, tapering it into the old line. Fasten any loose threads.

2. Pin the seam in the split area plus about 1 in. into the

Unpick a seam with embroidery scissors. Clip two or three threads on one fabric layer, at any point along the seam. Carefully separate the layers at the new "hole." Clip a couple of stitches, pull the layers apart, and continue till the seam is unpicked. If one fabric or trim layer is to be discarded, cut against it.

secure stitching on each side. If the fabric is slippery or heavy, or the area is hard to reach, baste and remove pins.

3. Sew along the pinned or basted line. If you can reach the area with a sewing machine, use a machine straight stitch—it's a bit more secure than hand sewing. Otherwise use a running or back stitch.

4. Overcast any unfinished edges. Remove pins or basting. Press.

REPAIRING GATHERS

Gathers that were sewn to a split seam often start to come undone. It's easiest to repair them by hand.

Press the area. With a double thread, make a single row of running stitches through the undone gathers (see figure 105). Draw up the thread to fit the seam. Pin and, if the area is large, baste. Restitch the seam.

Gauging and cartridge pleats are types of gathering used on Victorian garments, particularly skirts. They're rounded pleats that may be enclosed within the waistband (gauging) or stitched to it at the pleat fold (cartridge pleats).

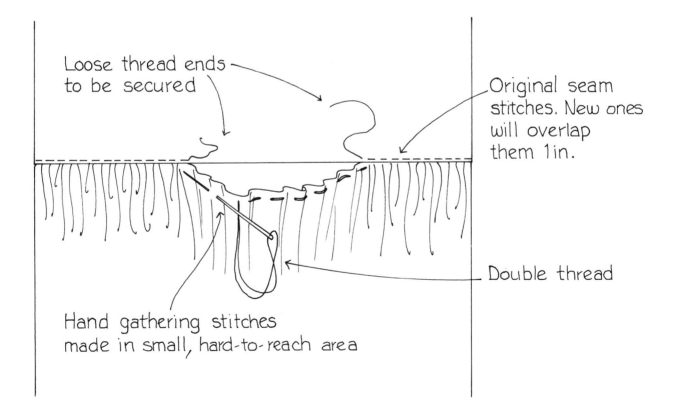

Figure 105: Gathers to be resewn to topstitched seam

1. Smooth, rather than press, the area to be gathered—old fold lines are helpful. You'll need two rows of large running stitches. Because precision is important, measure each stitch with a ruler and mark its location with a chalk dot.

   The rows should be located where the originals were. The stitches should be the same size as the originals; they will be longer on the wrong side if the pleat bulk hangs in back. The stitches on the top and bottom rows should match.

2. Using a double thread with a large knot, make the stitches at the dots.

3. Pull up the threads as tightly as possible—there should be no space between pleats. Fasten securely.

4. If pleats are enclosed, sandwich them between the waistband layers. Pin, baste, and remove pins. Sew the waistband to the wrong side of the skirt with a whipstitch. Then sew it to the right side with a slip stitch.

5. To attach pleats at the edge, butt the folds against the waistband in the original position (which will be below the top edge). Using double thread, whipstitch the top of each pleat to the waistband. Make three or four stitches each time.

6. Remove basting and press.

✺ MENDING TEARS

Straight tears can be mended by either hand or machine (see figure 106). Hand mending is best for cornered (L- and T-shaped) tears because it takes up less fabric.

To mend a straight tear by machine:

1. Pin (and if necessary baste) the edges together. Ease in any extra length on one side.

2. With a machine straight stitch sew a 1/4 in. "seam," tapering it into the fabric on each end.

3. Overcast the raw edges. Press the seam to one side.

To mend a straight tear by hand:

1. Pin the tear, baste, and remove pins. If you're experienced you can just hold the edges together instead.

2. Hold the tear vertically in the nonsewing hand. Insert the needle about 1/8 in. above the tear and 1/8 in. within its edges.

3. Make very fine, tight whipstitches, allowing the fabric to roll. Even out slight irregularities in the edges as you go.

You can sometimes restore gathers without the aid of gathering stitches, though this takes a good eye and some skill. Leave the area unpressed. Crunch the gathers along the original fold lines. Then pin and restitch the seam.

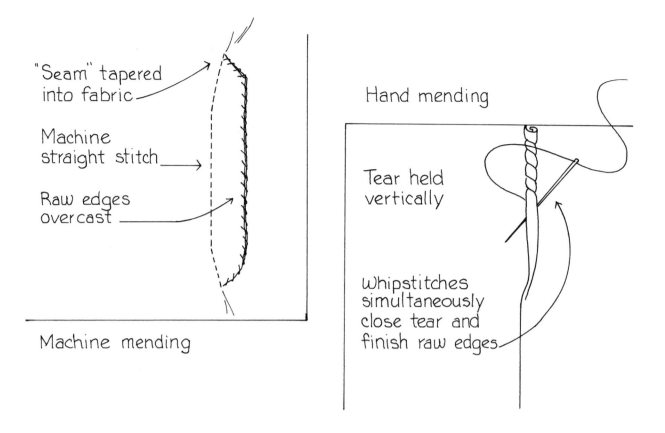

"Seam" tapered into fabric

Machine straight stitch

Raw edges overcast

Machine mending

Hand mending

Tear held vertically

Whipstitches simultaneously close tear and finish raw edges

Figure 106: Two ways to sew a tear

4. Check the right side. Any stitches that show were made deeper than the others. Even out the seam by working back up the tear at that depth, crossing the first stitches.

5. Remove basting and press.

Mend an L-shaped tear by working down one side; then turn the fabric and work down the other. Don't round off the corner. Mend a T-shaped tear like two separate straight tears; do the long side first.

A cornered tear in heavy fabric should be patched rather than mended.

✒ FIXING HOLES AND STAINS

Vintage garments frequently show small holes and irremovable stains. Most are easy to fix.

PATCHING

Holes, irregular tears, tears in weak fabric, and irremovable stains can all be patched. The area must be clean and pressed. The patch must be large enough to sew onto strong fabric beyond the hole. It should be the same weight as the garment fabric or slightly lighter, and cleanable by the same method.

If you can make the patch look like decoration it will be undetectable. This is easy if the garment is already highly decorated (see figure 107). The hole must be in a reasonable spot for decoration. The patch should blend in with any existing decoration. It may help to add another, symmetrically placed patch.

Suitable patches include:

- *Lace appliques and medallions.*

- *Small lace doilies and coasters.*

- *Crocheter's samples.* A standard crocheter's trick was/is to test thread size and stitches by making a little sample. To prevent raveling, run loose threads into the crochet with a large-eyed needle.

- *Motifs cut from a worn Irish (or other) crochet ground.* Pull connecting threads to test where raveling will cause the least damage. Clip away the motif, leaving connecting threads long enough to run in.

- *Motifs cut from tatting.* Because threads are knotted, tatting is less prone to ravel than hand lace or crochet.

I don't recommend dyeing to cover stains. The agitation weakens vintage garments even if you don't use a washer. A garment may turn several different shades because several fabrics, trims, or threads were used. And finally, dye can darken stains instead of concealing them.

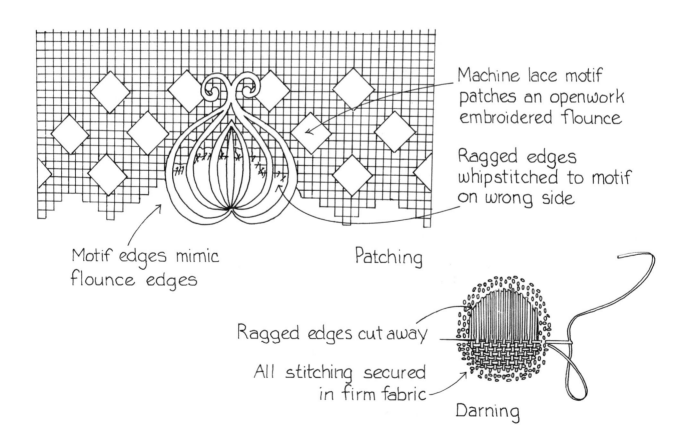

Machine lace motif patches an openwork embroidered flounce

Ragged edges whipstitched to motif on wrong side

Motif edges mimic flounce edges

Patching

Ragged edges cut away

All stitching secured in firm fabric

Darning

Figure 107: Two ways to mend a hole

- *Dense motifs cut from machine lace.* Overcast ragged edges.

- *Scraps of fine lace edging, insertion, and net.* Overcast edges.

- *Embroidered appliques.*

- *Embroidered areas of discarded garments and linens.* Turn under raw edges before attaching.

- *Contrasting fabric cut into applique shapes.* The shape should be appropriate for the period. Use a quilting template or other professional drawing as a pattern. Turn under edges.

- *Beaded motifs.* These must be strong. New ones are available as well as vintage.

Be sure all washable patch materials are preshrunk.

To sew on a decorative patch:

1. Measure the hole and choose a patch of the correct size.

2. Pin, then baste, the patch over the hole on the right side of the garment.

3. Sew with a fine whipstitch or machine zigzag stitch. If the fabric has unfinished edges, use a machine satin stitch.

4. Whipstitch the hole edges to the back of the patch, taking up one or two threads.

5. Remove basting and press.

Use a plain fabric patch if the garment is very plain or the hole is in an odd spot for decoration. If at all possible, use garment fabric cut off during alterations. Or use part of an inside hem or facing (which you'll then have to patch with another fabric). If you can't use garment fabric, find the best match you can.

To sew on a plain patch:

1. Measure the hole. Cut a square or rectangular patch a little larger than the hole plus 1/4 in. seam allowances. The patch should match the fabric grain and any nap or pattern.

2. Press under the seam allowances. Pin and baste the patch to the right side of the garment. Remove pins.

3. Sew with a slip stitch. Or use a machine topstitch, though this is more conspicuous.

4. Whipstitch the hole edges to the back of the patch.

5. Remove basting and press.

DARNING SMALL HOLES

Hand darning with running stitches is the most inconspicuous way to mend small holes in woolens. It's occasionally useful for

---

Machine zigzagging is technically a good substitute for whipstitching. However, it always looks more modern than a straight stitch or hand stitch.

Some Edwardian garments have heavy weights sewn to the hem. Remove weights immediately, because if they haven't torn the fabric yet they soon will.

Shirt cuff edges can be patched with a bias binding that matches the cuff. French cuffs can be reversed. Unpick the cuff and whipstitch over the frayed area. Reattach the cuff with the mended side out (when worn it will be hidden by the cuff fold).

other fabrics. Use thread that's the same weight and color as the garment thread—you may be able to pull some from a seam allowance. Work on the right side of the fabric, from one side of the hole to the other.

1. Cut away the ragged edges of the hole.

2. In the firm fabric, take several running stitches. Then lay a foundation thread vertically across the hole and take several stitches on the other side. From there, lay another foundation thread close to the first. Continue till you've laid a complete foundation.

3. Now work horizontally across the foundation. As before, start with a few running stitches in the fabric. Then alternately weave over and under the foundation threads. When you reach the other side of the hole, take a few running stitches and weave from that direction. Continue till you've covered the foundation.

4. Fasten the thread on the wrong side. Press.

Keep the darn as flat as possible—if you pull the thread too tight it will pucker.

REPLACING UNDERARMS

Stained or torn underarms are common in silk and rayon garments. Replace them with matching fabric. Because the underarm shape is complex, you'll need to make an insert pattern.

1. See which underarm is most damaged. Measure the damaged area.

2. Using a ruler and chalk, draw a geometric shape on each underarm that encompasses that area (see figure 108). This will be a triangle if only the bodice is damaged; a diamond if the sleeve is damaged too.

3. Cut out the damaged area along the chalk line, leaving only good fabric.

4. Unpick the seams. You'll have two or four pieces per underarm. Choose the least damaged ones for the pattern. Press under the seam allowances.

5. Pin the pieces onto pattern paper. Draw around them with a pencil, guessing at the outlines of badly damaged pieces. Even up the lines with a ruler and french curve.

6. Where the pieces were seamed, add 1/2 in. seam allowances by measuring out from the pattern line as described in chapter 4. Add 1 in. to the insert's outer edges.

7. Pin the pattern to the replacement fabric on the original grain line or the bias. Cut.

Worn edges on a wool or velvet coat can be patched with wide bias binding. Make your own from velvet or velveteen, in a matching or contrasting color. Wrap binding around all edges. Slip stitch each side or machine topstitch through all layers. For a more intentional look, cover some seams too. Or add velvet-covered buttons or frogs.

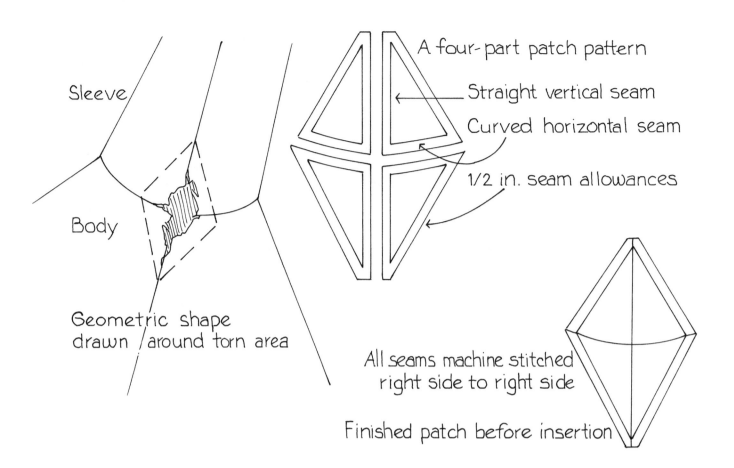

Sleeve

Body

Geometric shape
drawn around torn area

A four-part patch pattern

Straight vertical seam

Curved horizontal seam

1/2 in. seam allowances

All seams machine stitched
right side to right side

Finished patch before insertion

Figure 108: Underarm replacement

8. Pin the vertical insert seam(s) together right side to right side. Baste if necessary. Sew with a machine straight stitch. Remove any basting. Press in the same direction as on the garment. If there is a horizontal insert seam pin, sew, and press it. Overcast the seam allowances.

9. Press under the outer edges of the insert 1/2 in. Pin it to the right side of the garment, overlapping the cut edge 1/2 in. Baste and remove pins.

10. Slip stitch the insert to the garment. Or use a machine top-stitch, though this is more conspicuous. On the wrong side, overcast the raw edges together.

11. Remove basting. Press seams toward the insert.

Chapter 7 gives directions for enlarging an underarm with a gusset.

🦢 REPAIRING LACE

There are several basic types of lace and two approaches to lace repair. I'm using the term "lace" to cover needle lace, bobbin lace, battenberg lace, crocheted lace, knitted lace, machine net, and all other machine laces. And by "repair," I mean mending that can be done by the average sewer. The other approach, restoring the lace with lace-making techniques, takes expert knowledge and is unnecessary for most laces you're likely to acquire. Very old, valuable pieces should be taken to a professional restorer.

Late Victorian and Edwardian laces tend to be either very fine or very coarse. Fine valenciennes-type laces were heavily used on lingerie. Quantities of net (sometimes machine- or hand-embroidered) appeared on dresses. Heavy, often ecru-colored laces were thought to give an antique look. Bobbin and needle laces were generally used for trims. Battenberg and crochet were used for whole garments as well.

MENDING FINE LACE

It's easy to invisibly mend fine lace, even if the width or pattern is slightly changed. Mend seam splits and tears like fabric, with a whipstitch or machine zigzag stitch. Reattach trim to fabric by the same methods. Large holes can be sometimes be mended like tears, but if this causes too much distortion they need patching. Use a lace applique or bit of trim with a similar design. First turn under raw edges on the trim patch.

MENDING COARSE LACE

Bold needle and bobbin laces, and their machine counterparts, consist of motifs connected by finer bars. Generally a bar breaks near a motif (see figure 109). On the wrong side, whipstitch it to the motif with double sewing thread, repeatedly going over one or two stitches. Simultaneously tack down any loose threads.

If the bar has disappeared, check whether its absence is noticeable at wearing distance. If so, fill in the empty space with a thread "bar" of the correct length. Anchor it in the motifs and cross the empty space until the "bar" looks thick enough. Maintain an even tension and avoid pulling motifs together—any distortion is obvious.

Crocheted and knitted laces are prone to ravel. Connect motifs as for bobbin and needle lace, but pass your thread through the loose loops. Tack down or run in loose threads. Try to imitate the lace structure. Use either crochet or double sewing thread, whichever looks most natural. Frayed edges can be secured with fine whipstitches. Very badly frayed ones can be whipstitched, then covered with an edging.

Battenberg (tape) lace is joined by simple, large embroidery stitches that zigzag between motifs (which were created by arranging purchased tape). Repair it with embroidery thread of the same weight. You can usually figure out the stitch, but if you can't just zigzag (by hand) in the right places.

When you hand sew fine lace, don't fasten beginning threads with knots because they pull through the holes. Instead, leave at least 1/2 in. of thread free after inserting the needle, lay it in the direction you'll work, and whipstitch over it along with the lace. You can also do this when mending thin fabrics.

All-lace garments in good condition often have tattered silk linings. If the lining is attached only at the seams, cut it out next to them with embroidery scissors. Wear pretty silk undergarments instead of relining. If the lace garment isn't complete— that is the lining is integral in places—it may be worth adding lace motifs so you can do away with the lining.

Heavy missing bar can be filled in with thread

Light missing bar can be left as is if not noticeable

Detached bar can be resewn to motif

Figure 109: Coarse lace repairs

The seams of battenberg lace garments are usually joined with large running stitches. Repair them with either embroidery or sewing thread.

REPLACING LACE COLLARS AND YOKES

Several types of lace collars appear on vintage garments. One is the flat collar, which falls over the garment fabric. Another is the standing or high collar, which is fitted up around the neck. It may be attached to a lace yoke that fills in for some fabric, or there may be a yoke with no collar. A third type, which I call a neckline edging, is a cross between a collar and a yoke.

To replace a flat collar:

1. Unpick the original collar. Press the garment neckline on the wrong side.

2. Find a replacement collar that looks good on the garment. Its neckline should be the same shape and either the same size or slightly larger.

3. If the collar is large, either in one place or all over, run in hand gathering stitches (machine gathering doesn't work well on heavy collar lace).

4. Arrange the collar on the right side of the garment with the neckline edges even. Draw up the gathering thread till the collar lies flat. Pin, baste, and remove pins. Check flatness by trying on the garment.

5. Sew on the collar with a machine straight stitch (lace side up) or a running stitch. Original collars are often hand sewn, or even basted, onto dry-cleanable fabrics so they can be removed and washed separately. This is a good idea because lace doesn't dry clean well.

6. Remove basting. Cover the collar with a press cloth and press on the right side. Steam to ease in fullness.

To replace a high collar:

1. Unpick the original collar. Press the garment neckline on the wrong side.

2. If you don't have a replacement, it's easy to make one (see figure 110). Period collars are about 2 to 2 1/2 in. wide and made of straight lace trim. Often several lengths of narrow lace are pieced together, though sometimes one wide lace is used. Some collars have a slightly gathered edging.

If a high-necked garment is damaged, you can cut out a lower square or V neck. This can be filled in with a lace yoke, perhaps with an attached collar, or finished with an edging. First gather any excess fullness in the new neckline.

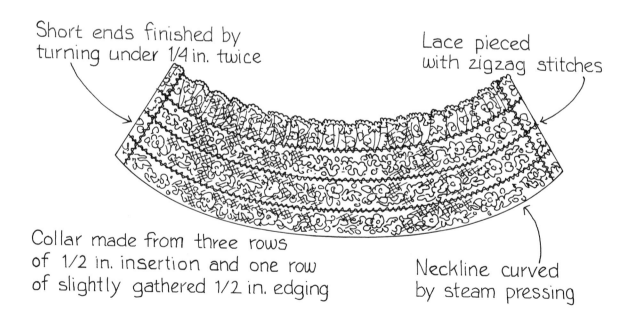

Short ends finished by turning under 1/4 in. twice

Lace pieced with zigzag stitches

Collar made from three rows of 1/2 in. insertion and one row of slightly gathered 1/2 in. edging

Neckline curved by steam pressing

Figure 110: Replacement high collar

Measure the neckline (including opening overlap) and cut the lace that length plus 1 in. Piece it by whipstitching or machine zigzagging. Then finish the collar's short ends by turning under 1/4 in. twice and sewing with a whipstitch or zigzag stitch. Press while forming the neckline edge into a slight curve.

3. On the right side, arrange the collar's neckline edge about 1/8 in. over the garment's. Pin, baste, and remove pins.

4. Sew with a fine whipstitch, or machine straight or zigzag stitch.

5. Remove basting and press.

6. Try the garment on yourself or a dress form, wrong side out. If the collar gaps at the top, pinch it into darts by the shoulder seams. Pin. Take off the garment. Baste darts and remove pins.

7. Sew down darts from the wrong side with a whipstitch or zigzag stitch.

8. Remove basting and press.

9. Attach enough small fasteners to keep the collar upright—three is a good number.

To replace a lace yoke, with or without an attached collar, on a dress or blouse:

1. The original yoke is usually sewn to a finished V or square neck. Unpick it. If you like the resulting neckline, don't bother replacing the yoke. You can fill in an overly low neck with an edging (see below).

2. A replacement can be another unpicked yoke, part of an old blouse or chemisette (dickey), a doily, or lace fabric. The yoke must have a finished neckline, open where the garment does (usually in back), and be at least 1/2 in. larger than the space to be filled in. It doesn't need to be exactly the right size or shape.

3. Arrange the yoke on a dress form as if it were being worn, including any opening overlap (see figure 111). (If you arrange it on yourself you'll need a helper.) If the opening isn't finished, trim to fit, fold under 1/4 in. twice, and pin closely. (If you wish you can finish the opening at this stage, then put the yoke back on the form.)

4. Put the garment on the form over the yoke. Pin it closely to the yoke around the neck.

5. Take off the yoke and garment together. Baste all pinned edges and remove pins.

6. Trim the yoke to 1/2 or 1 in. away from the neckline.

7. From the right side, sew the garment to the yoke with a slip stitch, whipstitch, or machine topstitch.

8. Overcast the yoke edges if they tend to ravel. Finish the opening edges as for a collar. Add fasteners.

9. Remove basting and press.

Of course, you could also sew the yoke over the garment and cover the join with lace edging, braid, or velvet ribbon.

To attach a neckline edging:

1. Examine the neckline. Usually the garment has a square or V neck and the edging extends above it. The edging is a straight length of lace that has been mitered (darted) to fit.

2. Unpick the old edging and press the neckline. You may need to reinforce the neckline, which is often overcast or narrow-hemmed. If the existing finish is weak, sew commercial bias binding to the right side, turn to the inside, and hem with a slip stitch.

3. Find lace edging or insertion of about the same width as the original and several inches longer than the neckline. Finish one end by turning over 1/4 in. twice and whip-stitching.

> On lingerie, fabric is gathered into the yoke bottom. Finish raw edges, gather, and attach with the yoke on top.

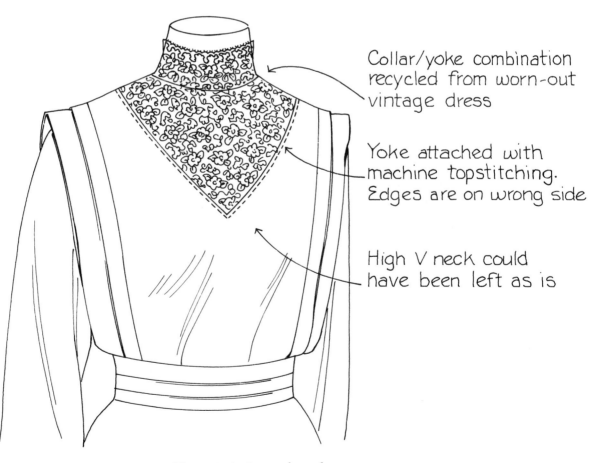

Collar/yoke combination recycled from worn-out vintage dress

Yoke attached with machine topstitching. Edges are on wrong side

High V neck could have been left as is

Figure 111: Lace yoke replacement

Repairing Lace

When adding bold lace to a garment, for example as a neckline edging or peplum, plan the positions of large motifs. Generally one should be centered at the focal point of the garment or section—often this is center front. Lace should never be seamed at a focal point, so pin it in the middle and work toward the ends.

4. Pin the edging to the right or wrong side of the garment (depending on whether you want the join to show), over- lapping the neckline 1/8 in. Start with the finished end. When you reach the other end, finish it.

5. The lace will bulge where you went around corners. Fold the bulges neatly to the inside so the edging lies flat (see figure 112). Pin these darts.

6. Baste and remove pins. Sew down the edging with a whip- stitch or machine topstitch. Whipstitch down the darts from the wrong side.

7. Remove basting and press.

✎ FIXING BEADED GARMENTS

Bead decoration was especially popular from the 1880s through the 1920s. Late Victorian clothes were generally bead- ed by sewing on purchased motifs or trim, usually black. Motifs and garment fabric are often still sturdy. Attach a motif with a running or basting stitch.

In the 1910s and 1920s, beads were usually sewn directly

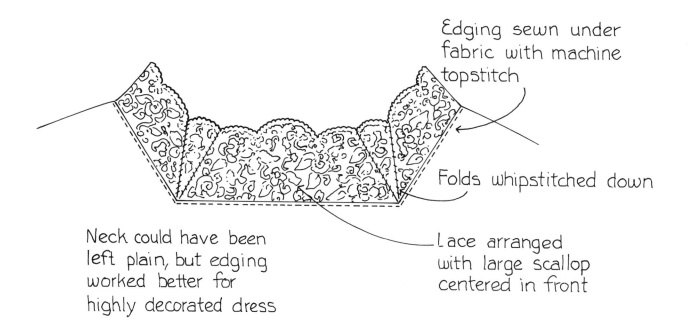

Edging sewn under fabric with machine topstitch

Folds whipstitched down

Neck could have been left plain, but edging worked better for highly decorated dress

Lace arranged with large scallop centered in front

Figure 112: Edging for shallow square neckline

to a thin fabric. Often the beading thread has broken or pulled through it, causing beads to drop off. Keep the garment in its own bag until mending to minimize bead loss. Beads come in many colors and shapes, which, except for faux pearls, are hard to match. Unless you're a perfectionist, you'll settle for securing what you have.

The beading thread can match either the fabric or the old thread—whichever shows less. A beading needle is best because most others won't fit through the holes. Note that hole size varies among beads of the same type.

To rebead:

1. Estimate whether you have enough beads to cover the pattern shown by the old holes. If not, simplify the pattern or leave some distance between beads.

2. Secure any thread ends.

3. Fasten your beading thread by taking a few stitches in one place.

4. Where the thread has broken and some beads are loose, reattach them by backstitching (see figure 113). Insert your needle from the wrong side. String a bead onto the thread

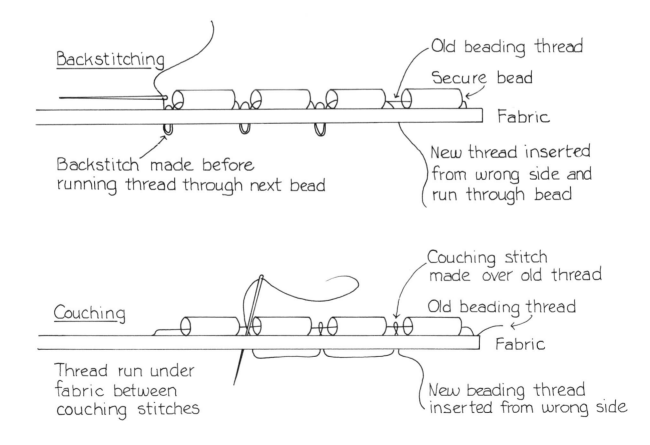

Figure 113: Two ways to rebead

and lay it on the fabric. Right at the end of the bead, reinsert the needle and take a stitch 1/16 to 1/8 in. long. Then backstitch that amount. Go under the fabric to the next bead position and repeat.

Instead of backstitching, you can string the loose beads and couch them as described below.

5. Where the thread has pulled through sheer fabric without breaking, reattach it by couching. Lay the threaded beads in position. Insert the needle from the wrong side between two beads. Make a stitch over, and at a right angle to, the beading thread. Go under the fabric to the next bead and repeat.

Handle the garment as gently as possible to keep more beads from loosening as you work.

Repairing beaded purses is a good deal more complex than repairing beaded garments. It's best to take them to an expert.

✒ REPLACING BONING

Boning was widely used to support turn-of-the-century bodices. It was usually steel, sometimes plastic, and occasionally whalebone. Sometimes bones are broken or rusty, or casings are worn. Or you've removed bones during alterations.

When to replace bones is a matter of judgement. I remove all bones from delicate garments because they poke holes, and from washable ones because they leave rust stains. Sometimes all bones on a sturdy dry-cleanable garment are damaged, or removed during alterations. I just leave them off if they're not essential to the look. But I will replace a few bones on a sturdy garment because it's less trouble than removing them all.

To replace boning:

1. Unpick bones. If they're sewn under facings, unpick facings where necessary.

2. Measure the bones. Cut yours to those lengths, adjusting for any alterations.

3. Cut casings 1/2 in. longer. For a lightweight garment, cut two per bone. There's no need to color-match existing casings—contrasting ones were intentionally used.

4. If you cut two casings per bone, sew bones between them with a whipstitch or (if you're skilled) a machine topstitch.

5. Turn under casings 1/4 in. at each end. Baste long sides to the garment.

6. Casings should be sewn to the seam allowances or underlining—never the outer fabric. Sew with a whipstitch, including one short end.

7. Insert bones. Stitch down the other end of the casings.

8. Restitch facings as necessary.

Wearing a corset under a deboned garment provides a fairly authentic silhouette—boning is a supplement.

ℳ RELINING A JACKET, COAT, OR CAPE

Typically, a period jacket or coat lining is made of a fragile silk that wears out long before the outer fabric. Replacing the lining rejuvenates the garment's appearance, maintains its shape, and makes it more comfortable. Be reassured that you'll get many more wearings out of the new lining than the old one.

Contrary to your natural inclination (or at least mine) you should replace a lining when it begins to show wear, rather than waiting till it falls apart. If the pieces are badly damaged it's a bit harder to make a pattern.

Choose a lining fabric following the instructions in chapter 2. But note that black satin (traditionally with gray-striped white silk sleeves) is the standard lining for men's formal jackets.

1. Turn the jacket inside out. Unpick the lining, trying not to stretch or tear it. Leave some thread ends in place to mark insertion, dart, and seam lines. If there are many pieces, label them with tailor's chalk.

2. If you need to mend or alter the jacket do it now. See whether newly exposed interfacing is coming loose. Reinforce as necessary, imitating the original stitches.

3. Undo the lining seams and press each piece, again without stretching. If you altered the jacket draw the alteration lines on the lining. If you'll make a paper pattern, press under the seam allowances.

4. Examine the pieces. Check for stretching by comparing left and right sides to each other and the garment. The least stretched and/or damaged version of a piece should form your pattern. You'll need to make a paper pattern for a piece if there is no undamaged version, if the seam allowances are very narrow or unevenly trimmed, or if you might want to copy the jacket sometime.

   Often jacket linings include small pockets. If you don't use these, don't bother replicating them. If you do, you can either copy the originals or use a commercial pattern (and its instructions). The new pockets can be a different size or style, but should not show outside bulges when full.

5. Whether or not you're making a paper pattern, you must mark a vertical grain line on each lining piece. Pull a sturdy-looking thread at the narrow end of the piece and follow it to the other end. Mark this grain line by basting. If the thread is too fragile to pull out, tear along the most damaged version of the piece and copy the line onto your lining or paper pattern piece.

6. To make a paper pattern piece, draw a grain line on paper and lay the lining on top, matching the grain (see figure

You can postpone relining by replacing only the most worn areas, for example the collar and lapels.

114). Secure the lining with weights or pins. Draw around it. You can draw freehand, then clean up the lines with a ruler and french curves. Or you can lay the curves by the lining edges and follow them. If two versions of a piece are damaged in different places, trace the best parts of each.

7. If both versions have an area too badly damaged for tracing, guess at its outline. Cut out the paper a good distance from your tentative line. Pin the paper to the garment inside along the more certain lines, working toward the uncertain one. Then pin that down and pencil-trace the garment seam onto your paper. Remove the paper and clean up the line.

8. Run a tracing wheel over the lining at dart and other inner lines, then pencil over the dents in the paper. Mark the beginning and end of gathered areas.

9. Take the lining off the paper. True seams and add seam allowances as described in chapter 4. Use an allowance of 1/2 in. if your original pieces were fairly intact; otherwise use 1 in. If a coat lining had a separate, free-hanging hem, add the original hem allowance.

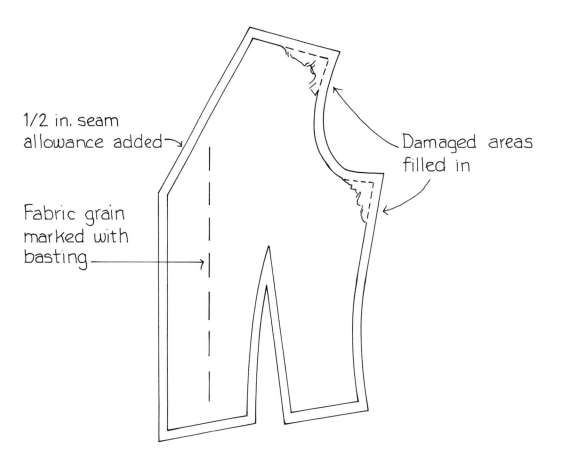

1/2 in. seam allowance added

Damaged areas filled in

Fabric grain marked with basting

Figure 114: Old lining front laid over paper pattern

10. Label, then cut out the paper pattern pieces. Save the original lining for reference till the end of the project.

11. Cut out the lining in a single layer, using a nap layout. To avoid pin marks, use weights or pin within the seam allowances. Transfer pattern marks. (Chapter 3 gives detailed instructions for cutting out.)

12. Stay stitch each lining piece. Run gathering threads where required. Press.

13. Now assemble the lining. First make any darts or stitched pleats and attach any pockets. If the front, back, and/or sleeve has multiple pieces, sew these together. (If you're relining a cape, skip steps involving sleeves.) Then sew the front to the back at the shoulder and side seams. Sew the sleeve underarm seam to create a tube, but don't sew the sleeve to the body.

    Press seams and clip curves as described in chapter 3. There's no need to finish the seams.

14. Press under all outer edges of the lining except the armholes. Baste.

15. With the jacket inside out, pin the lining to it wrong sides together (see figure 115). Pinning can be done flat or on a dress form or hanger (a dress form is best if you've done alterations or filled in pattern areas). Pin around all outer edges (except a separate coat hem) and the armholes, matching seams. (Some people also pin along the center back seam.) Where lining pieces don't match, smooth them onto the jacket and turn under outer edges as necessary. You may have to unpin the lining and restitch some seams.

16. Baste pinned edges and remove pins. Slip stitch around all basted edges except the armholes, where you should whipstitch. Remove basting and any thread ends. Press. If the lining is to be hemmed separately, leave a few inches free above it. Hand hem, slip stitch any loose edges, and press.

17. Press under the top and bottom of the sleeve lining. Pin the lining bottom to the sleeve bottom insertion line, which will be about 1/2 in. to 1 in. above the fold. Be sure to match seams. Baste, then slip stitch. Remove basting and press. Draw up any gathers in the sleeve head and arrange the pressed-under edge over the raw armhole edge, matching seams. Pin, baste, and slip stitch. Remove all basting and press.

Occasionally a lining has been discarded, or become too damaged to trace, before you buy the garment. Take the lining pattern from the outer garment, following the instructions in chapter 4.

To reline a vest, undo its side seams. Sew the lining to the vest around the outer edges and armholes. Pull lining to the inside and press. Pin and sew the side seams together, fabric to fabric and lining to lining, leaving a few inches of lining unstitched. Press, turning under the unstitched seam allowances. Then slip stitch those together.

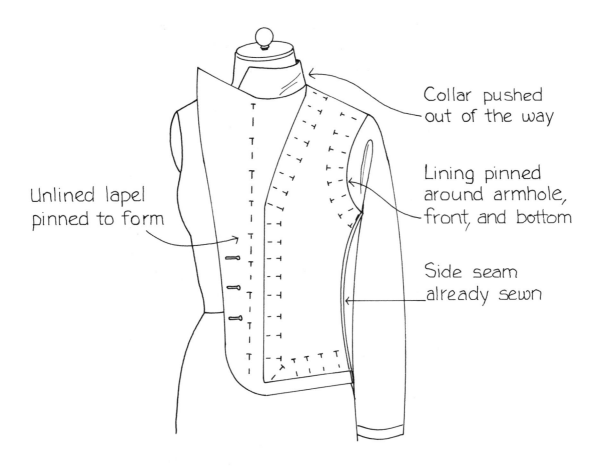

Collar pushed out of the way

Lining pinned around armhole, front, and bottom

Side seam already sewn

Unlined lapel pinned to form

Figure 115: Lining pinned to jacket on dress form

❧ WORKING WITH FURS

Although working with fur may seem intimidating, it's no harder than working with fabric. And given furriers' fees, it's sensible to repair inexpensive vintage furs yourself.

MENDING TEARS

You will need some special fur repair supplies.

- *Cold tape* is a narrow adhesive-backed cloth tape used to reinforce torn edges before sewing (the leather around tears is weak).

- *Sticky flannel* is a wider tape that can be used to cover and reinforce sewn tears, or even instead of sewing.

- *Sticky cloth* is a heavier product that serves the same purposes as sticky flannel on heavier furs.

- *Wedge-pointed fur needles, fur thread,* and *fur knives* are available. But a sharp hand-sewing needle, double sewing thread, and an X-Acto knife will do just fine.

Always work from the wrong, or skin, side. Unpick the lining just enough to get at the tear. Smooth the area flat.

To repair a tear with sticky flannel:

1. Cut a piece long enough to cover the tear and some undamaged skin.

2. Wipe any dirt off the skin. If it's too slick for the flannel to stick, rough it up slightly with an emery board.

3. Butt the tear edges together (overlapping creates lumps).

4. Press the flannel firmly over the tear with your hands (not an iron). Work carefully; pulling up the flannel to reposition it may worsen the tear.

5. Restitch the lining, without pressing the fur.

To repair a tear by sewing:

1. Cut two pieces of cold tape the length of the tear.

2. Press them over the edges with your hands (see figure 116).

3. Butt the tear edges together and sew with an overhand stitch. Don't catch hairs in the stitches because the repair will show on the right side. If you do, work them out with the needle point.

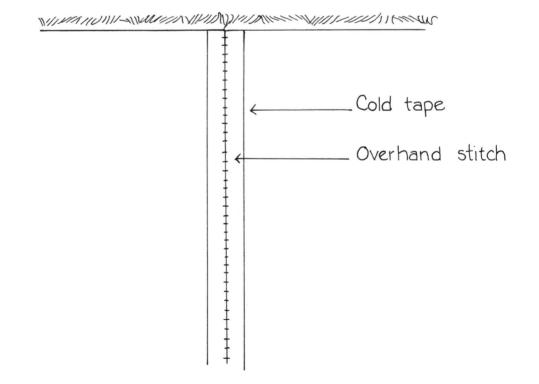

Cold tape

Overhand stitch

Figure 116: How to mend a tear in fur

4. If desired, press flannel over the mend.

5. Restitch the lining.

Tears with some fur missing must be patched. If you just pull the edges together they'll come apart under stress.

To patch:

1. Buy some matching fur. The best choice is an old fur collar from a thrift shop.

2. Draw a geometric shape around irregular tear edges with a ruler and chalk. Cut out with an X-Acto knife. Work from the skin side and push the hair out of the way.

3. Find an area on the patching fur that closely matches the color, texture, and nap of the torn area. Draw the patch outline on the skin side with a ruler and chalk.

4. Cut out the patch, making sure not to cut any hair.

5. Insert the patch by reinforcing and overhanding, or using sticky flannel.

6. Restitch the lining.

You can also patch bald spots that aren't too extensive.

REPLACING COLLARS AND CUFFS

Worn fur collars and cuffs on a cloth coat can easily be replaced. And you can glamorize a plain coat or suit by adding fur.

1. If there are fur pieces already, unpick them.

2. Make collar and cuff patterns by tracing the outlines of the fur pieces onto paper. If there are no fur pieces, pin the cloth collar and cuffs to paper and trace around them. Clean up the outlines with a ruler and french curves. Don't add seam allowances.

3. Buy a vintage collar and cuffs of the right size and shape. If necessary they can be larger anywhere except the neckline. Or make a collar and cuffs as described below.

4. Lay the fur pieces over your patterns, then over the coat. If they're a good size, just sew them to the coat as described.

5. If the fur pieces need taking in, mark the cutting lines on the lining with a ruler and chalk (see figure 117). Cut the lining with scissors. Unpick it enough to get at the skin. Cut the fur through the skin only. Turn under the cut lining edges and slip stitch together.

6. Arrange the wrong side of the fur pieces over the right side of the coat. Tack all edges to the coat with a largish running stitch. Holding the work in place with your hands,

roll back the fur piece slightly and take a stitch through its lining, then the coat fabric. Don't press.

Instead of buying a collar and cuffs, you can make them from the best portions of discarded furs, or from new skins.

To make a detachable collar and cuffs:

1. Make paper patterns as described above, but add 1/2 in. seam allowances. Draw a grain line down the middle of each pattern.

2. Fold under the seam allowances. Lay the patterns over your fur with the hair running parallel to the grain lines. Secure with pattern weights. Cut.

3. Unfold the seam allowances and press the pattern pieces. Cut linings from flannel or coat lining fabric.

4. Lay twill tape just over the fur edge on the hair side. Sew to the skin with an overhand stitch, trying not to include any hair.

5. Pull the tape to the skin side so it's concealed by the hair. Sew it to the skin with long running—but not basting—stitches. Make sure they don't show on the fur side.

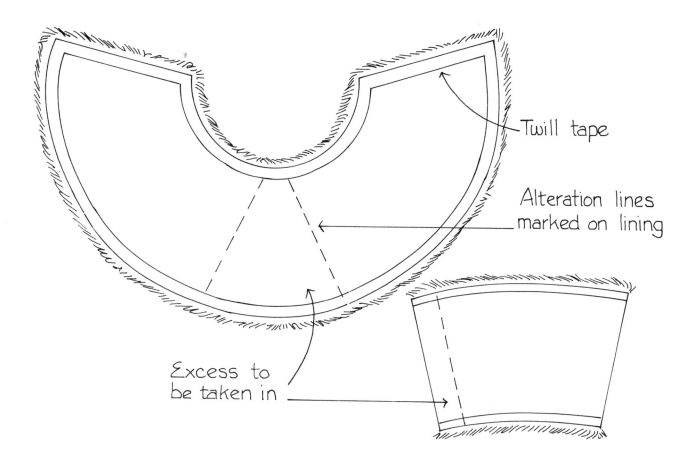

Figure 117: Fur collar and cuff marked for alterations

Appendix A lists fur supply sources.

A worn or mildewed fur coat lining can be replaced like a cloth coat lining.

6. Press under the lining edges with an iron. Baste.

7. Pin, then baste, the pressed-under edges to the twill tape. Don't insert pins or needles through the skin.

8. Slip stitch the linings to the tape. Remove all basting. Don't press.

❧ RESTORING HATS

An experienced milliner can do almost anything with a hat—clean it, repair it, refit it, reshape it, retrim it, even completely transform it. It would take another book to fully cover these techniques. I'm assuming you have a hat that needs just a little work.

BUYING TOOLS AND SUPPLIES

When restoring a hat you'll need the following supplies:

- *A hand-held garment steamer.* For removing dents and reviving trims. A tea kettle can be used in a pinch.
- *A hat block or wig stand.* To hold the hat while steaming. Optional, because you can substitute a bowl or pan the same size and shape as the crown, or a wadded hand towel.
- *A hat brush.* Use a small brush with camel hair bristles to remove surface dirt and to smooth felt while steaming.
- *Millinery or straw needles.* For sewing several thicknesses.
- *A thimble.* For protection when sewing thick, heavy hat materials.
- *Contact cement.* For gluing surfaces that will be under strain.
- *Millinery/bridal glue.* For permanently attaching fabric coverings and trims.
- *Small, clear or brown plastic millinery combs.* For securing a hat to your head.

Appendix A lists sources for millinery information and supplies.

Ordinary, doubled sewing thread is fine for hats.

STEAMING

Steaming can smooth out dents, restore a brim curve, and freshen battered trims. It works for straw, felt, and fabric-covered hats.

1. Brush the hat and trims well to remove surface dirt.

2. Place the crown over your hat block or substitute. I often wear a hat while steaming, but this does involve some contortions and the risk of steam burns. Sometimes you can just hold the hat inside the crown.

3. Steam the entire hat. At problem areas, hold the hat in the

correct shape or an exaggeration of it. Don't touch velvet on the outside or you'll leave finger marks. Brush felt in the nap direction. Fluff out trims. Be careful not to crush, or spatter boiling water on, delicate materials.

4. Leave the hat on the hat stand, or support the crown with wadded cloth. Allow to dry thoroughly.

If home steaming doesn't do the job, check your local phone book for professional hat blockers.

Spots not caused by liquid may be removable with an art gum eraser. Or by saturating with cornmeal, letting stand till cornmeal is absorbed (several hours), then brushing with a stiff brush. Dirty trims can be unpicked, then cleaned and ironed separately or replaced.

REPAIRING

Although a badly battered hat should be taken to a professional, simple repairs on small areas are feasible.

Slashes in felt, and cracks in straw, can be repaired by whip-stitching. Butt the edges together and sew as invisibly as possible.

Holes in felt can be patched on the inside with matching felt or similar fabric. Sew invisibly. Or glue with contact cement following the directions on the tube.

If the fabric covering a hat foundation is loose, resew it or reglue it with millinery glue.

If a damaged area still shows, cover it with trim. Hat trims include ribbon, braid, lace, net veiling, artificial flowers and fruit, feathers, fur, appliques, beaded motifs, buttons, and costume jewelry. Trims you might change should be sewn rather than glued. Although you can yank them off, remaining glue spoils the foundation's appearance.

Trims should look light and improvised. Don't sew them firmly, just tie tack here and there. To make a tie tack, insert the needle from the wrong side leaving a long, free thread end. Make one rather loose stitch and reinsert the needle. Tie the threads in a square knot, then clip.

A hidden safety pin or an ornamental brooch can be used instead of stitching.

Trim scraps that are too small for any other purpose can be used on hats.

KEEPING A HAT ON

Bonnets and some hats from before 1911 can be tied on with wide ribbons. Try on the hat to determine the correct tie placement (which is not necessarily over the ears) and length. Mark with chalk. Then sew the ribbon ends to the inside.

You can also sew thin, almost-invisible elastic cord to the hat sides, to be passed around the back of your head or under your chin (see figure 118).

Some turn-of-the-century hats have enormous crowns that were worn over heaped-up hairstyles. The hatpins that once secured them will be purely ornamental unless you have lots of hair. However, there is usually a silk bag inside the crown that can be stuffed with tissue paper to improve the fit. A damaged or missing bag can be duplicated (if necessary use another hat's bag as a pattern) and sewn on.

Many hats have a grosgrain ribbon band inside the crown. Sometimes you can dart this for a better fit without distorting the shape. You can reduce the hat size slightly by padding another piece of grosgrain with felt, then sewing or gluing it over the original.

Most styles can be secured with combs and/or loops. A comb is generally sewn to the front of the hat with the teeth pointing toward the back. But feel free to use more combs or a different placement. Try on the hat and mark the comb location. Then sew on the comb between the teeth.

Hat loops, like button loops, can be crocheted or made of cord or narrow braid. When you wear the hat you insert bobby pins through them into your hair. Try on the hat and mark the loop placement. It's usual to add one loop to each side, but do whatever works. Then sew the ends to the inside so the loops extend beneath the crown.

A wide-brimmed straw can be transformed into a motoring hat by wrapping a net or lace veil around the entire hat and tying it under the chin.

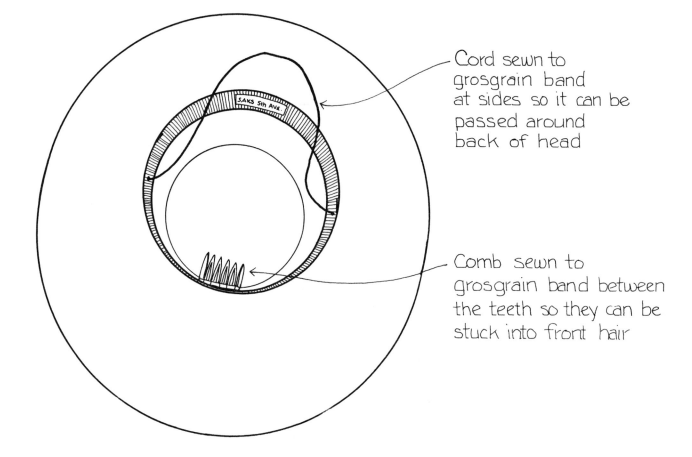

Figure 118: Hat with elastic cord and comb

Mending Garments

✒ REPAIRING SHOES

Most shoe repairs should be taken to a professional. Vintage soles and heel plates (the little soles on the heels) have always deteriorated. I have both replaced right after purchase. If you let heel plates go the heels wear down. Heel replacement is quite possible, but more expensive. Repair shops also clean leather and fabric-covered shoes. If some dirt remains the shoes can be dyed (even ones with color-contrasted sections).

One thing you can, and should, do yourself is periodically wipe smooth leathers with an oil-based cleaner/conditioner. (In my experience saddle soap damages vintage leather.) This prevents the cracks caused by drying. Shoe polish also provides some protection. Never condition or polish suede. Just brush off dirt—after it's dry—with a suede brush.

The lasts (forms) used to make shoes have changed over the years. You'll find pairs that fit some areas of your foot but not others. When shopping, first judge shoes by eye and select ones that look to be your modern size. Or lay the soles against your modern shoe soles. Then slip on the shoes. Carefully check the fit at the arch and the wide part of the foot. In my opinion these are the most important fitting areas and impossible to change successfully. However, long narrow toes are fine as long as yours are below the narrow part. Loose heels can be padded with heel liners, available at shoe repair shops, drug stores, and variety stores. Boots can be expanded at the ankle by lacing more widely than intended.

You can repair cracks in shoe uppers by gluing them to the lining or to an inside patch. The patch can be very thin leather or a firm medium-weight fabric. Use contact cement and allow to dry thoroughly.

It's also easy to replace inner sole liners. They're available where heel liners are sold, but you can make your own from fabric scraps. Take out the old ones and use them as a pattern. Cut new linings from a firm, slightly thick fabric like corduroy, wool, or felt. There's no need to finish the edges. Just glue down the new linings with contact cement.

Most shoe repair shops don't balk at, or charge extra for, vintage shoes. But if one says repairs can't be done, it may just mean they don't want to do them. I wanted shoulder straps added to some vintage clutch bags. A large, well-known shoe and purse repairer swore it was impossible. But one that repaired purses for a vintage clothing store had no problems.

Leather conditioner is good for purses, belts, and gloves as well as shoes. But shoe polish comes off accessories that rub against your clothes.

✣

7 Altering Garments

I have to admit I sometimes procrastinate on alterations. Like other sewers I take on more projects than I have time for, and alterations somehow look more formidable than they are. I use the following techniques to motivate myself:

- I resolve to make each garment wearable as soon as I buy it, while it seems new and exciting and my attention hasn't been drawn to other projects.

- If I slip up on this, I plan to wear the garment to a special event where I'd like to sport a new outfit.

- I do alterations between long sewing projects. Relining and taking in a coat seems like a breeze after making a complete Civil War ball gown ensemble.

My most important technique, however, is to think ahead. Before I buy a garment I decide what alterations must be done and, roughly, how to do them. If they're unfeasible, I don't buy it. That way I'm not afraid of ruining the garment—and I save time and money. After purchase I plan the alterations in detail and buy all the materials.

✠ PLANNING ALTERATIONS

Every vintage garment is unique and will fit you in a slightly different way. Try on the one you plan to alter and study yourself in a mirror. First ascertain that the garment really doesn't fit, not that you just aren't used to period fitting standards. For example, a properly fitting Edwardian camisole is long and blousy in front, but high in back. A properly fitting Victorian dress shirt has a tight collar, but a long, full body.

If you are still dissatisfied with the fit, identify the source of the problem. Is the jacket baggy all over, or just the sleeves? Is the dress too long in the skirt, the bodice, or both? Try pinning the garment in different places. Take it in, up, or let it out different amounts and study the effect.

Now, how will you fix the problem? Skim through the appropriate sections below and think out the steps. Which of several techniques will you choose? Which best preserves the original line and decoration? Do you need to adapt a technique to this garment?

Make sure the fabric is strong enough. Period silks especially may be too fragile for extensive alterations. Or perhaps you should replace one tightly fitting section, such as a waistband.

Will you need extra fabric or trim? These should match the

This chapter focuses on styles from 1890 to 1930, though many techniques are applicable to other periods. Garments from before 1890 are often too fragile to wear. And garments from after 1930 provide less scope for alteration.

Chapter 3 covers basic sewing operations, including fitting, pressing, finishing seams, gathering, pleating, cutting bias strips, and making plackets. Chapter 6 gives detailed instructions for hand stitches and mending.

If you don't have a dress form you usually don't have to wait till someone can help you fit a garment in back. Guess on the alteration, pin, try on, and look at yourself with the aid of an extra mirror. Take off the garment and repeat the process till the fit is correct. I do this all the time with excellent results.

garment or harmonize with it. They should be cleanable by the same method. Remember to preshrink. What about fasteners, bias tape, and other sundries? It's best to assemble everything now, rather than go shopping in the middle of a project—or find out too late that a technique won't work because it requires unavailable materials.

Once you've decided on an alteration technique, take exact measurements. Figure out how to divide amounts among seams, add seam allowances, and so forth. In most places you should use 1/2 in. seams. Check your arithmetic before cutting and/or use a calculator. Write measurements down.

Also make notes on alteration procedures and the original construction in case you're interrupted for a few days. Save cut-off pieces till the end of the project (and afterward if you might do further alterations or patching).

Press each seam as soon as you sew it (having tested the iron temperature on a scrap). Try on as you go and refit if necessary.

⚓ ALTERING A BODICE, BLOUSE, OR CAMISOLE

Late Victorian bodices are designed to fit closely and are often too small for the modern uncorseted figure. 1900s and 1910s styles are looser. Camisoles follow the period's bodice line.

MAKING SHOULDER TUCKS

The key to the fit of an Edwardian blouse is the shoulders. Slightly dropped shoulders look OK. In fact, they're more comfortable if the armhole is small. Larger shoulders can be taken in with tucks (see figure 119). Many Edwardian blouses already have shoulder tucks, so your alteration will be inconspicuous.

1. Try on the blouse and measure the amount to take in. Pin and test the fit. Make sure the armhole is comfortable.

2. Measure the width, depth, and placement of existing tucks. Also measure lace insertion and other decoration. Your tucks should be the same size as other elements and shouldn't conceal them if you can avoid it.

3. Measure the width, depth, and placement of your new tucks. Usually you will want released tucks (stitched part-way down the garment), though full-length ones can be used to take in the whole body. I usually extend tucks 2 to 3 in. down each side of the shoulder seam (that is, a total of 4 to 6 in. across the shoulders). The tuck width is the amount to be taken in divided by two (a 1/2 in. tuck takes in 1 in. of fabric). This, and the number of tucks, should harmonize

Wash never-worn, new/old clothes before altering. Sometimes they shrink. I once took in a silk slip and cut several inches off the hem, only to have it shrink to an unwearable size after washing. (And I did use cool water.)

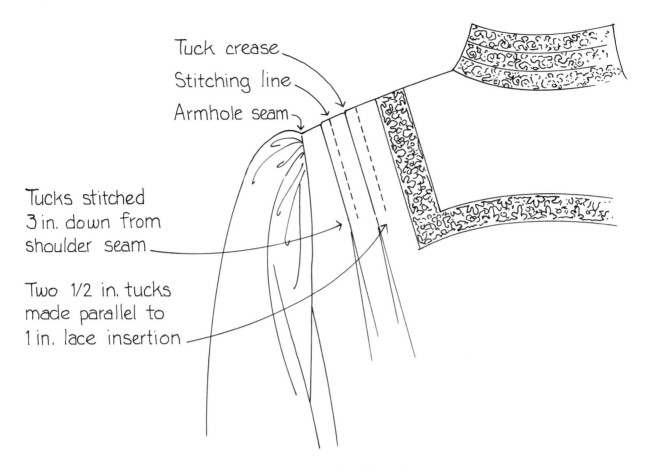

Tuck crease

Stitching line

Armhole seam

Tucks stitched
3 in. down from
shoulder seam

Two 1/2 in. tucks
made parallel to
1 in. lace insertion

Figure 119: Shoulder tucks

with the design. I generally use one or two 1/2 to 1 in. tucks. The wider the tucks, the more tailored the look.

Tucks should be parallel to a vertical line, such as lace insertion on the blouse front. The creases should fall toward the armhole seam.

4. Mark the tucks with tailor's chalk on the wrong side. Baste the marks through to the right side.

5. Pin the tucks, matching marks. Baste if the fabric is slippery. Sew carefully. With tucks, neatness counts. Remove any basting. Press toward the armhole.

Always do shoulder alterations before sleeve alterations because they affect the sleeve length.

PULLING IN THE NECKLINE

Sometimes a sleeveless or low-necked garment, such as a camisole, nightgown, or evening gown, has a neckline that is just too big. A drawstring can work wonders. In addition to pulling the neck in, it allows you to adjust the height and fullness for each wearing. This is useful for undergarments and many were designed this way. If yours wasn't, add lace beading or tatting to the outside of the neck and thread a pretty ribbon

Make sure the ribbon is narrower than the beading slots and use pliable silk ribbon, rather than synthetic. This reduces strain on the slots, an important consideration with vintage lace.

A crocheted or eyelet-edged garment may already have holes suitable for a ribbon, even if none was used originally.

You can also use this technique to pull in a loose camisole waist.

through it (see figure 120). An invisible casing of bias binding on the inside is usually better for formal dresses. The drawstring may be tucked inside after tying.

1. Try on the garment and play with the neck to make sure a drawstring is the correct solution. It isn't necessary to take precise measurements.

2. Take off the garment. Find lace beading or bias binding that harmonizes with it. I like narrow beading with closely spaced slots because this draws up the fabric evenly and smoothly. Pin the beading or binding all round the neck. Finish the ends at the opening by folding under twice. Miter lace beading at corners by folding it back on itself, then across at a right angle. Stretch bias binding instead.

3. Baste the lace or binding down and remove pins. Stitch by machine or hand. Remove basting. Press. Thread ribbon or narrow cord through the beading or casing.

ALTERING AT THE SIDE SEAMS

The side seams are the best place to alter a fitted bodice. Existing seam allowances may be extra wide to allow letting out or as the result of previous taking in. And alterations are less

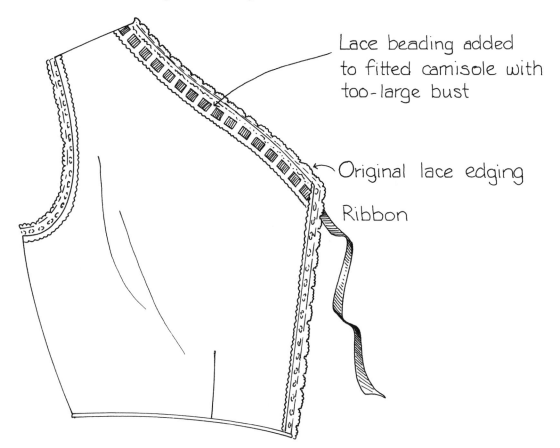

Figure 120: Lace beading and drawstring

visible at the sides than in front or back. They distort the line less. And people just don't notice your sides much.

Before letting out, check that there is extra fabric and that the color isn't too much darker. Almost always there is some color difference.

1. Try on the garment. If you are letting out, undo the side seams first. (If taking in, don't undo them till your new ones are sewn. They'll act as basting and as a reference to the original line.) Place pins vertically along the new seam line.

   Take off the garment. Measure the amount to take in or let out. This may differ at the chest and waist.

2. Draw the new seam line on the inside with tailor's chalk. If the garment has sleeves you must taper to the armhole because it is usually just large enough to allow movement. (See figure 121.) It may be OK to take in the armhole of a sleeveless garment.

   Pin along this line and try on again.

3. Pin new seams, placing pins at right angles to them, and machine sew. Press seams flat or to the side, however they

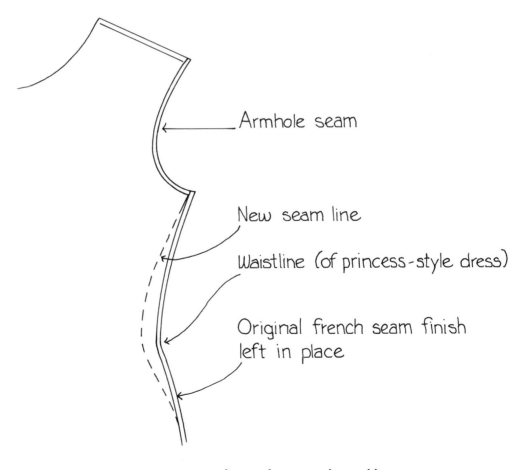

Armhole seam

New seam line

Waistline (of princess-style dress)

Original french seam finish left in place

Figure 121: New side seam line tapered into old

You can take in a camisole with a straight top and bottom by making 1/2 in. tucks on the outside. Make them near the side seams, right through the waistband. The creases should point toward the seams.

I recently saw a two-piece Victorian dress that had been altered with a dramatically contrasting brocade. The bodice was pieced with two straight front panels. Instead of letting out the skirt, the sewer inserted a front gore and pleated the excess skirt fabric in back. This alteration was effective, but would work best for 1880s and early 1890s styles.

Chapter 6 tells you how to replace a lace collar.

Occasionally you can let out wide turned-under plackets instead of adding extensions. Just unstitch them, press, and form new plackets by facing the inside with matching fabric or bias binding. Remember to let out both sides equally.

originally were. Undo the old seam allowances first if necessary. Note that some old seam lines can't be completely pressed out, even by a dry cleaner.

4. What about seam finishes? Don't trim off extra fabric because you may someday want to let the garment out again. The original seam finish will usually do. If not, imitate it. An underlined garment should be finished with overcasting or bias binding.

ADDING TO THE CENTER BACK

You can often add up to 4 in. to a back-closing dress or bodice without distorting the front fit. If it's gathered or tucked into a waistband, let out the fabric and waistband as described in the section on altering skirt waists.

If the garment doesn't have back fullness you can extend the center back following the steps below.

1. Try the garment on yourself or a dress form. Bring the edges as close together as possible and have someone measure the gap. Note whether its width is the same everywhere or whether it tapers from the waist to the neck. Even if the gap does taper, test the fit if the garment is let out the maximum amount all the way down the closure. (It's easiest not to taper the extensions.)

2. Take off the garment and examine its construction. If it has a collar you have three choices: to add fabric to the collar as well as the closure, to taper the extensions into the collar, or to replace the collar with a larger one that accommodates the extensions. The first method is easiest, but one of the others may look better.

   If the garment has a waistband this, and the skirt below it, should be let out the same amount as the bodice. (See the section on skirts.) But extensions should be tapered into the hip area of a princess dress (see figure 122). This also lets out the waist and hips.

3. Remove fasteners. If original buttonholes will be neither used nor covered by the extensions, whipstitch them closed. Remove back collar boning. Press garment edges.

4. Cut extensions from matching fabric or lace. Their length should allow for tapering into or extending the neck and hip areas, plus 1/2 to 1 in. for top and bottom seam allowances.

   Their width should not be tapered, but should be the maximum amount of the extension plus about 1 in. ease. Divide the total in half to determine how much to extend each edge. Add 1/2 in. for side seam allowances if using

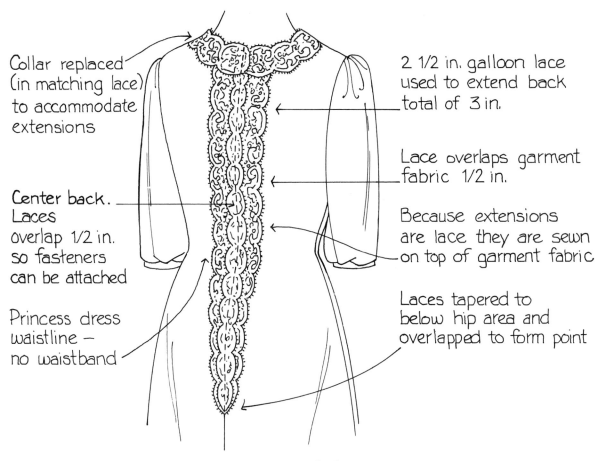

Collar replaced (in matching lace) to accommodate extensions

2 1/2 in. galloon lace used to extend back total of 3 in.

Lace overlaps garment fabric 1/2 in.

Center back. Laces overlap 1/2 in. so fasteners can be attached

Because extensions are lace they are sewn on top of garment fabric

Princess dress waistline — no waistband

Laces tapered to below hip area and overlapped to form point

Figure 122: Center back extensions

lace, or up to 1 in. for fabric that will be turned under. Also add at least 1/2 in. overlap for fasteners.

5. Determine whether the extensions will look better if sewn underneath or on top of the garment. Press fabric extension seam allowances toward the garment so they'll be hidden when attached.

6. Pin, then baste the extensions onto the garment. Taper them underneath or on top of the garment where necessary. (If extensions are tapered, it's best to do the pinning on a dress form.) Remember that in a woman's bodice the right side of the back overlaps the left. Try the garment on yourself or a dress form and adjust as necessary.

7. Sew the extensions to the garment at the seam allowances. Don't cut off extra fabric where you tapered. Just sew it down. For lace use a zigzag or whipstitch. For fabric use a machine straight stitch or slip stitch. Remove basting. Press.

8. Sew on fasteners. This is an excellent time to replace rusty or damaged ones, or change to a new type. Make new buttonholes or loops if necessary.

Some gathered 1900s bodices have a tight underlining. Add extensions to the underlining and let out extra fabric in the bodice.

Sometimes the high collar of a back-closing blouse is too tight even though the rest of it fits well. Add fabric, lace, or applique extensions to the collar only, tapering them into the back plackets. Move fasteners.

ALTERING SLEEVES

Even if there is lots of trim, sleeves can be shortened 1 to 4 in.

Shortening decorated sleeves

Many Edwardian blouses have horizontal bands of decoration (such as embroidery or tucks) near the cuffs or sleeve hems. You'll lose this if you cut off fabric and rehem the sleeves. However, you can take up the sleeves by adding still more tucks. This technique can also be used to take up plain sleeves, simultaneously adding decoration.

1. Try on the garment. Turn or pinch up excess fabric on one sleeve. Pin. See how it looks with your arms in different positions.

2. Take off the garment and determine tuck placement. Tucks look best if they're fairly narrow—about 1/2 in. But you may want them the same width as existing tucks or lace. If the sleeve must be shortened more than about 1 in., make several narrow blind tucks rather than one huge one. Remember that each 1/2 in. tuck takes up 1 in. of fabric, and that the crease of a blind tuck falls just over the top of the next. The crease of the lowest tuck should generally fall just above the highest band of decoration at the sleeve bottom (see figure 123).

3. Turn the sleeves inside out. Slip one over a sleeve board. Using a clear plastic ruler, mark top and bottom tucking lines with tailor's chalk. Baste marks through to the right side.

   To mark tucks accurately around the sleeve curve, measure each line from the sleeve hem or the decoration it falls above, not from the previous tuck line. Make many measurements close together, so that the lines almost connect themselves, rather than making just a few and connecting them with a ruler.

   For example, suppose you're making two 1/2 in. blind tucks above an embroidered band. Mark the first tucking line, which is the tuck bottom, 1/2 in. above the top of the band. Mark the next line, the tuck top, 1 1/2 in. above the band. Mark the second tuck bottom 2 in. above the band. Mark the final tuck top 3 in. above the band.

4. Turn the sleeve right side out. Closely pin the top and bottom of the lowest tuck together. Match sleeve seams. Sew. Remove basting thread. Use tweezers if any has caught in the machine stitching. Press before sewing the next tuck.

5. Wash blouse to remove tailor's chalk.

A full sleeve can sometimes be fitted to the wrist rather than shortened. Add lace beading as described in the section on pulling in a neckline.

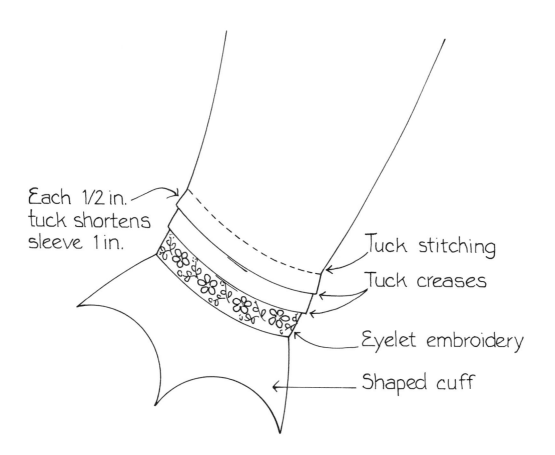

Each 1/2 in. tuck shortens sleeve 1 in.

Tuck stitching

Tuck creases

Eyelet embroidery

Shaped cuff

Figure 123: Sleeve tucks

Shortening lace sleeves

You may be afraid to alter the sleeves of a magnificent hand-made lace blouse. It is difficult, if not impossible, to shorten crochet—it ravels. However, you can often alter battenberg and other tape laces. These have woven tapes arranged to form motifs that are joined by large embroidery stitches.

1. Try the blouse on and measure the ideal amount to shorten.

2. Examine the lace. You'll notice that some motifs are larger and have a stronger horizontal line than others (see figure 124). Your goal is to cut the sleeve right below these motifs, so that just a few pieces of tape form the sleeve bottom. Find the motifs closest to where you measured.

3. Cut the embroidery threads below the new hem motifs, leaving long enough ends to tuck in.

4. Tuck in hanging threads and secure with a couple of stitches. If motifs don't hold together well at the hem, join them with embroidery stitches that imitate the originals. Tape lace stitches are so simple that you can imitate them even if you have no embroidery experience.

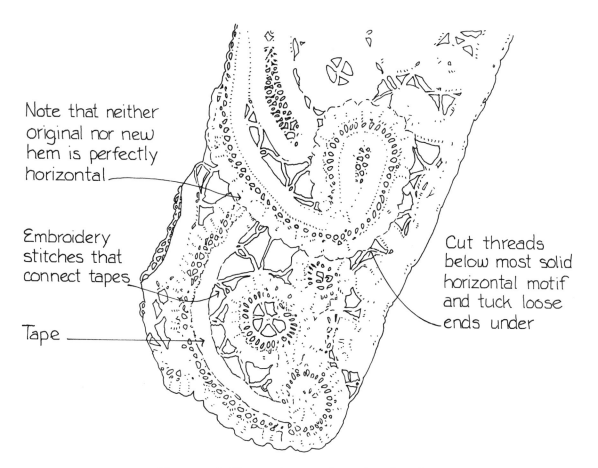

Note that neither original nor new hem is perfectly horizontal

Embroidery stitches that connect tapes

Tape

Cut threads below most solid horizontal motif and tuck loose ends under

Figure 124: How to shorten a battenberg lace sleeve

To lengthen any fancy blouse sleeve, sew lace edging (ungathered or gathered) to the hem.

Chapter 6 explains how to patch damaged underarms.

5. If the sleeve is slightly too short, or the edge seems too uneven, sew ungathered lace edging over the hem on the right side.

Adding sleeve gussets

Add underarm gussets to enlarge tight sleeves, as in figure 125.

1. Unpick the side and sleeve seams for a couple of inches on either side of the armhole seam. Try on the blouse. If it's still tight, unpick the seams till it fits. The split seams will form a diamond-shaped hole. Have someone measure its width while your arm is raised. Take off the blouse.

2. Find some fabric scraps that match the blouse as closely as possible. Draw two diamond-shaped gussets, using the length of the unpicked area and the width of the opening as guidelines. Add a 1/2 in. seam allowance all round. Cut.

3. Baste gussets into blouse underarms. Try on and adjust as necessary. Remove blouse.

4. Overcast raw gusset edges. Press gusset seam allowances under 1/4 in. Press garment seam allowances if they're wrinkled.

5. On the right side, pin and baste gussets 1/4 in. over the opening edges. Sew with a machine topstitch or slip stitch. Press on the wrong side.

LENGTHENING A BLOUSE

Edwardian blouses are often too short to stay tucked in. You can lengthen one 2 to 6 in. by adding a lace or fitted fabric peplum. The waist can simultaneously be let out if necessary. The blouse can have either a front or a back opening.

Either style of peplum can be used to lengthen a camisole.

Adding a lace peplum

A peplum made of pretty lace or eyelet edging is especially appropriate if the blouse is highly decorated or the peplum will be worn outside the skirt. I generally make peplums 3 or 4 in. wide, but they can be as wide as 6 in. A narrower edging is suitable for lengthening a blouse that already has a peplum.

1. Try on the blouse and measure how much to lengthen it. Most Edwardian blouses are intended to be higher in back. Make sure the back will be long enough, but don't try to even out the length.

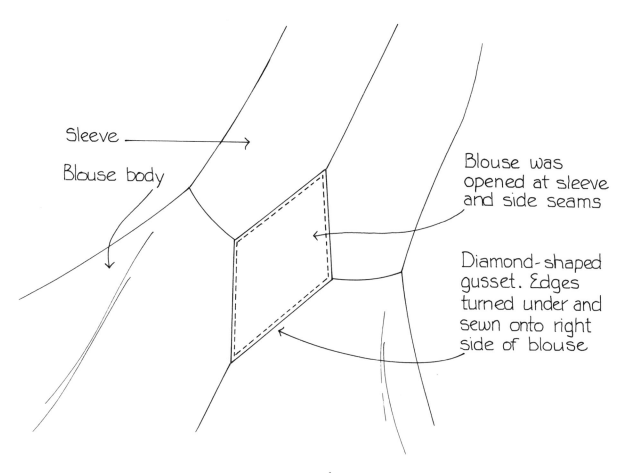

Sleeve

Blouse body

Blouse was opened at sleeve and side seams

Diamond-shaped gusset. Edges turned under and sewn onto right side of blouse

Figure 125: An underarm gusset

2. Examine the blouse construction. It may have a simple narrow hem, with waist ties to control the fullness; it may be gathered into a narrow band; or it may already be gathered into a peplum. If the blouse is one of the first two styles, undo all waistline gathers. Remove the ties or narrow band. Leave the hem in place. Press.

Don't remove an existing peplum unless you must let out the waist.

3. If the bottom edge is raw, hem following the directions for hemming a fitted peplum. For a heavy lace blouse or underlined bodice, finish the edge with narrow bias binding rather than a hem. Press.

4. Find a piece of lace or eyelet edging that harmonizes with the blouse. Its width should be the amount you want to lengthen plus about 1/4 in. Make sure there is ample length, but don't cut the edging till you've pinned it onto the peplum. First finish one short end by turning it under twice (1/4 to 1/2 in. altogether). Stitch with a straight machine stitch or whipstitch. Press.

5. On the right side, pin the edging around the hem (or existing peplum bottom), starting at the garment opening. When pinning around a curve, make little pleats in the top of the edging so that the bottom lies flat (see figure 126). Because pleats will be in the most curved areas they won't be evenly spaced. However, they should be symmetrical on each side of the center front or back (toward which the creases should point).

When you've gone almost all around, cut the edging. Leave enough to finish the remaining short end. Finish and press. Pin down, then baste.

6. Sew with a straight stitch. Remove basting. Press.

7. If you wish, sew narrow lace beading over the join and thread a ribbon through to draw up the peplum.

If you don't have a sufficiently wide edging, or want a richer effect, make the peplum by piecing several lengths of lace. To lengthen the garment waist, make the peplum from three lengths—lace insertion (the peplum top), lace beading (for drawing up the waist), and lace or eyelet edging (the peplum bottom).

Adding a fitted peplum

A fitted peplum made from a modern skirt pattern gives a finished look to a blouse (see figure 127). It should be 4 to 6 in. wide.

1. Try on the blouse and measure how much to lengthen. Ideally the existing hem is near your waist.

2. Undo any gathers. If necessary undo or trim the hem so that it's about 1 in. below your waist (1/2 in. is ease, 1/2 in. is a seam allowance). Press.

3. Find a modern fitted skirt pattern with a waistband, and

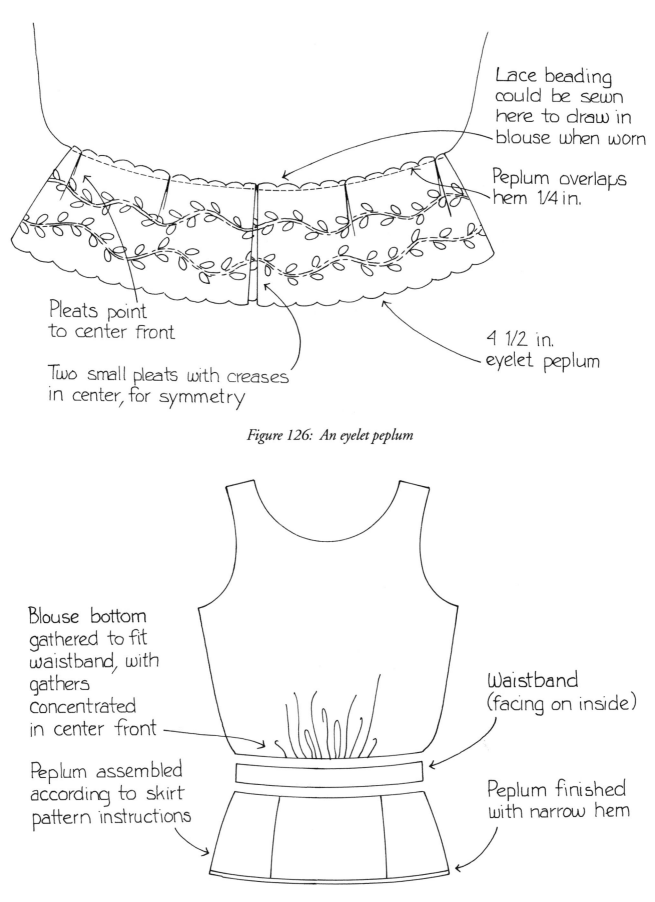

Lace beading could be sewn here to draw in blouse when worn

Peplum overlaps hem 1/4 in.

Pleats point to center front

Two small pleats with creases in center, for symmetry

4 1/2 in. eyelet peplum

Figure 126: An eyelet peplum

Blouse bottom gathered to fit waistband, with gathers concentrated in center front

Peplum assembled according to skirt pattern instructions

Waistband (facing on inside)

Peplum finished with narrow hem

Figure 127: A fitted peplum

some fabric that matches the blouse. Cut from the top of the pattern the amount you want to lengthen plus a 1/2 in. top seam allowance and 3/4 in. for a narrow hem. Cut two waistband pieces (one is a facing).

4. Pin and sew the skirt top following the pattern instructions. (For a more period look, substitute pleats or released tucks for darts.) Finish the front or back opening edges. This is your peplum.

5. Run gathering stitches to either side of the center front of the blouse, and to either side of the center back. Edwardian blouses are usually gathered only in these areas; gathering one all the way around looks less authentic and may make you look dumpy. Make the rows 3/8 and 1/2 in. from the blouse edge.

6. Press under the short ends of the waistband and facing, using the pattern seam allowance (which may not be 1/2 in.).

7. Lay the blouse edge over one (the outer) waistband piece, right side to right side. Draw up gathered areas to fit the waistband, distributing fullness equally between the center front and center back. Pin, then baste. Sew with a machine straight stitch. Remove basting. Press seam down toward the waistband.

8. Lay the peplum top over the other edge of the waistband, right side to right side. Pin and sew. Press seam up toward the waistband.

9. Press under one long seam allowance of the waistband facing. Pin the right side of the other long edge to the wrong side of the peplum. Sew. Press seam up toward the waistband.

10. On the wrong side, pin and baste the folded-under facing seam allowance to the waistband top. Slip stitch to the blouse/waistband seam allowance. Remove basting and press.

11. Press under 1/4 in. of the peplum edge. On the wrong side, press up 1/2 in. Pin and baste. Hem with a slip stitch or machine topstitch. Remove basting and press.

12. Sew a hook and eye to the waistband, or two if necessary. Or fasten with a button and buttonhole.

❦ ALTERING A MAN'S SHIRT OR WOMAN'S TAILORED BLOUSE

A properly fitting turn-of-the-century man's shirt seems wide and long by modern standards. Just tuck the excess in. The neck and (separate) collar, however, will be tight. Buy a size you can live with, and rely on the actual fit rather than the label's measurement—this is often not strictly accurate.

If you don't have a set of dress shirt studs and/or cuff links, or the sleeves are too long, it's easy to fix these problems.

A tailored turn-of-the-century blouse may require the same alterations as a man's shirt.

SUBSTITUTING FOR STUDS AND CUFF LINKS

You can substitute buttons for shirt studs, collar studs, and/or cuff links. These can easily be removed later if desired.

1. Sew together the buttonholes on the right side of the shirt (as you wear it), using a whipstitch or machine zigzag stitch. (For a woman's blouse, sew up the left buttonholes.) Then sew up the front and back neckband (collar stud) buttonholes and the back cuff buttonholes. (Refer to modern shirt cuffs if you become confused.) Press.

2. Find a matching set of buttons that fit through the remaining buttonholes, including those on your separate collar. You'll need two or three sizes. Mother-of-pearl in a round setting of gold- or silver-tone metal is a good choice.

3. Attach buttons over the sewn-up buttonholes.

You can enlarge a shirt neckband about 3/4 in. by fastening it with a hook and eye sewn as near the edges as possible. Sew the front buttonholes closed. Sew a button over the left one for attaching the collar (which will hide the alteration).

SHORTENING CUFFED SLEEVES

The simplest way to deal with an overly long man's shirt sleeve is to pull it up with sleeve garters around the upper arm. These can be purchased stocking garters or pieces of elastic cut to the arm circumference. But if the shirt will be worn without a jacket, the sleeves will look neater if shortened. Here's how.

1. Try on the shirt and measure how much to shorten the sleeves.

2. Unpick the cuff. Measure the sleeve placket. If it would be 4 in. or longer if you left it in place after cutting off the sleeve bottom, leave it in place. If not, unpick it, carefully noting how it was attached. Mark the unpicked cuff and placket "R" or "L" with tailor's chalk on the inside. Turn the sleeve inside out. Press the bottom.

3. Lay the sleeve bottom over a sleeve board or flat surface. Using a ruler and tailor's chalk, mark where to cut off the sleeve. Leave a 1/2 in. seam allowance even if the original one was smaller.

4. If you removed the placket, measure how long the new opening must be and extend the line. Cut. Reattach the placket following the original construction.

5. The sleeve bottom will have widened. Fullness is often

gathered into the cuff on men's shirts as well as women's blouses (see figure 128). Run machine gathering stitches 3/8 and 1/2 in. from the sleeve edge. If one side of the placket was turned under, stitch through it in that position.

6. Sandwich 1/2 in. of the sleeve between the two cuff layers. Draw gathers up evenly to fit the cuff. Pin, then baste. Sew with a machine topstitch. Remove basting and press.

7. Alter the other sleeve the same way.

❦ ALTERING A SKIRT OR PETTICOAT

When you buy skirts and petticoats you can be less particular about size than with other garments. Here are several methods for shortening, lengthening, and altering at the waist.

SHORTENING

Hem your skirt before doing waistband alterations or patching, so you can use the cut-off material.

A full-length skirt hem can be raised 1 to 8 in. Most skirts from before the 1910s are longer in back than in front. It's easiest, and most authentic, to leave them that way. Shorten the skirt an equal amount all the way around.

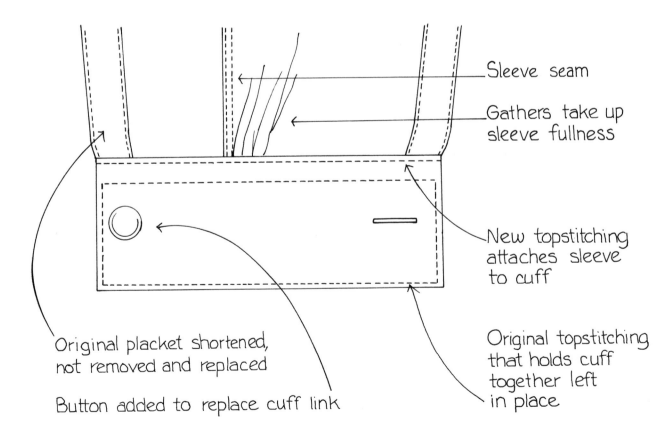

Sleeve seam

Gathers take up sleeve fullness

New topstitching attaches sleeve to cuff

Original placket shortened, not removed and replaced

Button added to replace cuff link

Original topstitching that holds cuff together left in place

Figure 128: Excess sleeve fullness gathered into cuff

When choosing an alteration method, consider both the skirt's construction and where its decoration will end up.

Hemming

A plain skirt or one with vertical decoration should be hemmed from the bottom. This is the easiest shortening method, and it removes stained and worn material.

1. Try on the skirt with the petticoats and shoes you'll wear. Determine how much to shorten by experimenting with different lengths and shoes.

2. Examine the skirt construction. Many skirts have a bias hem facing. You'll want one if your skirt is heavy or has damaged fabric near the hem. However, a light cotton skirt can just be hemmed up even if it currently has a facing.

3. Turn the skirt inside out. Unpick the facing or hem. Press the skirt bottom.

4. Figure out how much fabric to cut off. If you're using a facing you only need to leave 1/4 in. more than the finished length for a seam allowance. If not, you need to leave 2 or 2 1/2 in. for a hem. Lay the skirt on a big table and mark the cutting line on the inside with tailor's chalk, carefully preserving curves. Cut.

5. The original bias facing may well be too worn to use. Measure the hem circumference to see how much new facing you need. For a light skirt, get a commercial bias facing about 2 in. wide in the skirt color.

   For a heavy one, find a piece of light cotton velveteen. Using the instructions in chapter 3, make enough bias strips about 2 1/2 in. wide to face your hem, plus a little extra. Join into a straight length with 1/4 in. seams.

6. Press under one long edge of the facing 1/4 in. Pin and baste the other long edge to the skirt bottom, right side to right side. Lap the outer short end over the inner one and turn the raw edge under. Pin and baste.

   Machine sew the long edge with a 1/4 in. seam. Remove basting there. Press the facing to the inside, steaming it to conform to the skirt shape. Slip stitch or whipstitch the short ends down. Remove basting and press.

   Baste the hem about 1/4 in. up from the fold. Then pin and baste about 1/4 in. down from the (pressed-under) facing top.

7. For a skirt with no facing, mark the finished hemline on the inside with tailor's chalk. Baste marks through to the right side. Finish the raw edge by pressing it under 1/4 in.

Although velveteen is the most traditional facing fabric, you can use others of the same weight and flexibility. Because the facing will show at times, the color and pattern (if any) should be appropriate for the skirt. Lately I've been making facings from samples of light-weight brocade bought at an upholstery shop.

A hobble skirt narrows abruptly at the bottom. To make the hem wide enough to turn up, slash fabric and insert gussets.

Press the hem up and baste about 1/4 in. away from the fold. Lay brown paper between the skirt and hem. Steam out excess hem fullness. Pin and baste near the top.

8. Hand hem to the underlining only, or if there is none to the outer fabric. For heavy fabrics, use the basic hemming stitch. Use a slip stitch for light fabrics. Don't pull the thread too tight. Remove all basting and press.

Shortening from the waist

When you shorten a skirt or petticoat you don't want to lose flounces or other trim. One method is to take the skirt up from the waist. You can simultaneously alter the waist size. (See the section on altering skirt waists.)

1. Try on the skirt. Pull it up till the hem looks correct. Mark the new waistline with a pin.

2. Examine the skirt construction. First decide whether to finish the waist with a casing and drawstring or an attached waistband. A casing is easier and allows you to adjust the waist for each wearing (see figure 129). It is most appropriate for petticoats because it's more bulky and untidy than a waistband. A waistband is the best choice for a skirt.

   Now measure how much of the back opening will be left after you cut off the top. For a skirt with a waistband the finished back opening should be 7 in. or longer, so you can get the skirt over your hips. For a skirt with a casing the opening only needs to be an inch or so long. The wide, ungathered waist enables you to put on the skirt. If the opening will be large enough, don't bother moving the back placket.

3. Undo the existing waistband or casing, the back placket (if necessary), and gathering. Press the skirt top.

4. Lay the skirt on a table, wrong side out, and mark the new cutting line from the waist with tailor's chalk. Allow 3/4 to 1 in. for a casing or 1/2 in. for a waistband seam. Cut.

5. Try on the skirt. Open the back seam more if necessary. If there is a placket, reattach it. If not (and this is common) fold the former seam allowances in so no raw edges show, then slip stitch. Or make a facing from matching fabric, lace, or commercial bias binding.

If the skirt top is very curved, make the casing from commercial bias binding. Stitch one edge to the skirt, right side to right side. Press to stretch the other edge to the skirt shape. Pin and stitch.

6. To make a casing, first press the raw edge under about 1/4 in. Fold the skirt top down to form a 1/2 in. casing. Press. Pin and machine stitch. Press again. Thread twill tape through the opening (ribbon is so slippery it may come untied when you wear the skirt).

7. If the skirt will have a waistband, gather or pleat excess fabric and attach the waistband following the section on altering skirt waists.

Shortening above a flounce

There are two ways to shorten a skirt with a flounce: by unpicking the flounce and cutting the skirt, or by taking tucks above the flounce. The first method is easiest for a simple skirt. Tucking is best for petticoats and other garments with several layers of flounces. It's an authentic—and pretty—alteration method. I've made as many as eight tucks in my petticoats and everyone thinks the tucks are original.

To remove and reattach a flounce:

1. Try on the skirt and measure how much to shorten.

2. Carefully unpick the flounce. Undo gathers. Pull out loose threads. Press the flounce top.

3. Turn the skirt inside out. Using tailor's chalk, mark the amount to shorten from the bottom, leaving a 1/2 in. seam allowance. Cut. Press the skirt.

Sometimes you won't want to undo the original gathers. Take up excess fabric with little pleats at the center back. Or start pinning the flounce at a side seam. When you've pinned it all the way around, cut off the excess fabric except for a 1/2 in. seam allowance. Fold this over the other edge and press. Slip stitch edges together.

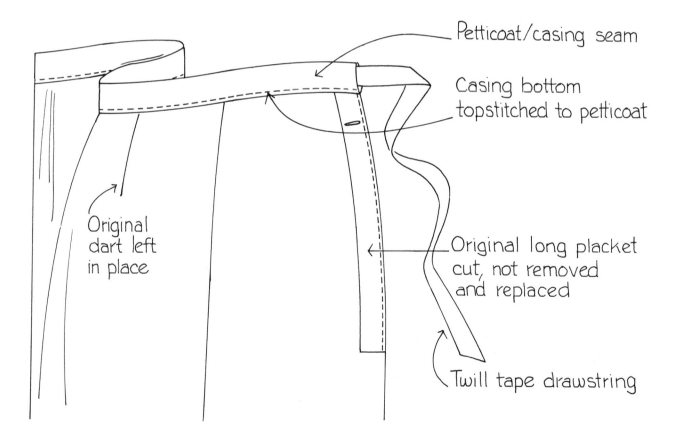

Figure 129: A bias binding petticoat casing

4. Measure the flounce length and mark the skirt at this point on the wrong side. Baste marks through and turn the skirt right side out.

5. Run gathering stitches 3/8 and 1/2 in. from the flounce top (see figure 130). It will be easier to distribute the gathers if you divide both flounce and skirt into fourths (or some number of sections determined by the skirt construction). Divide the gathering rows accordingly.

6. There are two ways to attach the flounce. If it has a finished top edge and you want this to be visible, attach the wrong side of the flounce to the right side of the skirt. If not, sew the right side of the flounce to the right side of the skirt. Lay the skirt on a table right side up and position the flounce for the method you'll use.

Starting at a seam, draw up gathers to fit the skirt and distribute them evenly. Pin the flounce on closely, baste, and machine stitch.

7. Remove basting. Press the new seam up, toward the skirt. Stitch bias binding over inside raw edges. If you wish you can cover a seam line or gathering stitches on the outside with velvet ribbon, ribbon-threaded lace beading or tatting, or other trim.

You can sometimes shorten a skirt by dividing a deep flounce in the middle, without harming the decoration. For example, you could divide a flounce made of horizontal rows of lace. Turn the cut-off part into an extra flounce.

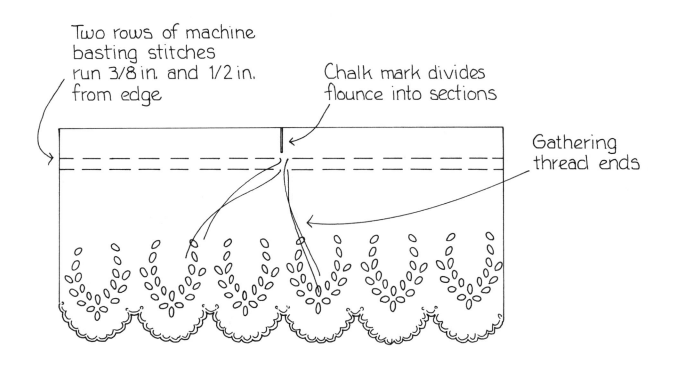

Two rows of machine basting stitches run 3/8 in. and 1/2 in. from edge

Chalk mark divides flounce into sections

Gathering thread ends

Figure 130: A flounce prepared for gathering

To take a skirt up with tucks:

1. Try on the skirt and measure how much to shorten. Now take it off and turn it inside out.

2. Determine tuck size and placement. The rules for this are similar to those for tucking a sleeve. The best tuck size is 1/2 in., blind tucks look better than widely spaced ones, and the crease of the lowest tuck should be just above the flounce. Mark tucks using a clear plastic ruler and tailor's chalk (see figure 131). Be very careful to maintain curves. Baste marks through to the right side.

3. Pin the lowest tuck closely, matching basting marks. To pin curved areas accurately, work from the sides of each section toward the middle.

4. Machine stitch. Examine the tuck closely all round to make sure there are no crooked lines or funny little pleats. If there are, redo those areas. Remove marking basting. Press.

5. Continue making tucks. After you've made the next-to-last one, try on the skirt. Sometimes I find the length is correct at this point. If not, make that last tuck.

6. Wash skirt to remove tailor's chalk.

I often unpick and resew shortening tucks made by the original owner. They tend to be basted, rather than sewn, and are likely to come undone. Also they're often too large for my taste.

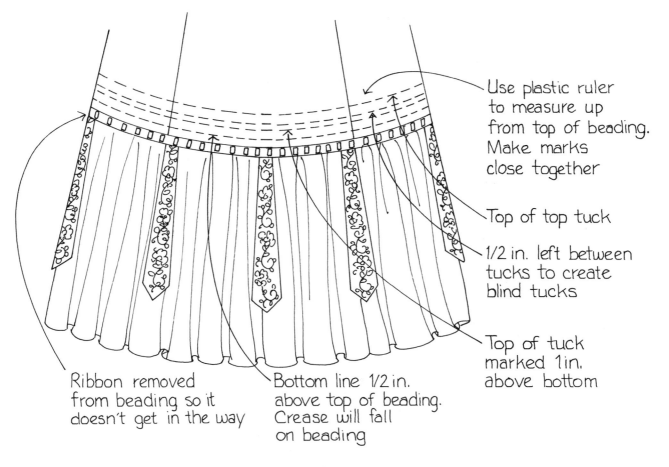

Use plastic ruler to measure up from top of beading. Make marks close together

Top of top tuck

1/2 in. left between tucks to create blind tucks

Top of tuck marked 1 in. above bottom

Ribbon removed from beading so it doesn't get in the way

Bottom line 1/2 in. above top of beading. Crease will fall on beading

Figure 131: Petticoat with two 1/2 in. tucks marked

LENGTHENING

Victorian and Edwardian skirts can't usually be let down and rehemmed, either because there isn't enough fabric or because there is a double bottom flounce. However, there are several other lengthening methods.

Adding fabric to the bottom

You can add fabric to the bottom of a skirt that has no flounce. The addition can be an ungathered border (best for adding small amounts and for tailored skirts) or a gathered flounce (best for adding large amounts and for decorated, feminine skirts).

Your hardest task will be finding coordinating fabric. Because you can seldom match colors accurately, choose an addition with enough contrast to be decorative. For example, if you have a light green satin skirt you might add a dark green velveteen border. If this is a dress, add some velveteen decoration to the bodice to tie the look together.

It's easier to add fabric to Edwardian whites because the difference in shades is less noticeable and most whites are already decorated with several trims. Eyelet is an excellent choice.

To lengthen a skirt by adding a border:

1. If you plan to undo the skirt hem to get a little extra length, or seam allowances for your addition, do this first. Press. (You may not be able to press out the original hemline.)

2. Try on the skirt and measure how much to add. Allow 1/2 in. for the seam allowance and 2 to 2 1/2 in. for the new hem. (If you plan to use a bias hem facing, don't add the 2 to 2 1/2 in. Follow the directions above on hemming a faced skirt.)

3. If the skirt bottom is straight, cut a fabric rectangle the right size. If the addition is only a few inches and the skirt isn't very flared, you might be able to use a rectangle cut on the bias.

Otherwise you'll have to draw an extension piece for each skirt section (see figure 132). Mark the grain near the center of each section by basting next to a vertical thread. Mark a grain line on the extension fabric or pattern paper. Lay the fabric or paper on a table. Lay the skirt above it. Align the skirt grain with the fabric/paper grain. Using a clear ruler or yardstick, extend the hem and seam lines to the depth of your addition, preserving the hem curve and seam slant. (The addition should be wider at the bottom.) Then add 1/2 in. seam allowances to the sides.

Label each piece and set aside.

Tucks may have been taken in the skirt for shortening or decoration. If they go all the way around you can lengthen the skirt by letting them out. Simply unpick tucks and press.

You can also use this technique to add fabric in the middle of a straight skirt, or to the top of a petticoat.

It's so common to cover a skirt-addition seam with braid that this can call attention to your alteration. Instead, sew on a wide, bold lace insertion. Cut away the fabric behind, overcast the edges, and press them away from the lace.

Altering Garments

If you used pattern paper, cut out the pieces in fabric.

4. Pin and machine sew the seam(s) of the addition. Finish them using the original method. Press.

5. Lay the addition over the skirt, right side to right side. Pin and sew. Press seam upward.

6. Hem the new skirt bottom.

To add a simulated hem to a skirt made of shaped border eyelet:

1. Try on the skirt and measure how much to add.

2. Following the directions above, cut a plain fabric border twice the desired addition plus 1/2 in. seam allowances. If the skirt is flared, omit excess fullness by drawing a pattern exactly the size of the addition, then drawing the other half in a mirror image.

3. Pin, machine sew, and finish the seams. Press.

4. Press under the long edges 1/2 in. Fold this "hem" in half wrong side to wrong side. Pin, then baste the top edges together.

The top of an extension can have scallops or another ornamental pattern. Turn under the edges and sew the extension over the skirt bottom wrong side to right side.

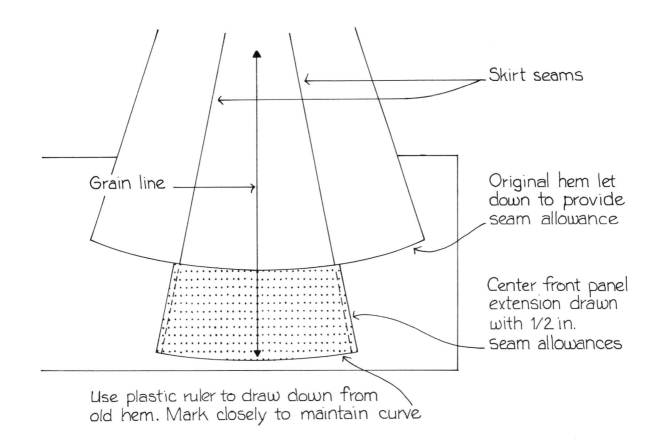

Figure 132: How to cut skirt extensions

You can also lengthen an eyelet skirt by sewing border eyelet trim underneath the original border.

5. Lay the basted edges just underneath the eyelet border. Pin, then baste through all layers. Machine or hand stitch. Remove basting. Press.

To lengthen a skirt by adding a flounce:

1. Try on the skirt and measure how much to add.

2. Undo the skirt hem if you plan to. Press. Measure the skirt circumference.

3. Cut out a rectangular flounce. The width should be 1 1/2 to 2 times your skirt circumference, depending on the desired fullness. Gather a scrap to test. (There will be enough extra to sew the ends together.) The length should be your addition plus a 1/2 in. seam allowance and a 2 to 2 1/2 in. hem allowance (no hem is needed for an eyelet border).

4. Sew the flounce ends together and finish the seam.

5. Gather and attach as described in the section on shortening a skirt with a flounce.

Piecing a skirt with a double flounce

Sometimes a petticoat or skirt has two deep flounces. The upper flounce is the most decorated. The bottom one is plainer, but usually has a short ruffle. You can lengthen the under flounce only to expose the ruffle and create a charming tiered effect. (See figure 133.)

1. Try on the skirt and measure how much to lengthen. Make sure the ruffle seam will still be hidden by the bottom of the top flounce. If more of the ruffle will be hidden, make sure the proportions look right.

2. Examine the skirt construction. You can add fabric either directly above the ruffle or at the flounce top. The second method is less likely to show but may be harder because the top and bottom flounces are often attached to the skirt with a single seam.

Sometimes there is a third, innermost flounce. Lengthen this the same amount as the second flounce if the second flounce needs support. You can lengthen it more if you need the extra length and the alteration will look good.

3. Unpick the ruffle or flounce. You'll simultaneously ungather it. Press.

4. Piece the flounce bottom (if you unpicked the ruffle) or the top (if you unpicked the flounce) using the technique for adding fabric to a skirt bottom. The top and bottom piecing seams should be 1/2 in. Press both seams up.

5. Regather and reattach the ruffle or flounce as described in the section on shortening a skirt with a flounce.

It's easy to enlarge a skirt or petticoat waist by letting out gathers, pleats, or tucks. To make one smaller, add gathers or pleats. How much you can alter depends on the garment construction. I have skirts I've let out 6 or 8 in., and one I took in 18 in. (after shortening it from the waist).

You don't need to replace the waistband unless you can't find enough matching fabric for enlargement or it's too fragile to withstand strain. (Even a well-fitting waistband is under strain.) Removing and replacing the waistband also allows you to adjust skirt fullness everywhere (though this is seldom necessary).

You can sometimes alter a waistband an inch or so simply by moving the fasteners.

Altering the waistband

Many skirts and dresses made before the 1920s have a back closure and more fullness in back. They can be altered there without removing the entire waistband.

To let out the waist:

1. Try on the garment over the undergarments you'll wear (note that a drawstring petticoat is bulkier than one with a waistband). Measure the gap at the waist.

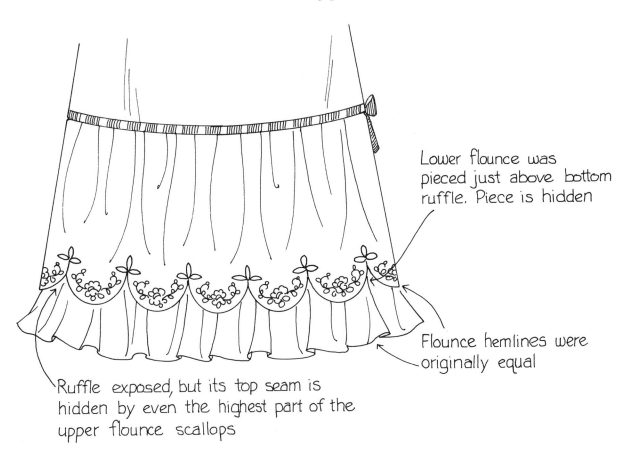

Lower flounce was pieced just above bottom ruffle. Piece is hidden

Flounce hemlines were originally equal

Ruffle exposed, but its top seam is hidden by even the highest part of the upper flounce scallops

Figure 133: Petticoat with under flounce let down

2. Look at the garment construction. Does it have tucks, pleats, or gathers? How many tucks or pleats should you let out to enlarge the waist? Letting out large pleats may release more than you need. You may have to make one pleat smaller rather than eliminating it. With gathering, assume that 1 in. of waistband controls 1 1/2 to 2 in. of skirt fabric.

3. Unpick the waistband from the garment at the center back where it controls fabric to be let out, plus about 2 in. extra per side. Unpick an equal amount on the right and left sides. Press.

4. Unpick pleats or tucks to be let out. Release gathers. Press, spraying washable fabrics with water to remove stitch marks.

5. To let out an unfaced (folded-over) skirt waistband, cut two small rectangles of matching fabric. Their width should be that of the original waistband before folding over. Their length should be the amount to be added plus about 1/2 in. to overlap the old waistband. And there should be 1/2 in. seam allowances all round.

   Finish the closure end of one extension by turning it inside out and machine stitching. Turn right side out and press. Press under the seam allowance of the overlap end. Fold the extension in half, wrong side to wrong side. On the right side of the garment, lay the overlap end 1/2 in. over the edge of the original waistband. Pin and baste. Machine topstitch through all layers. Or slip stitch on the inside and outside. Remove basting and press.

   Repeat for the other extension.

   To let out a faced dress or skirt waistband, cut four rectangles the width of the original waistband and the length of the extension, plus 1/2 in. seam allowances and 1/2 in. overlap. Don't finish the closure ends yet. Press seam allowances of the overlap ends under. On the inside of the garment, lay the overlap 1/2 in. over the old facing, wrong side to right side. Pin and baste. On the outside, pin and baste the waistband overlap over the old waistband, wrong side to right side. Pin and baste. Machine topstitch through all layers or slip stitch. (See figure 134.) Remove basting. Press.

6. Now attach the skirt. Press long waistband seam allowances in toward each other so they'll be hidden when the skirt is attached. Do the same for the closure edges of a faced waistband. Sandwich the skirt top between the long edges, arranging it to go right up to the closure edges. (If you unpicked a little too much fabric, pleat or gather it follow-

ing the instructions for taking in the waist.) Pin and baste all unsewn seams. For a faced waistband, do this first on the inside, then the outside.

7. Sew by the original method—machine topstitching, slip stitching, or some of both. Remove all basting. Press.

8. Reattach fasteners. If they're buttons, you'll have to make new buttonholes.

To take in the waist:

1. Try on the garment over the appropriate undergarments. Measure the overlap at the waist (minus fastener overlap).

2. Examine the garment construction. If fullness is controlled with gathers or pleats, use the same method. If neither is used, choose gathers for sheer fabrics and a dainty look. Choose pleats for heavier fabrics, less bulk, and a more tailored look. Personally I always substitute gathers or pleats for stitched-down tucks.

Heavy Victorian skirts sometimes have cartridge pleats, a rounded pleat that looks more like gathering. Imitate these even if they look bulky to you because other methods look wrong.

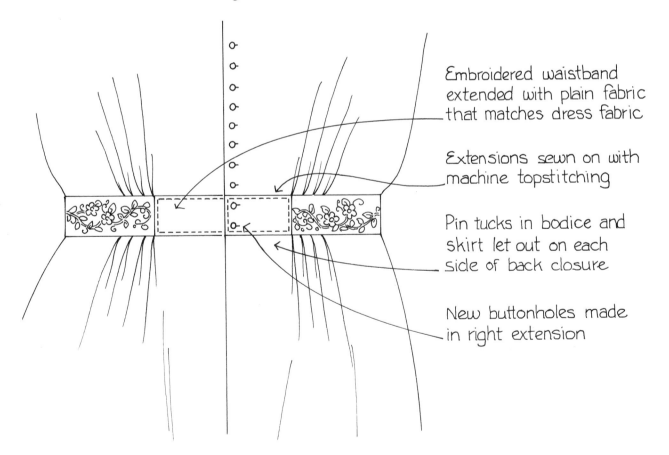

Figure 134: Dress with tucks let out and waistband extended

3. Unpick the waistband from the garment at the center back where it controls fabric to be taken in plus about 2 in. extra per side. Unpick an equal amount on the right and left sides.

4. To take in an unfaced waistband, turn it inside out and restitch the end seams. Turn right side out and press.

   To take in a faced waistband, cut off the excess fabric minus 1/2 in. seam allowances. Turn the end seam allowances toward each other and press. Don't sew yet.

5. Now take in the excess skirt fabric. When positioning gathers or tucks, concentrate them as close to the center back as possible. Fullness near the side seams makes your hips look bigger.

   If gathering, run machine basting through the fabric 3/8 and 1/2 in. from the top. Draw up to the waistband size, distributing gathers evenly. Baste.

   For cartridge pleats, hand gather with double thread, making stitches the same size as the originals. Draw up fabric as tightly as possible. Tie threads.

   When making pleats you first have to determine their size. Each pleat should be 1 1/2 to 2 1/2 in. wide at the top (and will take up twice that amount of fabric). Figure out how many you need on each side to fit the waist.

   To make a pleat, fold fabric toward the center back, forming the crease (see figure 135). Pin. Work from the center back pleat outward. Position pleat creases toward the center back (not the hips). The centermost creases should fall directly on the center back line where the skirt edges meet; they'll hide the opening.

   When making two or more pleats per side, overlap them so the creases are about 1/2 in. apart (and therefore closer to the center back). Keep measuring pleats as you go to regulate the size. When satisfied, baste them down.

6. Sew the skirt to the waistband as described in the section on letting out waists.

7. Replace fasteners.

Replacing the waistband

As with lengthening a skirt, the hardest part of making a new waistband is matching the fabric. A major skirt shortening sometimes provides enough. Pull a thread to find the straight grain and cut the waistband along it, piecing if necessary. Contemporary velveteen looks nice with Victorian silk skirts. Eyelet and sturdy lace work well with white dresses. And don't overlook the possibilities of heavy satin or grosgrain ribbon.

For a more controlled look, stitch pleats down at the creases. First put the skirt on a dress form (or wear it and have somebody help). Pin the pleat creases the way they hang—they get narrower and merge into the skirt. Machine stitch as close to creases as possible. Pull threads to the inside and tie, instead of machine backstitching.

A petticoat that won't show can be taken in about 2 in. by making two 1/2 in. pleats in the waistband. Pleat at center back if the petticoat has little back gathering; otherwise pleat at the side seams. The pleats can be either rectangles or short darts extending into the skirt. Machine stitch through all layers.

1. Take your waist measurement. Add 1/2 in. seam allowances and 1 in. for ease. Measure the opening overlap on the old waistband and add that much also. This is your waistband length.

   Measure the width of the old waistband. An unfaced skirt waistband consists of one piece that is double the finished width plus 1/2 in. seam allowances. A faced dress or skirt waistband consists of two pieces the finished width plus 1/2 in. seam allowances. An eyelet or lace waistband should be faced.

   For extra strength, you can add a fabric interfacing in the finished waistband width. However, many original waistbands aren't interfaced.

2. Draw a rectangle (or rectangles) the correct size on the wrong side of the fabric. The long edges should be parallel to the selvage. Cut.

3. If interfacing an unfaced waistband, pin, baste, and invisibly hemstitch one long edge to the middle of the waistband. Baste other edges down. If interfacing a faced waistband, baste all edges to the outer waistband piece.

If you want to change the waistband width of a Victorian or Edwardian skirt (perhaps to be the right size for eyelet you're using) use originals as a guideline. Skirt waistbands run 3/4 to 1 1/2 in.; dress waistbands, 1 to 2 in. A wider waistband changes the fit.

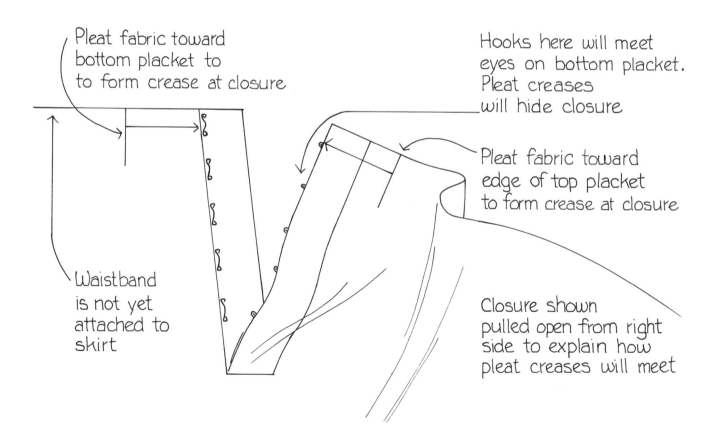

Pleat fabric toward bottom placket to to form crease at closure

Waistband is not yet attached to skirt

Hooks here will meet eyes on bottom placket. Pleat creases will hide closure

Pleat fabric toward edge of top placket to form crease at closure

Closure shown pulled open from right side to explain how pleat creases will meet

Figure 135: How to pleat skirt fabric

Grosgrain or petersham ribbon can make a good waistband for a silk skirt without much fullness. Cut two pieces of 1 in. wide ribbon to the length of the waist measurement plus 1 in. ease, 1/2 in. seam allowances, and overlap. Sew one piece of ribbon to the right side of the skirt about 1/2 in. below the raw edge, letting the short ends stick out 1/2 in. Place the second ribbon on top of the first, sew the short ends together, and flip the second ribbon to the inside, sandwiching the skirt top. Press. Machine stitch all around the waistband.

4. Press under one long edge of an unfaced waistband (the edge that isn't interfaced). Fold in half, right sides together, so the pressed edge is 1/2 in. away from the other long edge (see figure 136). Pin and machine stitch short ends. Turn right side out and press.

For a faced waistband, press short ends in toward each other, but don't sew yet.

5. Adjust skirt gathers or pleats as described in the section on taking in waists.

6. Now attach the skirt to the waistband. For an unfaced waistband, lay the unfolded edge over the skirt top, right side to right side. Pin, baste, and machine sew. Remove basting. Press seam up.

Turn the skirt inside out. Pin and baste the folded edge 1/2 in. down from the skirt top, so it's level with the seam you just made. Slip stitch to the seam allowance. Remove basting and press.

For a faced skirt waistband, sew the bottom of the outer waistband piece to the skirt, right side to right side. Remove basting and press seam up. Turn the garment inside out and repeat for the facing. Sew the upper and clo-

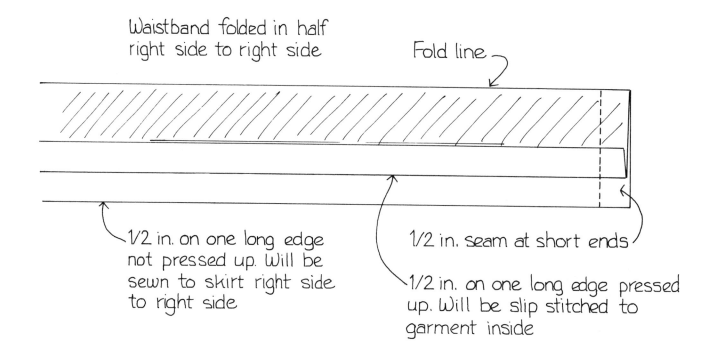

Waistband folded in half
right side to right side

Fold line

1/2 in. on one long edge
not pressed up. Will be
sewn to skirt right side
to right side

1/2 in. seam at short ends

1/2 in. on one long edge pressed
up. Will be slip stitched to
garment inside

Figure 136: An unfaced waistband turned inside out

sure edges together with a machine topstitch or slip stitch. If topstitching, you can also topstitch near the bottom seam for enhanced appearance and strength.

For a faced dress waistband, sew the bottom of the outer waistband to the skirt, then the top to the bodice (see figure 137). Turn the dress inside out and repeat for the facing.

7. Attach fasteners.

If a waistband fits well but is too fragile to support the skirt, consider covering it. This enables you to skip regathering or repleating.

To cover a waistband:

1. Unpick the fasteners.

2. Cut a new waistband 1/8 in. wider than the old one.

3. Press under both long ends, then baste. Sew the short ends and turn right side out.

4. Sandwich the old waistband with the new one. Slip stitch to the right side of the garment. Then slip stitch or whip-stitch to the wrong side.

5. Replace fasteners.

You can also cover or replace just the waist-band facing. Press under the seam allowances and slip stitch to the inside all round.

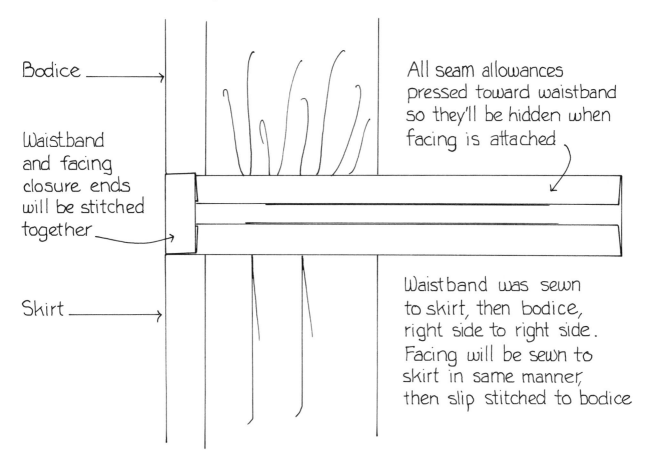

Bodice

Waistband and facing closure ends will be stitched together

Skirt

All seam allowances pressed toward waistband so they'll be hidden when facing is attached

Waistband was sewn to skirt, then bodice, right side to right side. Facing will be sewn to skirt in same manner, then slip stitched to bodice

Figure 137: Inside of faced dress waistband before facing is attached

❧ Altering a Dress or Long Slip

All the techniques I've described for altering blouses and skirts can be applied to dresses. Here are some additional ones for altering a one-piece dress.

CHANGING THE WAIST LENGTH

Whether you can shorten or lengthen a dress bodice depends on its construction. You can unpick and shorten it, replace the waistband with a wider one, and take up some dresses at the shoulders. Usually the waist length can only be altered an inch or so.

Shortening or lengthening from the waist

1. Try on the dress and measure how much to alter.

2. To shorten the bodice, unpick it from the waistband. Press both pieces. On the wrong side, measure and mark the amount to cut off, leaving 1/2 in. for the seam. Cut. If the bodice is gathered, run new gathering stitches in the original locations. Adjust gathers and baste.

3. Pin and baste the waistband to the bodice, right side to right side. Machine stitch. Pin and baste the pressed-under top of the facing to the inside. Slip stitch. Press.

To lengthen a bodice, replace the waistband with a wider, faced one as described in the section on replacing a waistband.

Taking up at the shoulders

Take up a collarless, sleeveless dress at the shoulders when it's too long between the shoulders and the bust and/or the neckline is too low.

1. Try on the dress and pinch it up at the shoulder seams till the fit is correct (see figure 138). You may want to take up different amounts at the neckline and armhole (changing the seam angle). Make sure the armhole will be large enough.

2. Do not unpick the existing seam. Pin and machine sew the new shoulder seam, through the neckline and armhole facings.

3. If you want to press the new seam open, unpick the old one. If necessary, trim excess fabric and finish the seam by overcasting. Otherwise just press it toward the back without unpicking and tack to the facings.

You may be able to take up a sleeved dress at the shoulders if the armhole is large. Pleat or gather excess sleeve fabric near the shoulder seam.

I often use this technique to shorten or improve the shoulder fit of a vest. After cutting, fold outside and lining seam allowances inward and press. Butt the front and back shoulders together and resew with a slip stitch on the outside and the lining.

To take up straps on a dress or slip, fold the strap to the inside to form a loop (in back where it's less visible). Sew down at the top of the loop (the new "seam") and the bottom (to hold the loop down). The extra length will be there if needed.

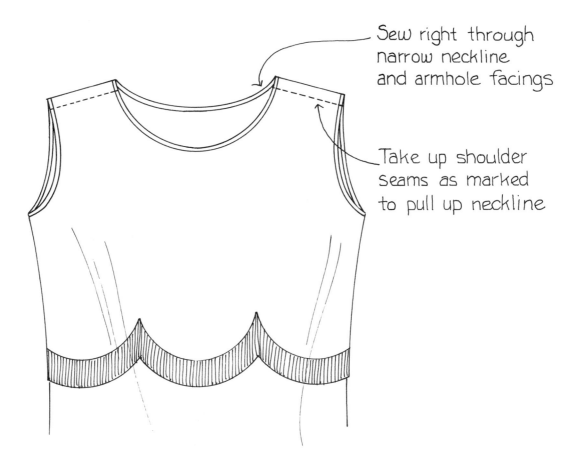

Sew right through
narrow neckline
and armhole facings

Take up shoulder
seams as marked
to pull up neckline

Figure 138: How to take a dress up at the shoulders

TURNING A DRESS INTO SEPARATES

There are several reasons to turn a dress into a separate blouse
and skirt. Maybe one part is wearable and the other seriously
damaged. Or you need to lengthen the bodice by piecing it. Or
complex alterations are needed for both the bodice and skirt. I
once turned a dress into separates when I had to extend the
back, lengthen the waist, add to the skirt waist, and take the
skirt up eight inches from the waist. (See figure 139.) It was
much easier to deal with two pieces. And I turned a closely fitted princess slip into a petticoat and camisole, rather than try
to move a hip area that was much too low.

Separation is generally too complex for dresses with an
entirely separate lining and for multiple-layer 1910s dresses. It
will work, however, when the bodice and skirt were underlined
separately, then sewn together.

1. If you're planning alterations, try on the dress and take the
   appropriate measurements.

2. Unpick the waist seam. If there's a waistband, leave the
   skirt attached.

Although figure 139
shows a bodice that has
been extended on the
left side only, you
should generally extend
both sides equally so as
not to change the
center back line.

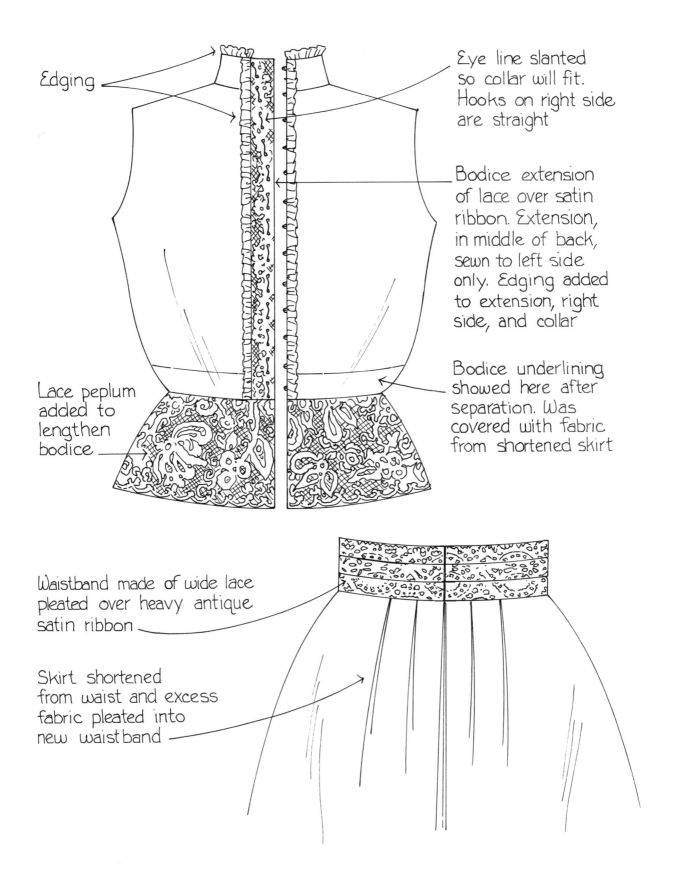

Edging

Eye line slanted so collar will fit. Hooks on right side are straight

Bodice extension of lace over satin ribbon. Extension, in middle of back, sewn to left side only. Edging added to extension, right side, and collar

Bodice underlining showed here after separation. Was covered with fabric from shortened skirt

Lace peplum added to lengthen bodice

Waistband made of wide lace pleated over heavy antique satin ribbon

Skirt shortened from waist and excess fabric pleated into new waistband

Figure 139: Alterations extensive enough to require separating dress

3. Do alterations other than lengthening the bodice and replacing the waistband.

4. The bodice must be lengthened to tuck in. Add a peplum as described in the section on lengthening a blouse.

5. The skirt needs a waistband. Finish the top of the original waistband by pressing raw edges in toward each other and slip stitching. Or add a new one as described in the section on replacing a waistband.

☙ ALTERING MEN'S TROUSERS

It's easy to alter vintage trousers at the hem and waist. Try them on with shoes and a belt or suspenders because these affect the fit.

ALTERING THE LENGTH

You hem trousers pretty much like a skirt except for the cuffs. Make sure cuff or hem fabric to be let down won't look too dark. Note that some turn-of-the-century trousers, like skirts of the same period, are intentionally cut lower in back.

Hemming up

Trousers can be hemmed up to remove damaged fabric even though they're the right length. If this is your goal, read both this section and the one on letting down.

1. Try on trousers and measure how much to shorten. Pin up and try on again. You can test different lengths by pinning up each leg a different amount. Take trousers off and measure how much you pinned with a ruler.

2. Turn the trousers wrong side out. Unpick the cuff and hem. Slip the leg over a sleeve board and press out the fold lines.

3. Mark the cutting line using a ruler and tailor's chalk. Leave 1 1/2 to 2 in. for the hem. Cut. Mark the hem fold line. Baste the mark through to the right side.

4. Press hem to the inside on the fold line, using the sleeve board again. The trouser leg may flare, so there is extra fabric in the hem. Slip a piece of brown paper between the leg and hem, and steam press to remove fullness. Or the leg may get narrower, so there isn't enough hem fabric. Let out a side seam in the hem area. If you can't, make a small, straight cut in the hem, where the outer fabric buckles, and spread to form a V shape (see figure 140). Press, gently stretching the hem.

5. Now finish the hem edge. Fold the hem down again tem-

I've also seen two garments—a bodice or blouse and a skirt, or a camisole and a petti-coat—combined into one dress or slip. Combining may change the style. But it's worth considering if you have two damaged garments whose good parts don't work as separates. Combining is most successful with Edwardian whites and with dresses that use multiple fabrics.

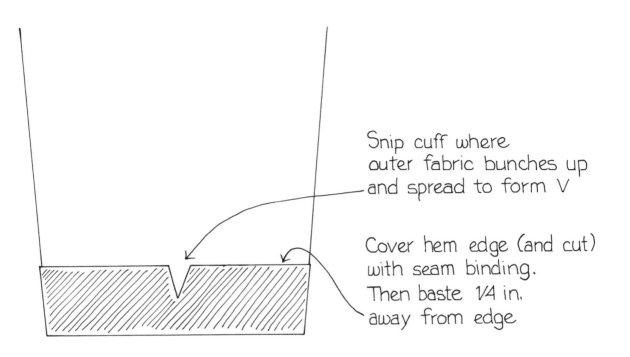

Snip cuff where
outer fabric bunches up
and spread to form V

Cover hem edge (and cut)
with seam binding.
Then baste 1/4 in.
away from edge

Hem turned up to inside

Figure 140: How to cut and spread a trouser hem edge

porarily (don't press) and turn the trousers right side out. Find some commercial seam or bias binding in a matching color. Starting at the side seam, pin seam binding over the raw edge. Neatly fold the last-pinned end over the first. Make sure to cover any cuts you made (use an extra, partial row of binding if necessary). Sew using a straight or zigzag machine stitch.

6. Turn the trousers inside out again. Press the hem up on the fold line. Pin finished edge to the trousers. (If there is still excess fullness, make tiny, nonbulky pleats at the hem edge.) Baste 1/4 in. away from the edge.

7. Hand hem using the basic hemming stitch. Remove basting. Press.

8. If there are cuffs, turn trousers right side out. Fold the cuff up evenly 1 1/2 in. (or however it was originally). Press, covering fabric with a press cloth. At the side seams, take a few tacking stitches to hold the cuff up. Bend about 1/4 in. of the cuff top down and sew through the inner layer and the trouser leg, much as you would sew on a button, taking care stitches don't show. Press up again.

Letting down

Your trousers may have a cuff folded up on the outside and a fairly narrow hem, or no cuff and a wider hem. You have two alteration choices for cuffed pants: to unpick the cuff and do without one, or to unpick the hem and fold up the fabric in a fake cuff. For uncuffed pants, you can let down the hem and face with bias binding.

To just unpick the cuff:

1. Unpick the cuff and press out fold lines from the wrong side. Try on trousers. If they're the right length, you're done.

2. If they're a bit long, hem them. If they're still too short, unpick the hem and face it (see below).

To create a false cuff:

1. Unpick the cuff and hem. Press out fold lines. Try on trousers. They should be the right length plus at least 1 1/2 in. Measure the excess.

2. On the right side, make a 1/2 in. tuck to simulate the cuff fold (this will take up 1 in. of fabric). Press upward, using a press cloth.

3. Turn trousers inside out. Press up the hem—it should be at least 1/2 in. wide. You don't need to finish the raw edge. Pin and baste.

4. Cut a facing from commercial bias binding. Its width should be the distance between the tuck bottom and the hem plus 1/2 in. seam allowances. Its length should be the trouser leg circumference plus 1/2 in. seam allowances.

5. Pin and stitch the short ends of the facing, right side to right side, to form a ring. Press seam open. Press remaining seam allowances under.

6. Turn facing right side out and slip over the wrong side of the trouser leg. Pin and baste to hem and trouser leg, letting most of the 1/2 in. hem show. Slip stitch. Remove basting and press.

To face the hem:

1. Try on trousers. They should be the right length plus at least 1/2 in. Measure the excess fabric.

2. Cut a length of commercial bias binding the circumference of the trouser leg plus 1/2 in. side seam allowances. Its width should allow for a 1 1/2 to 2 in. hem (at least 1/4 in. of this should be the trouser fabric) plus 1/4 in. top and bottom seam allowances.

3. Sew facing ends together to form a ring. Machine sew one edge to the trouser leg with a 1/4 in. seam. Press to the inside. Hem following the directions for taking up a hem.

ALTERING THE WAIST

You can take in (or let out) vintage trousers about 3 in. at the center back seam without distorting the pocket position. The seam goes right through the waistband, so you don't have to remove it. In some turn-of-the-century trousers, the top of this seam has a V-shaped opening.

1. It's hard to fit trousers in the seat by yourself, so get a helper. If letting out, first remove the center back belt loop. Remove suspender buttons if they'll get in the way. Unpick the center facing seam. Unpick stitching at the top and bottom several inches to each side of the center seam. Then unpick the trouser seam most of the way to the crotch.

   Put on the trousers wrong side out. Have your helper pin a new seam starting at the waistband and gradually tapering to join the old one (some trousers must be pinned further down than others). Place pins vertically.

   Move around in front of a mirror to check fit and comfort.

2. If taking in, undo the waistband facing (but not the trouser seam) after trying on.

   Remove pins one at a time and replace them on one side only through the pin holes. Mark the new seam line by rubbing tailor's chalk over the pin positions, fixing it up a little if necessary (see figure 141). Remove pins.

3. Pin the center back seam through the chalk line, placing pins horizontally. Carefully adjust trousers so the seam is the same on both sides. Machine stitch. If taking in, unpick the old seam to where it joins the new one. Press seam open.

   Leave a large seam allowance in place unless its bulk shows on the right side—you may want to let the trousers out again someday. If you must cut off part, finish the raw edges by overcasting.

4. Press facing edges. Fold them under till they butt at the back seam—again, don't cut off extra fabric. Pin and baste the edges, top, and bottom. Slip stitch or whipstitch the edges and top. If there is machine topstitching at the bottom, turn the trousers right side out and follow the old topstitching lines. Remove basting and press.

5. Reattach suspender buttons. Press belt loop ends under and invisibly hand or machine sew to trousers.

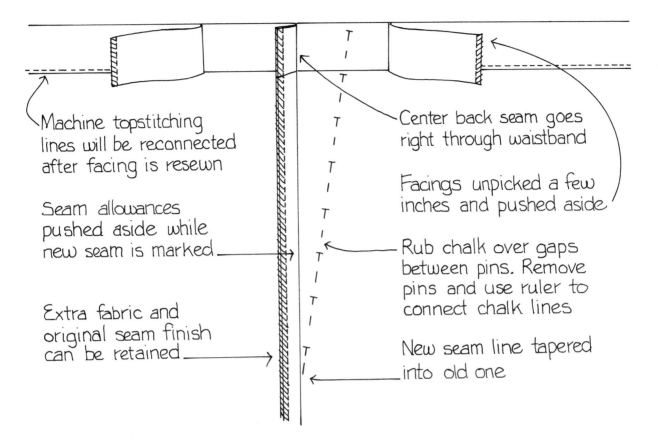

Machine topstitching lines will be reconnected after facing is resewn

Seam allowances pushed aside while new seam is marked

Extra fabric and original seam finish can be retained

Center back seam goes right through waistband

Facings unpicked a few inches and pushed aside

Rub chalk over gaps between pins. Remove pins and use ruler to connect chalk lines

New seam line tapered into old one

Figure 141: Trousers being marked for taking in

☙ FITTING A TAILORED JACKET OR COAT

These alterations are appropriate for any jacket or coat, whether it's a suit jacket, evening tails, or winter coat—and whether it belongs to a man or woman.

If you plan to reline the jacket, remove the lining and do alterations first. Remember to transfer alterations to the new lining.

HEMMING THE BOTTOM OF A LINED JACKET

To help retain hemline curves, trace them onto cardboard before undoing the hem. Use this pattern to draw the new hemline.

1. Try on the jacket and measure how much to hem.

2. Turn the jacket inside out. Unpick the place the lining is sewn to the outer fabric.

3. Fold up the lining and mark the cutting line on the wrong side of the lining and outer fabric. Take the same amount off both (some linings are intentionally cut longer for ease). Leave 1/2 in. seam allowances. Cut.

Some unlined
Edwardian women's
jackets have narrow
machine-stitched hems.
Leave about 1/2 to 1 in.
for the hem plus 1/4 to
1/2 in. for turning
under the raw edge.
Press under edge, turn
up on the inside, and
pin. Machine topstitch
through all layers, or
slip stitch.

4. Press the lining seam allowance under. Press the outer fabric edge up to create a margin that shows on the bottom (see figure 142). Lay the lining over the outer fabric to hide the outer fabric seam allowance. Pin and baste. Remove pins.

5. Slip stitch lining to fabric. Remove basting. Press from the inside, using a press cloth.

ALTERING SLEEVES

Jacket sleeves can be shortened, lengthened, or taken in for a less baggy fit.

Shortening cuffed sleeves

To hem a lined, uncuffed sleeve, follow the steps for hemming a jacket bottom, removing and replacing sleeve buttons. (Treat a jacket sleeve with a seam a few inches from the bottom, but no turned-up cuff, like an uncuffed sleeve.) These instructions are for hemming a sleeve with a separate, turned-up cuff.

I always hem one sleeve at a time, leaving the other intact as a construction reference.

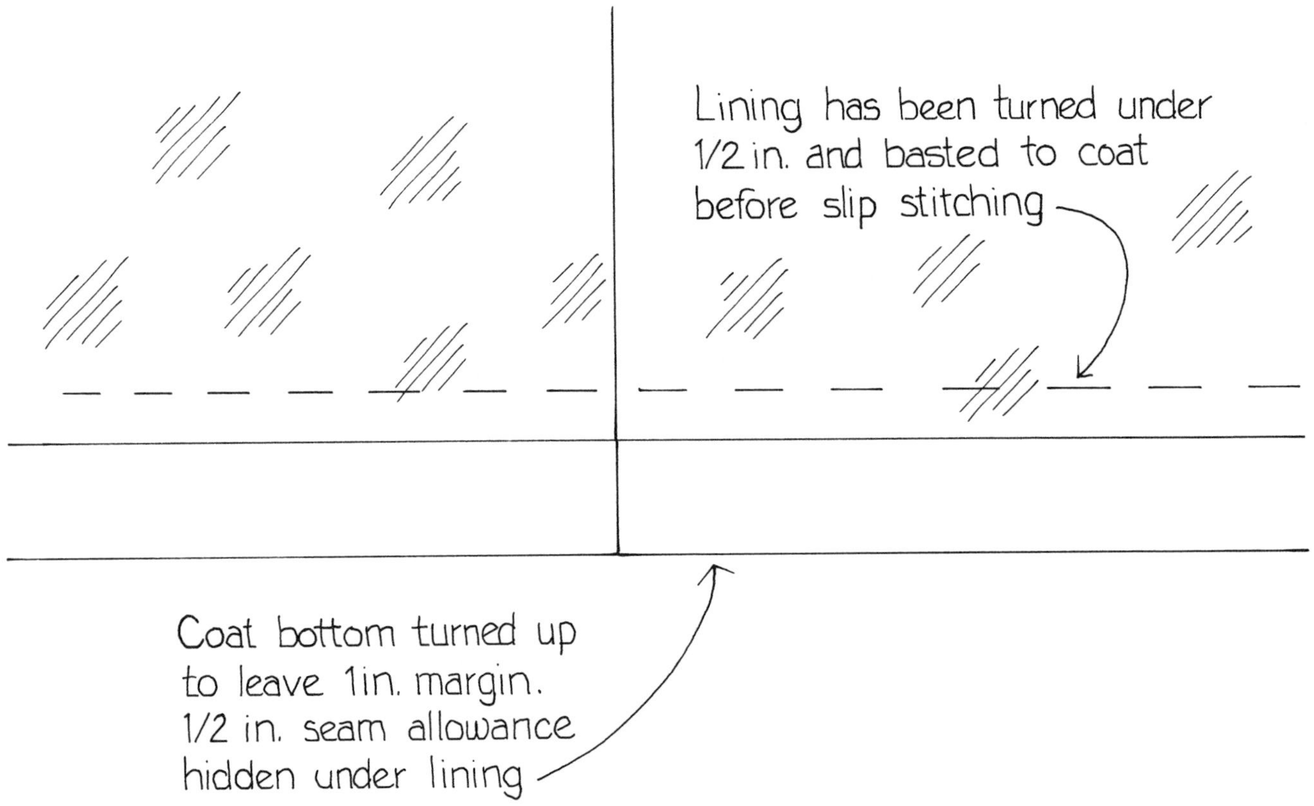

Lining has been turned under 1/2 in. and basted to coat before slip stitching

Coat bottom turned up to leave 1in. margin. 1/2 in. seam allowance hidden under lining

Figure 142: Lined coat prepared for rehemming

1. Try on the jacket and figure out how much to shorten the sleeves.

2. Unpick the cuff seam, and the lining seam if any. Label cuffs "R" or "L" if working on both sleeves at once. Remove cuff buttons if they'll get in the way.

3. While you unpick you'll see the sleeve construction. With an unlined sleeve, the sleeve bottom and cuff may have been sewn togther right side to right side, with the seam hidden under the turned-up cuff.

   With a lined sleeve, the lining edge may first have been finished by pressing under, then sewn up over the outside of the sleeve edge. The cuff is slip stitched to the lining on the inside, then turned up on the outside to hide the bit of lining.

   Or double cuff edges may have been turned under and the sleeve edge (plus the lining edge, if any) sandwiched between them, then stitched. (See the section on adding a cuff.)

4. After figuring out how to reattach the cuff, mark the cutting line on the wrong side of the sleeve and lining. Use seam allowances the same width as the originals. Cut.

5. Slip the cuff over the sleeve. If the sleeve buckles, the cuff is now too small (the sleeve widens toward the shoulder). If the cuff has decorative edges tacked together, carefully split these to create a flared cuff (see figure 143). If not, you can take in the sleeve and lining seams (fold the sleeve and lining away from each other to get to the seam).

6. Reattach cuff following the original construction—usually you'll use a slip stitch.

7. Bend back flared cuff edges about 1/4 in. and tack the inner layer to the sleeve to keep the cuff upright. Resew buttons if necessary.

Lengthening sleeves

You can lengthen a plain jacket sleeve about 2 1/2 to 3 1/2 in. by adding a cuff (see figure 144). You might use largish garment scraps left over from hemming. Or a contrasting material such as velvet. To make the alteration fabric blend in, sew some of it onto the collar and perhaps the pockets. Adding a couple of buttons to each cuff on the front side of the cuff seam also gives an authentic look.

If there's already a cuff, you can piece the sleeve an inch or so under it, as long as the turned-up cuff hides the piece (see figure 145). This works best with an unlined jacket.

Occasionally a previous owner who has shortened the sleeves leaves extra fabric under the lining, which you can let down.

To add a cuff:

1. Try on the jacket and measure how much to lengthen the sleeves. Find cuff fabric, and cuff facing fabric if this will be different.

2. Turn the jacket inside out. Unpick the sleeve hem and press. Cut so that the sleeve and lining edges are even. Baste together.

3. For most jackets you'll want a faced cuff, so the wrong side doesn't show when you wear the jacket. The facing can be made from a lightweight fabric like the lining, or from the cuff fabric.

   Measure the sleeve circumference 1/2 in. up from the edge. On pattern paper, draw a horizontal line this length plus 1/2 in. side seam allowances. This is the cuff top. Measure 3 1/2 to 4 1/2 in. down—however wide you want your cuff plus 1/2 in. top and bottom seam allowances. Draw the cuff bottom. If the sleeve narrows considerably from the shoulder, or you're fitting a small wrist, make the cuff bottom a little narrower than the top.

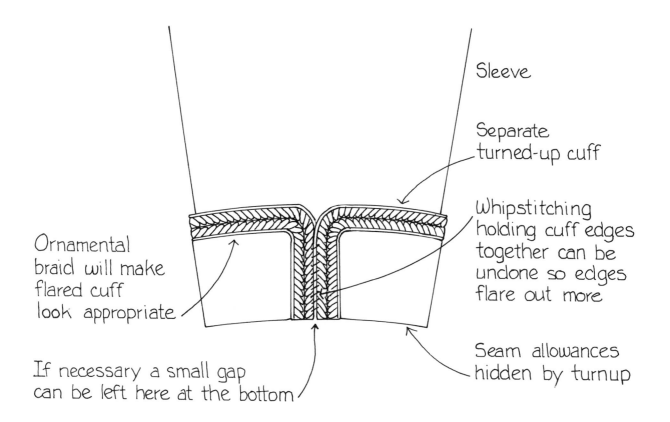

Figure 143: A cuff that can be split to create a larger flared cuff

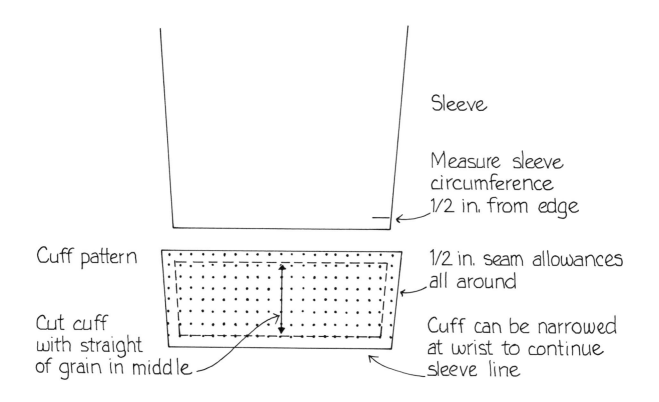

Sleeve

Measure sleeve circumference 1/2 in. from edge

Cuff pattern

1/2 in. seam allowances all around

Cut cuff with straight of grain in middle

Cuff can be narrowed at wrist to continue sleeve line

Figure 144: How to add a cuff

If you do this, fold the cuff pattern in half and draw a grain line in the middle.

4. Pin the pattern to the right side of the fabric with the grain parallel to the selvage. Cut two cuffs and two facings. For napped fabrics, mark the cuff top on the wrong side with tailor's chalk.

5. Press the edges of the cuff and facing tops under 1/2 in. Pin each side seam together right side to right side (baste slippery fabrics). Machine stitch. Press seam open over a sleeve board.

   Pin each cuff to its facing on the bottom, right side to right side. Machine stitch. Turn cuffs right side out. Press on the facing side with a press cloth, manipulating seam so it doesn't fall on the cuff side.

6. Sandwich the sleeve and lining edges between the turned-in cuff edges. Pin and baste. Slip stitch on both sides or machine topstitch through all layers. Remove basting. Press.

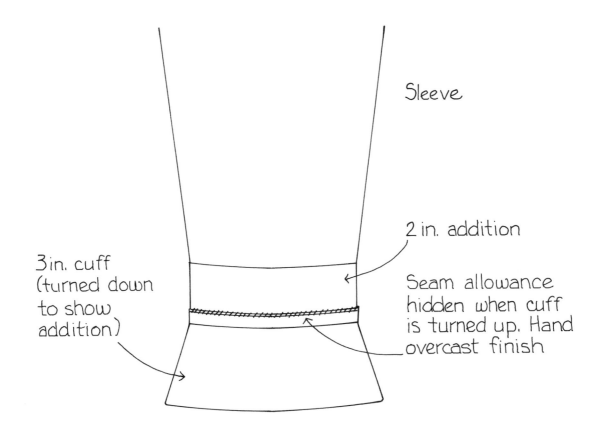

Figure 145: Jacket sleeve pieced under the cuff

To piece under a cuff:

1. Try on the jacket and measure how much to lengthen the sleeves. Find fabric from a previous alteration or a matching remnant.

2. Unpick cuffs and label "R" and "L."

3. Cut a piece of fabric the sleeve bottom circumference plus a 1/2 in. side seam allowance. The addition shouldn't be too wide to be covered by the cuff—probably about 2 in. Leave 1/2 in. top and bottom seam allowances.

   For better conformation to the sleeve shape, cut the addition on the bias.

4. Sew the short ends of the addition right side to right side to form a ring. Press seam open.

5. Sew the top of the addition to the sleeve bottom, right side to right side. Turn sleeve inside out and press seam down. Overcast raw edges. Turn right side out again.

6. Attach cuff by the original method. Press up.

Taking in sleeves

Sometimes a jacket looks too big even though you've taken in the side and back seams. Try taking in the sleeves too, preferably when you hem them up.

1. Pin in the sleeve seam, tapering from the armhole (which should not be altered) to the wrist. Try on the jacket and adjust pins as necessary. Take off the jacket. Measure how much you took in at the sleeve hem.

2. Turn the sleeves inside out. Unpick the lining at the sleeve hem and pull it up to expose the sleeve and lining seams on the wrong side.

3. Slip the sleeve over a sleeve board. At the sleeve hem, mark how much to take in. Use a yardstick to draw a line that tapers to the armhole (see figure 146). Repeat for the sleeve lining.

4. Pin the new seam and machine stitch. Undo the old seam. Press open.

5. Pull the lining back down. Reattach to the sleeve as described in the section on hemming a sleeve.

6. Repeat for the other sleeve.

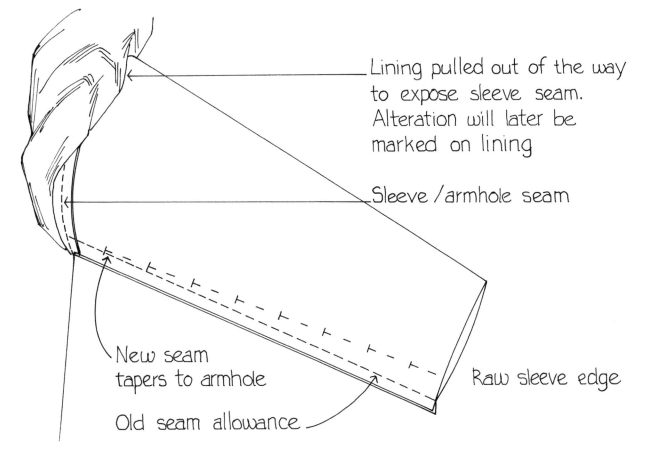

Lining pulled out of the way to expose sleeve seam. Alteration will later be marked on lining

Sleeve / armhole seam

New seam tapers to armhole

Old seam allowance

Raw sleeve edge

Figure 146: Sleeve seam marked for taking in

TAKING IN AND LETTING OUT

Sometimes you can take in a jacket an inch or so by moving the buttons. First make sure this won't distort the neckline or pocket position.

For a small alteration, unpick the lining at the seam only plus a couple of inches to either side at the hem and neckline. Machine sew outer seam. Press lining seam allowances under and slip stitch together.

A Victorian bodice with no fabric to let out may be wearable as an open jacket (over a blouse). The best candidates are plain, close-fitting styles with enough body not to droop. The bodice must fit across the back.

You can alter a jacket at the side seams and the center back seam—as long as you don't alter the armholes or neckline. Before you start to let out, feel the seam allowances through the lining to see if they're wide enough. Ideally you should do this before purchase. At a vintage clothing show, I bought a Victorian winter coat that many customers had passed up because of its impossibly small waist. When I felt the side seams I discovered four inches of invisible fabric that I let out to make the coat fit perfectly.

1. If you're letting out the jacket, first undo the lining hem to reach the inside of the lining. Undo the lining and outer side seams. Pin, tapering the seam from the waist to the armhole. Place pins vertically. Try on the jacket. If this doesn't do the trick, repeat for the center back seam, tapering to the neckline (see figure 147).

   If you're taking in, pin the outer fabric without undoing the lining. You'll still try the side seams first and taper from the waist to the armhole or neck.

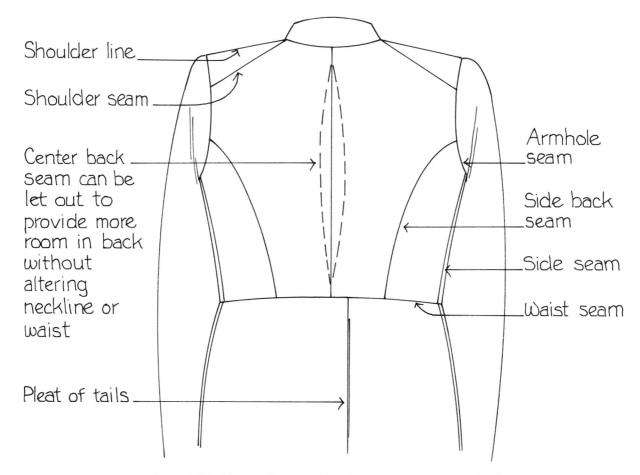

Figure 147: Man's tail coat marked for letting out at center back

2. On the wrong side of the outer fabric and lining, draw new seam lines that follow the pins. Maintain any fitting curves. Pin the seams and machine sew. Undo old seams if taking in. Press new seams flat on the wrong side. Press on the right side, using a press cloth, to remove old seam marks.

3. Resew the lining hem following the instructions for hemming a jacket.

Resources

For many years I've built a library of costume books. I also maintain a resource list. It includes booksellers, reenactment and sewing suppliers, vintage clothing dealers, and costuming and reenactment organizations.

I continually scout ads and other lists for new sources. I send for every catalog that intrigues me. I update address and product information every time I deal with a business or notice their ad has changed. And I delete the listing if they go out of business.

In choosing listings for this book, my main concerns were usefulness and accessibility. Most sources are directly related to costuming, collecting, or reenactment. All businesses sell by mail, so are accessible no matter where you live. All sell retail, to the public. Some also have stores or sell wholesale; contact them and ask. Anybody can participate in the events and join the organizations.

Now for the caveats. I can't know about every source. I can't guarantee anybody's products or service. And enough time may have elapsed since publication for a listing to be outdated.

The listings are organized in sections so you can easily find what you're looking for. Listings appropriate for more than one section are cross-referenced. Alphabetization is by the author's last name or the business name. Contact names for businesses are given first, the way letters are addressed.

One final note: when you send an inquiry to any source, a long, self-addressed stamped envelope (LSASE) is appreciated.

⚑ BOOKS

This section is a combined bibliography and resource list. I own all the books in it and refer to them frequently. Most are in print and/or crop up often in used costume book dealers' catalogs. If you can't find a book in any store or catalog, go to a bookstore and leaf through their desk copy of *Books in Print*. Ask them to order the book if it's in print. If it isn't, ask a used costume book dealer to do a search.

HISTORIES OF COSTUME

Barton, Lucy. *Historic Costume for the Stage.* Boston: Walter H. Baker, 1963.

> Oriented toward theater costumers. Includes men's and women's clothes for different social classes and occupations, materials, and accessories. Detailed and practical. There's a companion volume of scale drafts, *Period Patterns.*

Boucher, Francois. *20,000 Years of Fashion: The History of Costume and Personal Adornment.* New York: Harry N. Abrams, n.d.

> A broad, but solid survey of costume with lots of illustrations.

Payne, Blanche. *History of Costume: From the Ancient Egyptians to the Twentieth Century.* New York: Harper & Row, 1965.

> A detailed history of men's and women's clothes, including accessories and hairstyles. My edition also has scale drafts of 43 garments from the 14th to the late 19th centuries. In the second edition these were replaced by text on 20th-century costume.

HISTORIES OF SPECIFIC PERIODS OR TOPICS

Adburgham, Alison. *Shops and Shopping 1800–1914: Where, and in What Manner the Well-Dressed Englishwoman Bought Her Clothes.* London: George Allen and Unwin, 1981.

Shopping and dressmaking in the 19th and early 20th centuries.

Alexander, Helene. *Fans.* London: B. T. Batsford, 1984.

History of the fan from the 17th century to the 20th.

Arnold, Janet. *Queen Elizabeth's Wardrobe Unlock'd.* Leeds: W. S. Maney & Son, 1988.

Compares and analyzes portraits of the queen and others, the inventory of robes, tallies of gifts to and from the queen, and other sources. Includes chapters on Elizabethan women's fashions, how they were made, and jewelry and embroidery designs. Contains 460 photos, mostly black-and-white, of paintings, original garments, and details. A magnificent book.

Ashelford, Jane. *Dress in the Age of Elizabeth I.* New York: Holmes & Meier, 1988.

Detailed work on Elizabethan fashions. Includes men's and women's garments, accessories, materials, masque dress, class distinctions, and shopping.

Buck, Anne. *Dress in Eighteenth-Century England.* London: B. T. Batsford, 1979.

Detailed information on what was worn by men and women of each social class, and how clothes were bought and made.

Buck, Anne. *Victorian Costume and Costume Accessories.* Carlton: Ruth Bean, 1984.

Mostly women's clothes, with a chapter each on men and children.

Byrde, Penelope. *The Male Image: Men's Fashion in England 1300–1970.* London: B. T. Batsford, 1979.

A very good history of men's fashion.

Useful for construction because it pays attention to details.

Byrde, Penelope. *Nineteenth-Century Fashion.* London: B. T. Batsford, 1992.

Equally devoted to men's and women's clothes. The information on men's clothes is slightly different from *The Male Image.*

Cincinnati Art Museum. *With Grace & Favour: Victorian & Edwardian Fashion in America.* Cincinnati: Cincinnati Art Museum, 1993.

An exhibit catalog with photos, mostly color, of 66 dresses from 1837 to 1912. Includes a style history with construction details and essays on acquiring a French wardrobe, reform dress, and the fabric scrapbooks of a Midwestern school-teacher.

Clark, Fiona. *Hats.* London: B. T. Batsford, 1982.

History of men's and women's hats from 1600 to the 1970s.

Coleman, Elizabeth Ann. *The Opulent Era: Fashions of Worth, Doucet, and Pingat.* New York: Thames and Hudson, 1989.

A luxurious book on late 19th-century couture.

Crowfoot, Elisabeth, Frances Pritchard, and Kay Staniland. *Textiles and Clothing 1150–1450.* London: HMSO Publications, 1992.

The fourth volume of the Medieval Finds from Excavations in London series, which also includes *Knives and Scabbards, Shoes and Pattens,* and *Dress Accessories.* A thoroughly scholarly work.

Cumming, Valerie. *Gloves.* London: B. T. Batsford, 1982.

History of gloves from 1600 to the 1970s.

Cunnington, C. Willett and Phillis Cunnington. *The History of Underclothes.* London: Faber and Faber, 1981.

Men's and women's underclothes from

the Middle Ages to 1950. Reprinted by Dover Publications.

de Courtais, Georgine. *Women's Headdress and Hairstyles: In England from A.D. 600 to the Present Day.* London: B. T. Batsford, 1986.

Contains descriptions of styles and their development, as well as drawings.

de Marly, Diana. *Dress in America: The New World 1492–1800.* New York: Holmes & Meier, 1990.

A history of American colonial dress.

de Marly, Diana. *Fashion for Men: An Illustrated History.* New York: Holmes & Meier, 1985.

Has more social/cultural and less technical information than *The Male Image.*

Earnshaw, Pat. *Lace in Fashion: From the Sixteenth to the Twentieth Centuries.* London: B. T. Batsford, 1985.

A solid, well-illustrated history of what different laces looked like and how they were worn by men and women. Includes machine lace.

Ewing, Elizabeth. *History of Children's Costume.* New York: Charles Scribner's Sons, 1977.

From the Middle Ages to the 1970s.

Ewing, Elizabeth. *Underwear: A History.* New York: Theater Arts Books, 1972.

Focuses on women's underclothes, largely Elizabethan to the 1940s.

Farrell, Jeremy. *Socks & Stockings.* London: B. T. Batsford, 1992.

History of men's and women's hose from 1600 to 1990.

Farrell, Jeremy. *Umbrellas and Parasols.* London: B. T. Batsford, 1985.

History of umbrellas and parasols from 1600 into the 1980s.

Foster, Vanda. *Bags and Purses.* London: B. T. Batsford, 1982.

History of bags and purses from 1600 to 1980.

Gibbings, Sarah. *The Tie: Trends and Traditions.* New York: Barron's Educational Series, 1990.

Men's neckwear from the 17th century into the 1980s. Popular but solid. Lots of sidebars on minitopics like stickpins, bandannas, women's ties, and tie collecting.

Ginsburg, Madeleine. *The Hat: Trends and Traditions.* New York: Barron's Educational Series, 1990.

Men's and women's hats from the Middle Ages into the 1980s. Has the same format and quality as *The Tie.*

Goldthorpe, Caroline. *From Queen to Empress: Victorian Dress 1837–1877.* New York: Metropolitan Museum of Art, 1988.

Victorian women's dress, including day, evening, wedding, mourning, and court.

Herald, Jacqueline. *Renaissance Dress in Italy 1400–1500.* Atlantic Highlands: Humanities Press, 1981.

Well researched with lots of technical detail and lushly illustrated.

Holland, Vyvyan. *Hand Coloured Fashion Plates 1770–1899.* London: B. T. Batsford, 1988.

History of the fashion plate with 134 illustrations (5 in color). Oriented toward collectors.

Kennett, Frances. *The Collector's Book of Fashion.* New York: Crown Publishers, 1983.

Really a history of 20th-century women's fashion with a short conservation chapter and a list of museums tacked on.

Kidwell, Claudia. *Cutting a Fashionable Fit: Dressmaker's Drafting Systems in the United States.* Washington: Smithsonian Institution Press, 1979.

A history and analysis of 19th-century patent drafting systems. Also throws light on commercial patterns and custom dressmaking.

Kidwell, Claudia. *Suiting Everyone: The Democratization of Clothing in America.*

Washington: Smithsonian Institution Press, 1974.

History of the manufacture and distribution of clothing in America from the 18th century to the 1960s.

Kraatz, Anne. *Lace: History and Fashion.* New York: Rizzoli International Publications, 1989.

Many books on lace promote a "romantic" mystique, without providing much information. Others mystify with a profusion of technical and foreign terms. This book strikes a nice balance.

Kyoto Costume Institute. *Revolution in Fashion 1715–1815.* New York: Abbeville Press, 1989.

Gorgeous photos, many in color, of 150 men's and women's costumes. The seven essays include one by Janet Arnold on cut and construction, with three scale patterns.

Levey, Santina M. *Lace: A History.* Leeds: W. S. Maney & Son, 1983.

From the early 16th century to World War I. A detailed, scholarly work with 500 large black-and-white plates of laces and costumes.

Levitt, Sarah. *Victorians Unbuttoned: Registered Designs for Clothing, their Makers and Wearers, 1839–1900.* London: George Allen & Unwin, 1986.

Indicates when technical innovations were first used in clothes and accessories. Ties in with the history of ready-to-wear.

Los Angeles County Museum of Art. *An Elegant Art: Fashion and Fantasy in the Eighteenth Century.* New York: Harry N. Abrams, 1983.

An exhibit catalog with informative essays on fashionable and fancy dress, fabrics, decoration, and deportment. Men's and women's clothes.

Mackrell, Alice. *Shawls, Stoles, and Scarves.* London: B. T. Batsford, 1986.

History of shawls, stoles, and scarves from 1600 into the 1980s.

Mills, Betty. *Calico Chronicle: Texas Women and Their Fashions, 1830–1910.* Lubbock: Texas Tech Press, 1985.

What pioneers wore and how they obtained it.

Mosconi, Davide and Riccardo Villarosa. *The Book of Ties.* London: Tie Rack, 1985.

A clever book containing pictures of 188 knots and tying instructions. Although some knots are jokes, many are historic. I bought my copy at the Tie Rack in the local mall.

Newton, Stella Mary. *Fashion in the Age of the Black Prince: A Study of the Years 1340–1365.* Woodbridge: Boydell Press, 1980.

A scholarly, in-depth work.

Ribeiro, Aileen. *Dress in Eighteenth-Century Europe 1715–1789.* New York: Holmes & Meier, 1985.

Men's and women's fashionable and fancy dress, how clothes were bought and made, and the etiquette of dress.

Ribeiro, Aileen. *Fashion in the French Revolution.* New York: Holmes & Meier, 1988.

Men's and women's fashions, and their political implications, from 1789 to 1799.

Scarisbrick, Diana. *Jewellery.* London: B. T. Batsford, 1984.

History of jewelry from 1600 to 1980.

Scott, Margaret. *Late Gothic Europe, 1400–1500.* Atlantic Highlands: Humanities Press, 1980.

Combines solid research, technical detail, and lovely illustrations.

Steele, Valerie. *Paris Fashion: A Cultural History.* New York: Oxford University Press, 1988.

A history of Parisian fashion and its influence abroad from the Middle Ages to the 1980s.

Swann, June. *Shoes.* London: B. T. Batsford, 1982.

> History of shoes from 1600 into the 1970s.

Walker, Richard. *Savile Row: An Illustrated History.* New York: Rizzoli International Publications, 1989.

> History of the English center of custom tailoring from the late 17th century to the late 20th.

Walkley, Christina. *The Ghost in the Looking Glass: The Victorian Seamstress.* London: Peter Owen, 1981.

> A vivid account of sweated labor and the social/economic conditions that forced women to submit to it.

Walkley, Christina and Vanda Foster. *Crinolines and Crimping Irons: Victorian Clothes, How They Were Cleaned and Cared For.* London: Peter Owen, 1978.

> Period methods for washing clothes and lace, cleaning accessories and trims, dealing with men's clothes, stain removal, and storage.

Wallace, Carol McD., et al. *Dance: A Very Social History.* New York: Rizzoli International Publications, 1986.

> Published to accompany a Metropolitan Museum of Art exhibit. Contains four essays on social dance and dance wear from the 18th century well into the 20th.

ANTHOLOGIES OF PICTURES

Period pictures include fashion plates and drawings, mail-order catalogs and excerpts, and photographic portraits. Books containing modern photos of period garments are mostly museum catalogs.

Period pictures

Bloomingdale Brothers. *Bloomingdale's Illustrated 1886 Catalog.* New York: Dover Publications, 1988.

> Reprint showing fashions (mostly women's), dry goods, and housewares.

Blum, Stella, ed. *Ackermann's Costume Plates: Women's Fashions in England, 1818–1828.* New York: Dover Publications, 1978.

Blum, Stella, ed. *Eighteenth-Century French Fashion Plates in Full Color: 64 Engravings from the "Galerie des Modes," 1778–1787.* New York: Dover Publications, 1982.

Blum, Stella, ed. *Everyday Fashions of the Thirties: As Pictured in Sears Catalogs.* New York: Dover Publications, 1986.

Blum, Stella, ed. *Everyday Fashions of the Twenties: As Pictured in Sears and Other Catalogs.* New York: Dover Publications, 1981.

Blum, Stella, ed. *Fashions and Costumes from Godey's Lady's Book.* New York: Dover Publications, 1985.

Blum, Stella, ed. *Paris Fashions of the 1890s.* New York: Dover Publications, 1984.

Blum, Stella, ed. *Victorian Fashions and Costumes from Harper's Bazar: 1867–1898.* New York: Dover Publications, 1974.

> These seven books are anthologies of period fashion plates or catalog illustrations, plus essays on the period's styles.

Bryk, Nancy Villa, ed. *American Dress Pattern Catalogs, 1873–1909.* New York: Dover Publications, 1988.

> Reprints of four complete catalogs plus a short essay.

Cunnington, C. Willett. *English Women's Clothing in the Nineteenth Century.* New York: Dover Publications, 1990.

> Over 400 pages of fashion plates, drawings of garments and hairstyles, and period quotes.

Gernsheim, Alison, ed. *Victorian and Edwardian Fashion: A Photographic Survey.* New York: Dover Publications, 1963.

> Over 230 illustrations, plus fashion history.

Gibbs-Smith, Charles H., ed. *The Fashionable Lady in the 19th Century.* London: HMSO Publications, 1960.

Contains 219 black-and-white fashion plates and cartoons of styles from 1800 to 1900.

Ginsburg, Madeleine, ed. *Victorian Dress in Photographs.* New York: Holmes & Meier, 1983.

Photos of men, women, and children with substantial captions. Introduced with an essay on "clothes in camera."

Ishiyama, Akira, ed. *The Charm of Art Nouveau: Fashion Plates of the Late 19th Century.* Tokyo: Graphic-sha Publishing, 1986.

European fashion plates from 1880 to 1902, all in color. Introduction and captions are in both English and Japanese. Although the plates have no special relationship to Art Nouveau, they are charming.

Jno. J. Mitchell Co. *Men's Fashion Illustrations from the Turn of the Century.* New York: Dover Publications, 1990.

Plates from *The Sartorial Art Journal,* 1900–1910.

Johnson, Judy M., ed. *French Fashion Plates of the Romantic Era in Full Color: 120 Plates from the "Petit Courier des Dames,"* 1830–34. New York: Dover Publications, 1991.

The title says everything, except that there's also a two-page essay on styles and materials.

Jordan, Marsh & Co. *Jordan Marsh Illustrated Catalog of 1891.* New York: Dover Publications, 1991.

Reprint of catalog for women's clothes, fabrics, and trimmings, plus a few men's clothes.

La Barre, Kathleen M. and Kay D. La Barre. *Reference Book of Men's Vintage Clothing 1900–1919.* Portland: La Barre Books, 1992.

La Barre, Kathleen M. and Kay D. La Barre. *Reference Book of Women's Vintage Clothing 1900–1919.* Portland: La Barre Books, 1990.

These two books contain illustrations from fashion magazines pasted up by category—bags, bathing suits, belts, and so on. Alongside runs text that probably summarizes the original descriptions.

Lambert, Miles, ed. *Fashion in Photographs 1860–1880.* London: B. T. Batsford, 1991.

Photos of men, women, and groups from the National Portrait Gallery. Each is captioned with several paragraphs on the subject(s) and his/her/their clothes. The introduction covers the early history of portrait photography.

Lepape, Georges, George Barbier, et al. *French Fashion Plates in Full Color from the Gazette du Bon Ton (1912–1925).* New York: Dover Publications, 1979.

Fifty-eight color plates of designer styles.

Levitt, Sarah, ed. *Fashion in Photographs 1880–1900.* London: B. T. Batsford, 1991.

Has the same format as *Fashion in Photographs 1860–1880.* The introduction covers photographic techniques, social currents, and how society affected dress.

National Cloak & Suit Co. *Women's Fashions of the Early 1900s: An Unabridged Republication of "New York Fashions, 1909."* New York: Dover Publications, 1992.

Reprint of a mail-order catalog showing suits, day and lingerie dresses, wrappers, blouses, skirts, coats, lingerie, and accessories.

Olian, JoAnne, ed. *Authentic French Fashions of the Twenties: 413 Costume Designs from "L'Art et la Mode."* New York: Dover Publications, 1990.

Fashion drawings of women's couture clothes, plus an essay.

Perry, Dame & Co. *Women's and Children's Fashions of 1917: The Complete Perry, Dame & Co. Catalog.* New York: Dover Publications, 1992.

Shows most components of an average woman's wardrobe.

Robinson, Julian. *Fashion in the '30s.* New York: Two Continents Publishing Group, 1978.

Photos and drawings of women's clothes from 1930s fashion magazines.

Rowley, Katrina, ed. *Fashion in Photographs 1900–1920.* London: B. T. Batsford, 1992.

Has the same format as *Fashion in Photographs 1860–1880,* plus an informative introduction.

Modern pictures of period garments

Bradfield, Nancy. *Costume in Detail: Women's Dress 1730–1930.* Boston: Plays Inc., 1983.

Drawings of clothes and accessories with construction details and some measurements.

Byrde, Penelope. *Museum of Costume.* Bath: Museum of Costume, 1984.

Shows displays from one of the great English collections.

Cincinnati Art Museum. *With Grace & Favour: Victorian & Edwardian Fashion in America.*

See under Histories of Specific Periods or Topics.

Coleman, Elizabeth Ann. *Changing Fashions 1800–1970.* New York: Brooklyn Museum, 1972.

Contains 34 photos, 7 in color, of women's garments.

Coleman, Elizabeth Ann. *The Opulent Era.*

See under Histories of Specific Periods or Topics.

Fischbach, Friedrich. *Historic Textile Patterns in Full Color.* New York: Dover Publications, 1992.

Reprint of drawings, some with adapted color schemes, from a late Victorian work. Shows textile patterns from the Middle Ages to the 18th century.

Goldthorpe, Caroline. *From Queen to Empress: Victorian Dress 1837–1877.*

See under Histories of Specific Periods or Topics.

Hornbostel, Wilhelm et al. *Voilà: Glanzstücke Historischer Moden 1750–1960.* Munchen: Prestel-Verlag, 1991.

An exhibit catalog format showing clothes, mostly 1750–1930, with descriptions on opposite pages. In German. The dates and some other identification information are intelligible to English readers.

Kyoto Costume Institute. *Revolution in Fashion 1715–1815.*

See under Histories of Specific Periods or Topics.

Kyoto Costume Institute and Metropolitan Museum of Art. *Evolution of Fashion 1835–1895.* Kyoto Costume Institute and Metropolitan Museum of Art, 1980.

Color photos of women's outfits and undergarments with captions in English and Japanese.

Los Angeles County Museum of Art. *An Elegant Art: Fashion and Fantasy in the Eighteenth Century.*

See under Histories of Specific Periods or Topics.

Rothstein, Natalie, ed. *Four Hundred Years of Fashion.* London: Victoria and Albert Museum, 1984.

Documents the museum's famous collection with photos of men's and women's garments from about 1600 to 1983. Photos are both large and small; some are color. Accompanying text describes how the museum built the collection.

Thieme, Otto Charles. *Simply Stunning: 200 Years of Fashion from the Cincinnati Art Museum.* Cincinnati: Cincinnati Art Museum, 1988.

Color photos of 51 women's outfits from 1770 to 1985.

Tozer, Jane and Sarah Levitt. *Fabric of Society: A Century of People and Their Clothes 1770–1870.* Manchester: City of Manchester Cultural Services, 1983.

Not a history, but a series of short essays on such topics as "the Gent," "love and marriage," and "fine linen." (No, those titles are not the story of someone's engagement.) Many photos of garments and close-ups of fabrics.

Tsukamoto, Koichi, Richard Martin, et al. *The Undercover Story.* Fashion Institute of Technology and Kyoto Costume Institute, 1982.

An exhibit catalog with photos of women's lingerie and some dresses. Mostly Victorian and Edwardian.

Western Reserve Historical Society. *Costume.* Cleveland: Western Reserve Historical Society, 1986.

An exhibit catalog with photos of about 70 women's garments from 1810 to 1968.

WORKS ON PATTERN MAKING AND SEWING

This section lists modern books on flat pattern and other patterning techniques. It also lists modern books containing scale drafts and reprints with scale drafts and/or drafting instructions. Finally it lists sewing, needlework, and millinery manuals, mostly period.

Flat pattern alteration

Alexander, Lyn. *Pattern Designing for Dressmakers.* Denver: Lyn Alexander Designs, 1988.

An introduction to modern flat pattern work with an orientation toward late Victorian/Edwardian styles. For women's or dolls' clothes.

Kopp, Ernestine, Vittorina Rolfo, and Beatrice Zelin. *Designing Apparel Through the Flat Pattern.* New York: Fairchild Publications, 1971.

Kopp, Ernestine, Vittorina Rolfo, and Beatrice Zelin. *New Fashion Areas for Designing Apparel Through the Flat Pattern.* New York: Fairchild Publications, 1972.

These two books are standard garment design texts. They contain step-by-step instructions for designing modern women's styles from a sloper. Techniques can be adapted to historic garments.

Scale drafts and drafting instruction

Andersen, Ellen. *Moden 1790–1840.* Copenhagen: Nationalmuseet, 1986.

Danish history of costume that contains scale drafts, close-ups of period garments, and period illustrations. Worthwhile even if you don't read Danish.

Arnold, Janet. *Patterns of Fashion: The Cut and Construction of Clothes for Men and Women 1560–1620.* New York: Drama Book Publishers, 1985.

Arnold, Janet. *Patterns of Fashion 1: Englishwomen's Dresses and Their Construction 1660–1860.* New York: Drama Book Publishers, 1972.

Arnold, Janet. *Patterns of Fashion 2: Englishwomen's Dresses and Their Construction 1860–1940.* New York: Drama Book Publishers, 1972.

These three books are essentials for the costumer's library. They contain scale drafts of period garments with detailed notes on the original construction. The drawings of garments and details are exquisite. The 1560–1620 volume also has photos.

Bech, Viben. *Moden 1840–1890.* Copenhagen: Nationalmuseet, 1989.

The sequel to Ellen Andersen's *Moden 1790–1840,* with the same format.

Burnham, Dorothy K. *Cut My Cote.* Toronto: Royal Ontario Museum, 1973.

Scale drafts of geometric garments, including chemises and shirts from the 12th through the 19th centuries. A small book, but definitely worth having.

Croonborg, Frederick T. *The Blue Book of Men's Tailoring.* New York: Van Nostrand Reinhold, 1977.

Reprint of a 1907 tailor's drafting manual.

Davis, R. I. *Men's Garments 1830–1900: A Guide to Pattern Cutting.* London: B. T. Batsford, 1989.

Modern scale drafts and drafting instructions.

de Alcega, Juan. *Tailor's Pattern Book.* Carlton: Ruth Bean, 1979.

A facsimile plus English translation of a 1589 tailor's manual. The drafts are not to scale.

Devere, Louis. *The Handbook of Practical Cutting on the Centre Point System.* Mendocino: R. L. Shep, 1986.

Reprint of an 1866 tailor's drafting manual.

Dreher, Denise. *From the Neck Up.*

See under Sewing, Needlework, and Millinery Manuals.

Edson, Doris and Lucy Barton. *Period Patterns.* Boston: Walter H. Baker, 1970.

The companion to *Historic Costume for the Stage.* Contains scale drafts for men's and women's garments from 1575 to 1912, plus some photos. The patterns were taken from original garments or publications, then drawn to standard sizes.

Gehret, Ellen J. *Rural Pennsylvania Clothing.* York: Liberty Cap Books, 1976.

Scale drafts, hand-sewing instructions, and information on materials for colonial clothes.

Giles, Edward B. *The Art of Cutting and History of English Costume.* Mendocino: R. L. Shep, 1987.

Reprint of an 1896 technical history of men's wear from ancient Britain into the 1880s. Includes drafts and drafting instructions from 1589 to 1887.

Gordon, S. S. *Ladies' Tailor-Made Garments.* Berkeley: Lacis Publications, 1993.

Reprint of a 1908 drafting manual.

Hecklinger, Charles. *Dress and Cloak Cutter: Women's Costume 1877–1882.* Mendocino: R. L. Shep, 1987.

Reprint of an 1882 tailor's drafting manual.

Hill, Margot Hamilton and Peter A. Bucknell. *The Evolution of Fashion: Pattern and Cut from 1066 to 1930.* New York: Drama Book Publishers, 1967.

Modern scale drafts for men's and women's outfits. Includes notes on materials and construction. Illustrated by modern costume plates.

Hochfelden, Brigitta and Marie Niedner. *Das Buch der Wäsche.* Hannover: Th. Schafer Druckerei GmbH, 1983.

Reprint of an Edwardian manual on sewing lingerie and household linens. In German. The illustrations and accompanying pattern sheets (with overlapping patterns) are intelligible to English readers.

Hopkins, J. C. *Edwardian Ladies' Tailoring: The Twentieth Century System of Ladies' Garment Cutting.* Mendocino: R. L. Shep, 1990.

Reprint of a 1910 drafting manual.

Hunnisett, Jean. *Period Costume for Stage & Screen: Patterns for Women's Dress 1500–1800.* Studio City: Players Press, 1991.

Hunnisett, Jean. *Period Costume for Stage & Screen: Patterns for Women's Dress 1800–1909.* Studio City: Players Press, 1991.

These two books contain modern scale drafts for foundation garments, lingerie, and clothes. Garment shapes and dates were thoroughly researched. The assembly instructions are terse but valuable. There's also information on what it's like to wear the clothes and how that affects construction.

Jno. J. Mitchell Co. *"Standard" Work on Cutting: A Complete Treatise on the Art and Science of Garment Cutting.* Berkeley: Lacis Publications, 1990.

Reprint of an 1886 tailor's drafting manual.

Kohler, Carl. *A History of Costume.* New York: Dover Publications, 1963.

Reprint of a 1928 book. History of costume from the ancient Egyptians to 1870. Contains scale drafts (though more than one scale is used) for all periods. Beginning in the 11th century, Kohler based some patterns on original garments.

Kyoto Costume Institute. *Revolution in Fashion 1715–1815.*

See under Histories of Specific Periods or Topics.

Lady, A. *The Workwoman's Guide.* Guilford: Opus Publications, 1986.

Reprint of an 1838 manual on cutting out and sewing. Many patterns, mostly for men's and women's undergarments and household linens. Although not to scale they can be drafted easily. Clearly written and organized.

Minister, Edward & Son. *The Complete Guide to Practical Cutting.* Mendocino: R. L. Shep, 1993.

Reprint of an 1853 manual, with drafts for men's and some women's tailored clothes.

Niedner, Marie. *Beyers Grozes Lehrbuch der Wäsche.* Hannover: Th. Schafer Druckerei GmbH, 1983.

Reprint of a 1927 German manual on sewing lingerie and household linens. Illustrations and patterns like those in *Das Buch der Wäsche.*

Niedner, Marie. *Das Buch der Haus-Schneiderei.* Hannover: Th. Schafer Druckerei GmbH, 1983.

Reprint of a 1910 German manual on making everyday women's clothes. Illustrations and patterns like those in *Das Buch der Wäsche.*

Norris, Herbert. *Costume and Fashion Volume Two: Senlac to Bosworth 1066–1485.* London: J. M. Dent and Sons, 1927.

Norris, Herbert. *Costume and Fashion Volume Three: The Tudors Book I 1485–1547.* London: J. M. Dent and Sons, 1938.

Norris, Herbert. *Costume and Fashion Volume Three: The Tudors Book II 1547–1603.* London: J. M. Dent and Sons, 1938.

To my surprise, no one seems to have written an exhaustive, construction-oriented book on medieval dress since these three books were published. On the good side, they contain a great many descriptions, drawings, and diagrams that can be used as drafting guides. On the bad, Norris's historical attitudes and some of his information are antiquated. Until recently his books were available only in libraries. But they've been reprinted in photocopy form by Falconwood Press and are sold by Raiments.

Payne, Blanche. *History of Costume: From the Ancient Egyptians to the Twentieth Century.*

See under Histories of Costume.

Shep, R. L., ed. *Civil War Ladies: Fashions and Needle-Arts of the Early 1860s.* Mendocino: R. L. Shep, 1987.

Engravings, pattern diagrams, needlework projects, and piano music from the 1861 and 1864 issues of *Peterson's Magazine.* Diagrams are not to scale.

Shep, R. L., ed. *Late Georgian Costume.* Mendocino: R. L. Shep, 1991.

Two reprints in one volume. One is a drafting manual, *The Tailor's Friendly Instructor,* written by J. Wyatt in 1822. The other is *The Art of Tying the Cravat,* written by H. LeBlanc (and attributed to Honoré de Balzac) in 1828.

Vincent, W. D. F. *Tailoring of the Belle Epoque: Vincent's Systems of Cutting All Kinds of Tailor-Made Garments.* Mendocino: R. L. Shep, 1991.

Reprint of a 1903 drafting manual.

Waugh, Norah. *Corsets and Crinolines.* New York: Theatre Arts Books, 1970.

Waugh, Norah. *The Cut of Men's Clothes 1600–1900.* New York: Theatre Arts Books, 1964.

Waugh, Norah. *The Cut of Women's Clothes 1600–1930.* New York: Theatre Arts Books, 1968.

These three books contain scale drafts of period garments, period drafts, information on materials and construction, quotes from period sources, and period portraits and fashion plates. They're a must for the costumer's library.

Wright, Merideth. *Put on Thy Beautiful Garments: Rural New England Clothing, 1783–1800.* East Montpelier: The Clothes Press, 1990.

Reprinted by Dover Publications as *Everyday Dress of Rural America, 1783–1800.* Information on materials, scale drafts, and hand-sewing instructions. The patterns are very similar to those in Waugh's, Arnold's, and Burnham's books, plus Kidwell's article on shortgowns in *Dress.*

Other aspects of pattern making

Cassidy, Christine. *Patterntaking.* Sausalito: Christine Cassidy, 1991.

A small book on copying modern garments by the cloth method.

Price, Jeanne and Bernard Zamkoff. *Grading Techniques for Modern Design.* New York: Fairchild Publications, 1974.

How to change a standard modern pattern size to another standard modern pattern size.

Tarrant, Naomi. *Collecting Costume: The Care and Display of Clothes and Accessories.*

See under Books on Collecting and Restoring Vintage Clothes.

Sewing, needlework, and millinery manuals

Ben-Yusuf, Anna. *Edwardian Hats: The Art of Millinery.* Mendocino: R. L. Shep, 1992.

Reprint of a 1909 millinery guide.

Butterick Publishing Co. *The Dressmaker.* New York: Butterick Publishing, 1916.

This Edwardian sewing manual often appears in used costume book dealers' catalogs. I have an almost identical 1911 edition.

Cabrera, Roberto and Patricia Flaherty Myers. *Classic Tailoring Techniques: A Construction Guide for Men's Wear.* New York: Fairchild Publications, 1983.

Cabrera, Roberto and Patricia Flaherty Myers. *Classic Tailoring Techniques: A Construction Guide for Women's Wear.* New York: Fairchild Publications, 1984.

These two books contain information on molding and shaping garments, which can be adapted to period styles.

Caulfeild, S. F. A. *Encylopedia of Victorian Needlework.* New York: Dover Publications, 1972.

Two-volume reprint of an 1887 "dictionary." Contains definitions and instructions for all types of handwork, in alphabetical order.

Coates, Lydia Trattles. *American Dressmaking Step by Step.* New York: Pictorial Review Co., 1917.

Clearly written and cross-referenced between sections. Gives assembly orders for common garments. This is my favorite Edwardian/ragtime manual. It often appears in used costume book dealers' catalogs.

Dreher, Denise. *From the Neck Up: An Illustrated Guide to Hatmaking.*

Minneapolis: Madhatter Press, 1981.

Thorough instruction in millinery techniques plus over 60 modern scale patterns for historic hats.

Hartley, Florence. *The Ladies' Hand Book of Fancy and Ornamental Work.* Mendocino: R. L. Shep, 1991.

Reprint of an 1859 needlework manual.

Ingham, Rosemary and Liz Covey. *The Costumer's Handbook.* Englewood Cliffs: Prentice-Hall, 1980.

Oriented toward theater costumers. Basic sewing techniques and how to adapt modern accessories. A revised edition titled *The Costume Technician's Handbook* has been published by Heinemann Educational Books.

Kaye, Georgina Kerr. *Millinery for Every Woman.* Berkeley: Lacis Publications, 1992.

Reprint of a 1926 millinery guide.

Mansfield, Evelyn A. and Ethel L. Lucas. *Clothing Construction.* Boston: Houghton Mifflin, 1974.

This manual comes from when home dressmakers emulated couture rather than factory techniques. Lots of information on hand sewing and decorative details.

Pullen, Martha. *Antique Clothing: French Sewing by Machine.* Huntsville: Martha Pullen Co., 1990.

An idea book for reproducing Edwardian whites. Contains modern drawings of originals and redrawings of pattern catalog pictures. Somewhat oriented toward transmuting women's designs into little girls'. Gives instructions for lace insertion, pin tucking, and decorative details.

Shep, R. L., ed. *The Ladies' Self Instructor in Millinery and Mantua Making, Embroidery and Appplique, Canvas-Work, Knitting, Netting and Crochet-Work.* Mendocino: R. L. Shep, 1988.

Reprint of an 1853 needlework manual.

Vogue Patterns. *The Vogue Sewing Book.* New York: Butterick Publishing Co., 1975.

I like this manual so much that when my first copy wore out I replaced it with the same edition. However, it's been updated several times since 1975.

Women's Institute of Domestic Arts and Sciences. A dressmaking manual published as a series of booklets with no apparent series title. Several editions, from the 1910s through the 1930s.

BOOKS ON COLLECTING AND RESTORING VINTAGE CLOTHES

Earnshaw, Pat. *The Identification of Lace.* Aylesbury: Shire Publications, 1980.

A small guide that focuses on hand lace from the 17th through the 19th centuries.

Finch, Karen and Greta Putnam. *The Care and Preservation of Textiles.* London: B. T. Batsford, 1985.

Museum techniques for cleaning, mending, display, and storage.

Funaro, Diana. *The Yestermorrow Clothes Book: How to Remodel Secondhand Clothes.* Radnor: Chilton Book Co., 1976.

Step-by-step instructions for altering vintage clothes. Emphasis on 1930s and 40s clothes, and for adapting them to 70s styles.

Ginsburg, Madeleine, ed. *The Illustrated History of Textiles.* New York: Portland House, 1991.

An informative survey of many types of textiles (woven, printed, embroidered, knitted, lace, carpets, tapestries). The buying section is for English collectors.

Haertig, Evelyn. *Antique Combs & Purses.* Carmel: Gallery Graphics Press, 1983.

Haertig, Evelyn. *More Beautiful Purses.* Carmel: Gallery Graphics Press, 1990.

Although these books would benefit from editorial work and more detailed dating information, they contain many beautiful color photos.

Holland, Vyvyan. *Hand Coloured Fashion Plates 1770–1899.*

See under Histories of Specific Periods or Topics.

McCormick, Terry. *The Consumer's Guide to Vintage Clothing.* New York: Dembner Books, 1987.

Practical guide to buying, wearing, and caring for vintage. The most informative and least dated book I've found.

Reigate, Emily. *An Illustrated Guide to Lace.* Woodbridge: Antique Collectors' Club, 1986.

A large guide that focuses on hand lace from the 17th to the early 20th centuries.

Tarrant, Naomi. *Collecting Costume: The Care and Display of Clothes and Accessories.* London: George Allen & Unwin, 1983.

For the serious amateur collector. Chapters on building a collection, storage, cleaning and mending, inventory, dating/identification, display, and research. Includes information on garment copying.

SOURCE BOOKS

Dick, Karen, ed. *The Whole Costumer's Catalogue.* Beallsville: Karen Dick, 1993.

An annual, book-length resource list for historic and other costumers. Reviews include candid opinions. Very valuable. However, listings aren't consistently verified before republication, so some are out of date.

McRae, Bobbi A. *The New Fiberworks Sourcebook.* Austin: Fiberworks Publications, 1993.

Lists almost 1,000 resources for all areas of the fiber arts. An updated edition of *The Fiberworks Sourcebook* and *The Fabric & Fiber Sourcebook.*

✍ BOOK DEALERS

Fortunately there are many excellent dealers in new and used costume books. Most general dealers print several good-sized catalogs a year. Some publishers like to sell directly to the public and some don't. Most of the ones listed here do. But that doesn't mean you shouldn't try to order from others. If they want you to work through a bookstore they'll tell you.

GENERAL NEW AND USED

Amazon Drygoods
See under Reproduction and Restoration Supplies.

Charles B. Wood III
Antiquarian Booksellers
PO Box 2369
Cambridge, MA 02238
(617) 868-1711

Carries some tailoring and costume books. Write for catalog.

Nancy Garcelon
Antiques and Otherwise
10 Hastings Ave.
Millbury, MA 01527
(508) 754-2267

Used books on costume, sewing, knitting, crochet. Some vintage patterns and pattern catalogs. $5 for one year of catalogs.

Fred Struthers
Books on Cloth and Related Subjects
PO Box 2706
Ft. Bragg, CA 95437
(707) 964-8662

New and used books on all areas of costume. Catalog, $2.50.

Campbell's
See under Reproduction and Restoration Supplies.

Clotilde
See under Reproduction and Restoration Supplies.

Drama Books
134 Ninth St.
San Francisco, CA 94103
(415) 255-0604

New books on costume, plus other the-
ater-related subjects. Catalog, $4.50 plus
$1.50 shipping.

Golden Legend, Inc.
7615 Sunset Blvd.
Los Angeles, CA 90046
(213) 850-5520

Out-of-print, rare, and antiquarian the-
ater-related books. Free catalog.

G Street Fabrics
Mail Order Service
12240 Wilkins Ave.
Rockville, MD 20852

Send $5 for a thick printout of new books
on sewing, needlework, and costume.

Joslin Hall Rare Books
PO Box 516
Concord, MA 01742
(508) 371-3101

Books on costume and textiles. Catalog,
$1.

Bette S. Feinstein
Hard-to-Find Needlework Books
96 Roundwood Rd.
Newtown, MA 02164
(617) 969-0942

New and used books on many types of
needlework. Send $1 for catalog.

George Robert Kane Books
252 Third Ave.
Santa Cruz, CA 95062
(408) 426-4133

Used books on costume, textiles, and interior decoration. Free list.

Lacis
See under Reproduction and Restoration
Supplies.

Gloria Montlack
12 Harrow Ln.
Old Bethpage, NY 11804
(516) 249-5632

Used books, including books on costume
and fashion. Free catalog.

Raiments
See under Reproduction and Restoration
Supplies.

The Unicorn
1338 Ross St.
Petaluma, CA 94954
(707) 762-3362
(800) 289-9276

New books on costume, fashion design,
sewing, and fiber arts. Catalog, $2.50.

Lois Mueller
Wooden Porch Books
Route 1, Box 262
Middlebourne, WV 26149
(304) 386-4434

Vintage dressmaking, tailoring, and etiquette books, and modern books on costume and textile arts. Send $3 for the next
three catalogs.

PUBLISHERS

Lyn Alexander Designs
PO Box 8341
Denver, CO 80201

Publishes *Pattern Designing for Dressmakers,*
plus doll patterns.

Art Book Services, Inc.
PO Box 360
Hughsonville, NY 12537
(800) 247-9955

Beautiful books on high-end collectibles,
including lace, textiles, and jewelry. Free
catalog.

B. T. Batsford Ltd.
4 Fitzhardinge St.
London W1H 0AH
England

Publishes a number of books on costume. Service is amazingly rapid. Ordering by credit card avoids currency conversion hassles. Free brochure.

Christine Cassidy
10 Libertyship Way, Suite 152
Sausalito, CA 94965

Publishes *Patterntaking.*

Karen Dick
Box 207, Main Street
Beallsville, PA 15313
(412) 769-3242

In conjunction with many contributors, publishes the *Whole Costumer's Catalogue.*

Dover Publications, Inc.
31 E Second St.
Mineola, NY 11501

Books on clothing and needlework, mostly reprints. Ask for the needlecraft and pictorial archives catalogs. They're free.

Drama Book Publishers
260 Fifth Ave.
New York, NY 10001
(212) 725-5377

Books on costume and theater. Distributes a number of standard English books. Free catalog.

Fiberworks Publications
PO Box 49770
Austin, TX 78765
(512) 454-7160

Publishes fiber arts source books.

Gallery Graphics Press
PO Box 5457
Carmel, CA 93921

Publishes *Antique Combs & Purses* and *More Beautiful Purses.*

Holmes & Meier
30 Irving Pl.
New York, NY 10003

Books on costume history. Free catalog.

La Barre Books
7136 SE 87th
Portland, OR 97266

Anthologies of fashion drawings from period magazines. Free list.

Lacis
See under Reproduction and Restoration Supplies.

Madhatter Press
PO Box 7480
Minneapolis, MN 55407

Publishes *From the Neck Up.*

Players Press, Inc.
PO Box 1132
Studio City, CA 91614

Publishes *Period Costume for Stage & Screen.*

Martha Pullen Co.
See under Reproduction and Restoration Supplies.

R. L. Shep
44473 Fernwood
Box 668
Mendocino, CA 95460
(707) 937-1436

Reprints of dressmaking/tailoring manuals, plus needlework and etiquette books. Free brochure.

✄ PERIODICALS

I don't understand why there aren't more magazines devoted to costuming and/or vintage clothes. Luckily, you can also find information in sewing, antiques, and "country" magazines. My favorites are listed here. Also see the list of organizations. Most publish periodicals for their members.

Many periodicals allow you to subscribe for more or less than a year, at a different subscription rate. Only the basic annual rate is given here. For more information, contact the publisher.

Antiques & Collecting Hobbies
1006 S Michigan Ave.
Chicago, IL 60605
(800) 762-7576
(312) 939-4767 (in Illinois)

A monthly antiques magazine that periodically features articles on vintage clothes and accessories. Subscription, $24.

Antique Trader Weekly
PO Box 1050
Dubuque, IA 52004
(319) 588-2073

A thick weekly newspaper on antiques/collectibles. Includes articles on vintage clothes and textiles, plus ads for all types of collectibles. Subscription, $29.

AntiqueWeek
27 N Jefferson St.
PO Box 90
Knightstown, IN 46148
(800) 876-5133

Weekly newspaper devoted to antiques/collectibles that includes articles on vintage clothes. Two editions, Central (subscription $25.95) and Eastern ($21.95).

Costume
See under Organizations, Costume Collecting and Making.

Costumer's Quarterly
See under Organizations, Costume Collecting and Making.

Country Folk Art
Subscription Dept.
8393 E Holly Rd.
Holly, MI 48442

A "country decorating" magazine that sometimes has articles on vintage clothes, accessories, and lace. Subscription $14.95/year (four issues).

Cutter's Research Journal
USITT
10 W 19th St., Suite 5A
New York, NY 10011

A technical publication on historic and

theater costume. Includes full-size and scale patterns, plus in-depth reviews of patterns published elsewhere. $16/year (four issues).

Dress
See under Organizations, Costume Collecting and Making.

The Lace Collector
The Lace Merchant
PO Box 222
Plainwell, MI 49080
(616) 685-9792

A quarterly newsletter on buying, identifying, repairing, and using antique lace. $20/year. Also sells a catalog of color slides.

The MidAtlantic Antiques Magazine
Henderson Daily Dispatch Co., Inc.
PO Box 908
Henderson, NC 27536
(919) 492-4001

Monthly newspaper devoted to antiques/collectibles that includes articles on vintage clothes. Subscription, $12.

PieceWork
Interweave Press
201 E 4th St.
Loveland, CO 80537
(800) 645-3675

A bimonthly magazine on ethnic and historic textiles, with a mixture of description and small projects. Subscription, $21.

Sew News
1 Fashion Center
PO Box 11291
Des Moines, IA 50340

Monthly magazine that focuses on modern fashions, sewing techniques, and technology. $19.94/year.

Smoke & Fire News
PO Box 166
Grand Rapids, OH 43522
(419) 832-0303

Monthly newspaper listing upcoming

reenactment events for most eras in most parts of the country, plus articles and book reviews. $15/year. Also runs a sutlery specializing in French and Indian War period clothing. Free quarterly catalog.

Threads
The Taunton Press
63 S Main St.
Newtown, CT 06470

Bimonthly magazine that focuses on modern sewing techniques. Occasionally has articles on vintage and theater clothing, and on fiber arts other than sewing. $26/year.

Vintage Fashion and Costume Jewelry
Lucille Tempesta and Davida Baron
PO Box 265
Glen Oaks, NY 11004
(718) 969-2320
(718) 939-3095

Quarterly newsletter on vintage costume jewelry. $15/year.

✄ REPRODUCTION AND RESTORATION SUPPLIES

Regular fabric stores abound. But most cater to modern fashion sewers. This section lists sources for historic patterns, natural-fiber trims and fabrics, hard-to-find notions, and professional sewing tools. It also includes conservation supplies.

Janet Burgess
Amazon Drygoods
2218 E 11th St.
Davenport, IA 52803
(319) 322-6800
(309) 786-3504
(800) 798-7979 (orders only)

Supplies and books for reproductions, ready-made reproductions, and accessories. General catalog, $3. Pattern catalog, $7. Shoe catalog, $5.

Angelsea
PO Box 4586
Stockton, CA 95204
(209) 948-8428

Antique-looking ribbons in silk and silk-alikes, brocades, velvet, and grosgrain. Catalog with some pictures and swatches, $3.

Baer Fabrics
515 E Market St.
Louisville, KY 40202
(502) 583-5521

Large store that carries fabrics, trims, and costume shop supplies. For swatching service, please be specific about the desired color, fiber, and texture.

Samuel Bauer & Sons, Inc.
135 W 29th St.
New York, NY 10001
(800) 762-2837

Professional supplies for working with fur. Free catalog.

Britex Fabrics
146 Geary St., 147 Maiden Ln.
San Francisco, CA 94108
(415) 392-2910

A huge store that carries high-quality, natural-fiber fabrics. Send $5 for their swatching service. Explain what you want and any price restrictions.

Campbell's
PO Box 400
Gratz, PA 17030

Send $5 for catalog of several hundred historic and ethnic patterns, plus extensive book selection.

Cherish
PO Box 941
New York, NY 10024

Conservation supplies, including a range of padded hangers. Free list.

Clotilde
1909 SW First Ave.
Fort Lauderdale, FL 33315
(305) 761-8655
(800) 772-2891 (order line)

Carries an enormous selection of sewing gadgets. Also books on quilting, machine embroidery, and other special techniques. Free catalog.

Conservation Resources International
8000-H Forbes Pl.
Springfield, VA 22151
(703) 321-7730

Acid-free tissue and boxes.

The Costume Connection, Inc.
PO Box 4518
Falls Church, VA 22044
(703) 354-7711
(703) 237-1373

Distributes Medieval Miscellanea patterns. These are men's and women's patterns, with multiple "views," for styles from 650 to 1610, plus headwear and purses. Catalog, $1.50.

Dixie Gun Works, Inc.
See under Reproduction Clothes, Accessories, and Weapons.

Elsie's Exquisiques
513 Broadway
Niles, MI 49120
(616) 684-7034
(800) 742-SILK (orders)

Victorianesque braids, trims, silk ribbons, and ribbon roses. Say explictly you want to buy retail. Catalog, $5.

Harriet Engler Tailoring and Custom Sewing
See under Reproduction Clothes, Accessories, and Weapons.

Victoria Faye
PO Box 640
Folsom, CA 95763
(916) 983-2321

Heirloom sewing supplies—lace trims and motifs, embroidery, ribbons, and silk fabrics. $5 for catalog, $2.50 for ribbon color guide.

Folkwear
The Taunton Press
63 S Main St.
PO Box 5506
Newtown, CT 06470
(800) 888-8286

Send $3 for catalog of historic and ethnic patterns.

Greenberg & Hammer, Inc.
24 W 57th St.
New York, NY 10019
(212) 246-2835
(800) 955-5135

Boning, busks, hoop wire, millinery wire, interfacings, and professional sewing supplies. Free catalog.

Heidi's Pages and Petticoats
810 El Caminito
Livermore, CA 94550

Women's and men's patterns for the Civil War era, plus some reproduction accessories. Send $3 for catalog.

Hollinger Corp.
PO Box 8360
Fredericksburg, VA 22404
(800) 643-0491

Acid-free tissue and boxes.

Kannik's Korner
PO Box 1654
Springfield, OH 45501
(513) 325-8385

Sells an 18th-century chemise pattern and a booklet on hand sewing. Also makes custom reproductions.

Lacis
2982 Adeline St.
Berkeley, CA 94703
(510) 843-7178

Books, patterns, and reproduction supplies. General and pattern catalog, $1. Book catalog, $4.

Ladish Pearl Button Co.
1601 E Central
Wichita, KS 67214

Unused vintage mother-of-pearl buttons. Send $1 for information and samples.

Ledgewood Studio
6000 Ledgewood Dr.
Forest Park, GA 30050
(404) 361-6098

Fine, mostly narrow cotton and cotton/rayon laces. Suitable for Victorian and Edwardian reproductions. Catalog, $2.

Light Impressions
Box 940
Rochester, NY 14603
(800) 828-6216

Acid-free tissue and textile storage boxes. Free catalog.

Mary Ellen & Co.
29400 Rankert Rd.
N Liberty, IN 46554
(219) 656-3000
(800) 669-1860

Patterns, books, and accessories for period living.

Northern Society of Costume and Textiles
c/o Bolling Hall Museum
Bowling Hall Rd.
Bradford, West Yorks, BD4 7LP
England

Patterns of period garments, including a dress that belonged to Charlotte Bronte and a French working-class dress of 1789.

Old World Enterprises
29036 Kepler Ct.
Cold Spring, MN 56320

Over 30 patterns for men and women, from 1805 to the 1890s. Send $2 for catalog.

Ornamental Resources, Inc.
1427 Miner St.
Box 3010
Idaho Springs, CO 80452
(303) 279-2102

Focuses on jewelry supplies and beads. Also carries sew-on jewels and some hat-pins, tassels, and miscellaneous items. Many vintage materials. Large catalog with bimonthly supplements, $25.

Past Patterns
PO Box 7587
Grand Rapids, MI 49510
(616) 245-9456

Patterns for the 1830s to the 1930s. Catalog, $3. Also copies of patterns from 1900 to 1950 in original sizes. Selected Attic Copies catalog (1900–1949), $4.25. Teens Attic Copies catalog, $3. Twenties Attic Copies catalog, $3.

Period Impressions
1320 Dale Dr.
Lexington, KY 40517

Men's and women's patterns from the 18th century through the 1880s, mostly for the Civil War and Revolutionary eras. Catalog, $2.

Martha Pullen Co.
518 Madison St.
Huntsville, AL 35801
(205) 533-9586

Fine laces suitable for Edwardian reproductions.

Janet Wilson Anderson
Raiments
PO Box 6176
Fullerton, CA 92634
(818) 791-9195

Catalog of reproduction patterns, books, and some supplies, $5.

Richard the Thread
8320 Melrose Ave., #201
Los Angeles, CA 90069
(213) 852-4997
(800) 748-5830

Costuming supplies, including professional sewing supplies, dyes, sew-on jewels, and a line of historic patterns. Free color catalog.

Rocking Horse Farm
PO Box 735
Chardon, OH 44024

Men's and women's patterns, from the periods 1740–1820 and 1880–1950. Catalog, $2.

Kathleen B. Smith & Co. Textile Reproductions
PO Box 48
West Chesterfield, MA 01084
(413) 296-4437

Supplies and books for 18th-century reproductions. Send $3 for catalog, additional $12 for swatch book.

Smoke & Fire Co.
See under Periodicals.

Talas
213 W 35th
New York, NY 10001
(212) 736-7744

Catalog of conservation supplies, $5.

Emile L. Thomas, Jr.
G. F. Thomas cleaners
859 14th St.
San Francisco, CA 94114
(415) 861-0969

Experienced in hand cleaning antique garments. Will clean by mail. Specify hand cleaning, the garment's age, and (if possible) cause of stains.

Jas. Townsend & Son, Inc.
See under Reproduction Clothes, Accessories, and Weapons.

University Products
Catalog Dept.
PO Box 101
Holyoke, MA 01041
(800) 336-4847

Free catalog of conservation supplies.

Leslie Walstrom
6136 Wrigley Way
Fort Worth, TX 76133

Sells period sewing patterns and plans to publish reprints.

Maurie Welsh
211 Read Ave.
Crestwood, NY 10707
(914) 793-2138

Vintage lace fabric and trim (mostly machine); collars, cuffs, etc.; and woven fabric. From 1900 through the 1950s. Also wedding and party clothes for women, mostly 1890–1930. Has several lists costing $1–$3; contact for information. Requires full prepayment.

✍ REPRODUCTION CLOTHES, ACCESSORIES, AND WEAPONS

Even if you're an accomplished sewer there will be things you can't make—or don't have time to. And some items, such as weapons, wigs, and living goods, are usually made by specialists. So here are sources for ready-made and custom reproductions. Many also sell reproduction supplies.

Amazon Drygoods
See under Reproduction and Restoration Supplies.

J. S. Schroter
Antique Arms
PO Box 10794
Costa Mesa, CA 92627

Period weapons; transferring emphasis from swords to firearms. Catalog, $3.

Buffalo Enterprises
308 W King St.
PO Box 183
East Berlin, PA 17316
(717) 259-9081

Reproductions of 18th-century clothes and shoes, for men and women. Also a variety of living goods. Some Civil War style items. Catalog, $4.

Circa Costumes Corp.
PO Box 654
Rockville Centre, NY 11571
(516) 536-7990

Reproductions of mid 19th-century everyday clothes. Free catalog.

Rod Casteel
Colonial Armory
106 Lynnbrook
Eugene, OR 97404
(503) 688-0607

Custom makes a wide variety of swords and daggers, at several grades and price ranges. Illustrated catalog, $2.

Charles Childs
County Cloth
13797-C Georgetown St., NE
Paris, OH 44669
(216) 862-3307

Reproductions of garments for the Confederate enlisted man. Catalog, $3.

Dixie Gun Works, Inc.
PO Box 130
Gunpowder Ln.
Union City, TN 38261
(800) 238-6785 (orders only)

Send $4 for Sears-sized illustrated catalog of black powder guns, antique gun parts, shooting supplies, and related books. Also carries regimental buttons and other reproduction supplies.

Deborah Jarrett
The 18th-Century Seamstress
1475 Sumneytown Pike
Harleysville, PA 19438
(215) 287-6939

Carries men's, women's, and children's garments. Send SASE for illustrated price list.

Susan K. Elseth
See under Vintage Clothes and Accessories, Mail-Order Dealers.

Harriet Engler Tailoring and Custom Sewing
PO Box 1363

Winchester, VA 22601
(703) 667-2541

Patterns and custom-made 19th-century reproductions. Send $7 for adult catalog, $3 for children's.

The Hat/Cap Exchange
PO Box 377
Betterton, MD 21610
(410) 348-2244

A branch of Hatcrafters (see below).

Hatcrafters, Inc.
20 N Springfield Rd.
Clifton Heights, PA 19018
(215) 623-2620

Felt hats for many eras, with minimal trimmings. Emphasis on men's and military hats. Two illustrated catalogs, for Hatcrafters and the Hat/Cap Exchange, $5.

His Lady and the Soldier Sutlery
851 Kaypat Dr.
Hope, MI 48628
(517) 435-3518

Natural-looking synthetic hairpieces and wigs. For 18th- and 19th-century hairstyles. Send $2 for catalog.

Karalee Tearney
La Pelleterie
Highway 41 N
PO Box 127
Arrow Rock, MO 65320
(816) 837-3261

Custom-made clothes and accessories for the Revolutionary War period, in settler and Native American styles. Leather a specialty. Catalog, $5.

Legendary Arms, Inc.
PO Box 20198
Greeley Square Station
New York, NY 10001

Large selection of weapons from many eras, plus a few shields and uniforms. Color catalog, $5.

Museum Replicas Ltd.
2143 Gees Mill Rd.
Box 840
Conyers, GA 30707
(800) 241-3664

Arms and armor from the Viking period to the French and Indian War. Catalog, $2.

Joseph S. Covais
New Columbia
PO Box 524
Charleston, IL 61920
(217) 348-5927

Reproductions of 19th-century American clothes, mostly military uniforms. Catalog, $3.75.

Rocky Mountain Mercantile
Box 31241
Aurora, CO 80041

Simple custom-made clothes, accessories, and living goods for the Civil War era. Catalog, $2.

G. Gedney Godwin
Sutler of Mount Misery
2139 Welsh Valley Rd.
Valley Forge, PA 19481
(215) 783-0670

Supplies, many hand crafted, for the American Revolutionary War period. Firearms, swords, camping equipment, men's and women's clothes, and shoes. Catalog, $4.95.

Jas. Townsend & Son, Inc.
133 N First St.
PO Box 415
Pierceton, IN 46562
(219) 594-5580

Supplies for the Revolutionary War period. Men's and women's clothes, accessories, jewelry, books, patterns, sewing supplies, and around-the-campfire gear. Free catalog.

✈ VINTAGE CLOTHES AND ACCESSORIES

I've bought from most of these mail-order dealers and keep in touch with the rest. All sell on approval or have a fair return policy. Some also have stores and/or sell at shows.

Vintage clothing shows are my favorite buying venue because the selection is incredible. Most managers hold several shows a year in different geographic areas. Ask for this year's calendar.

I like auctions less because they're a gamble. But many people love them for exactly that reason. The large auction houses listed can send you a calendar and auction catalogs.

MAIL-ORDER DEALERS

Mary Ann McClelland
The Antiquarian/Mail-Order Memories
800 1/2 Pontiac St.
Rochester, IN 46975
(219) 223-5339

Women's 19th- and early 20th-century clothes and accessories. Sells on approval.

Charlotte Dart
Barb's Vintage Rose
927 Massachusetts St.
Lawrence, KS 66044
(913) 841-2451

Women's and men's clothes and accessories, 1890–1950. Sells on approval.

Veronica Trainer
Bayhouse
PO Box 40443
Bay Village, OH 44140
(216) 871-8584

Beaded and metal mesh purses. Payment in advance. Illustrated catalog, $3.

Barbara Pare
Bird 'n Hand
123 Nagonoba
PO Box 813
Northport, MI 49670
(616) 386-7104

Specializes in women's hats, mostly

1890s–1920s, many retrimmed. Also carries clothes. Requires 50 percent deposit or credit card number.

Barbara Bulla, Antiques
6330 King Mountain Rd.
Asheboro, NC 27203
(919) 381-3554

Women's clothes from 1910 to 1930. Also accessories, buttons, trims, and cosmetics containers. Sells on approval with 50 percent deposit.

Lynell Schwartz
The Curiosity Shop
PO Box 964
Cheshire, CT 06410
(203) 271-0643

Catalog of beaded and metal mesh purses, and catalog of costume jewelry. $3 each. Requires full prepayment.

Susan K. Elseth
9574 Landbreeze Row
Columbia, MD 21045
(410) 964-0872

Women's clothes, Victorian–1920s. Also custom reproductions of vintage hats. Send SASE for list. Sells on approval. Requires $50 deposit from first-time customers.

Caralee Smith
Fashions of Yesteryear
11424 Northview Dr.
Aledo, TX 76008
(817) 560-4372

Women's and men's clothes and accessories, 1880s–1940s. Contact with want list. Sells on approval; requires a $50 deposit from first-time customers.

Pat Stephens and Pat O'Brien
Flapper Alley Ltd.
1518 N Farwell
Milwaukee, WI 53202
(414) 276-6252

Victorian–1940s clothes and accessories. Also large selection of antique buttons. Send want list. Requires full prepayment from new customers.

Judy Herscovitch
The Gallery of Costume
5 Hillhouse Rd.
Winnipeg, Manitoba
Canada R2V 2W1
(204) 338-8877
(204) 586-2222

Clothes and accessories, mostly Victorian–1920s. Women's clothes and a smaller but reasonable selection of men's. Illustrated catalog, $4. Prepayment required. Visa is accepted and convenient for international orders.

Pahaka
19 Fox Hill
Upper Saddle River, NJ 07458
(201) 327-1464

Women's and men's vintage clothes, mostly 1900–1940. Some laces and accessories. Send wants with SASE. Requires 50 percent deposit for an approval box.

Joanne Haug
Reflections of the Past
PO Box 40361
Bay Village, OH 44140
(216) 835-6924

Clothes and accessories, mostly women's and from the early 19th through the early 20th centuries. More collectibles than wearables. Also lace and small textiles, some very old. Illustrated catalog, $4 ($5 in Canada). Requires full prepayment.

Susan and Suzanne
Suzi's Antiques, Inc.
235 N Main St.
Farmville, VA 23901
(804) 392-4655

Women's and men's clothes and accessories. Mostly 1860–1920. Sends list and photos if possible. Requires a deposit or full prepayment.

Priscilla Washco
The Victorian Lady
102 S Main St.
PO Box 424
Waxhaw, NC 28173

(704) 843-2917
(704) 843-4467
(800) 786-1886

Small accessories, needlework tools, cosmetics containers, mirrors, and other dresser items. 1880–1950. Catalog, $3. Requires full prepayment.

Nancy L. Haugh
Victorian Whites
7 Winterbrook Ct.
York Village, ME 03909
(207) 363-8111

Edwardian white lingerie and dresses, 1920–1940 party dresses and lingerie, accessories, linens, lace, and trims. Send LSASE for brochure listing general types and $1 apiece for photos. Requires full prepayment.

Art and Janene Fawcett
Vintage Silhouettes
1301 Pomona St.
Crockett, CA 94525
(510) 787-7274

Victorian–1950s clothes and accessories, for men and women. Sells on approval. Requires a credit card number for security.

Lindy Moore
Vintage Vogue
1301 Pomona St.
Crockett, CA 94525
(510) 787-2260

Victorian–1950s clothes and accessories. Sells on approval. Requires a credit card number for security.

Maurie Welsh
See under Reproduction and Restoration Supplies.

Elaine Wilmarth
5715 Sir Galahad Rd.
Glenn Dale, MD 20769
(301) 464-1567

Edwardian whites and linens. Sends photos or drawings. Prepayment required.

AUCTIONS AND EXPOSITIONS

Barrows Show Promotional, Ltd.
PO Box 141
Portland, CT 06480
(203) 342-2540

Holds three vintage clothing shows a year in West Hartford, Connecticut.

Jack Black Enterprises
PO Box 61172
Phoenix, AZ 85082
(602) 943-1766
(800) 678-9987

Holds an annual show in Phoenix, Arizona.

Butterfield West
164 Utah St.
San Francisco, CA 94103
(415) 861-7500

Holds about one auction a year that consists largely of vintage clothes. Allows absentee bids. Prices available by touch-tone phone after the sale.

Caddigan Auctioneers, Inc.
1130 Washington St. (Rt. 53)
Hanover, MA 02339
(617) 826-8648

Holds auctions of vintage clothes, accessories, and textiles.

Caskey Lees
PO Box 1637
Topanga, CA 90290
(310) 455-2886

Holds shows featuring textiles, costumes, and clothes in Southern California.

Christie's East
219 E 67th St.
New York, NY 10021
(212) 606-0400

Holds auctions, which include vintage clothes, in New York and London. Accepts mail bids.

Creative Management Productions
Box 343

Holt, MI 48842
(517) 676-2079

Holds several large Midwestern antiques/
collectibles shows that include textiles,
quilts, and vintage clothes.

Molly Turner
Molly's Vintage Promotions
194 Amity St.
Amherst, MA 01002
(413) 549-6446

Holds four vintage clothing shows a year,
two in Massachusetts and two in New
York. Also publishes a quarterly newsletter,
the *Vintage Gazette;* subscription $10.

Nadia Professional Management
PO Box 156
Flourtown, PA 19034
(215) 643-1396

Holds about 2 vintage clothing and 24
general antique shows per year.

Somewhere in Time Promotions
PO Box 88892
Seattle, WA 98138
(206) 848-5420

Holds two vintage clothing shows a year,
in Seattle.

Joan Tramontano
Stella Show Management Co.
163 Terrace St.
Haworth, NJ 07641
(201) 384-0010

Holds 14 antiques fairs a year, 5 of which
include vintage clothes, in New York and
New Jersey.

Vintage Expositions
PO Box 391
Alamo, CA 94507
(510) 653-1087

Holds about five vintage clothing shows a
year in California. Joining their Federation
of Vintage Fashion ($10) gets you two
show tickets for the price of one and a
quarterly newsletter, *Vintage!*.

The Young Management Co.
PO Box 1538
Waterbury, CT 06721
(203) 758-3880

Holds 2 shows a year that focus on vintage
clothes, plus 11 others.

❧ ORGANIZATIONS

Organizations offer events, meetings, group
outings, and information sharing. If an organization has no chapter in your area you can
probably start one. And some organizations
are worth joining for their publications.

Different membership dues may be
charged for students, seniors, couples, businesses, or institutions. Only basic individual
dues are given here. Contact the organization
for more information.

COSTUME COLLECTING AND MAKING

California Purse Collectors Club
PO Box 572
Campbell, CA 95009
(408) 866-6250

Holds bimonthly meetings and publishes a
newsletter. Membership, $20.

Anne Brogden
Membership Secretary
The Costume Society
63 Salisbury Rd.
Garston, Liverpool L19 OPH
England

Publishes an annual journal, *Costume,* and
some books. Has meetings, trips to
exhibits, etc. (in England). Worth joining
for the journal. Membership is £17 for
"overseas ordinary members."

The Costume Society of America
55 Edgewater Dr.
PO Box 73
Earleville, MD 21919
(410) 275-2329

Publishes an annual journal, *Dress,* a
national newsletter, *CSA News,* and

regional newsletters. Organizes meetings, talks, and trips to exhibits. There are eight regional chapters. Membership is $55.

Bruce MacDermott
Greater Bay Area Costumers Guild
(Dreamers of Decadence)
2801 Ashby Ave.
Berkeley, CA 94705
(415) 469-7602
(415) 864-5511
(510) 486-8232

A chapter of the International Costumer's Guild. Puts on costume events and workshops. Members receive a monthly newsletter, *The Costumer's Scribe,* as well as the *Costumer's Quarterly.* Membership, which includes membership in the ICG, is $20.

Institute of Textiles and Needle Arts
Newbury College
129 Fisher Ave.
Brookline, MA 02146
(617) 730-7067

Holds an annual summer workshop that focuses largely on historic topics. In past years these have included history of costume, clothing restoration, lace identification, Victorian pattern making, and Hollywood costumes.

Lillian Baker
International Club for Collectors of Hatpins and Hatpin Holders
15237 Chanera Ave.
Gardena, CA 90249
(310) 329-2619

Holds biannual conventions. Publishes the *Pictorial Journal* annually and the *Points* newsletter monthly. Membership, $35.

Debbie Jones
Corresponding Secretary
International Costumer's Guild
144 Arona St.
St. Paul, MN 55108

An organization for historic and science fiction costuming. Publishes the *Costumer's Quarterly* (nonmember subscription $10) and sponsors an annual CostumeCon.

There are 16 regional chapters, who have their own events and publications. Dues vary with the chapter.

Lois Pool
Secretary
National Button Society
2733 Juno Pl.
Akron, OH 44333

Publishes five annual national bulletins and holds shows. Membership is $15.

REENACTMENT/LIVING HISTORY

James Flack
Membership Director
Art Deco Society of California
Shell Building
100 Bush St., Suite 511
San Francisco, CA 94104
(415) 982-DECO

Holds events that focus on 1920s–40s fashions and culture. Publishes a quarterly magazine, the *Sophisticate,* and monthly mailers on events. Membership is $45.

Bay Area English Regency Society (BAERS)
See under Vintage Dance, Organizations and Events.

Georgian Society
See under Vintage Dance, Organizations and Events.

Greater Bay Area Costumers Guild
See under Costume Collecting and Making.

Barry Wells
Membership Director
Living History Association
PO Box 578
Wilmington, VT 05363
(802) 464-5569
(802) 464-0535

Covers reenactments of all time periods. Membership, $15. Publishes a quarterly newsletter, *Living Historian.* Nonmember subscription, $8.

Robert Fox
Medieval Studies and Restorations
133-33 120th St.
South Ozone Park, NY 11420
(212) 848-3364

Recreates the spirit and times of the high Middle Ages.

Midwest Open Air Museums
Coordinating Council
c/o Judith Sheridan
8774 Rt. 45 NW
North Bloomfield, OH 44450
(216) 685-4410

A professional organization for people interested in interpreting history, including administrators, interpreters, curators, historians, and reenactors. Publishes the *Midwest Open Air Museums Magazine.* Membership is $15.

National Civil War Association
PO Box 70084
Sunnyvale, CA 94086
(408) 927-7651

Holds battle reenactments, encampments, and other events. Publishes a newsletter, the *Dispatch.* Membership is $30.

Society for Creative Anachronism
PO Box 360743
Milpitas, CA 95036
(408) 263-9305

Holds Middle Ages and Renaissance reenactments. Has chapters all over the U.S. and in some other countries. Publishes *Tournaments Illuminated,* chapter newsletters, and the Compleat Anachronist pamphlet series. Membership is $25.

Mary Hafner-Laney
Membership Secretary
Somewhere in Time, Unlimited
22107 103rd Pl. NE
Kent, WA 98031
(206) 852-1760

Has parties in costume, including vintage dances. Publishes a newsletter five times a year. Membership is $5.

VINTAGE DANCE

This section lists organizations that give vintage dances to which historic costume is worn. It also lists teachers who can help you prepare for them. You don't have to be registered at a university or in a performing group to take their classes.

Organizations and events

Art Deco Society of California
See under Reenactment/Living History.

Alan Winston
Bay Area English Regency Society (BAERS)
380 Curtner, Apt. 7
Palo Alto, CA 94306
(415) 856-2259

Gives "Regency" dance lessons and balls. The dances are simplified English country dances rather than authentic Regency.

Country Dance and Song Society of America
12 New South St.
Northampton, MA 01060
(413) 584-9913

A national organization that promotes the teaching of English country dance. Contact them for the name of your regional chapter. Some chapters have annual Playford balls for which baroque or Regency costume is appropriate.

Elaine Pelz
Friends of the English Regency
15931 Kalisher St.
Granada Hills, CA 91344
(818) 366-3827

Similar to the Bay Area English Regency Society.

Linda Peterson
The Georgian Society
PO Box 4234
Albuquerque, NM 87196

Similar to the Bay Area English Regency Society.

Hilary Powers
Gaskell Occasional Dance Society
(510) 834-1066

Gives a bimontly Victorian ball in Oakland, CA.

James and Cathleen Myers
Period Events and Entertainments
Recreation Society (PEERS)
949 E St., Apt. 3
Belmont, CA 94002
(415) 593-2940

Holds bimonthly balls in the San Francisco Bay Area. Concentrates (but not exclusively) on Victorian and early 20th century.

Somewhere in Time, Unlimited
See under Reenactment/Living History.

Instruction

Jim X. Borzym
American Vernacular Dance
2221 Columbine Ave.
Boulder, CO 80302
(303) 449-5962

Holds ragtime classes and events.

Desmond Strobel
Antique Academy of Genteel Dance
6350 Deep Dell Pl.
Hollywood, CA 90068
(213) 469-0267

Teaches dance from late baroque through 1920s in local classes and workshops around the country. Also holds balls.

Thomas Baird
850 Amsterdam Ave., #6F
New York, NY 10025
(212) 932-0694

Teaches baroque dance.

Cincinnati Court Dancers
PO Box 23320
Cincinnati, OH 45223
(513) 281-7039

Holds local Renaissance workshops and

balls. Send $5 to subscribe to their newsletter, *Variations.*

Carol Teten
Dance Through Time
50 Oak St., Suite 501
San Francisco, CA 94102
(415) 621-3627

Teaches local classes and workshops around the country. Specializes in 19th-century and ragtime dance.

Angene Feves
70 Karol Ln.
Pleasant Hill, CA 94532
(510) 943-1356

Teaches Renaissance and baroque dance in private lessons, public classes, and workshops around the country.

Flying Cloud Academy of Vintage Dance
PO Box 862
Cincinnati, OH 45201
(513) 733-3077

Holds an annual one-week workshop, plus events throughout the year. Send $6 to subscribe to their newsletter, the *Flying Cloud Gazette.*

Randy Lumb
Friends of Traditional Dance
PO Box 64
Fort Collins, CO 80522
(303) 493-8277

Holds classes in Victorian and early 20th-century dance. Also two Viennese balls and two or three big band swing dances per year.

Wendy Hilton
330 W 28th St., Apt. 18E
New York, NY 10001
(212) 727-2098

Teaches baroque dance to advanced students in private or open classes.

Elizabeth Aldrich and Charles Garth
Historical Dance Foundation, Inc.
31 Union Square W, Suite 15-D
New York, NY 10003

(212) 255-5545

The directors hold an annual two-week workshop for periods from Renaissance through 1920s. They also teach at workshops around the country.

Walter and Nancyanna Dill
Living Traditions
2442 NW Market St., #168
Seattle, WA 98107
(206) 781-1238

Teach 1880s–1920s dances, plus 30s–50s swing, lindy, and fox-trot. Hold quarterly special events with guest instructors.

Stan Isaacs and Karen Kalinsky
The Pomander Club
210 E Meadow Dr.
Palo Alto, CA 94306
(415) 856-8044

Hold weekly classes in vintage dance from authentic Regency through 1920s. Also a monthly ragtime–1920s ball. Act as dance masters for balls held by other organizations.

Richard Powers
c/o Dance Division
Stanford University
375 Santa Teresa Ave.
Stanford, CA 94305
(415) 723-1234

Teaches dance, mostly Victorian and early 20th century, and organizes workshops and events.

Patri Pugliese and Hannah Artuso
39 Capen St.
Medford, MA 02155
(617) 396-2870

Teach 19th-century and ragtime dance. Also sell photocopies of original dance manuals from the early 18th through the early 20th centuries.

Dance Division
Stanford University
375 Santa Teresa Ave.
Stanford, CA 94305
(415) 723-1234

In some years, holds a one-week workshop focusing on a range of periods. Also gives an annual ragtime ball.

Department of Music
Braun Music Center
Stanford University
Stanford, CA 94305
(415) 723-3811

Holds an annual two-week baroque dance workshop, with classes for all levels.

Robert Morris and Katherine Terzi
Steppin' Out
86 E Stewart Ave.
Lansdowne, PA 19050
(215) 259-1642

Teach Victorian and ragtime dance. Also sell vintage clothes at dance workshops and events.

Marc Casslar
Vintage Dance Society
PO Box 832
Bloomfield, CT 06002
(203) 286-9191

Teaches dances from 1840 to 1925, holds period dance events, and organizes them for others. Publishes a newsletter, *The Society Page;* subscription $5.

Paige Whitley-Baugess
713 Pollock St.
New Bern, NC 28562
(919) 636-0476

Teaches baroque dance.

Metric Conversion Table

This table is at the back of the book so you can refer to it while reading any chapter. It contains the English and metric equivalents of measurements often used in sewing. It also defines a few archaic units you'll see in old sources. Numbers running to several decimal places and (usually) fractions under 1/16 in. have been rounded for easy use.

English measurement	Metric equivalent	Metric measurement	English equivalent
1/8 in.	3.2 mm	1 mm	1/32 in.
1/4 in.	6.4 mm	2 mm	1/16 in.
3/8 in.	9.5 mm	3 mm	1/8 in.
1/2 in.	1.3 cm	4 mm	5/32 in.
5/8 in.	1.6 cm	5 mm	7/32 in.
3/4 in.	1.9 cm	6 mm	1/4 in.
7/8 in.	2.2 cm	7 mm	9/32 in.
1 in.	2.5 cm	8 mm	5/16 in.
1 1/4 in.	3.2 cm	9 mm	11/32 in.
1 1/2 in.	3.8 cm	10 mm (1 cm)	13/32 in.
1 3/4 in.	4.4 cm	2 cm	3/4 in.
2 in.	5.1 cm	3 cm	1 3/16 in.
2 1/4 in. (1 nail)	5.7 cm	4 cm	1 9/16 in.
2 1/2 in.	6.4 cm	5 cm	2 in.
2 3/4 in.	7.0 cm	6 cm	2 3/8 in.
3 in.	7.6 cm	7 cm	2 3/4 in.
3 1/4 in.	8.3 cm	8 cm	3 1/8 in.
3 1/2 in.	8.9 cm	9 cm	3 1/2 in.
3 3/4 in.	9.5 cm	10 cm	3 15/16 in.
4 in.	10.2 cm	15 cm	5 7/8 in.
4 1/2 in.	11.4 cm	20 cm	7 7/8 in.
5 in.	12.7 cm	25 cm	9 13/16 in.
5 1/2 in.	14.0 cm	30 cm	11 13/16 in.
6 in.	15.2 cm	35 cm	13 3/4 in.
6 1/2 in.	16.5 cm	40 cm	15 3/4 in.

English measurement	Metric equivalent	Metric measurement	English equivalent
7 in.	178 cm	45 cm	17 11/16 in.
7 1/2 in.	19.1 cm	50 cm	19 11/16 in.
8 in.	20.3 cm	55 cm	21 5/8 in.
8 1/2 in.	21.6 cm	60 cm	23 5/8 in.
9 in. (1/4 yd.)	22.9 cm	65 cm	25 9/16 in.
9 1/2 in.	24.1 cm	70 cm	27 9/16 in.
10 in.	25.4 cm	75 cm	29 1/2 in.
10 1/2 in.	26.7 cm	80 cm	31 1/2 in.
11 in.	27.9 cm	85 cm	33 7/16 in.
11 1/2 in.	29.2 cm	90 cm	35 7/16 in.
12 in. (1 ft.)	30.5 cm	95 cm	37 3/8 in.
1/2 yd. (18 in.)	45.7 cm	100 cm (1 m)	39 3/8 in.
3/4 yd. (27 in.)	68.6 cm		
1 yd. (36 in.)	91.4 cm		
1 English ell (45 in.)	114.3 cm		

The old Dutch or Flemish ell was about 27 in. (68.6 cm), and the old Scotch ell about 37 in. (94 cm).

Afterword

Future editions of this book will be updated as I research more techniques and discover more sources. You are invited to contribute information. Although I can't guarantee inclusion in the resource appendix, I welcome announcements of new businesses and address/policy changes in old ones.

Index

pressing
    vintage clothes, 198–199, 202
    while sewing, 134–135
purses
    buying, 192
    conditioning, 247
    storing, 206–207
    styles, 32, 56

R

reproductions. *See* costumes
robes, 14
ruffs, 18–21, 32, 123

S

sack coats, 33, 40, 46, 51
scale patterns. *See under* patterns
seams
    altering, 252–254, 286–287, 293–295
    finishing, 114–116
        binding, 115–116
        clipping, 114
        flat–fell, 115–116
        french, 115–116
        french whipped, 115–116
        grading, 114–115
        mock french, 115–116
        notching, 114–115
        overcasting, 115, 214–215
        topstitching, 116
        trimming, 114
    mending, 221–224
    piping, 132–134
    stay stitching, 112–113
    unpicking, 222
shawls, 32, 39, 78
shirts
    altering, 262–264
    drafting, 177–179
    mending, 226
    styles, 3, 18, 30, 35, 40, 45–46, 51, 53,
        167, 201
    wearing, 201
shoes. *See* footwear
silverfish, 207
skirt lifters, 203–204
skirts

altering waist
    letting out, 273–275
    taking in, 275–276
    waistband, 276–279
lengthening
    with border, 270–271
    with false hem, 271–272
    with flounce, 272
    under flounce, 272
shortening
    above flounce, 267–268
    hemming, 265–266
    tucking, 269
    from waist, 266–267
sleeves
    enlarging underarms, 258–259
    fitting to wrist, 256
    lengthening
        blouse, 258
        under cuffs, 292
        with cuffs, 290–291
    shortening
        cuffed jacket, 288–289
        cuffed shirt, 263–264
        decorated, 256–257
        lace, 257–258
    taking in, 293
slips
    altering neckline, 251–252
    altering shoulders, 280
    separating, 281–283
    See also bodices; skirts
snaps, 218
stains
    covering, 224–228
    evaluating, 190–191
    removing, 197–198, 213, 245
stay stitching, 112–113
stockings
    buying, 192
    styles, 18, 23, 39, 48, 55
suits
    men's
        American Revolution, 22–23, 25
        Art Deco, 51–52
        buying, 42
        Civil War, 33–34
        Elizabethan, 17–19
        Gay Nineties, 40–41
        ragtime, 45–47

About the Author

Frances Grimble has collected, restored, and reproduced historic clothes since 1972. She owns over 650 original garments and accessories dating from the 1810s to the 1930s. Ms. Grimble has read extensively on the history of costume; her library includes over 700 related books. After receiving her B.A. in history, she graduated from the UC Berkeley publishing program. She has also taken formal courses in clothing design, sewing, and textile arts.

Ms. Grimble has done folk and historic dance since 1974. She currently concentrates on historic dance including Renaissance, baroque, Regency, Victorian, ragtime, and 1920s. When attending events, she wears appropriate reproductions or vintage clothes.

Ms. Grimble has been a professional writer and editor since 1983. Over 50 of her articles on vintage clothes have appeared in national magazines, including *Threads, Sew News, Vintage Fashions, Antique Trader Weekly, Americana,* and many others. She has considerable experience in writing how-to material, having coauthored the *dBASE IV User's Instant Reference* and been the sole author of four book-length computer manuals. In her most recent in-house position, she was a project editor for a computer book publisher. She currently works as a freelance writer in San Francisco, California.

About the Artist

Deborah Kuhn combines professional illustration experience with a thorough understanding of costume construction. Since completing her art studies in 1974, she has done fashion illustration for clients that include Nordstrom and Folkwear. In 1989 she entered a college apparel design program. She spent two years studying design, pattern making, and construction. This led to work in the Seattle Opera costume shop. Ms. Kuhn lives in Seattle, Washington, where she continues both aspects of her career.

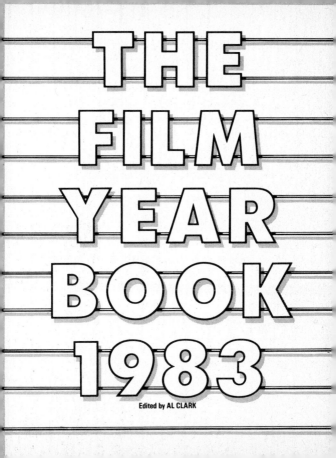

THE FILM YEAR BOOK 1983

Edited by AL CLARK

COVER & BOOK DESIGN BY
JOHN GORDON

ASSISTED BY   AND   SUB EDITORS   AND
MANDY OLLIS · GILLIAN SERMON · CATHERINE CARDWELL · CAT LEDGER

FIRST PUBLISHED IN GREAT BRITAIN IN 1982 BY
VIRGIN BOOKS LTD, 61-63 PORTOBELLO ROAD, LONDON W11 3DD

FIRST EVERGREEN EDITION PUBLISHED IN 1983
ISBN: 0-394-62465-3

PRINTED IN THE UNITED STATES OF AMERICA

GROVE PRESS, INC., 196 WEST HOUSTON STREET, NEW YORK, N.Y. 10014

ACKNOWLEDGEMENTS

FOR THEIR HELP IN SUPPLYING PICTURES AND INFORMATION, MANY THANKS TO THE FOLLOWING FILM
DISTRIBUTORS, PRODUCTION COMPANIES, PUBLICITY FIRMS, ARCHIVES AND PUBLICATIONS, AND
PARTICULARLY TO THE INDIVIDUALS WITHIN THEM WHO SET THINGS IN MOTION: ALPHA, AMANDA,
AMBASSADOR, ARTIFICIAL EYE, BARBER INTERNATIONAL, BAVARIA ATELIER, BLUE DOLPHIN, BORDEAUX,
BRENT WALKER, BRITISH FILM INSTITUTE, CANNON, CINEGATE, COLUMBIA, CONNOISSEUR, CONTEMPORARY,
CURZON, DENNIS DAVIDSON ASSOCIATES, EAGLE, EMI, ENTERPRISE, ENTERTAINMENT, EVENT, FACELIFT,
FILMWAYS, FLASHBACKS, GALA, GTO, HANDMADE, ITC, JAC PUBLICITY, JAY JAY, JOEL FINLER COLLECTION,
THE KOBAL COLLECTION, LONDON INTERNATIONAL, LORIMAR, MAINLINE, MGM, MICHAEL WHITE LTD, MIKE
WHEELER ASSOCIATES, MIRACLE, MOON PICTURES, NEW REALM, OSIRIS, THE OTHER CINEMA, PARAMOUNT,
PIC PUBLICITY, PRODUCTION ASSOCIATES, RALLY, RANK, REBEL, ROGERS & COWAN, ROSIER PICTURES,
SCREEN INTERNATIONAL, SOREN FISHER ASSOCIATES, TIGON, 20TH CENTURY FOX, TWIN CONTINENTAL, UIP,
UNITED ARTISTS, UNIVERSAL, WALT DISNEY PRODUCTIONS AND WARNER BROTHERS.

THANKS ALSO TO JOHN WALKER, STEVE GRANT, CHRIS PEACHMENT AND GIOVANNI DADOMO, WHO
PROVIDED EMERGENCY SUPPORT AT A MOMENT'S NOTICE, AND TO TONY CRAWLEY, WHOSE ADVICE WAS
ALWAYS EITHER USEFUL OR ENTERTAINING; SOMETIMES BOTH. THERE WERE NUMEROUS OTHERS WHOM I
PROBABLY BORED INTO SOMETHING RESEMBLING A CATATONIC TRANCE AT ONE STAGE OR ANOTHER
DURING THE FIVE HUNDRED YEARS OR SO THAT I SPENT ON THE JOB. THEIR PATIENCE IS REMEMBERED,
EVEN IF THEIR NAMES AREN'T.

DEE THORNE WAS INDISPENSABLE THROUGHOUT IT ALL: PHOTO RESEARCH, TYPING, CO-ORDINATING,
PHONE CALLS THAT PESTERED, PERSUADED, BULLIED AND CAJOLED. MARY VOLK HELPED FOR AS LONG AS
SHE COULD STAND IT. ROB MACKIE DID SOME VALUABLE SUPPLEMENTARY SUBBING. NO THANKS AT ALL TO
THE MISGUIDED PEDANT WHO CHANGED *VICTOR/VICTORIA* (RIGHT) TO *VICTOR, VICTORIA* (WRONG)
THROUGHOUT PAGES 104 AND 105.

FINALLY AT THE RISK OF SOUNDING LIKE MICHAEL PARKINSON, I WOULD LIKE TO DEDICATE THIS BOOK TO
THE TWO PEPE DÁVILAS, WHO RAN THE CINE CORRALES AND GAVE ME MY FIRST TASTE OF FILMS. THEY
DIDN'T KNOW WHAT THEY WERE LETTING THEMSELVES IN FOR; BUT THEN, NEITHER DID I.   A.C.

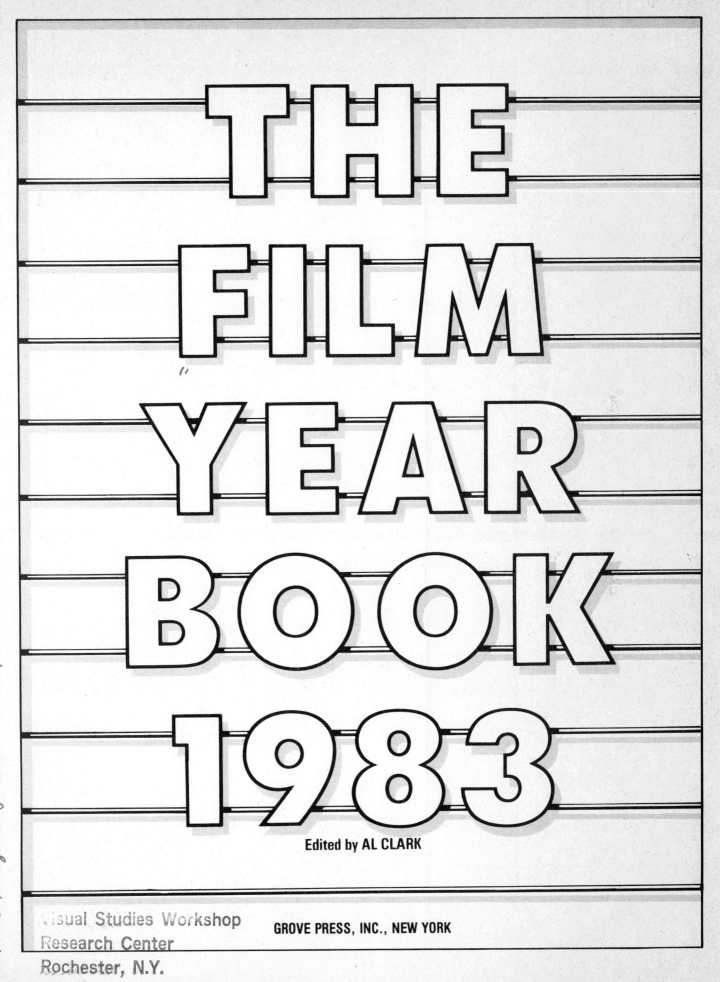

THE FILM YEAR BOOK 1983

Edited by AL CLARK

GROVE PRESS, INC., NEW YORK

EDITOR

AL CLARK IS THE AUTHOR OF *RAYMOND CHANDLER IN HOLLYWOOD*.
HE SEES TOO MANY FILMS FOR COMFORT AND WRITES ABOUT THEM WHEN DUTY OR INCLINATION CALLS.

CONTRIBUTORS

TONY CRAWLEY, AUTHOR OF *THE FILMS OF SOPHIA LOREN*, *BEBÉ: THE FILMS OF BRIGITTE BARDOT* AND THE NEW AMERICAN BOOK, *SCREEN DREAMS: THE HOLLYWOOD PIN-UP*, HAS WRITTEN ON FILMS FOR PUBLICATIONS THROUGHOUT THE WORLD. HE NOW LIVES IN FRANCE, FROM WHERE HE CONTINUES TO CONTRIBUTE TO PERIODICALS AS DIVERSE AS *CLUB INTERNATIONAL*, *RITZ*, AND THE *SUNDAY TELEGRAPH MAGAZINE*, AS WELL AS BEING FOREIGN EDITOR OF *STARBURST* AND *CINEMA*.

RAYMOND DURGNAT TEACHES FILM HISTORY AND THEORY IN THE DEPARTMENT OF CULTURAL HISTORY AT THE ROYAL COLLEGE OF ART IN LONDON. HIS BOOKS ON FILM INCLUDE *FILMS AND FEELINGS*, *THE CRAZY MIRROR*, *THE STRANGE CASE OF ALFRED HITCHCOCK*, *JEAN RENOIR*, *LUIS BUNUEL*, *FRANJU*, *DURGNAT ON FILM*. HE WRITES FOR *FILMS ON SCREEN AND VIDEO*, *PRIMETIME*, *STUDIO INTERNATIONAL*, AND *THE QUARTERLY REVIEW OF FILM STUDIES*.

DAVID EHRENSTEIN IS THE FILM EDITOR OF THE *LOS ANGELES READER*. HE HAS CONTRIBUTED TO THE *VILLAGE VOICE*, *ROLLING STONE*, *CAHIERS DU CINEMA*, *FILM CULTURE*, *FILM COMMENT*, *FILM QUARTERLY*, *DECEMBER*, AND THE ANTHOLOGIES *JEAN-LUC GODARD* AND *THE NEW AMERICAN CINEMA*. HE IS ALSO THE CO-AUTHOR, WITH BILL REED, OF *ROCK ON FILM*.

QUENTIN FALK IS THE CO-EDITOR OF THE TRADE MAGAZINE *SCREEN INTERNATIONAL*. A CONTRIBUTOR TO THE ANTHOLOGY *ANATOMY OF THE MOVIES*, HE ALSO WRITES FOR *SIGHT AND SOUND* AND THE LONDON *STANDARD*, AND DISCUSSES FILMS ON BBC, LBC AND CAPITAL RADIO.

JON STEPHEN FINK, SOURED BY THE PARANOID SILENCE WHICH GREETED PUBLICATION OF HIS BOOK *CLUCK!* HAS TURNED HIS BACK ON LITERATURE. HE HAS SINCE FOUND A NICHE AS A SCREENWRITER IN HOLLYWOOD.

BJ FRANKLIN HAS BEEN THE HOLLYWOOD-BASED AMERICAN EDITOR OF *SCREEN INTERNATIONAL* SINCE 1978. AFTER A SUCCESSFUL CAREER AS A MODEL AND TV HOSTESS, SHE ENTERED JOURNALISM AS ASSOCIATE EDITOR OF *ADWEEK* (THEN CALLED *MAC*), THE WEST COAST'S LEADING ADVERTISING PAPER, BEFORE BECOMING EDITOR OF THE *HOLLYWOOD REPORTER*.

ADRIAN HODGES IS A FILM WRITER AND TV EDITOR WITH *SCREEN INTERNATIONAL*, AND IS THE VIDEO CORRESPONDENT OF *THE SUN*. HE HAS CONTRIBUTED TO NUMEROUS NEWSPAPERS AND MAGAZINES, AND IS CURRENTLY WRITING A BOOK ABOUT THE VIDEO MARKET.

DAVID McGILLIVRAY HAS, SINCE 1970, WRITTEN AND APPEARED IN 16 FILMS, THE BEST KNOWN OF WHICH ARE *HOUSE OF WHIPCORD* AND *FRIGHTMARE*. HE ALSO DABBLES IN OTHER BRANCHES OF THE MEDIA, NOTABLY RADIO (OVER 600 BROADCASTS SINCE 1973) AND THEATRE (HE RUNS THE TOURING COMPANY *ENTERTAINMENT MACHINE*). HE IS THE AUTHOR OF *THE HISTORY OF BRITISH SEX MOVIES 1957-1981*.

DAVE MARSH WAS A FOUNDING EDITOR OF *CREEM*, A MUSIC CRITIC AT *NEWSDAY* AND AN EDITOR AT *THE REAL PAPER* IN BOSTON BEFORE JOINING *ROLLING STONE* AS AN ASSOCIATE EDITOR IN 1975. HIS BOOKS INCLUDE *ELVIS*, *BORN TO RUN: THE BRUCE SPRINGSTEEN STORY*, *THE BOOK OF ROCK LISTS* AND *THE ROLLING STONE RECORD GUIDE*.

MYRON MEISEL IS A LOS ANGELES-BASED PRODUCER, WRÍTER AND LAWYER. HE PRODUCED *I'M A STRANGER HERE MYSELF: A PORTRAIT OF NICHOLAS RAY* AND *FINAL EXAM*, AND WAS ASSOCIATE PRODUCER OF *TOUCH-ME-NOT*. A MEMBER OF THE NATIONAL SOCIETY OF FILM CRITICS, HE HAS WRITTEN ON FILM AND THE MOVIE INDUSTRY FOR MANY PERIODICALS, INCLUDING *ROLLING STONE*, *FILM COMMENT* AND *AMERICAN FILM*.

BART MILLS WRITES ABOUT FILMS AND TELEVISION FROM HOLLYWOOD FOR SUCH PUBLICATIONS AS *THE GUARDIAN*, THE *LOS ANGELES TIMES* AND *AMERICAN FILM*. HIS SURVEY OF THE UNITED STATES CULTURAL SCENE *KEEPING PEOPLE STUPID* WILL BE PUBLISHED NEXT YEAR.

CHRIS PEACHMENT IS THE FILM EDITOR OF *EVENT*. HE HAS WRITTEN FOR *TIME OUT* AND HAS WORKED AS A FEATURE WRITER ON A MIDDLE-EASTERN JOURNAL.

DILYS POWELL WAS THE FILM CRITIC OF THE *SUNDAY TIMES* FROM 1939-1976, AND HAS SINCE WRITTEN FOR THE SAME NEWSPAPER ABOUT FILMS ON TELEVISION. SHE IS ALSO THE FILM CRITIC OF *PUNCH*, A FREQUENT BROADCASTER AND THE AUTHOR OF SEVERAL BOOKS ABOUT GREECE.

MIKE SARNE IS A FREQUENT CONTRIBUTOR TO FILM MAGAZINES AND LECTURES ON FILM AND THE VISUAL ARTS. HE IS ALSO A FILM-MAKER (*JOANNA*, *MYRA BRECKINRIDGE*, *VERA VERÃO*), ACTOR, SINGER, COMPOSER AND PHOTOGRAPHER. IN THE THEATRE HE HAS PRODUCED FOR THE WEST END AS WELL AS THE FRINGE AND MAKES PERIODIC FORAYS INTO OTHER RELATED AREAS.

ANDREW SARRIS IS FILM CRITIC AND SENIOR EDITOR OF THE *VILLAGE VOICE* IN NEW YORK. HE IS THE AUTHOR OF *THE FILMS OF JOSEF VON STERNBERG*, *THE AMERICAN CINEMA*, *CONFESSIONS OF A CULTIST*, *THE PRIMAL SCREEN*, *THE JOHN FORD MOVIE MYSTERY*, AND, MOST RECENTLY, *POLITICS AND CINEMA*. HE HAS BEEN REVIEWING MOVIES FOR A QUARTER OF A CENTURY.

PAUL TAYLOR IS A LONDON-BASED FREELANCE WRITER AND RESEARCHER ON FILM, TELEVISION AND FOOTBALL, CONTRIBUTING REGULARLY TO *TIME OUT*, *MONTHLY FILM BULLETIN* AND OTHER PUBLICATIONS. A FORMER FILM PROGRAMMER AT LONDON'S ICA CINEMA AND BIRMINGHAM ARTS LAB, HE WRITES SCRIPTS FOR SCOTTISH TELEVISION'S *FESTIVAL CINEMA* PROGRAMME.

COLIN VAINES IS A REPORTER AND FEATURE WRITER WITH *SCREEN INTERNATIONAL*. A CONTRIBUTOR TO THE ANTHOLOGY *ANATOMY OF THE MOVIES*, HE WRITES FOR SEVERAL FILM MAGAZINES — INCLUDING *PHOTOPLAY*, *BIOGRAPH* AND *MOVIE STAR* — AND ALSO BROADCASTS ON RADIO LONDON.

JOHN WALKER CAN BE GLIMPSED BRIEFLY AND BULKILY IN THE BOB DYLAN DOCUMENTARY *DON'T LOOK BACK*, MAKING ONE OF THE FILM'S MOST PERTINENT COMMENTS, "WHY?", A QUESTION HE HAS GONE ON ASKING EVER SINCE. A FORMER FEATURES EDITOR AND SHOWBUSINESS EDITOR OF *THE MAIL ON SUNDAY*, HE HAS WORKED AS A FILM AND THEATRE CRITIC FOR BRITISH AND AMERICAN NEWSPAPERS AND MAGAZINES.

CONTENTS

THE FILMS

by *Al Clark*

Like the book in general, this covers the year between **July 1 1981** and **June 30 1982** and, excepting re-issues and 16mm movies, chronicles all the feature films released in the United Kingdom during this time. With a few notable discrepancies (*Fort Apache the Bronx*, released in the US before the period documented here, falls well within it in the UK, while with *Chariots of Fire* and *Gregory's Girl* the position is reversed, which explains their absence), most major films open in both countries within the same year. Some American movies take their time in crossing the ocean. Others — more than ever before, it would seem — are considered "unsuitable" for British audiences and are never shown in the UK. These are listed separately at the end of the section.

Abbreviations used are as follows: *dir* director *pro* producer *exec pro* executive producer *scr* screenplay *ph* director of photography *ed* editor *pro des* production designer *art dir* art director *cert* British Board of Film Censors certificate. The others are self-explanatory. The production company and UK distributor of each film are in brackets after the title. Many of the principal distributors have amalgamated to form British distribution outlets such as Columbia-EMI-Warner and UIP, which represents Universal, Paramount, MGM and United Artists. To avoid confusion for American readers, the individual company concerned is named whenever possible.

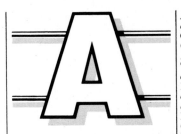

ABSENCE OF MALICE (Mirage Enterprises/Columbia)
dir-pro Sydney Pollack *exec pro* Ronald L. Schwary *scr* Kurt Luedtke *ph* Owen Roizman, in DeLuxe colour *ed* Sheldon Kahn *pro des* Terence March *music* Dave Grusin *r time* 116 mins *cert* A *UK opening* Feb 25.
cast Paul Newman, Sally Field, Bob Balaban, Melinda Dillon, Luther Adler, Barry Primus, Josef Sommer, John Harkins, Don Hood, Wilford Brimley, Arnie Ross, Anna Marie Napotes, Shelley Spurlock, Shawn McAllister, Joe Petrullo, Rooney Kerwin, Oswaldo Calvo, Clardy Malugen, Sharon Anderson, Jody Wilson, Ilse Earl, Alfredo Alvarez Colderon, Pat Sullivan, Bill Hindman, John Archie, Timothy Hawkins, Ricardo Marquez, Patricia Matzdorff, Diane Zolten, Kathy Suergiu, Jeff Gillen, Ted Bartsch, Sugar Ray Mann, Richard O'Feldman, Chuck Lupo, John DiSanti, Laurie V. Logan, Jack McDermott, Mark Harris, Bobbie-Ellyne Kosstrin, Lynn Parraga, Lee Sandman, Barry Hober, Gary Van Auken.

Worthy, entertaining, impeccably liberal but ultimately unpersuasive power-of-the-press saga which examines journalistic ethics, the destructiveness of inadequate research and the dangers of speculative publication. Sally Field, excessively cute, is the ambitious Miami reporter whose appetite for a story exceeds her good sense. Paul Newman, effectively virtuous, is the honest liquor merchant at the receiving end of a planted report about the murder of a local union leader. The soiled (but just about to be laundered) singlet under 'All The President's Men'.

ABSOLUTION (Bulldog/Enterprise)
dir Anthony Page *pro* Danny O'Donovan, Elliott Kastner *exec pro* George Pappas, Alan Cluer *scr* Anthony Shaffer *ph* John Coquillon, in Technicolor *ed* John Victor Smith *pro des* Natasha Kroll *music* Stanley Myers *r time* 95 mins *cert* X *UK opening* Nov 5.
cast Richard Burton, Dominic Guard, Dai Bradley, Andrew Keir, Billy Connolly, Willoughby Gray, Hilda Fenemore, Sharon Duce, Hilary Mason, Robert Addie, Trevor Martin, Robin Soans, Preston Lockwood, James Ottaway, Brook Williams, Jon Plowman, Brian Glover, Dan Meaden, Kevin Hart, Philip Leake, Michael Crompton, Andrew Boxer, Charles Rigby, Richard Willis, Michael Bell, Michael Parkhouse, Martin Stringer, Richard Kates, Francis Fry, Martyn Hesford, Julian Firth, Clive Gehle, Tim Short.

Three years on the shelf, and available as a video cassette suspiciously soon after its theatrical release, this lame dog of a murder mystery has Richard Burton, who had just cast off his robes following the disastrous 'Exorcist II', as a teacher-priest at a Catholic public school who goes through all kinds of ecclesiastical torment after giving absolution to (he thinks) a bright, mischievous boy he favours who seems to be going off the rails in a serious way. Literally scripted, and full of showy narrative tricks, it still manages to work itself up into a fair old lather without ever persuading the audience that it should do likewise.

ALLIGATOR (Group 1/Alpha)
dir Lewis Teague *pro* Brandon Chase *scr* John Sayles *ph* Joseph Mangine, in DeLuxe colour *ed* Larry Bock, Ronald Medico *art dir* Michael Erler *music* Craig Hundley *r time* 91 mins *cert* AA *UK opening* Feb 11.
cast Robert Forster, Robin Riker, Michael Gazzo, Dean Jagger, Sidney Lassick, Jack Carter, Perry Lang, Henry Silva, Bart Braverman, John Lisbon Wood, James Ingersoll, Robert Doyle, Patti Jerome, Angel Tompkins, Sue Lyon, Leslie Brown, Buckley Norris, Royce D. Applegate, Tom Kindle, Jim Brockett, Simmy Bow, Jim Boeke, Stan Haze, James Arone, Peter Miller, Pat Petersen, Micol, Frederick Long, Ed Brodow, Larry

Margo, Philip Luther, John F. Goff, Elizabeth Halsey, Barry Chase, Richard Partlow, Jeradio de Cordovier, Dick Richards, Vincent de Stefano, Jo Jo D'Amore, Bella Buck, Kendall Carly Browne, Danny Baseda, Tink Williams, Corky Ford, Charles R. Penland, Anita Keith, Michael Mazurki, Margaret Muse, Michael Misita, Harold Greene, Margie Platt, Nike Zachmanoglou, Gloria Morrison.

Part ecology tract, part political metaphor, but mainly a brisk and funny exploitation thriller about a pet alligator, flushed down the toilet as a baby, who, nourished into a colossus by scoffing anyone who comes into view while it prowls undiscerningly around the sewers, goes on the rampage both below and above ground level. John Sayles, tongue very confidently in cheek after his witty 'Piranha' script, hardly puts a foot wrong, even if he does leave several of his characters literally legless.

ALTERED STATES (Warner)
dir Ken Russell *pro* Howard Gottfried *exec pro* Daniel Melnick *scr* Sidney Aaron, from the novel by Paddy Chayevsky *ph* Jordan Cronenweth in Technicolor *ed* Eric Jenkins *pro des* Richard McDonald *music* John Corigliano *r time* 102 mins *cert* X *UK opening* Jul 9.
cast William Hurt, Blair Brown, Bob Balaban, Charles Haid, Thaao Penghlis, Miguel Godreau, Dori Brenner, Peter Brandon, Charles White Eagle, Drew Barrymore, Megan Jeffers, Jack Murdock, Frank McCarthy, Deborah Baltzell, Evan Richards, Hap Lawrence, John Walter Davis, Cynthia Burr, Susan Bredhoff, John Larroquette, George Gaynes, Ora Rubinstein, Paul Larson, Eric Forst, Adriana Shaw, Martin Fiscoe, Olivia Michelle.

A pretentious, protracted bad trip of a film in which research scientist

William Hurt goes ape (literally) as his experiments in regression, with the help of magic mushrooms and an isolation tank, go wrong. This is all tarted up in a characteristically numbing and excessive style by Russell and his special effects team, and compounded by a great deal of jargon and waffle. For chemically-aided late night shows only.

AMERICAN POP (Columbia)
dir-pro Ralph Bakshi, Martin Ransohoff *exec pro* Richard R. St Johns, Maggie Abbott *scr* Ronni Kern *ph* Frances Grumman, in colour *ed* David Ramirez *music* Lee Holdridge *r time* 96 mins *cert* AA *UK opening* Aug 20.

Spanning four generations of Russian immigrants, not to mention the history of American popular music and the appropriate social backdrop for each period, Bakshi can hardly be accused of allowing the problems of animation to discourage his ambitious intentions. Whether or not a ponderous, would-be naturalistic epic is a suitable vehicle for the cartoon form is another matter.

AMERICAN RASPBERRY
(Chartwell/Cannon)
(US TITLE: PRIME TIME)
dir Bradley R. Swirnoff *pro* Marc Trabulus *exec pro* Robin French *scr* Stephen Feinberg, John Baskin, Roger Schulman, Bradley R. Swirnoff *ph* Matthew Leonetti, in Metrocolor *ed* Geoff Rowland *art dir* Dan Lomino *music* Ken Lauber *r time* 64 mins *cert* X *UK opening* Apr 18.
cast Paul Ainsley, Wil Albert, Royce D. Applegate, Meredith Baer, Gene Borkan, Jordan Brian, Bumper, Marianne Bunch, Twinkie Caplan, Mel Carter, Joanna Cassidy, Dort Clark, Katherine Dunfee Clark, Beatrice Colen, Dee Cooper, Ken Davitian, Hal K. Dawson, Susan Doukas, Fred Dryer, Murphy Dunne, John Fain, Laura Fanning, Art Fleming, Aaron Fletcher, Connie Fox, Fred Franklyn, Dick Frattali, Kinky Friedman, Ben Frommer, Stephen Furst, George Furth, Mousie Garner, Larry Gelman, Gertrude Graner, Bradley Greene, Laurence Haddon, Mary Hamill, Sandy Helberg, Basil Hoffman, Peter Kastner, Rosanne Katon, Suzanne Kent, Carl La Fong, Hap Lawrence, Carole Mallory, Arvid Malnaa, James McCabe, Ira Miller, Marvin Miller, Bret Morrison, Micky Morton, Craig Richard Nelson, Warren Oates, Maria O'Brian, Jack O'Leary, Ken Olfson, Dick O'Neil, Nancy Parsons.

Gossamer-flimsy, four-year-old amalgam of inferior parody, advertising breaks and miscellaneous TV trivia. Old hat, utterly pointless in that the medium it seeks to deflate is its own best showcase, it is almost entirely devoid of anything which might recommend it.

AN AMERICAN WEREWOLF IN LONDON (Polygram/Barber International)
dir-scr John Landis *pro* George Folsey Jr. *exec pro* Peter Guber, Jon Peters *ph* Robert Paynter, in Technicolor *ed* Malcolm Campbell *art dir* Leslie Dilley *music* Elmer Bernstein *r time* 98 mins *cert* X *UK opening* Nov 12.
cast David Naughton, Jenny Agutter, Griffin Dunne, John Woodvine, Brian Glover, Lila Kaye, David Schofield, Paul Kember, Frank Oz, Don McKillop, Joe Belcher, Paddy Ryan, Rik Mayall, Sean Baker, Anne-Marie Davies, Colin Fernandes, Albert Moses, Kermit the Frog, Miss Piggy, Michele Brisigotti, Mark Fisher, Gordon Sterne, Paula Jacobs, Claudine Bowyer, Johanna Crayden, Nina Carter, Geoffrey Burridge, Brenda Cavendish, Christopher Scoular, Mary Tempest, Cynthia Powell, Sydney Bromley, Frank Singuineau, Will Leighton, Michael Carter, Elizabeth Bradley, Rufus Deakin, Lesley Ward, George Hilsdon, Gerry Lewis, Dennis Fraser, Alan Ford, Peter Ellis, Denise Stephens, Christine Hargreaves, Brenda Bristols, Lance Boyle, Chris Bailey, Georgia Bailey, Linzi Drew, Lucienne Morgan, Gypsy Dave Cooper, Susan Spencer, Bob Babenia, Ken Sicklen, John Salthouse, John Altman, Keith Hodiak, John Owens, Roger Rowland.

Beginning with some amusing, leisurely scene setting in a Transylvania-like English North Country — where the eponymous hero and his friend are attacked by some unspecified monster on the moors — and moving to London, where he discovers the irreversible truth about his condition (full moon equals lycanthropic rampage), this witty, stylish, enjoyable film is a rare species in itself: a horror movie which mixes traditional virtues with knowing humour and gets it right.

AMIN — THE RISE AND FALL
(Intermedia/Twin Continental)
dir-pro Sharad Patel *scr* Wade Huie *ph* Harvey Harrison, in Technicolor *ed* Keith Palmer *art dir* David Minty *music* Christopher Gunning *r time* 101 mins *cert* X *UK opening* Sept 3.
cast Joseph Olita, Geoffrey Keen, Denis Hills, Leonard Trolley, Andre Maranne, Diane Mercer, Tony Sibbald, Thomas Baptiste, Louis Mahoney, Ka Vundla, Sophie Kind, Marlene

Dogherty, Martin Okello, Nicky Giles, Anne Wanjuga, Norbert Okare, Fred Ynanga, Victor Riitho, June Kikumu, Roy Leask.

Brisk, crude but efficient chronicle of Idi Amin's seven-year reign of terror in Uganda, which began as a big party and ended as a catalogue of murder and mutilation, with a creditable (and credible) performance from Amin lookalike Joseph Olita amidst all the predictable carnage.

ARTHUR (Orion/Warner)
dir-scr Steve Gordon *pro* Robert Greenhut *exec pro* Charles H. Joffe *ph* Fred Schuler, in Technicolor *ed* Susan E Morse *pro des* Stephen Hendrickson *music* Burt Bacharach *r time* 97 mins *cert* AA *UK opening* Dec 17.
cast Dudley Moore, Liza Minnelli, John Gielgud, Geraldine Fitzgerald, Jill Eikenberry, Stephen Elliot, Ted Ross, Barney Martin, Thomas Barbour, Anne De Salvo, Marjorie Barnes, Dillon Evans, Maurice Copeland, Justine Johnson, Paul Vincent, Mary Alan Hokanson, Paul Gleason, Phyllis Somerville, Irving Metzman, Joe Doolan, John Doolan, Melissa Ballan, Florence Tarlow, Lou Jacobi, Gordon Press, Bob Maroff, Marcella Lowry, Jerome Collamore, Mark Fleischman, Helen Hanft, John Bentley, Raymond Serra, Peter Evans, Dominic Guastaferro, Phil Oxman, Richard Hamilton, George Riddle, Lawrence Tierney, Bobo Lewis, B. Constance Barry, Kurt Schlesinger.

Transparently thin, eye-washingly sentimental, intermittently funny and, by the end, thoroughly charming

Left: An American Werewolf in London. Above: Amin — The Rise and Fall

comedy about a drunken, retarded millionaire playboy (Dudley Moore, relying heavily on his routines), engaged to an heiress, who risks disinheritance when he falls for poor-girl Liza Minnelli. Despite its general patchiness and a massively overrated performance by John Gielgud as the plummy, acidic valet who favours the stagey epigram, it is a film, like 'Heaven Can Wait' and 'Bronco Billy', which has you coming out believing that the world is a funny place and people are good. Even if it is easier when you're rich.

THE AVIATOR'S WIFE (Les Films du Losange/Artificial Eye)
dir-scr Eric Rohmer *pro* Margaret Menegoz *ph* Bernard Lutic, in Eastman Color *ed* Cécile Decugis *music* Jean-Louis Valero *r time* 106 mins *cert* A *UK opening* Jul 9.
cast Philippe Marlaud, Marie Rivière, Anne-Laure Meury, Matthieu Carrière, Philippe Caroit, Coralie Clément, Lise Hérédia, Haydée Caillot, Mary Stephen, Neil Chan, Rosette, Fabrice Luchini.

Engaging, stylish, characteristically lightweight Rohmer comedy, supposedly the first of a "comedies and proverbs" series and blunted by the same tweeness which affected his 'Moral Tales'. Lots of improvisation and day-in-the-life "naturalism". Less than meets the eye.

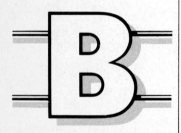

BACK ROADS (CBS/Rank)
dir Martin Ritt *pro* Ronald Shedlo *scr* Gary Devore *ph* John A. Alonzo, in Panavision, DeLuxe colour *ed* Sidney Levin *pro des* Walter Scott Herndon *music* Henry Mancini *r time* 95 mins *cert* AA *UK opening* Nov 5.
cast Sally Field, Tommy Lee Jones, David Keith, Miriam Colon, Michael Gazzo, Dan Shor, M. Emmet Walsh, Barbara Babcock, Nell Carter, Alex Colon, Lee de Broux, Ralph Seymour, Royce Applegate, Bruce M. Fischer, John Dennis Johnston, Don "Red" Barry, Bill Jacoby, Eric Laneuville,

Brian Frishman, Diane Sommerfield, Henry Slate, Matthew Campion, Tony Ganios, Lee McLaughlin, Arthur Pugh, Gerry Okuneff, Louie Nicholas, Cherie Brantley, Jim Bailey, Fred Baldwin, Billy Holliday, Barbara Thompson, Buddy Thompson, Phil Gordon, Mike Barton, Richard Charles Boyle, Sherrie Whitman, Lupita Cornego, Bob E Hannah, David Powledge, Eliott Keener, David Pellette, David Dahlgren, John Jackson, John Wilmot, Jack Shadix, Leonardo J. Noriega, Joe Ford, Woody Watson, Duke Alexander.

Ritt is hardly renowned as a director with the light touch, but here he is at the helm of a wispy, sentimental road movie about the difficulties encountered by a couple of casualties with aspirations — a tart with a heart and a simple but quick-witted ex-boxer — on an eventful odyssey from Alabama to California. Warm but vacuous, it has the asset of an engaging performance from Tommy Lee Jones and the liability of an unbearably winsome one from Sally Field.

THE BEADS OF ONE ROSARY (PRF-Zespol/Cinegate)
dir-scr Kazimierz Kutz *ph* Wieslaw Zdort, in colour *ed* Jozef Bartczak, Miroslawa Filipiak *art dir* Andrzej Plocki, Miroslaw Krelik, S. Burzynski *music* Wojciech Kilar *r time* 116 mins *cert* A *UK opening* Mar 11.
cast Augustyn Halotta, Marta Straszna, Ewa Wisniewska, Franciszek Pieczka, Jan Bogdol, Stanislaw Zaczyk, Jerzy Rzepka, Ryszard Jasny, Roza Richter, Wladyslaw Gluch, Antoni Wolny, Maksymilian Baron.

Leisurely, wordy, touching and funny account of how a stroppy old retired miner (who looks rather like a Polish Art Carney) refuses to move from his demolition-doomed house to a new high-rise flat and is prepared to resist both persuasion and intimidation by the authorities — for a while anyway. Exquisite performances from the two principals, both, remarkably, non-professionals.

BELOW THE BELT (Productions Associates)
dir-pro Robert Fowler *exec pro* Joseph Miller *scr* Robert Fowler, Sherry Sonnett, based on the novel 'To Smithereens' by Rosalyn Drexler *ph* Alan Metzger, in colour *ed* Steven Zaillon *art dir* Eugene Gurlitz, Sterling von Franck *music* Jerry Fielding *r time* 95 min *cert* AA *UK opening* May 20.

cast Regina Baff, John C. Becher, Mildred Burke, James Gammon, Annie McGreevey, Billie Mahoney, Ric Mancini, Jane O'Brien, Titi Paris, Sierra Pecheur, Gregory Rozakis, Frazer Smith, Shirley Stoler, Dolph Sweet, K.C. Townsend, Paul Brennan, Ray Scott.

Deftly scripted, confidently performed account of a no-hoper New Yorker who isn't much good at anything but is persuaded to try her hand at women's wrestling and becomes a big success (as a "Mexican Spitfire") in a touring circus. Modest in both budget and intention, with the inevitable resemblance to 'The California Dolls' in its portrayal of road boredom and ring activity, it doesn't really go anywhere — except, of course, to a climactic confrontation in the ring — but it is both likeable and well made. Shirley Stoler, the big girl in 'The Honeymoon Killers', puts in an appearance, still reassuringly colossal.

THE BEYOND (Fulvia Film/Eagle)
dir Lucio Fulci *pro* Fabrizio De Angelis *scr* Lucio Fulci, Giorgio Mariuzzo, Dardano Sacchetti *ph* Sergio Salvati, in Technicolor *ed* Vincenzo Tomassi *pro des* Massimo Lentini *music* Fabio Frizzi *r time* 85 mins *cert* X *UK opening* Nov 19.
cast Katherine McColl, David Warbeck, Sara Keller, Antoine Saint John, Michele Mirabella, Veronica Lazar, Anthony Flees, Giovanni De Nava, Al Cliver, Giampaolo Saccarola, Maria Pia Marsala, Laura De Marchi.

A girl inherits a hotel in Louisiana and finds zombies in the cellar and menacing corpses in the bathroom before discovering that the place is built over one of the seven gateways to hell, through which, in her torment, she eventually goes. Risible and grisly in about equal measures, with numerous picturesque deaths and ideas amalgamated from every horror source, the message is spelt out in neon-lit capitals: check the cellar.

BEYOND REASONABLE DOUBT (Endeavour/Enterprise)
dir John Laing *pro* John Barnett *scr* David Yallop, based on his book *ph* Alun Bollinger, in colour *ed* Michael Horton *art dir* Kai Hawkins *music* Dave Fraser *r time* 108 mins *cert* A *UK opening* Apr 29.
cast David Hemmings, John Hargreaves, Tony Barry, Martyn Sanderson, Grant Tilly, Diana Rowan, Ian Watkin, Terence Cooper, Marshall Napier, John Bach, Bruce Allpress, Bruno Lawrence, Peter Hayden, Mark Hadlow, Robert Shannon, Kate Harcourt, Heather Lindsay, Michael Booth, John Givins, John Batstone, Karl Bradley, Patrick Smythe, Alba, Gray Syms, Lex Calder, Clyde Scott, Jack Bongard, Hazel Cole, Philip Laing, Ian Harrop, Bill Johnston, Gil Cornwall, Bernard Moodie, Dawn Blair, Laurie Dee, Desmond Locke, Allan Nixon, Tristar Amos, Michael Kent, Brian Saipe, Timothy Lee, Mike Gill, Ken Haris, Noel Appleby, Fred James.

Tightly constructed, skilfully paced amalgam of thriller and dramatised documentary, based on a court case which extended over nine years from initial charge to eventual pardon, in which the police of a rural area of New Zealand assemble a labyrinth of circumstantial evidence to charge a local farmer with murder. Unsensational, in both senses of the word, but sound, it has an impressive performance from John Hargreaves as the hapless victim of police manipulation, and a persuasive one from David Hemmings, whose portrayal of the corrupt inspector suggests that he hasn't completely wasted the 16 years since 'Blow Up'.

BLACKOUT (Dal-Les-Maki/Miracle)
dir Eddy Matalon *pro* Nicole M. Boisvert, Eddy Matalon, John Dunning *exec pro* Andre Link, Ivan Reitman, John Vidette *scr* John C.W. Saxton *ph* Jean-Jacques Tarbes, in colour *ed* Debra Karen *art dir* Jocelyn Joly *music* Didier Vasseur *r time* 92 mins *cert* AA *UK opening* Feb 4.
cast Jim Mitchum, Robert Carradine, Belinda J. Montgomery, June Allyson, Jean-Pierre Aumont, Ray Milland, Don Granberry, Terry Haig, Victor B. Tyler, Jimmy Loftus, Gwen Tolbart, Fred Doederlein, Camille Ange, Maurice Attias, David Bairstow, Thor Bishopric, David Bloom, Norris Domingue, Anna Dorland, Claudie Duckworth, George Fonseca, Sony Forbes, Henry Gamer, Alexander Godfrey, Dick Grant, Arthur Grosser, Marek Lehman, Judy London, Peter MacNeill, Doris Malcolm, Jim Murchison, Louis Negin, Malcolm Nelthorpe, Allan Neumann, Candace O'Connor, Jarvis Oree, Arlaigh Peterson, Mary Pinatel, Marguerite Sidhom, Norman Taviss, Vlasta Vrana, Jim Walton, Len Watt, John Wildman, Roy Witham, Bill Zaget.

A five-year-old Canadian-French co-production about four psychos who escape during a blackout in New York and rape, kill and pillage their way around an entire budget-saving apartment block. The presence of June Allyson, Jean Pierre Aumont and Ray Millant in the cast is an indication of how slim pickings must be these days for veterans who still need to work.

BLOOD WEDDING (Artificial Eye)
dir Carlos Saura *pro* Emiliano Piedra *ph* Teodoro Escamilla, in Eastman

Right: The Beyond

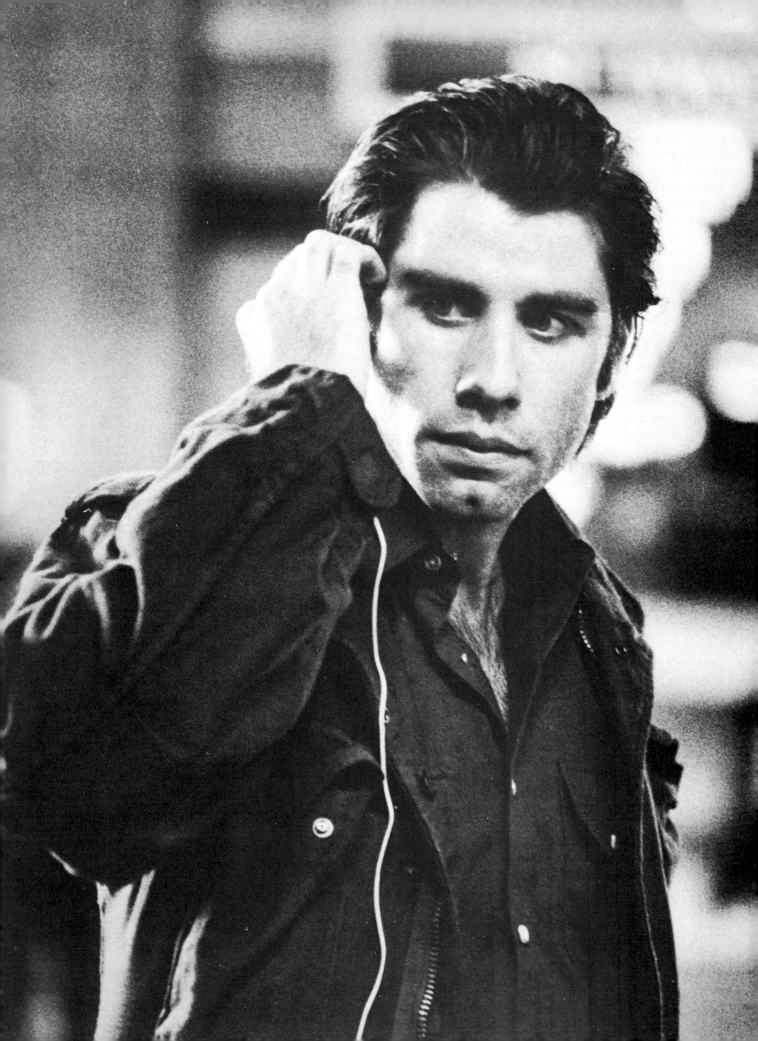

Color *ed* Pablo del Amo *art dir* Rafael Palmero *music* Emilio de Diego *r time* 71 mins *cert* U *UK opening* Feb 11.
cast Antonio Gades, Cristina Hoyos, Juan Antonio Jimenez, Pilar Cardenas, Carmen Villena, El Guito, Lario Diaz, Enrique Esteve, Elvira Andres, Azucena Flores, Cristina Gombau, Marisa Neila, Antonio Quintana, Quico Franco, Candy Roman, Emilio de Diego, Antonio Solera, Jose Merce, Gomez de Jerez.

Garcia Lorca's passion-and-revenge play transformed into a Flamenco ballet by the great dancer/choreographer Antonio Gades and filmed by Carlos Saura at a dress rehearsal, complete with backstage preparations, interview footage and final briefing. If this makes it sound like some dreary arts programme, nothing could be further from the truth. It is absolutely riveting, its minimal set and absence of trimmings placing the emphasis quite rightly on the remarkable dancing by Gades and his company. The choreography extends to the filming itself, which is extraordinarily evocative and exciting. The dance film of the decade so far.

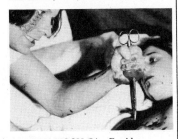

BLOODY MOON (Lisa-Rapid-Metro/Amanda)
dir Jesus Franco *pro* Wolf C. Hartwig *scr* Rayo Casablanca *ph* Juan Soler, in colour *ed* Karl Aulitzky *art dir* Klaus Haase *music* Gerhard Heinz *r time* 83 mins *cert* X *UK opening* May 6.
cast Olivia Pascal, Christoph Moosbrugger, Nadja Gerganoff, Alexander Waechter, Jasmin Losensky, Corinna Gillwald, Ann-Beate Engelke, Peter Exacoustos, Antonia Garcia, Beatriz Sancho Nieto, Maria Rubio, Otto W. Retzer.

Having walked the line between softcore corn and splatter horror for many years now, Jesus Franco — who in more self-consciously "international" days was known as Jess Franco and even Jess Frank — must surely now be in his element. The only curious detail about this weary West German action replay of all the time-honoured ingredients is that a cast dominated by German names should all play characters with Spanish ones.

BLOW OUT (Filmways/Columbia)
dir-scr Brian De Palma *pro* George Litto *exec pro* Fred Caruso *ph* Vilmos Zsigmond, in Panavision, Technicolor *ed* Paul Hirsch *pro des* Paul Sylbert *music* Pino Donaggio *r time* 107 mins *cert* X *UK opening* Oct 22.
cast John Travolta, Nancy Allen, John Lithgow, Dennis Franz, John Aquino, Peter Boyden, Curt May, John McMartin, Deborah Everton, J. Patrick McNamara, Amanda Cleveland, Roger Wilson, Lori-Nan Engler, Cindy Manion, Missy O'Shea, Marcy Bigelman, Ann Kelly, Dean Bennett, John Coppolino Jr, Archie Long, Dave Roberts, Claire Carter, Maurice Copeland, John Hoffmeister, David De Felice, Barbara Sigel, Tom McCarthy, Reginald M. Wallace, Robert L. Penrose, Larry Woody, Dick McGarvin, Michael Borghese, Rosanna

Fichera, James Jeter, Luddy Tramontana, Sid Doherty, Milt Fields, Bud Seese, Maureen Sullivan, Brian Corrigan, Elaine Filoon, Robin Sherwood, Tim Choate, B. J. Cyrus, Dave De Angelis, Thomas Finn, Tony Devon, Henry Cohen, Bernie Rachelle, William Tarman, Michael Tearson.

Clever, ironic, stylish thriller, full of characteristic De Palma flourishes, about a low-budget sound man, in search of wind effects and the perfect scream for the porno-carnage movie on which he's working, who becomes an audio witness to murder when he inadvertently records the moments preceding a politician's watery death. Part conspiracy drama, part study of doomed attachment, it has an impressively mature performance from Travolta and an attractively casual one from the under-employed Nancy Allen as the good-natured hooker he rescues from the submerged vehicle. The concluding pursuit across the Liberty Day celebrations in Philadelphia is one of the most perfectly choreographed sequences in any film of recent memory.

THE BOAT (PSO-Bavaria Atelier/Columbia)
dir-scr Wolfgang Petersen *pro* Gunter Rohrbach *exec pro* Mark Damon, Edward R. Pressman, John W. Hyde *ph* Jost Vacano, in Fujicolor *ed* Hannes Nikel *pro des* Rolf Zehetbauer *art dir* Gotz Weidner *music* Klaus Doldinger *r time* 128 mins *cert* AA *UK opening* Apr 8.
cast Jurgen Prochnow, Herbert Gronemeyer, Klaus Wennemann, Hubertus Bengsch, Martin Semmelrogge, Bernd Tauber, Erwin Leder, Martin May, Heinz Honig, U.A. Ochsen, Claude-Oliver Rudolph, Jan Fedder, Ralph Richter, Joachim Bernhard, Oliver Stritzel, Konrad Becker, Lutz Schnell, Martin Hemme, Roger Barth, Christian Bendomir, Albert Kraml, Peter Pathenis, Christian Seipolt, Ferdinand Schaal, Rolf Weber, Lothar Zajicek, Rita Cadillac, Otto Sander, Gunter Lamprecht.

Almost as out of favour as Viking adventures or biblical epics, submarine movies are unlikely to enjoy a return to favour as a consequence of this noisy, claustrophobic, sweatily intense big-budget underwater drama. Immaculately made and largely restricted to the interior of a U-boat patrolling the Atlantic in 1941 — with plenty of virtuoso Steadicam photography whenever battle stations is called — it is too self-conscious, and more significantly too late, an attempt to provide a German version of futility-of-war heroics to make much difference either way.

BODY AND SOUL (Cannon)
dir George Bowers *pro* Menahem Golan, Yoram Globus *scr* Leon Isaac Kennedy, based on the original screenplay by Abraham Polonsky *ph* James Forrest, in colour *ed* Samuel D. Pollard, Skip Schoolnik *art dir* Bob Ziembicki *music* Webster Lewis *r time* 122 mins *cert* X *UK opening* Apr 18.
cast Leon Isaac Kennedy, Jayne Kennedy, Muhammad Ali, Michael Gazzo, Perry Lang, Kim Hamilton, Gilbert Lewis, Nikki Swasse, Peter Lawford, Danny Wells, Johnny Brown, Azizi Johari, Rosanne Katon, Chris Wallace, Robbie Epps, J.B. Williamson, Al Denavo, Mel Welles, Deforrest Covan, Al Garcia, Jimmy Lennon, Mike Garfield, Howard Zazove, Cheryle Tyre Smith, James Carter, John Isaacs, Eddie Mustafos, Lonnie Bennett, Al Chavez, John Liechty, Andy Price, Lonnie Epps, Leonard Bailey, John Sherrod, Rita Minor, Regina Clayton, Noel Chacon,

Janice Lester, Edgy Lee, Deborah Willis Lacey, Ola Ray, Ingrid Greer, Laurie Senit, Mark Isaacs.

Completely pointless remake of Rossen's 1947 classic, to which it bears little qualitative resemblance. Muhammad Ali, once an aspiring film star, gets to play himself.

BODY HEAT (Ladd Company/Warner)
dir-scr Lawrence Kasdan *pro* Fred T. Gallo *ph* Richard H. Kline, in Panavision, Technicolor *ed* Carol Littleton *pro des* Bill Kenney *music* John Barry *r time* 113 mins *cert* X *UK opening* Jan 21.
cast William Hurt, Kathleen Turner, Richard Crenna, Ted Danson, J.A. Preston, Mickey Rourke, Kim Zimmer, Jane Hallaren, Lanna Saunders, Carola McGuinness, Michael Ryan, Larry Marko, Deborah Lucchessi, Lynn Hallowell, Thom J. Sharp, Ruth Thorn, Diane Lewis, Robert Traynor, Meg Kasdan, Ruth P. Strahan, Filomena Triscari, Bruce A. Lee, Ramiro Velasco, Tomas Choy, Servio T. Moreno.

No sooner has gullible small-time Florida lawyer William Hurt been shown the wind-chimes on bored predatory wife Kathleen Turner's porch than he's in her bed and plotting to murder her husband. Kasdan's first film as a director is the traditional film noir cocktail — murder, lust, avarice, betrayal — presented in the customary glass — sunlight through shutters, shadows, neon, night fogs. An old-style potion ('Double Indemnity', 'The

Left: Blow Out. Above: The Boat

The Bogey Man

Postman Always Rings Twice') with
new-style aspirations ('Night Moves').
It's marvellously atmospheric,
beautifully written and looks terrific. It
has plenty of sex, sweat and smart
talk. And lots of smoking, even
immediately after jogging. Ultimately
though, it is a little too knowing to be
a great film but certainly not too
knowing to be a very good one.

THE BOGEY MAN (Interbest/Miracle)
(US TITLE: THE BOOGEYMAN)
dir-pro Ulli Lommel *exec pro* Wolf
Schmidt *scr* Ulli Lommel, Suzanna
Love, David Herschel *ph* David
Sperling, Jochen Breitenstein, in
Metrocolor *ed* Terrell Tannen *art dir*
Robert Morgan *music* Tim Krog *r time*
83 mins *cert* X *UK opening* Feb 4.
cast Suzanna Love, Ron James, John
Carradine, Nicholas Love, Raymond
Boyden, Felicite Morgan, Bill
Rayburn, Llewelyn Thomas, Jay
Wright, Natasha Schiano, Gillian
Gordon, Howard Grant, Jane Pratt,
Lucinda Ziesing, David Swim, Katie
Casey, Ernest Meier, Stony Richards,
Claudia Porcelli, Catherine Tambini.

*Low-budget, medium-efficiency horror
movie in which a dead man has his
telekinetically-powered vengeance with
the pieces of broken glass from a
mirror in the bedroom where he was
murdered. Inexplicably re-titled, unless
the distributors thought its potential
audience might mistake it for a film
about a boring American hard rock
band.*

THE BOOGENS (Taft International/
Sunn Classic)
dir James L. Conway *pro* Charles E.
Sellier Jnr. *scr* David O'Malley, Bob
Hunt *ph* Paul Hipp, in colour *ed*
Michael Spence *pro des* Paul Staheli
art dir Linda Kiffe *music* Bob
Summers *r time* 95 mins *cert* X *UK
opening* Apr 18.
cast Rebecca Balding, Fred McCarren,
Anne-Marie Martin, Jeff Harlan, John
Crawford, Med Flory, Jon Lormer, Peg
Stewart, Scott Wilkinson, Marcia
Reider.

*The re-opening of a silver mine after
many years reveals the creatures
responsible for the cave-in which led to
its closure. A pretty dreary lot they are
too, befitting the film to which they
give their name.*

THE BORDER (Universal-RKO)
dir Tony Richardson *pro* Edgar
Bronfman Jnr. *exec pro* Neil Hartley

The Border

scr Deric Washburn, Walon Green,
David Freeman *ph* Ric Waite, Vilmos
Zsigmond, in Panavision, Technicolor
ed Robert K. Lambert *pro des* Toby
Rafelson *art dir* Richard Sawyer *music*
Ry Cooder *r time* 108 mins *cert* X *UK
opening* Apr 22.
cast Jack Nicholson, Harvey Keitel,
Valerie Perrine, Warren Oates, Elpidia
Carrillo, Shannon Wilcox, Manuel
Viescas, Jeff Morris, Dirk Blocker,
Mike Gomez, Lonny Chapman, Stacey
Pickren, James Jeter, William Russ,
Gary Sexton, William McLaughlin,
Floyd Levine, Alan Fudge, Gary
Grubbs, Billy Silva, David Beecroft,
Esther Sylvey, Luis Mejia, Roberto
Rivera, Jay Thurman, Craig Terry,
Juan Ramirez, Adalberto Cortez,
Concepcion Palmares, Juan Salas,
Norma Mayo, Paula Ruiz, Carlos
Bruno Villanueva, Ronne Drummond,
Richard Watts, Bernice E. Shamaley,
Kenna Espersen, Glenda Meadows, Joe
Zizik, Maria Delgado, Lupe Ontiveros,
Francisco Farias, Edmundo Alonzo,
Alan Gibbs.

cast Leonard Rossiter, Graham Crowden, Joan Plowright, Jill Bennett, Marsha Hunt, Malcolm McDowell, Robin Askwith, John Bett, Frank Grimes, Peter Jeffrey, Fulton Mackay, John Moffatt, Dandy Nichols, Brian Pettifer, Vivian Pickles, Marcus Powell, Barbara Hicks, Catherine Willmer, Mary MacLeod, Dave Atkins, Mark Hamill, Peter Machin, Marcus Powell, Gladys Crosbie, Rufus Collins, Ram John Holder, Jim Findlay, Pauline Melville, Kevin Lloyd, Robert Pugh, Robbie Coltrane, Glen Williams, Brian Glover, Mike Grady, Tony Haygarth, Jagdish Kumar, Patrick Durkin, Passy Joyce, Richard Griffiths, Dave Hill, Charmian May, Valentine Dyall, Roland Culver, Betty Marsden, Adele Strong, Ted Burnett, Gabrielle Lloyd, Barbara Flynn, Val Pringle, Robert Lee, Errol Shaker, Alan Penn, Liz Smith, Robin Davies, Alan Bates, Arthur Lowe, T.P. McKenna.

For the first hour-and-a-bit, up to when the Queen Mother figure arrives on a royal visit, it's great fun. Anderson's periodic assessment of the state of the nation is as splenetically grumpy as ever, but even the laboriousness of the metaphor — Britain viewed as a chaotic hospital populated by ineffectual management and pedantic unions, with the demonstrators baying outside the gates — can't deflate the succession of effective comic moments. Caricature is the ammunition and everybody is at the receiving end; it is as utterly non-partisan in its targets as a 'Carry On' film and almost as broad in its humour. Then the moralistic finger-wagging starts. Having little time for soapbox oratory, however worthy the intention, I was on my way. Dilys Powell feels otherwise: see Films of the Year.

BUDDY BUDDY (MGM)
dir Billy Wilder pro Jay Weston exec pro Alain Bernheim scr Billy Wilder, I.A.L Diamond, based on a play and story by Francis Veber ph Harry Stradling Jr, in Panavision, Metrocolor ed Argyle Nelson pro des Daniel A. Lomino music Lalo Schifrin r time 96 mins cert AA UK opening May 6.
cast Jack Lemmon, Walter Matthau, Paula Prentiss, Klaus Kinski, Dana Elcar, Miles Chapin, Michael Ensign, Joan Shawlee, Fil Formicola, C.J. Hunt, Bette Raya, Ronnie Sperling, Suzie Galler, John Schubeck, Ed Begley Jr., Frank Farmer, Tom Kindle, Biff Manard, Charlotte Stewart, Neile McQueen, Myrna Dell, Gene Price, Ben Lessy, Patti Jerome, Gary Allen, Frances Bay, Dean Bruce, Rod Gist, Steve Hirshon, John Cutler, Billy Beck, David Carlile, Archie Lang, Regina Leeds, Frank Dent, Timothy Sullivan, Troy Melton, June Smaney, Lorna Thayer, Jennifer Fajardo, Patrick Bishop, Wendell Titcomb.

This writer would crawl over hot coals and eat shit to defend Billy Wilder, and on occasion has done so, but this slow, stagey would-be black comedy, accomplished so much better by Edouard Molinaro as 'L'Emmerdeur'

Buddy Buddy

in 1973, would give little reason for facing the full inquisition, An obvious attempt to capitalise on pre-disposed audience expectations from 'The Fortune Cookie', 'The Odd Couple' and 'The Front Page', it has Walter Matthau lining himself up for a big hit in one hotel room while Jack Lemmon, upset that his wife has run off with a sex therapist, tries very hard to commit suicide in the neighbouring one. A few good lines, too much back projection, an excessively extended joke in which Matthau assembles and separates the components of a rifle and, above all, a general air of weariness and desperation in which everybody tries that little bit too hard.

THE BURNING
(Miramax/Handmade)
dir Tony Maylam pro Harvey Weinstein exec pro Jean Ubaud, Michael Cohl, Andre Djaoui scr Peter Lawrence, Bob Weinstein, based on story by Harvey Weinstein, Tony Maylam, Brad Grey ph Harvey

Harrison, in colour ed Jack Sholder art dir Peter Politanoff music Rick Wakeman r time 91 mins cert X UK opening Nov 5.
cast Brian Matthews, Leah Ayres, Brian Backer, Larry Joshua, Jason Alexander, Ned Eisenberg, Carrick Glenn, Carolyn Houlihan, Fisher Stevens, Lou David, Shelly Bruce, Sarah Chodoff, Bonnie Deroski, Holly Hunter, Kevi Kendall, J.R. McKechnie, George Parry, Ame Segull, Jeff De Hart, Bruce Kluger, Keith Mandell, Jerry McGee, Mansoor Najee-Ullah, Willie Reale, John Roach, K.C. Townsend, John Tripp, James Van Verth.

Torpid action replay of 'Friday the 13th' and its ilk, with a brutish camp caretaker, burnt to a crisp some years earlier, on the traditional revenge rampage. His victims are the usual teenagers who populate such films as victims — usually when alone or having sex. You know the stuff.

BUSTIN' LOOSE (Universal)
dir Oz Scott pro Richard Pryor, Michael S. Glick exec pro William Greaves scr Roger L. Simon, based on story by Richard Pryor ph Dennis Dalzell, in Technicolor ed David Holden, Skip Lusk, Harry Keramidas art dir Charles R. Davis, John Corso music Mark Davis, Roberta Flack r time 94 mins cert A UK opening Sept 17.
cast Richard Pryor, Cicely Tyson, Angel Ramirez, Jimmy Hughes, Edwin DeLeon, Edwin Kinter, Tami Luchow, Janet Wong, Alphonso Alexander, Kia Cooper, Robert Christian, George Coe,

Tony Richardson's first film for what seems like an eternity follows Sam Goldwyn's famous dictum by beginning with an earthquake and working its way up to a climax, although the old ogre would never have tolerated an ending as wet as the one on display here. Accompanied by his good-hearted but pea-brained consumerist wife (Valerie Perrine, perfect), Jack Nicholson becomes a border patrolman in El Paso and finds just about everyone on the take, smuggling in Mexican workers paid for by cheap-labour businessmen while dutifully hounding the others. Treading the traditional tightrope between conscience and corruption, he finds redemption by helping out a real madonna of a Mexican girl and her baby. Some effective action sequences, impressive use of the wide screen and one marvellous moment when Perrine ravishes Nicholson on the new waterbed while he looks up to check the price tag. But also a lot of clumsy cross-cutting, some obtrusively heavy-handed songs from Ry Cooder and a needlessly confusing narrative. I believe the term is "interesting failure".

BRITANNIA HOSPITAL (EMI)
dir Lindsay Anderson pro Davina Belling, Clive Parsons scr David Sherwin ph Mike Fash, in colour ed Michael Ellis pro des Norris Spencer music Alan Price r time 116 mins cert AA UK opening May 27.

Bustin' Loose

Bill Quinn, Roy Jenson, Fred Carney, Peggy McCay, Luke Andreas, Earl Billings, Mathew Clark, Nick Dimitri, Les Engel, Michael A. Elser, Paul Gardner, Ben Gerard, Gary Goetzman, Joe Jacobs, Paul Mooney, Lee Noblitt, Inez Pedroza, Morgan Roberts, Vern Taylor, Rick Sawaya, Shila Turna, Gloria Jewel Waggener, Jonelle White, Jewell Williams, Sunny Woods.

Richard Pryor is a very funny man and for some of this mawkish comedy about a small-time thief, a schoolteacher and a bus load of multiracial, maladjusted children he manages to remain so. What defeats him, and the viewer, is his apparent compulsion to be cute and lovable as well. There is no need for him to do this. And certainly there is no need for us to watch him do it.

BUTTERFLY (New Realm)
dir-pro Matt Cimber *exec pro* Tino Barzie *scr* John Goff, Matt Cimber, based on the novel by James M. Cain *ph* Eddy Van Der Enden, in Metrocolor *ed* B.A. Schoenfeld, Stan Siegel *art dir* Dave De Carlo *music* Ennio Morricone *r time* 108 mins *cert* X *UK opening* Apr 29.
cast Stacy Keach, Pia Zadora, Orson Welles, Lois Nettleton, Edward Albert, Stuart Whitman, Ed McMahon, June Lockhart, James Franciscus, Paul Hampton, Buck Flower, Ann Dane, Greg Gault, John O'Connor White, Peter Jason, Kim Ptak, Leigh Christian, Dr. Abraham Rudnick, John Goff, Dylan Urquidi.

Comically over-wrought adaptation of Cain's lust-and-incest novella, with the action transferred to the Nevada desert where Pia Zadora, spilling out of her dress, turns up at a disused silver mine and informs its caretaker Stacy Keach that she is his daughter. If one had not already decoded it from the abundance of posture-striking, supplemented by numerous variations on a pout, Zadora's sensual disposition is spelled out in neon when she takes a ladle full of milk straight from the cow and laps it up. "I like it warm, with froth on top," she purrs. From then on, it's only a matter of time before Keach has his hand in her bath — and he's not looking for the soap. Increasing in its ludicrousness with every scene, it reaches its apex in a courtroom finale of pure farce presided over by Orson Welles, looking weary and ill, as well he might.

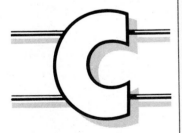

THE CALIFORNIA DOLLS (MGM)
(US TITLE: ...ALL THE MARBLES)
dir Robert Aldrich *pro* William Aldrich *scr* Mel Frohman *ph* Joseph Biroc, in Metrocolor *ed* Irving C. Rosenblum, Richard Lane *pro des* Carl Anderson *art dir* Beala Neel *music* Frank De Vol *r time* 113 mins *cert* X *UK opening* Dec 26.
cast Peter Falk, Vicki Frederick, Laurene Landon, Burt Young, Tracy Reed, Ursaline Bryant-King, Claudette Nevins, Richard Jaeckel, John Hancock, Lenny Montana, Charlie Dell, Chick Hearn, Joe Greene, Cliff Emmich, Clyde Kusatsu, Marlene

The California Dolls

Petrilli, Karen McKay, Jon Terry, Alvin Hammer, Angela Aames, Stanley Brock, Susan Mechsner, Leslie Henderson, Taemi Hagiwara, Ayumi Hori, Faith Minton, Irma Eugenia Aguilar, Martha Louisa Coello, Gustavo Torres, Paul Greenwood, Adolfo Plascencia, William J. Kulzer, Don Brodie, Lennie Bremen, Gloria Hayes, Perry Cook, Charles Anderson, Randy McClane, Ray Homesley, Steve White, Cosmo Sardo, Ernie Fuentes, Johnnie Decker, Nicholas Shields, Dan Magiera, Susan Barnes, Chuck Hicks, Gary McLarty, Joseph Margo, Ivan Ditmars.

A welcome return to form for Aldrich in this nicely observed account of female tag wrestlers (whose team name provides the film's British title) and their quick-witted manager competing around the grim industrial towns of the American mid-west, eating poorly and living on their wits. Funny, touching and completely assured — both in and out of the ring.

CAMERA BUFF (Cinegate)
dir-scr Krzysztof Keislowski *ph* Jacek Petrycki, in colour *ed* Halina Nawrocka *art dir* Rafal Waltenberger *music* Krzysztof Knittel *r time* 112 mins *cert* A *UK opening* Dec 31.
cast Jerzy Stuhr, Malgorzata Zabkowska, Ewa Pokas, Stefan Czyzewski, Jerzy Nowak, Tadeusz Bradecki, Marek Litewka, Boguslaw Sobczuk, Krzysztof Zanussi, Andrzej Jurga.

Amusing, pointedly acid Polish comedy about a factory worker whose

life is transformed after he buys a cine camera — particularly when he graduates from home movies to investigative documentaries — and the effect this obsession has on his wife (who leaves him) and the factory authorities (who pressure him towards conformity). Both intriguing and revealing, it is also critical in a way one suspects is no longer possible in its country of origin.

THE CANNONBALL RUN (Golden Harvest/Fox)
dir Hal Needham *pro* Albert S. Ruddy *exec pro* Raymond Chow *scr* Brock Yates *ph* Michael Butler, in Technicolor *ed* Donn Cambern, william D. Gordean *art dir* Carol Wenger *music* Al Capps *r time* 95 mins *cert* A *UK opening* Jul 16.
cast Burt Reynolds, Roger Moore, Farrah Fawcett, Dom DeLuise, Dean Martin, Sammy Davis Jr, Jack Elam, Adrienne Barbeau, Terry Bradshaw, Jackie Chan, Bert Convy, Jamie Farr, Peter Fonda, George Furth, Michael Hui, Bianca Jagger, Molly Picon, Jimmy 'The Greek' Snyder, Mel Tillis, Rick Aviles, Warren Berlinger, Tara Buckman, John Fiedler, Norman Grabowski, Joe Klecko, Grayce Spence, Bob Tessier, Alfie Wise, Johnny Yune, Lois Areno, Simone Burton, Finele Carpenter, Susan McDonald, Janet Woytak, Ben Rogers, Jim Lewis, Fred Smith, Roy Tatum, Dudley Remus, Hal Carter, Brock Yates, Kathleen M. Shea, Nancy Austin, Samir Kamoun, John Megna, Linda McClure, Laura Lizer Sommers, Richard Losee, Richie Burns Wright.

Brisk, noisy, coarse, lightweight comedy from the actor-director team responsible for 'Hooper' and both 'Smokey and the Bandits' films. Using a race across America as a backdrop for innumerable pile-ups it is the kind of movie for which the term "routine" might have been invented.

CAVEMAN (United Artists)
dir Carl Gottlieb *pro* Lawrence Turman, David Foster *scr* Rudy de Luca, Carl Gottlieb *ph* Alan Hume, in

Left: Butterfly. Above: The Cannonball Run

Technicolor *ed* Gene Fowler *pro des* Philip M. Jefferies *art dir* Jose Rodriguez Granada *music* Lalo Schifrin *r time* 91 mins *cert* A *UK opening* Jul 23.
cast Ringo Starr, Barbara Bach, Dennis Quaid, Shelley Long, Jack Gilford, Cork Hubbert, Mark King, Paco Morayta, Evan Kim, Ed Greenberg, Carl Lumbly, Jack Scalici, Erica Carlson, Gigi Vorgan, Sara Lopez Sierra, Esteban Valdez, Juan Ancona Figueroa, Juan Omar Ortiz, Anais de Melo, John Matuszak, Avery Schreiber, Miguel Angel Fuentes, Tere Alvarez, Ana de Sade, Gerardo Zepeda, Hector Moreno, Pamela Gual.

Grunts-and-loincloths comedy full of tired visual gags and budget monsters.

CELESTE (Artificial Eye)
dir Percy Adlon *pro* Eleonore Adlon *scr* Percy Adlon, based on the book 'Monsieur Proust' by Celeste Albaret *ph* Jurgen Martin, Horst Becker, Helmo Sahliger, Hermann Ramelow, in Eastman Color *ed* Clara Fabry *art dir* Hans Gailling, Marlies Frese, Kurt Diell, Esther Wenger *music* Cesar Franck *r time* 106 mins *cert* AA *UK opening* Mar 25.
cast Eva Mattes, Jurgen Arndt, Norbert Wartha, Wolf Euba, Joseph Manoth, Leo Bardischewski, Horst Raspe, Andi Stefanescu, Rolf Illig.

Proust's last years — tubercular, bed-ridden, crotchety — recalled by his tirelessly patient housekeeper. Funereally slow, incredibly heavy going.

THE CHALLENGE (CBS/Rank)
dir John Frankenheimer *pro* Robert L. Rosen, Ron Beckman *exec pro* Lyle Poncher *s cr* John Sayles, Richard Maxwell, Ivan Moffat *ph* Kozo Okazaki, in DeLuxe colour *ed* Jack Wheeler *pro des* Yoshiyuki Ishida *music* Jerry Goldsmith *r time* 109 mins *cert* X *UK opening* Apr 22.
cast Scott Glenn, Toshiro Mifune, Donna Kei Benz, Atsuo Nakamura, Sab Shimono, Miiko Taka, Calvin Jung, Clyde Kusatsu, Shogo Shimada, Seiji Miyaguchi, Yoshio Inaba, Kenta Fukasaku, Kiyoaki Nagai, Naoto Fujita, Kazunaga Tsuji, Hisashi Osaka, Kusuo Kita.

With 'French Connection 2' Frankenheimer made one of the best films of the Seventies, but generally his prodigy status of the previous decade has not held up well. One of the

problems lies in the subjects he chooses. The current American fascination with all things Japanese (just count those Sushi bars!) does not prove a profitable avenue for his rather solemn, though unquestionable, talent. For a start, it means that John Sayles' co-authored screenplay — which superimposes US thriller conventions on an Oriental swordplay movie, contrasting the old Japan of honour and Samurai combat and the new one of space invaders and capitalist gangsters — is so punctuated by plodding philosophical interludes that it barely has a chance to work on any level. While no great fan of Sydney Pollack, one has to concede that he did it all better in 'The Yazuka'.

CHANEL SOLITAIRE (Gardenia-Todrest/Handmade)
dir George Kaczender *pro* Larry Spangler *exec pro* Eric Rochat *scr* Julian More, based on the novel by Mme. Claude Delay *ph* Ricardo Aronovich, in colour *ed* Georges Klotz *art dir* Jacques Saulnier *music* Jean Musy *r time* 135 mins *cert* AA *UK opening* Feb 11.
cast Marie-France Pisier, Timothy Dalton, Rutger Hauer, Karen Black, Brigitte Fossey, Brenda Vaccaro, Leila Frechet, Catherine Alcover, Albert Augier, Corine Blue, Lyne Chardonnet, Yvonne Dany, Isabelle Duby, Huguette Faget, David Gabison, Louba Guertchikoff, Philippe Mareuil, Nicole Maurey, Jean-Gabriel Nordmann, Lionel Rocheman, Violetta Sanchez, Jimmy Shuman, Jean Valmont, Louise Vincent, Sylvia Zerbib, Philippe Nicaud, Alexandra Stewart, Catherine Allegret, Helene Vallier, Marie-Helene Daste, Jeremy Child, Yves Brainville, Jean-Marie Proslier, Lambert Wilson, Virginie Ogouz, Humbert Balsan.

When it comes to English language turkeys, Marie-France Pisier really does pick them. First 'The Other Side of Midnight' — generally acknowledged as the unintentional-laughs-per-minute champion of recent years — now this. So flimsy that it barely exists, this Anglo-French biopic about fashion designer Coco Chanel, immaculately rags-to-riches, is the customary succession of affairs (both ways, naturellement) and high life (riding, sex, restaurants), all framed by random soft focus and plenty of suspect French accents. Sufficiently risible to be recommendable.

CHARLES AND LUCIE (Avon Films)
dir Nelly Kaplan *pro* Claude Makovski *scr* Jean Chapot *ph* Gilbert Sandoz, in colour *ed* Nelly Kaplan, Jean Chapot *music* Pierre Perret *r time* 97 mins *cert* AA *UK opening* Jun 24.
cast Daniel Ceccaldi, Ginette Garcin, Jean-Marie Proslier, Samson Fainsilber, Georges Claisse, Guy Grosso, Marcel Gassouk, Albert Konan-Koffi, Henri Tissot, Albert Lerda, Robert Beauvais, Julie Turin, Josy Andrew, Feodor Atkine, Pierre Repp, Jacques Mauny, Pierre Charras, Renee Duncan, Belen, Sylvain Curtel, Lili Cox, Tania Sourseva, Jean Panisse, Albert Manachi.

A couple of weary, middle-aged Parisian dreamers — a hypochondriac no-hoper junk seller and a minor singer turned concierge — are the victims of an elaborate confidence trick and end up destitute in the south of France, pursued by the police, adrift in a picaresque world of criminals, palm readers and con-men. A charming, gossamer fairy tale, it evaporates from the memory within minutes.

THE CHOSEN (Contemporary)
dir Jeremy Paul Kagan *pro* Edie Landau, Ely Landau *exec pro*

Jonathan Bernstein *scr* Edwin Gordon, based on the novel by Chaim Potok *ph* Arthur Ornitz, in colour *ed* David Garfield, Howard Smith *pro des* Stuart Wurtzel *music* Elmer Bernstein *r time* 108 mins *cert* A *UK opening* Jun 17.
cast Maximilian Schell, Rod Steiger, Robby Benson, Barry Miller, Hildy Brooks, Kaethe Fine, Ron Rifkin, Robert Burke, Lonny Price, Evan Handler, Douglas Warhit, Jeff Marcus, Stuart Charno, Richard Lifschutz, Clement Fowler, John Pankow, Richard Ziman, Bruce MacVittie, E.D. Miller, Jack Hollander, Elaine Goren, Kathryn Conners, Iva March, Val Avery, Danton Stone, Mark Nelson, Stephen Hanan, Naama Potok, Laura Delano, Carol Levy, David Ellin, Tony Munafo, Chaim Potok, Rabbi Eli Webberman, Ed Herlihy, Frank Maxwell, Bob Drew, Abraham Kate, Zvee Scooler.

Suffocatingly earnest, numbingly sentimental study of how a friendship between two Jewish adolescents in post-war New York is torn apart by the opposing political and religious beliefs of their fathers (one is a Zionist campaigner, the other a Hassidic Rabbi). As the latter, Rod Steiger, eyes rolling and a breathy homily never far from his lips, gives his hammiest performance ever in a career not exactly noted for its moderation.

CHRIST STOPPED AT EBOLI (Artificial Eye)
dir Francesco Rosi *pro* Franco Cristaldi, Nicola Carraro *scr* Francesco Rosi, Tonino Guerra, Raffaele La Capria, based on the book by Carlo Levi *ph* Pasqualino De Santis, in colour *ed* Ruggero Mastroianni *art dir* Andrea Crisanti *music* Piero Piccioni *r time* 152 mins *cert* A *UK opening* Apr 29.
cast Gian Maria Volonte, Paolo Bonacelli, Alain Cuny, Lea Massari, Irene Papas, Francois Simon, Luigi Infantino, Accursio De Leo, Francesco Callari, Vincenzo Vitale, Antonio Allocca, Vincenzo Licata, Muzzi Loffredo, Lidia Bavusi, Francesco Capotorto, Maria Antonia Capotorto, Antonio Jodice, Francesco Palumbo, Paolo Di Sabato, Tommaso Polgar, Giuseppe Persia, Giacomo Giardino, Stavros Tornes, Frank Raviele, Francesca Massaro, Rocco Sisto.

Exiled by Mussolini to a forgotten corner of southern Italy in 1935, a Turin doctor, upon whose autobiographical account this is based, finds himself in a remote wilderness of poverty, oppression and superstition. A departure from Rossi's customary style, and a backdated companion in location terms alone to 'Three Brothers', it lingers on every detail in its portrayal of a universe apart. Beautifully photographed, minutely observed and enormously rewarding for people who aren't in a hurry.

Above: Chanel Solitaire. Right: Caveman

Christiane F

CHRISTIANE F (Solaris/Fox)
dir Ulrich Edel *pro* Bernd Eichinger, Hans Weth *scr* Herman Weigel, based on the book by Kai Hermann, Horst Rieck *ph* Justus Pankau, Jurgen Jurges, in colour *ed* Jane Seitz *music* Jurgen Knieper, David Bowie *r time* 131 mins *cert* X *UK opening* Dec 17.
cast Natja Brunckhorst, Thomas Haustein, Jens Kuphal, Rainer Wolk, Jan Georg Effler, Christiane Reichelt, Daniela Jaeger, Kerstin Richter, Peggy Bussieck, Kerstin Malessa, Cathrine Schabeck, Andreas Fuhrmann, Lutz Hemmerling, Uwe Diderich, Lothar Chamski, Christiane Lechle, Ellen Esser, Stanislaus Solotar, Eberhart Auriga, David Bowie.

Powerful, pessimistic dramatisation, filmed in an effective semi-documentary style, of a true story about a 13-year-old girl in West Berlin who drifts into prostitution and heroin addiction. Well performed by a cast of unknowns, and horrifically graphic, it is mandatory viewing for anyone still harbouring glamorous ideas about drugs. Regrettably its (understandable) X certificate prevents it from reaching precisely the age group at which it is aimed.

CIRCLE OF DECEIT (Bioskop-Artemis-Argos/UIP)
dir Volker Schlondorff *pro* Eberhard Junkersdorf *scr* Volker Schlondorff, Jean-Claude Carriere, Margarethe von Trotta, Kai Hermann, based on the novel by Nicolas Born *ph* Igor Luther, in Eastman Color *ed* Suzanne Baron *art dir* Alexandre Riachi, Tannous Zougheib *music* Maurice Jarre *r time* 109 mins *cert* X *UK opening* Apr 15.
cast Bruno Ganz, Hanna Schygulla, Jerzy Skolimowski, Gila von Weitershausen, Jean Carmet, Martin Urtel, John Munro, Fouad Naim, Josette Khalil, Khaled El Saeid, Ghassan Mattar, Sarah Salem, Rafic Najem, Magnia Fakhoury, Jack Diagilaitas, Roger Assaf, Hakmeh Abou Ali, Hassan Husseiny, Isaaf Husseiny, Wasim Soubra, Wally Nachaby, Mohamed Kalach, Isabella, Jeanne, Hans Hackermann, Hans Peter Orff, Joachim Dieter Mues, Wolfgang Karven, Eric Spitella, Bamby Nucho, Peter Kamph, Nick Dobree, Philip Padfield, Rick Panzarella, Toni Maw, Mohamed Chouly, Youssef Raad, Dina Haidar, Sousso Abdel Mafiz, Ghassan Fadlallah, Imad Hammoudi, Hussein Kaouk.

War correspondent Bruno Ganz — his marriage on the rocks, the pressures closing in — arrives in Beirut with his photographer - commentator - rationaliser Jerzy Skolimowski and finds that all his predisposed ideas about the kind of report he should file on the Middle East war dissolve in the face of grisly experience. A powerful, haunting film, made all the more convincing by its on-the-spot locations.

CITY OF WOMEN (Opera-Gaumont/Artificial Eye)
dir Federico Fellini *scr* Federico Fellini, Bernardino Zapponi *ph* Giuseppe Rotunno, in Technovision, Eastman Color *ed* Ruggero Mastroianni *art dir* Dante Ferretti *music* Luis Bacalov *r time* 139 mins *cert* X *UK opening* Sept 17.
cast Marcello Mastroianni, Anna Prucnal, Bernice Stegers, Iole Silvani, Donatella Damiani, Ettore Manni, Fiammetta Baralla, Catherine Carrel, Marcello Di Falco, Silvana Fusacchia, Gabriella Giorgelli, Dominique Labourier, Stephane Emilfork, Nadia Vasil, Sylvie Mayer, Meerberger Nahyr, Helene G. Calzarelli, Sylvie Wacrenier, Sibilla Sedat, Alessandra Panelli, Loredana Solfizi, Rosaria Tafuri, Carla Terlizzi, Katren Gebelein, Fiorella Molinari, Jill Lucas, Viviane Lucas, Valeria Moriconi.

Self-referential as ever, Fellini casts Marcello Mastroianni adrift in a surreal countryside of his imagination where he confronts his attitudes to women. For all the characteristically impressive imagery, a long, empty masturbatory fantasy which he could have spared his audience and told to his shrink.

CLASH OF THE TITANS (MGM)
dir Desmond David *pro* Charles H. Schneer, Ray Harryhausen *scr* Beverley Cross *ph* Ted Moore, in Dynarama, Metrocolor *ed* Timothy Gee *pro des* Frank White *art dir* Don Picton, Peter Howitt, Giorgio Desideri, Fernando Gonzalez *music* Laurence Rosenthal *r time* 118 mins *cert* A *UK opening* Jul 2.
cast Laurence Olivier, Claire Bloom, Maggie Smith, Ursula Andress, Jack Gwillim, Susan Fleetwood, Pat Roach, Harry Hamlin, Judi Bowker, Burgess Meredith, Sian Phillips, Flora Robson, Freda Jackson, Anna Manahan, Tim Pigott-Smith, Neil McCarthy, Donald Houston, Vida Taylor, Harry Jones.

Big colourful digest of Greek mythology full of togas, ancient-speak and the customary range of Harryhausen special effects, some that work well (the Medusa, the flying horse), others which merely elicit sniggers (the vulture that carries off Judi Bowker). Thin on characterisation but redeemed by its sense of fun.

CLEAN SLATE (Curzon)
dir Bertrand Tavernier *pro* Adolphe Viezzi *scr* Jean Aurench, Bertrand

Tavernier, based on the novel 'Pop 1280' by Jim Thompson *ph* Pierre William Glenn, in colour *ed* Armand Psenny *pro des* Alexandre Trauner *art dir* Frankie Diago *music* Philippe Sarde *r time* 128 mins *cert* AA *UK opening* May 6.
cast Philippe Noiret, Isabelle Huppert, Jean-Pierre Marielle, Stephane Audran, Eddy Mitchell, Guy Marchand, Irene Skobline, Michel Beaune, Jean Champion, Victor Garrivier, Gerard Hernandez, Abdoulaye Diop, Daniel Langlet, Francois Perrot, Raymond Hermantier, Mamadou Dioum, Samba Mane, Irenee Martin.

In transferring Jim Thompson's acclaimed pulp novel from the American South to a French colonial outpost in Africa just before World War II, Tavernier also transforms Thompson's sheriff-as-avenging-angel figure into a cheerful slob of a police chief, turning a blind eye to everything, who begins finding it simpler to deal with his problems by killing the poeple who cause them, demolishing his victims with brisk, dispassionate precision. Effective as a black comedy, evocative as an observation about automatic-pilot racism and people going round the bend in the heat, it is finally deflated by its laboured symbolism and excessive length.

COME WITH ME MY LOVE (First Decameron/Tigon)
(US TITLE: TAKE TIME TO SMELL THE FLOWERS)
dir-pro Chris Caras *scr* Allen Raskow *ph* John W. Huston, in colour *ed* Ron Palmer *music* Chris Shrantakis, Gerald Liebmann *r time* 64 mins *cert* X *UK opening* Jul 30.
cast Viju Krem, David Anthony, Greta Hartog, Richard Salamon, Harrington Smith, Thea Caradino, Fred L. Cherrick, Richard Alexander, Rance Patrick, Turk Cakovsky, Lois Ashmeyer, Richard Thierney, Jack Halliday, Elizabeth Martin, Ed Bursk, Ellen Irons.

Dreary portmanteau in which a couple planning to make a film tell each other stories between cool-as-a-mountain-stream sexual encounters. These are enacted by the usual exhibitionist dullards.

CONDORMAN (Walt Disney)
dir Charles Jarrott *pro* Jan Williams *exec pro* Ron Miller *scr* Marc Stirdivant, Glen Caron, Mickey Rose, based on the novel 'The Game of X' by Robert Sheckley *ph* Charles F. Wheeler, in Panavision, Technicolor *ed* Gordon D. Brenner *pro des* Albert Witherick *art dir* Marc Frederix *music* Henry Mancini *r time* 90 mins *cert* U *UK opening* Jul 2.

cast Michael Crawford, Oliver Reed, Barbara Carrera, James Hampton, Jean-Pierre Kalfon, Dana Elcar, Vernon Dobtcheff, Robert Arden.

Resembling some bizarre amalgam of Superman, James Bond and his television character Frank Spencer, Michael Crawford, with wobbly American accent, plays a comic strip writer who tests the feasibility of his hero's exploits in real life. That this should involve location hopping, cartoon villains, chase scenes, wrecked cars and a beautiful defecting spy should come as no surprise. That it should all be done so heavy handedly does.

THE CONDUCTOR (PRF-Zespol/Cinegate)
dir Andrzej Wajda *scr* Andrzej Kijowski, based on conversations with Andrzej Markowski *ph* Slawomir Idziak, in Orwocolor *ed* Halina Prugar *pro des* Allan Starski *music* Beethoven *r time* 101 mins *cert* A *UK opening* Oct 22.
cast John Gielgud, Krystyna Janda, Andrzej Seweryn, Marysia Seweryn, Anna Lopatowska, Mavis Waler, Jan Ciecierski, Jozef Fryzlewicz, Janusz Gajos, Mary Ann Krasiniski, Tadeusz Czechowski, Marek Dabrowski, Stanislaw Gorka, Jerzy Kleyn, Elzbieta Strzalkowska, Jerzy Szmidt, Wojciech Wysocki, Stanislaw Zatloka.

Dense, multi-faceted pre-'Man of Iron' Wajda with John Gielgud (dubbed into Polish some of the time, with far from satisfactory results) giving a superb if familiar performance as the veteran conductor returning from New York to his native Poland to guest-conduct the orchestra in which his dead sweetheart's daughter, married to the resident conductor, is one of the principal violinists.

THE CONSTANT FACTOR (PRF-Zespol/Cinegate)
dir-scr Krzysztof Zanussi *ph* Slawomir Idziak, in Eastman Color *ed* Urszula Sliwinska, Ewa Smal *art dir* Tadeusz Wybult, Maciej Putowski *music* Wojciech Kilar *r time* 91 mins *cert* A *UK opening* Sept 24.
cast Tadeusz Bradecki, Zofia Mrozowska, Malgorzata Zajaczkowska, Cezary Morawski, Witold Pyrkosz, Ewa Lejczak, Jan Jurewicz, Juliusz Machulski, Jacek Strzemzalski, Edward Zebrowski, Marek Litewka.

Fragmented, allusive but visually impressive moral tale about destiny and small-time corruption in contemporary Poland. Similar in its range of concerns, though very different in mood from...

THE CONTRACT (PRF-Zespol/Cinegate)
dir-scr Krzysztof Zanussi *ph* Slawomir Idziak, in colour *ed* Urszula Sliwinska, Ewa Smal *art dir* Tadeusz Wybult, Maciej Putowski, Teresa Gruber, Gabriela Allina, Joanna Lelanow *music* Wojciech Kilar *r time* 111 mins *cert* AA *UK opening* Feb 4.
cast Maja Komorowska, Tadeusz Lomnicki, Magda Jaroszowna, Krzysztof Kolberger, Nina Andrycz, Zofia Mrozowska, Beata Tyszkiewicz, Janusz Gajos, Edward Lubaszenko, Ignacy Machowski, Christine Paul, Peter Bonke, Leslie Caron, Irena Byrska, Jolanta Kozak, Maciej Robakiewica, Jerzy Swiech, Bozena Dykiel, Lilianna Glabczynska, Krystyna Sznerr, Laura Lacz, Eugeniusz Priwiezencew, Jan Jurewicz.

In this characteristic — though rather more obviously comic than usual — satirical portrait of Polish life, Zanussi has as his catalysts a couple about to be married through parental pressure. When the bride refuses to go through with the church wedding and vanishes, the groom's father goes ahead with the reception regardless. The film, therefore, is largely about what happens at a party celebrating a wedding that has not taken place: the drunken insults, the sexual indiscretions, the petty rivalries. The lightest and funniest of Zanussi's films, with a particularly enjoyable performance from Leslie Caron as the puffed-up kleptomaniac symbol of Western decadence.

Clash of the Titans

Countryman

COUNTRYMAN (Island)
dir Dickie Jobson *pro* Chris Blackwell *exec pro* Stephan Sperry *scr* Dickie Jobson, Michael Thomas *ph* Dominique Chapuis, in Technicolor *ed* John Victor Smith, Peter Boyle *art dir* Bernard Leonard *music* Wally Badarou *r time* 102 mins *cert* AA *UK opening* Apr 29.
cast Countryman, Hiram Keller, Kristina St Clair, Carl Bradshaw, Basil Keane, Ronnie McKay, Ronald Gossop, Oliver Sammuels, Chin, Jahman, Buster Jameson, Freshey Richardson, Bobby Russell, Lucien Tai Ten Quee, Claudia Robinson, Papa Three-Cards, Monair Zacca, Peter Packer, Dee Anthony, Jim Newman, Kingsley Rose, Honey Fernandez, Duncan Booth.

Punctuated as it is by an excess of rasta homilies, random Jamaicana and a soundtrack which works too hard, and too obviously, at underlining each moment in musical terms, this exuberant, enjoyable film still succeeds — well, most of the time it does — in amalgamating elements of a political thriller with the trappings of a simple-minded adventure movie. The story itself is pretty thin: Countryman, a

The Crazy Horse of Paris

nature-boy fisherman with mystical powers and a fluent line in philosophical patter — part Superman, part Aristotle with added ganga — rescues an American couple whose plane has crashed, then hides them as they are hunted and used to political advantage, all this against a background of election paranoia and corruption. But at the heart of it is a genuinely engaging performance from Countryman himself and photography which bathes the whole thing, particularly the night scenes, in a fairy-tale glow befitting its central character.

THE CRAZY HORSE OF PARIS
(Crazy Horse Productions/Productions Assoc)
dir-scr Alain Bernardin *ph* Roland Pontoizeau in Eastman Color *ed* Yvonne Martin *music* Jacques Morali *r time* 95 mins *cert* X *UK opening* Nov 19.
cast John Lennox, Dickie Henderson, Alain Bernardin, George Carl, Senor Wences, Milo and Roger, Lova Moor, Rosa Fumetto, Lily Paramount, Sofia Palladium, Kiki Zanzibar, Baba Moleskine, Goody Pentagone, Polly Underground, Trucula Bonbon, Moony

Trafalgar, Norma Picadilly, Greta Farenheit, Loida Calumet, Galia Paderewska, Malika Preambule, Lussa Matchbox, Usha Starlight, Vanilla Banana, Victoria Rodeo, Prima Symphony, Eva de Bratislava, Miko Miku, Supra Galaxy.

A protracted visit to the nightclub of the same name. Made four years ago, it appears to last that long.

CUTTER'S WAY (United Artists)
dir Ivan Passer *pro* Paul R. Gurian *scr* Jeffrey Alan Fiskin, based on the novel 'Cutter and Bone' by Newton Thornburg *ph* Jordan Cronenweth, in Technicolor *ed* Caroline Ferriol *art dir* Josan Russo *music* Jack Nitzsche *r time* 109 mins *cert* X *UK opening* Jan 14.
cast Jeff Bridges, John Heard, Lisa Eichhorn, Ann Dusenberry, Stephen Elliott, Arthur Rosenberg, Nina Van Pallandt, Patricia Donahue, Geraldine Baron, Katherine Pass, Frank McCarthy, George Planco, Jay Fletcher, George Dickerson, Jack Murdock, Essex Smith, Rod Gist, Leonard Lightfoot, Julia Duffy, Randy Shepard, Roy Hollis, Billy Drago, Caesar Cordova, Jon Terry, William Pelt, Ron Marcroft, Ted White, Tony Epper, Andy Epper, Chris Howell, H.P. Evetts, Ron Burke.

Originally titled 'Cutter and Bone' before being withdrawn, re-titled and

re-launched, 'Cutter's Way' is the year's best example of an old-time mainstream American thriller dressed up in new-time art-movie paranoia. An engaging Santa Barbara layabout, Bone (Jeff Bridges), sees a dead woman's body being thrown into a trashcan and thinks he recognizes a local oil tycoon as the murderer. A crippled, embittered Vietnam war veteran, Cutter (John Heard, with eyepatch and wooden leg), decides on a campaign of retribution despite his friend's escalating doubts, with predictably apocalyptic results. Nothing much is explained but in this kind of film — as rivetingly cryptic as Penn's 'Night Moves', though not quite as good — it doesn't matter.

D

DEAD AND BURIED (GTO)
dir Gary A. Sherman *pro* Ronald Shusett, Robert Fentress *exec pro* Richard R. St. Johns *scr* Ronald Shusett, Dan O'Bannon *ph* Steve Poster, in colour *ed* Alan Balsam *art dir* Bill Sandell, Joe Aubel *music* Joe Renzetti *r time* 96 mins *cert* X *UK opening* Nov 1.
cast James Farentino, Melody Anderson, Jack Albertson, Dennis Redfield, Nancy Locke Hauser, Lisa Blount, Robert Englund, Bill Quinn, Michael Currie, Christopher Allport, Joe Medalis, Macon McCalman, Lisa Marie, Estelle Omens, Barry Corbin, Linda Turley, Ed Bakey, Glen Morshower, Robert Boler, Michael Pataki, Jill Fosse, Mark Courtney, Michael Courtney, Renee McDonell, Dottie Catching, Colby Smith, Judy Ashton.

It is curious that James Farentino (who is in 'Dead and Buried') and James Franciscus (who isn't) should share the same first name, the same initials and almost the same number of syllables, since everything they touch turns to turkey. This one, from the writers of 'Alien' as the publicity proudly announces, is the turkey in which bizarre inhabitants of an isolated small town are given to appearing out of nowhere and killing any hapless outsiders who happen to be around. A hideously graphic and very violent death follows. Clue: the coroner/undertaker is one of the living dead.

DEADLY BLESSING
(Polygram/Barber International)
dir Wes Craven *pro* Micheline Keller, Max Keller, Pat Herskovic *exec pro* William Gilmore *scr* Glenn M. Benest, Matthew Barr, Wes Craven *ph* Robert

Jessup, in Metrocolor *ed* Richard Bracken *pro des* Jack Marty *music* James Horner *r time* 102 mins *cert* X *UK opening* Feb 4.
cast Maren Jensen, Susan Buckner, Sharon Stone, Jeff East, Lisa Hartman, Lois Nettleton, Ernest Borgnine, Coleen Riley, Doug Barr, Michael Berryman, Kevin Cooney, Bobby Dark, Kevin Farr, Neil Fletcher, Jonathon Gulla, Chester Kulas Jnr, Lawrence Montaigne, Lucky Mosley, Dan Shackelford, Annabelle Weenick, Jenna Worthen.

Set in an Eastern Pennsylvanian Hittite farming area (funny hats, beards, superstition) but filmed in Texas (wide open spaces for added menace), this potentially routine amalgam of supernatural thriller and orthodox blood-letter of the gorgeous-terrorised-women school is given what little persuasiveness it has by Craven's stylish direction, particularly in the dream sequences. Already assured of some kind of immortality after 'The Hills Have Eyes', if only on the part of drunken sicko-perverts who can't resist late night shows, Craven looks as if he might build on it.

DEAR BOYS (Sigma/Rosier)
dir Paul de Lussanet *pro* Matthijs van Heijningen *scr* Chiem van Houweninge, Paul de Lussanet, based on the novels 'Taal Der Liefde', 'Lieve Jongens' and 'Lieve Leven' by Gerard Revé *ph* Paul van den Bos, in colour *ed* Hans van Dongen *art dir* Gebr. Goedemans *music* Laurens van Rooyen *r time* 88 mins *UK opening* Mar 5.
cast Hugo Metsers, Hans Dagelet, Bill van Dijk, Albert Mol, Pleuni Touw, Marina de Graaf, Astrid Nijgh, Gerard Cox, Jan Hopman, Hans Cornelissen, Jaap Hoogstra, Jan Staal, Mevrouw de Meijer, Wim Barry, Herman Ouwersloot, Bert Kiene.

Dutch homosexual soft-corn soft-porn, embellished by a few weary gags and the prescribed proportion of "meaningful" statements.

DEATH IS MY TRADE (WDR-Iduna/Contemporary)
dir Theodor Kotulla *pro* Fred Ilgner *exec pro* Volker Canaris, Nils Nilson *scr* Theodor Kotulla, based on the novel by Robert Merle *ph* Dieter Naujeck, in colour *ed* Wolfgang Richter *art dir* Wolfgang Schunke *music* Eberhard Weber *r time* 145 mins *cert* A *UK opening* Mar 18.
cast Gotz George, Kai Taschner, Elisabeth Schwarz, Kurt Hubner, Hans Korte, Sigurd Fitzek, Peter Franke, Wilfried Elste, Matthias Fuchs.

Detached, unsensationalist account — subdivided by chapters and making no attempt to steer the audience's responses — of the rise of a young German patriot from minor World War I hero to commandant of the Auschwitz concentration camp where he dispassionately murders thousands of Jews every day and treats it with the abstracted air of a bureaucrat trying to keep up with target totals. Chilling stuff, made all the more effective by Gotz George's hypnotically po-faced performance as the man who never questions an order.

DEATH WISH II (Golan-Globus/Columbia)
dir Michael Winner *pro* Menahem Golan, Yoram Globus *exec pro* Hal

Death Wish II

Landers, Bobby Roberts *scr* David Engelbach, based on characters created by Brian Garfield *ph* Richard L. Kline, Tom Del Ruth *ed* Arnold Crust, Julian Semilian *pro des* William Hiney *music* Jimmy Page *r time* 92 mins *cert* X *UK opening* Feb 11.
cast Charles Bronson, Jill Ireland, Vincent Gardenia, J. D. Cannon, Anthony Franciosa, Ben Frank, Robin Sherwood, Silvana Gillardo, Robert F. Lyons, Michael Prince, Drew Snyder, Paul Lambert, Thomas Duffy, Kevyn Major Howard, Stuart K. Robinson, Laurence Fishburne, E. Lamont Johnson, Paul Comi, Frank Campanella, Hugh Warden, James Begg, Melody Santangello, Robert Sniveley, Steffen Zacharias, Don Moss, Charles Cyphers, Peter Pan, David Daniels, Don Dubbins, James Galante, Buck Young, Karsen Lee, Leslie Graves, Teresa Baxter, Cindy Daly, Susannah Darrow, Henry Capps, Joshua Gallegos, Paul McCallum, Roberta Collins, Diane Markoff, Cynthia Burr, Michael Tavon, Ezekiel Moss, Ranson Walrod, Gary Boyle, Ava Lazar, Fred Saxon, Henry Youngman, Ginny Cooper, Lesa Weis, Twyla Littleton, Diane Manzo.

Not so much a sequel as a Los Angeles edition of its eight-year-old predecessor, with taciturn avenger Charles Bronson, one step ahead of the police as ever, roaming the streets gunning down the cartoon hoodlums who raped and murdered his already traumatised teenage daughter. Vacuous, gloating and predictable, it lacks a single redeeming factor.

DEEP THOUGHTS (Spectacular Trading Co/Jay Jay)
dir Jack Regis *pro* Dick Randall *ph* Francois Abount, in colour *ed* Claude Guerin *r time* 81 mins *cert* X *UK opening* Oct 15.
cast John Holmes, Louise Lovelace, Ajita Wilson, Kevin Cowans, Shirley Alan, Dominique Saint Clair, Claude Valmont.

Rooted in the premise of showing what people are really thinking, this is full of familiar characters thinking familiar things, all of them to do with sex. Come in Sigmund!

DRAGONSLAYER (Paramount/Walt Disney)
dir Matthew Robbins *pro* Hal Barwood *exec pro* Howard W. Koch *scr* Hal Barwood, Matthew Robbins *ph* Derek Vanlint, in Panavision, Metrocolor *ed* Tony Lawson *pro des* Elliot Scott *art dir* Alan Cassie *music* Alex North *r time* 109 mins *cert* A *UK opening* Feb 11.
cast Peter MacNicol, Caitlin Clarke, Ralph Richardson, John Hallam, Peter Eyre, Albert Salmi, Chloe Salaman, Sydney Bromley, Emrys James, Roger

Dragonslayer

Kemp, Ian McDiarmid, Ken Shorter, Jason White, Yolanda Palfrey, Douglas Cooper, Alf Mangon, David Mount, James Payne, Chris Twinn.

The problem for Disney these days, with or without Paramount's collaboration, is to keep treading the line between what the studio has traditionally done best — imaginative, convincing fantasies for the young and their dutiful parents — and keeping up with a world which rapidly turns it all into camp. This sombre sword-and-sorcery-plus-myth-and-magic tale, for all its striking special effects (among which Ralph Richardson's strange performance must qualify), does not really answer the problem. Animation might have done so.

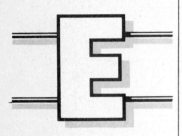

EATEN ALIVE (Dana/Eagle)
dir-scr Umberto Lenzi *pro* Luciano Martini, Mino Loy *ph* Federico Zanni, in colour *ed* Eugenio Alabiso *pro des* Massimo Antonello Gelene *music* Budy Maglione *r time* 85 mins *cert* X *UK opening* Nov 8.
cast Mel Ferrer, Robert Kerman, Janet Agren, Ivan Rassimov, Paola Senatore, Me Me Lai, Mag Fleming, Franco Fantasia, Gianfranco Coduti, Alfred Joseph Berry, Michele Schiegelm.

One of several Jonestown-inspired quickies that appeared during the year, this one is set in New Guinea and strains the parallel by calling its villain Reverend Jonas. In case you were wondering, he is not played by Mel Ferrer.

ELECTRIC BLUE THE MOVIE
(Scrip Glow/Tigon)
dir-pro Adam Cole *exec pro* Tony Power, Roger Cook *ph* various, in colour *r time* 94 mins *cert* X *UK opening* Jan 14.
cast Marilyn Chambers, Desiree Cousteau, Brigitte Lahaie, Mandy Miller, Joanna Lumley, Marilyn Monroe, Jayne Mansfield.

...As opposed to Electric Blue the Building Site of course. Long a ritual part of the video-buff's dirty-night-in, the Electric Blue series' only redeeming feature was a crude resemblance to the kind of home movie one speculates might have been produced in suburbia after a boozy outing. Indeed, the best moments of this dreadful compilation — blown up to 35mm and presented as a sort of de-luxe wanker's digest — are the final scenes in which a succession of housewives rather awkwardly represent some received notion of

centrefold behaviour. Otherwise, it's the traditional ingredients: nude disco dancing, massage, masturbation, fun in the sun and, of course, "candid" celebrity footage.

EMMANUELLE IN SOHO (Roldvale/Tigon)
dir David Hughes *pro* John M. East *exec pro* David Sullivan *scr* Brian Daly, John M. East *ph* Don Lord, in colour *ed* David Woodward *r time* 67 mins *cert* X *UK opening* Jul 9.
cast Mandy Miller, Julie Lee, John M. East, Keith Fraser, Gavin Clare, Tim Blackstone, Geraldine Hooper, Anita Desmarais, Georges Waser, Erika Lea, Cathy Green, Suzanne Richens, John Roach, Vicki Scott, Louise London, Natalie Newport, Linzi Drew, Marie Harper, Samantha Devonshire, Carla Lawrence, Ruth Chapman, Kalla Ryan.

Tired, tawdry little farce which 20 years earlier might have been made with less nudity, but a good deal more charm, as a 'Carry On' film.

EMMANUELL'S SILVER TONGUE
(Summit/Jay Jay)
dir-scr Mauro Ivaldi, Guido Leoni *ph* Gino Santini, in Panavision, Technicolor *ed* Carlo Reali, Anna D'Angelo *art dir* Franco Calabrese, Edoardo Puoti *music* Alberto Baldan Bembo *r time* 92 mins *cert* X *UK opening* Jul 5.
cast Carmen Villani, Nadia Cassini, Roberto Cenci, Gianfranco D'Angelo, Huberta Shaw, Enzo Andronico, Ali' Zaiem.

Yet another spelling of Emmanuelle (which has already enjoyed several variations on the number of m's and l's) camouflages a dismally uninviting Tunisian romp. In this one she is a hypnotherapist.

ENDLESS LOVE (Polygram/Barber International)
dir Franco Zeffirelli *pro* Dyson Lovell *exec pro* Keith Barish *scr* Judith Rascoe, based on the novel by Scott Spencer *ph* David Watkin, in Technicolor *ed* Michael J. Sheridan *pro des* Ed Wittstein *art dir* Ed Pisoni *music* Jonathan Tunick *r time* 116 mins *cert* AA *UK opening* Oct 22.
cast Brooke Shields, Martin Hewitt, Shirley Knight, Don Murray, Richard Kiley, Beatrice Straight, Jimmy Spader, Ian Ziering, Robert Moore, Penelope Milford, Jan Miner, Salem Ludwig, Leon B. Stevens, Vida Wright, Jeff Marcus, Patrick Taylor, Jamie Bernstein, Tom Cruise, Jeffrey

B. Versalle, Jami Gertz, Maria Todd, Douglas Alan-Mann, Steve Calicchio, Robert Kahn, Jeremy Bar-Illan, Scott Cushman, David Willis, Barry Pruitt, Amy Whitman, Kenneth Cory, Teri Shields, Sylvia Short, Ethelmae Mason, Anna Berger, Joan Glasco, Mark Hopson Arnold, Kathy Bernard, Philip Lenkowsky, Arthur Epstein, Leonard H. Pass, Lawrence Sellars, Ron Perkins, Gilbert Stafford, Marvin Foster, Millidge Mosley, Walt Gorney, Willie Wenger, Robert Altman, Ruth Last, George Kyle, Lee Kimball, Martin Pinckney, Duffy Piccini.

The agony and the ecstasy of teenage romance. Part one: the agony. Pretty, soppy (and pretty soppy), this tastefully voyeuristic Romeo and Juliet revival is so slow and lingers so long over each detail that one can climb a mountain, have a shower, enjoy a three-course meal and make a return journey to Guam while waiting for the next incident.

THE END OF AUGUST
(Sewanee/Enterprise)
dir Bob Graham *pro* Warren Jacobson, Sally Sharp *exec pro* Martin Jurow *scr*

Eula Seaton, Leon Heller, based on the novel 'The Awakening' by Kate Chopin *ph* Robert Elswit, in Metrocolor *ed* Jay Lash Cassidy *pro des* Warren Jacobson, Erin Jo Jurow, Fred Baldwin *art dir* Joe Wertheimer *music* Shirley Walker *r time* 105 mins *cert* A *UK opening* Nov 19.
cast Sally Sharp, Lilia Skala, David Marshall Grant, Kathleen Widdoes, Paul Roebling, Paul Shenar, John McLiam, Mark Linn-Baker, Patricia Falkenhain, Ray Poole, William Meisle, Saundra Santiago, Miles Mutchler, Adrian Boyes, Andrew Chambers, Brown Wallace, Jenna Worthen, Sally Maloney, Robert Harper, Pearly Donald, Andrea Tyner, Angela Tyner, Theola Ostes, Father Zoghby, Nancy Miles, Sara Jo Roush, Judy Corcoran.

Cool, elegant, empty study of married woman's genteel frustration and disgruntlement set in turn-of-the-century New Orleans, full of gorgeous period detail and postcard-like definition yet almost entirely devoid of interest.

ENTER THE NINJA (Cannon/Columbia)
dir Menahem Golan *pro* Judd Bernard, Yoram Globus *scr* Dick Desmond, Judd Bernard, Menahem Golan *ph* David Gurfinkel, in colour *ed* Mark Goldblatt, Michael Duthie *art dir* Robert Lee *kusic* W. Michael Lewis, Laurin Rinder *r time* 94 mins *cert* X *UK opening* Oct 1.
cast Franco Nero, Susan George, Sho Kosugi, Christopher George, Alex Courtney, Will Hare, Zachi Noy, Constantin De Goguel, Dale Ishimoto, Jonee Gamboa, Leo Martinez, Ken Metcalfe, Subas Herrero, Alan Amiel, Doug Ivan, Bob Jones, Jack Turner, Derek Webster, Konrad Waalkes, James Gaines, Don Gordon, Isolde Winter, Lucy Bush.

Giving new dimensions to boredom, this rather suspect late arrival on the martial arts front tests credulity

Endless Love

Enter the Ninja

beyond straining point by having Franco Nero as the Ninjutsu graduate (*that makes him a Ninja*) *who defends a pal's coconut plantation in Manilla from the terrorism of an unpleasant tycoon with his own Ninja. Intended to be exciting, it is merely inciting — to demand back one's money.*

ESCAPE FROM NEW YORK (Avco Embassy/Barber International)
dir John Carpenter *pro* Larry Franco, Debra Hill *scr* John Carpenter, Nick Castle *ph* Dean Cundey, in Panavision,

Metrocolor *ed* Todd Ramsey *pro des* Joe Alves *music* John Carpenter, Alan Howarth *r time* 99 mins *cert* AA *UK opening* Sept 24.
cast Kurt Russell, Lee Van Cleef, Ernest Borgnine, Donald Pleasence, Isaac Hayes, Season Hubley, Tom Atkins, Charles Cyphers, Harry Dean Stanton, Adrienne Barbeau, Joe Unger, Frank Doubleday, Jon Strobel, John Cothran Jnr, Garrett Bergfeld, Richard Cosentino, Robert John Metcalf, Joel Bennett, Vic Bullock, Clem Fox, Tobar Mayo, Nancy Stephens, Steven Gagon, Steven Ford, Michael Taylor, Lonnie Wun, Dale House, David R. Patrick, Bob Minor, Wally Taylor, James O'Hagen, James Emery, Tom Lillard, Borah Silver, Tony Papenfuss, John Diehl, Carmen Filpi, Buck Flower, Clay Wright, Al Cerullo, Ox Baker, Lowmoan Spectacular, Ronald E. House, Alan Shearman, Joseph A. Perrotti, Roger Bumpass, Ron Vernan.

Like some bizarre mating of a futuristic Western, a George Romero movie and a sequel to 'The Warriors', Carpenter's graduation to big-budget film-making (by his standards) is set at the end of the century when Manhattan island has become a walled prison where criminals are simply abandoned to finish each other off. Into this menacing ghost town goes Kurt Russell, looking like an extra from 'Cruising', with a couple of implanted electrodes ready to explode if he fails to rescue American President

Donald Pleasence within the required 24 hours. Speedy, simple and effective, it is accomplished with Carpenter's customary flair.

ESCAPE TO VICTORY (Lorimar/ITC)
(US TITLE: VICTORY)
DIR John Huston *pro* Freddie Fields *exec pro* Gordon McLendon *scr* Evan Jones, Yabo Yablonsky *ph* Gerry Fisher, in Panavision, Metrocolor *ed* Roberto Silvi *pro des* J. Dennis Washington *music* Bill Conti *r time* 115 mins *cert* A *UK opening* Sept 4.

cast Sylvester Stallone, Michael Caine, Max von Sydow, Pele, Bobby Moore, Osvaldo Ardiles, Paul Van Himst, Kazimierz Deyna, Hallvar Thorenson, Mike Summerbee, Co Prins, Russell Osman, John Wark, Soren Linsted, Kevin O'Callaghan, Gary Waldhorn, George Mikell, Laurie Sivell, Arthur Brauss, Robin Turner, Michael Wolf, Jurgen Andersen, David Shawyer, Werner Roth, Amidou, Benoit Ferreux, Jean Francois Stevenin, Jack Lenoir, Folton Gera, Carole Laure, Tim Piggott-Smith, Julian Curry, Clive

Escape to Victory

Merrison, Maurice Roeves, Michael
Cochrane, Jack Kendrick, Daniel
Massey, Anton Diffring, Gunter
Wolbert, Capacci Eolo, Michael Drhey.

*Prompted by soccer-crazy camp
commandant Max von Sydow, a team
of POWs — among them a podgy
Michael Caine (as a former West Ham
and England football star!) and a
slimline Sylvester Stallone who turns
out to be a tolerable goalkeeper — take
on the Nazis in a Paris stadium, and
develop an escape plan with the help of
the French Resistance. An unlikely
venture for Huston but one that works
well as the exciting, comic-strip
jingoistic yarn he clearly intended.*

EVIL UNDER THE SUN (EMI)

dir Guy Hamilton *pro* John
Brabourne, Richard Goodwin *scr*
Anthony Shaffer, based on the novel
by Agatha Christie *ph* Christopher
Challis, in Panavision, Technicolor *ed*
Richard Marden *pro des* Elliot Scott
art dir Alan Cassie *music* Cole Porter
r time 116 mins *cert* A *UK opening*
Mar 23.
cast Peter Ustinov, Jane Birkin, Colin
Blakely, Nicholas Clay, James Mason,
Roddy McDowall, Sylvia Miles, Denis
Quilley, Diana Rigg, Maggie Smith,
Emily Hone, John Alderson, Paul
Antrim, Cyril Conway, Barbara Hicks,
Richard Vernon, Robert Dorning,
Dimitri Andreas.

*The fourth of the Brabourne/Goodwin-
produced series adapted from Agatha
Christie novels, the third to feature her
detective Hercule Poirot, and the
second to have Peter Ustinov playing
him, reveals a formula in such an
advanced state of decay that it is
virtually pleading to be put out of its
rickety and protracted misery. With an
amalgam of Cole Porter tunes to knock
up the nostalgia count, and a leadenly
overstated Anthony Shaffer
screenplay, a bunch of all-star clothes
horses amble through some backdated
notion of Cowardish wit by exchanging
a dutiful succession of contrived
epigrams. By the time it finally
happens, the murder of the bitchy
Broadway star is almost a relief. By
the time Poirot reveals who did it —
years later, it feels — nobody cares.*

EXCALIBUR (Orion/Warner)

dir-pro John Boorman *exec pro* Edgar
F. Gross, Robert A. Eisenstein *scr*
Rospo Pallenberg, John Boorman,
based on 'Le Morte d'Arthur' by
Thomas Malory *ph* Alex Thomson, in
Technicolor *ed* John Merritt *pro des*
Anthony Pratt *art dir* Tim
Hutchinson *music* Trevor Jones *r time*
140 mins *cert* AA *UK opening* Jul 2.
cast Nigel Terry, Helen Mirren,
Nicholas Clay, Cherie Lunghi, Paul
Geoffrey, Nicol Williamson, Robert
Addie, Gabriel Byrne, Keith Buckley,
Katrine Boorman, Liam Neeson, Corin
Redgrave, Niall O'Brien, Patrick
Stewart, Clive Swift, Ciarin Hinds,
Liam O'Calloghan, Michael Muldoon,
Charley Boorman, Mannix Flynn,
Garrett Keogh, Emmet Bergin,
Barbara Byrne, Brid Brennan, Kay
McLaren, Eammon Kelly.

021-2

Boorman's long-gestating Camelot epic about the rise and fall of Arthur finally surfaces as a handsome but self-consciously mythic amalgam of history, legend and whimsy. Its lesser moments remind one irresistibly of 'Monty Python and the Holy Grail', an impression exacerbated by Nicol Williamson's eccentric portrayal of Merlin, all sudden mood changes and funny voices.

AN EYE FOR AN EYE (Avco Embassy/Barber International)
dir Steve Carver *pro* Frank Capra Jnr. *exec pro* Robert Rehme *scr* William Gray, James Bruner *ph* Roger Shearman, in colour *ed* Anthony Redman *art dir* Vance Lorenzini *music* William Goldstein *r time* 104 mins *cert* X *UK opening* May 6.
cast Chuck Norris, Christopher Lee, Richard Roundtree, Matt Clark, Mako, Maggie Cooper, Rosalind Chao, Professor Toru Tanaka, Stuart Pankin, Terry Kiser, Mel Novak, Richard Prieto.

You know the stuff if you know any Californian Kung Fu at all. The San Francisco cop who leaves the force to avenge the death of a pal who was on the trail of a drugs ring; the high kicks, the low dives, the falls from windows, the exploding cars. And, as it's Chuck Norris, the blond hair, the discreetly casual outfits, the terrific success against improbable odds — particularly where they involve a climactic showdown with an Oriental colossus. People keep going to see it, though: mock-Easterns have replaced pretend-Westerns as the favoured undemanding night out. Christopher Lee, who has not developed any significant talents in the martial arts, wears his best "Is this what I went to Hollywood for?" expression throughout.

EYE OF THE NEEDLE (United Artists)
dir Richard Marquand *pro* Stephen Friedman *scr* Stanley Mann, based on the novel by Ken Follett *ph* Alan Hume, in Technicolor *ed* Sean Barton *pro des* Wilfred Shingleton *art dir* Bert Davey, John Hoesli *music* Miklos Rozsa *r time* 112 mins *cert* AA *UK opening* Dec 17.
cast Donald Sutherland, Kate Nelligan, Ian Bannen, Christopher Cazenove, Stephen MacKenna, Philip Martin Brown, Goerge Belbin, Faith Brook, Barbara Greley, George Lee, Arthur Lovegrove, Colin Rix, Barbara Ewing, Chris Jenkinson, William Merrow, Patrick Connor, David Hayman, Rupert Frazer, Jonathan Nicholas, Alex McCrindle, John Bennett, Sam Kydd, John Paul, Stephen Phillips, Richard Graydon, Michael Mellinger, Alan Surtees, Don Fellows, Stuart Harwood, Rik Mayall, Rory Edwards, Ellis Dale, Bill Fraser, Michael Joseph,

Left: Excalibur

Eye of the Needle

John Rees, John Grieve, Bruce White, David Ashton, Bill Nighy.

Old-hat-with-new-trimmings World War II thriller with Donald Sutherland as a Nazi spy (stern father, of course) who ends up on a Scottish island with an attractive woman and her crippled ex-Spitfire pilot, and finds that romance complicates invasion plans. Sound, moderately exciting emphatically traditional film-making, embellished with a few knife murders.

EYES OF A STRANGER (Warner)
dir Ken Wiederhorn *pro* Ronald Zerra *scr* Mark Jackson, Eric L. Bloon *ph* Mini Rojas, in colour *ed* Rick Shaine *art dir* Jessica Sack *music* Richard Einhorn *r time* 83 mins *cert* X *UK opening* Jul 2.
cast Lauren Tewes, Jennifer Jason Leigh, John DiSanti, Peter Dupré, Gwen Lewis, Kitty Lunn, Timothy Hawkins, Ted Richert, Toni Crabtree, Bob Small, Stella Rivera, Dan Fitzgerald, José Bahamande, Luke Halpin, Rhonda Flynn, Tony Federico, Alan Lee, Amy Krug, Tabbetha Tracey, Sarah Hutcheson, Jillian Lindig, George DeVries, Melvin Pape, Robert Goodman, Herb Goldstein, Sonia Zomina, Joe Friedman, Pat Warren, Kathy Suergiu, Michael de Silva, Richard Allen, Madeline Curtis.

Another opportunistic thriller in the terrorised women series, which reveals the killer from the start and then gloats in his homicidal unpleasantness. Full of silly people and bad sociology, as these films tend to be.

F

FASTER, PUSSYCAT! KILL! KILL!
(Eve Prods./Tigon)
dir-ed Russ Meyer *pro* Eve Meyer, Russ Meyer *scr* Jack Moran *ph* Walter Schenk *music* Paul Sawtelle, Bert Shefter *r time* 83 mins *cert* X *UK opening* Oct 29.
cast Tura Satana, Haji, Lori Williams, Susan Bernard, Stuart Lancaster, Paul Trinka, Dennis Busch, Ray Barlow, Mickey Foxx.

There are few things in the cinema on which you can always rely. One of them is that whether a Russ Meyer film was made last week or 17 years ago, as this one was, it will feature the same amalgam of massive mammaries, elementary sadomasochism and hilariously solemn moralising. Here a trio of go-go girls in hipsters and plastic boots speed across the desert looking for trouble, and of course finding it. Recommended viewing for anyone who has not yet surrendered to terminal sensitivity.

THE FINAL CONFLICT (Fox)
dir Graham Baker *pro* Harvey Bernhard *exec pro* Richard Donner *scr* Andrew Birkin, based on characters created by David Seltzer *ph* Robert Paynter, Phil Meheux, in Panavision, DeLuxe Colour *ed* Alan Strachan *pro des* Herbert Westbrook *art dir* Martin Atkinson *music* Jerry Goldsmith *r time* 108 mins *cert* X *UK opening* Sept 17.
cast Sam Neill, Rossano Brazzi, Don Gordon, Lisa Harrow, Barnaby Holm, Mason Adams, Robert Arden, Tommy Duggan, Leueen Willoughby, Louis Mahoney, Marc Boyle, Richard

Oldfield, Milos Kirek, Tony Vogel, Arwen Holm, Hugh Moxey, William Fox, John Baskcomb, Norman Bird, Marc Smith, Arnold Diamond, Eric Richard, Richard Williams, Stephen Turner, Al Matthews, Larry Martyn, Frank Coda, Harry Littlewood.

Forgoing the usual star line-up in favour of a largely anonymous cast, the concluding chapter of the 'Omen' trilogy has charismatic Antichrist Damien as not only the head of a large corporation but also US ambassador to the UK, ideal positions from which to

sustain his battle against Christianity in general and the Second Coming in particular. Rossano Brazzi and six priests are his opposition. Complete tosh, of course, but entertaining enough.

FIRST MONDAY IN OCTOBER
(Paramount)
dir Ronald Neame *pro* Paul Heller, Martha Scott *scr* Jerome Lawrence, Robert E. Lee, based on their own play *ph* Fred J. Koenekamp, in Panavision, Metrocolor *ed* Peter E. Berger *pro des* Philip M. Jefferies *art dir* John V. Cartwright *music* Ian Fraser *r time* 98 mins *cert* AA *UK opening* Jan 14.

cast Walter Matthau, Jill Clayburgh, Barnard Hughes, Jan Sterling, James Stephens, Joshua Bryant, Wiley Harker, F.J. O'Neil, Charles Lampkin, Lew Palter, Richard McMurray, Herb Vigran, Edmund Stoiber, Noble Willingham, Richard McKenzie, Ann Doran, Dallas Alinder, Olive Dunbar, High Gillin, James E. Brodhead, Arthur Adams, Nick Angotti, Jeanne Joe, Christopher Tenney, Richard Balin, Martin Agronsky, Ray Colbert, Bob Sherman, Carol Coggin, Sig Frohlich, Kenneth Du Main, Stanley Lawrence, Dick Winslow, Joe Terry, Sandy Chapin, Dudley Knight, Edwin M. Adams, Sergeant Ronnie Thomas, Jeff Scheulen, Jordan Charney, Mary Munday, Bebe Drake-Massey, Richard de Angeles, Jim Vanko, William G. Clark, Wendy E. Taylor.

Self-consciously literate, intermittently amusing courtroom comedy — based on, and sounding like, a very wordy play — founded on the increasingly suspect principle that all one needs to bring such films to life is a female sparring partner for Matthau's genially grumpy charm. In this one, Jill Clayburgh plays the first woman to be appointed to the US Supreme Court (a conservative too), with Matthau as the liberal judge who argues with her in and out of court. Little more than a protracted debate punctuated by the occasional stagey aphorism, it rarely rises above the routine. Clayburgh, in particular, is urgently in need of some good material.

FLYING SEX (Golden Era)
dir Franco Martinelli *scr* Romano Scandariato *ph* Sergio Salvati, in colour *ed* Alberto Moriani *music* Walter Rizatti *r time* 80 mins *cert* X *UK opening* Aug 20.
cast Eveline Barnett, Al Cliver, Franz Muller, Brenda Shington, Venantino Venantino, Linda Fumis.

The one about the woman who, because her first orgasm was achieved with the help of a toy plane, can only reach one when airborne. To this end she becomes a hostess. Her novelist husband, poor sod, becomes a steward to keep her company in the galley.

FORCE: FIVE (United Artists)
dir-scr Robert Clouse *pro* Fred Weintraub *ph* Gil Hubbs, in Technicolor *ed* Bob Bring *art dir* Richard Lawrence *music* William

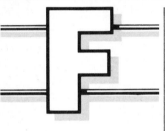

Goldstein *r time* 93 mins *cert* X *UK opening* Dec 3.
cast Joe Lewis, Bong Soo Han, Sonny Barnes, Richard Norton, Benny Urquidez, Ron Hayden, Bob Schott, Pam Huntingdon, Peter McLean, Mandy Wyss, Mel Novak, Michael Prince, Tom Villard, Matthew Tobin, Dennis Mancini, Patricia Alice Albrecht, Edith Fields, Kathryn Greer, Glenn Morrissey, Bill Ryusaki, Dolores Cantu, Phil Rubenstein, Addison Randall, Loren Hanes, Michael Gates, Kelly Greer, Susan Santelli, Rubin Moreno, Nora Denney, John G. Becher, John Vincent Schumman, Phil Chong, Jason Randal, Pat Johnson, Stephen L. Meek, Don Charles McGovern.

More Hollywood kung-fu as a religious cult leader in the Jonestown tradition, a bit careless with his acupuncture needles and able to get his well-to-do disciples to sign over their inheritance, is exposed and defeated by a multi-racial martial arts team. Exuberant, colourful, simple-minded, endlessly sadistic, enormously entertaining. To be avoided by the easily upset, who avoided it in large numbers.

FORT APACHE THE BRONX (Time-Life/Rank)
Dir Daniel Petrie *pro* Martin Richards, Tom Fiorello *exec pro* David Susskind *scr* Heywood Gould, suggested by the experiences of Thomas Mulhearn, Pete Tessitore *ph* John Alcott, in DeLuxe colour *ed* Rita Roland *pro des* Ben Edwards *art dir* Christopher Nowak *music* Jonathan Tunick *r time* 123 mins *cert* AA *UK opening* Jan 21.
cast Paul Newman, Edward Asner, Ken Wahl, Danny Aiello, Rachel Ticotin, Pam Grier, Kathleen Beller, Tito Goya, Miguel Pinero, Jaime Tirelli, Lance William Guecia, Ronnie Clanton, Clifford David, Sully Boyar, Michael Higgins, Rik Colitti, Irving Metzman, Frank Adu, John Aquino, Norman Matlock, John Ring, Tony Di Benedetto, Terence Brady, Randy Jurgenson, Marvin Cohen, Paul Gleason, Reinaldo Medina, Darryl Edwards, Donald Petrie, Thomas A. Carlin, Frederick Allen, Cominic Chianese, Mike Cichetti, Apu Guecia, Kim Delgado, Reyno, Dadi Pinero, Cleavant Derricks, Dolores Hernandez, Santos Morales, Ruth Last, José Rabelo, Gilbert Lewis, Lisa Loomer, Sandi Franklin, Eric Mourino, Jessica Costello, Gloria Irizarry, Manuel Santiago, Joaquin La Habana, Fred Strothers, Sylvia "Kuumba" Williams, Patricia Dratel, Thomas Fiorello.

Within half an hour from the start of this amalgam of glorified sub-plots, genial, moral South Bronx patrolman Paul Newman has, with his sidekick Ken Wahl, rescued a hysterical queen from a suicide leap, defended a homicidal hooker against her pimp, disarmed a maniac with a knife (by the simple expedient of Newman pulling

funny faces) and delivered a baby. This episodic all-in-a-day's-work approach works to a degree (the film is never boring) but all too often degenerates into a glib series of fragmented cameos (it is never that interesting). It is well known that Newman can carry a film on his own. It is neither necessary nor desirable that he should.

THE FOUR SEASONS (Universal)
dir-scr Alan Alda *pro* Martin Bregman *exec pro* Louis A. Stroller *ph* Victor J. Kemper, in Technicolor *ph* Michael Economou *pro des* Jack Collins *music* Antonio Vivaldi *r time* 108 mins *cert* AA *UK opening* Sept 3.
cast Alan Alda, Carol Burnett, Len Cariou, Sandy Dennis, Rita Moreno, Jack Weston, Bess Armstrong, Elizabeth Alda, Beatrice Alda, Robert Hitt, Kristi McCarthy, David Stackpole.

Suffocatingly soft-centred analysis of group friendship chronicled through a year in the life of three rather tiresome married couples and punctuated by their seasonal encounters. A moderately funny first half gives way, in the tradition of "thoughtful" American comedies, to a more serious

examination of the moralistic, self-regarding central characters. Nevertheless, an assured debut as a director by Alda.

THE FOX AND THE HOUND (Walt Disney)
dir Art Stevens, Ted Berman, Richard Rich *pro* Wolfgang Reitherman, Art Stevens *exec pro* Ron Miller *scr* Larry Clemmons, Ted Berman, Peter Young, Steve Hulett, David Michener, Burny Mattinson, Earl Kress, Vance Gerry, based on the novel by Daniel P. Mannix *ph* not credited, in Technicolor *ed* James Melton, Jim Koford *art dir* Don Griffith *music* Buddy Baker *r time* 83 mins *cert* U *UK opening* Oct 22.

Doggedly traditional Disney cartoon about an abandoned fox cub and a young hound puppy who grow up as friends and then find custom and instinct dictating that they be adversaries. High on the sugar, low on the laughs, but clearly enjoyed by the audience at which it is aimed, it could have been made at any time in the 45 years since 'Snow White and the Seven Dwarfs'.

Fort Apache the Bronx

THE FRENCH LIEUTENANT'S WOMAN (United Artists)

dir Karel Reisz *pro* Leon Clore *scr* Harold Pinter, based on the novel by John Fowles, in Technicolor *ed* John Bloom *pro des* Assheton Gorton *art dir* Norman Dorme, Terry Pritchard, Allan Cameron *music* Carl Davis *r time* 123 mins *cert* AA *UK opening* Oct 15.
cast Meryl Streep, Jeremy Irons, Leo McKern, Patience Collier, Hilton McRae, Emily Morgan, Charlotte Mitchell, Lynsey Baxter, Jean Faulds, Peter Vaughan, Colin Jeavons, Liz Smith, John Barrett, Arabella Weir, Ben Forster, Catherine Willmer, Anthony Langdon, Edward Duke, Richard Griffiths, Graham Fletcher-Cook, Richard Hope, Michael Elwyn, Toni Palmer, Cecily Hobbs, Doreen Mantle, David Warner, Alun Armstrong, Gerard Falconetti, Penelope Wilton, Joanna Joseph, Judith Alderson, Cora Kinnaird, Orlando Fraser, Fredrika Morton, Alice Maschler, Matthew Morton, Vicky Ireland, Claire Travers-Deacon, Harriet Walter, Janet Rawson, Mia Soteriou, Mary McLeod, Peter Fraser, Rayner Newmark.

Starchy but impressive adaptation of the Fowles best-seller, with the author's device of punctuating the narrative with an analysis of Victorian England replaced by a parallel story involving the actors themselves as participants in a film. When in costume, Jeremy Irons is the gentleman panteontologist who spots mournful, mysterious Meryl Streep staring out to sea in Lyme Regis and develops an obsessive passion. Neatly scripted by Pinter, and successful up to a point, it is too fussily self-conscious an attempt to make a great film to be one.

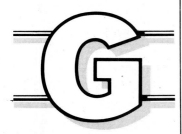

GALLIPOLI (Associated R & R Films)

dir Peter Weir *pro* Robert Stigwood, Patricia Lovell *exec pro* Francis O'Brien *scr* David Williamson *ph* Russell Boyd, in Panavision, Eastman Color *ed* William Anderson *art dir* Herbert Pinter *music* Brian May *r time* 111 mins *cert* A *UK opening* Dec 10.
cast Mark Lee, Mel Gibson, Bill Hunter, Robert Grubb, Tim McKenzie, David Argue, Bill Kerr, Ron Graham, Harold Hopkins, Charles Yunupingu, Heath Harris, Gerda Nicholson, Brian Anderson, Reg Evans, Jack Giddy, Dane Peterson, Paul Linkson, Jenny Lovell, Steve Dodd, Harold Baigent, Robyn Walwey, Don Quin, Phyllis Burford, Marjorie Irving, John Murphy, Peter Ford, Diane Chamberlain, Ian Govett, Geoff Parry, Clive Bennington, Giles Holland-Martin, Moshe Kedem, John Morris, Don Barker, Kiwi White, Paul Sonkkila, Peter Lawless, Saltbush Baldock, Les Dayman, Stan Green, Max Wearing, Graham Dow, Peter R. House.

Not so much a tale of men engaged in pointlessly sacrificial warfare —

Left: The French Lieutenant's Woman. Above: Gallipoli

although the Australian participation in the Dardanelles campaign of 1915 provides the film with its backdrop and climax — as a study of the friendship between two young runners in Western Australia who enlist for different reasons. In the spirited, patriotic tradition of 'Chariots of Fire', it shares its assets and liabilities by being handsome and touching yet trying a little too hard to pull the right heartstrings.

GEORGIA'S FRIENDS (Filmways/Fox)
(US TITLE: FOUR FRIENDS)

dir Arthur Penn *pro* Arthur Penn, Gene Lasko *exec pro* Michael Tolan, Julia Miles *scr* Steven Tesich *ph* Ghislain Cloquet, in Technicolor *ed* Barry Malkin, Marc Laub *pro des* David Chapman *art dir* Dick Hughes *music* Elizabeth Swados *r time* 115 mins *cert* AA *UK opening* Jun 17.
cast Craig Wasson, Jodi Thelen, Michael Huddleston, Jim Metzler, Scott Hardt, Elizabeth Lawrence, Miklos Simon, Michael Kovacs, Beatrice Fredman, Pier Calabria, Zaid Farid, David Graf, Felix Shuman, George Womack, Todd Isaacson, Sharon Kemp, Reed Birney, Harlan Hogan, Elizabeth Goldstein, Julia Murray, Dick Sollenberger, Lois Smith, James Leo Herlihy, Ramiro Carrillo, Merceded Ruehl, James

Maxwell, Glenne Headly, Paul Greco, Petrea Burchard, Natalija Nogulich, Branko Vasich, Ruzica Markovic, Helen Nogulich, Linh Thanh Ly Nguyen, Thu Anh Ly Nguyen, Nga Bich Thi Duong, Brandon Green, William Salatich, Alice Elliott.

Penn's first film since the remarkable 'Missouri Breaks' turns out to be the kind of wet, self-important, quasi-analytical tosh which characterised the worst excesses of the Sixties, a decade employed here both as catalyst and backdrop, with bits of period detail floating in and out like so many old calendar pages. The action itself follows the changing attitudes and fortunes of a group of high school friends, three of whom become infatuated with the fourth, a tiresome brat who gets pregnant by one, marries another and finally ends up with the immigrant steelworker's son who loved her all along (and who is the film's central character). It is hard to believe that such a heavy-handed exuberance-and-disillusion parable could come from as gifted a team as Penn and writer Steve Tesich, whose screenplay for 'Breaking Away' was the highlight of its year. Mawkish and melodramatic by turns, its statements about the American condition spelt out in neon, 'Friends' has all the awesome significance and penetrating awareness of a Simon and Garfunkel reunion concert.

THE GERMAN SISTERS (Bioskop-Film/Miracle)

dir-scr Margarethe von Trotta *pro* Eberhard Junkersdorf *ph* Franz Rath, in Fujicolor *ed* Dagmar Hirtz *art dir* Georg von Kieseritzky, Barbara Kloth *music* Nicolas Economou *r time* 107 mins *cert* AA *UK opening* May 13.
cast Jutta Lampe, Barbara Sukowa, Rudiger Vogler, Doris Schade, Verenice Rudolph, Luc Bondy, Franz Rudnick, Julia Biedermann, Ina

Robinski, Patrick Estrada-Pox, Samir Jawad, Barbara Paepcke, Rebecca Paepcke, Margit Czenki, Carola Hembus, Anna Steinmann, Wulfhild Sydow, Ingeborg Weber, Satan Deutscher, Karin Bremer, Rolf Schult, Anton Rattinger, Lydia Billiet, Hannelore Minkus, Wilbert Steinmann, Felix Moeller, Christoph Parge, Michael Sellmann.

Known principally for her collaborations with husband Volker Schlondorff, von Trotta is acquiring a substantial reputation of her own as a consequence of this slow, reflective study, inspired by a real-life parallel, of two sisters, a feminist journalist and a Baader-Meinhof terrorist. Immaculately made but incredibly heavy going, as such films tend to be.

GHOST STORY (Universal)

dir John Irvin *pro* Burt Weissbourd *scr* Lawrence D. Cohen, based on the novel by Peter Straub *ph* Jack Cardiff, in Technicolor *ed* Tom Rolf *art dir* Norman Newberry *music* Philippe Sarde *r time* 111 mins *cert* X *UK opening* Jan 28.
cast Fred Astaire, Melvyn Douglas, Douglas Fairbanks Jr, John Houseman, Craig Wasson, Patricia Neal, Alice Krige, Jacqueline Brookes, Miguel Fernandes, Lance Holcomb, Mark Chamberlin, Tim Choate, Kurt Johnson, Ken Olin, Brad Sullivan, Guy Boyd, Robert Burr, Helena Carroll, Robin Curtis, Breon Gorman, Cagle D. Green, Kyra Carleton, James Greene, Ruth Hunt, Deborah Offner, Michael O'Neil, Virginia P. Bingham, William E. Conway, Russell R. Bletzer, Terrance Mario Carnes, Alfred Curven, Edward F. Dillon, Alvin W. Fretz, Hugh Hires, Raymond J. Quinn, Barbara von Zastrow.

Swimming commendably against the predominant tide of terror movies by substituting as its victim figures a quartet of elderly men for the customary bunch of promiscuous teenagers, this adaptation of Straub's best seller is more of a ghost ramble really, leading its audience through a labyrinth of subplots and flashbacks as the four old lags are haunted by the vengeful spirit of a young girl who once died through their neglect. Shorn by a quarter of its length, and livened up by the vulgar exploitative touch of a William Castle, it might have made an agreeable enough support feature.

A GIRL FROM LORRAINE (Phenix-Gaumont-SSR/Gala)

dir Claude Goretta *pro* Yves Peyrot, Raymond Pousaz *scr* Claude Goretta, Jacques Kirsner, Rosina Rochette *ph* Philippe Rousselot, in colour *ed* Joele Van Effenterre *art dir* Jacques Bufnoir *music* Arie Dzierlatka *r time* 112 mins *cert* AA *UK opening* Feb 4.
cast Nathalie Baye, Angela Winkler, Bruno Ganz, Pierre Vernier, Patrick Chesnais, Dominique Paturel, Roland Monod, Jean Obe, Henri Poirier, Robert Rimbaud, Jean Davy, Jacques Lalande.

Thoughtful, nicely observed if rather po-faced film about an unemployed provincial woman (a persuasive and engaging performance from Nathalie Baye) who goes to Paris looking for a job and finds instead the things wide-eyed outsiders always seem to be up against: loneliness, disappointment, alienation and of course other people who come from somewhere else. Considering the liabilities of movies founded on incorruptible innocents adrift in the big city, it all works rather well, although Goretta could now do with a change of gear.

THE GODS MUST BE CRAZY (Mimosa Films/New Realm)

dir-pro-scr-ed Jamie Uys *exec pro* Boet Troskie *ph* Buster Reynolds, Jamie Uys, Robert Lewis, in colour *art dir* Caroline Burls *music* John Boshoff *r time* 108 mins *cert* A *UK opening* Apr 8.
cast Xao, Marius Weyers, Sandra Prinsloo, Nic de Jager, Louw Verwey, Michael Thys, Fanyana Sidumo, Joe Seakatsie, Brian O'Shaughnessy, Vera Blacker, Ken Gampu, Jamie Uys.

A Coca-Cola bottle (very symbolic) is dropped from a passing plane into the Kalahari desert, disrupting life among the tribe of Bushmen who find it; one of them is sent to throw if off the edge of the world. Despite a departure point which would have discouraged anyone except the person who wrote it, 'The Gods Must Be Crazy' is, for all its slapstick excess (plentiful) and occasional tweeness (the voice-over), one of the most unassumingly enjoyable comedies of the year. Much disliked by the touchy white consciences who have become the new custodians of black culture, it is a real banana-skin fairy-tale, terribly flimsy but enormously winning.

GOODBYE PORK PIE (New Zealand Film Commission/Brent Walker)

dir Geoff Murphy *pro* Nigel Hutchinson, Geoff Murphy *scr* Geoff Murphy, Ian Mune *ph* Alaun Bollinger, in Eastman Color *ed* Mike Horton *art dir* Kal Hawkins, Robin Outterside *music* John Charles *r time* 105 mins *cert* AA *UK opening* Oct 15.
cast Tony Barry, Kelly Johnson, Claire Oberman, Shirley Gruar, Jackie Lowitt, Don Selwyn, Shirley Dunn, Paki Cherrington, Christine Lloyd, Maggie Maxwell, John Ferdinand, Clyde Scott, Steven Tozer, Phil Gordon, Bruno Lawrence, Adele Chapman, Ian Watkin, Frances Edmond, Marshall Napier, Bill Juliff, John Bach, Liz Simpson, Alan Wilke, Paul Watson, Timothy Lee, Michael Woolf, Andrew Dungan, Frank Prythetch, Linus Murphy, Matthew

Nieuwlands, Danny O'Connel, Paul Paino, David Pottinger, Keith Richardson, Roy Sanders, Gene Saunders, Doug Aston, Charles Barlow, Len Bernard, Mike Booth, Morris Bruce, Bill Carson, Norman Fairley, Norman Fletcher, Ged Sharp, Peter Sledmere, Kevin Simpson, The Wizard, Brain Ward, John Galvin, Dee Kelly, Max Kennard, Melissa Lawrence, Chris Lines, Jim Woodfine.

Exuberant, affectionate New Zealand road movie in which two joyriders in a stolen Mini are pursued by the police from one end of the country to the other. Fuelled by its great vitality and engaging lack of pretension, the only liability is a slight tendency towards self-conscious zaniness.

THE GRASS IS SINGING (Chibote-Swedish Film Institute/Mainline)

dir Michael Raeburn *pro* Mark Forstater *scr* Michael Raeburn, from the novel by Doris Lessing *ph* Bille August, in colour *ed* Thomas Schalm *pro des* Disley Jones *music* Lasse Dahlberg, Bjorn Isfalt, (African) Temba Tana *r time* 110 mins *cert* A *UK opening* Apr 22.
cast Karen Black, John Thaw, John Kani, John Moulder-Brown, Patrick Mynhardt, Bjorn Gedda.

Making the most of its scenic Zambian locations, but drowning them in an Afro-European soup of a score, Lessing's tale of an insecure woman who marries a farmer and goes round the bend in the Bush becomes a routine exercise in over-wrought melodrama: decent, passionate but somehow off the mark. John Thaw, whose accent lies somewhere between Golders Green and the Transvaal, spends much of the time suffering from malaria.

THE GREAT MUPPET CAPER (ITC)

dir Jim Henson *pro* David Lazer, Frank Oz *exec pro* Martin Starger *scr* Tom Patchett, Jay Tarses, Jery Juhl, Jack Rose *ph* Oswald Morris, in Technicolor *ed* Ralph Kemplen *pro des* Harry Lange *art dir* Leigh Malone *music* Joe Raposo *r time* 97 mins *cert* U *UK opening* Jul 30.
cast Diana Rigg, Charles Grodin, John Cleese, Robert Morley, Peter Ustinov, Jack Warden, Erica Creer, Kate Howard, Della Finch, Michael Robbins, Joan Sanderson, Peter Hughes, Peggy Aitchison, Tommy Godfrey, Katia Borg, Valli Kemp, Michele Ivan-Zadeh, Chai Lee, Christine Nelson, Rodney Lovick, Suzanne Church, Ian Hanham, David Ludwig, Mary Mazstead, Patti Dalton, Cynthia Ashley, Lynn Latham, Susan Backlinie, Cynthia Leake, Sherrill Cannon, Kahren Lohren, Christine Cullen, Tricia McFarlin, Susie Guest, Denise McKenna, Wendy Holker, Melina Lee Phelps, Linda Horn, Denise Potter, Lee Keenan, Ann Rynne, Darine Klega, Roberta Ward, Peter Falk.

Enjoyable, lively, greatly improved follow-up to 'The Muppet Movie' with a "proper" story (Kermit and Fozzie are investigative reporters in pursuit of jewel thieves) and numerous nods to Hollywood musicals, most tellingly when Miss Piggy does a water ballet in the style of Esther Williams with the spirit of Busby Berkeley. The humans, needless to say, are left at the starting post.

GROUND ZERO (James Flocker Enterprises/London International)

dir-pro James T. Flocker *scr* Samuel Newman *ph* David P. Flocker, in colour *ed* David E. Jackson *music* Phil Comer, Frank Vierra, Mike Sedlak, Mark Comer, Delano Damron *r time* 86 mins *cert* A *UK opening* Jul 16.
cast Ron Casteel, Melvin Belli, Augie Treibach, Kim Friese, John Waugh, Yvonne D'Angiers, Hal Stein, Dominic Guzzo, Anthony Curcio, Mike Maurantonio, Lia Belli, Charles Granata, David Button, Vincent Turturici, Ernest Arata, Mike Loring, Larry Higgins, Gary Adams, Leo Hutchison, Norman Nelson, Gerald French, Henry Eslick, John Dunn, Gary Ellis, David Flocker.

A nuclear bomb placed by a gang of terrorists in a tower on San Francisco's Golden Gate Bridge. A secret service agent with a limp and a propensity for philosophising at unlikely moments. These are the principal ingredients of this utterly implausible, thoroughly enjoyable turkey, buried for eight years (it was released in the US in 1973) and disinterred for reasons which remain a mystery.

Right: The Great Muppet Caper

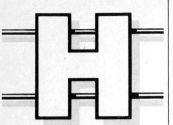

HALLOWEEN II (Dino De Laurentiis/EMI)

dir Rick Rosenthal *pro-scr* Debra Hill, John Carpenter *exec pro* Irwin Yablans, Joseph Wolf *ph* Dean Cundey, in Panavision, Metrocolor *music* John Carpenter, Alan Howarth *r time* 92 mins *cert* X *UK opening* Feb 25.
cast Jamie Lee Curtis, Donald Pleasence, Charles Cyphers, Jeffrey Kramer, Lance Guest, Pamela Susan Shoop, Hunter von Leer, Dick Warlock, Leo Rossi, Gloria Gifford, Tawny Moyer, Ana Alicia, Ford Rainey, Cliff Emmich, Nancy Stephens, John Zenda, Catherine Bergstrom, Alan Haufrect, Lucille Bensen, Howard Culver, Dana Carvey, Bill Warlock, Jonathan Prince, Leigh French, Ty Mitchell, Nancy Loomis, Pamela McMyler, Dennis Holahan, Nichole Drucker, Ken Smolka, Adam Gunn, Roger Hampton, Robin Coleman, Jack Verbois, Tony Moran, Kyle Richards, Brian Andrews, Anne Bruner.

The first half hour is far from promising. The end of Carpenter's original is dutifully re-enacted, the old victims are found while new ones are being lined up, rather a lot of philosophical waffle is dispensed and the subjective camera stalks around in the prescribed manner. However, things improve immeasurably once the action has moved to the hospital where Jamie Lee Curtis is recovering from her earlier ordeal while the seemingly indestructible killer wanders the corridors, and Rosenthal makes skilful use of all the tricks which keep an audience on the boil. 'Halloween III', needless to say, has already been announced.

HEAVEN'S GATE (United Artists)

dir-scr Michael Cimino *pro* Joann Carelli *ph* Vilmos Zsigmond, in Panavision, Technicolor *ed* Tom Rolf, William Reynolds, Lisa Fruchtman, Gerald Greenberg *art dir* Tambi Larsen, Spencer Deverill, Maurice Fowler *music* David Mansfield *r time* 148 mins (first showing 205 mins) *cert* X *UK opening* Sept 10.
cast Kris Kristofferson, Christopher Walken, John Hurt, Sam Waterston, Brad Dourif, Isabelle Huppert, Joseph Cotten, Jeff Bridges, Ronnie Hawkins, Paul Koslo, Geoffrey Lewis, Richard Masur, Roseanne Vela, Mary C. Wright, Nicholas Woodeson, Stefan Shcherby, Waldemar Kalinowski, Terry O'Quinn, John Conley, Margaret

Heaven's Gate

Benczak, James Knobeloch, Erika Petersen, Robin Bartlett, Tom Noonan, Marat Yusim, Aivars Smits, Gordana Rashovich, Jarlath Conroy, Allen Keller, Caroline Kava, Mady Kaplan, Anna Levine, Pat Hodges, Mickey Rourke, Kevin McClarnon, Kai Wulff, Steve Majstorovic, Gabriel Walsh, Norton Buffalo, Jack Blessing, Jerry Sullivan.

Cut by an hour following its disastrous American opening, and still failing miserably at the box office (budget $36m, US rentals $1.5m), Cimino's folly turned out to be neither the all-eclipsing masterwork he clearly intended nor the irredeemable turkey his critics dismissed. Ravishingly photographed (misty browns for the interiors, cloud formations and far horizons for the exteriors) in the self-conscious 'painterly' style of 'Ryan's Daughter' and 'Barry Lyndon', with touches of 'McCabe and Mrs Miller', it is a triumph of style over content: marvellous set pieces, millions of authentic looking extras and a real sense of small bloody struggles in a big country (the Johnson County War in Wyoming) without at any stage making one interested in the people who participate in them. There is a snow-capped mountain behind the town which looks just like the one in the Paramount logo. You can almost hear it breathe a sigh of relief that the bill wasn't theirs.

HEAVY METAL (Columbia)

dir Gerald Potterton *pro* Ivan Reitman *exec pro* Leonard Mogel *scr* Dan Goldberg, Len Blum, based on original art and stories by Richard Corben, Angus McKie, Dan O'Bannon, Thomas Warkentin, Berni Wrightson *ph* in Metrocolor *ed* Janice Brown *pro des* Michael Gross *music* Elmer Bernstein *r time* 90 mins *cert* AA *UK opening* Dec 17.

Cinema cartoons for 'adults', even if they are inspired by a noted sci-fi magazine and feature a thousand artists, tend to be highly avoidable. Whimsical, would-be mystical and full of all the customary time-space travel themes, they are best enjoyed by people who either went to Woodstock or wish they had; people who are 'into' rock'n'roll. Indeed, the soundtrack here, with the exception of the effortlessly unclassifiable Devo, is a real heavy-metallurgist's convention. These films are twee and tiresome. Avoid them, and avoid this one.

HELL NIGHT (BLT/Miracle)

dir Tom De Simone *pro* Irwin Yablans, Bruce Cohn Curtis *exec pro* Joseph Wolf, Chuck Russell *scr* Randolph Feldman *ph* Mac Ahlberg, in Metrocolor *ed* Tony Di Marco *art dir* Steven G. Legler *music* Dan Wyman *r time* 100 mins *cert* X *UK opening* Feb 4.
cast Linda Blair, Vincent Van Patten, Peter Barton, Kevin Brophy, Jenny Neumann, Suki Goodwin, Jimmy Sturtevant, Hal Ralston, Cary Fox, Ronald Gans, Gloria Hellman.

Drumming his fingers on the table in the interval between producing 'Halloweens' I and II, Yablans clearly decided to keep his hand in with this fancy-dress variation on 'Friday the 13th', in which the usual college students (this time in costume on account of a fraternity party) are terrorised by the usual twisted mutant (this time in a haunted mansion). Or maybe there are two mutants. In films of this kind, it doesn't matter much. This one is better than many, although still not a patch on 'Halloween'.

HERBIE GOES BANANAS (Walt Disney)

dir Vincent McEveety *pro* Ron Miller *scr* Don Tait, based on characters created by Gordon Buford *ph* Frank Phillips, in Technicolor *ed* Gordon D. Brenner *art dir* John B. Mansbridge, Rodger Maus, Augustin Ytuarte *music* Frank De Vol *r time* 93 mins *cert* U *UK opening* Jul 23.

cast Cloris Leachman, Charles Martin Smith, John Vernon, Stephan W. Burns, Elyssa Davalos, Joaquin Garay III, Harvey Korman, Richard Jaeckel, Alex Rocco, Fritz Feld, Vito Scotti, Jose Gonzalez Gonzalez, Rubin Moreno, Tina Melard, Jorge Moreno, Allan Hunt, Tom Scott, Hector Morales, Iris Adrian, Ceil Cabot, Patricia Van Patten, Jack Perkins, Henry Slate, Ernie Fuentes, Antonio Trevino, Dante D'Andre, Alma Beltran, Dolores Aguirre, Aurora Coria, Alex Tinne, Don Diamond, Warde Donovan, Ray Victor, Bert Santos, Buddy Joe Hooker, Steve Boyum, Kenny Endoso, Mario Cisneros, Jeff Ramsey, John C. Meier.

Cheerful Disney pot-boiler with attractive location work framing a familiar story about what happens after a junior Mexican pickpocket gets his wallets mixed up. Herbie himself is as cute as ever but must be due for a visit to the scrapyard soon.

THE HERD (Guney Film/BFI)

dir Zeki Okten *scr* Yilmaz Guney *ph* Izzet Akay, in Eastman Color *ed* Ozdemir Aritan *pro des* Rauf Ozangil, Sabri Aslankara *music* Zulfu Livaneli *r time* 118 mins *cert* AA *UK opening* May 27.
cast Tarik Akan, Melike Demirag, Tuncel Kuritz, Levent Inanir, Meral Niron, Erol Demiroz, Yaman Okay, Savas Yurttas, Sener Kokkaya, Fehmi Yasar, Gokturk Demirezen, Suayip Adlig, Guler Okten, Turgut Okutman, Gulten Kaya, Ekrem Erkek, Resmiye Yilmaz, Cemile Talan, Zeliha Bekan, Cevahir Civelek.

Handsomely filmed, impressively sustained drama, made in 1978, about the gradual disintegration of old shepherd-family ways as they become exposed to the ravaging effects of modern Turkey. Written in a prison cell by Yilmaz Guney who, until his recent escape, had spent most of the past decade in jail.

HISTORY OF THE WORLD PART I (Brooksfilms/EMI)

dir-pro-scr Mel Brooks *ph* Woody Omens, Paul Wilson, in Panavision, DeLuxe Colour *ed* John C. Howard, Danford B. Greene *pro des* Harold Michelson, Stuart Craig *art dir* Norman Newberry, Bob Cartwright *music* John Morris *r time* 92 mins *cert* AA *UK opening* Oct 8.
cast Mel Brooks, Dom DeLuise, Madeline Kahn, Harvey Korman, Cloris Leachman, Ron Carey, Gregory

History of the World Part I

Hines, Pamela Stephenson, Andreas Voutsina, Shecky Greene, Sid Caesar, Howard Morris, Rudy DeLuca, Mary-Margaret Humes, J.J. Barry, Sammy Shore, Michael Champion, Earl Finn, Leigh French, Richard Karron, Susette Carroll, Suzanne Kent, Bea Arthur, Charlie Callas, Dena Dietrich, Paul Mazursky, Rod Haase, Ron Clark, Jack Riley, Art Metrano, Diane Day, Henny Youngman, Hunter Von Leer, Fritz Feld, Hugh Hefner, Pat McCormick, Barry Levinson, Sid Gould, Jim Steck, Ronny Graham, John Myhers, Lee Delano, Robert B. Goldberg, Alan U. Schwartz, Jay Burton, Robert Zappy, Ira Miller, Milt Freedman, Johnny Silver, Charles Thomas Murphy, Eileen Saki, Molly Basler, Christine Dickinson, Deborah Dawes, Lisa Sohm, Michele Drake, Jeana Tomasino, Lisa Welch, Janis Schmitt, Heidi Sorenson, Karen Morton, Kathy Collins, Lori Sutton, Lou Mulford, John Hurt, Henry Kaiser, Zale Kessler, Anthony Messina, Howard Mann, Sandy Helberg, Mitchell Bock, Gilbert Lee, Jackie Mason, Phil Leeds, Eddie Heim, David Chavez, John Frayer, Dennon

Rawles, Rick Mason, Stan Mazin, Dom Salinaro, Jim Roddy, Ted Sprague, Spencer Henderson, Bill Armstrong, John King, Jack Carter, Jan Murray, Spike Milligan, John Hillerman, Sidney Lassick, Jonathan Cecil, Andrew Sachs, Fiona Richmond, Nigel Hawthorne, Bella Emberg, Geoffrey Larder, George Lane Cooper, Stephanie Marrian, Royce Mills, Mike Cottrell, Gerald Stadden, John Gavin, Rusty Goff, Monica Teama, Cleo Rocos, Jilly Johnson.

A great comic mind with a wayward sense of judgment, Brooks seems to have settled for throwing an abundance of tired scatological jokes at the camera and seeing what sticks. Simply, it works too hard to little effect, its attempt to do for historical epics what 'Airplane!' did for disaster movies falling increasingly flat, its bawdiness merely tiresome. Most depressing of all, the big production number, obviously intended to eclipse the memory of 'Springtime for Hitler', fails to raise much more than a knowing smile. If he'd made it all in England 15 years ago with Sid James and the gang, it might have worked.

HOG WILD (Bordeaux)
dir Les Rose *pro* Claude Heroux *exec pro* Victor Solnicki, Pierre David, Stephen Miller *scr* Andrew Peter Marin *ph* Rene Verzier, in colour *ed* Dominique Boisvert *pro des* Carol Spier *art dir* Ninkey Dalton *music* Paul Zaza *r time* 95 mins *cert* AA *UK opening* Jun 24.
cast Patti D'Arbanville, Michael Biehn, Tony Rosato, Angelo Rizacos, Martin Doyle, Claude Phillipe, Matt Craven, Jack Blum, Keith Knight, Michael Zelnicker, Robin McCulloch, Sean McCann, John Rutter, Bronwen

Mantel, Karen Stephen, Stephanie Miller, Mitch Martin, Jacoba Knaapen, Thomas Kovacs, Matt Birman-Feldman, Susan Harrop, Norman Taviss, Bena Singer, Len Watt, Rolly Nincheri, Rudy Stoeckel, Alexander Godfrey, Richard Rebiere, Stephen Bloomer, Thom Haverstock, Timothy Webber, Andrew Semple, Stephen Mayoff, Helen Udy, Erik Kalacis, Marilyn Rosell.

Leadenly paced, utterly charmless biker comedy about how the mild-mannered high school boys (some of them looking near retirement age) stop getting sand kicked in their faces by a gang of sneering bad-asses in leather. A turgid hybrid of 'Animal House' and 'American Graffiti', its only redeeming factors are a cartoon of a performance from Tony Rosato as the biker big-boy (although he can't decide whether to be Belushi or Brando, and goes for both) and a scene in which his girlfriend and the principal wimp consummate their suppressed passion in a giant vat of honey. The soundtrack, incidentally, is one of those that, by commenting on the action all the time, assumes the audience is as dumb as the film.

— 35 —

HONEYSUCKLE ROSE (Warner)
dir Jerry Schatzberg *pro* Gene Taft
exec pro Sydney Pollack *scr* Carol
Sobieski, William D Wittliff, John
Binder, based on the story by Gosta
Steven, Gustav Holander *ph* Robby
Muller in Panavision, Technicolor *ed*
Aram Avakian, Norman Gay, Marc
Laub, Evan Lottman *pro des* Joel
Schiller *r time* 119 mins *cert* A *UK
opening* Aug 20.
cast Willie Nelson, Dyan Cannon, Amy
Irving, Slim Pickens, Joey Floyd,
Charles Levin, Priscilla Pointer,
Mickey Rooney Jr, Pepe Serna, Lane
Smith, Diana Scarwid, Emmylou
Harris, Rex Ludwick, Mickey Raphael,
Bee Spears, Chris Ethridge, Paul
English, Bobby Nelson, Jody Payne,
Randy ''Poodie'' Locke, T. Snake,
Johnny Gimble, Kenneth Threadgill,
Grady Martin, Hank Cochran, Jeannie
Seely, Gene Rader, Frank Stewart, Lu
Belle Camp, A.L. Camp, Bernedette
Whitehead, Jackie Ezzell, Harvey
Christiansen, Hackberry Johnson,
Kenneth Eric Hamilton, Nelson
Fowler, Guy Houston Garrett, Centa
Boyd, Cara Kanak, Augie Myers,
Robert Gotschall, Emilio Gonzales,
Mary Jane Valle, Randy Arlyn
Fletcher, Ray Liberto, Sam Allred,
Bob Baty, John Meadows, Crody
Hubach, Dick Gimble, Maurice
Anderson, Ray D. Hollingsworth, Bill
Mounce, Kenny Frazier.

*Old-fashioned, heart-on-its-sleeve
romantic drama about Willie Nelson's
interior tug of war between the
pleasures of domesticity with Dyan
Cannon and the lure of the road with
his country-and-western group. It is
also about the perils of singing lovey-
dovey duets on stage with your ex-
guitarist's daughter while your wife is
watching.*

HONKY TONK FREEWAY (EMI)
dir John Schlesinger *pro* Don Boyd,
Howard W. Koch Jr. *scr* Edward
Clinton *ph* John Bailey, in Technicolor
ed Jim Clark *art dir* Edwin O'Donovan
music George Martin, Elmer Bernstein
r time 107 mins *cert* AA *UK opening*
Oct 15.
cast William Devane, Beau Bridges,
Teri Garr, Beverly D'Angelo, Hume
Cronyn, Jessica Tandy, Howard
Hesseman, Paul Jabara, Daniel Stern,
George Dzundza, Joe Grifasi, Deborah
Rush, Geraldine Page, David Rasche,
Frances Lee McCain, Sandra McCabe,
Renny Roker, Celia Weston, Jenn
Thompson, Peter Billingsley, Ron
Frazier, Jerry Hardin, John Ashton,
John C. Becher, Alice Beardsley, Davis
Roberts, Loretta Tupper, Francis Bay,
Rollin Moriyama, Kimiko Hiroshige,
James Staley, Shelley Batt, Jason
Keller, Shane Keller, Kelly Lange,
Kent Williams, Arnold Johnson,
Nancy Parsons, Jessica Rains, Ann
Risley, Helen Hanft, Don Morgan,
Paul Keenan, Robert Stoneman,
Randy Norton, Al Corley, Murphy
Dunn, Leo Burmester, Jeffrey Combs,
Jack Murdock, Ann Coleman, Gordon

Right: Honky Tonk Freeway

Haight, Jack Thibeau, Martha Gehman, George Solomon, Dick Christie, Anita Dangler, Mags Kavanaugh, Gloria Leroy.

Cheerfully overstated satire-on-wheels as a cross-section of state-of-America stereotypes inadvertently end up in a small Florida town which is struggling to get a freeway exit. Populated by enough characters to accommodate several sittings of the cabin scene in 'A Night at the Opera', and with an episodic framework reminiscent of Kramer's 'Mad World', the main problem is that it spreads its laughs too broadly. But unlike many comedies this year, it has some laughs to spread. Greatly disparaged on release, rather enjoyable in retrospect.

HOT BUBBLEGUM (Noah Films-Planet/Cannon)
dir Boaz Davidson *pro* Menahem Golan, Yoram Globus *exec pro* Sam Waynberg *scr* Eli Tavor, Boaz Davidson *ph* Amnon Solomon, in colour *ed* Jhon Koslowsky *art dir* Ariel Roshko *r time* 94 mins *cert* X *UK opening* Jul 5.
cast Yiftach Katzur, Zacki Noy, Jonathan Segal, Devora Kadar, Menashe Warshansky, Ariela Rabinovitch, Orna Dagan, Rachel Steiner, Avi Hadash, Sybille Roach, Christina Schmittmer, Joshua Loof, Amos Levy, Chaya Cohen, Raveet Lithman, Irit Barak, Olga Spondorf, Myriam Fuks.

Witless, formulaic third instalment, following 'Lemon Popsicle' and 'Going Steady', of the tepid Israeli series, itself a shallow reproduction of 'American Graffiti'. The traditional range of Fifties songs is dutifully wheeled out on the soundtrack.

HOW TO BEAT THE HIGH COST OF LIVING (Filmways-AIP/New Realm)
dir Robert Scheerer *pro* Jerome M. Zeitman, Robert Kaufman *exec pro* Samuel Z. Arkoff *scr* Robert Kaufman *ph* James Crabe, in colour *ed* Bill Butler *pro des* Lawrence G. Paull *music* Patrick Williams *r time* 97 mins *cert* AA *UK opening* Nov 15.
cast Susan Saint James, Jane Curtin, Jessica Lange, Richard Benjamin, Eddie Albert, Cathryn Damon, Dabney Coleman, Sybil Danning, Michael Bell, Susan Tolsky, Byron Morrow, Allan Warnick, Art Metrano, Ronnie Schell, Garrett Morris, Fred Willard, Al Checco, David Lunney, Michael K. Daly, James "Izzy" Whetstine, Jack Krupnick, James Aday, Wesley Baldwin, Sarah Leonard, Robin Hickman, Daniel Maves, Tom Morrison, Jonathan Schwartz, Jane

Van Boskirk, Jon Dickman, Bill Ritchie, Robert Canaga, Colleen Murff, Stan Boyd, Jerry Zinnamon, Tom Gressler, Philip Miller, Ralph Garrett, Robert W. Talbot, Harvey Lewis, Nanci Westerland, Joan Schumacher, Scott Barkhurst, Linda Hall, Craig Jackson, Larry Woodruff, Wendy Shawn, Carmen Zapata, Dru Wagner.

Engaging and enjoyable female heist movie in which three friends with financial problems decide to steal the money they need. Well performed, wittily scripted and devoid of further pretensions.

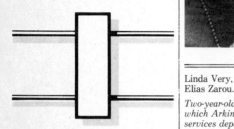

I'M COMING YOUR WAY (SNPC-Arturo Gonzalez/Tigon)
dir Tony Moore *pro* Mario Alabiso *scr* Sergio Chiusi, Robert Estevez, Tony La Penna *ph* Valverde Mateos Manuel, in Telecolor *ed* Gianfranco Amicucci *art dir* Gumersindo Andrea Lopez *music* Marcello Giombini *r time* 67 mins *cert* X *UK opening* Dec 3.
cast Ajita Wilson, Cristina Lai, Anthony Steffen, Luciano Rossi, Stelio Candelli, Aldo Minardi, Franco Daddi, Maite Micott, Serafino Profumo, Agota Gobertina, Zaira Zoccheddu, Adelaide Cendra, Valeria Magrini, Maristella Greco, Anna Maria Panaro.

Great (completely irrelevant) title, terrible (completely irrelevant) film.

IMPROPER CHANNELS (Paragon/Rank)
dir Eric Till *pro* Alfred Pariser, Morrie Ruvinsky *exec pro* Jon Slan *scr* Morrie Ruvinsky, Ian Sutherland, Alan Arkin *ph* Anthony Richmond, in colour *ed* Thom Noble *art dir* Ninkey Dalton, Charles Dunlop *music* Micky Erbe, Maribeth Solomon *r time* 93 mins *cert* A *UK opening* Nov 8.
cast Alan Arkin, Mariette Hartley, Monica Parker, Harry Ditson, Benjamin Gordon, Kate Lynch, Jane Mallett, Sarah Stevens, Danny Higham, Leslie Yeo, Richard Farrell, Martin Yan, Ruth Springford, Tony Rosato, Philip Akin, Harvey Atkin, Richard Blackburn, Jessica Booker, Ken Camroux, Les Carlson, Eugene Clark, Eric Clavering, Gillie Fenwick, Vanya Frank, Paul Emile Frappier, Angelo Fusco, Joyce Gordon, Luba Goy, Lynda Mason Green, Tim Henry, Alfred Humphreys, Sandy Kovack, Sylvia Llewellyn, David Main, Al Maini, Kate McDonald, Marianne McIsaac, Harry McWilliams, Patrick Patterson, Wayne Robson, Patrick Rose, Stephanie Shouldus, Ted Turner,

In God We Trust

Linda Very, Mary Charlotte Wilcox, Elias Zarou.

Two-year-old Canadian comedy in which Arkin fights a city's social services department and its computer centre to regain custody of his daughter. It has its moments but there aren't many of them.

IN GOD WE TRUST (Universal)
dir Marty Feldman *pro* Howard West, George Shapiro *exec pro* Norman T. Herman *scr* Marty Feldman, Chris Allen *ph* Charles Correll, in Technicolor *ed* David Blewitt *pro des* Lawrence G. Paull *music* John Morris *r time* 97 mins *cert* AA *UK opening* Aug 13.
cast Marty Feldman, Peter Boyle, Louise Lasser, Wilfrid Hyde-White, Richard Pryor, Andy Kaufman, Severn Darden, Eddie Parkes, Barbara Ann Walters, David Burton, Kaisen Chu, Chuck Hicks, Rose Mitchom, Sue Angelyn Strain, Terry L. Finch, David Francis Banks, Stephanie Ross, Richard A. Roth, John J. Koshel, Peter Koshel, Lynda Chase-Chankin, Brayton "Bob" Yerkes, David Bond, Norman Bartold, Len Lawson, Peter Nyberg, Paul Baxley, Larri Thomas.

Hideously unfunny would-be blasphemous comedy, in the tradition of Mel Brooks and Monty Python, about a monk sent into a world of hookers, tricksters and religious charlatans to raise money for the monastery. Lots of sniggering innuendo and heavy-handed satire. Hardly a laugh raised.

THE INQUISITOR (Ariane-TF1/Gala)
dir Claude Miller *pro* Georges Dancigers, Alexandre Mnouchkine *scr* Claude Miller, Jean Herman, Michel Audiard, based on the novel 'Brainwash' by John Wainwright *ph* Bruno Nuytten, in Eastman Color *ed* Albert Jurgenson *art dir* Eric Moulard *music* Georges Delerue *r time* 90 mins *cert* AA *UK opening* Apr 8.
cast Lino Ventura, Michel Serrault, Guy Marchand, Romy Schneider, Didier Agostini, Patrick Depeyrat, Pierre Maguelon, Serge Malik, Jean-Claude Penchenat, Yves Pignot,

Mathieu Schiffman, Michel Such, Elsa Lunghini, Mohammed Bekireche.

Superficially little more than a shifting cat-and-mouse dialogue for two against a backdrop of New Year's Eve festivities and dark bourgeois secrets — and rarely moving from the room in the French town police station where an inspector interrogates a wealthy lawyer suspected of child murder — this riveting psychological thriller, far from conveying the static staginess one might anticipate, is full of exciting detail and subtly changing balances of sympathy, suspicion and guilt. An excellent script superbly acted by all concerned, particularly Ventura and Serrault.

INSATIABLE (Amanda)
dir-pro Godfrey Daniels *ph* J.R. Baggs, in colour *art dir* Skip Davis *r time* 67 mins *cert* X *UK opening* Feb 25.
cast Marilyn Chambers, John C. Holmes, Serena, Jesie St. James, John Leslie, Mike Ranger, David Morris, Richard Pacheco, Joan Turner.

An orphaned nymphomaniac with a modelling career, a large inheritance and a colossal sex drive recalls how she acquired it, punctuated by fantasies, flashbacks and several chats with her aunt. Using a lot of redundant split-screen effects, and apparently cut by several significant minutes, satiation is reached quite rapidly and with all the empty drama of a premature ejaculation.

I, THE JURY (Warner)
dir Richard T. Heffron *pro* Robert Solo *scr* Larry Cohen, based on the novel by Mickey Spillane *ph* Andrew Laszlo, in Technicolor *ed* Garth Craven *pro des* Robert Gundlach *music* Bill Conti *r time* 109 mins *cert* X *UK opening* May 13.
cast Armand Assante, Barbara Carrera, Laurene Landon, Alan King, Geoffrey Lewis, Paul Sorvino, Judson Scott, Barry Snider, Julia Barr, Jessica James, Frederick Downs, Mary Margaret Amato, F.J. O'Neil, William Schilling, Robert Sevra, Don Pike,

Timothy Myers, Lee Anne Harris, Lynette Harris, Gwynn Gillis, Mike Miller, Alex Stevens, Bobbi Burns, M. Sharon Madigan, Richard Russell Ramos, Norm Blankenship, Daniel Faraldo, H. Richard Greene, Felicity Adler, Jodi Douglas, Lee H. Doyle, Cheryl Henry, Michael Fiorello, Herb Peterson, Richard Dahlia, Aaron Barsky, Ernest Harada, Larry Pine, Joe Farago, Alan Dellay, Jack Davidson, Loring Pickering, Corrinne Bohrer.

Plagued by production problems (including an early bath for director Larry Cohen), the second film version of Spillane's celebrated first novel is punctuated with numerous grisly deaths, a surfeit of random sadism and the full complement of miscellaneous unpleasantness, which it details with ostentatious relish. It's the comic-strip update with added gore, the traditional tale of revenge fencing for prominence with the CIA references and the sex clinic jokes. And it provides further evidence of the fact that, with the exception of Aldrich's masterful 'Kiss Me Deadly', Spillane has not transferred well to the screen, worst of all when he was daft enough to play his own central character in 'The Girl Hunters'. It is not without its redeeming factors, however: pace, occasional wit ("Try not to kill more than two or three people today", the rueful police captain advises Hammer) and self-parody on overtime.

IT HURTS ONLY WHEN I LAUGH (Columbia)
(US TITLE: ONLY WHEN I LAUGH)
dir Glenn Jordan *pro* Roger M. Rothstein, Neil Simon *scr* Neil Simon, based on his play 'The Gingerbread Lady' *ph* David M. Walsh, in Metrocolor *ed* John Wright *pro des* Albert Brenner *art dir* David Haber *music* David Shire *r time* 120 mins *cert* AA *UK opening* Jan 28.
cast Marsha Mason, Kristy McNichol, James Coco, Joan Hackett, David Dukes, John Bennett Perry, Guy Boyd, Ed Moore, Byron Webster, Peter Coffield, Mark Schubb, Ellen La Gamba, Venida Evans, John Vargas, Nancy Nagler, Dan Monahan, Michael Ross, Tom Ormeny, Ken Weisbrath, Henry Olek, Jane Atkins, Kevin Bacon, Ron Levine, Rebecca Stanley, Dick La Padula, Phillip Lindsay, Birdie Hale, Wayne Framson.

A little of Neil Simon goes a very long way. One of the acknowledged masters of comedy dialogue in the last two decades, and co-producer of this self-adaptation from one of his conveyor-belt sequence of plays, Simon's idea of a good line is a succession of suffocatingly self-conscious wisecracks-by-numbers delivered by whoever happens to be around at the time. There is no question about his wit, although it is interesting to note that his material works better in the theatre, where audiences are conditioned to accept artificiality more

Right: Insatiable

— 38 —

The Janitor

easily. This one is the customary laughter-and-tears saga, with wife Marsha Mason as an alcoholic actress just back from drying out, whose teenage daughter decides to move in with her. It is also about the whining homosexual actor and the neurotic narcissist she has as friends. Simon's problem may well be rooted in the kind of people he writes about: silly, self-analytical New Yorkers who talk too much, mainly about themselves. A change of climate might blow out the automatic pilot and act as a catalyst for something worthwhile.

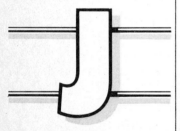

THE JANITOR (Fox)
(US TITLE: EYEWITNESS)
dir-pro Peter Yates *scr* Steve Tesich *ph* Matthew F. Leonetti, in Technicolor *ed* Cynthia Scheider *pro des* Philip Rosenberg *music* Stanley Silverman *r time* 108 mins *cert* AA *UK opening* Oct 8.
cast William Hurt, Sigourney Weaver, Christopher Plummer, James Woods, Irene Worth, Kenneth McMillan, Pamela Reed, Albert Paulsen, Steven Hill, Morgan Freeman, Alice Drummond, Sharon Goldman, Chao-Li Chi, Keone Young, Dennis Sakamoto, Henry Yuk, Mikhail Bogin, Moshe Geffen, Jo Davidson, Bill Mazer, John Roland, James Ray Weeks, Milton Zane, Richard Murphy, Dow McKeever, Jhoe Breedlove, Kimmy Wong, Alex Rosa, Mark Burns, Irish Whitney.

Oblique, atmospheric thriller about a night-shift janitor in a New York office block, who feigns knowledge about a murder to elicit the interest of a television journalist on whom he has a crush. A little improbable —

particularly in its sub-plot about an escape organisation for Russian jews — but wittily scripted, well paced and fortified by William Hurt's winning performance.

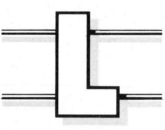

LADY CHATTERLEY'S LOVER
(Cannon/Columbia)
dir Just Jaeckin *pro* Christopher Pearce, Andre Djaoui *exec pro* Menahem Golan, Yoram Globus *scr* Christopher Wicking, Just Jaeckin, from the novel by D.H. Lawrence *ph* Robert Fraisse, in colour *ed* Eunice Mountjoy *pro des* Anton Furst *music*

Stanley Myers, Richard Harvey *r time* 103 mins *cert* X *UK opening* Dec 17.
cast Sylvia Kristel, Nicholas Clay, Shane Briant, Ann Mitchell, Elizabeth Spriggs, Pascale Rivault, Anthony Head, Frank Moorey, Bessie Love, John Tynan, Michael Huston, Fran Hunter, Ryan Michael, Mark Colleano.

Encouraged to take a lover by her crippled husband, and prescribed "fresh air and healthy activity" by his knowing nurse, a bored (and dubbed) Sylvia Kristel masturbates in a veil, dreams about a white stallion and finds him in gamekeeper Nicholas Clay. A risible, cliché-ridden adaptation, with any suggestion of eroticism in the frequent sexual encounters deflated by a comically soupy score which equates crescendo with orgasm.

THE LAST HUNTER (Flora Film-Gico Cinematografica/Eagle)
dir Anthony M. Dawson *pro* Gianfranco Couyoumdjian *scr* Dardano Sacchetti *ph* Riccardo Pallottini, in

Lady Chatterley's Lover

Technicolor *ed* Alberto Moriani *pro des* Bartolomeo Scavia *music* Franco Micalizzi *r time* 96 mins *cert* X *UK opening* Nov 1.
cast David Warbeck, Tisa Farrow, Tony King, Bobby Rhodes, Margi Eveline Newton, John Steiner, Massimo Vanni, Alan Collins, Dino Conti, Gianfranco Moroni.

Pacey, cut-price spaghetti 'Apocalypse Now', thin on characterisation, thick on exploding guts, mangled limbs and general jungle madness. Crude, gloating and excessive, it is the kind of film that will literally make you lose your dinner.

LAST MOMENTS (Cineproduzioni Daunia 80/GTO)
dir Mario Gariazzo *exec pro* Armando Novelli *scr* Luisa Montagnana, Massimo Franciosa, Tony La Penna *ph* Claudio Racca, in Telecolor *ed* Amedeo Giomini *art dir* Francesco Cuppini *music* Stelvio Cipriani *r time* 100 mins *cert* A *UK opening* Jan 10.
cast Renato Cestie, James Whitmore, Marina Malfatti, Lee J. Cobb, Maurizio Arena, Lina Volonghi, Cyril Cusack, Silvano Tranquilli, Carlo Romano, Umberto D'Orsi, Gianni

Agus, Tony Norton, Gabriella Andreini, Pupo de Luca, Paolo Nelli, Giacomo Furia, Giustino Durano, Franco Pesce, Giordano Albertoni, Alfredo Adami, Luciano Bonnanni, Spartaco Battisti, Flora Carosello, Anna Di Leo, Cesare Di Vito, Vittorio Fanfoni, Sandra Mantegna, Fullvio Pelegrino, Lorenzo Piani, Derio Pino, Sven Valsecchi, Pietro Zardini.

It's eight-years-old, it's Italian and it's a real turkey. Present and correct to pull heartstrings are the broken-hearted father, abandoned by his wife and drinking himself to a standstill; the plucky, enterprising son who provides for them both before going down with fatigue and malnutrition; the father and mother reunited to give their dying son a happy send-off; and, most extraordinary of all, Cyril Cusack as a balloon seller with a direct line to God. Where do they dig up this stuff? Why? And what are Cusack, James Whitmore and Lee J. Cobb doing in it?

LAURA (Les Films de l'Alma-cora/Bordeaux)
dir David Hamilton *pro* Serge Laski, Malcolm James Thomson *exec pro* Alain Terzian *scr* Joseph Morhaim, Andre Szots *ph* Bernard Daillencourt,

in colour *ed* Joele Van Effenterre *art dir* Eric Simon *music* Patrick Juvet *r time* 90 mins *cert* X *UK opening* Jun 3.
cast Maud Adams, Dawn Dunlap, James Mitchell, Maureen Kerwin, Piere Londiche, Thierry Redlet, Louise Vincent, William Millic.

As a film-maker, David Hamilton makes a great collection of soft-focus wall hangings if you happen to like underage girls framed in dreamy still life. 'Laura', like the dreadful 'Bilitis', is almost continuous still life, the ultimate decorative cool-as-a-mountain-stream experience, so numbingly devoid of anything which makes cinema interesting that one wonders how any of the participants kept themselves awake. For the audience it is much the same problem.

THE LEGEND OF THE LONE RANGER (ITC)
dir William A. Fraker *pro* Walter Coblenz *exec pro* Martin Starger *scr* Ivan Goff, Ben Roberts, Michael Kane, William Roberts, based on characters created by George W. Trendle, Fran Striker *ph* Laszlo Kovacs, in Panavision, Technicolor *ed* Thomas Stanford *pro des* Albert Brenner *art dir* David M. Haber *music* John Barry *r time* 97 mins *cert* A *UK opening* Aug 6.
cast Klinton Spilsbury, Michael Horse, Christopher Lloyd, Matt Clark, Juanin Clay, John Bennett Perry, David Hayward, John Hart, Rick Traeger, James Bowman, Kit Wong, Daniel Nunez, Jason Robards, Richard Farnsworth, Lincoln Tate, Ted Flicker, Marc Gilpin, Patrick Montoya, David Bennett, R.L. Tolbert, Clay Boss, Jose Rey Toledo, Max Cisneros, Ted White, Chere Bryson, James Lee Crite, Jim Burke, Jeff Ramsey, Bennie Dobbins, Henry Wills, Greg Walker, Ben Bates, Mike Adams, Bill Hart, Larry Randles, Robert Hoy, Ted Gehring,

Buck Taylor, Tom R. Diaz, Chuck Hayward, Tom Laughlin, Terry Leonard, Steve Meador, Joe Finnegan, Roy Bonner, John M. Smith.

Not a patch on Fraker's debut as a director, 'Monte Walsh', although beautifully photographed and obviously striving after similar "classical" qualities, this may as well have been subtitled 'The Early Years' since a lengthy prologue precedes the eventual transformation into the masked avenger. One suspects the intention of a sequel which, since this failed to make cash registers sing, is unlikely to materialize.*

LIGHT YEARS AWAY (Phénix-Slotint/Artificial Eye)
dir Alain Tanner *pro* Pierre Heros *exec pro* Bernard Lorain *scr* Alain Tanner, based on the novel 'La Voie Sauvage' by Daniel Odier *ph* Jean-Francois Robin, in Eastman Color *ed* Brigitte Sousselier *art dir* John Lucas *music* Arie Dzierlatka *r time* 107 mins *cert* AA *UK opening* Jan 7.
cast Trevor Howard, Mick Ford, Odile Schmitt, Louis Samier, Joe Pilkington, John Murphy, Mannix Flynn, Don Foley, Jerry O'Brien, Vincent Smith, Gabrielle Keenan, Bernice Stegers, Henri Virlogeux.

Dreamy, good-looking back-to-nature fable set in the year 2000, partly in a city but mainly in the middle of bleak (Irish) countryside where Jonas (Mick Ford), a character who has served time under Tanner before, goes through the peculiar initiation tests demanded by a crabby old garage owner (Trevor Howard) whose interest in birds is a prelude to flying. Thoughtful and well made, but very light on the action and unremittingly heavy on the imagery and the meaningful exchanges.

LIGHTNING OVER WATER (Road Movies-Viking Film/Cinegate)
dir Nicholas Ray, Wim Wenders *pro* Chris Sievernich, Pierre Cottrell *exec pro* Renee Gundelach *scr* Nicholas Ray, Wim Wenders *ed* Peter Przygodda *music* Ronee Blakley *r time* 91 mins *cert* AA *UK opening* Oct 8.
cast Gerry Bamman, Ronee Blakley, Pierre Cottrell, Stefan Czapsky, Mitch Dubin, Tom Farrell, Becky Johnston, Tom Kaufman, Maryte Kavaliauskus, Pat Kirck, Ed Lachman, Martin Muller, Craig Nelson, Peter Przygodda, Nicholas Ray, Susan Ray, Tim Ray, Martin Schafer, Chris Sievernich, Wim Wenders.

Wenders' tribute to Nicholas Ray who died of cancer in 1979 after 16 years away from Hollywood. Chronicling his last months with a mixture of imagery, conversation and footage of Ray at work, it is inevitably harrowing stuff but accomplished with just the right balance of unselfconscious hero-worship and pragmatic distance.

LILI MARLEEN (Roxy-CIP-Rialto/Alpha)
dir Rainer Werner Fassbinder *pro* Luggi Waldleitner *scr* Manfred Purzer, Joshua Sinclair, Rainer Werner Fassbinder *ph* Xaver Schwarzenberger, in colour *ed* Franz Walsch, Juliane Lorenz *pro des* Rolf Zehetbauer *art dir* Herbert Stravel *music* Peer Raben *r time* 120 mins *cert* AA *UK opening* Jan 7.
cast Hanna Schygulla, Giancarlo Giannini, Mel Ferrer, Karl Heinz von Hassel, Erik Schumann, Hark Bohm, Gottfried John, Karin Baal, Christine Kaufmann, Udo Kier, Roger Fritz, Rainer Will, Raul Giminez, Adrian Hoven, Willy Harlander, Barbara Valentin, Helen Vita, Elisabeth Volkman, Lilo Pempeit, Traute Hoss, Brigitte Mira, Herb Andress, Michael McLernon, Jurgen Drager, Rudolf Lenz, Toni Netzle.

Although advertised as if it were some Nazi-chic mating of 'Cabaret' and 'The Damned', the apposite copyline for 'Lili Marleen' is more along the lines of "The story of a song!" In other words, it's a knowing (but not too knowing) nod to the romantic melodramas and tarted-up biopics which Hollywood once produced with metronomic regularity, the song itself, delivered on innumerable occasions, serving as a linking device, general backdrop and convenient punctuation mark to what can only be described as an entertaining yarn. Two young people torn apart by powerful, interfering father; stranded girl records song and becomes celebrity-darling of Third Reich big-boys; boyfriend jailed by Nazis; eventual, but fruitless, re-

Lili Marleen

acquaintance across a crowded concert-hall. Familiar stuff of course, but given real flourish by Fassbinder. If any of his snootier followers thought he should be above this kind of enjoyable "mainstream" film-making, that was their problem. And probably still is.

LION OF THE DESERT (Falcon International/Enterprise)
dir-pro Moustapha Akkad *scr* H.A.L. Craig *ph* Jack Hildyard, in Panavision, Eastman Color *ed* John Shirley *pro des* Mario Garbuglia, Syd Cain *art dir* Giorgio Desideri, Maurice Cain, Bob Bell *music* Maurice Jarre *r time* 163 mins *cert* AA *UK opening* Aug 27.
cast Anthony Quinn, Oliver Reed, Irene Papas, Raf Vallone, Rod Steiger, John Gielgud, Andrew Keir, Gastone Moschin, Stefano Patrizi, Adolfo Lastretti, Sky Dumont, Takis Emmanuel, Rodolfo Bigotti, Robert Brown, Elenora Stathopoulou, Luciano Bartoli, Claudio Gora, Giordano Falzoni, Franco Fantasia, Ihab Werfaly, Ewen Solon, Loris Bazoki, Alec Mango, Filippo Degara, George Sweeney, Luciano Catenacci, Victor Baring, Pietro Brambilla, Pietro Tordi, Pietro Gerlini, Massimiliano Baratta, Mario Feliciani, Gianfranco Barra, Lino Capolicchio.

Factually based, handsomely filmed battle of wits in the desert between a wily Bedouin guerilla (Quinn, simple courage) and a supercilious Italian general (Reed, military might) as Mussolini's armies massacre their way across Libya. Cliché-ridden and over-long, it was one of the year's most notable failures at the box office. Maurice Jarre does variations on his 'Lawrence of Arabia' theme.

LOLA (Rialto-Trio/Miracle)
dir-exec pro Rainer Werner Fassbinder *pro* Horst Wendlandt *scr* Peter Marthesheimer, Pea Frohlich, Rainer Werner Fassbinder *ph* Xaver Schwarzenberger, in colour *ed* Juliane Lorenz *art dir* Rolf Zehetbauer *music* Peer Raben *r time* 115 mins *cert* AA *UK opening* Mar 25.
cast Barbara Sukowa, Armin Mueller-Stahl, Mario Adorf, Matthias Fuchs, Helga Feddersen, Karin Baal, Ivan Desny, Elisabeth Volkmann, Hark Bohm, Karl-Heinz von Hassel, Rosel Zech, Sonja Neudorfer, Christine Kaufmann, Y Sa Lo, Gunther Kaufmann, Isolde Barth, Harry Baer, Rainer Will, Karsten Peters, Herbert Steinmetz, Nino Korda, Raul Giminez, Udo Kier, Andrea Heuer, Ulrike Vigo, Helmut Petigk, Juliane Lorenz, Marita Pleyer, Maxim Oswald.

Filming his political allegories as if he were working at Universal in the mid-Fifties (this one has particularly odd and effective use of garish old-movie colour), Fassbinder was, for all his self-consciousness, the European film-maker who most skilfully trod the tightrope between reverence towards Hollywood and a regard for his own country's cinema. 'Lola', another of his German-history-examined-through-the-eyes-of-a-female-protagonist movies, is an update of 'The Blue Angel' set in a provincial city in 1954, when Adenauer had a smile on his face, the economic miracle was very much on the horizon and a council building commissioner falls for a whorehouse singer against a background of petty corruption where it is difficult to find anyone who isn't in someone else's pocket. A bit over-long, as most films tend to be these days, but endlessly watchable.

Love Camp

LOVE CAMP (Chranders Film Produktion/Tigon)
dir-pro-scr Christian Anders *ed* Renate Engelmann *music* Christian Anders *r time* 88 mins *cert* X *UK opening* Sept 17.
cast Laura Gemser, Christian Anders, Gabriele Tinti, Sacha Borisenko, Simone Brahmann, Maximilian Wolters, Fini, Veronika Schecker, Bob Burrows.

Yet another religious cult film, the down-market counterpart of the women-under-threat strain, with Laura Gemser, having graduated from the Black Emanuelle series, presiding over a "free love" commune in Cyprus in which orgies are commonplace, people get whipped for being monogamous and those who try to leave are thrown down a ravine. Hilariously unpleasant, utterly pointless, it is a questionable personal triumph for Christian Anders who did virtually everything including appear in it. Let's say it's not exactly 'Reds'.

LOVE LUST AND ECSTASY (Andromeda International/Tigon)
dir Ilia Milonako *pro* Vagelis Fournistakis *exec pro* Panayotis Ioannidis *scr* Suzy Astor *story* Evangelos Fournistakis *ph* Vasilis Cristomoglou, in colour *ed* Daniele Alabiso *music* Giovanni Ullu *r time* 77 mins *cert* X *UK opening* Jul 30.
cast Ajita Wilson, Mireille Damien, Danilo Micheli, Massimo Sadurny, Stratos Zamidis, George Minter, Nadia Danezi, Charles Colin.

The mixture as advertised — plus blackmail and murder.

LOVING COUPLES (Time-Life/Rank)
dir Jack Smight *pro* Renee Valente *scr* Martin Donovan *ph* Philip Lathrop, in Metrocolor *ed* Greyfox, Frank Urioste *art dir* Jan Scott *music* Fred Karlin *r time* 98 mins *cert* AA *UK opening* Oct 15.
cast Shirley MacLaine, James Coburn, Susan Sarandon, Stephen Collins, Sally Kellerman, Nan Martin, Shelly Batt, Bernard Behrens, Anne Bloom, Fred Carney, Helena Carroll, Marilyn Chris, Pat Corley, Michael Curry, John Davis, John Delancie, Edith Fields, Peter Hobbs, Paula Jones, Art Kassul, Hap Lawrence, Bob Levine, John Medici, David Murphy, Estelle Omens, June Sanders, Tony Travis, Sam Weisman.

Clumsy, charmless would-be satirical comedy, all jacuzzis and psychobabble, about partner-swopping in Southern California. With the exception of Susan Sarandon, whose perpetual expression of vague bewilderment makes her appear above it all, everybody is on ham-overdrive while trying hard to be endearing and contemporary. It is difficult to form even the beginnings of an idea of what could have attracted gifted actors like Coburn and MacLaine to flimsy nonsense like this.

LUNCH WAGON (Seymour Borde & Associates/Bordeaux)
dir Ernest Pintoff *pro* Mark Borde *exec pro* Seymour Borde *scr* Leon Phillips, Marshall Harvey, Terrie Frankle *ph* Fred Lemler, in DeLuxe colour *ed* Ed Salier *music* Richard Band *r time* 88 mins *cert* AA *UK opening* Jun 24.
cast Pamela Bryant, Rosanne Katon, Candy Moore, Rick Podell, James Van

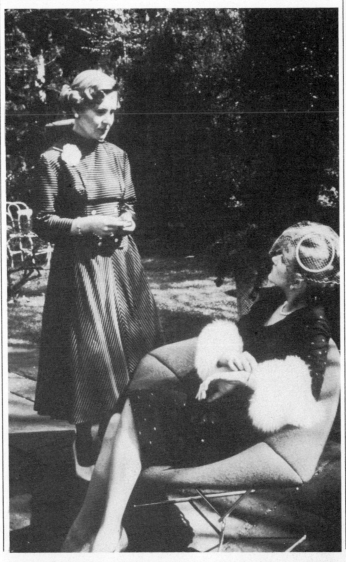
*Left: Lion of the Desert
Right: Lola*

Patten, Chuck McCann, Rose Marie, Michael Tucci, Louisa Moritz, Vic Dunlop, Anthony Charnota, George Memmoli, Michael Mislove, Nels Van Patten, Maurice Sneed, Gary Levy, Biff Manard, Peggy Mannix, John Thompson, Dale Bozzio, Peter Marc, Steve Tannen, Bobby Sandler, Odis McKinney, Debrah Kelly, Terry Bozzio, Warren Cucurullo.

In the days of 'Where the Boys Are', swinging college girls spent the summer sitting around places like Fort Lauderdale picking up boys. Now they have to work. Here a couple of very unlikely garage attendants are fired from their jobs and become unexpected recipients of the lunch wagon in question, which they paint pink and call (surely not) Love Bites. When they are joined by another curvy co-ed, who just happens to be a keen cook, they can begin driving towards the rest of the plot: crooks and chases and travelling musicians and even a stolen diamond. Agreeable enough in a simple-minded way, it supported the perfectly dreadful 'Hog Wild'. What all these new would-be "teen film" directors need is a night locked in a cinema showing 'How to Stuff a Wild Bikini'.

MADAME OLGA'S PUPILS
(Balcazar/Amanda)
dir-scr Joseph L. Bronstein *ph* Hans Burman, in Eastman Color *music* Raymond Balcazar *r time* 82 mins *cert* X *UK opening* May 6.
cast Helga Line, Marye Harper, George Gonce, Lynn Andersen, Eva Lyberten, Anthony Smith, Jazmine Venturini.

Dubbed Spanish sexploiter set in London, where Madame Olga's pupils turn out to be teenage girls hired out to wealthy clients with a piano school as camouflage. Serious wearers of raincoats should be warned that there is a substantial sub-plot involving young love and eventual redemption.

MAD MAX 2 (Warner)
(US TITLE: THE ROAD WARRIOR)
dir George Miller *pro* Byron Kennedy *scr* Terry Hayes, George Miller, Brian Hannant *ph* Dean Semler, in Panavision, Technicolor *ed* David Stiven, Tim Wellburn, Michael Chirgwin *art dir* Graham Walker *music* Brian May *r time* 95 mins *cert* A *UK opening* Mar 4.
cast Mel Gibson, Bruce Spence, Vernon Wells, Emil Minty, Mike Preston, Kjell Nilsson, Virginia Hey, Syd Heylen, Moira Claux, David Slingsby, Arkie Whiteley, Steve J. Spears, Max Phipps, William Zappa, Jimmy Brown, David Downer, Tyler Coppin, Max Fairchild, Kristoffer Greaves, Guy Norris, Tony Deary, Anne Jones, James McCardell, Kathleen McKay.

One of the few sequels which completely eclipses its predecessor, and set in the same vast unspecified desert, where the all-consuming quest for petrol continues to monopolise the survivors of some oil-war apocalypse and the self-styled warlords of the wasteland go around with dead bodies strapped to the front of their vehicles. Brilliantly filmed and full of sly, artful humour as well as the customary surfeit of improvised vehicles and mangled bodies. A winning performance from Bruce Spence in the tradition of Donald Sutherland and a stolid Bronsonesque one from Mel Gibson.

MAKING LOVE (Indieprod/Fox)
dir Arthur Hiller *pro* Allen Adler, Daniel Melnick *scr* Barry Sandler *ph* David M. Walsh, in DeLuxe colour *ed* William H. Reynolds *pro des* James D. Vance *music* Leonard Rosenman *r time* 112 mins *cert* X *UK opening* Jun 10.
cast Michael Ontkean, Kate Jackson, Harry Hamlin, Wendy Hiller, Arthur Hill, Nancy Olson, John Dukakis, Terry Kiser, Dennis Howard, Asher Brauner, John Calvin, Gwen Arner, Gary Swanson, Ann Harvey, Stanley Kamel, Chip Lucia, Doug Johnson, Ben Mittleman, Mickey Jones, Joe Medalis, Erica Hiller, Michael Shannon, Arthur Taxier, Phoebe Dorin, Mark Schubb, Carol King, Camilla Carr, Lili Haydn, Paul Sanderson, David Knell, David Murphy, Michael Dudikoff, John Starr, Charles Zukow, Scott Ryder, Joanne Hicks, Stacy Kuhne, Stephanie Segal, Kedren Jones, Alexander Lockwood, Andrew Harris, Michael Harris, Robert Mikels, Jason Mikels.

Hollywood's first big-budget movie about homosexuality turns out to be a familiar story of a marriage breaking up, with boy-meets-boy variations. The characters in the triangle are the

Right: Mad Max 2

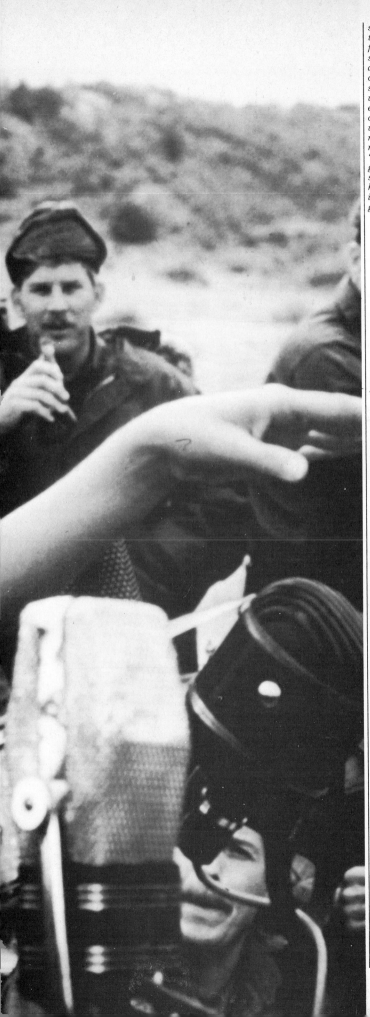

sensitive physician husband, the rising television executive wife and the freewheeling gay novelist, to whom the sensitive physician husband is attracted: beautiful, childless people, conforming to Californian standards of sophistication, who are wonderfully understanding about one another's emotional problems. The moral is the conventional West Coast one: those who are casual about meaningful relationships must expect to suffer (but not too much). Hiller, who directed 'Love Story', is adept at this kind of glossy nonsense, the sort of sentimental tosh that used to be known as "a woman's picture" and is, in its updated version, no more than gay glib.

MANGANINNIE (Tasmanian Film Corp/Contemporary)
dir John Honey pro Gilda Baracchi exec pro Gil Brealey, Malcolm Smith scr Ken Kelso, based on the novel by Beth Roberts ph Gary Hansen, in Eastman-Color ed Mike Woolveridge art dir Neil Angwin music Peter Sculthorpe r time 90 mins cert U UK opening Jan 28.
cast Mawuyul Yathalawuy, Anna Ralph, Phillip Hinton, Elaine Mangan, Buruminy Dhamarrandji, Reg Evans, Jonathan Elliott, Timothy Latham, Barry Pierce, Tony Tapp, Paddy Garritty, Brian Duhig, Barrie Muir, Lex Clark, Peter Thompson, Brian Young, Allen Harvey, Don Evans, Bill McCluskey, Leone Dickson, Tas Burns.

Slow, dreamy, lyrical account — like 'Walkabout' deprived of its sting and framed in the rosy visual focus of Disney anthropology — of how the only survivor of a massacred Aboriginal tribe teams up with a small white girl on a trek across the bush, with the now traditional conclusion: death for one, a difficulty in re-adjusting for the other. Well made, but a little too cute for comfort.

MAN OF IRON (PRF-Zespol/Artificial Eye)
dir Andrzej Wajda scr Aleksander Scibor-Rylski ph Edward Klosinski, part in colour ed Halina Prugar art dir Allan Starski, Maja Chrolowska music Andrzej Korzynski r time 152 mins cert A UK opening Sept 24.
cast Jerzy Radziwilowicz, Krystyna Janda, Marian Opania, Irena Byrska, Wieslawa Kosmalska, Boguslaw Linda, Franciszek Trzeciak, Janusz Gajos, Adrezej Seweryn, Marek Kondrat, Jerzy Trela, Krysztof Janczar, Krystyna Zachwatowicz-Wajda, Boguslaw Sobczuk, Wojciech Alaborski, Halina Labonarska, Bozena Dykiel, Lech Walesa.

Topical, discursive sequel to 'Man of Marble', set in and around the shipyards of Gdansk at the time Solidarity was founded, where fear and

Left: Marilyn the Untold Story

harassment rule and a drunken, disenchanted radio producer discovers where his loyalties lie while attempting to build up incriminating evidence against a young strike leader. A marvellous film, made all the more poignant by the events since it was made.

MARILYN THE UNTOLD STORY (Time-Life/Rank)
dir John Flynn, Jack Arnold pro Lawrence Schiller scr Dalene Young ph Terry K. Meade, in colour ed Jack Gleason, Patrick T. Roark art dir Jan Scott, Sydney Z. Litwack music William Goldstein r time 120 mins cert A UK opening Nov 12.
cast Catherine Hicks, Richard Basehart, Frank Converse, John Ireland, Viveca Lindfors, Jason Miller, Sheree North, Kevin Geer, Tracey Gold, Priscilla Morrill, John Christy Ewing, Howard Caine, Larry Pennell, Bill Vint, Brad Blaisdell, J.P. Bumstead, Carole Tru Foster, Paul Larson, Anne Ramsey, John Steadman, Janus Blythe, Sima Conrad, E. Brian Dean, Michael Fairman, Jim Greenleaf, James Hayden, Mae Marmy, Jessamine Milner, John Moskoff, Frank Pesce, Alex Romero, Lance Rosen, George Skaff, Cecily Walper.

Preceded, predictably enough, by another airing of Elton John's awful 'Candle in the Wind', the untold story turns out to be a routine re-run of familiar biographical details borrowed from Norman Mailer, padded with a lot of paperback Freud, and wheeled out in an efficiently anonymous manner. Cut by 30 minutes in the change-over from television to cinema, one wonders if the full-length version is less random in the amount of time it allocates to each episode. Not quite "There's a guy bashing away on a typewriter upstairs, says his name is Arthur Miller", but well on its way.

MEMOIRS OF A SURVIVOR (Memorial/EMI)
dir David Gladwell pro Michael Medwin, Penny Clark scr Kerry Crabbe, David Gladwell, based on the novel by Doris Lessing ph Walter Lassally, in Technicolor ed William Shapter pro des Keith Wilson music Mike Thorn r time 115 mins cert X UK opening Sept 24.
cast Julie Christie, Christopher Guard, Leonie Mellinger, Debbie Hutchings, Nigel Hawthorne, Pat Keen, Georgina Griffiths, Christopher Tsangarides, Mark Dignam, Alison Dowling, John Franklyn-Robbins, Rowena Cooper, Barbara Hicks, John Cromer, Adrienne Byrne, Marion Owen Smith, Tara MacGowran, Mark Farmer, John Altman, David Squire, Jeanne Watts, Pamela Cundell, Bryan Matheson, Ann Tirard, Jeillo Edwards, Arthur Lovegrove, John Rutland.

Slow, earnest, over-literal adaptation of Lessing's clumsily symbolic novel about urban decay and blurred realities after the holocaust, with Julie Christie watching the collapse of society from one end of her flat while cultivating a Victorian fantasy world at the other.

Mephisto

MEPHISTO (Mafilm-Manfred Durniok Prod/Cinegate)
dir Istvan Szabo *scr* Peter Dobai, Istvan Szabo, based on the novel by Klaus Mann *ph* Lajos Koltai, in Eastman Colour *ed* Zsuzsa Csakany *art dir* Jozsef Romvari *music* Zdenko Tamassy *r time* 144 mins *cert* AA *UK opening* Nov 5.
cast Klaus Maria Brandauer, Ildiko Bansagi, Krystyna Janda, Rolf Hoppe, Gyorgy Cserhalmi, Peter Andorai, Karin Boyd, Christine Harbort, Tamas Major, Ildiko Kishonti, Maria Bisztrai, Sandor Lukacs, Agnes Banfalvi, Judit Hernadi, Vilmos Kun, Ida Versenyi, Istvan Komlos, Sari Gencsy, Zdzislaw Mrozewski, Stanislava Strobachova, Karoly Ujlaky, Professor Martin Hellberg, Katalin Solyom, Gyorgy Banffy, Josef Csor, Christian Grasshof, Hedi Temessy, David Robinson, Geza Kovacs, Teri Tordai, Hans Ulrich Laufer, Margrid Hellberg, Kerstin Hellberg.

An extraordinary film, rooted in a striking, sustained performance from Klaus Maria Brandauer as a radical but fame-craving actor whose career rises at the same pace as the Nazis, and who learns to live with his compromises as friends recede into exile or oblivion, until he becomes little more than a political puppet.

MISSING (Universal)
dir Costa-Gavras *pro* Edward Lewis, Mildred Lewis *exec pro* Peter Guber, Jon Peters *scr* Costa-Gavras, Donald Stewart, based on the book by Thomas Hauser *ph* Ricardo Aronovich, in Technicolor *ed* Francoise Bonnot *pro des* Peter Jamison *art dir* Agustin Ytuarte, Lucero Isaac *music* Vangelis *r time* 122 mins *cert* AA *UK opening* May 27.
cast Jack Lemmon, Sissy Spacek, Melanie Mayron, John Shea, Charles Cioffi, David Clennon, Richard Venture, Jerry Hardin, Richard Bradford, Joe Regalbuto, Keith

Left: Mommie Dearest

Szarabajka, John Doolittle, Janice Rule, Ward Costello, Hansford Rowe, Tina Romero, Richard Whiting, Martin Lasalle, Terry Nelson, Robert Hitt, Felix Gonzalez, M.E. Rios, Jorge Russek, Edna Nochoechea, Alan Penwrith, Alex Camacho, M. Avilla Camacho, Kimberly Farr, Elizabeth Cross, Piero Cross, Gary Richardson, Josefina Echanove, Robert Johnstreet, Linda Spheeris, Jorge Mancilla, Gerardo Vigil, Mario Valdez, Jaime Garza, Joe I. Tompkins, John Fenton, Jacqueline Evans, Jorge Santoyo, Juan Vazquez, Antonio Medellin, Albert Cates.

Costa-Gavras's first American movie is, like his other political thrillers, marvellously persuasive, brilliantly filmed and ethically unbalanced. There are no shades of opinion or moral complexities in his universe. Based on a true story of a young American who was murdered in Chile during the anti-Allende coup, possibly with American connivance, the movie is too schematic to convince intellectually, but still carries considerable emotional weight, particularly in the scenes including Lemmon's distraught father who is gradually educated in the devious ways of governments. The coup's casual slaughters and official repression are convincingly depicted, and there is one brilliant surrealist image of a white horse galloping wildly through dark, deserted streets pursued by a jeepful of trigger-happy soldiers which confirms Costa-Gavras as one of the great contemporary film-makers; bold, adventurous and totally in control of his medium.

MOMMIE DEAREST (Paramount)
dir Frank Perry *pro* Frank Yablans *exec pro* David Koontz, Terence O'Neill *scr* Frank Yablans, Frank Perry, Tracy Hotchner, Robert Getchell, based on the book by Christina Crawford *ph* Paul Lohmann, in Metrocolor *ed* Peter E. Berger *pro des* Bill Malley *art dir* Harold Michelson *music* Henry Mancini *r time* 129 mins *cert* AA *UK opening* Nov 26.
cast Faye Dunaway, Diana Scarwid, Steve Forrest, Howard da Silva, Mara Hobel, Rutanya Alda, Harry Goz, Michael Edwards, Jocelyn Brando, Priscilla Pointer, Joe Abdullah, Gary Allen, Selma Archerd, Adrian Aron, Xander Berkeley, Matthew Campion, Carolyn Coates, Jerry Douglas, Margaret Fairchild, Phillip R. Allen, James Kirkwood, Michael D. Gainsborough, Matthew Faison, Peter Jason, Ellen Feldman, Robert Harper, Cathy Lind Hayes, Victoria James, Dawn Jeffory, Virginia Kiser, S. John Launer, Russ Marin, Nicholas Mele, Belita Moreno, Warren Munson, Alice

Nunn, Norman Palmer, David F. Price, Jeremy Scott Reinbolt, Michael Talbot, Arthur Taxier, Joseph Warren, Erica Wexler.

"The biggest mother of them all," as the US distributors decided to call her when they saw the people standing in line carrying wire coat hangers, is unswervingly competitive, zealously disciplined and fetishistically clean. She also hacks down rose bushes when her career does a nosedive and beats her small daughter with the aforementioned hangers for failing to observe wardrobe protocol. The childhood miseries recollected by Christina Crawford (represented persuasively by Mara Hobel and Diana Scarwid) turn out to be very much in the style of one of her mother's films, and Faye Dunaway rises to the occasion with a hilariously over-wrought performance: all lips, eyebrows and flared nostrils.

MONTENEGRO (Viking-Europa-Smart Egg/New Realm)
dir-scr Dusan Makavejev *pro* Bo Jonsson *ph* Tomislaw Pinter, in Eastman Color *ed* Sylvia Ingermarsson *art dir* Radu Borusescu *music* Kornell Kovach *r time* 96 mins *cert* X *UK opening* Nov 12.
cast Susan Anspach, Erland Josephson, Bora Todorovic, Per Oscarsson, Patricia Gelin, Svetozar Cvetkovic, Lisbeth Zachrisson, Nikola Janic, John Zacharias, Lasse Aberg, Marianne Jacobi, Jamie Marsh, Marina Lindahl, Dragan Ilic, Milo Petrovic, John Parkinson, Jan Nygren, Kaarina Harvistola, Ewa Gisslen, Elsie Holm, Paul Smith, Bo Ivan Peterson.

Extraordinary study of debauchery and derangement with Susan Anspach as an American wife, going to pieces with boredom in Sweden, who ends up in a bizarre drinking club with a bunch of wild Yugoslav immigrants who use the place to fight, dance, have sex and generally "express" themselves, much like the animals Makavejev uses rather heavy-handedly as occasional visual punctuation marks. After all that, it need hardly be added, she goes completely off the rails. Bawdy, funny, erotic, utterly compelling.

MOSCOW DISTRUSTS TEARS (Mosfilm/Rank)
dir Vladimir Menshov *scr* Valentin Chernykh *ph* Igor Slabnevich, in Sovcolor *ed* Mikhailovoi *art dir* Said Menyalshchikov *music* Sergei Nikitin *r time* 148 mins *cert* A *UK opening* Oct 1.
cast Vera Alentova, Alexei Batalov,

Irina Muraveva, Alexandr Fatiushin, Raisa Ryazanova, Boris Smorchkov, Yuri Vasilyer, Natalya Vavilova, Oleg Tabakov, Yevgeniya Khanayeva, Valentina Ushakova, Viktor Uralsky, Zoya Fedorova, Lia Akhedzhakova, Tatyana Koniukhova, Innokenti Smoktunovsky.

The Oscar winner for 1981's best foreign film turns out to be a gently humorous, inoffensively conventional romantic comedy about the aspirations of three provincial girls sharing a room in 1958 Moscow and their circumstances 20 years later. Dammit, the Academy voters clearly concluded, these Russkies are just like you and me!

THE MOUSE AND HIS CHILD (Ambassador)
dir Fred Wolf, Charles Swenson *pro* Walt deFaria *exec pro* Warren Lockhart, Shintaro Tsuji *scr* Carol Mon Pere, based on the novel by Russell Hoban *ph* Wally Bulloch, in DeLuxe colour *pro des* Vincent Davis, Sam Kirson, Bob Mitchell, Al Sheah *art dir* David McMacken *music* Roger Kellaway *r time* 83 mins *cert* U *UK opening* Apr 7.

One of the less desirable consequences of that combination of whimsy and philosophy which characterised 'enlightened' young Americans in the late Sixties and early Seventies is that it attracted them to the cartoon form. I haven't read the Russell Hoban book on which this is based, but I doubt that it could have been as self-conscious and preachy as this. Like 'The Point', which involved many of the same animators, the film's skilfulness (which is beyond question) is eclipsed by its preciousness (which is suffocating), although it is interesting to observe that Neville Brand — several times as nasty as Jack Elam where B-movie heavies are concerned — does one of the voices.

THE MOUSE AND THE WOMAN (Alvicar/Facelift)
dir Karl Francis *pro* Hayden Pearce, Karl Francis *exec pro* Alfred J. Gooding, Vincent Kane *scr* Vincent Kane, Karl Francis, based on the short story by Dylan Thomas *ph* Nick Gifford, in colour *ed* Neil Thomson *art*

dir Hayden Pearce *music* Alun Francis *r time* 105 mins *cert* AA *UK opening* Jul 30.
cast Dafydd Hywel, Karen Archer, Alan Devlin, Patricia Napier, Peter Sproule, Howard L. Lewis, Ionette Lloyd Davies, Beti Jones, Basil Painting, Dafydd Havard, John Pierce Jones, John Lehmann, Bob Mason, Huw Ceredig, Robert Blythe, Simon Coady, Brian Lee, John Cassady, Steve James, Glyn Davies, Ozi and Glesnè, Joffre Swales Quartet.

Strikingly photographed, soundly performed tale of lust, class conflict and the effects of war, expanded from Dylan Thomas's short story and set in Wales before and after World War One.

MY DINNER WITH ANDRÉ (André Co/Cinegate)
dir Louis Malle *pro* George W. George, Beverley Karp *scr* Wallace Shawn, André Gregory *ph* Jeri Sopanen, in colour *ed* Suzanne Baron *pro des* David Mitchell *art dir* Stephen McCabe *music* Allen Shawn *r time* 111 mins *cert* A *UK opening* May 6.
cast André Gregory, Wallace Shawn, Jean Lenauer, Roy Butler.

The dinner, to adopt the vernacular of the film it frames, is more symbolic than actual. Certainly food is served, and a waiter wanders in and out of view occasionally, but not much is

The Mouse and his Child

eaten. What happens instead is that André Gregory, who was and may still be an avant-garde theatre director, bends the ear of his playwright friend Wallace Shawn for what seems like several years. Wally and André haven't seen each other for a while and Wally, the way people do, asks him what he's been up to. André, self-absorbed to a point well beyond tedium, has been around the world

"discovering" himself and he spares no detail in his account of his transcendental experiences: group encounters, tree hugging, eating sand, being buried alive, and the rest of a familiar litany. Wally, when he can get a word in, expresses a preference for minor earthly comforts: a morning newspaper, a cup of coffee, an electric blanket. It is the escalating surrealism of their exchange which makes this peculiar, funny, irritating film so engaging in the end. It is, as André might have declared, beyond boredom.

The Mouse and the Woman

No Mercy No Future

THE NIGHT THE LIGHTS WENT OUT IN GEORGIA (Avco Embassy/New Realm)

dir Ronald F. Maxwell *pro* Elliot Geisinger, Howard Kuperman, Howard Smith, Ronald Saland *exec pro* William Blake, Carole Blake *scr* Bob Bonney, based on the song by Bobby Russell *ph* Bill Butler, in Technicolor *ed* Anne Goursaud *pro des* Gene Rudolf *music* David Shire *r time* 101 mins *cert* AA *UK opening* Nov 15.
cast Kristy McNichol, Dennis Quaid, Mark Hamill, Don Stroud, Sunny Johnson, Arlen Dean Snyder, Barry Corbin, Lulu McNichol, Royce Clark, Jerry Rushing, Jerry Campbell, Maxwell Morrow, Bill Gribble, Lonnie Smith, Elaine Falone, Terry Browning, Barrie Geisinger, Ellen Saland, J. Don Ferguson, S. Victoria Marlowe, William Phillips, Fred Covington, Ralph Pace, Nikola Colton, Cindy Partlow, Wanda Strange, Harry Wilcox, Rita Teeter, Bobby Leroux, Debbie Strudas, Lit Connah, Elsie Sligh, Roger Teeter, Marilyn Hickey, Charles Franzen, Luther McLaughlin, Anne Haney, Joan Riordan, Anita Haynes, Danny Nelson, R.P. Noren, White Trash Band, Michael Massey, Linda Stephens, Wayne Sharpnack, Keith Allison, Jim Stabile, Robert "Bubba" Dean, Scott MacLellan, Kirk Johnson, Ruth Cameron, John Edson, Ron Maxwell.

Flimsy, good-natured highroads-and-byroads comedy-drama, in which country singer Dennis Quaid and his lively sister-manager Kristy McNichol (delightful as ever) make their way, very slowly, to Nashville and intended stardom. Cut by 16 minutes from its original running time, it still seems to last an eternity.

NO MERCY NO FUTURE (Mainline)

dir-pro-scr Halma Sanders-Brahms *ph* Thomas Mauch, in colour *ed* Ursula West, Hanni Lewerenz *music* Manfred Opitz, Harald Grosskopf *r time* 100 mins *cert* X *UK opening* May 6.
cast Elisabeth Stepanek, Hubertus von Weyrauch, Irmgard Mellinger, Nguyen Chi Canh, Erich Koitzsch-Koltzack, George Stamkowski, Curt Curtini, Karl Heinz Reimann, Abdel Wahed Askar, Hasan Hasan, Nabil Beiroumi, Harald Hoedt, Jorge Reis, Erika Dannhoff, Gunther Ehlert, Carola Regnier.

Grim, unyielding account of a suicidal, schizophrenic woman, wandering the streets of Berlin when she hasn't been committed to hospitals by her parents, who enjoys (or rather fails to enjoy) religious visions, casual sex and a wide range of personal suffering. Initially involving, cumulatively exhausting, it is difficult to speculate on who, other than admirers of the director, would choose to see a film as unremittingly depressing as this.

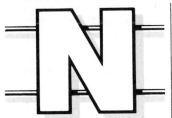

The Night the Lights Went Out in Georgia

THE OBERWALD MYSTERY (RAI-Polytel Int/Artificial Eye)

dir Michelangelo Antonioni *pro* Sergio Benvenuti, Alessandro von Norman, Giancarlo Bernardoni *scr* Michelangelo Antonioni, Tonino Guerra, from the play 'L'aigle a deux tetes' by Jean Cocteau *ph* Luciano Tovoli, in colour *ed* Michelangelo Antonioni, Francesco Grandoni *art dir* Mischa Scandella *music* Strauss, Schoenberg, Brahms, *r time* 129 mins *cert* A *UK opening* Jul 23.
cast Monica Vitti, Franco Branciaroli, Luigi Diberti, Elisabetta Pozzi, Amad Saha Alan, Paolo Bonacelli.

Antonioni's first film for six years, shot on videotape later transferred to film and resulting in a tiresomely arty blur which, allied to his insistent use

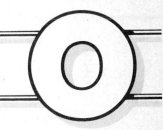

On Golden Pond

of unusual colour effects, becomes a bit like watching a light show through a smoke haze. Monica Vitti, as the queen of a Middle European state who falls in love with an assassin who resembles her dead husband, is in great form.

ON GOLDEN POND (ITC/IPC)
dir Mark Rydell *pro* Bruce Gilbert *scr* Ernest Thompson, based on his play *ph* Billy Williams, in colour *ed* Robert L. Wolfe *pro des* Stephen Grimes *music* Dave Grusin *r time* 109 mins *cert* AA *UK opening* Mar 4.
cast Katharine Hepburn, Henry Fonda, Jane Fonda, Doug McKeon, Dabney Coleman, William Lanteau, Chris Rydell.

Leisurely, sentimental study of old age and the New England countryside around the ever-twinkling lake where crusty octogenarian Henry Fonda and his resilient wife Katharine Hepburn spend their summers. Dominated by its central performances, with strong understated support from Jane Fonda and a marvellous cameo by Dabney Coleman (whom she helped to string

Out of the Blue

up in 'Nine to Five') as her Californian dentist boyfriend.

OUT OF THE BLUE (Robson Street Prods/Cinegate)
dir Dennis Hopper *pro* Leonard Yakir, Gary Jules Louvenat *exec pro* Paul Lewis *scr* Leonard Yakir, Brenda Nielson *ph* Marc Champion, in colour *ed* Doris Dyck *art dir* David Hiscox *music* Tom Lavin *r time* 93 mins *cert* X *UK opening* Oct 1.
cast Linda Manz, Dennis Hopper, Sharon Farrell, Raymond Burr, Don Gordon, Eric Allen, Fiona Brody, David Crowley, Joan Hoffman, Carl Nelson, Francis Ann Pettit, Glen Pfeifer, David Ackridge, Jim Byrne, Glen Fyfe, Louis Gentle, Murdine Hirsch, John Anderson, Howard Taylor, Ron Charter, Ray Wallis, Trevor Wilkins, Nancy Gould, Michele Little, Valentina Fierro, Ray Isabelle, Sid Albina de Silva, Wayne McLeod, Eve Humber, Mike Spencer.

Hopper's first work as a director since 'The Last Movie' — reputedly fuelled by cocaine and now seemingly lost in

the realms of myth — is appropriately a study of a generation gone sour: the browning, rather than the greening, of small-town America. Linda Manz is the teenage daughter of an alcoholic former convict and a junkie waitress, on whom, adrift between rock 'n' roll and punk (she idolises Elvis Presley and Sid Vicious), she takes her revenge. Improvisational zeal gives way to mannered naturalism too often for comfort, but it's still powerful, persuasive stuff.

OUTLAND (Ladd Company/Warner)
dir-scr Peter Hyams *pro* Richard A. Roth *exec pro* Stanley O'Toole *ph* Stephen Goldblatt, in Panavision, Technicolor *ed* Stuart Baird *pro des* Philip Harrison *art dir* Malcolm Middleton *music* Jerry Goldsmith *r time* 109 mins *cert* AA *UK opening* Aug 27.
cast Sean Connery, Peter Boyle, Frances Sternhagen, James B Sikking, Kika Markham, Clarke Peters, Steven Berkoff, John Ratzenberger, Nicholas Barnes, Manning Redwood, Pat Starr, Hal Galili, Angus MacInnes, Stuart Milligan, Eugene Lipinski, Norman Chancer, Ron Travis, Anni Domingo, Bill Bailey, Chris Williams, Marc Boyle, Richard Hammat, James Berwick, Gary Olsen, Isabelle Lucas, Sharon Duce, P.H. Moriarty, Doug Robinson, Angelique Rockas, Judith Alderson, Rayner Bourton, Julia Depyer, Nina Francoise, Brendon Hughes, Philip Johnston, Norri Morgan.

Thinly veiled galactic 'High Noon', with the western town replaced by a lunar mining colony where new marshal Sean Connery sets out to eliminate the officially-sanctioned drug abuse which has prompted numerous suicides as well as increasing productivity. Left by his wife and child, he awaits the imported hit men as time ticks (or rather flickers) by on the giant digital clock. Superbly designed and solidly acted, it loses its bearings when the action sequences give way to the slow, wordy interludes.

P

PARASITE (Entertainment)
dir-pro Charles Band *exec pro* Irwin Yablans *scr* Alan Adler, Michael Shoob, Frank Levering *ph* Mac Ahlberg, in 3D, Metrocolor *ed* Brad Arensman *art dir* Pamela B. Warner *music* Richard Band *r time* 85 mins *cert* X *UK opening* May 27.

cast Robert Glaudini, Demi Moore, Luca Bercovici, James Davidson, Al Fann, Tom Villard, Scott Thomson, Cherie Currie, Vivian Blaine, James Cavan, Joanelle Romero, Freddie Moore, Natalie May, Cheryl Smith, Joel Miller.

First of a whole rash of 3D features to reach Britain from the US drive-ins, in turn occasioned by the sudden success of 'Comin' At Ya', a brutal and cheapskate attempt to make a spaghetti western without any heart, soul or a leading man who can act. This isn't a great deal better, involving a scientist with a growth in his belly, and his battle to kill it before it multiplies and takes over the world. A gang of teen thugs intervenes, and reaps the familiar just rewards. The 3D effects are adequate without being any real improvement on Fifties' versions of the technique and the story has been taken further with far more horrifying results by David Cronenberg, most notably in 'Shivers', whose horrible intestinal creatures the 'parasite' resembles more than a little.

PASSIONE D'AMORE (Massfilm-Marceau Cocinor/Connoisseur)
dir Ettore Scola *pro* Franco Committeri *scr* Ruggero Maccari, Ettore Scola, based on the novel 'Fosca' by Iginio Ugo Tarchetti *ph* Claudio Ragona, in Eastman Color *ed* Raimondo Crociani *art dir* Fiorenzo Senese *music* Armando Trovajoli *r time* 117 mins *cert* AA *UK opening* Apr 22.
cast Bernard Giraudeau, Valeria D'Obici, Laura Antonelli, Jean-Louis Trintignant, Massimo Girotti, Bernard Blier, Gerardo Amato, Sandro Ghiani, Alberto Incrocci, Rosaria Schemmari, Francesco Piastra, Saverio Vallone, Franco Committeri.

Costume drama set in 19th century Italy, which allows plenty of room for both the requisite picturesque detail and an unlikely tale about a young cavalry officer, separated from his mistress when he is posted to a remote border garrison in the mountains, who finds himself drawn into a bizarre web of passion and hysteria when the

Right: Outland

colonel's cousin, an ugly hysteric with a terminal illness, falls for him irreversibly, with disastrous consequences — death for her, disintegration for him. The kind of absurd, over-wrought film which would be laughed off the screen if it weren't Italian. As it is, forelocks were tugged dutifully.

PATERNITY (Paramount)
dir David Steinberg *pro* Lawrence Gordon, Hank Moonjean *exec pro* Jerry Tokofsky *scr* Charlie Peters *ph* Bobby Byrne, in colour *ed* Donn Cambern *pro des* Jack Collis *art dir* Pete Smith, Howard Barker *music* David Shire *r time* 93 mins *cert* AA *UK opening* Oct 29.
cast Burt Reynolds, Beverly D'Angelo, Norman Fell, Paul Dooley, Elizabeth Ashley, Laruen Hutton, Juanita Moore, Peter Billingsley, Jacqueline Brookes, Linda Gillin, Mike Kellin, Victoria Young, Elsa Raven, MacIntyre Dixon, Murphy Dunne, Toni Kalem, Alfie Wise, Kathy Bendett, Carol Locatell, Kay Armen, Tony Di Benedetto, Dick Wieand, Eugene Troobnick, Ken Magee, Elaine Giftos, Sydney Daniels, Hector Troy, Roger Etienne, Susanna Dalton, Jason Delgado, Aaron Jessup, Frank Bongiorno, Frank Hamilton, James Harder, Irena Ferris, Lee Ann Duffield, Clotilde, Brad Trumbull, John Gilgreen, Jeff Lawrence, Robin Blake, Paula Holland, Laura Grayson, Buddy Micucci, Derek Thompson, Joseph Hamer, Bob Maroff, Kevin Rigney, Natalie Priest, Jane Cecil.

Flat, flimsy attempt to make an old-fashioned light comedy with new-fashioned trappings, padded out with plenty of New York sightseeing. The engagingly self-deflating Reynolds is the prosperous Manhattan bachelor (the manager of Madison Square Garden no less) who spots middle age on the horizon and decides he wants a child without the restrictions of a wife.

Beverly d'Angelo, a cornet player and part-time waitress who needs the money, takes the job and moves in so that Reynolds can supervise the pregnancy. You know the rest.

THE PATRIOT (Kairos-Film/The Other Cinema)
dir-pro-scr Alexander Kluge *ph* Thomas Mauch, Jorg Schmidt-Reitwein, Werner Luring, Gunther Hormann, part in colour *ed* Beate Mainka-Jellinghaus *r time* 120 mins *UK opening* Oct 1.
cast Hannelore Hoger, Alfred Edel, Alexander von Eschwege, Hans Heckel, Beate Holle, Kurt Jurgens, Dieter Mainka, Willi Munch, Gunther Keidel, Marius Muller-Westernhagen, Wolf Hanne, Judith Krichbaum, Roland Reuff.

Suffocatingly pretentious, irritatingly fragmented wander through the German experience as history teacher Hannelore Hoger attempts to examine his country's past, present and

possible future in a series of tiresome parables. The unacceptable face of European cinema, and virtually a commercial for not thinking too much.

PAUL RAYMOND'S EROTICA (Norfolk International/Brent Walker)
dir-scr Brian Smedley-Aston *pro* James Kenelm Clarke *exec pro* Paul Raymond *ph* Alan Hall, in colour *ed* Jim Connock *music* Steve Gray *r time* 86 mins *cert* X *UK opening* Aug 27.
cast Brigitte Lahaie, Diana Cochran, Raymond Revue Bar Girls, Paul Raymond.

Inflated commercial for Paul Raymond, his Revuebar, his magazines and his staff, disguised as a story about an insatiable French photo-journalist doing the rounds of the empire.

PENNIES FROM HEAVEN (MGM)
dir Herbert Ross *pro* Nora Kaye, Herbert Ross *exec pro* Richard McCallum *scr* Dennis Potter, based on his television series *ph* Gordon Willis, in Metrocolor *ed* Richard Marks *art dir* Fred Tuch, Bernie Cutler *music arr* Marvin Hamlisch, Billy May *r time* 108 mins *cert* AA *UK opening* May 20.
cast Steve Martin, Bernadette Peters, Christopher Walken, Jessica Harper, Vernel Bagneris, John McMartin, John Karlen, Jay Garner, Robert Fitch, Tommy Rall, Eliska Krupka, Frank McCarthy, Raleigh Bond, Gloria Leroy, Nancy Parsons, Toni Kaye, Shirley Kirkes, Jack Fletcher, Hunter Watkins, Arell Blanton, George Wilbur, M.C. Gainey, Mark Campbell, Mart Martinez, Duke Stroud, Joe Medalis, Richard Blum, William Frankfather, James Mendenhall, Jim Boeke, Robert Lee Jarvis, Luke Andreas, Will Hare, Joshua Cadman, Paul Valentine, Bill Richards, John Craig, Alton Ruff, Karla Bush, Robin Hoff, Linda Montana, Dorothy Cronin, Twink Caplan, Lillian D'Honau, Barbara Nordella, Dean Taliaferro.

Dennis Potter's acclaimed TV serial

given a touch of old Hollywood gloss (in the Mitty-style hero's fantasy sequences anyway), a more marketable star in the gawky but finally amiable Martin, and some stunning Edward Hopper-derived Depression sets. Those who saw Bob Hoskins in the altogether broodier TV version will not find their memories wiped easily by this altogether more lightweight treatment of the same material. On the other hand, there remains a great contemporary soundtrack, more than a few superb set pieces and, of course, the Potter signature, never really allowing for simple sentiment to take over where a more world-weary and knowing conclusion can be drawn.

POLYESTER (New Line Productions/GTO)
dir-pro-scr John Waters *exec pro* Robert Shaye *ph* David Insley, in colour *ed* Charles Roggero *art dir* Vincent Perano *music* Chris Stein, Michael Kamen *r time* 86 mins *cert* X *UK opening* May 13.

cast Divine, Tab Hunter, Edith Massey, Mink Stole, David Samson, Joni Ruth White, Mary Garlington, Ken King, Hans Kramm, Stiv Bators, Rick Breitenfeld, Michael Watson, Derek Neal, Jean Hill, Jim Hill, John Brothers, Mary Vivian Pearce, Sharon Niesp, Cookie Mueller, Susan Lowe, Tom Diventi, George Hulse, Tony Parkham, Paul Holland, Alberto Panella, Frank Tamburo, Nancy Morgan, Keats Smith, Gordon Kamka, David Klein, George Stover, Steve

Pennies From Heaven

Left: Passione D'Amore. Above: The Patriot

Yeager, Mary Egoff, John De La Vega, Chuck Yeaton, George Udell.

Waters' biggest budget to date enables him to move his gross TV star into better lodgings for this Middle-American comedy-romance with a difference. The difference is 'Odorama', a younger relative of 'Smellovision' (used so disastrously in 'Scent of Mystery' 25 years ago), utilising "scratch and sniff" cards instead of pumping smells into the cinema. Those familiar with Waters' work won't anticipate too many perfumes, but the film will probably disappoint those who like his pictures for their more degenerate aspects. Here they're toned down somewhat, and the results border on respectability. It's all still a million miles from a Doris Day film, however — Divine's son is a punk foot fetishist, hubby runs a porno palace — and there are several extremely funny moments. Hunter acquits himself without too much embarrassment considering the company he's forced to keep, and the ending will bring a contented tear to the most jaundiced eye.

POSSESSION (Oliane-Marianne-Soma/New Realm)
dir-scr Andrzej Zulawski *pro* Marie-Laure Reyre *ph* Bruno Nuytten, in Eastman Color *ed* Marie-Sophie Dubus, Suzanne Lang-Willar *art dir* Holger Gross *music* Andrzej Korzynski *r time* 122 mins *cert* X *UK opening* Jun 24.
cast Isabelle Adjani, Sam Neill, Margit Carstensen, Heinz Bennent, Johanna Hofer, Shaun Lawton, Michael Hogben, Carl Duering, Maximilian Ruethlein, Thomas Frey, Leslie Malton, Gerd Neubert, Kerstin Wohlfahrt, Ilse Bahrs, Karin Mumm, Herbert Chwoika, Barbara Stanek, Ilse Trautschold.

Exempted from closer examination as a turkey only by its proximity to the end of the year under review, 'Possession' defines new heights in awfulness, with a plotline staggering under the increasing weight of ludicrous incident. Isabelle Adjani wanders around Berlin in a catatonic trance, slicing herself up with an electric carver, killing policemen to feed to the fungus she keeps in a deserted flat, and having a massive haemorrhage in the subway involving Krakatoa-like eruptions of blood and pus. Zulawski shoots the whole charade with a bewildering series of vertiginous camera angles, mismatched shots and giddy tracking. The slurping tentacular creature which Adjani finally persuades to lie on top of her, is, by comparison with the surrounding mess, quite engaging.

PRIEST OF LOVE
(Ronceval/Enterprise)
dir Christopher Miles *pro* Christopher Miles, Andrew Donally *exec pro* Stanley J. Seeger *scr* Alan Plater, based on the book by Harry T. Moore and the letters and writings of D.H. Lawrence *ph* Ted Moore, in colour *ed* Paul Davies *pro des* Ted Tester, David Brockhurst *music* Joseph James *r time* 125 mins *cert* AA *UK opening* Feb 18.
cast Ian McKellen, Janet Suzman, Ava Gardner, Penelope Keith, Jorge Rivero, Maurizio Merli, John Gielgud, James Faulkner, Mike Gwilym, Massimo Ranieri, Marjorie Yates, Wendy Alnutt, Jane Booker, Elio Pandolfi, Shane Rimmer, Sarah Brackett, Adrienne Burgess, Patrick Holt, Derek Martin, Burnell Tucker, Mary Gifford, John Hudson, Daniel Chatto, Roger Sloman, Gareth Forwood, Frank Marcus, Indian Dancers from the Taos Pueblo, Paco Mauri, La Marimba, Hermanos Lugunas, Adrian Montano, Herminio Carrasco, Mike Morris, Natasha Buchanan, Anne Dyson, Julian Fellowes, Graham Faulkner, Niall Padden, Andrew McCulloch, Andrew Lodge, Sarah Miles, Sean Mathias, Francesco Carnellitti, Cyrus Elias, Madeleine Todd, Wolf Kahler, Graziana Cappellini, Andrea Occhipinti, John Flint, Brian McDermott, Duccio Dogone, Roberto Bonnanni, Roy Herrick, David Glover, Mellan Mitchell.

Flying backwards and forwards over the more salacious episodes of D.H. Lawrence's life, this film turns an already eventful career into the stuff of banner headlines; sensationalising what was trivial, and then trivialising what was really important, which was, by any standards, a unique contribution to literature. One major problem is the theatre-trained English cast, whose general lack of cinematic savvy is shown up by the Grand Dame presence of Ava Gardner. Far worse is the appalling, portentous dialogue. But worst of all is the moving spirit behind the whole thing: it's exactly the kind of spineless, snivelling liberalism that Lawrence himself denounced in the English and spent half his life trying to escape.

PRINCE OF THE CITY
(Orion/Warner)
dir Sidney Lumet *pro* Burtt Haris *exec pro* Jay Presson Allen *scr* Jay Presson Allen, Sidney Lumet, based on the book by Robert Daley *ph* Andrzej Bartkowiak, in Technicolor *ed* John J. Fitzstephens *pro des* Tony Walton *art dir* Edward Pisoni *music* Paul Chihara *r time* 167 mins *cert* X *UK opening* Dec 17.

Above: Possession. Right: Priest of Love

cast Treat Williams, Jerry Orbach, Richard Foronjy, Don Billett, Kenny Marino, Carmine Caridi, Tony Page, Norman Parker, Paul Roebling, Bob Balaban, James Tolkan, Steve Inwood, Lindsay Crouse, Matthew Laurance, Tony Turco, Ron Maccone, Ron Karabatsos, Tony Di Benedetto, Tony Munafo, Robert Christian, Lee Richardson, Lane Smith, Cosmo Alegretti, Bobby Alto, Michael Beckett, Burton Collins, Henry Ferrantino, Carmine Foresta, Conrad Fowkes, Peter Friedman, Peter Michael Goetz, Lance Henriksen, Eddie Jones, Don Leslie, Dana Lorge, Harry Madsen, E.D. Miller, Cynthia Nixon, Ron Perkins, Lionel Pina, Jose Santana.

Long, harrowing bio-pic, in the tradition of Lumet's own 'Serpico', about friendship, loyalty and police corruption in New York with Treat Williams (excellent) as a narcotics detective in a successful high-living "special investigating unit" who walks the tightrope of conflicting loyalties when he agrees to become an informer for an investigating commission which turns out to be just as shifty as its intended victims. Soundly scripted, well paced, utterly persuasive.

Psychopath

PRIVATE LESSONS *(Sunn Classic)*
dir Alan Myerson *pro* R. Ben Efraim *exec pro* Jack Barry, Dan Enright *scr* Dan Greenburg, based on his novel 'Philly' *ph* Jan de Bont, in Metrocolor *ed* Fred Chulack *art dir* Linda Pearl *r time* 85 mins *cert* X *UK opening* Apr 29.
cast Sylvia Kristel, Howard Hesseman, Eric Brown, Patrick Piccininni, Ed Begley Jr., Pamela Bryant, Meredith Baer, Ron Foster, Peter Elbling, Dan Barrows, Dan Greenburg, Marian Gibson.

Prince of the City

One of the occupational hazards of acquiring fame at a young age for on-screen sexual dallying, as Sylvia Kristel most emphatically did, is that once you've dallied with your contemporaries for what the film world considers to be a suitable time, you are inevitably called upon to be the older woman who gives a 15-year-old American boy his much-needed initiation — often, as is the case here, punctuated by dreadful music on which some AOR consultant has misguidedly advised. Dreadfully coy, but seemingly enormously profitable, this has a blackmail sub-plot to camouflage the flimsy voyeurism. Myerson, incidentally, directed the memorable 'Steelyard Blues' ten years ago. 'Private Lessons' will already have made him more money but will be forgotten by next week. In fact, it already has been.

THE PROUD ONES (Production Bela-TFI/Gala)
dir Claude Chabrol *pro* Georges de Beauregard *scr* Daniel Boulanger, Claude Chabrol, based on the book 'The Horse of Pride' by Pierre-Jakez Helias *ph* Jean Rabier, in Eastman

Color *ed* Monique Fardoulis *art dir* Hilton McConnico *music* Pierre Jansen *r time* 118 mins *cert* A *UK opening* May 20.
cast Jacques Dufilho, Bernadette Lesache, Francois Cluzet, Ronan Hubert, Arnel Hubert, Paul Leperson, Pierre Le Rumeur, Michel Blanc, Dominique Lavanant, Bernard Dumaine, Pierre Dumeniaud, Jacques Chailleux, Yves Morgan.

One of the problems inherent in beautifully photographed films about rural poverty — and 'The Proud Ones' is certainly not alone in this respect — is that they encourage a disparity between how one suspects an audience is supposed to respond and what it actually sees. This account of peasant life in Brittany before and during the First World War is a good example. On the one hand, it rubs your face in the minutiae of field labour; on the other, it surrounds the poverty in such a seductive cocoon of national costumes, benevolent myth and rustic ideal-homes that one searches around the corners of every frame for lurking colour-supplement photographers in search of the perfect picture.

PSYCHOPATH (Larry Brown Prods/London International)
dir-pro Larry Brown *exec pro* Thomas P. Richardson *scr* Walter C. Dallenbach *ph* Jack Beckett, in colour *ed* John Williams, Dennis Jakob *music* Country Al Ross *r time* 84 mins *cert* AA *UK opening* Sept 27.
cast Tom Basham, Gene Carlson, Gretchen Kanne, Dave Carlile, Barbara Grover, Lance Larson, Jeff Rice, Pete Renoudet, Jackson Bostwick, John D. Ashton, Mary Rings, Margaret Avery, Sam Javis, Brenda Venus, Carol Ann Daniels, Bruce Kimball.

The host of a children's television programme goes around murdering child-battering parents. Made in 1973, where it should have stayed.

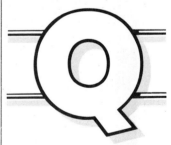

QUARTET (Merchant Ivory-Lyric Int/Fox)
dir James Ivory *pro* Ismail Merchant, Jean Pierre Mahot de la Querantonnais *exec pro* Hubert Niogret *scr* Ruth Prawer Jhabvala, from the novel by Jean Rhys *ph* Pierre Lhomme, in colour *ed* Humphrey Dixon *art dir* Jean-Jacques Caziot *music* Richard Robbins *r time* 101 mins *cert* X *UK opening* Jul 16.
cast Alan Bates, Maggie Smith, Isabelle Adjani, Anthony Higgins, Sheila Gish, Pierre Clementi, Suzanne Flon, Daniel Mesguish, Armelia McQueen, Wiley Wood, Daniel Chatto, Bernice Stegers, Virginie Thevenet,

Sebastien Floche, Paulita Sedgwick, Isabella Canto Da Maya, Francois Viaur, Dino Zanghi, Michel Such, Jean-Pierre Dravel, Annie Noel, Maurice Ribot, Pierre Julien, Humbert Balsan, Serge Marquand, Muriel Montosse, Caroline Loeb, Jeffrey Kime, Shirley Allan, Anne-Marie Brissonière, Marie-France de Bourges, Brigitte Hermetz, Joceline Comellas, Romain Bremond, Arlette Spetelbroot, Monique Mauclair.

Cool, thoughtful, leisurely film set in a picture-book Paris in the late 1920s, where a stranded Isabelle Adjani enjoys — or rather fails to enjoy — the patronage of Alan Bates and Maggie Smith. Attractively photographed, with an immaculate sense of period, it somehow fails to stir the blood.

QUEST FOR FIRE (ICC-Fox)
dir Jean-Jacques Annaud *pro* John Kemeny, Denis Heroux *exec pro* Michael Gruskoff *scr* Gerard Brach, based on the novel 'La Guerre de Feu' by J.H. Rosny *ph* Claude Agostini, in Panavision, Bellevue-Pathé colour *ed* Yves Langlois *pro des* Guy Comtois, Brian Morris *art dir* Clinton Cavers *music* Philippe Sarde *r time* 100 mins *cert* AA *UK opening* Apr 8.

cast Everett McGill, Ron Perlman, Nameer El-Kadi, Rae Dawn Chong, Gary Schwartz, Naseer El-Kadi, Frank Olivier Bonnet, Jean-Michel Kindt, Kurt Schiegl, Brian Gill, Terry Fitt, Bibi Caspari, Peter Elliott, Michelle Leduc, Robert Lavoie, Matt Birman, Christian Benard, Joy Boushell, Mary Lou Foy, Robert Gondek, Sylvie Guilbault, Steve Ramanuskas, Lydia Chaban, Dena Francis, Helene Gregoire, Lloyd McKinnon, Georgette Rondeau, Rod Bennett, Jacques Demers, Michel Drouet, Michel Francoeur, Charles Gosselin, Bernard Kendall, Benoit Levesque, Joshua Melnick, Jean-Claude Meunier, Alex Quaglia, The Great Antonio, Jacques Caron.

The first wholly prehistoric epic in a decade by-passes the usual pitfalls of ancient-speak quite simply: it doesn't have any. Improving marginally on the lines he — or one of his three Italian co-scriptwriters — contributed to 'Moses the Lawgiver' ("Where are you taking the children of Israel, Moses?" — "To the Holy Land, where else?"), Anthony Burgess is credited with 'special languages' while fellow expert Desmond Morris is on 'body language and gestures'. All this brings a needless dimension of academic correctness to what works best as a yarn about three grunting primitives wearing bits of old fur who set out on the quest in question after their fire has been put out by another even more primitive tribe. Often very funny if rarely very exciting, it is an entertaining mixture of high adventure and low anthropology populated by endearingly monosyllabic characters. Some of Desmond's 'body language',incidentally, involves the discovery of the missionary position.

RAGTIME (EMI)
dir Milos Forman *pro* Dino De Laurentiis *exec pro* Michael Hausman, Bernard Williams *scr* Michael Weller, based on the novel by E.L. Doctorow *ph* Miroslav Ondricek, in Todd-AO, Technicolor *ed* Anne V. Coates, Antony Gibbs, Stanley Warnow *pro des* John Graysmark *art dir* Patrizia Von Brandenstein, Anthony Reading

music Randy Newman *r time* 155 mins *cert* AA *UK opening* Feb 18.
cast James Cagney, Brad Dourif, Moses Gunn, Elizabeth McGovern, Kenneth McMillan, Pat O'Brien, Donald O'Connor, James Olson, Mandy Patinkin, Howard E. Rollins Jr., Mary Steenburgen, Debbie Allen, Jeff Demunn, Robert Joy, Norman

Mailer, Bruce Boa, Hoolihan Burke, Edwin Cooper, Jeff Daniels, Fran Drescher, Bessie Love, Herman Meckler, Jenny Nichols, Max Nichols, Eloise O'Brien, Don Plumley, Ted Ross, Norman Chancer, Zack Norman, Bill Reimbold, Frankie Faison, Samuel L. Jackson, Calvin Levels, Dorsey Wright, Hal Galili, Christopher Malcolm, Richard Griffiths, Billy J. Mitchell, Robert Arden, Robert Boyd.

Milos Forman's European sensibility should have been ideally suited to filming E.L. Doctorow's overrated bestseller, a panorama of turn-of-the-century American life, mixing fact and fiction, which drew much of its narrative strength from Heinrich von Kleist's 'Michael Kohlhaas'. But he gives neither impetus nor cohesion to the epic original, which he has restructured on a more intimate scale, switching between domestic problems and public upheavals, confusing more than he clarifies. If there is no central focus to the film, there are many incidental pleasures, notably in the quality of acting from its large cast, particularly Howard E. Rollins Jr., who gives one of the year's most riveting performances. The principal disappointment is James Cagney, making a much-publicised return to acting. Arthritic and rigid in old age, he seems more embalmed than alive, a failing that applies to much else in the movie.

RAIDERS OF THE LOST ARK
(Lucasfilm/Paramount)
dir Steven Spielberg *pro* Frank Marshall *exec pro* George Lucas, Howard Kazanjian *scr* Lawrence Kasdan *story* George Lucas, Philip Kaufman *ph* Douglas Slocombe, in Panavision, Metrocolor *ed* Michael

Quest for Fire

Raiders of the Lost Ark

Kahn *pro des* Norman Reynolds *art dir* Leslie Dilley *music* John Williams *r time* 115 mins *cert* A *UK opening* Jul 30.
cast Harrison Ford, Karen Allen, Paul Freeman, Ronald Lacey, John Rhys-Davies, Denholm Elliott, Alfred Molina, Wolf Kahler, Anthony Higgins, Vic Tablian, Don Fellows, William Hootkins, Bill Reimbold, Fred Sorenson, Patrick Durkin, Matthew Scurfield, Malcolm Weaver, Sonny Caldinez, Anthony Chinn, Pat Roach, Christopher Frederick, Tutte Lemkow, Ishaq Bux, Kiran Shah, Souad Messaoudi, Terry Richards, Steve Hanson, Frank Marshall, Martin Kreidt, George Harris, Eddie Tagoe, John Rees, Tony Vogel, Ted Grossman.

The knowing dissolve from the Paramount mountain to its real-life Peruvian counterpart is the first clue to the spirit of this exuberant, jokey, skilfully paced adventure yarn with the narrative of an old serial and a budget that would fund a small country for six months. An effective performance from Harrison Ford as the heroic archaeologist who runs the usual gauntlet in trying to prevent the power-giving Ark of the title from falling into the hands of the Nazis. One of the most uniformly enjoyable films of the year — and, unsurprisingly, one of the most successful.

REDS (Paramount)
dir-pro Warren Beatty *exec pro* Simon Relph, Dede Allen *scr* Warren Beatty, Trevor Griffiths *ph* Vittorio Storaro, in Technicolor *ed* Dede Allen, Craig McKay *pro des* Richard Sylbert *art dir* Simon Holland *music* Stephen

Sondheim, Dave Grusin *r time* 196 mins *cert* AA *UK opening* Feb 25.
cast Warren Beatty, Diane Keaton, Edward Herrmann, Jerzy Kosinski, Jack Nicholson, Paul Sorvino, Maureen Stapleton, Nicolas Coster, M. Emmet Walsh, Ian Wolfe, Bessie Love, MacIntyre Dixon, Pat Starr, Eleanor D. Wilson, Max Wright, George Plimpton, Harry Ditson, Leigh Curran, Kathryn Grody, Brenda Currin, Nancy Duiguid, Norman Chancer, Dolph Sweet, Ramon Bieri, Jack O'Leary, Gene Hackman, Gerald Hiken, William Daniels, Dave King, Joseph Buloff, Stefan Gryff, Denis Pekarev, Roger Sloman, Stuart Richman, Oleg Kerensky, Nikko Seppala, John J. Hooker, Shane Rimmer, Jerry Hardin, Jack Kehoe,

Reds

Christopher Malcolm, Tony Sibbald, R.G. Armstrong, Josef Sommer, Jan Triska, Ake Lindman, Pertti Weckstrom, Nina Macarova, Jose De Fillippo, Andreas La Casa, Roger Baldwin, Henry Miller, Adela Rogers St. Johns, Dora Russell, Scott Nearing, Tess Davis, Heaton Vorse, Hamilton Fish, Isaac Don Levine, Rebecca West, Will Durant, Will Weinstone, Oleg Kerensky, Emmanuel Herbert, Arne Swabeck, Adele Nathan, George Seldes, Kenneth Chamberlain, Blanche Hays Fagen, Galina Von Meck, Art Shields, Andrew Dasburg, Hugo Gellert, Dorothy Frooks, George Jessel, Jacob Bailin, John Ballato, Lucita Williams, Bernadine Szold-Fritz, Jessica Smith, Harry Carlisle, Arthur Mayer.

Warren Beatty could end up as the Cecil B. De Mille, or even the Irving Thalberg, of the 1980s. His enormously ambitious film about the life of journalist-revolutionary John Reed reveals him as a producer-director of surprising sensitivity, as well as an actor of continuing charm. If 'Reds' fails, as it ultimately does, it is an honourable failure and one that would have seemed a success in a smaller talent. Beatty uses the camera well, in a manner that owes much to David Lean, has provided his cast with an intelligent script and orchestrated the effective device of having actual witnesses to Reed's life and times provide a wayward chorus of such vitality that it almost overshadows the fiction.

REMEMBRANCE (Channel 4/Mainline)
dir-pro Colin Gregg *scr* Hugh Stoddart *ph* John Metcalfe, in Eastman Color *ed* Peter Delfgou *art dir* Jamie Leonard *r time* 117 mins *cert* AA *UK opening* Jun 3.
cast John Altman, Al Ashton, Martin Barrass, Nick Dunning, Sally Jane Jackson, David John, Peter Lee-Wilson, Gary Oldman, Ewan Stewart, Timothy Spall, Kim Taylforth, Michele Winstanley, Kenneth Griffith, Roger Adamson, Dawn Archibald, Sean Arnold, Dicken Ashworth, Sheila Ballantine, John Barrett, Derek Benfield, Jesse Birdsall, Mark Drewry, Roger Booth, Jon Croft, Alison Dowling, Nicola Wright, Nick Ellesworth, Peter Ellis, Myra Frances, Michael Godley, Dave Hill, Peter Jonfield, Wolf Kahler, Marjie Lawrence, Doel Luscombe, Tony

Mathews, Lisa Maxwell, Anna Rees, Don Munday, Eileen Page, Robert Pitman, John Price, Lawrie Quayle, John Rutland, Flip Webster.

A distinctly unpromising and old-fashioned departure point — the last 24 hours ashore of a group of sailors — overstated in a way which spells television sponsorship in neon-lit capitals, does little to deflate the intentions of this striking, unyieldingly grim portrait of the English present: a world of rain, boring evenings, heavy drinking, casual violence, discos and Indian restaurants. It will not export well and people who see it will book holidays abroad the following morning.

RETURN OF THE SECAUCUS SEVEN (Salsipuedes Prods/Osiris)
dir-scr-ed John Sayles *pro* Jeffrey Nelson, William Aydelott *ph* Austin DeBesche, in colour *music* Mason Daring *r time* 110 mins *cert* AA *UK opening* Oct 29.
cast Bruce MacDonald, Adam Lefevre, Gordon Clapp, Karen Trott, David Strathaim, Marisa Smith, Carolyn Brooks, Nancy Mette, Cora Bennett, Steven Zaitz, Brian Johnston, Ernie Bashaw, Jessica MacDonald, Jeffrey Nelson, Maggie Renzi, Maggie Cousineau, Jean Passanante, Mark Arnott, John Sayles, Amy Schewel, Eric Forsythe, Betsy Julia Robinson, John Medillo, Jack LaValle, Benjamin Zaitz.

Writer of much of Roger Corman's recent stylish trash, Sayles' directorial debut is a likeable, funny, verbose view of a septet of former Sixties activists, drifting towards conformity and

realising it, whose annual reunion weekend teaches them a few lessons. Some great lines, some intentionally dreadful songs, some attractive performances from a cast of unknowns.

RICH AND FAMOUS (MGM)
dir George Cukor *pro* William Allyn *scr* Gerald Ayres, based on the play 'Old Acquaintance' by John Van Druten *ph* Don Peterman, Peter Eco, in Metrocolor *ed* John F. Burnett *pro des* Jan Scott *art dir* Fred Harpman, James A. Taylor *music* Georges Delerue *r time* 117 mins *cert* X *UK opening* Jan 14.
cast Jacqueline Bisset, Candice Bergen, David Selby, Hart Bochner, Steven Hill, Meg Ryan, Matt Lattanzi, Daniel Faraldo, Nicole Eggert, Joe Moross, Kres Mersky, Cloyce Morrow, Cheryl Robinson, Allan Warnick, Michael Brandon, Ann Risley, Damion Sheller, Haley Fox, Fay Kanin, Tara Simpson, Herb Graham, Charlotte Moore, William Schilling, John Perkins, Herb Bress, Alan Berliner, Don Bachardy, Ruth Conte, Marsha Hunt, Christopher Isherwood, Pola Miller, Paul Morrissey, Jennifer Naim-Smith, Karen Somerville, Roger Vadim, Sandra Smith Allyn, Frances Bergen, Ray Bradbury, Ellen Brill, Gwen Davis, Frank De Felitta, Michael Dewell, Nina Foch, Elizabeth Forsythe-Hailey, Oliver Hailey, Randal Kleiser, Gavin Lambert.

The original film adaptation of John Van Druten's play 'Old Acquaintance' was just as camp as this but nowhere near as wet, and had at least the advantage of casting Bette Davis and Miriam Hopkins as the two writers

whose paths keep crossing and dividing. There are two problems here. One is that yesterday's drama has, rather unconvincingly, been tarted up to conform to today's expectations — sex, bad language, a journalist from 'Rolling Stone' etc. The other is that Bisset (the intellectual one who talks in "thinking woman" cartoon balloons) and Bergen (the cheerful pragmatic one who makes a fortune from exploitative trash) seem barely capable of writing each other a letter. One of the most unintentionally funny films in recent memory, and recommendable for that reason, 'Rich and Famous' is just a lot of window dressing in search of a convincing dummy.

ROAD GAMES (Avco Embassy/Barber International)
dir-pro Richard Franklin *exec pro* Bernard Schwartz *scr* Everett De Roche *ph* Vincent Monton, in Panavision, Eastman Color *ed* Edward McQueen-Mason *pro des-art dir* Jon Dowding *music* Brian May *r time* 93 mins *cert* AA *UK opening* May 6.
cast Stacy Keach, Jamie Lee Curtis, Marion Edward, Grant Page, Bill Stacey, Thaddeus Smith, Stephen Millichamp, Alan Hopgood, John Murphy, Robert Thompson, Angie La Bozzetta, Colin Vancao.

Stacy Keach is rapidly becoming one of those good actors who (an exception in his case for Huston's 'Fat City') is rarely in good movies. Here he is the lone trucker, heaving his 18-wheeler across Australia, reading John Donne and worrying about the hostile locals, his dingo and the maniac who's slicing up hitch-hikers; an action replay, in

Rich and Famous

Rosemary's Killer

other words, of every road movie theme imaginable, from the malevolence of 'Duel' and 'Slither' to the occupational boredom of 'Kings of the Road'. This is crossed with the women-in-peril vein of the customary nastiness, represented by the ubiquitous Jamie Lee Curtis, who is surely due for a change of pace. There is an ironic touch in the fact that the final chase in Perth gets slower rather than faster, but otherwise the film just seems like two dead genres enclosed in one coffin and badly in need of a good send-off.

ROAR (Alpha)
dir-pro-scr Noel Marshall *exec pro* Banjiro Uemura *ph* Jan de Bont, in Panavision, Technicolor *pro des* Joel Marshall *music* Terence P. Minogue *r time* 101 mins *cert* A *UK opening* Apr 1.
cast Tippi Hedren, Noel Marshall, Melanie Griffith, John Marshall, Jerry Marshall, Kyalo Mativo, Frank Tom, Steve Miller, Rick Glassey.

Belying its $17 million budget and five years in the making, this wispy propagandist nature study — built on the slenderest of stories and failing to

capitalise on even the most elementary excitement — suggests a film made up as it went along in accordance with the general mood of the considerable number of wild animals which populate it. Principally lions, the most irrepressibly cute even having the benefit of their own credit, they overplay their limited charm to the point of tedium and well beyond. The humans — an animal-loving scientist living in the African (well, Californian) bush, his visiting family, a local friend and a couple of nasty game hunters — wander through it cheerfully, weighed down by vacuous homilies. Undeniably good-hearted and well-photographed, it still manages to define new dimensions in tedium.

ROSEMARY'S KILLER (Carolco/Entertainment)
dir Joseph Zito *pro* Joseph Zito, David Streit *exec pro* James Bochis *scr* Glenn Leopold, Neal F. Barbera *ph* Raul Lomas, in colour *ed* Joel Goodman *pro des* Lorenzo Mans *art dir* Roberta Neiman *music* Richard Einhorn *r time* 87 mins *cert* X *UK opening* Jun 3.
cast Farley Granger, Vicky Dawson, Christopher Goutman, Lawrence Tierney, Cindy Weintraub, Lisa Dunsheath, David Sederholm, Bill Nunnery, Thom Bray, Diane Rode, Bryan Englund, Donna Davis, Carlton Carpenter, Joy Glaccum, Timothy Wahrer, John Seitz, Bill Hugh Collins, Dan Lownsberry, Douglas Stevenson, Susan Monts, John Christian, Richard Colligan, Steven Bock, Matthew Iddings.

Advertised rather desperately as "the film that shocked America!" — suggesting that America is now so desensitised to the succession of movies in which attractive women are stalked or slaughtered that this in itself might carry some distinction — 'Rosemary's Killer', it has to be said, is just more of the same with added roses, its only peculiarity being the casting of Farley Granger, 30 years after his handsome, tennis-playing hero of 'Strangers on a Train', as the villain.

Roar

RUST NEVER SLEEPS (Shakey Pictures/Blue Dolphin)

dir-ed Bernard Shakey *pro* L.A. Johnson *exec pro* Elliot Rabinowitz *ph* Paul Goldsmith, Jon Else, Robby Greenberg, Hiro Narita, Richard Pearce, Daniel Pearl, in DeLuxe colour *r time* 108 mins *cert* U *UK opening* Aug 27.

Straightforward representation of a Neil Young and Crazy Horse concert directed and edited by a pseudonymous Neil Young. There are those who view this self-regarding whiner as a minor deity. This writer is not among them.

THE SECRET POLICEMAN'S OTHER BALL (Amnesty International/UIP)
dir Julien Temple *pro* Martin Lewis, Peter Walker *ph* Oliver Stapleton, in colour *ed* Geoff Hogg *music* various *r time* 99 mins *cert* AA *UK opening* Mar 18.
cast Rowan Atkinson, Jeff Beck, Alan Bennett, John Bird, Tim Brooke-Taylor, Graham Chapman, Eric Clapton, John Cleese, Phil Collins, Billy Connolly, Donovan, Johnny Fingers, John Fortune, Bob Geldof, Chris Langham, Griff Rhys Jones, Alexei Sayle, Pamela Stephenson, Sting, The Secret Police, John Wells, Victoria Wood, Michael Palin, David Rappaport, Daryl Stuermer, Danny Thompson, Maynard Williams.

Efficient, straightforward account of Amnesty's 1981 fund-raising show, featuring the now customary cocktail of music and humour. It's an effective if predictable format which works particularly well when, taking their cue from Pete Townshend in a previous gala, "popular" performers like Sting, Phil Collins and Bob Geldof sing stripped-down versions of songs with which they are closely identified. The comedy content varies according to taste: there is an excess of old lags going through their paces, compounded by the audience's easy-to-please big-occasion acquiescence, but Billy Connolly's protracted drinking story, delivered with winning relish, is both funny to hear and impressive to watch. Among the relative newcomers, Chris Langham makes everything seem easy while Alexei Sayle, bursting with splenetic huff and puff, makes it all seem very difficult.

SEVERAL DAYS IN THE LIFE OF I.I. OBLOMOV
(Mosfilm/Contemporary)
dir Nikita Mikhalkov *scr* Aleksandr Adabashyan, Nikita Mikhalkov, based on the novel 'Oblomov' by Ivan A. Goncharov *ph* Pavel Lebeshev, in Sovcolor *ed* E. Praksinoi *art dir* Aleksandr Adabashyan, Aleksandr Samulekin *music* Eduard Artemiev *r time* 140 mins *cert* U *UK opening* Sept 10.
cast Oleg Tabakov, Yuri Bogatyryov, Andrei Popov, Yelena Solovei, Avangard Leontiev, Andrei Razumovsky, Oleg Kozlov, G. Shostko, Gleb Strizhenov, Y. Kleshchevskaya, Yevgeny Steblov, Yevgenia Glushenko,

Right: The Secret Policeman's Other Ball

Several Days in the Life of I.I. Oblomov

Nikolai Pastukhov, O. Basilashvili, A. Kharitonov, L. Sokolova, I. Kashintsev, P. Kadoshnikov, N. Tengayev, E. Romanov, N. Gorlov, R. Akhmetov, V. Gogolyev, N. Terenteva, N. Burlyaev, A. Ovchinnikov, V. Novikova, M. Dorofeyev, K. Mikhailova, Fedya Stukov.

The interminable Russian novel adapted into a film not quite as interminable, but near enough.

SEX ON THE ROCKS (Lisa-Film/Amanda)
dir Siggi Götz *exec pro* Erich Tomek *scr* Florian Burg *ph* Heinz Hölscher, in colour *ed* Eva Zeyn, Gisela Winkel *music* Gerhard Heinz *r time* 87 mins *cert* X *UK opening* Jul 2.
cast Regis Porte, Tanja Spiess, Michael Gspandl, Beate Gränitz, Margit Geissler, Gesa Thoma, Heidi Stroh, Jan Hopman, Karl Heinz Maslo, Rafael Molina, Manel Aragones, Jean Henké, Carlos "Carla" Delgardo.

Fun (and lack of it) in the Ibiza sun. The usual catalogue of parties, discos, nudity and motorcycle rides, trotted out with dreary uniformity. The intriguingly named Carlos "Carla" Delgardo is Carlos below the waist, Carla above.

SHARKY'S MACHINE
(Orion/Warner)
dir Burt Reynolds *pro* Hank Moonjean *scr* Gerald Di Pego, based on the novel by William Diehl *ph* William A. Fraker, in Technicolor *ed* William Gordean *pro des* Walter Scott Herndon *music* Al Capps *r time* 120 mins *cert* X *UK opening* Apr 1.
cast Burt Reynolds, Vittorio Gassman, Brian Keith, Charles Durning, Earl Holliman, Bernie Casey, Henry Silva, Richard Libertini, Darryl Hickman, Rachel Ward, Joseph Mascolo, Carol Locatell, Hari Rhodes, John Fielder, James O'Connell, Val Avery, Suzee Pai, Aarika Wells, Tony King, Dan Inosanto, Weaver Levy, May Keller Pearce, Sheryl Kilby, James Lewis, Scott Newell, Glynn Ruben, Bennie Moore, Alveda King Beale, Gayle Davis, Atim Kweli, Brenda Bynum, Gus Mann, William Diehl, Elaine Falone, Wanda Strange, Barbara Stokes, John Greenwell, John Arthur, Terrayne Crawford, Mary Beth Busbee, J. Don Ferguson, Monica Kaufman, Dave Michaels, Wes Sarginson, Forrest Sawyer, Colonel Beach, Danny Melson, Lamar Jackson, El Mongol, Sue Cockrell, Lisa Hall, Pam Newman, April Reed, Susan Williamson, Diana Szlosberg.

Visually lively, verbally leaden cop thriller in which incorruptible Reynolds uncovers all kinds of mayhem in mobland and falls for high-class hooker Rachel Ward after spending what seems like years surveying her in action through binoculars. Rather an excess of self-conscious tough-guy talk, but the action sequences are impressive — the opening itself is brilliant — and there are strong performances from Henry Silva as a pilled-up hit man contracted by smooth mobster Vittorio Gassman, who even manages to make 'My Funny Valentine' sound sinister. Jokingly referred to by Reynolds as "Dirty Harry Goes to Atlanta", which is not far from the truth.

SHOCK TREATMENT (Fox)
dir Jim Sharman *pro* John Goldstone *exec pro* Lou Adler, Michael White *scr* Richard O'Brien, Jim Sharman *ph* Mike Molloy, in Technicolor *ed* Richard Bedford *pro des* Brian Thomson *art dir* Andrew Sanders *music* Richard Hartley, Richard O'Brien *r time* 95 mins *cert* A *UK opening* Jan 14.
cast Jessica Harper, Cliff De Young, Richard O'Brien, Patricia Quinn, Charles Gray, Nell Campbell, Ruby Wax, Barry Humphries, Rik Mayall, Darlene Johnson, Manning Redwood, Wendy Raebeck, Jeremy Newson, Betsy Brantley, Perry Bedden, Rufus Collins, Chris Malcolm, Ray Charleson, Eugene Lipinski, Barry Dennen, Imogen Claire, Gary Shail, Donald Waugh, Claire Toeman, Sinitta Renet, David John, Gary Martin.

One of the most thoroughly unpleasant experiences of my life was watching 'The Rocky Horror Show' at wherever it became a resident in the Kings Road surrounded by braying, sycophantic trendies. It was full of horribly derivative early-Seventies pop-pastiche for people who don't really like any kind of music that isn't connected to banal memories and backdated fashion; it was shallow satire for people who thought they understood its source. It, and the subsequent film, got the audience it deserved. 'Shock Treatment' is the stubbed-out fag-end of the same tradition, retaining the central couple from its predecessor, and directing its heavy-handed parody at (wait for it) American television, game shows in particular. It is a film for people who regret the passing of stack-heels, and who still use the word "decadent" with a straight face.

SHOGUN (Paramount)
dir Jerry London *pro* Eric Bercovici *exec pro* James Clavell *scr* Eric Bercovici, based on the novel by James Clavell *ph* Andrew Laszlo, in colour *ed* Jack Tucker, Bill Luciano, Donald R. Rode *pro des* Joseph R. Jennings *music* Maurice Jarre *r time* 150 mins *cert* A *UK opening* Nov 20.
cast Richard Chamberlain, Toshira Mifune, Yoko Shimada, Frankie Sakai, Alan Badel, Michael Hordern, Damien Thomas, John Rhys-Davies, Vladek Sheybal, George Innes, Leon Lissek, Yuki Meguro, Hideo Takamatsu, Nobuo Kaneko, Edward Peel, Steve Ubels, John Carney, Neil McCarthy, Eric Richard, Stewart MacKenzie, Ian Jentle, Morgan Sheppard, Masumi Okada, Yosuke Natsuki, Seiji Miyaguchi, Rinichi Yamamoto, Hiroshi Hasegawa, Toru Abe, Miiko Taka,

Left: Sharky's Machine. Above: Shock Treatment

Mika Kitagawa, Shin Takuma,
Shizuko Azuma.

*Cut by nine-and-a-half hours from its
original form as a TV series — and
still managing to last forever as it
confuses the audience with narrative
jumps — this is the one about the
shipwrecked English navigator, the
feudal wars in 17th century Japan, and
the assimilation of oriental culture
through the attentions of a local
woman. Handsomely filmed, and
thankfully allowing the Japanese to
speak in their own language, finally it
seems little more than an excuse for
Richard Chamberlain to model
kimonos.*

SHOGUN ASSASSIN (Katsu/Facelift)
dir Kenji Misumi, (American version,
Robert Houston) *pro* Shintaro Katsu,
Hisaharu Matsubara, David Weisman
exec pro Peter Shanaberg *scr* Kazuo
Koike, Robert Houston, David
Weisman, based on a story by Kazuo
Koike, Goseki Kojima *ph* Chishi
Makiura, in Tohoscope, Fujicolor *ed*
Toshio Taniguchi, Lee Percy *art dir*
Akira Naito *music* Hideakira Sakurai,
W. Michael Lewis, Mark Lindsay
r time 84 mins *cert* X *UK opening*
Nov 19.
cast Tomisaburo Wakayama, Masahiro
Tomikawa, Kayo Matsuo, Minoru
Ohki, Shoji Kobayashi, Shia Kishida,
Akihiro Tomikawa.

*Seeking revenge after the murder of
his wife, an all-purpose slaughterhouse
on legs disguised as a samurai
swordsman achieves satisfaction by
wiping out an abundance of the mad
shogun's Ninja warriors: heads roll,
blood spurts, throats, hands and feet
all go with relentless frequency. His
small son counts the bodies. The
dialogue is American. The bloodshed is
plentiful.*

SHOOT THE MOON (MGM)
dir Alan Parker *pro* Alan Marshall
exec pro Edgar J. Scherick, Stuart
Millar *scr* Bo Goldman *ph* Michael
Seresin, in Metrocolor *ed* Gerry
Hambling *pro des* Geoffrey Kirkland
art dir Stu Campbell *r time* 124 mins
cert AA *UK opening* Jun 3.
cast Albert Finney, Diane Keaton,
Karen Allen, Peter Weller, Dana Hill,
Viveka Davis, Tracey Gold, Tina
Yothers, George Murdock, Leora
Dana, Irving Metzman, Kenneth
Kimmins, Michael Alldredge, Robert
Costanzo, David Landsberg, Lou
Cutell, James Cranna, Nancy Fish,
Jeremy Schoenberg, Stephen Morrell,
Jim Lange, Georgann Johnson, O-Lan
Shepard, Helen Slayton-Hughes,
Robert Ackerman, Eunice Suarez,
Hector M. Morales, Morgan Upton,
Edwina Moore, Kathryn Trask, Bill
Reddick, Bonnie Carpenter, Margaret
Clark, Jan Dunn, Rob Glover.

*Recommended above all to leisured,
sensitive sorts who like to discuss
"relationships", 'Shoot the Moon' is
about what happens when a well-to-do
Marin County couple — he a successful
writer bored with marriage and having*

Right: Shoot the Moon

an affair, she a prickly, demoralised housewife who knows it — split up after 15 years. It is also about how it affects the eldest of their four noisy daughters and about their parents' difficulty in avoiding contact over the months that follow, despite the fact that he spends much of his time mooning about on the Pacific beach outside his new girlfriend's house, and that she falls for the bloke building her tennis court. It has some warmly observed moments (Keaton's tears in the bath, a broadly comic restaurant scene, anything involving the children, who are all terrific), but the cumulative effect is wearying, leading to a finale which tries to be cathartic and just seems contrived.

S.O.B. (Lorimar/ITC)
dir-scr Blake Edwards *pro* Blake Edwards, Tony Adams *exec pro* Michael B. Wolf *ph* Harry Stradling, in colour *ed* Ralph E. Winters *pro des* Rodger Maus *art dir* William Craig Smith *music* Henry Mancini *r time* 121 mins *cert* AA *UK opening* Jul 2.
cast Julie Andrews, William Holden, Richard Mulligan, Robert Vaughn, Robert Webber, Robert Preston, Larry Hagman, Shelley Winters, Marisa Berenson, Loretta Swift, Katherine MacMurray, Craig Stevens, Robert Loggia, Jennifer Edwards, Stuart Margolin, Paul Stewart, Benson Fong, John Pleshette, John Lawlor, Larry Storch, Ken Swofford, Bert Rosario, Hamilton Camp, Joe Penny, Stiffe Tanney, Mimi Davis, David Young, Virginia Gregg, Paddy Stone, Byron Kane, Rosanna Arquette, Stephen Johnson, Erica John, Gene Nelson, Charles Lampkin, Pat Colbert, Joseph Benti, Kevin Justrich, Kimberly Woodward.

Edwards settles a few old scores with Hollywood through this enjoyable but over-long and overstated satirical comedy about a deranged film producer with a $30 million flop on his hands which he turns into gold-dust through the wonder of a little soft-core pornography. Bilious, anal, impeccably tasteless, it is just about sustained by the jokes that do work and by sound, reliable performances from William Holden and Robert Preston. The rest of the cast hams it up agreeably but excessively. Ironically it will probably become best known as the film in which Julie Andrews' tits got their first airing.

SO FINE (Warner)
dir-scr Andrew Bergman *pro* Mike Lobell *ph* James A. Contner, in Technicolor *ed* Alan Heim *pro des* Santo Loquasto *art dir* Paul Eads *music* Ennio Morricone *r time* 91 mins *cert* AA *UK opening* Jan 7.
cast Ryan O'Neal, Jack Warden, Mariangela Melato, Richard Kiel, Fred Gwynne, Mike Kellin, David Rounds, Joel Steadman, Angela Pietro Pinto, Michael Lombard, Jessica James, Bruce Millholland, Merwin Goldsmith, Irving Metzman, Louis de Banzie, Rick Lieberman, Anthony Siricco Jr., Michael Laguardia, Chip Zien, Bill Luhrs, Dick Boccelli, Lydia Laurans,

Margaret Hall, Sally Jane Heit, Henry Lawrence, James Hong, Danny Kwan, Paul Price, Tyra Farrell, Joseph Montabo, Jose Machado, Sophie Schwab, Jerome Binder, Hy Mencher, Maria Tai, Beda Elliot, Joseph Ilardi, John Bentley, Herb Schlein, Alma Cuervo, John Stockwell, Beverly May, P.K. Fields, Webster Whinery, Kathie Flusk, Randy Jones, Christopher Loomis, Hyla Marrow, Gail Lawrence, Martha Gaylord, Bernie McInerny, Alan Leach, Pamela Lewis, Jim Jansen, Pierre Epstein, Tony Aylward, Todd Isaacson, Adam Stolarsky, Judith Cohen.

It begins with university professor Ryan O'Neal helping out his father's clothing business after the latter falls into debt to a menacing colossus. It ends with a campus performance of Verdi's 'Otello' invaded by several of the principal characters. In between O'Neal rips his (or rather the menacing colossus' racy wife's) jeans across the buttocks while making his escape after a night of passion and succeeds in starting a new trend which, needless to say, rescues the family business. O'Neal is an effective light comedian who, like George Segal, has not had much luck (or judgment) in his choice of material. Andrew Bergman is a gifted screenwriter who has chosen the wrong directorial debut. Any way you look at it, it's a tired, coy, frantic farce for the very easily amused.

SOUTHERN COMFORT (Phoenix-Cinema Group/EMI)
dir Walter Hill *pro* David Giler *exec pro* William J. Immerman *scr* Michael Kane, Walter Hill, David Giler *ph* Andrew Laszlo, in DeLuxe colour *ed* Freeman Davies *pro des* John Vallone *music* Ry Cooder *r time* 105 mins *cert* X *UK opening* Oct 29.
cast Keith Carradine, Powers Boothe, Fred Ward, Franklyn Seales, T.K. Carter, Lewis Smith, Les Lannom, Peter Coyote, Carlos Brown, Brion James, Sonny Landham, Allen Graf, Ned Dowd, Rob Ryder, Greg Guirard, June Borel, Jeanne Louise Buillard, Orel Borel, Jeannie Spector, Marc Savoy, Frank Savoy, Dewey Balfa, John Stelly.

'Deliverance' meets 'Apocalypse Now' Louisiana-style as a squad of National Guardsmen — enthusiastic part-timers adrift in the swamps with army clothes but civilian attitudes — make use of some unattended Cajun canoes and discover how tenacious primitive revenge can be. A bit heavy on the slow-motion violence, but beautifully photographed in subtly desaturated colours, with a distinctive score and a mood of menacing, oppressive finality.

STRIPES (Columbia)
dir Ivan Reitman *pro* Ivan Reitman, Dan Goldberg *sc* Len Blum, Dan Goldberg, Harold Ramis *ph* Bill Butler, in Metrocolor *ed* Eva Ruggiero, Michael Luciano, Harry Keller *pro des* James H. Spencer *music* Elme Bernstein *r time* 106 mins *cert* AA

Left: So Fine

UK opening Sept 10.
cast Bill Murray, Harold Ramis, Warren Oates, P.J. Soles, John Larroquette, Sean Young, John Diehl, Roberta Leighton, Lance LeGault, Conrad Dunn, John Voldstad, Judge Reinhold, Antone Pagan, Glenn-Michael Jones, John Candy, Bill Lucking, Fran Ryan, Joseph P. Flaherty, Nick Toth, Dave Thomas, Robin Klein, Robert J. Wilke, Lois Areno, Samuel Briggs, Joseph X. Flaherty, Hershel B. Harlson, Timothy Busfield, Solomon Schmidt, Gino Gottarelli, Gene Scherer, Dawn Clark, Juanita Merrritt, Susan Mechsner, Sue Bowser, Linda Dupree, Leslie Henderson, Craig Schaefer, Arkady Rakhman, Pamela Bowman, Gerald J. Counts, Yetim Buntsis, Semyon Veyts, Larry R. Gillette, Glen Leigh Marshall, Dale Prince, Larry Odell Lane, Joyce D. Helmus, David A. Mullins, Bruce E. Ellis, David D. Platko, Phillip A. Urbansky, William R. Sykes, Bill Paxton, J.A. Crawford, Michael Flynn, Norman Mont-Eton, Mark S. Markowicz, Jeff Viola, Robert Dulaine.

From the same team as the dreadful 'Meatballs', a heavy-handed smart-alec comedy about a couple of disenchanted iconoclasts who enlist in the army, join the inevitable platoon of misfits (complete with tyrannical drill sergeant and oafish company commander) and accidentally become heroes. For all its philosophical good humour, there is little here that can't be found portrayed more winningly in a 'Sgt Bilko' re-run.

Supersnooper

A SUMMER AFFAIR (Renn Prods-Societe Francaise de Production/Gala)
dir-scr Claude Berri *exec pro* Pierre Grunstein *ph* André Neau, in Panavision, Eastman Color *ed* Jacques Witta *music* Michel Stelio
r time 84 mins *cert* AA *UK opening* Oct 1.
cast Jean-Pierre Marielle, Victor Lanoux, Christine Dejoux, Agnès

Soral, Martine Sarcey, Robert Bahr, Tiburce Fauretto, Tessa Bouche, Marc Raine, Jacques Le Breton, Peter Bouke, Michel Stelio and musicians, Les Caribes Steel Band, Smile Orchestra, Les Flagada Stompers.

Intermittently amusing, gently whimsical generation gap morality tale — with plenty of homilies about sexual freedom — about a couple of middle-aged Frenchmen, on holiday with their teenage daughters, whose hypocrisy becomes evident after one has sex with the other's daughter.

SUPERSNOOPER (Trans-Cinema TV/Columbia)
dir Sergio Corbucci *exec pro* Maximilian Wolkoff *scr* Sergio Corbucci, Sabatino Giuffini *ph* Silvano Ippoliti, in Technicolor *ed* Eugene Ballaby *pro des* Marco Dentici *music* La Bionda *r time* 94 mins *cert* A *UK opening* Aug 6.
cast Terence Hill, Ernest Borgnine, Joanne Dru, Marc Lawrence, Julie Gordon, Lee Sandman, Herb Goldstein, Don Sebastien, Sal Borghese, Claudio Ruffini, Sergio Smacchi, Woody Woodbury, Dow Stout, Jack McDermott, Charles D. Thomas, Charles Buie, Bobby Gale, Ben Taylor, Florence McGee.

Engagingly inept cut-price spaghetti 'Superman', with Terence Hill (aka

Mario Girotti) as the Miami patrolman who develops supernatural powers after being exposed to radiation. With these he flies, sees through walls, defies attempts to execute him and, inevitably, brings a counterfeiting gang to justice. A laugh a minute — well, a laugh every five minutes.

SWEDISH EROTIC SEXATIONS
(Jay Jay)
dir Michael Thomas *scr* Manfred Gregor, Mel Quinones *ph* Peter Baumgartner, in colour *music* Walter Baumgartner *r time* 80 mins *cert* X *UK opening* Sept 3.
cast Brigitte Lahaie, Jane Baker, Nadine Pascal, Francette Maillol.

Swedish school leavers run a service station in Switzerland. Male customers, if they're quick about it, get more than petrol. A few good (if familiar) jokes about television presenters who can see their viewers. Not much else.

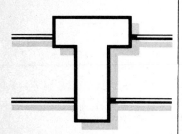

TAKE IT OR LEAVE IT (Nutty Stiff Prods/GTO)
dir-pro Dave Robinson *scr* Madness, Philip McDonald, Dave Robinson *ph* Nic Knowland, in colour *ed* Michael Ellis *art dir* Bert Davey *music* Madness *r time* 82 mins *cert* A *UK opening* Oct 15.
cast Graham McPherson, Mark Bedford, Lee Thompson, Carl Smith, Dan Woodgate, Christopher Foreman, Mike Barson, John Hasler, Simon Birdsall, Andrew Chalk, Ian Tokins, Sue Foreman, Gary Dovey, Clive Langer, Steve O'Brien, Susan Barson, Polly Perkins, Carl Howard-Walsh,

Wilfred Grove, Gerard Kelly, Paul Stacey, Jeremy Stacey, Oswald Lindsay, Alfie Curtis, Ted Burnett, Arthur Whybrow, Keith Bell, Zoot Money, Barry Linehan, Doreen Keogh, Bob Curtiss, Sean Curry, Charles Cork, Mike Smart, John Simpkin, Simon Bates, Steve Holloway.

The formation (amidst turbulently comical comings and goings) and eventual rise of Madness chronicled, not with the surreal ingenuity of the group's promotional films but in the style of a structured home movie, with all the concomitant liabilities. Excessive improvisation of dialogue is one of them (untrained actors asked to be "natural" sound and look more mannered), but this is counteracted by the film's generally attractive, unpretentious air.

TAPS (Fox)
dir Harold Becker *pro* Stanley R. Jaffe, Howard B. Jaffe *scr* Darryl Ponicsan, Robert Mark Kamen, from the novel 'Father Sky' by Devery Freeman *adap* James Lineberger *ph* Owen Roizman *ed* Maury Winetrobe *art dir* Stan Jolley, Alfred Sweeney *music* Maurice Jarre *r time* 126 mins *cert* A *UK opening* Feb 25.
cast George C. Scott, Timothy Hutton, Ronny Cox, Sean Penn, Tom Cruise, Brendan Ward, Evan Handler, John P. Navin Jr., Billy Van Zandt, Giancarlo Esposito, Donald Kimmel, Tim Wahrer, Tim Riley, Jeff Rochlin, Rusty Jacobs, Wayne Tippett, Jess Osuna, Earl Hindman, James Handy, Steven Ryan, Michael Longfield, Jay Gregory, Karen Braga, Ralph Drischell, Jane Cecil, Thomas Medearis, Amelia Romano, Sheila Marra.

Earnest, wordy, moralistic tale of honour, duty, tradition and hero-worship in a military academy occupied by its cadets in defiance of an attempt to close it down. A great performance from newcomer Sean Penn and a solid, sustained one from Timothy Hutton who is rarely off the screen. George C. Scott follows the Brando tradition of getting top billing for little more than a cameo.

TARZAN, THE APE MAN
(Svengali/MGM)
dir John Derek *pro* Bo Derek *scr* Tom Rowe, Gary Goddard, based on characters created by Edgar Rice Burroughs *ph* John Derek, in Metrocolor *ed* James B. Ling *art dir* Alan Roderick-Jones *music* Perry Botkin *r time* 112 mins *cert* AA *UK opening* Sept 24.
cast Bo Derek, Richard Harris, John Phillip Law, Miles O'Keeffe, Akushula Selayah, Steven Strong, Maxime Philoe, Leonard Bailey, Wilfrid Hyde-White, Laurie Mains, Harold Ayer.

Or rather Jane The Body, since the Dereks' version of the familiar story, sold in the UK with the copy-line "The most exciting pair in the jungle", is little more than a gloatingly extended view of Bo's anatomical salients in a

Tarzan, the Ape Man

variety of wet, clinging semi-costumes on attractive Sri Lankan locations. Everybody else, including the film's luckless Tarzan Miles O'Keeffe, is subordinate to the main attraction, which is just as well in the case of Richard Harris, who gives the hammiest, most embarrassing performance of the year.

TATTOO (Joseph E. Levine/Handmade)
dir Bob Brooks *pro* Joseph E. Levine, Richard P. Levine *scr* Joyce Bunuel, based on story by Bob Brooks *ph* Arthur Ornitz, Michael Seresin, in Technicolor *ed* Thom Noble *pro des* Stuart Wertzel *music* Barry De Vorzon *r time* 103 mins *cert* X *UK opening* Oct 15.
cast Bruce Dern, Maud Adams, Leonard Frey, Rikke Borge, John Getz, Peter Iacangelo, Alan Leach, Cynthia Nixon, Trish Doolan, Anthony Mannino, Lex Monson, Patricia Roe, Jane Hoffman, Robert Burr, John Snyder, B.J. Cirell, Kevin O'Rourke, Sally-Jane Heit, Gavin Reed, Henry Dibling, Alan Brasington, Anne Anderson, Winnie, John Granger, Sam Schacht, Orlando Dole, Jonathan Hogan, Robert Hitt, Kate McGregor-Stewart, Don Jay, Jack Davidson, E. Katherine Kerr, Daniel Suchar, David Suchar, Shunshin Kan, Richard McGonagle, Harold Mandel, Frank Santos.

The weird in pursuit of the unobtainable, or you can only tattoo the one you love. Puritanical tattooist Bruce Dern, eyes working overtime, develops an obsessive attachment to model Maude Adams, kidnaps and drugs her, and gradually etches out his masterwork on her before the big consummation. Unpleasant and voyeuristic, which is just about tolerable; dull, which isn't.

TAXI ZUM KLO (The Other Cinema)
dir-scr Frank Ripploh *pro* Laurens Straub, Frank Ripploh, Horst Schier *ph* Horst Schier, in colour *ed* Marina Runne, Mathias von Gunten *music* Hans Wittstatt *r time* 94 mins *UK opening* Jan 7.
cast Frank Ripploh, Bernd Broaderup, Orpha Termin, Peter Fahrni, Dieter Godde, Klaus Schnee, Vernd Kroger, Markus Voigtlander, Irmgard Lademacher, Gregor Becker, Marguerite Dupont, Eberhard Freudenthal, Beate Springer, Millie Buttner, Gitta Lederer, Hans Gerd Mertens, Ulla Topf, Franco Papadu, Tabea Blumenschein, Magdalene Montezuma, Jurgen Moller, Valeska Gerstenberg, Brigitte Knigge, Hans Kellner, Ric Schachtebeck.

Made on a flimsy budget of £25,000, this engagingly full-frontal tale of homosexual life has been one of the runaway successes of the year at the small cinemas that it has played in Great Britain and the US. Unashamedly autobiographical in content, it has Frank Ripploh portraying himself trying to enjoy the comforts of a conventional domestic set-up with his boyfriend Bernd Broaderup (who also plays himself), while also indulging in his predilection for cruising leather bars and public lavatories. The casual sex brings its

punishments — Frank finds himself with a bout of hepatitis (cue for an unflinching rectal examination) and a spell in hospital, while the film's title refers to his break for freedom when he quits his sickbed and takes a taxi to his favourite pick-up cottage. The film's candour and lack of inhibition (there are S&M and golden shower sequences) won over many people, although there was some dissent within the audience at which it was directed about the film's possible lack of revolutionary zeal.

Terror Eyes

TERROR EYES (Lorimar/Rank)
dir Kenneth Hughes *pro* Larry Babb,
Ruth Avergon *exec pro* Marc Gregory
Comjean, Bernard Kebadjian *scr* Ruth
Avergon *ph* Mark Irwin, in colour *ed*
Robert Reitano *pro des* William F.
DeSeta *music* Brad Fiedel *r time* 89
mins *cert* X *UK opening* Jul 2.
cast Leonard Mann, Rachel Ward,
Drew Snyder, Joseph R. Sicari,
Nicholas Cairis, Karen MacDonald,
Annette Miller, Bill McCann, Margo
Skinner, Elizabeth Barnitz, Holly
Hardman, Meb Boden, Leonard
Corman, Belle McDonald, Ed Higgins,
William McDonald, Kevin Fennessy,
Ed Chalmers, John Blood, Lisa Allee,
Elizabeth Allee, Patricia Pellows, J.J.
Wright, Ted Duncan, Patricia Rust,
Jane-Leah Bedrick, Wally Hooper Jnr.,
Kevin King, Nancy Rothman.

*Beware of directors like Ken Hughes
who suddenly decide to elongate their
names. It usually means that they're
about to move into a new, pretentious,
self-regarding phase of their work. All
it appears to have produced in his case
is an efficiently tricksy, nasty thriller
about a leather-clad motorcyclist who
decapitates college girls in Boston.
Familiar to the point of tedium, it is a
formula which must soon plead for
clemency.*

THIS IS ELVIS (Warner)
dir-pro-scr Malcolm Leo, Andrew Solt
exec pro David L. Wolper *ph* Gil
Hubbs, in Technicolor *ed* Bud
Friedgen *music* Walter Scharf *r time*
101 mins *cert* A *UK opening* Jul 9.
cast David Scott, Paul Boensch,
Johnny Harra, Lawrence Koller,
Rhonda Lyn, Debbie Edge, Larry
Raspberry, Furry Lewis, Liz Robinson,
Dana MacKay, Knox Phillips, Cheryl
Needham, Andrea Cyrill, Jerry
Phillips, Emory Smith.

*Engaging, superficial, occasionally
riveting Presley biography assembled*

*from film clips and reinforced, rather
unsatisfactorily, with scenes of
"dramatised" reconstruction. Even as
the bloated balladeer who at the end
staggers through the prophetic
bombast of 'My Way' and the
grandiose sentimentality of 'An
American Trilogy', Presley himself is
never less than a colossus among
singers.*

TICKET TO HEAVEN (Miracle)
dir Ralph L. Thomas *pro* Vivienne
Leebosh *exec pro* Ronald I. Cohen *scr*
Ralph L. Thomas, Anne Cameron,
based on the novel 'Moonwebs' by
Josh Freed *ph* Richard Leiterman, in
colour *ed* Ron Wisman *pro des* Susan
Longmire *art dir* Jill Scott *music*
Micky Erbe, Maribeth Solomon *r time*
107 mins *cert* AA *UK opening* Jan 28.
cast Nick Mancuso, Saul Rubineck,
Meg Foster, Kim Cattrall, R.H.
Thomson, Jennifer Dale, Guy Boyd,
Dixie Seatle, Paul Soles, Harvey
Atkin, Robert Joy, Stephen Markle,
Timothy Webber, Patrick Brymer,
Marcia Diamond, Michael Zelnicker,
Denise Naples, Angelo Rizacos, Cindy
Girling, Gina Dick, Christopher
Britton, Margot Dionne, Claire
Pimpare, Lynne Kolber, Lyn Harvey,
Josh Freed, Candace O'Conner,
Michael Wincott, Doris Petrie, Judy,
David Main, Les Rubie, Sandra Gies,
Susan Hannon, Marie Lynn
Hammond, Paul Booth, Charlie Gray,
Brian Leonard, Ron Nigrini, Craig
Stephens, Grant Slater.

*I don't know about you but, much as I
enjoy the cordiality of strangers, I find
those people who stand around in
Californian airports just gleaming
good vibes when they know you've
just got off an eleven-hour flight a bit
unsettling. It's not what they say so
much as the way they, well,* package *it.*

*In 'Ticket to Heaven', Nick Mancuso,
nursing a few bruises after his
girlfriend has left him, goes to San
Francisco and doesn't take long to
respond to the packaging. Once his
breakdown and brainwashing are
complete, the rest of the film concerns
his capture, rescue and deprogramming
by the people he left behind. Beware-of-
religious-cults movies have been
almost as abundant as women-in-peril
routines this year. This, for all its
melodramatic simplicity, is one of the
better ones.*

THREE BROTHERS (Iter Film-
Gaumont/Artificial Eye)
dir Francesco Rosi *pro* Georgio Nocell,

Ticket to Heaven

Antonio Macri scr Francesco Rosi, based on the story 'The Third Son' by A. Platonov ph Pasqualino de Santis, in Technicolor ed Ruggero Mastroianni art dir Andrea Crisanti music Piero Piccioni r time 111 mins cert A UK opening Oct 18.
cast Philippe Noiret, Charles Vanel, Michele Placido, Vittorio Mezzogiorno, Andrea Ferreol, Maddalena Crippa, Sara Tafuri, Marta Zoffoli, Tino Schipinzi, Simonetta Stefanelli, Pietro Biondi, Ferdinando Greco, Accursio Di Leo, Cosimo Milone, Luigi Infantino, Gina Pontrelli, Girolamo Marzano, Maria Antonia Capotorto, Ferdinando Murolo, Francesco Capotorto, Cristofaro Chiapparino.

Thoughtful, lyrical account of three brothers — teacher, magistrate and factory worker — returning to their childhood village in Southern Italy, and what they reveal of themselves (and Italian life in general) while coming to terms with their loss.

THREE IMMORAL WOMEN (Films du Jeudi/Entertainment)
dir-scr Walerian Borowczyk pro Pierre Braunberger exec pro Michel de Vidas ph Bernard Daillencourt, in Fujicolor ed Kadicha Basiha art dir Jacques d'Ovidio music Olivier Dassault, Philippe d'Aram r time 89 mins cert X UK opening Jul 9.
cast Marina Pierro, Gaelle Legrand, Pascale Christophe, Francois Guetary, Jean-Claude Dreyfus, Jean Martinelli, Pierre Benedetti, Philippe Desboeuf, Noel Simsolo, Roger Lefrère, Gérard Falconetti, Mathieu Rivolier, Robert Capia, Daniel Marty, Jacky Baudet, Sylvain Ramsamy, Jean Boullu, Assan Fall, France Rumilly, Yves Gourvil, Lisbeth Arno, Gérard Ismael, Henri Piegay.

Much cut three-year-old triple-decker, featuring a dog, a rabbit, an emasculation, a couple of cut throats and a range of sexual activity.

TIME BANDITS (Handmade)
dir-pro Terry Gilliam exec pro George Harrison, Denis O'Brien scr Michael Palin, Terry Gilliam ph Peter Biziou, in Technicolor ed Julian Doyle pro des Millie Burns art dir Norman Garwood music Mike Moran r time 113 mins cert A UK opening Jul 16.
cast John Cleese, Sean Connery, Shelley Duvall, Katherine Helmond, Ian Holm, Michael Palin, Ralph Richardson, Peter Vaughan, David Warner, David Rappaport, Kenny Baker, Jack Purvis, Mike Edmonds, Malcolm Dixon, Tiny Ross, Craig Warnock, David Baker, Sheila Fearn, Jim Broadbent, John Young, Myrtle Devenish, Brian Bowes, Leon Lissek, Terence Bayler, Preston Lockwood, Charles McKeown, David Leland, John Hughman, Derrick O'Connor, Declan Mulholland, Neil McCarthy, Peter Jonfield, Derek Deadman, Jerold Wells, Roger Frost, Martin Carroll, Marcus Powell, Winston Dennis, Del Baker, Juliette James, Ian Muir, Mark Holmes, Andrew MacLachlan, Chris Grant, Tony Jay, Edwin Finn.

A great comic idea developed with ingenuity and imagination: six disgruntled dwarfs steal a map of the universe and, with the suburban schoolboy in whose bedroom they appear one night, time travel through the holes left in the cosmos by its careless creator. Inevitably, there are occasional lapses into the familiar absurdist potpourri favoured by former members of the Monty Python gang when there's no one looking after quality control. To the film's considerable credit, you hardly notice.

TOMORROW'S WARRIOR (Cyprian/Cinegate)
dir-pro-scr-ed Michael Papas ph John McCallum, in Techniscope, Technicolor art dir Stephan Athienites, Angelos Angeli music Nicos Mamangakis r time 95 mins cert AA UK opening Jun 10.
cast Christos Zannides, Aristodemos Fessas, Dimitri Andreas, Jenny Lipman, Joanna Shafkali, Antonis Katsaris, George Zenios, Omiros Lambrakis, Maria Mitsi, Margarita Solomou, George Vatiliotis, Nikias Nikolaides, Costas Demetriou, Doros Kyriakides, Andreas Markou, Nana Georghiou, Pericles Theodorides, Andreas Papanicholas, Nikos Kouroussis.

Set in Cyprus before, during and after the Turkish invasion of 1974 — and as unswervingly partisan as Papas' first film 'The Private Right', which dealt with the British occupation of the same island — 'Tomorrow's Warrior' is a decent, passionate, well-made film with some dazzling (and deafening) action sequences. It has one considerable liability: in making the central character a small boy (a handsome and brave one at that), it capitalises on the resultant sentimentality with a regularity which rapidly becomes wearying.

Above: Time Bandits. Right: True Confessions

TORN BETWEEN TWO LOVERS (Alan Landsburg Productions/GTO)
dir Delbert Mann pro Linda Otto, Joan Barnett exec pro Tom Kuhn scr Doris Silverton ph Ron Lautore, in colour ed Gene Milford, Lloyd Nelson art dir David Jaquest music Ian Fraser r time 97 mins cert A UK opening Jan 10.
cast Lee Remick, Joe Bologna, George Peppard, Giorgio Tozzi, Murphy Cross, Jess Osuna, Lois Markle, Martin Shakar, Molly Cheek, Derrick Jones, Mary Long, Sean McCann, Kay Hawtry, Andrea Martin, Tom Harvey, Murray Westgate, David Hughes, Rocco Bellusci.

Made for American television and "suggested" by the soppy song it retains as a title, 'Torn Between Two Lovers' probably has more backdated romantic clichés per minute than any other film released this year. The happily married woman stranded at an airport; the confident and sophisticated architect who becomes her fellow ship-in-the-night; their affair, conducted largely in front of a big open fire; and, of course, the choice she has to make at the end. More fun than it's supposed to be, and directed with some assurance, if not much inspiration, by one of Hollywood's old reliables.

THE TRAGEDY OF A RIDICULOUS MAN (Ladd Company/Warner)
dir-scr Bernardo Bertolucci pro Giovanni Bertolucci ph Carlo Di

Palma, in Technicolor ed Gabriella Cristani pro des Gianni Silvestri music Ennio Morricone r time 116 mins cert AA UK opening Nov 26.
cast Ugo Tognazzi, Anouk Aimée, Laura Morante, Victor Cavallo, Olympia Carlisi, Riccardo Tognazzi, Vittorio Caprioli, Renato Salvatori, Don Backy, Cosimo Cinieri, Margherita Chiari, Gaetano Ferrari, Gianni Migliavacca, Ennio Ferrari, Franco Trevisi, Pietro Longari Ponzoni.

Inverting his customary son-in-search-of-father theme against the inevitable (in an Italian film) background of terrorism, Bertolucci goes for the open-ended approach in this sombre, verbose but visually splendid examination of a dairy farmer coming to terms with the disappearance of his son, who may or may not have been kidnapped. Highly ambiguous, richly rewarding.

TRUE CONFESSIONS (United Artists)
dir Ulu Grosbard pro Irwin Winkler, Robert Chartoff scr John Gregory Dunne, Joan Didion, based on the novel by John Gregory Dunne ph Owen Roizman, in colour ed Lunzee Klingman pro des Stephen S Grimes art dir W. Stewart Campbell music George Delerue r time 108 mins cert AA UK opening Nov 19.
cast Robert De Niro, Robert Duvall, Charles Durning, Kenneth McMillan, Ed Flanders, Cyril Cusack, Burgess Meredith, Rose Gregorio, Dan Hedaya, Gwen Van Dam, Tom Hill, Jeanette Nolan, Jorge Cervera Jnr, Susan Myers, Louisa Moritz, Darwyn Carson, Pat Corley, Matthew Faison, Richard Foronjy, Joe Medalis, Louis Basile, Louise Fitch, Margery Nelson, James Hong, Ron Ryan, Frederic Cook, Kirk Brennan, Fred Dennis, Shelly Batt, Mary Munday, Colin Hamilton, Amanda Cleveland, Pierrino Mascarino, Michael Callahan, Harry Pavelis, Luisa Leschin, Bob Arthur, Bill Furnell, Sig Frohlich, Steve Arvin, Paul Valentine, Steve Powers, Dr Joseph H. Choi, Sharon Miller, Kevin Breslin, Jeff Howard, Harry Duncan.

Haunting, leisurely adaptation by Dunne and Didion of the former's superb novel about two brothers — one an upwardly mobile monsignor who raises funds and does deals, the other a downwardly mobile homicide detective who examines corpses and pursues criminals — whose complex relationship is thrown out of gear when a grisly murder reveals all kinds of suspect mutual backscratching between the Catholic church and far-from-sinless local businessmen in 1948 Los Angeles. Although trimmed of numerous sub-plots and some significant characters, it is played to such perfection by De Niro, Duvall and much of the supporting cast that its distinguished origins become simply that: distinguished origins.

TWO STAGE SISTERS (Tianma Film Studio/BFI)
dir Xie Jin *scr* Lin Gu, Xu Jin, Xie Jin *ph* Zhou Daming, in colour *ed* Zhang Liqun *art dir* Ge Schicheng *music* Huang Zhun *r time* 114 mins *cert* U *UK opening* Sept 10.
cast Xie Fang, Cao Yindi, Feng Ji, Gao Yuansheng, Shen Fengjuan, Xu Caigen, Shangguan Yunzhu, Ma Ji, Luo Zhengyi, Wu Baifang, Li Wei, Deng Nan, Shen Hao, Dong Lin, Ding Ran.

1964 Chinese film, supposedly one of the last films made there before the Cultural Revolution, about the shifting associations within a theatre company.

U

AN UNSUITABLE JOB FOR A WOMAN (Boyd's Co/Goldcrest)
dir Christopher Petit *pro* Michael Relph, Peter McKay *exec pro* Don Boyd *scr* Elizabeth McKay, Brian Scobie, Christopher Petit, based on the novel by P.D. James *ph* Martin Schafer, in Gevacolor *ed* Mick Audsley *pro des* Anton Furst *art dir* John Beard *music* Chas Jankel *r time* 94 mins *cert* AA *UK opening* May 13.
cast Billie Whitelaw, Paul Freeman, Pippa Guard, Dominic Guard, Elizabeth Spriggs, David Horovitch, Dawn Archibald, Bernadette Short, James Gilbey, Kelda Holmes, Margaret Wade, Alex Guard.

An Unsuitable Job for a Woman

Petit's remarkable second film is a cryptic, distorted, looking-glass thriller which combines elements of English murder mysteries, European "investigation" movies and plain old skeletons-in-the-closet melodrama and then subtly turns them on their heads. I have written about it at greater length on page 106.

URGH! A MUSIC WAR
(Lorimar/Osiris)
dir Derek Burbidge *pro* Michael White *ph* John Metcalfe, Kate Humphreys, Dick Pope, David Scott, John Simmons, Mike Metcalf, David Anderson, Patrick McCann, in colour *ed* Jim Alderton *r time* 124 mins *cert* A *UK opening* Oct 22.
cast The Police, Wall of Voodoo, Toyah, John Cooper Clarke, Orchestral Manoeuvres in the Dark, Chelsea, Oingo Boingo, Echo and the Bunnymen, Jools Holland, XTC, Klaus Nomi, Athletico Spizz '80, The Go Go's, The Dead Kennedys, Steel Pulse, Gary Numan, Joan Jett, Magazine, Surf Punks, The Members, The Au Pairs, The Cramps, Invisible Sex, Père

Ubu, Devo, The Alley Cats, John Otway, The Gang of Four, 999, The Fleshtones, X, Skafish, Splodgenessabounds, UB40.

Far from the apocalyptic intimations of its title, this tiresomely protracted 34-group variety show masquerading as an introduction to 'New Wave' has the effect of a promotional clip that goes on forever.

V

VENOM (Handmade)
dir Piers Haggard *pro* Martin Bregman *exec pro* Richard R. St. Johns *scr* Robert Carrington, based on

Venom

the novel by Alan Scholefield *ph* Gil Taylor, in Technicolor *ed* Michael Bradsell *art dir* Tony Curtis *r time* 93 mins *cert* AA *UK opening* Mar 11.
cast Sterling Hayden, Klaus Kinski, Sarah Miles, Oliver Reed, Cornelia Sharpe, Nicol Williamson, Susan George, Lance Holcomb, Mike Gwilym, Rita Webb, John Cater, John Forbes-Robertson, Hugh Lloyd.

An asthmatic boy with a roomful of pets is at the receiving end of an abortive kidnap attempt — engineered by saucy cockney maid Susan George and psycho chauffeur Oliver Reed in league with grumpy criminal Klaus Kinski — at around the time his mistakenly received killer black mamba goes on the loose. One of those hilariously tepid non-thrillers in which everybody says things twice to spin out a scenario so crucifyingly banal that it virtually pleads for a comfortable bed and a bottle of sleeping pills. Highspots: the snake crawling up Reed's trouser leg and the overseas sales department view of London — a view of the bridge from the Tower Hotel and a genial gor-blimey cabby, the like of which the city hasn't known for about 20 years.

VICE SQUAD (Francos Films/New Realm)
dir Jacques Scandelari *pro* Francis Cosne *scr* Pierre Germont, Jacques Scandelari *ph* Francois About, in colour *ed* Pierre-Alain Beauchard *music* Cerrone *r time* 92 mins *cert* X *UK opening* Oct 15.
cast Patrice Valota, Odile Michel, Florence Cayrol, Jean-Pol Brissart, Patrick Olivier, Marie-George Pascal, Marianne Comtell, Jacques Berthier, Jacques Dacqmine, Jean Turlier, Bernard Bireaud, Denis Seurat, Danièle Croisy, Jean-Marie Arnoux, Philippe Castelli.

Three-year-old porno-policier of little consequence.

VICTOR/VICTORIA (MGM)

dir-scr Blake Edwards *pro* Blake Edwards, Tony Adams *ph* Dick Bush, in Panavision, Metrocolor *ed* Ralph E. Winters, Alan Killick *pro des* Rodger Maus *art dir* Tim Hutchinson, William Craig Smith *music* Henry Mancini *r time* 134 mins *cert* AA *UK opening* Apr 1.
cast Julie Andrews, James Garner, Robert Preston, Lesley Ann Warren, Alex Karras, John Rhys-Davies, Graham Stark, Peter Arne, Sherloque Tanney, Michael Robbins, Norman Chancer, David Gant, Maria Charles, Malcolm Jamieson, John Cassady, Mike Tezcan, Christopher Good, Matyelock Gibbs, Jay Benedict, Olivier Pierre, Martin Rayner, George Silver, Joanna Dickens, Terence Skelton, Ina Skriver, Stuart Turton, Geoffrey Beevers, Sam Williams, Simon Chandler, Neil Cunningham, Vivienne Chandler, Bill Monks, Perry Davey, Elizabeth Vaughan, Paddy Ward, Tim Stern.

Let's do the show right here! Snooty British critics tend not to approve of Blake Edwards for all kinds of suspect reasons. One of them is that, at a time monopolised by self-conscious nostalgia and heavy-handed pseudery, he has the light touch and makes sly, funny, good-looking traditional Hollywood movies without singing too many arias about it. Putting the bile of 'S.O.B.' on hold for the moment, here he has Julie Andrews as a destitute light opera singer in mid-Thirties Paris who keeps the wolf from the door, and unintentionally draws one to it, by pretending to be a Polish count pretending to be a female impersonator. Far from faultless — some of the anachronistic language is pure California encounter group and the sexual caricatures are a little over-drawn — it still wipes the floor with most of the competition with its wit, style, running jokes and consistently sound comic performances. If Edwards weren't so damned busy being himself, he would've made a great Billy Wilder.

VIOLENT STREETS (United Artists)
(US TITLE: THIEF)

dir-exec pro Michael Mann *pro* Jerry Bruckheimer, Ronnie Caan *scr* Michael Mann, based on the novel 'The Home Invaders' by Frank Hohimer *ph*

Donald Thorin, in Astro Color *ed* Dov Hoenig *pro des* Mel Bourne *art dir* Mary Dodson *music* Tangerine Dream *r time* 122 mins *cert* X *UK opening* Sept 17.
cast James Caan, Tuesday Weld, Willie Nelson, James Belushi, Robert Prosky, Tom Signorelli, Dennis Farina, Nick Nickeas, W.R. (Bill) Brown, Norm Tobin, John Santucci, Gavin MacFadyen, Chuck Adamson, Sam Cirone, Spero Anast, Walter Scott, Sam T. Louis, William LaValley, Lora Staley, Hal Frank, Del Close, Bruce Young, John Kapelos, Mike Genovese, Joan Lazzerini, Beverly Somerman, Enrico R. Cannataro, Mary Louise Wade, Donna J. Fenton, Thomas Giblin, Willie Hayes, Conrad Mocarski, Benny Turner, William L. Peterson, Steve Randolph, Nancy Santucci, Nathan Davis, Thomas O. Erhart Jnr, Fredric Stone, Robert J. Kuper, Joene Hanhardt, Marge Kotlisky, J.J. Saunders, Susan McCormick, Karen Bercovici, Michael Paul Chan, Tom Howard, Richard Karie, Oscar Di Lorenzo, Patti Ross, Margot Charlior.

A pointless change of title for this sombre, hypnotic philosophical crime thriller with James Caan (excellent) as a professional safe-breaker whose independence becomes an inconvenience to both the police and the syndicate with which he has become involved. Tightly scripted, meticulously detailed and dazzling visually — all rainswept streets and phantasmagoric neon — it is one of the year's most riveting films.

VISITING HOURS (Filmplan Int/Fox)

dir Jean Claude Lord *pro* Claude Heroux *exec pro* Pierre David, Victor Solnicki *scr* Brian Taggert *ph* Rene Verzier, in Panavision, colour *ed* Jean Claude Lord, Lise Thouin *art dir* Michel Proulx *music* Jonathan Goldsmith *r time* 104 mins *cert* X *UK opening* Apr 15.
cast Michael Ironside, Lee Grant, Linda Purl, William Shatner, Lenore Zann, Harvey Atkin, Helen Hughes, Michael J. Reynolds, Kristen Bishopric, Debra Kirschenbaum, Elizabeth Leigh Milne, Maureen McRae, Dustin Waln, Neil Affleck, Damir Andrei, Dorothy Barker, Steve Bettcher, Walker Boone, Richard Briere, Terrance P. Coady, Richard Comar, Dora Dainton, Sylvie Desbois, Yvan Ducharme, Sarita Elman, Kathleen Fee.

Taking a leaf out of 'Peeping Tom' (the maniac with the knife likes to photograph his victims as he kills them), adding a bit of elementary psychology (he had a disturbed childhood), mixing it in with a bit of facile topicality (the principal intended victim is a campaigning female journalist) and a touch of 'Halloween II' (much of the action takes place in a hospital which mysteriously becomes depopulated when the heroine is under threat), 'Visiting Hours' delivers its shocks with some skill but no taste. Finally, it suffocates in the mess of its borrowings, signalling, one hopes, the end of a genre much in need of being shown to the door.

WARM NIGHTS, HOT PLEASURES
(MRC-Balcasar-Gama/Tigon)

dir-scr Hubert Frank *pro* Roland Kovac *exec pro* Robert Russ *ph* Franz X. Lederle in Eastman Color *art dir* Nino Borghi *music* Roland Kovac *r time* 99 mins *cert* X *UK opening* Nov 12.
cast Anne Parillaud, Sascha Hehn, Roland Kovac, Brigitte Stein, Paca Gabaldon, Jose Luis de Villalonga, Jose Antonio Ceinos, Carlos Martos, Molino Rojo, Eva Lyberten, Maria Rey, Jennifer Jones, Maite.

A racing driver, an heiress and assorted financial predators convene in Spain for sex, hully-gullying and conspiracy while the old chap whose will they are debating, and whom they think is dead, watches all the activities on closed-circuit television upstairs. At least he enjoys himself.

WHOSE LIFE IS IT ANYWAY?
(MGM)

dir John Badham *pro* Lawrence P. Bachmann *exec pro* Martin Schute, Ray Cooney *scr* Brian Clark, Reginald Rose, based on the play by Brian Clark *ph* Mario Tosi, in Metrocolor *ed* Frank Morriss *pro des* Gene Callahan *art dir* Sydney Litwack *music* Arthur Rubinstein *r time* 119 mins *cert* AA *UK opening* Mar 11.
cast Richard Dreyfuss, John Cassavetes, Christine Lahti, Bob Balaban, Alba Oms, Kaki Hunter, Thomas Carter, Janet Eilber, Ken McMillan, George Wyner, Mel Stewart, Ward Costello, Kathryn Grody, Lyman Ward, Lissa Layng, Dorothy Meyer, Tony Simotes, Betty Cole, Alston Ahern, Jeffrey Combs, Steve Bourne, Alan Stock, Michael-Steve Jones, Robert Telford, John

Garber, Abigail Hepner, Roberta Williams, Juli Andelman, Sebastian DeFrancesco, Thomas Collette, Duane F. Johnson, Larry D. Callaghan, William E. Townsend.

Speechy, stagey adaptation of the speechy, stagey (and successful) play, with Richard Dreyfuss as the sculptor who decides he has a right to end his own life after a car crash has left him paralysed, and John Cassavetes, sporting a new hairdo, as the imperious doctor who opposes him. A worthy film, but for all its eloquently pointed dialogue, too full of sententious moralising (about equal parts sarcasm and self-pity) to be a particularly interesting one, despite a showy, sustained performance from Dreyfuss and effective ones from Christine Lahti and Bob Balaban who, if he isn't actually in everything this year, appears to be.

WILD WOMEN OF WONGO
(Tropical Pictures/Pathe Alpha)

dir James L. Wolcott *pro* George R. Black *scr* Cedric Rutherford *ph* M. Walsh, in Pathecolor *ed* D.J. Cazale *r time* 80 mins *cert* AA *UK opening* Mar 19.
cast Pat Crowley, Jean Hawkshaw, Johnny Walsh, Ed Fury, Mary Ann

Warm Nights, Hot Pleasures

Webb, Rex Richards, Cande Gerrard, Adrienne Bourbeau.

The women in question are not especially wild, but they are cute and comely while their men are merely ugly oiks with poorly styled executive hairdos. The nearby Goona tribe men are hairless and handsome but their women are lumpy and lardy. It is inevitable, in this Teenage-Confidential-in-loin-cloths scenario that the right people should end up in one another's arms — as indeed they do when collectively married by a priestess with a joke-shop lizard attached to her wrist and a propensity for doing the watusi in a frenziedly God-fearing manner. This hilariously awful dating movie for racy primitives, whose characters employ a bizarre amalgam of ancientspeak and Fifties' teen talk, is set on a tropical island somewhere on the United States mainland, where an all-knowing parrot follows the action, the crocodiles are all plastic and a girl can spend an eternity underwater wrestling with one without coming up for air. Be warned — or encouraged.

WINTER OF OUR DREAMS (Vega Film Prods/Enterprise)
dir-scr John Duigan *pro* Richard Mason *pro* Tom Cowan, in Eastman Color *ed* Henry Dangar *pro des* Lee Whitmore *music* Sharyn Calcraft *r time* 90 mins *cert* X *UK opening* Feb 11.
cast Judy Davis, Bryan Brown, Cathy Downes, Baz Luhrmann, Peter Mochrie, Mervyn Drake, Mercia Deane-Johns, Joy Hruby, Margie McCrae, Kim Deacon, Caz Lederman, Jenny Ludlam, Virginia Duigan, Rosemary Lenzo, Alex Pinder.

Significantly different in both subject matter and treatment from most of the Australian films seen here, this leisurely, introspective study of a Sydney prostitute trying to break out

of her vicious circle of junk and despair has the benefit of a lively, assertive performance from Judy Davis, who can hardly put a foot wrong these days.

WOLFEN (Orion/Warner)
dir Michael Wadleigh *pro* Rupert Hitzig *exec pro* Alan King *scr* David Eyre, Michael Wadleigh, based on the novel by Whitley Strieber *ph* Gerry Fisher, in Panavision, Technicolor *ed* Chris Lebenzon, Dennis Dolan, Martin Bram, Marchall M. Borden *pro des* Paul Sylbert *art dir* David Chapman *music* James Horner *r time* 115 mins *cert* X *UK opening* Nov 12.
cast Albert Finney, Diane Venora, Edward James Olmos, Gregory Hines, Tom Noonan, Dick O'Neill, Dehl Berti, Peter Michael Goetz, Sam Gray, Ralph Bell, Max M. Brown, Anne Marie Photamo, Sarah Felder, Reginald Vel Johnson, James Tolkan, John McCurry, Chris Manor, Donald Symington, Jeffery Ware, E. Brian Dean, Jeffery Thompson, Victor Arnold, Frank Adonis, Richard Minchenberg, Ray Serra, Thomas Ryan, Tony Latham, David Connell, Jery Hewitt, Ray Brocksmith, Michael Wadleigh.

Pretentious, muddled ecological thriller, with the requisite socio-mystical overtones, in which maverick New York detective Albert Finney (very much at ease with the best of the dialogue) is called in to investigate a murder the police attribute to terrorists. Instead it turns out to be Nature's revenge as mutated American Indian descendants roam the Bronx in a distinctively lupine manner. Comparable to 'Altered States' in its excess of effects, and to 'Heaven's Gate' in its budget-to-returns ratio, it also suffered the misfortune of opening in England in the same week as the rather more modest, and infinitely more enjoyable, 'An American Werewolf in London'. Prediction: to be rediscovered and revered by the late-night cinema contingent.

THE WOMAN NEXT DOOR (Les Films du Carrosse-TFI/Gala)
dir Francois Truffaut *scr* Francois Truffaut, Suzanne Schiffman, Jean Aurel *ph* William Lubtchansky, in Fujicolor *ed* Martine Barraque *art dir* Jean-Pierre Kohut-Svelko *music* Georges Delerue *r time* 106 mins *cert* AA *UK opening* Jan 21.
cast Gerard Depardieu, Fanny Ardant, Henri Garcin, Michele Baumgartner, Veronique Silver, Roger Van Hool, Philippe Morier-Genous, Olivier Becquaert, Nicole Vauthier, Muriel Combe.

After enduring continued accusations of sentimentality, Truffaut finally returns to the torments of hopeless love that underlined his early successes like 'Jules et Jim' and turns in his most assured movie for years. Much of the film's success is rooted in its two excellent central performances. Depardieu is the suspended adolescent, working with toy boats and enjoying a contented marriage in the bourgeois midi of central France, who is unhinged by the reappearance of his

former lover Ardant with whom he revives an intense, destructive affair. The acting of these two, supplemented by a drier script than usual, emphasises the idea with which Truffaut has too often simply flirted: that love matters and that its results are often devastating: the walking wounded in this film are left picking their way through the dead.

ZORRO THE GAY BLADE (Melvin Simon Prods/Fox)
dir Peter Medak *pro* George Hamilton, C.O. Erickson *exec pro* Melvin Simon *scr* Hal Dresner *ph* John A. Alonzo, in DeLuxe colour *ed* Hillary Jane Kranze *pro des* Herman A. Blumenthal *art dir* Adrian Gorton *music* Max Steiner, Joaquin Turina *r time* 93 mins *cert* A *UK opening* Dec 31.
cast George Hamilton, Lauren Hutton, Brenda Vaccaro, Ron Leibman, Donovan Scott, James Booth, Helen Burns, Clive Revill, Carolyn Seymour, Eduardo Alcaraz, Carlos Bravo, Roberto Dumont, Jorge Bolio, Dick Balduzzi, Ana Eliza Perez Bolanos, Francisco Mauri, Julian Colman, Francisco Morayta, Pilar Pellicer, Owen Lee, Gustavo Ganem, Armando Duarte, Norm Blankenship, Frank Welker.

Wolfen

After 20 years of playing rich cads and wet heroes, George Hamilton finally struck the motherlode with 'Love at First Bite' in 1979. Its skilful mixture of knowing satire and broad farce is repeated here with a change of costume and a discernible increase in hammy overstatement. The new twist is that Don Diego/Zorro has a foppish limp-wrist of a twin brother, also played, needless to say, by Hamilton, who goes some way towards compensating for the film's formulaic excesses with his unselfconscious good humour.

THE OTHER FILMS

The following films opened in the United States or Canada during the July 1981-June 1982 year. None of them, at the time of going to press, have been shown in Great Britain. Some of them will certainly appear sooner or later. A few others might. Most of them won't, for a variety of reasons. Check the list again in July 1983: it should make revealing reading.

The Amateur *(Fox)* dir. Charles Jarrott with John Savage, Christopher Plummer, Marthe Keller, Arthur Hill.
Author! Author! *(Fox)* dir. Arthur Hiller with Al Pacino, Dyan Cannon, Tuesday Weld, Alan King.
Barbarosa *(Universal-AFD)* dir. Fred Schepisi with Willie Nelson, Gary Busey, Isela Vega, Gilbert Roland.
Basket Case *(Analysis)* dir. Frank Henenlotter with Kevin Van Hentenryck, Terri Susan Smith, Beverly Bonner, Robert Vogel.
Battletruck *(New World)* dir. Harley Cokliss with Michael Beck, Annie McEnroe, James Wainwright, John Ratzenberger.
The Beast Within *(MGM/UA)* dir. Philippe Mora with Ronny Cox, Bibi Besch, Paul Clemens, Don Gordon.
Bloodsucking Freaks *(Troma)* dir. Joel M. Reed with Seamus O'Brien, Louie De Jesus, Nils McMaster, Viju Krim.
Breakdown *(Pioneer)* dir. Kathryn Bigelow with Willem Dafoe, Robert Gordon, Marin Kanter, J. Don Ferguson.
The Bushido Blade *(Aquarius)* dir. Tom Kotani with Richard Boone, Sonny Chiba, Frank Converse, Laura Gemser.
Cannery Row *(MGM/UA)* dir. David S. Ward with Nick Nolte, Debra Winger, Aura Lindley, Frank McRae.
Carbon Copy *(Avco Embassy)* dir. Michael Schultz with George Segal, Susan Saint James, Jack Warden, Danzel Washington.
Chu Chu and the Philly Flash *(Fox)* dir. David Lowell Rich with Alan Arkin, Carol Burnett, Jack Warden, Danny Aiello.
Cold River *(Pacific International)* dir. Fred G. Sullivan with Suzanne Weber, Pat Petersen, Richard Jaeckel, Robert Earl Jones.
Comin' at Ya *(Filmways)* dir. Ferdinando Baldi with Tony Anthony, Gene Quintano, Victoria Abril, Ricardo Palacios.
Continental Divide *(Universal)* dir. Michael Apted with John Belushi, Blair Brown, Allen Goorwitz, Carlin Glynn.
Cries in the Night *(Frontier Amusements)* dir. William Fruet with Lesleh Donaldson, Kay Hawtrey.
Dead Men Don't Wear Plaid *(Universal)* dir. Carl Reiner with Steve Martin, Rachel Ward, Reni Santoni, Carl Reiner.
Deathtrap *(Warner)* dir. Sidney Lumet with Michael Caine, Christopher Reeve, Dyan Cannon, Irene Worth.
Death Valley *(Universal)* dir. Dick Richards with Paul Le Mat, Catherine Hicks, Stephen McHattie, A. Wilford Brimley.
Demonoid *(American Panorama)* dir. Alfred Zacharias with Samantha Eggar, Stuart Whitman, Roy Cameron Jexson, Narciso Busquets.
Diner *(MGM/UA)* dir. Barry Levinson

with Steve Guttenberg, Daniel Stern, Mickey Rourke, Kevin Bacon.
Don't Cry, It's Only Thunder *(Sanrio Communications)* dir. Peter Werner with Dennis Christopher, Susan Saint James, Lisa Lu, Thu Thuy.
Dr. Jekyll's Dungeon of Death *(New American)* dir. James Wood with James Mathers, John Kearney, Tom Nicholson, Dawn Carver.
Drive-In Massacre *(New American)* dir. Stuart Segall with Jake Barnes, Adam Lawrence, Douglas Gudbye, Newton Naushaus.
The Escape Artist *(Orion/Warner)* dir. Caleb Deschanel with Griffin O'Neal, Raul Julia, Teri Garr, Joan Hackett.
E.T.: The Extra-Terrestrial *(Universal)* dir. Steven Spielberg with Dee Wallace, Henry Thomas, Peter Coyote, Robert MacNaughton.
Evilspeak *(Moreno Co.)* dir. Eric Weston with Clint Howard, R.G. Armstrong, Joseph Cortese, Claude Earl Jones.
Fast-Walking *(Pickman Film)* dir. James B. Harris with James Woods, Tim McIntire, Kay Lenz, Robert Hooks.
Fighting Back *(Paramount)* dir. Lewis Teague with Tom Skerritt, Patti LuPone, Michael Sarrazin, Yaphet Kotto.
Forbidden World *(New World)* dir. Allan Holzman with Jesse Vint, June Chadwick, Dawn Dunlap, Linden Chiles.
Forty Deuce *(Island)* dir. Paul Morrissey with Orson Bean, Kevin Bacon, Mark Keyloun, Harris Laskaway.
Galaxy of Terror *(New World)* dir. B.D. Clark with Edward Albert, Erin Moran, Ray Walston, Bernard Behrens.
Gas *(Paramount)* dir. Les Rose with Donald Sutherland, Susan Anspach, Howie Mandel, Sterling Hayden.
Goin' All the Way *(Saturn International)* dir. Robert Freedman with Dan Waldman, Deborah Van Rhyn, Joshua Cadman, Sherie Miller.
Hanky Panky *(Columbia)* dir. Sidney Poitier with Gene Wilder, Gilda Radner, Kathleen Quinlan, Richard Widmark.
Harry Tracy — Desperado *(IMC/Isram)* dir. William A. Graham with Bruce Dern, Helen Shaver, Michael C. Gwynne, Gordon Lightfoot.
Health *(Fox)* dir. Robert Altman with Lauren Bacall, Glenda Jackson, James Garner, Carol Burnett.
Heartbeeps *(Universal)* dir. Allan Arkush with Andy Kaufman, Bernadette Peters, Randy Quaid, Kenneth McMillan.
The High Country *(Crown International)* dir. Harvey Hart with Timothy Bottoms, Linda Purl, George Sims, Jim Lawrence.
The House Where Evil Dwells *(MGM/UA)* dir. Kevin Connor with Edward Albert, Susan George, Doug McClure, Amy Barrett.
I Ought to Be in Pictures *(Fox)* dir. Herbert Ross with Walter Matthau, Ann-Margret, Dinah Manoff, Lance Guest.
If You Could See What I Hear *(Jensen Farley)* dir. Eric Till with Marc Singer, R.H. Thomson, Sarah Torgov, Shari Belafonte.
I'm Dancing as Fast as I Can

(Paramount) dir. Jack Hofsiss with Jill Clayburgh, Nicol Williamson, Dianne Wiest, Joe Pesci.
Kill Squad *(Summa Vista)* dir. Patrick G. Donahue with Jean Glaude, Jeff Risk, Jerry Johnson, Bill Cambra.
Kings and Desperate Men *(pro. co. Kineversal)* dir. Alexis Kanner with Patrick McGoohan, Alexis Kanner, Andrea Marcovicci, Margaret Trudeau.
The Kinky Coaches and the Pom-Pom Pussycats *(Summa Vista)* dir. Mark Warren with John Vernon, Norman Fell, Robert Forster.
A Little Sex *(Universal)* dir. Bruce Paltrow with Tim Matheson, Kate Capshaw, Edward Herrmann, John Glover.
Looker *(Ladd Co./Warner)* dir. Michael Crichton with Albert Finney, James Coburn, Susan Dey, Leigh Taylor-Young.
Loose Shoes *(Atlantic)* dir. Steno with Lewis Arquette, Danny Dayton, Murphy Dunne, Howard Hesseman.
Love & Money *(Paramount)* dir. James Toback with Ray Sharkey, Ornella Muti, Klaus Kinski, Armand Assante.
Madman *(Jensen Farley)* dir. Joe Giannone with Alexis Dubin, Tony Fish, Harriet Bass, Seth Jones.
Melanie *(Embassy)* dir. Rex Bromfield with Glynnis O'Connor, Burton Cummings, Paul Sorvino, Trudy Young.
Modern Problems *(Fox)* dir. Ken Shapiro with Chevy Chase, Patti D'Arbanville, Mary Kay Place, Nell Carter.
Mystique *(pro. co. Televicine International)* dir. Bobby Roth with Yvette Mimieux, Christopher Allport, Cindy Pickett, John Considine.
Neighbors *(Columbia)* dir. John G. Avildsen with John Belushi, Dan Aykroyd, Kathryn Walker, Cathy Moriarty.
Night Crossing *(Walt Disney/Buena Vista)* dir. Delbert Mann with John Hurt, Jane Alexander, Glynnis O'Connor, Dough McKeon.
Nobody's Perfect *(Columbia)* dir. Peter Bonerz with Gabe Kaplan, Alex Karras, Robert Klein, Susan Clark.
One from the Heart *(Zoetrope/Columbia)* dir. Francis Coppola with Frederic Forrest, Teri Garr, Nastassia Kinski, Raul Julia.
Paradise *(Embassy)* dir. Stuart Gillard with Willie Aames, Phoebe Cates, Richard Curnock, Tuvia Tavi.
Penitentiary II *(MGM/UA)* dir. Jamaa Fanaka with Leon Isaac Kennedy, Ernie Hudson, Mr. T., Glynn Turman.
Personal Best *(Universal)* dir. Robert Towne with Mariel Hemingway, Scott Glen, Patrice Donnelly, Kenny Moore.
The Prowler *(Sandhurst Corp.)* dir. Joseph Zito with Vicki Dawson, Christopher Goutman, Cindy Weintraub, Farley Granger.
The Pursuit of D.B. Cooper *(Universal)* dir. Roger Spottiswoode with Robert Duvall, Treat Williams, Kathryn Harrold, Ed Flanders.
Raggedy Man *(Universal)* dir. Jack Fisk with Sissy Spacek, Eric Roberts, William Sanderson, Tracey Walter.
Roommates *(Platinum Pictures)* dir. Chuck Vincent with Samantha Fox, Veronica Hart, Kelly Nichols, Jamie Gillis.
Saturday the 14th *(New World)* dir. Howard R. Cohen with Richard

Benjamin, Paula Prentiss, Severn Darden, Jeffrey Tambor.
Screamers *(New World)* dir. Sergio Martino with Barbara Bach, Claudio Cassinelli, Richard Johnson, Joseph Cotten.
The Seduction *(Embassy)* dir. David Schmoeller with Morgan Fairchild, Michael Sarrazin, Vince Edwards, Andrew Stevens.
Silence of the North *(Universal)* dir. Allan Winton King with Ellen Burstyn, Tom Skerritt, Gordon Pinsent, Jennifer McKinney.
Silent Rage *(Columbia)* dir. Michael Miller with Chuck Norris, Ron Silver, Steven Keats, Toni Kalem.
The Slumber Party Massacre *(Pacific)* dir. Amy Jones with Michele Michaels, Robin Stille, Michael Villela, Andre Honore.
Smokey Bites the Dust *(New World)* dir. Charles B. Griffitih with Jimmy McNichol, Janet Julian, Walter Barnes, Patrick Campbell.
Soup for One *(Warner)* dir Jonathan Kaufer with Saul Rubinek, Marcia Strassman, Gerrit Graham, Teddy Pendergrass.
St. Helens *(Parnell)* dir. Ernest Pintoff with Art Carney, David Huffman, Cassie Yates, Ron O'Neal.
A Stranger Is Watching *(MGM/UA)* dir. Sean S. Cunningham with Kate Mulgrew, Rip Torn, James Naughton, Shawn Von Schreiber.
Student Bodies *(Paramount)* dir. Mickey Rose with Kristen Riter, Matthew Goldsby, Richard Brando, Joe Flood.
Surfacing *(Pan-Canadian)* dir. Claude Jutra with Joseph Bottoms, Kathleen Beller, R.H. Thomson, Margaret Dragu.
Swamp Thing *(Embassy)* dir. Wes Craven with Louis Jourdan, Adrienne Barbeau, Ray Wise, David Hess.
Tag *(New World)* dir. Nick Castle with Robert Carradine, Linda Hamilton, Bruce Abbott, Kristine DeBell.
They All Laughed *(Fox, then UA Classics)* dir. Peter Bogdanovich with Audrey Hepburn, Ben Gazzara, John Ritter, Colleen Camp.
Threshold *(pro. co. Paragon)* dir. Richard Pearce with Donald Sutherland, John Marley, Sharon Ackerman, Mare Winningham.
Too Far to Go *(Zoetrope)* dir. Fielder Cook with Michael Moriarty, Blythe Danner, Glenn Close, Ken Kercheval.
Tulips *(Avco-Embassy)* dir. Stan Ferris with Gabe Kaplan, Bernadette Peters, Henry Gibson, Al Waxman.
Under the Rainbow *(Orion/Warner)* dir. Steve Rash with Chevy Chase, Carrie Fisher, Billy Barty, Eve Arden.
The Unseen *(World Northal)* dir. Peter Foleg with Barbara Bach, Sydney Lassick, Stephen Furst, Leia Goldoni.
White Dog *(Paramount)* dir. Samuel Fuller with Kristy McNichol, Paul Winfield, Burl Ives, James Parker.
The Woman Inside *(Fox)* dir. Joseph Van Winkle with Gloria Manon, Dane Clark, John Blondell, Michael Champion.
Wrong Is Right *(Columbia)* dir. Richard Brooks with Sean Connery, George Grizzard, Robert Conrad, Katharine Ross.
Zoot Suit *(Universal)* dir. Luis Valdez with Daniel Valdez, Edward James Olmos, Charles Aidman, Tyne Daly.

THE US YEAR

There has long been a theory that the cinema prospers in recessionary times. The 1981-82 year at the American and Canadian box offices gave further credence to it.

Going to a movie is still a relatively inexpensive form of entertainment, even with ticket prices in the US escalating to $4.50 or $5 — and up to a record $6 for Columbia's big, expensive *Annie* when it opened in selected theatres in May 1982.

As the country plunged into its worst recession since before World War II, box office returns rocketed skyward. Comedy and adventure reigned supreme, and the champion was an action adventure film spiced with plenty of comedy, *Raiders of the Lost Ark*.

Launched in June 1981, *Raiders* was still running in many of its original engagements a year later, and has so far taken in over $200 million in box office grosses for the production company, Lucasfilm, and its distributor, Paramount.

Thanks to three pictures hitting the movie screens in summer 1982 with an immediate and tremendous impact — with a few others close behind — two record breaking summers were chalked up during that July 1981 to June 1982 year. In only two or three weeks, *E.T. : The Extra Terrestrial*, *Star Trek II: The Wrath of Khan* and *Rocky III* had each passed the box office grosses of all but seven of the preceding year's films (and 1981 had been the biggest summer — and year — in industry history).

At the end of June 1982, after taking in almost $60 million for Universal in its first 17 days, Steven Spielberg's *E.T.* was still earning an average of $3 million a day from 1245 theatres, and showing no signs of slowing down. Running neck and neck behind it were Paramount's *Star Trek II* and MGM/UA's *Rocky III*, both of which broke opening week records for their studios' pictures. Single theatre records were being

'Arthur': close to $100 million at US box office

bettered everywhere. Meanwhile, "Trekkies", the highly organised fans of the *Star Trek* television series, unanimously proclaimed the latest outing of their heroes of the Starship Enterprise to be much better than the original *Star Trek* feature. Spielberg was hands down the man of the year. He not only produced and directed *E.T.*, but also co-wrote and co-produced *Poltergeist* and directed *Raiders of the Lost Ark*, which had dominated the summer 1981 scene.

As the July-to-June year ended, *Star Trek II* and *Rocky III* were proving even further that sequels can be successful. One of the biggest successes of summer 1981 was a sequel, *Superman II*, which pulled in grosses of $130 million before fading from the lists. In addition, the top sequel of all time, *The Empire Strikes Back*, was reissued in July 1981 and added another $14 million or so to the coffers of its distributor, 20th Century Fox.

That 14 million is a "film rental" figure, not "box office gross". The theatre owners' previously negotiated percentages and house expenses are taken out of the money from ticket sales, and what is left goes to the distributing studio — usually about half, depending on many factors, including how the deals were set up. The distributor's share of the

"gross" is called the "rental". The financers, the producers and all those holding profit points in the movie are paid after the studio subtracts its marketing and distribution costs from the rental.

The other big winners during the record-setting 1981 summer season were Orion/Warner Brothers' *Arthur*, which was close to the $100 million mark a year later and still running in many places; *Stripes*, a Bill Murray comedy from Columbia, which did not last as long as *Arthur* but nevertheless had earned over $85 million at the ticket wickets by the end of the year; and *For Your Eyes Only*, latest of the James Bond series from United Artists (now MGM/UA).

There were no blockbusters among the pictures released at Christmas time. The Hollywood major studios presented a string of downbeat pictures about depressing subjects, and the public stayed away in droves. MGM, in particular, was hit by the public's apathy toward the group of movies the studio was hoping would help finance its recent $380 million purchase of United Artists.

According to a March 1982 story in the *Los Angeles Times*, MGM/UA released ten films in 1981 and early 1982 at a total production and marketing cost of $178.7 million and realised only $50.2 million return in film rentals for the lot.

Furthermore, one MGM/UA release, *Pennies From Heaven*, was one of the Top Ten box office turkeys of the year, bringing back around $2.5 million in rentals after costing the studio either $24 million (if we take the word of the producer, Herbert Ross) or $31 million (if we believe the newspaper's figure).

Hollywood studio executives consider cost and earnings figures on individual movies to be proprietary information, and do not reveal these figures even in their annual reports for stockholders. Nor do they give them to the industry organisation, the Motion Picture Association of America. The "creative

'The Cannonball Run': an $80 million gross

bookkeeping" that is sometimes done with a movie's profit figures in Hollywood is legendary.

Another MGM/UA film, Alan Parker's *Shoot the Moon*, also failed at the box office, earning only about the same as *Pennies* and costing around $21 million for production and marketing.

MGM/UA's other Christmas losers were the Jack Lemmon/Walter Matthau starrer, *Buddy Buddy* — a special disappointment in that it was expected to do well because it at least was a comedy among all the serious holiday fare — and *Whose Life is it, Anyway?* based on a successful Broadway play, but an instant bomb on the silver screen.

Fortunately, MGM and UA traditionally have derived more than half of their theatrical earnings in the overseas market, so some of their domestic losers will make money from their foreign theatrical runs. A prime example is UA's *For Your Eyes Only*, which had a very respectable domestic gross of $51 million in 1981 and returned rentals of $25,439,479. One problem; its cost was between $28 and $29 million. However, James Bond pictures are very popular internationally, and it will undoubtedly end up earning good money.

The biggest surprise of the year was *Porky's*, Canadian director Bob Clark's raunchy little sex comedy about a horny group of Fifties adolescents, produced for only $4.2 million by Melvin Simon Productions and Astral Bellevue Pathe of Canada. Released by 20th Century Fox in March 1982, it gave the entire US box office a shot of adrenalin that led to the largest March theatrical gross in history; then the biggest April and May; then it was on its way to breaking the record again for the entire summer.

A real Cinderella story, *Porky's* had hit a £100 million gross by early July. And speaking of *Cinderella*, Disney's Buena Vista reissued that animated classic at Christmas 1981 and garnered another $20 million (gross) for the studio.

Paramount was lucky to have *Raiders* running on and on, because the studio's two mega-million-dollar holiday releases, *Reds* and *Ragtime*, were evidently never going to take in enough at the wickets even to cover their costs. In 80 days, *Reds* had taken in around $32 million gross, but Paramount admitted that Warren Beatty's epic had cost $35 million to produce — and informed sources estimated the figure was closer to $53 million.

With hundreds of films released every year by Hollywood, there are, of course, many losers — and many big and small winners. *On Golden Pond*, taken over by Universal when AFD folded, was not an expensive movie to make, but it passed the $100 million benchmark in grosses. And *The Cannonball Run*, a Golden Harvest/20th Century Fox feature, ran up an $80 million gross in a fast, wide release in over 1600 theatres.

Most of the losers (like John Schlesinger's $25 million *Honky Tonk Freeway*), just opened and then sank fast without much fanfare. But two of them, Francis Coppola's *One From the Heart* and Filmways' *Blow Out*, received a lot of attention because the fate of their respective studios was riding on their successes.

Coppola shopped his $23 million *One From the Heart* around to the studios very dramatically, making Columbia feel like a victor in winning distribution rights. But the general public couldn't have cared less about it. Columbia yanked it after only a few disastrous weeks and wrote it off as a total loss.

Blow Out was given a well-ballyhooed $9 million marketing launch (on top of its estimated $18 million cost), but it blew out fast, bringing in only $8 million in rentals.

Listed below are the Top Ten box office winners and losers of the July-June year, according to available information. B.J. Franklin

WINNERS	LOSERS
Raiders of the Lost Ark	*One From the Heart*
Superman II	*Reds*
On Golden Pond	*Ragtime*
Porky's	*Blow Out*
Arthur	*Honky Tonk Freeway*
Stripes	*Dragonslayer*
The Cannonball Run	*Condorman*
E.T.: The Extra Terrestrial	*Pennies From Heaven*
Rocky III	*Shoot The Moon*
Star Trek II: The Wrath of Khan	*All the Marbles* (almost a tie with *Cannery Row* and *Whose Life is it, Anyway?*)

THE UK YEAR

It is a curious and ultimately revealing irony that, thanks to the startling Óscar success of *Chariots Of Fire*, 1981-82 may in years to come be seen as a triumphant year for the British film industry, although a closer and more sober look behind the win reveals an industry in disarray and apparently irreversible decline.

The success of *Chariots* and to a lesser extent *Gregory's Girl*, as well as the welcome boost of Channel Four production and British-made-but-American-financed movies such as *Raiders of the Lost Ark*, *The French Lieutenant's Woman* and *Superman II*, only obscured much more lasting and damaging facts such as dwindling attendances (British people now go the the cinema less than twice a year on average), closing cinemas and the disappearance of Rank and ITC as major film production houses. The only remaining British major, Thorn-EMI, have also shown an increasing emphasis on production in the US. The once powerful triumvirate of Rank, ITC and EMI have all floundered in recent months thanks to a series of terrible flops at the box office, both at home and, much more significantly, overseas.

Certainly, by the mid-summer of 1981 the writing was on the wall. Rank, whose commitment to the film industry had in recent years become increasingly and obviously half-hearted, had already pulled out of film production, and they followed this in June with the closure of 29 cinemas, with indications of more to follow. Although a considerable fuss was generated and there was much talk of how the shade of J. Arthur Rank would return to haunt his less bold successors, nobody was very surprised. Rank, after all, the argument ran, had been a spent force for some time, their ambition blunted by a nearly invisible and certainly unimaginative film management team.

But cracks beneath the surface of Lord Grade's flamboyant ACC empire, including the film arm ITC, were much more significant.

The summer had already started badly for the seemingly indestructible Lew, media darling and former dance expert, whose nimble footwork had kept his company buoyant, or at least afloat, despite a succession of box office disasters. But there was one disaster even Lew couldn't escape: *Raise The Titanic*, a 40 million dollar adventure, including special effects which made those of *Thunderbirds* look like an

— 79 —

'Gregory's Girl': one of the year's most notable successes

extreme in sophistication, had left the company with an industry joke and a cash deficit it was to prove unable to survive.

ACC's first calamity of the year, the announcement of the closure of ATV Elstree Studios, was not directly connected. Independent Broadcasting Authority regulations stipulating that ATV (now Central TV) activities should be centred in the Midlands put paid to the home of such Grade money-spinners as *The Muppets* and many others.

But Lew, his familiar cigar and equally familiar quote ("I will never retire. I'm at work every morning by 5.30") still always to hand, denied that anything else was wrong. Pledging a continuing commitment to production, he bravely maintained that future ITC product such as *The Legend of the Lone Ranger* and particularly *The Great Muppet Caper* would rectify the problems. It would be a cruelty to labour how unfortunately his optimism would rebound in his face. *The Lone Ranger* and then, most damagingly, *The Great Muppet Caper* were released to a bemused and supremely indifferent British public who stayed away in droves.

Desperately wheeling and dealing, Lew clinched deals with Universal in America for the distribution of new ITC product, which included a modest middlebrow weepie called *On Golden Pond*. The joint ACC/EMI American distribution set-up AFD having by now fallen by the wayside, Grade sold most of

his rights to future profits on his own films to Universal in return for upfront money. It was an entirely typical if desperately unlucky twist of fate which later saw *On Golden Pond* break the 100 million dollar earnings mark for its new proprietors.

The depth of the ITC problem burst into the open in September with the departure from ITC of Jack Gill, considered for years the heir apparent to the Grade empire. The full facts of his resignation or dismissal have never been fully revealed, but all the evidence points to a failed boardroom plot during which Gill found himself without promised support only at the final moments. Gill's departure with his by now celebrated £750,000 golden handshake (still unpaid, thanks to legal wrangles, at the time of going to press) left Grade supreme but also supremely alone, and it was not long before he was back in the headlines.

October saw the disintegration of the ITC film sales arm and the first mentions of a shadowy Australian financier named Robert Holmes a'Court, who rapidly established himself on the ACC board.

During the next few months ITC's Classic cinema chain of 126 screens came up for sale, eventually to go to an up-and-coming Israeli company, Cannon Films; Holmes a'Court consolidated his position before launching an inevitable takeover bid for the entire ACC organisation, promising a new "executive position" for Grade. The battle for ACC,

which was quickly joined by the oil-based Heron organisation, was to drag on for another six months before being finally settled in the Australian's favour. All Lew's vainglorious but curiously attractive boasting about both his own and his company's longevity finally came to nothing, leaving him perhaps the saddest figure at this year's Cannes Film Festival, for so long his special domain — alone, and finally the victim of the power politics he loved so much.

The disintegration of ACC, boasting a plot marginally more interesting than most of Lew's films, is easy to treat as a real-life soap opera, but the loss of the company is genuinely sad for the British industry. With Lew's departure vanishes much of the swagger and fun that used to be an integral part of the business. Although his decisions in production (or more likely those of his advisers) were often outdated and catastrophic, his departure leaves a gap that is unlikely to be filled.

Elsewhere the story was, for the most part, little better. As the video industry gained in strength and ambition, so the film business went into seemingly corresponding decline. The industry trade paper *Screen International* mildly predicted that admissions for UK cinemas in 1981 would reach an all-time low of around 90 million — only to find its prediction, branded at the time as pessimistic and even defeatist, as uncomfortably prescient. The actual figure, released by the board of trade in April, revealed an ugly figure of 86 million in which not even the most optimistic could find any sign of recovery.

The causes of this steady decline from a post-war peak of around 500 million are easy to find — television, video, poor facilities in cinemas, economic decline — but solutions are in short supply. If the decline continues then there is little doubt that the exhibition industry faces what could be its final crisis.

The last remaining major, EMI, had its own problems. In common with other English companies they had gone all out to conquer the lucrative US market. To this end their production activity, instigated by Barry "Smiler" Spikings, was centred in America. Their flagship was a $25 million "road" movie to be directed,

rather incongruously, by John Schlesinger. In common with most other massively overbudgeted movies this year, it was an artistic and financial mess that Spikings reportedly only just survived. EMI's other product fared little better, and their current, mostly American-based production roster almost certainly carries with it the future of the company's film-making arm.

Earlier in October 1981, the company's appointment of former Burton Menswear chief Brian North ("I have no knowledge of the film industry and therefore hopefully arrive without any bias") as their new managing director caused the industry no little hilarity; but the joke may turn sour when what are seen as inevitable redundancies and cost savings come into effect.

It would be a rabid optimist who looked to a British government for support in these difficult times, and sure enough the Conservative administration reacted to the problems of the film industry with a traditional mixture of ignorance and contempt. Indeed, Chancellor Sir Geoffrey Howe's brilliant answer to the problems of production in the UK was to close, in his April budget, the tax loophole which had facilitated much of what little production there had been in the previous year. Films minister Sally Oppenheim, famous in previous incarnations for her hairstyles and her protection of the consumer (although in which ways is not entirely evident), was clearly bewildered by the conflicting demands of the UK industry and retired prematurely. Her successor, one Iain Sproat, appears equally inert, although one can only remain hopeful. Sir Harold Wilson's Interim Action Committee, which has been considering the problems of the industry for what seems a lifetime, appears increasingly redundant and pointless.

On the production front the UK suffered its worst ever year, with most of the studios — Pinewood, Shepperton, Lee International, EMI Elstree, Twickenham, Bray — being consistently underused. Were it not for the presence of prestige American pictures such as Barbra Streisand's *Yentl*, MGM's *The Hunger*, and Columbia's *Krull* the situation would be bleak indeed. Mercifully signs are more optimistic for the rest of

1982, with far more home-based production announced, and the total number of films made in the UK in the first half of the year already outstripping the entire number for the previous year.

British facilities and particularly technicians have long been acknowledged as probably the best in the world, but it would only be a true patriot who ascribed the Americans' continued presence here to much beyond the favourable dollar exchange rate which enables US productions to be made much more cheaply in the UK.

And yet despite it all the British film industry, for so long confined to insular excellence on the TV screen suddenly fought back in magnificent style in 1982, a fight which culminated in the extraordinary Oscar triumph of the David Puttnam-produced Hugh Hudson-directed *Chariots of Fire*.

Released in early Summer in the UK, there was little indication at first of the phenomenon about to be unleashed. Although successful enough, *Chariots* seemed unlikely to set the world on fire, particularly when its own partial backers, 20th Century Fox, refused to release it in America. Eventually the rather more adventurous Ladd Company distributed through Warner Brothers in the US. Good reviews were followed by a fine performance at the box office, apparently a sufficient reward for producer David Puttnam's determination in getting his seven-million-dollar baby off the ground. But gradually the feeling grew that something remarkable was happening. After receiving only a screenplay award (for Colin Welland) at the parochial London *Evening Standard* awards in December, by March it had scooped four awards, including best film at the British Academy of Film and Television Arts annual beano — with a handful of Oscar nominations into the bargain.

Popular opinion was that Warren Beatty's epic *Reds*, combined with the traditional sympathy vote for the ageing stars of *On Golden Pond* (Henry Fonda and Katharine Hepburn), would pip *Chariots* at the post. The rest, as they say, is history: *Chariots* won Oscars for best film, best screenplay, best costume design and best music. An epic evening for the British.

The long-term effects of the film's success are harder to fathom. Certainly it leaves Puttnam as one of the world's most in-demand producers, and Hugh Hudson seems equally well set. It is greatly to their credit that their next films (*Local Hero* and *Greystoke* respectively) are being made in Britain. But beyond that lie the traditional problems, which will resurface as soon as the euphoria is over. Ironically the triumph may even have made the prospect of government aid — by common agreement the only real remedy for the industry's ills — even more remote. As one observer put it at the time, "Now the Government can turn round and say — 'there you are, we told you you could do it without any help from us'".

Puttnam's success should not overshadow the determined contribution of other producers to the British year. Davina Belling and Clive Parsons, who in previous years had come up with subjects as diverse as *Rosie Dixon Night Nurse* and *Breaking Glass*, this year made, with director Bill Forsyth, the surprise hit *Gregory's Girl*. A charming comedy made for something less than £200,000, it has now run for exactly a year at London's Cinecenta, and is, to scale, the most successful film distributed by ITC. Forsyth has now teamed up with Puttnam to make *Local Hero*.

Don Boyd, recovering from his venture to the US for *Honky Tonk Freeway*, returned his attention to his own company which produced and part-financed Chris Petit's *An Unsuitable Job for a Woman* and Mai Zetterling's *Scrubbers*.

Another surprise hit was *Time Bandits*, written by Michael Palin and directed by Terry Gilliam for Handmade Films, one of the most enterprising of the independents currently on the scene. Handmade have also branched out with new films by Michael Palin (*The Missionary*) and Michael Blakemore (*Privates on Parade*).

As in past years the only ray of light on the exhibition side was the performance of art houses, which for the most part kept and, particularly in the provinces, expanded their audiences. But even there problems arose. The double strain of VAT and Eady Levy payments (Eady Levy is the amount extracted from ticket sales at all cinemas, which is later redistributed to the industry) brought many small cinemas close to financial crisis, the only solution being conversion to club status, a move undertaken by Romaine Hart's "Screen" cinemas and the "Gate" chain, among others. This was all very well, but customer resistance to cinema clubs is well known, mainly because of their association with the seedier side of the industry.

Smash success of the year on the art house circuit was the Hungarian *Mephisto*, which ran for months at the Gate Camden. Other notable foreign film successes were Eric Rohmer's *The Aviator's Wife*, Truffaut's *The Last Metro* and Makavejev's *Montenegro*.

Mainstream hit of the year, for the umpteenth time, was the latest Bond film *For Your Eyes Only*, which sat serenely at the head of the *Screen International* Top Ten for most of the summer and autumn of 1981. Although it lost out to *Superman II* for the whole of 1981, there is little doubt it will still be featured strongly by the time 1982 comes to an end. Other successes were more or less predictable; Steven Spielberg's knockabout *Raiders of the Lost Ark*, *Flash Gordon*, *Clash of the Titans* and Clint Eastwood's *Any Which Way You Can*. A welcome success was Roman Polanski's elegiac *Tess*, which sat on the shelf for two years before Columbia finally screwed up the courage to release it.

The reverse side of the coin, the box office turkeys, were possibly of more interest to the collector, and indeed one or two of them could well grace bad film festivals in years to come. The size of the British exhibition system generally means that real financial disasters can usually be pulled before they do too much damage. But a glance back over the year reveals a number of artistic and monetary stinkers that the distributors would rather forget about. In no particular order these included:
The Legend of the Lone Ranger
Heaven's Gate
Caveman
The Great Muppet Caper
Escape to Victory
Buddy Buddy
Ghost Story
Loving Couples
Priest of Love
Rich and Famous
These broke down into intriguing categories. The failed lavish-budget spectacular (*Rich and Famous, Muppet Caper, Escape to Victory, Heaven's Gate*), the attempted nostalgia piece (*Ghost Story, Lone Ranger*) the would-be artistic crossover (*Priest of Love*) and the failed formula comedies (*Buddy Buddy, Loving Couples*). Of all these only one is unique: *Caveman*, a hideously unfunny comedy with Ringo Starr, is a unique example of a film that not only should never have been made but should also have been suppressed instantly on its release. Highly recommended for people who go to the dentist for fun.

The rest of 1982 appears a little more promising, and certainly there are enough major movies waiting in the wings for the next year, including the third part of the *Star Wars* saga. But overall the lingering memory of the last 12 months will be the euphoria over *Chariots* hiding a multitude of problems and uncertainties in every area of the film industry.

ADRIAN HODGES

UK TEN TOP 1981 — Chart by Screen International			
Superman 2 (Columbia-EMI-Warner)	A	British
For Your Eyes Only (United Artists)	A	British
Flash Gordon (Columbia-EMI-Warner)	A	British
Snow White and the Seven Dwarfs (Disney)	U	American
Any Which Way You Can (Columbia-EMI-Warner)	AA	American
Clash of the Titans (CIC)	A	British
Private Benjamin (Columbia-EMI-Warner)	AA	American
Raiders of the Lost Ark (CIC)	A	American
The Elephant Man (Columbia-EMI-Warner)	AA	British
Tess (Columbia-EMI-Warner)	A	Franco-British

FILMS OF THE YEAR
TRUE CONFESSIONS

True Confessions is a strange movie to watch, and to think through. Its storyline is a sprawling matter which mixes strong meat with anti-climaxes whose dissatisfactions loiter to haunt us. It's dry and sour. No character is loveable and the only consolation for pain is the energy in their respect, anger and duty.

It's a murder mystery, among other things. Quite apart from the routine complications of that theme, it does to genre expectations what Thelonious Monk did to modern jazz. The notes you expect are replaced by pointed gaps and the story juts into strange tangents, chunks and zig-zags.

My hunch is that it's a crucial film of the decade and the clearest marker yet of a new mode in popular American thought.

Robert Duvall and Robert de Niro play not its heroes, but its protagonists. Their story opens in the 1960s. Tom Spellacy (Duvall) is a detective retired from the Los Angeles Police Department. His brother Des (de Niro), a Catholic priest, fulfils his duties as pastor of a low-class desert parish, though fatally ill. (Two other conspicuous characters have the Big C.) Reunited, the brothers recall the 1940s. How another priest, Father Mickey, died of a cardiac arrest while screwing a brothel's black pearl. How the Madam, a Jewess, had carried a torch for Tom ever since the 1930s, when they both worked for a racketeer known as Jack Amsterdam. Now (1948) Amsterdam is an honest building contractor, and happy to build a church school at cost in exchange for the seal of respectability: a Papal audience. Des, a clever, ambitious Monsignor, is aide and fixer for the Cardinal (Cyril Cusack). He drives a hard bargain . . .

Complicated, isn't it? The discreet brothel, the obliging cop, the clergymen with balance-sheet minds, all slot into a tortuous system which no-one planned and which no-one needs to understand as a whole. But then the body of a Christian Scientist girl from St. Louis is found nude and bisected in a vacant lot. In her stomach an undigested eggroll fixes the hour of her death. Another clue points to a stagfilm director with a fine old WASP name. He's already dead, in a car-crash — a fate which fits the film's pattern of deaths. It's as natural as cancer. It's also as sudden, and as conducive to damnation, as death by orgasm. Swiftly the whodunnit interest yields to questions of tolerance and corruption, with connivance as their disquieting common factor.

It's a film in the key of C. C for confession and corruption. For cancer, car-crash and cash. For Cardinal and Communion. For Conception (Immaculate) and for "cutters" (hookers' word for johns who like watching them bleed). The biggest C in this crazy quilt of creeds and colours is moral confusion. However scathing we may want to be about clerical wheeler-dealing and priestly carnality, the film's casuistry and moral nostalgias generate a powerful respect for the Catholic faith. Indeed, the film's last shots — and an earlier joke about an Irish Navvy — scoop a faith-shaped hole out of this dirty world.

In French terms its moral spirit is close to Melville and to Bresson (who recently described himself as a "Christian atheist"). But its social canvas is richer. It's the least private, the least auteurist, of films. Grosbard's style, as impersonal as a kaleidoscope, gears into the new Hollywood's interest in America's swirl of subcultures. It whisks us between a fashionable wedding, with its green lawns and off-white bridal dress; a grubby Hispanic church off a sweltering highway; headlines screaming about "the werewolf killer of the virgin tramp". The visual style is a swizzle-stick of bright distractions and sardonic reactions, that routinely dislocate the sense of a scene, whether it's the horror of a nude half-body lying in the sunshine, or the priest's unspoken confession to his brother in a lunch-counter. The script (by husband-and-wife Joan Didion and John Gregory Dunne, decanted from his even more complicated novel) crackles with ironies of every kind. Over Chinese food Tom grimly says, "I busted this joint fourteen times when I was in Vice. Now I eat here every day." When a nun bars his way to his mother's hospital bed he snarls, "May all your sons be Jesuits, Sister."

The Forties' action of *True Confessions* evokes the heyday of Chandler's Marlowe, his stamping-ground (Southern California), and his genre, *film noir*. The Marlowe ethos has had a good long run, and maybe it once was a cutting-edge of America's post-mortem on its puritan ideals. But

wasn't he archaic, even for the 1940s, with his knight-errant's soul? His wisecracks didn't disguise his chivalrous sentiments, and his loner's trenchcoat was a magic shield against the spirit of the mean streets. That is to say, that Chandler never threw the really insidious temptations Marlowe's way. Even Altman in *The Long Goodbye* went easy on this much-loved, over-literary, figure. For the private eye has become a sacred cow of film culture, with his very convenient combination of reformism and private enterprise, casualness and 90 per cent justice, virtue and toughness, all in one handy package. There's a converging line of *noir*-look complacency in organisation-man cops (from Dick Tracy via *Dragnet* and Kojack). But Tom Spellacy lives, moves and has his being within a spiritual ecology that eclipses those options.

From another angle, *True Confessions* may seem to draw a bead on the Hitchcock vision. It's easy to catalogue the echoes: *I Confess, Family Plot,* the two brothers as Strangers-On-A-Case whose guilts criss-cross. But I doubt if these themes indicate Hitchcock's influence, whether by imitation or *homage*, parody or rejoinder. They're shared ideas transformed by a very different vision.

Suspense is a kind of lyricism, based on moral certainty, at least insofar as we care for characters who stand for something. Probably it's related to poetic realism, like which it inherits something from a humanist tradition. Hence directors as different as Hitchcock and Renoir are "poetic", in the sense that even their suspense and sadness postulates the possibility of some bond between man and nature or God or "the way things are." *True Confessions* has no such confidence. Faces and settings are at daggers and distractions drawn. Social life is a jungle of plots, counterplots, and accidents. Given the disparities between any two people, no overall lyrical mood is possible: only a weary mixture of sympathy and suspicion, tolerance and despair. Taken further, nihilism looms, and fear of that subtends everything in this movie, quietly but very suspensefully indeed.

It refuses to be amoral or immoral. But it also refuses that traditional suspense whereby some order can repel

threats to it. This colder, sadder, stoic vision knows it can't. Depriving itself of either-or excitements, it works to a both-and pattern, with its constant, obsessive anxiety. No man can know the snakes from the ladders, nor which way he's moving on the board.

In tracing systems of covert power and selfishness it's like a Rosi film (and Rosi converged on certain themes in his American movie, *Lucky Luciano,* unfortunately wrecked by studio re-cuts). It's very close to that phase of neo-realism. Its muckraking is political, not at all in the same way as Rosi's Marxist commitment, but in an equally serious one. We could talk of alienation and anomie, but they're sociologists' words, and hardly fit this film's sensibility about some three-way-split between soul, man and social system. "Religion" comes from *religio,* a bond, whose absence is what this film's about. Only the girl's body can be stitched together again.

The jagged storyline and dramatics are mainstream, American, terms for the avant-garde pessimism of Robbe-Grillet and Duras. (And both these writers are fascinated by atrocity, mystery and reassembling corpses.) Quite

possibly their formalist extremism excludes most human responses, and it's *True Confessions* which makes the truest confession, about how the common man can neither deny nor accept a certain nihilism. The cop and the priest are two sides of the common man: one forgives too little, the other too much . . .

Hence some critical misunderstandings. The film's scepticism requires, not flatness exactly, but a deadpan uncertainty. Hints and information matter more than "style", or rather, they *are* its style. Tom's rage and Des's blandness are opposite options, and both right, both wrong. No judgement of a man can be made to stick. Father Mickey dies in orgasm (his second), but most spectators would agree with Catholic dogma, that we still can't know if he's damned. Nor what "damned" means. A similar equivocation seethes within Duvall's mean smiles with the Madam who either loves him or is just lonely. None of all this makes wrong right, or forgiveable. If the film seems flat it's only because it bristles with sharp edges.

Its quiet sad tension is a writer's quality which reminds me of Simenon. And there's a Simenon-like proportion of

depth to *breadth.* By *depth* I mean psychology, sociology, moral causality, ideology, and other *explanatory* things. By *breadth* I mean the action, in the sense of the overt interaction between people and situations, issues and feelings. Critics love to reduce breadth to depth, action to explanation. Yet no deep-level factors can explain the action, because it involves them all. Each works only in the context of the others, and it's the *breadth* which controls the *depth.* Stories don't exist to explain life; they exist to depict it.

Obviously one can speculate about the brothers' Oedipal rivalries and so on, but the terms which this film, like Simenon, emphasises, are the rough, practical, ideas used by cops and priests and whores and other operators in the real, unpredictable world. Things like how the brothers' vocations have sharpened and warped their minds, how one has become a berserker because the other uses smoothie strategies (and vice versa). *True Confessions,* like Simenon, expresses a very modern philosophy: materialism and indeterminacy, absurdity and probability, routine and faith, social systemics and moral protest. RAYMOND DURGNAT.

RICHARD PRYOR LIVE ON THE SUNSET STRIP

It may be argued that *Richard Pryor Live on the Sunset Strip* is not a bona fide movie, but, rather, a piece of canned, if pizzazz, vaudeville. Nonetheless, it is *the* most exhilarating screen entertainment I have experienced in the past year.

There is nothing formally innovative about it. Pryor did much the same thing three years ago in a very successfully marketed film attraction entitled *Richard Pryor Live in Concert*. At that time I was jolted into an awareness of Pryor as a comic genius and not just the fringe comedian he was able to reveal previously in the circumscribed "white bread" routines demanded by the mass media. His language in *Concert* was foul and cleansing at the same time, because with Pryor the dirt was a bass accompaniment to shrieking riffs of pain and fear and self-recognition. After a "Get Whitey" opening that established the total blackness of his humour, Pryor burst through to universality by treating the most horrifying experiences as part of nature's dialectic. He was as outrageous as Lenny Bruce but infinitely more graceful as a performer, particularly when

parodying his heart in the midst of a seizure or when slinking across a stage into the raunchy precincts of animal kingdom. Pryor was and remains an uncanny mimic with a finely tuned ear to the nuances of power struggles in speech, and in unexpurgated form his raging unconscious was triumphantly unlocked.

We might note at this point that Richard Pryor's rise to superstardom is not without its paradoxes. For one thing, Pryor's emergence as a "crossover" performer — i.e. as a black entertainer popular with white audiences — comes at a time when racism is perceived to be on the upswing in Ronald Reagan's America. Similarly, his status as a counterculture figure embodying a radical lifestyle *vis-à-vis* sex and drugs coincides with the increasing fulminations of the so-called Moral Majority and other manifestations of fanatical fundamentalism across the length and breadth of America. Pryor is peaking also in a period when black-made movies are in a state of decline and virtual extinction.

On the other hand, Pryor has profited from certain occurrences in the entertainment industry that

have paved the way for his uniquely emancipated form of self-expression. Hence, the decline in the supply and popularity of comparatively conventional narrative movies has opened the way for "concert" attractions that would have seemed forbiddingly freakish only a few years ago. And though black film-making may be moribund, black inner city audiences remain to supply a hardcore, rock-bottom cushion for the ultimate box-office receipts. Pryor's astounding liberties with language, liberties that encompass the frankest street terms for sexual, scatalogical, racial and ethnic taboos, would not have been permissible on the nation's screens before the cable revolution made it possible for the most daring modern comedians to perform their acts without censorship or the inhibitions of "good taste". Robin Williams and Steve Martin are only the best known of a group of singularly irreverent comics who have broken through the self-imposed restrictions of network television to reach a considerably larger audience for their raunchy routines than was possible before in "live" clubs and arenas.

Then there is the matter of profit margins. A one-man show with minimal "production values" cannot help but be a bonanza if it achieves wide theatrical distribution. At a time when the costs of making movies have soared astronomically both *Richard Pryor Live in Concert* and *Richard Pryor Live on the Sunset Strip* are marvellous bargains for Pryor's producers. But then why has this ultra-economical idea not worked with other popular entertainers, white and black? Why, for the most part, has it not even been tried? Why not a Steve Martin Live in Concert, or a Robin Williams, or a Barbra Streisand, or a Diana Ross, or a Dolly Parton, or a Lily Tomlin? What does Richard Pryor have that these luminaries lack? What indeed

is the magic ingredient in his extraordinarily successful formula?

We might say for starters that Pryor has become a public figure of sufficient notoriety to give his act a certain *frisson* of true confessions. He is reportedly a hot-tempered individual given to acts of violence against wives, women

friends, colleagues, and other associates and acquaintances. On one occasion, he actually shot a car in order to punish its owner. The tabloid accounts of such escapades figure prominently in his act, not as part of any mean-spirited process of getting even, but, rather, as a way of exorcising the evil spirits within him that have taken him time and again close to the edge. In this regard, Pryor follows the advice of Yeats in making poetry out of his quarrel with himself, rather than making rhetoric out of his quarrel with others.

Yet, as controversial a celebrity as Pryor may have been at the time of *Richard Pryor Live in Concert*, he had become quite literally a flaming legend before the filming of *Richard Pryor Live on the Sunset Strip*. Even the word "Live" took on an ironically celebratory connotation in the light of his blazing misadventure with the "free basing" of cocaine, an activity that sent him racing

out of his house in flames. This catastrophic accident occurred in an era when many pop stars have died of drugs at tragically young ages. Pryor survived his horrible ordeal, and was, in a sense, comically reborn in *Richard Pryor Live on the Sunset Strip*. It is *his* life and *his* near death to which audiences respond so emotionally both live and on film.

There are several audiences to be considered in the playing out of the Pryor phenomenon. There is the predominantly hip audience for the concert itself, and the predominantly street audience for the movie. Pryor has a special talent for bridging the gap between the hipsters and the street people by being subtle without being tentative, and by being vigorous without being vulgar.

Far from being a freakish film attraction, therefore, Richard Pryor's *Live on the Sunset Strip* restores to screen laughter a class-crossing unity that is in particularly short supply with today's increasingly fragmented audiences. An extraordinary mimic with an ability to shift gears between an authoritarian baritone and a whiney falsetto, Pryor can construct hilarious dialogues between himself and his drug habit, between himself and the woman in his life, and between himself and the various parts of his body. Because he is so scathingly honest about the excesses of black or "nigger" existence, the latter a term he announces he has foresworn since a humbling trip to Africa, he can do an extended "Mafia" routine and fully integrate it into his apparent autobiography.

It has been reported that when Pryor first performed his *Sunset Strip* concert, he impulsively started out with the climactic, traumatic routine about his accident, and then had nowhere to go as a performing act, with the result that he left the stage after a few moments with his fans in a state of befuddlement, and he in a state of hysteria. On a second try he held off on the accident material until the end of the evening, at which point he leaves his audience on the crest of an emotional epiphany.

I suppose that in 30 years some film historian will choose to analyse Pryor not merely on the basis of his two remarkable concert films, but also on his comedy performances in such high-grossing farces as *Silver*

Streak and *Stir Crazy*, in both of which he formed an uneasy partnership with the excruciatingly hammy Gene Wilder. My own feeling is that though Pryor has sparkled from time to time in conventional screen comedies, he has found his ultimate fulfilment only in his concert films. No hack scenario or frantic slapstick from the brutish movies of his time can compare with the farcical intrigues Pryor concocts within his own remarkably multi-viewpointed comic persona. The laughter he inspires goes beyond doctrinaire platitudes about "tolerance" and "liberation" to a perceptive contemplation of the hopelessly goofy times in which he and we live. He confronts his own celebrity and status without cutting off his roots or unduly sentimentalising them either.

There is a certain morbidity, I suppose, in watching a performer with a certifiable tendency toward self-destruction. Yet it is a privilege to experience an art that is remarkably free of malice and egomania, and yet unmistakably drawn from the darkest depths of the soul. Richard Pryor's art preserved in movie concert form is clearly for the ages.
ANDREW SARRIS

OUT OF THE BLUE

1955. *Rebel Without a Cause*. James Dean, a complex compendium of moody angst and alienation, a casualty of the American Family, a quizzical star-gazer moved by planetarium visions. A landmark film, an iconic role, a mythic character. Footnoted in the supporting cast, Dean's buddy Dennis Hopper.

1980. Hopper, an interim rebel with good cause, a Hollywood victim-cum-American Friend to young European cineastes and cinemas, applies himself to turning around a flailing, failing Canadian quickie into a sustained, 25-years-on, critical reflection on Nicholas Ray's film, on Dean's screen persona, and on the generation for whom both inspired nascent visions of a necessary counter-culture. Unexpectedly, from nowhere: *Out of the Blue*.

The title comes from Neil Young's sourly ironic rock anthem 'Hey Hey My My (Out of the Blue),' used here as constant abrasive commentary and back-and-forth referent to images of another American Family at degree zero, and counterposed with Elvis' 'Heartbreak Hotel,'

repetitive cassette-borne accompaniment for a new "rebel". Jim Backus' Middle-American straightman Pop has mutated into Hopper himself, ex-easy-riding prodigal father to lost punkette Linda Manz (in the Dean role), now star-gazing herself — at Elvis, Sid Vicious and a faded photo of clay-footed Dad in his old be-leathered Wild One incarnation.

Dad's home from six years' imprisonment for drunkenly totalling a crowded school bus with his truck, which sits as a macabre play-pen for Cindy (Manz) beyond the house. Mom (Sharon Farrell), a fast-food roadhouse waitress, has become a promiscuous, harassed junkie. Don Gordon is the slimy "uncle" in an unbearably intense triangle of sex, booze and high-pitched duplicitous emotional war. Cindy, a scarred-early teenage veteran of this family battlescape, takes out her muddlement on the CB airwaves and a bedroom drum-kit, or sucks her thumb. Five-foot-nothing of reactive aggression, and a regular truant from both home and know-nothing school, she could be the archetypal

Problem Child.

But psychologist Raymond Burr, for all the solve-it-all connotations he trails from his Perry Mason/Ironside past, gets only two scenes to prove his incomprehension and impotence in the face of Cindy's "disturbance".

Triggered into recall of mutually repressed nightmare memories (the real traumatic skeletons in this family closet) by her father, it is Cindy who has to come up with the answers — bleak, vicious and spectacularly final — that eventually (and all too shocking for some) tip the movie right out of the blue, into the black. Her self-styled "punk gesture" explosively and suicidally annihilates the family. Over the end credits and the aftermath of Cindy's mini-apocalypse, Neil Young baits us again that 'it's better to burn out than to fade away'. We can sing along with "Hey Hey My My, rock'n'roll will never die" and wonder . . .

Out of the Blue is a head-on, no-compromise assault, on its audience (sadly small, and definitely split) as much as on its sordidly faded cases from the Sixties and the lost generation they've spawned

and betrayed. While the adults are desperately trying to sustain the trippy irresponsibility of their counter-culture roots (turned to obscene parody in a neo-redneck milieu), the kid is stuck with dying heroes and nihilist sloganeering. It's an extremist vision, but controlled with a tautly-sprung, risky, non-exploitative intelligence and integrity. And not a little black irony. We see Dad's wipe-out of the school bus in an edgy, tone-setting prologue that jolts the film's hysteria into action with sharply violent surprise, yet when we spool forward to his release we discover his first job as rehabilitee to be driving a garbage-dump bulldozer!

Hopper's signature is all over the movie. The Method is pushed into the Eighties as the nervily "laid-back" tics of ageing hippies grate ceaselessly against the primary self-dramatising of Manz's remarkable Cindy, aping a distorted vision of her father as a prototype punk. Ensemble hysterics dominate the dialogue, while Hopper fragments the rushing, downward, downbeat spiral with bizarre backgrounds for Cindy's truant excursions, glorying self-amusedly in the rough edges of mock-*verité* street cinema. The performances are all superb, repelling cliché sympathies, and Manz is absolutely credible as a daughter of Hopper's. The resonant tensions between soundtrack and narrative are maintained with a rigour that suggests possible recompense for the loose equations Hopper had encouraged with his earlier ground-breaking *Easy Rider* compilation.

The strongest, strangest ironies, though, are that Hopper only ended up directing the film by accident, and that all this might well have turned into the stuff of the year's appalling generic equivalent, *Ordinary People*. *Out of the Blue* started out as a tax-sheltered Canadian project, dependent for advantageous financing

arrangements on the involvement of Canadian nationals in key positions on both sides of the camera. Then entitled *CeBe* (Cindy's nickname in the film), it was to have been the feature debut as director of Leonard Yakir, who had co-authored the script with his wife Brenda Nielson and was also co-producing what was in effect to be a routine family problem drama — a delinquent case history to be narrated omnisciently by Burr's psychologist. Hopper had simply taken the acting role as a favour to executive producer Paul Lewis, a long-time associate, and had been sitting out the first fortnight of shooting near Vancouver when he was first warily approached by the backers to look over two-and-a-half hours' worth of apparently unusable footage that Yakir had shot.

Hopper was under no illusions that he had been either first or unanimous choice to take over direction when Yakir was fired, but leapt at the first chance to direct since a vengeful Hollywood had buried his 1971

Venice Festival prize-winner *The Last Movie* without release, and virtually blackballed his chances of working since — hence the subsequent succession of exile acting roles and appearances for American mavericks.

It took him the one weekend available to rewrite, recast and relocate the picture. Some of the Canadian actors had walked off with Yakir, and Hopper brought in Don Gordon, who had appeared in *The Last Movie*. He also contacted Neil Young, who was willing to provide a complete, original soundtrack, but the backers ran scared on allowing too many of Hopper's "notorious" buddies into the project, and limited Young's contribution to the now-essential title track, despite the rocker's handy Canadian passport. A hectic schedule of four weeks and two days' shooting, and six weeks' editing, followed, including five days (at the producers' insistence) with Raymond Burr, still the nominal star, but in fact now almost superfluous to Hopper's requirements. The

narration, needless to say, went.

This troubled production history was still but the prelude to the real panic with the film, which originated in a farcical necessity to reassign "points" for the changed levels of Canadian participation in crewing and casting, and had the effect of leaving the movie in a literally stateless limbo by the time it was premiered at Cannes, when its cost was still in doubt because the tax loss financing system was being queried by the Canadian government. Though some European critical reaction was enthusiastic, the American majors predictably shied away from the combination of subject, treatment and the director's reputation. British distribution, through the independent company Cinegate, has been only sporadic since the movie's Edinburgh Film Festival showcase and London run, though directly attributable spin-offs to date include the promised unveiling of the hitherto hidden glories of *The Last Movie*, and the first ever

British exhibition of Hopper's still photographs (the products of a career that sustained the director through one of his two periods on the unofficial Hollywood "blacklist").

What it should prompt, of course, is suitable acclaim for a unique and totally original talent (of the sort guiltily gushed out and then abruptly denied the director of *Easy Rider*), in the form of the opportunity for Hopper to build on its abrasive vision with some sort of regularity. But, of course, it won't. Acting roles in Spain and Germany, and an ongoing collaboration on the long-gestating *Human Highway* film with Neil Young, Russ Tamblyn and Dean Stockwell, seem inadequate reward for a filmmaker whose work places the respectably Oscar-laden *Ordinary People* in an even more belittling perspective, and catches precisely the provocative punk ethos of its period in a way that mainstream efforts like *Foxes* or *Times Square* can only palely, punily mimic.
PAUL TAYLOR

MISSING

Like the snake observed swallowing its tail, Hollywood is so all-devouring it cares little whether its films are anti-Hollywood or even anti-American. If a film company can hustle a buck denouncing capitalism, that's what the free-enterprise system is all about. *Reds* and *Pennies from Heaven* offered strong critiques of the American way of life. Those were period films, however. *Missing*, set just nine years ago, offers the best picture this year of the snake gulping itself.

Missing shows Jack Lemmon going to Chile a few days after Pinochet's bloody 1973 coup. The Lemmon character is searching for one of the coup's innocent victims, his son. The plot of the film becomes Lemmon's lesson in the consequences of voting for Nixon: America got Watergate and the world got Kissingerism. The murder of the son of the Lemmon character was a matter of vast indifference to the front-line practitioners of realpolitik in the American Embassy in Santiago. In fact, the film alleges, they probably signed the young man's death warrant. Even more scandalous, Washington probably played the invisible puppet-master behind Pinochet himself.

The director and co-scriptwriter of *Missing*, the Greek-born French citizen Constantine Costa-Gavras, has been making political cinema since 1969. Costa-Gavras' *Z* explored the

Lambrakis Affair, a political murder which foreshadowed the Colonels' takeover in Greece. He went on to depict the Stalinist purges in Czechoslovakia in *The Confession* in 1970. *State of Siege* in 1972 showed a CIA man engineering political torture in Uruguay. *Special Section* in 1975 exposed the eagerness of French officials to cooperate with the Nazis in killing Jews in 1941.

That's not a likely background for employment at Universal Studios, a Hollywood production factory so commercially minded that it devotes unused sound stages to a tourist trap called "the Universal tour". It turns out that Universal thought

Missing was a warm, emotional account of a man's belated reconciliation with his son, who died tragically of leukemia, or in a car accident, or something like that. After all, there isn't a line in the film that specifically ties the events depicted in it to Chile. Costa-Gavras went along with the gag. He told me, "The political drama of *Missing* is only the background of the story. While the young man's father and son's widow (played by Sissy Spacek) are investigating the young man's disappearance, they aren't interested in the coup. They're interested only in their personal tragedy, not in the fate of the country".

Jack Lemmon, a political liberal but never one to shout from a soapbox, agrees that *Missing* isn't a "message" film. "It's a true story, and the man I play, Ed Horman, has become my friend. His emotions are the subject of the film, not his politics. That's why the film is a hit in America — because it's about people. Otherwise you might as well stand on a street corner distributing leaflets."

The gaff was blown three days before the film's release in America last February. The American Secretary of State, "Excitable Al" Haig, issued a

three-page denunciation of the film. Point by point, Haig and Co. contested the film's allegations. No, America didn't connive in Horman Junior's death. No, America didn't obstruct Horman Senior's efforts to find out what happened. And no, America didn't engineer the coup in which at least 20,000 civilians died. Lemmon, who seems at 57 more effective now when he's not seeking laughs, skilfully shows Horman's transformation from staunch Republican through half a dozen gradations of doubt to implacable opposition to the United States government's actions. Costa-Gavras, as in *Z*, has succeeded in encapsulating a nation's politics in the dilemma of a single man. In semi-documentary style, the film seems literally snatched from among fast-moving events. The most memorable shot in the film — a white horse racing through the darkened streets with a truckload of troops in trigger-happy pursuit — is such a powerful symbol of the coup's haphazard violence because it appears to be something that just ran into a lucky cameraman's viewfinder. Costa-Gavras uses *Panorama's* techniques to make an agitprop point, rivetting even the politically apathetic.

The State Department couched its rebuttal in unassailable legalisms like, "There is no evidence that..." Costa-Gavras was forced to admit that the film is a conjecture, not the literal, provable, exact documentary truth. Based on a book written by Thomas Hansen (*The Execution of Charles Horman*), the film tells the truth as Ed Horman saw it. If America killed his son while toppling the socialist Allende government, and if America isn't prepared to admit it yet, then obviously there will be "no evidence" to that effect, the director pointed out.

Lemmon, too, comes heatedly to the defence of the film: "I'm not really a political animal. I'm a middle-of-the-road liberal. But I would stake my children's lives on the truth of the allegations in the film. Yet the allegations can never be proved because the American government will never release the documents that could prove it. The State Department says it gave Horman hundreds of documents relating to his son's death. What the State Department didn't say is that it also refused to give up hundreds of other documents — the ones that would have proved Horman's point".

The State Department's response to *Missing* is a testimony to the power of the cinema. The American government hadn't even bothered to comment when the book was published in 1978. The government's response to Horman's 1977 lawsuit had been equally low-key: delay, deny, delay, deny. Eventually, just before filming started, the lawsuit was withdrawn by Horman. "Once there was a firm start-date for the film, the suit had to be withdrawn," Lemmon explains. "It's such an accusatory film that any judge would have ruled the suit out of order."

The $9.5 million film was shot in Mexico, accompanied by a total absence of the usual on-location hoopla. There were no studio press releases and no junkets for journalists to kiss the stars' rings. In the trade papers' listing of films in

production, *Missing* was referred to mystifyingly as "An Untitled Story", Lemmon and Spacek as stars sounded like an odd couple indeed.

It was Costa-Gavras who had nixed the customary pre-release hype. "I made *Missing* exactly the same way I have made all my films — either I make the film entirely without interference, or I don't make the film." In 1972 Costa-Gavras had been offered the chance to direct *The Godfather* but Paramount wouldn't allow him to show Brando and Pacino as drug-dealers. In 1979, Costa-Gavras was on the verge of starting to film Andre Malraux's *Man's Fate* in Shanghai, but he cancelled the project when the Chinese government wanted him to soften even further the book's already highly sympathetic view of the Communist Party.

Costa-Gavras demands total independence because he suffered the mutilation of his second film, *One Man Too Many*, in 1967 at the hands of the US distributor. "Since then, I have never left the final cut to others. Also, I have never taken orders on casting — making the bad guys sweating and fat or evil Jack Palance types." One of the most convincing aspects of *Missing* is its depiction of middle- and low-level American diplomats. Smooth, bland and far from stupid, they perform their duties

without a qualm, as if they were stamping passports.

Costa-Gavras' own politics are anybody's guess. He has remained credible as the West's foremost maker of political cinema because his films, taken as a whole, jerk no knees in favour of either Right or Left. He seems to be broadly sympathetic to socialism, but if the Communists came to power his head would probably be among the first to fall into the basket.

He is drawn to political subjects, he says, "because politics is the mixture of people and power. Politics is not just what politicians do. My

ancestors used to go out into the agora, the marketplace, and speak of politics. For Greeks, personal life is always inextricably linked to political life".

In America, political life is generally limited to election-time mutterings of "A plague on both your houses". Costa-Gavras says, "All of our culture pushes us to just accept what we have been told. Information about America's involvement in the Chilean coup was easy for most Americans to resist. Some people also reject this movie for that reason. Others, I hope, see the movie and go home and read about the events in El Salvador and Poland in a new way". Slyly, Costa-Gavras extends Ronald Reagan's philosophy of international politics: "Let Poland be Poland. Let Chile be Chile. Let El Salvador be El Salvador. I believe in freedom. We all speak of freedom, but sometimes we mean only our own freedom. I feel we should respect others' freedom as much as our own".

As for the Haigists who said of *Missing* that, "Oh, it's a bunch of Commies making an anti-American movie," Costa-Gavras argues, "I don't think it's an anti-American movie. It's anti- a small part of American policy. It attacks a way of thinking — that because we have seen what Communism has done to people in Russia, we should accept any kind of repression. It attacks the idea that we should accept repression even worse than in Poland now, where at least very few have been killed so far, in order to avoid Communism."
BART MILLS

BLOW OUT

Brian De Palma's *Blow Out* is the most eccentric successful film anyone has made recently, not because its subject or approach are particularly odd, but because all of the movie's achievements are made in spite of itself. *Blow Out* is a picture with almost everything going against it: an adult thriller in the midst of a vogue for adolescent fantasy; a star (John Travolta) cast radically against type, with dialogue that's never more than serviceable; a typically derivative De Palma script (an aurally-oriented remake of *Blow Up* with Watergate overtones); a score that's maudlin, obvious and annoying.

Despite all of this, *Blow Out* works — not all of it, and not always, but often enough to make De Palma's underlying vision compelling. For all of its flaws (and sometimes, because of them), *Blow Out* is a tribute to the richness of Brian De Palma's visual imagination.

Of course, Hollywood will never see it that way. *Blow Out* cost about $18 million — more than twice as much as any other De Palma film, and it grossed only about half that much. It's the kind of failure that especially hurts a director like De Palma, who is an outsider (and almost a renegade) because he lives and works on the East Coast, and prefers elevating trashiness to the level of art to fiddling with tony, respectable subjects.

But there's another side to

this issue. De Palma makes pop movies — big, colourful, narrative films which seek wide audiences. So *Blow Out* needs big grosses to justify its ambitions — cinematic, social and political. De Palma is most obviously compared with his erstwhile, New York-based, Italian-American sidekick, Martin Scorsese, but he would never be as comfortable working as marginally as Scorsese always has. The difference between *Blow Out* and *Raging Bull* isn't just the difference between film-makers who get caught in their pilfering and those who escape such judgement (since Scorsese owes as much or more to Rossellini and the neo-realists as De Palma does to Antonioni and Hitchcock), but between a film which actively pursues some sort of dialogue with an audience and a movie which lives in such a narrow world that it becomes self-referential.

The least that can be said for *Blow Out* is that it ceaselessly reaches out to involve us in its attempt to divine the difference between art and paranoia and reality. And one of its attractions is that, while it comes to no conclusions about where the boundaries between those qualities finally are drawn, it insists upon the importance of creating some maps. In the end, *Blow Out* is about a world in which such distinctions have collapsed (or been exploded), about what it means for the game to be rigged against common

decency. It is a theme to which De Palma has returned before — in *Phantom of the Paradise, Carrie, The Fury, Home Movies*, in all of which the protagonists are undone by their unwillingness to believe exactly how depraved the rest of the world has become.

Jack Terry (Travolta) is a sound technician for the kind of sleazy horror film that uses its thin plot as an excuse for shots of unclad coeds — a

genre convention De Palma perfected in *Carrie*, and which he satirises in *Blow Out*'s opening sequence.

Jack Terry is a kind of Hawksian figure — or as close as we're liable to come to one these days — who is not so much immersed in his job, which is clearly demeaning, as captivated by the work itself, its subtleties and disciplines. In one of the film's most effective set pieces, De Palma lingers on the minutiae of Jack's recordings and equipment — the spools of tape, the recorders themselves, the splicing decks, the microphones — and we see Jack out on location, taping various noises (cars hissing by in the rain, water sloshing under a bridge, an owl hooting, a couple whispering lovers' small talk in the night), later cutting off sections of the tape, labelling and storing them. Always fascinated by technology, De Palma seems especially engrossed this time, perhaps because Jack's tools are the equipment of a voyeur, that shadowy figure who

always dominates in his movies.

Voyeurism is such an obvious metaphor for the film-maker's trade that it seems corny to dwell on it. But no-one (save perhaps Michael Powell) has operated nearly so productively from this pathological perspective. *Home Movies*, De Palma's experimental sex farce of 1980, is the most personal version of this voyeuristic obsession, a

spurious biography, not only for its protagonist but for De Palma himself, who based the story on his own family. In *Dressed to Kill*, the theme takes a more social twist, though one which remains rooted in individual pathology, suggesting the devastating energies lurking behind the outwardly calm and objective eye of the spy.

Blow Out tackles voyeurism at the outer limit, creating (or exposing) an entire world in which everyone is either a voyeur or a victim. De Palma gives us not only Travolta, the tape-recording eavesdropper, but Nancy Allen's Sally and Dennis Franz's Manny Karp, who snoop for divorce evidence, and John Lithgow's Burke, the fanatically paranoid secret-agent-cum-hitman. Each of these characters, around whom the whole film revolves, is in turn spied upon (or, at least, Burke suspects he might be, which is why he uses pay phones). Meanwhile, civilians and police march innocently onward, refusing to

acknowledge the dimensions of the conspiracy, celebrating a land of freedom and opportunity while Burke and his bosses cheat them of those very things, distracted by gaudy fireworks displays while genuine life-and-death struggles take place just above their heads.

This is a genuinely radical (and far from inaccurate) portrait of American society. If De Palma's story were stronger, or if he did not take such delight in his visual inventiveness that the narrative is sometimes abandoned, he might have created a political masterpiece, a movie which perfectly summarised his nation and its illusions and discontents. As it is, his meanings have to be sifted out from his own distractions, and the substance of what he is trying to say remains not just oblique but in many ways opaque.

What sustains the film, then, is what is beyond plot: the fine performances De Palma draws from Travolta (in his first genuinely adult role), Allen, Franz and Lithgow; the extraordinary exterior night-time cinematography of Vilmos Zsigmond; and De Palma's own series of set pieces, from the pre-credit horror movie in-joke to the climactic chase through the Philadelphia streets. At the same time that these undermine the narrative flow of *Blow Out*, they are also what turn it into such a vivid, memorable and impressively confident piece of work.

It's silly to argue that De Palma's set pieces — no matter how dazzling — justify his narrative weaknesses; his ambitions preclude any justification for his liabilities as a story-teller. On the other hand, the set pieces themselves work as a kind of subplot: it's easy to imagine that Burke's random, Son-of-Sam-style

killing of prostitutes was included simply to give De Palma the opportunity to film the elaborate tracking and slaying of his first victim. It's obvious, again, that the scene in which Travolta describes his catastrophic career as a police technician is included precisely so that De Palma can steal a march on the most graphic incident in *Prince of the City*, a film he felt cheated out of directing. (And De Palma renders this scene so much more effectively than Sidney Lumet, that comparing the two is probably worth a semester of film school.)

More importantly, De Palma nails his point down best with a pair of plot-connected set pieces. In the first, Jack Terry returns to his studio to find all

of his tapes erased; as he checks out one reel after another, the camera swoops above, sweeping the room in consecutive 360 degree pans as this confirmation of conspiracy sinks in, and also in emulation of the whirling of the tapes themselves. Again, De Palma has entered the delirium of the voyeur, but this time with an added degree of complicity. If the illusion of voyeurism is that it grants distance from emotional involvement, its most sobering reality is its final induction of the voyeur into psychic responsibility for what he observes.

This theme recurs in the scene in which Sally and Manny confront one another, and their parts in the conspiracy, in Manny's squalid hotel room. Manny's fumbling, futile attempt at seduction, Sally's brutal awakening, the sordidness of the environment are brought home in our final view of them, huddled helplessly on the bed, again witnessed from far above them. Yet what one feels (and what one is meant to feel) is not sardonic aloofness but compassion.

In these scenes, demonstrating the vulnerability of his characters without flinching, De Palma reveals his compassion without irony or

condescension. Though he always maintains a hard-boiled exterior, and must continually distance himself by means of comedy and gross gore from his poor fools, ultimately De Palma identifies himself (and us) with them.

In the end, then, it is pointless merely to celebrate De Palma the master cinema technician. Doubtless, he has a more painterly vision than any of his American contemporaries. But without this deeply rooted compassion, his visual genius wouldn't mean much. In the end, it is because De Palma feels so deeply for his characters that he so carefully burnishes the armour of his technique, and it is because he is so relentlessly honest in his dealings with them that he must show us their (and our) most sordid, gruesome and abject qualities.

Blow Out's final, most sickening joke is that even such carefully nurtured lives may ultimately be meaningless or trivial, reduced to nothing more than a whimper or a scream. Yet even this may be preserved: it's what keeps Jack Terry (and maybe Brian De Palma) going. And it is in keeping this part of our lives, however mean and ugly, that *Blow Out* transcends itself. Like all of Brian De Palma's films, it has soul. DAVE MARSH

VIOLENT STREETS

There is hardly anything natural in *Violent Streets*. Eight or nine times in the movie, a small red electronic blip appears, endlessly cycling across a scope. It can usually be glimpsed on a walky-talky fitted in James Caan's top right-hand breast pocket, but can also be seen in a police tail car, and on the hi-fi system in Caan's new suburban home. The device does not seem to have any particular significance; it is more like a simple shorthand signature, taking its place alongside all the many other pieces of equipment which glitter on the movie's surface. For Caan operates in the pure white heat of contemporary urban life. His city has become a kind of mechanical netherworld through which he travels on a passport which is a combination of technical skill and hard-won integrity. His skill is certainly never in doubt.

The ten-minute speechless opening sequence is a robbery (cf the long silent robbery sequence in *Rififi*), played out to the sound of Tangerine Dream's nerveless score and the whine of vault-cutting machinery. Clothed in blue overalls, rendered anonymous by goggles and gloves, Caan has temporarily become a robot, a mechanical extension of the complex tools that he is using. Repeated cutaway shots to the magnetic drill slicing through the safe suggest not only the visually abstract nature of urban life, but also the extreme skill required to navigate the complexity of modern high technology.

The theme of dehumanisation even extends to the "placing" of Willie Nelson, ostensibly the most humane of the movie's characters. The natural warmth of Nelson's own persona, is undercut by his being placed in positions where he is hampered by inhuman mechanisms. The first time, he is behind the screen of a prison visiting room; the second time, he is hooked up to a life support system in hospital. His second and last speech is not even heard, but whispered to Caan who later repeats it.

Caan himself is prey to the same process; he deals in used cars (dead pieces of machinery) as a front for his "magic act". The local mafia use an electro-plating company as a front and also as a convenient way of disposing of dead bodies. Even the child that Caan and Weld take on is acquired through the mafia, rather than born to them. The whole city has been reduced to a series of Mondrian-like pure colour abstractions. There are hardly any horizon shots in the film, the camera frequently being tilted down to avoid the skyline. Neon blue and green reflect from the rain-slicked sidewalks, from the smelting yards, from the freeways and used car lots that dominate the film's scenery. Everywhere in these violent streets, nature has been excluded, life has become dehumanised and made subordinate to the sovereignty of machinery. *Violent Streets* may well be the first high-tech movie.

Running counter to this extreme process of dehumanisation however, is Caan's well-defined existential stance. "I'm a thief," he shouts at Weld, with a defiance partly born out of the fact that she has never bothered to ask him what he does. "I wear 150 dollar slacks. I wear silk shirts. I wear 800 dollar suits. I change cars like other guys change shoes... I'm a thief." This is less a confession than an existential declaration and it stands at the very heart of the movie (US title: *Thief*), coming as it does just before the central 15-minute dialogue between Caan and Weld in the coffee shop above a freeway.

In this sequence of sustained intensity, Caan relates how he reached the bottom line of existence in prison. Having taken on the king rat of the jail (the darkly named Captain Morphus) and half killed him, he hits the yard the next day knowing that he's a dead man; but nothing happens. He has reached that dangerous point, recognised by the other cons, of not caring any more about life or death, a point where "nothing means nothing". It is from this base of nihilism that he builds his life, most graphically on a postcard built up as a montage of pictures cut from magazines. This sense of having reached a personal point of no return, is underscored by perhaps the warmest shot of the film, that of Weld reaching across the table to clasp his hand.

It is only later that his choice to opt for dependence on a family and family life turns out to have been a fatal error. And it is significant that his two wrong moves — his attachment to Weld and his agreement to work for the local mafia chief, Leo — should follow on from one another in strict sequence, not logically connected perhaps, but juxtaposed as if betrayal invoked a logical sequence of error.

To underline just how pure is this film's concern with the absolute limit of individual integrity, it is worth looking at what the movie has left out, rather than put in. There are no scenes of everyday "straight" life, with which to compare the characters' life of illegitimacy. As in Mann's first film *The Jericho Mile*, which took place completely

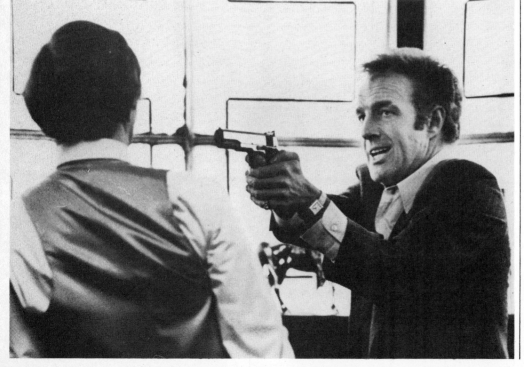

inside Folsom jail, the subterranean milieu has become a microcosm of life itself; not a place to compare with the "normal" world, but the whole world itself. The dilemmas of any individual, facing up to the corporate nightmare of any large organisation, are exactly these, the movie is saying, despite the criminal setting.

Nor is the film concerned with the traditional chase or detection themes of the thriller genre. The sole appearance of the police is to underline Caan's attitude toward co-operation with them (or with anyone). They want their cut of his take; his personal code forbids such compromise, such invasion of his privacy, They beat him half to death; he still won't budge. And when they stake him out with two tail cars and electronic surveillance gear, it is his superior savvy and technical skill which successfully ditches them, never to be seen again. Just as "straight" life is absent from the film, so too are traditional police procedures.

What is centrally, defiantly, *there*, is Caan's sheer expertise, and nowhere is it more forcefully presented as in the film's other long sequence: some 20 minutes of drilling his way through to an apparently impregnable bank safe. After cutting his way through the roof of the building and down a lift shaft, by-passing six different alarm systems, he then tackles the vault with a huge thermal lance. With a dark filter on the camera lens to offset the white heat of the cutting sparks, and the roar of melting metal, the whole scene takes on an infernal aspect, grating on the nerves and physically exhausting. When it is finally over, the camera rests on Caan for a single quiet moment, as he sits back, removes his welding mask, and lights a cigarette. One can taste the relief.

The following jump cut to Caan and Weld swimming in the Pacific looks like a signal for the end of the film, but is in fact a false suggestion. Caan has yet to collect his money. Leo returns only part of it, having hived off the rest into local business ventures, in an attempt to incorporate Caan into the mafia's family (it is ironic that Leo sometimes refers to Caan as "Sonny", not only suggesting his own father figure image, but harking back to Caan's role as Sonny Corleone in *The Godfather*). Caan realises that he has

reached that irreversible nadir again. He dissolves his family by sending Weld and the child away with his getaway driver, then methodically destroys the structure of his present life, blowing up his home and his regular haunt the "Green Mill" Bar, setting fire to his used car park lot and even discarding his encoded life-picture-postcard in the gutter. This dismissal of all his possessions, in an equivalent of a viking's funeral, looks less suicidal than something like an arrival, once more, at the point where "nothing means nothing". So extreme is this mood of nihilism, that his

arrival at Leo's with a gun carries no intimation of success or failure. Whether Caan will end dead or alive is not only impossible to predict but also somehow irrelevant.

In a movie as good as this, it seems churlish to suggest that the ending is not good enough, but its failure seems to be as much technical as anything else. The use of slow motion violence raises unwelcome, outdated comparisons with Peckinpah, and seems impelled less by a clearcut design than by a lack of invention. One cutaway shot to Leo finding his gun in a drawer and hiding behind the

corner is a serious mistake, destroying the suspense by revealing too much, and breaking the tension of the sequence.

And the final crane shot, through the leaves of a tree, of a wounded Caan limping away down the pavement, leaves an uncertain mixture of reactions, less relief at his survival or triumph at his victory, more like a certain bewilderment at what he now faces — the banal conclusion of a walk through the suburbs. A man who has already walked through hell deserves rather better.
CHRIS PEACHMENT

THEY ALL LAUGHED

In Peter Bogdanovich's new film, *They All Laughed*, every shot has a beauty of its own, not in the pictorial sense but in terms of its functional meaning. Made for the now defunct feature film division of Time-Life, the film suffered from a lack of enthusiasm on the part of its American distributor, 20th Century Fox, and might never have been theatrically released in the US if Bogdanovich had not undertaken to buy the film back, risking his own money. Bogdanovich's own company, Moon Pictures, self-distributed to good notices and initial business, but such a small company was unable to compete with other Christmas releases, so the film has now been licensed to UA Classics, with UK rights going to the Rank Organisation. It will open in London "in due course," they say.

They All Laughed is certainly, to my mind, the Best Film of the Year, but it's more important that, even though it's obviously a film towards which Bogdanovich has been working all his career as a director, in a way it might be called his first film as a major artist, notwithstanding *The Last Picture Show*, *What's Up, Doc?*, *Paper Moon* and *Targets*. It not only synthesizes the various strands of his work to date, but it also represents an advance into a thematic and emotional richness that he hitherto had only hinted at, and then skirted. In *Daisy Miller*, a

courageous film, he had confronted his own coldness. In *They All Laughed*, nothing separates him from the characters he loves with infectious generosity but without indulgence.

It helps that the three central male characters are likely all projections of various of Bogdanovich's self-images, and that three central female characters each embody distinctive traits he admires in women (significantly post-Hawksian). Working out of deep identification and love can be a salutary enterprise for an artist. The elaborate farcical developments are never mechanical, however artificial, when each wrinkle represents a further advance in the artist's investigation of his own feelings, toward himself and others.

The film merits consideration with the best of Lubitsch, Renoir or Sturges, with which it shares strategies and attributes. It must be strongly emphasized though that in no sense can *They All Laughed* be regarded as a derivative work, as could *What's Up, Doc?* despite its formidable accomplishment. Indeed, the film seems to me the most original and expressive work in the American cinema since '*10*' and *Dawn of the Dead*, and with Spielberg's *E.T.*, the first glimpse at an expression of the *zeitgeist* of the Eighties.

The movie's essential subject is the way people play today, marking it as a romp with serious business on its mind. It could be called a more-than-doubled quadrille, as five men and five women pursue one another, each in his fashion. The original title for *At Long Last Love* had been *Quadrille*, and the current film achieves everything at which that unjustly maligned, ambitious work failed.

Ben Gazzara, John Ritter and Blaine Novak are three easy-going private detectives working for George Morfogen's agency in Manhattan. Throughout the film they become romantically entangled with the women

they are assigned to follow. Though no one seems to take their professional responsibilities seriously, in fact the conflict between those duties and their passions (however deep or fleeting) animates most of the action.

Bogdanovich's screenplay deftly juggles relationships and complications with consummate ease, but little of the film's profundity derives from the literary material. Instead, *They All Laughed* accomplishes its storytelling by predominantly visual means, conveying depth of emotion not by dialogue or situation so much as through the visual elaboration of character and feeling. The architecture of the movie mirrors the new Manhattan it celebrates: supple, modern, functional, dedicated to both high ideals and private ends.

The movie opens with a jarring contrast, as country and western music is heard over skyscraper vistas. Cabby Patti Hansen is driving a nervous Morfogen to a rendezvous with a helicopter on the waterfront. Hansen, a model, gives a remarkably fresh, laconic, sexy performance, but Bogdanovich does more than elicit attractive, natural qualities from her. Like Hawks, his framing decisively creates the context for the characterisation. Throughout, he identifies certain compositions with each role. The framing tends to be strong around Hansen: she knows who she is, and she doesn't change during the movie.

The introductory scene at the dock provides a masterful example of analytic cutting typical of the entire film, in which every character seems to be watching everyone else and in which relationships are suggested which are not as yet defined. We wonder who Gazzara is, as he eyes Morfogen, the arrivals by air, and even Hansen with a sinister insouciance.

When Gazzara turns away from the scene, Bogdanovich uses a shot that he will repeat many times, but only with Gazzara. He has the actor walk towards the lens slightly and then rolls the camera out in a panning motion as Gazzara leaves the frame. I wish there were a single technical word to describe this kind of shot, which isn't particularly novel in itself, although Bogdanovich has found incredibly resonant ways of using it. It tends to resolve the energy that has been accumulating during the intense cutting preceding it and to associate that resolution with Gazzara. It establishes Gazzara not only as a potential balance for the frenetic passions racing around the plot but also as a visual loner, causing the audience to identify with him as a man of private feelings and also to set him apart from the action.

Gazzara gets picked up by Hansen and they banter in self-consciously neo-Hawksian style until he asks to be let off to join his two small daughters. Walking with his kids (played by Bogdanovich's own children), Gazzara achieves a certain continuity that will be permitted only rarely in this film: the camera trucks along with them, cutting only when the shot necessitates it. The long, extended movements continue until Gazzara ends their conversation, when Bogdanovich once again employs the rolling pan shot that is already beginning to accumulate definite emotional force.

The film's focus then shifts to Ritter and Novak, who are

tailing the appealingly attractive Dorothy Stratten at the behest of her jealous husband. Ritter is unabashedly smitten by his quarry and himself jealous of any prospective boyfriend she may have found. His quandary juxtaposes sexual desire and personal independence, a central conflict that will be elaborated in many ways. Meanwhile, Gazzara stops off at a country and western music bar to see a long-term girl friend, rising singing star Colleen Camp (in a daring, courageously self-effacing performance), who berates him with a slough of perfectly reasonable canned homilies about commitment and her demands for that kind of consideration, which are deftly parried by Gazzara without being genuinely responsive. From this scene, Bogdanovich cuts to Ritter pursuing Stratten on roller skates at a fashionable rink. Ritter, like Gazzara, is also trying to avoid a confrontation, but unlike Gazzara, he is in conflict, wanting to make contact with his blonde venus.

By this point, the contrasts between the three detectives have been established. Ritter is bumbling, physically clumsy, moony, idealistic, engaged. Novak is hip, smooth, confident, rapacious. Gazzara is disengaged, cool, professional, vulnerable but self-contained. (It's lucky they're all friends.) In this context, the myriad ways in which the characters "meet cute" becomes an expression of profound contact. *They All Laughed* takes the form of a dating movie in which relationships are struck for whatever short-term heat they can generate. Significantly, although spouses, ex- and otherwise, figure prominently throughout, none of them appears more than glancingly; they are generally viewed in long shot, talked about in absentia, or only heard over the telephone. Marriage is banished from the arena, and the movie suggests that such exclusion may be a necessary corollary to the possibilities for romance remaining in our time.

They All Laughed purveys the new morality without judgments: the philosophical challenge posed is how it can be a morality at all without making judgments? Bogdanovich only makes tentative stabs at this core issue. Part of his answer

involves a needed solicitude for the feelings of others, including an honesty about one's own. The only characters who are deceived in the film are those who, as Gazzara acerbically observes, suspect others of the transgressions they themselves commit.

The truth seems to lie in the pursuit of genuinely felt impulses, which often requires an agile balancing act, morally and logistically. From this perspective, it might be possible to call *They All Laughed* a profoundly immature film, except that it has the courage to plumb the implications of its despairing prognosis for deep relationships and weigh

what's gained against what's lost. It also exhibits such a heartfelt appreciation for the grace required to live one's life on the edge between hedonism and responsibility that one must grant the complexity of Bogdanovich's vision even as one can question the ultimate consequences of his position.

Ritter's obsessive crush on Stratten plays pointedly like a parody version of *Vertigo*, just as some of the shots observing Stratten and husband through their apartment window recall *Rear Window*. These are not just in-joke references: the invocation of themes from these films bears direct relevance to the development of this movie's themes. Bogdanovich uses

Hitchcockian angles throughout: when Stratten discovers Ritter staked outside her flat, or when Ritter is seen from overhead as he races into the courthouse, having lost Stratten. This may be the first Hitchcockian farce since the Master's own *Mr. and Mrs. Smith* (1941), which had its share of curious angles (I exempt *The Trouble With Harry*, which seems more of a Shakespearean pastoral).

Bogdanovich also adopts a Hitchcockian attitude towards his use of kisses as revealing the nature of a relationship. In a key love scene between Gazzara and Audrey Hepburn, Bogdanovich cuts to a reverse angle at the instant of the kiss, presaging the inevitable interruption of the connection between them. For that matter, when Ritter and Stratten first kiss, you expect that this time Bogdanovich will not cut. To our dismay, he does, suddenly, though only to a set-up slightly to one side, suggesting that he understands the Ritter-Stratten love in the same realistic terms that Gazzara would, choosing to permit them their moment without any endorsement of their future. It's worth noting that Gazzara and Hepburn are accorded the privileged space of a long love scene without a cut or even the disruption of a moving camera (after a pan down to them to the strains of Sinatra singing 'These Foolish

Things'!). One senses throughout that Bogdanovich is making careful distinctions between the many sorts of romantic involvement possible to people who have forsaken any faith in the possibility of commitment. All feeling must be evanescent, because passion contains the seeds of its own inevitable loss.

The final scene, which formally mirrors the first, once again has Gazzara walking out of the frame, even as Hepburn flies off, trapped inside the helicopter as it makes its way back towards the skyline. Bogdanovich provides him with the consolation of a good drink with a sympathetic redhead, suggesting that for all the magnitude of personal loss he just suffered, every heartbreak must be accounted part of the accumulated pain of daily living. In other hands, it might have been a flip ending; for Bogdanovich, its stoicism has the tone of sincere gravity, not posture. *They All Laughed* may not expect too much of emotions, but it treasures every one of them to the full.

For all its underlying seriousness, *They All Laughed* proves that great slapstick needn't be stupid, although only Blake Edwards and Bogdanovich seem to understand that anymore. I think it breaks new ground as both art and entertainment.
MYRON MEISEL

BODY HEAT

Time magazine's Richard Corliss definitively captured the essence of *Body Heat's* crystallisation of *film noir* when he began his review: "It is 1946; it is 1981."

Eight months later, when discussing the arrival of a new French firebrand with *Diva*, Corliss said rather more about the stylish Lawrence Kasdan than Jean-Jacques Beinex did during a ten-point guide to style and flair in film making. Style, ran the coda, seems simple, insinuates, is witty and advances a story. Flair looks facile, asserts, is clever and replaces a story.

Corliss, who knows cinema and Kasdan well, left out the perhaps overly obvious

beyond the superficially obvious (Cain, Chandler, Hammett, Aldrich) to sift through Godard, Fuller, Spillane and Robert Towne, more than Polanski, for *Chinatown*, in a masterly mélange that bows to all without interrupting the shimmering flow of educated originality.

Body Heat simply sizzles with story, settings, sets and setpieces, topped by a novitiate writer-director in total control of subject, forever shifting camera and scenario, actors and above all himself. He allows himself one self-indulgent moment, the rather heavy-handed symbolism of the clown driving a red car

have known it all first time around. *Indemnity* is just one of the varying antecedents *Body Heat* touched upon, embraced here and there, then left alone to get on with the job. However, as it is so close to Cain in murderous action, suspenseful excitement, final retribution and, assuredly, eroticism (and such assured eroticism for Hollywood), Kasdan made the kind of movie one had the right to expect from Rafelson with *The Postman Always Rings Twice*.

There comes a point in any film-maker's life (their stars', too) when they're blown away by the whole Hollywood crap-shoot. That battle fatigue was wholly evident in *Postman* (apart from the still revved-up Jessica Lange). Kasdan's film instead, was fresh and refreshing. Lively and alive.

"I wanted this film to have the intricate structure of a dream," Kasdan has stated, "the density of a good novel and the texture of recognisable people in extraordinary circumstances." That's Hitchcockian without being Hitchcock. Kasdan sets his ball rolling with sparkling dialogue that deserves audience participation far more than the *Rocky* (or *Mommie Dearest*) horror shows. You know the passages. If you don't, they'll be in every tome of Hollywood quotes from hereon. They begin with William Hurt's first meeting with Kathleen Turner.
She: You're not so smart. I like that in a man.
He: What else do you like? Lazy. Ugly. Horny. I got them all.
She: You don't look lazy. Second meeting.
He: You shouldn't dress like that.
She: This is a blouse and a skirt. I don't know what you're talking about.
He: You shouldn't wear that body.
She: My temperature runs a couple of degrees higher than normal. About a hundred. I don't mind. I guess it's the engine or something. Runs a little fast.
He: Maybe you need a tune-up.

She: Don't tell me — you've got just the right tool.
He: I don't talk like that. Third meeting; second trysting.
He: I like this place. It's got a nice feel.
She: You were on top.

It's part Tracy and Hepburn, part Bogie and Bacall, and all Kasdan who admits he is working on returning to the cinema that which he has been missing. Language. "*Noir* was rich in it. The dialogue crackles. It has bite," he told David Chute. His double-entendres work more than both ways. Most of her lines are keys to the drama, as well as the foreplay. She doesn't like smart men, she has to be on top. As mother told her, knowledge is power. She found her most powerful knowledge for herself. "Some men when they get a whiff of it, follow you like a hound. Most men are like little boys."

William Hurt's Ned Racine is no match for her considerable wiles. Racine is a two-bit lawyer; incompetence is his winning ploy in court. He doesn't *look* a loser. But this *is* America 1981 where rotten lawyers can live well. He is little boyish enough to screw around with air stewardesses, nurses, meter-maids, who appear to pick up their chat, like him (or from him) in pulp fiction. He sees his own history burning up on the horizon of the opening shot (his use of the expression "torched" about this fire sets us, early on, in 1981 not 1946). Apart from his stud appeal, he doesn't know which way is up anymore.

He's ripe as the sucker required by Kathleen Turner's Matty Walker, a cat on a hot thin hoof, who aims to be rich and live in an exotic land. She (seemingly) chances upon him as the 1981 crowd sit back to a big band swinging through 'That Old Feeling' and cueing that old, biting repartee. Matty is "well-tended". Racine needs tending. She arouses him easily with her spilt ice-cream — "you don't want to lick it off?" — and vanishes into the steamy night. As Racine's black cop pal later imparts,

summation. Style says, I can. Flair yells, I could . . . I'm sure.

Even without his scripts for the runaway mega-hits of the Lucasfilm faculty in Marin County, Lawrence Kasdan, at 33, is (like *Body Heat*) the Hollywood highspot of the year under review. While his first film as a director is not quite worthy of David Chute's award as "perhaps the most stunning debut movie ever", it is clearly the complete movie-brat's work, including Coppola's. In both super script and finished film (the two don't always match), it is influenced by the mass of conscious and unconscious flotsam and jetsam of a film buff's mental archives. These linear connections range

past William Hurt as he swops his murder-plan rental-car for his own red convertible.

On first viewing, the film is well nigh perfect: deft, polished, honed, together, co-ordinated and, as the saying goes about good rock, tight. Apart from that clown, every scene, every word is vital to the developing jigsaw. On second and third viewings, months apart, the opening two-thirds of the ritualistic three acts (plus pro and epilogues) held up extraordinarily well. If the climax was weaker, it was simply a matter of familiarity with the twist in the tale. Had *Body Heat* been, as some critics dismissively tagged it, just an uncredited re-tread of *Double Indemnity*, we would

when it gets hot on the Florida gold coast, people try to kill each other; "everything is just a little askew".

The trap is set; between her legs. The bait is hooked; same place. The affair is molten, mercurial, *Tango*-ish. All limbs and limbo. Sure enough, it is the lawyer who says, he thinks without being harried, that they'll kill Matty's husband. He, who "only comes up at weekends". There's a lot of penile thrust to Kasdan's dialogue. This suits Racine's image as a bit of a prick in search of a condom. "I know sometimes the shit comes down so heavy, I should wear a hat." Matty gives him one as a present in one of many cross-weave shots. Cut! And hubby arrives with a present for her, their niece; part of the shit, and the ultimate penile gag, coming down on Ned. He later tells his buddies that Matty might well fuck him to death. Just as hubby, seduced into prolonged sex to stop him wandering around the house before his killer comes, grasps for time out and asks Matty,

"You trying to kill me?"

If Kasdan won all the praise, he deserves it for his visuals and orals, plus an adept selection of cast and crew. None is wasted, like his text. Richard H. Kline's atmospheric camera, Bill Kenney's production design and John Barry's score are all lush, without being plush. Actors include Ted Danson, from the under-rated *Onion Field*, as the dancing toed and

fingered assistant-DA; J.A. Preston, a new black face, as the cop who couldn't leave things alone. And the two notables: Mickey Rourke's street, explosive and rock-wise Bowery Boy of 1981 and Kathleen Turner's sinous Matty. She has more in common with *Bad Timing's* Theresa Russell (or the everlastingly wasted Michelle Phillips) than the overdone, inevitable *film noir*

comparison with Bacall.

There was also a hint of an in-joke in Richard Crenna playing the hubby. He played the adulterer-killer in the last tele-rehash of *Double Indemnity* in 1973. That was four years before Michigan University's Larry Kasdan sold his first script, *Continental Divide*... He has since written *Star Wars III* (*Revenge of the Jedi*), is part connected with the sequel to *Raiders of the Lost Ark*. From then on, as *Body Heat* signals, he's on his own.

Despite all the *noir* nuances, this is Kasdan's first wholly original. Aside from some jokey visual references to Hurt's two other films, there is, for example, no repetition of scenes as in *Raiders* and *Continental Divide*. This is a new work, pulsing like the blood in the engorged couplings, for a neat 113 minutes, without trying to be too neat. The other major difference between style and flair, of course, is: flair shows off. Style simply shows.
TONY CRAWLEY.

BRITANNIA HOSPITAL

One may respect the British cinema and yet feel it is lacking in attack — attack in the sense of an unhesitating approach to a subject. Lindsay Anderson's *Britannia Hospital* doesn't lead up to its theme, it goes in fighting. The ambulance drives up to the hospital, the attendants decide to take the expiring patient in and, after a colloquy with a nurse who is going off duty and has no intention of being held up by the dying, leave him to breathe his last in the deserted reception hall. The film makes no bones about it; the hospital staff and the ancillaries are callous in a supposedly humanitarian profession. They work to rule.

The scene ought to be distressing. On the contrary, it is wickedly funny. One may not actually laugh, but one relishes a black joke. And there we have another element rare in the British cinema: *Britannia Hospital* is unadulterated satire. It is one long savage joke. But it is a joke which is serious.

If you examine the film you will find few aspects of our contemporary society untouched: royalty and the Establishment, the unions, the police, medicine, the Church, the public services; all are bound together in a day in the life of a London hospital. It is, it ought to be, a day of celebration. The institution has lived four hundred years, and today royalty is coming to open the new wing (one can't

expect Lindsay Anderson and his writer David Sherwin to miss the possibility that the new key may be reluctant to turn in the lock).

But uproar rules the Britannia. The kitchen staff are on strike against privilege; the private patients aren't going to get their grilled kidneys for breakfast and plates of orange are served instead. Workmen are still painting the walls where royal feet are to mount the stairs. The gates are picketed; demonstrators are massing outside. Bombs have been thrown, and visitors, even royal visitors, are going to find difficulty in getting in. *Britannia Hospital* joins the growing catalogue of disaster movies.

This series of misadventures and mistimings and misfortunes is transformed into an assault both on the people who have created the crisis and on the people who are trying to preserve the status quo. A key figure is the Senior Administrator of the hospital: nothing, he feels, must be allowed to dislocate the running of the great day. The kitchen staff are in chaos, his assistant can't quiet them. What will placate these fighters for democracy, these opponents of class? Perhaps an invitation for a representative to attend the royal luncheon? Even a hint,

half a promise, of some kind of decoration, an MBE, perhaps an OBE?

The hospital Branch Secretary of the National Union of Public Employees is won over: the royal luncheon will be served all right (though those intolerable private patients will be trundled out of the place). Gradually there are more additions to the select assembly; the upholders of democracy, equality and no privilege betray a positively bourgeois eagerness to sit at table with aristocracy. Meanwhile as the aspirants practise their curtseys the exponents of morale struggle on: the hospital disc jockey offers good cheer and over the public address system the padre won't be denied, despite the desperate situation, the chance of a prayer.

But *Britannia Hospital*, though it is consistently funny, has a serious core. Satire reverses the normal movement of happy narrative and offers contradictions; satire veils seriousness under absurdity. It is not the first time Lindsay Anderson has attacked the hideous extravagances of modern science. In *O Lucky Man* a volunteer for experimental research, you may remember, was turned into a pig. This time the experiment is even more ambitious — and more open to public appreciation.

The new wing of the hospital, devoted to advanced surgery, is the domain of a pioneer in human transplants. He works with the newly dead and the precariously living. He may need some section of the human frame — but it must be fresh, and the patient, moribund but obstinately clinging to life, may have to be helped on his way out of this world if his organs, his limbs, his very head are to be of service.

It is here that satire, while remaining superficially jocular, takes on a grisly severity. A television spy, peering through windows or smuggled into the institution by allies, is ready to report on the procedures of medicine. At the same time a television team follows the great surgeon as, outlining his plans, he walks through the grounds: still follows him as to applauding cries of "super!" he backs into the conference called to make final arrangements for the royal visit. But in the laboratory there is delay, and as I say the materials for transplant must be fresh. If it isn't — well, science is ready to seize its opportunities. That unwary television spy can be cornered...

True satire has no compunction: one remembers Swift's *Modest Proposal* which set out a scheme for using the superfluous progeny of the Irish as food. The surgeon's transplant is not only successful, it is manifold. The victim, ready to be recalled to life from the operating table, is a patchwork. Arms, thighs, chest, stomach have been stitched together from various sources; the legs will kick to demonstrate the triumph of the surgeon's needlework, the teeth will bite, the hands — but let's not go on. For this is another Frankenstein's Monster; the sutures will leak, the patchwork creature will rouse himself from his post-operation coma, and science will have to defend itself from its own triumph...

Smartly edited, *Britannia Hospital* whisks its audience away from horror to farce,

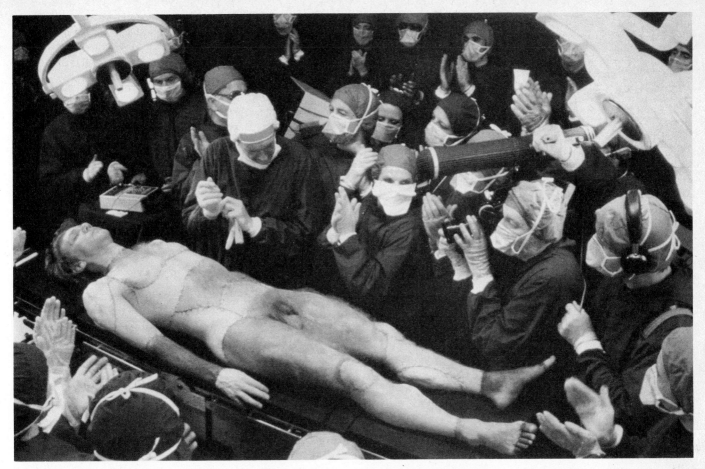

from the ferocity of the attack on scientific megalomania to the absurdities of snobbery or the irrational actions of the mob. The Palace entourage, even the Visitor herself will be smuggled into the hospital under the guise of stretcher cases. One must not make the mistake of thinking that Royalty is the central target of Lindsay Anderson's attack on a society at once servile and cantankerous. On the contrary, the Royal Visitor, wearing a Queen Mum's hat and smiling graciously and continuously in appalling circumstances, wins one's heart. At the reception after the Press show of the film she appeared in her screen costume, and really one felt that a curtsey would not be out of place in honour of the character's blameless good manners. But in the film it takes more than an august presence to quiet the democratic mob. It takes — and this is the true target of the movie — the monstrous hubris of science.

For transplanting organs and limbs is not enough. The great surgeon must create a new being, a sublimation of the human species; he must substitute for the flawed being which is mankind a thing all brain, a machine. Each time I

have seen the film a kind of frustration has settled over the audience at the point where this mechanism is unveiled. Possibly some spectators have shrunk from the film's riotous disregard of sensibilities, from the refusal to observe the niceties of well-bred social warfare. Some of us, on the other hand, have been thankful for the all-out assault, no holds barred.

Nationally we are short these days of satirists, and there have been times when one feared that Lindsay Anderson might be lost to the British cinema. The silence which in the last few minutes of *Britannia Hospital* descends over an audience previously responsive does not proceed from reluctance to share a brutal joke. It is, I think, a kind of disappointment, a longing not for an intellectual prophecy of a detestable future but for some stirring finale, some further explosion of farce. But then one must remember that Lindsay Anderson is a serious film maker, a satirist because he feels, because he cares.

And *Britannia Hospital* is a director's film, a writer's film. Resoundingly well acted, its successes cannot be ascribed to any central figure. One can appreciate, though, the

ensemble playing and the happy interaction of a multitude of performers ready to submerge themselves in a general effect. Some of them have appeared before in Anderson's movies. One remembers, for instance, Graham Crowden, the surgeon here, and Malcolm McDowell, now playing the television reporter; one welcomes the nucleus of an Anderson stock company (and the music once again is by Alan Price). The sly sidelong look of Leonard Rossiter is put to good use in the character of the placating Administrator, and Brian Pettifer as his assistant wears

harassment as if it were a skin. Vivien Pickles' Matron, Joan Plowright as a union leader insistent on her rights, Jill Bennett as the surgeon's adoring aide and Gladys Crosbie as the Royal Visitor keep beautifully within the bounds of the plausible. Certainly the casting deserves a word of praise.

One laughs gratefully and almost continuously. But let's not forget the title of this foray into the social condition of the country. Lindsay Anderson sees Britain as ailing. Britannia, his film says, is one large hospital.
DILYS POWELL

REDS

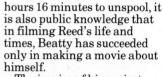

Warren Beatty's *Reds* is indisputably among the cinematic events of the year. A vast and ambitious epic about a little remembered American hero, it marks a new stage in the career of an actor who seems driven, or even tormented, by desires out of the ordinary.

In the absence of the old Hollywood studio system, actors have gained an unexpected power. It is their personalities that sell films, and they know it. Consequently some have used this power to acquire greater influence as producers and directors. But most have been content to star themselves in the same kind of films in which they made their names. The Clint Eastwood of a spaghetti Western is laconic kin to the Eastwood of *Firefox*.

But Beatty wants more. He desires not just fame and fortune (for he already has that), but acknowledged greatness. *Reds* is his bid for glory. It was made over a long period — nearly two years — and at vast expense — estimates of the cost begin at $34 million. Its shooting was notable for hard work and a dogged perfectionism that resulted in endless takes, tantrums and tempers.

The result is a long, complex film which, in the terms by which Beatty would wish to be judged, is a failure. Nor was it a commercial success. Had Beatty been willing to promote it, by personal appearances and interviews, it might have been more successful at the box office.

Reds' most arresting image is of Beatty, as John Reed, chasing a truck to carry him to battle. It is repeated twice, for Beatty uses symmetry to make his points, and in the end Reed is left behind.

Beatty, too, seems stranded, unable to escape from the environment that has sustained him ever since he arrived to make *Splendour in the Grass* 21 years ago. Over the years he has diligently learned his craft. But his technique as a director is to manipulate those aspects of film he has learned from other Hollywood hands. There are cosy domestic sequences in *Reds* — Louise Bryant with her lover Eugene O'Neill, or spending Christmas with John Reed — which recall romantic comedies of the 1930s. There are scenes of Louise Bryant struggling across the snows of Finland (an event invented by Beatty) which suggest nothing so much as *Dr Zhivago*. *Reds* is an anthology of Hollywood directorial approaches.

The film's fascination is in its revelation of the inadequacies of this approach, of the inability of the dream machine that Hollywood has become to treat the actualities of living. Hollywood cinema has long been the opium of the people. Its conventions are just that: conventional means of conveying reassurance. The radical content of *Reds* is betrayed by the safeness of its directorial style. And if I ignore its occasional virtues, it is only to emphasize the increasing distance of the big-budget American movie from life and its escape into myth.

It is no secret that for more than a decade Beatty was obsessed by the middle-class, Harvard-educated radical journalist John Reed, the man Upton Sinclair once accused of being a playboy revolutionary. Since *Reds* exists as 17,616 feet of film, which takes three hours 16 minutes to unspool, it is also public knowledge that in filming Reed's life and times, Beatty has succeeded only in making a movie about himself.

The ironies of his project cannot have been lost on Beatty who is a producer and director of intelligence and apparently overwhelming ambition. One is encapsulated in the small print assigning the copyright of the film to Barclays Mercantile Industrial Finance Limited. Capitalism does not finance revolutions, only right-wing coups, but it does love a movie star.

The contradictions involved must have been brought home to him when he filmed Reed's speech to the revolutionary congress of the Peoples of the East in Spain, with local extras playing Arabs. *Rolling Stone* reported that after Beatty had explained to them that Reed was against the exploitation of the working man by American capitalism, the extras struck for higher wages, which they got.

But Beatty recognised that Reed was a perfect subject for him to film. As the producer, director and star he must have recalled Orson Welles' *Citizen Kane*, for *Reds* stands in a dialectical relationship to the earlier masterpiece. Where Welles investigated a monster of capitalism, he would celebrate, by similar means, a saint of radicalism.

Self-identification with Reed has bedevilled many who have investigated his life. Reed himself seems to have been aware of his legendary qualities and to have exaggerated them. He was a romantic figure: a big, handsome, impulsive golden boy, wild lover, boozy poet, great journalist. He fought and suffered for his beliefs and died young, his life incomplete.

After his death in Moscow, one of his many lovers, Mabel Dodge, complained that Reed was being used as "a tool" to carve other people's prejudices into a satisfactory form. "I feel that anyone so lovable and so amorphous as he was is destined to be kicked back and

forth like a football," she wrote.

Beatty has succumbed to this tendency to remake Reed in his own image. He, too, is a man whose love affairs have often obscured his achievements, who takes politics seriously and who wants to put his talents at the service of his commitments. But he has fallen into the Hollywood trap of believing that a "big" subject demands the big treatment. A Hollywood epic is a clearly defined genre; it used to mean Cecil B. De Mille showgirls in ancient Rome. In these leaner times, it is a matter of images — small figures dwarfed by the landscape, as in *Dr Zhivago* — and themes — the individual altering the course of history, as in *Lawrence of Arabia* — which put individuals at the centre of historical processes.

It is a view of history directly opposed to Marx's dialectic where the forces of historical change are impersonal. But in Hollywood, where Irving Thalberg is still revered as a great man and individuals do have awesome powers, it makes perfect sense.

Reed becomes the perfect paradigm of the romantic revolutionary, a man who fought all bureaucratic systems, whether American capitalism or Soviet communism. In his battle with the Comintern can be read Beatty's own struggles with the studio bosses that began when he wanted to produce

Bonnie and Clyde. In *Reds*, Reed is subsumed into Beatty's own personality and concerns, which may be the reason why his performance is so low key. He does not have to act the part; he is it.

By the standards of Hollywood, Beatty took risks. (The scale of values there, as Blake Edwards' witty *S.O.B.* made clear, depends upon one absolute: the box office returns. I can remember one producer boasting to me of his daring because he had signed Paul Scofield — "an actor who doesn't mean a nickel outside Britain" — for a major role in his film.) He persuaded the British playwright Trevor Griffiths to work on the script with him. But later, of course, he hired Elaine May to add some jokes.

"What do I come as?" says Louise Bryant to Reed when he asks her to follow him to New York. "It's nearly Thanksgiving, why not come as a turkey," replies Reed in lines only Miss May can have written. It's a nice line, but it totally distorts the relationship between Bryant and Reed, although it may reflect that between Beatty and Diane Keaton.

Beatty has at least opened up for rediscovery America's radical past. But he has done so in a way which emphasizes that it is past. The political issues explored by *Reds* are dated and irrelevant to our times: splits over ideology in the American Communist

Party, power struggles during the early days of the Russian revolution. Issues concerning class, wealth and power are never discussed. And politics becomes subsidiary to the film's love story.

Reds states rather than explores the love triangle of Reed, Bryant and Eugene O'Neill. The pain and anguish Bryant and Reed caused each other through their various affairs, the strength of their feelings for one another are suggested only through the clichés of romantic films, in a sequence of cosy domestic scenes.

If Reed becomes a mirror of

Beatty's own personality, then Diane Keaton's Louise Bryant is never anything other than Keaton. Who else could this figure be, forever on the verge of hysteria, blinking back the tears while trying to smile? The sensibility portrayed is specifically modern. So specific indeed that she is a casebook study of a late 1970s New York neurotic, a bundle of confusions without a self to hold them together.

Keaton gives the performance her admirers have come to know and love from Woody Allen's movies. However, in a period film, it is a curious aberration, only re-emphasizing the personal nature of Beatty's film. The actual direction of the film, though, eschews individuality. Beautifully photographed, it nevertheless lacks any real flair. It demonstrates only that Beatty is a director who could take his place on any Hollywood production line.

The film's one concession to individuality is Beatty's use of real people, old, tough survivors in his chorus of witnesses to the events the film portrays. Their purpose is to show the impossibility of knowing what happened in history, thus justifying Beatty's treatment of the past in terms of the present. But so vivid is the individuality of these unidentified people that it undercuts the reality of Beatty's fictional recreations.

Reds has little reference outside itself, except to other films. The only life it touches is that of its producer, director and star. The cult of the personality has claimed another victim. JOHN WALKER

RAIDERS OF THE LOST ARK

My son has seen it five times. Or it may be three. He can't remember. All we know is that he'd just as soon see it again as anything else that's on. The film is a continuation of the Coppola Clan's infancy indulgence that started with *American Graffiti.* And yet, there's a difference.

Early films in a director's career tend to be like first novels: they contain a lot of heartfelt truth. *Auteur* cinema is all about this truth and European directors conventionally like to make films about subjects they understand or have lived through. In Hollywood films have always been made for one purpose only — money. And if there has been a film since *Gone With the Wind* that epitomises perfectly this frame of reference it is *Raiders of the Lost Ark.*

With Spielberg we have a director who (a) likes to scare the hell out of his public and (b) doesn't mind them knowing that the joke is on them. Apart from which, he is technically the most able of his generation.

In an *auteur* film the subject evolves out of something real with a point of view that the director feels strongly about. Here, on the other hand, we get the feeling that no expense was spared in having fun. To put a picture like this together you must work on the understanding that you are only going to give the audience what it wants. The originality comes with the treatment. But how can you tell what an audience wants if they haven't seen it yet? That's simple: you take the best bits from all the ones they liked before and represent the meal predigested and redigested. It will feel new and taste better than it did the last time.

And so, despite loving, admiring and enjoying it I must confess to a certain sour grapesy, dog-in-the-manger ambivalence to *Raiders* that has nothing to do with its brilliance. It is the movie that has everything: adventure, a love interest, immaculate technique, chauvinism, patriotism, religion, mystique, tension, humour, a handsome hero, disgusting villains, big bangs, a thousand snakes, special effects, a great script (action packed). In fact, it has absolutely nothing wrong with it. So, if there is anything wrong with it that's what it is. It's too good.

Of course, it's incredible. You might say it's a series of pastiches of James Bond, Humphrey Bogart, Hammer horror and so on, but that would only be saying that Lucas and Spielberg see and remember a lot of films. I have news for you: they have seen every single film ever made.

We film reviewers are mere amateurs at moviegoing, those guys see everything. But the strongest influence is the memory of the innocent enjoyments of childhood. It was the root cause of *Star Wars.* Lucas there wanted to give us the feeling he had watching *Flash Gordon.* So he became Luke Skywalker. With Spielberg, a Hitchcock disciple although far more sophisticated than the odious De Palma, he wants to retransmit the delicious feeling of fear when it's fun, when it's not really happening to you.

Close Encounters was based on the superstitious prejudice of extra-terrestrial life; *Duel* on the impossible idea that an old beat-up truck can go faster than a modern car; *Jaws* on an exaggerated respect for a fish's intelligence. *1941* didn't work, although based on prejudices that have worked before — it was just that he let his mocking sense of humour show through. It is to Spielberg's credit that while *Raiders* is an equally expensive venture it comes off so magnificently.

I will reveal my provincialism — although Hollywood is a suburb, anything not from there is known as "parochial" — when I confess that on seeing the Ark of the Covenant being guyed as a "radio transmitter to God" my hackles rose somewhat prudishly. But then, I reasonably considered, Spielberg and Lucas have a perfect right to deal with the Bible as they see fit; who am I to object? The cavalier use of the Almighty's selective powers are shown to be on the right side, that is to say, ours. Heaven opens up in a way it never could have during *Star Wars.* But there I go again, mixing up movies. You can't say it looks bad on the screen. I'm sure if Lucas and Spielberg did the Old Testament sometime they'd make a marvellous job parting the Red Sea.

Some people don't take this film seriously and they're not supposed to. The only serious thing about it is how much

money it makes and deserves. I once heard Coppola explaining how he put together *Apocalypse Now*. He said he never thought of a plot. His idea was to put in everything he wanted in the film and a plot would work itself out. It's the theory (Western) of more is more, as opposed to Eastern where less is more. The more the merrier, more bangs, more punches, more noise, more action, everyone's a kid at heart — an old movie maxim — and don't let's pretend it's easy. It's one of the hardest things in the world to do right.

No one can deny the nastiness of Nazis — just the people to punch if you're a hero and an educated hero who's really a schoolteacher and an archaeologist during the vac. Sex is suggested in the way the Hays Commission liked it, before it got physical and messy and, anyhow, it has no place here — puppy love will do. With *Raiders* we are plumbing the past in more ways than one. We are feeding off the moral certitude of our parents' generation, protected in our cocoon of pre-teenage innocence. The real world — whatever that may be — is never there. The real world is what you meet when you leave the cinema, an imaginary

sixgun still at your hip, a whip that somehow reminds you of snakes that remind you of the Garden of Eden, the halcyon days before you knew what was what.

Of course, it's a formula picture, a formula of formulae. The plot equals the action equals the development of character equals dialogue equals technique. All the balls are in the air and not one must drop. It's an American art form, movies. We make films, sometimes we work in the cinema. But movies are about the barely credible, that you participate in and it makes you feel good. The English try it and fail — we don't have the chutzpah.

Do you really want 30 million dollars? Use our studio and our technicians but don't ask *us* to make one of those super colossal expensive jobs ourselves unless you're Richard Attenborough, and we all know what happened to him. More than once.

It's like Coppola says. He puts all the things in he wants to see and then links them up. The plot makes sense; we've seen it all before when we were young, not as good, or was it? And so there's a sense of déjà vu which my son hasn't yet heard about. I'll be seeing

Raiders again in a couple of days, no doubt. There's nothing on for kids to see and Herbie the human VW ran out of steam some time back. So, I'll be back in the age of innocence with all the other dads. After the seventh viewing, I'm told, you get to like it all over again. I'll see. When you know a movie off by heart, it's hard to tell if you like it. Familiarity breeds a certain respect in this instance,

though. I still can't see the joins, the flow is just as fast and terrific. The actors and their reactions become old friends. But do I like it? Or them? That's a tough one to answer. I admire it, love it, respect it, even laugh in a couple of places — Spielberg does catch you off-guard — but like it? I don't know what that means any more. My kid could tell you. He likes it. A lot.
MIKE SARNE

VICTOR, VICTORIA

If the success of Blake Edwards' *Victor, Victoria* can be said to represent anything in particular, then it has to be the triumph of old-fashioned Hollywood savvy over new-fangled Hollywood mechanics. Hardly a camera turns these days before a major studio's top brass has consulted the crystal balls of computer-processed consumer surveys and research polls. Once the elements supposedly guaranteed to attract the interests of the so-called "core" audience has been accounted for, then smooth production sailing is considered possible.

Edwards' sophisticated comedy-with-music wasn't made that prepackaged way. Its story of a penniless *chanteuse* who becomes the toast of Paris in the Thirties by posing as a female impersonator may strike a trendy chord or two (gay and women's liberation, the success of *La Cage Aux Folles*, etc.), but as written and directed by Edwards, *Victor, Victoria* is a smoothly crafted piece of traditional Hollywood film making.

Combining equal parts of high and low comedy, romantic interludes, production numbers and specialty turns, it's a film organised along the resolutely sane principle that if you give an audience a decent amount of sufficiently varied material in an overall spirit of general goodwill, then you're sure to please someone some of the time, while not getting on anyone's nerves the rest of the time. There's a bracingly simple logic to this approach, but in recent years with films geared to exclusive sets of viewers (*Animal House* for teenagers and young adults, *Kramer Vs. Kramer* for the Carriage Trade, and so forth) the concept of trying to appeal to the largest numbers of movie-goers in a single film has gone out the window. That *Victor, Victoria* accomplishes this goal with a cast of actors well into their forties, whose box office appeal is decidedly limited, is unusual. The fact that this success is in the musical comedy form (a genre that, with the exception of *Grease*, has proved largely unpopular in recent years) is astonishing.

That Edwards should be the film maker to make such a breakthrough, should, however, be no surprise to anyone familiar with his long career. As the last Hollywood artist in the gloss and glamour tradition of Vincente Minnelli and Stanley Donen, Edwards is ideally suited to exploit the smooth surfaces and svelte surroundings which something like *Victor, Victoria* requires. From the Manhattan chic of *Breakfast at Tiffany's*, through the melodrama of *Experiment in Terror*, *Days of Wine and Roses* and *Gunn*, to the burlesque pratfalls of the *Pink Panther* series, Edwards has consistently demonstrated a proficiency in most mainstream film making styles. In his best film in the slapstick vein, *The Party*, he displayed an understanding of sound and image gag-craft that at moments rivals the best of Jacques Tati. More recently in *10* and *S.O.B.*, Edwards has harnessed this physical skill and moulded it into a richer structure of verbal wit (in the style of Billy Wilder) and dramatic interplay (very remindful of Minnelli).

In *Victor, Victoria* this richer Edwards *mise en scène* comes together more forcefully than ever. The low-keyed legato opening of the film perfectly sets the tone for what's to follow. The camera pans slowly across the landscape of a soot and snow-covered Paris street — as if the film were a bittersweet romance of another era on the order of Borzage's *Seventh Heaven*. Shortly thereafter, we meet two of the residents of this squalid byway, a destitute homosexual nightclub performer played by Robert Preston, and an exceedingly bedraggled British singer played by Julie Andrews. The mood is one of melancholy desperation, but even in these sorry straits Edwards manages to score one of his most brilliant comic coups in a scene where the starving Andrews faints at the sight of a man eating a whipped cream desert as she stands before the window of a posh restaurant. The gag itself is as old as a Chaplin two-reeler, but Edwards' skilful editing (knowing the precise moment when to cut between the man and Andrews' reaction) makes this tiny moment a triumph of comedy montage.

From this point on, shifts between giddiness and pathos accelerate, climaxed by a well-staged set piece in which Preston and Andrews cause havoc at a restaurant by letting loose a cockroach in order to avoid paying the check. Again, the basic idea behind the scene doesn't sparkle with originality — it's Edwards' sure comic touch that makes it work.

Slapstick gives way to sophisticated farce as the film's plot moves into high gear at the halfway point. Throwing in her lot with the enterprising Preston, Andrews decides to go along with an incredible scheme he's thought up and becomes a transvestite nightclub star — a *woman* playing a *man* playing a *woman*. It's a thoroughly outrageous idea, but Edwards, through Preston's character, disarms all objections. According to Preston, since the idea of her going through with such a deception is "too unbelievable" it logically follows that "no one will believe it".

In a crazy world, the only way to get ahead is to act crazier than anyone else. And when the results are as entertaining as they are in *Victor, Victoria*, few spectators

are disinclined to go along with the joke. Moreover, in terms of the plot, the wisdom of Preston's world-view becomes increasingly apparent as three new characters are added to the farcical stew: a Chicago nightclub owner played by James Garner; his dizzy, brassy girlfriend, wisecracked in the grand Jean Hagen tradition by Lesley Ann Warren; and his roly-poly bodyguard, neatly played by former football pro Alex Karras.

Entranced by Andrews' act, man's man Garner is stunned to discover that the Victoria he found so alluring on stage is supposed to be a Victor when off it. Smelling a rat, and determined to uncover the truth, Garner sneaks into Andrews' hotel suite late one evening to get a glimpse of him/her in the buff. The resulting comic chaos expands the jest of the earlier restaurant scene, while laying the groundwork for Andrews' and Garner's eventual romance.

The characters played by Karras and Warren, meanwhile, neatly dovetail into the film's overall sexual hellzapoppin. With her fizzy blonde hair, screechy voice, and exaggerated gestures, Warren's character is far more of a female impersonation than that of any transvestite. In the same way Karras's tough exterior serves to disguise the fact that he (as disclosed in one of the film's most hilarious comic pay-offs) is actually a homosexual.

Between the extremes of

these two stand Andrews and Garner, she delighted to reap the benefits (social as well as monetary) from this sexual deception, he mortified at the prospect of having his sexual certainty undermined. Even after Garner learns the truth, he and Andrews can't proceed in a traditional boy/girl manner. She's got to keep up the deception for the sake of her job, and as a result he must keep their romance in the shadows — just like a closeted homosexual couple.

Edwards touches on a number of serious areas in this off-beat coming together of lovers (and in the less troubled, though just as sincere, friendship between Preston and Andrews) but he never loses sight of his main objective — entertainment. After slapstick and farce, romantic comedy is *Victor, Victoria*'s final destination. But along the way, Edwards has managed to slip in several full-scale musical production numbers as well.

The successful interpolation of these musical turns is perhaps *Victor, Victoria*'s most singular triumph. After the success of *The Sound of Music* in 1966, Hollywood fell all over itself producing big-budget musicals. But none of the productions that followed — *Dr. Dolittle*, *Paint Your Wagon*, *Camelot*, *Star* — ever captured the fancy of the public the way the Rodgers and Hammerstein musical did.

Edwards came a cropper with his *Darling Lili* (1970), an extremely elaborate and expensive flop starring

Andrews that nearly brought both their careers to a halt. Now some 12 years later, Edwards and Andrews reprise the neo-Ophuls spirit they touched on in *Lili*. 'Crazy World', as sung by Andrews in *Victor, Victoria*, beautifully reprises the lovely 'Whistling Away the Dark' number in *Darling Lili*, gracefully swirling camera movements and all.

The final magic ingredient of *Victor, Victoria*'s success is that despite the many costly failures of the Sixties, the public's love of the musical form has never really died. All it needed was the proper venue to make it palatable. *Grease*, by appealing to teenagers, slipped song and dance through in one direction. Bob Fosse's show-biz-drama-with-music, *All That Jazz*, did much the same thing in another way — beating Broadway hit *Chorus Line* to the movie making punch.

Victor, Victoria splits the difference between the pop commercialism of the former and the New York-style sophistication of the latter. Edwards, Andrews and company slip a musical right under the eyes of the public through comedy and romance, and in the process reawaken a taste for song-and-dance excitement. The grace and professionalism with which this very difficult task is accomplished testifies to the strength of show biz tradition in the face of new-style special effects. The only special effect on view in *Victor, Victoria* is talent. DAVID EHRENSTEIN

AN UNSUITABLE JOB FOR A WOMAN

For reasons more connected with a suspect metabolism than with any deeply rooted Philistinism, I never saw Chris Petit's first film *Radio On*. Everybody said that it was very good but described it in a way which suggested that it went on forever very slowly. As I often fell asleep during art movies, and still do when inclination gets the better of obligation, I decided instead to go to something fast and noisy.

His second, *An Unsuitable Job for a Woman*, is a remarkable film, the best British movie of a year lamentably barren of candidates: part English murder mystery story (it is adapted from the novel by P.D. James), part detective thriller (the central character is an assistant who assumes the role of a partner when her detective agency boss commits suicide), part skeletons-in-the-closet melodrama (the family which employs her turns out to have more than their fair share of them).

So far, so ordinary. Indeed, the only superficial difference between this film and an orthodox whodunnit of the Cluedo-board school is that it takes an imaginative film-maker's delight in emphasising details and then lingering on them for a few seconds longer than tradition dictates. Petit's cameraman Martin Schafer is a perfect match for the style: the interiors are shadowy and menacing, the exteriors vivid

to the point of being hallucinatory, heightened colours depicting a bleak countryside where rain clouds gather over telephone booths in the middle of nowhere and silence is not so much the random backdrop to some pressured townie's idea of a rural reverie as the soundtrack to an escalating obsession.

But, much like Pippa Guard, who is in every scene yet makes no effort to monopolise them, *An Unsuitable Job for a Woman* is ordinary in an extraordinary way. Guard is ordinary enough in appearance not to draw too much attention to herself but extraordinary enough to be worthy of the camera's constant surveillance. She looks like a late-developer English rose who loosened up at her 21st

birthday party and still has Sunday lunch with her parents. Possibly she spent six months on a belated stint as a hippy in the West Country in the mid-Seventies. It's difficult to tell, and it's important that you shouldn't be able to do so. She wears sweaters, shirts and jeans; occasionally, when funeral or professionalism calls, a trouser suit.

As she pursues her investigation of the circumstances behind the apparent suicide-by-hanging of a property tycoon's son, the way she looks (or the way Petit chooses to make her look) changes subtly, almost imperceptibly. At the beginning she is formal, nervous and ingenuous, trying hard to convey the air of practised authority she considers must be part of her trade. Then, staying in the derelict cottage where the boy spent his last days, she begins to look increasingly haunted by his presence in her life. When she puts her toothbrush in the same jar as his, the identification is complete. In flesh-and-blood terms, she gets even closer by having sex with his father. Finally, after she has struggled out of the garden well with the help of the belt which supposedly hanged him and certainly almost hanged her, she takes on the appearance of an

avenging angel. It is Guard's very anonymity which makes her such a perfect choice for the part in this marvellously cryptic, distorted, looking-glass thriller.

An Unsuitable Job for a Woman is, above all, the model film adaptation, transforming James's labyrinth of obsession, revenge and family secrets into a genuinely cinematic experience. If it looks terrific, it sounds even better. There is hardly a redundant line of dialogue, and it is delivered with particular relish by Billie Whitelaw as the character with the most devastating secret of all. To paraphrase Raymond Chandler's description of Humphrey Bogart, all she has to do to dominate a scene is to enter it. There is one moment at the beginning when the old lady who found the body delivers a rather soap-boxy generation-gap monologue which seems unnecessarily stagey in the context of what surrounds it. There is another at the end, when Paul Freeman is trying to exorcise his guilt and grief before being shot, which strikes a similar anomalous note. Between these two exchanges is dialogue which, had Petit not written most of it himself, would have required a mating of Harold Pinter and Robert Towne to produce.

Inevitably, Petit's interest in European cinema has prompted comparisons with Chabrol, Melville and the other critics' pets. But what makes *An Unsuitable Job for a Woman* so enjoyable is how much of his own film it is: leisurely paced (it does take its time), modestly budgeted (a toy car knocked into a fish tank pre-echoes a cut-price finale involving precisely that), agreeably stylish and, most important of all, utterly hypnotic. It is a film for all seasons.

As for the kind of fast and noisy film I went to see in preference to *Radio On*, my other favourite movie this year was *Mad Max II*. It doesn't matter why you like that one as long as you like it. AL CLARK

TURKEYS of THE YEAR
VENOM

At least it's British, that's what I say. English to the quick and proud of it. It's times like these that you know who your friends are.

Venom is about a small snake that gets the odd close-up to make it look larger. We think it's a he but in an exciting last-minute plot dénouement/coda that I won't bore you with, it turns out to have been a she. There, now I've told you, you won't bother to see it. But you must. Write to your MP, *The Times*. Have it on at your local if it's come off. We must lend our support in these trying times and buy British. That's what I'm going on about. The company that made *Venom* is Handmade Films which, in a word, gives a thumbnail sketch of the British cottage film industry. While our American cousins come over here making *Superman* and suchlike in our studios using our technicians and taking our Eady money that we could well use, the home-grown product rests its entire reputation on one small heroic reptile that bites Susan George in the face (how bitchy!) and Oliver Reed in the balls (how apt!) and Klaus Kinski, token Kraut fresh from Dracula, all over. The animal is selective in the extreme, leaving the goodies, Sterling Hayden, Nicol Williamson, Sarah Miles, Michael Gough and others untouched. Now, a snake that can do this and lay eggs must have its heart in the right place.

I suppose if the Yanks made this film they'd get a big motorised shark and call it *Jaws* or three thousand snakes and call it *Raiders of the Lost Ark* or something. But we, brave embattled Brits, make do with the Dunkirk spirit and tell it like it is. Or isn't.

The confusion starts in the first reel when a kidnap is botched because of this snake. There's this asthmatic American kid, see, whose grandfather is a pusillanimous easy-going oldster called Sterling Hayden and they get this snake by mistake while the chauffeur (Ollie) and the nanny (Susan) and international terrorist (Klaus) keep bumping into each other in his small house off Eaton Square someplace. Ollie shoots a policeman for no reason on earth. Klaus sets up a meeting with Sterling in the Tower Hotel so we can see Tower Bridge in the background (yes, it's that sort of flick, film fans), and Susan takes off her dress once before she gets bitten in the face by this snake I told you about.

Nicol Williamson is there with his hands in his pockets most of the time; you can see it was cold when they shot it. Sarah Miles is very flirtatious for some reason or other, batting her eyelids indiscriminately at heroes and villains alike and the whole film is a disaster movie on a small scale. There, that's it in a nutshell.

Of course, I haven't mentioned other featured elements such as tracking shots from the snake's point of view. And then, wait for it, wide-angle shots where the lens gets all misty after Ollie and Sue get bitten. You get this uncanny feeling of the snake's remorse, as if the little thing is crying over what it has had to do. This is quite touching.

I could say that the film might have been made in such a way as to scare the living daylights out of you. But, in that case, one would have had to show the snake from the victim's point of view, the victim then being a leading player, say the asthmatic kid or Sarah or Nicol, one of the goodies — the goodies are the ones the audience is supposed to like as opposed to the baddies which they're supposed not to. Now, this is all elementary 11-plus info that we Brits taught the Yanks first, so why am I saying it?

The simple answer to that is, if *Venom* is anything to go by, we don't seem to know what we're doing. But, at least it's British, this film, there's no getting away from that. Probably the first since *The Blue Lamp*. I mean, you can't really count *Chariots of Fire*. That David Puttnam gets his money from shady Levantines and swarthy Continentals. Or some of it anyway. *Venom* is British, I tell you, the money had the portrait of Her Majesty on it. Alf Garnett would have been proud of this film, if he'd known about it.

And the snake is a great little actor. I mean actress. She keeps the whole thing together. They even named the film after her, sort of. The bit where she bites Klaus while Klaus is being shot by the police while being filmed in slow motion as he wraps the snake around his arm and falls from the balcony while entangled in lace curtains is . . . well, words fail me. Times like this you're glad you're British and not a Kraut like Klaus who's stuck with that kind of part. That isn't to say that Ollie and Sue don't do sterling work, and Sterling is the token Yank to make the flick attractive to his compatriots across the great water.

And Sarah is there too, of course. Have I missed anyone? Let me think . . . asthmatic kid, American mother, absent father, British bobbies, Eaton Square, Rolls Royce, snake, Klaus, Ollie, Sue. . . That seems to be everybody.

A swinging London story, then folks, about this great little snake who hates Krauts, chauffeurs and nannies and sets out to rid the world of them. This snake is good to children and Americans and dies doing its duty against the Hun as, locked in a death struggle Holmes and Moriarty-style they fall from the first floor of an elegant desirable residence in a fashionable part of Mayfair while Nicol Williamson protects his nether regions with his pockets full of hands.

That's about it. MIKE SARNE

LEGEND OF THE LONE RANGER

Since no Western has been a significant hit since *Butch Cassidy and the Sundance Kid* in 1969 (unless one counts Mel Brooks' spoof, *Blazing Saddles*, in 1974), it's hard to imagine that as recently as 15 years ago, Westerns were still among the most popular of movie and television genres. Nowadays, marketing departments scramble to avoid creating any impression that a film may have Western elements — many theorised that the weak business generated by Clint Eastwood's *Bronco Billy* and the John Travolta-starrer *Urban Cowboy* was caused by public perception that those films may have been Westerns, even though they weren't. I doubt it. It isn't that the public is turned off to Westerns: I suspect the movie-going audience really doesn't know what one is anymore, at least not in traditional cowboy drag. *Star Wars* and *Outland* gave indications that the frontier has irrevocably shifted to outer space.

Although the Western is certifiably dead, instant ephemera like *The Legend of the Lone Ranger* only drive the nails into the coffin. The Lone Ranger was always dully formulaic, but I still recall how as a child I had eagerly awaited for what seemed an eternity for the annual re-run of the television show explaining how the Lone Ranger assumed his secret identity, to become a cut-rate gringo Zorro. Although my memory of that programme itself is perforce fuzzy, for all its elementary television

dramaturgy, it had to be more effective than this indecisive, uncertain shade of re-make. It takes 50 minutes for the man to don his mask, and thereafter the character isn't even exploited, ambling through a matter-of-fact climax without a jot of tension or suspense. Moreover, I can't recall another film in this budget class (apparently about $17 million) where so much of the dialogue has been dubbed. Lead Klinton Spilsbury must have been unimaginably wooden if the dubbed voice we hear on film was considered an improvement. In this context, the customarily dusty exteriors of Lazslo Kovacs (presumably in collaboration with director William A. Fraker, more often a cinematographer) only emphasise the picturesque aspects of boredom.

Mostly the film is content to trade on mechanical tirades of fundamentalist right-wing rhetoric which would be reprehensible if the film had any punch; instead, the audience-pandering Reagan-age homilies are so mechanical as to seem insincere. Once again law and order is exalted as a code for virulent vigilantism, and the easy cynicism assumes that all politicians are crooks. Still, the film does represent an obviously serious effort to tackle the material, although nearly every decision seems dead wrong. Sometimes, Fraker aims for comic gravity, sometimes for an operatic flourish, still others for a fake-lyrical passage redolent of

Muybridge's motion studies, only far less illuminating. There's the sure giveaway for uncertain stylistic intentions: the half-hearted stab at parody with send-ups of conventions done with a breeziness that could only have gusted in from Mel Brooks' campfire.

In this stultifying context, one fixes on the odd moment of arousal. Several of the stunts are classically well-done, though rarely do any of them have any discernible relationship to the central action. And crass as the scene is played, there's some outlandish nonsense about concocting a smoking-car assemblage out of a celebrity magazine, circa 1870, gathering none other than President Ulysses S. Grant, Wild Bill Hickok, Buffalo Bill Cody and **General George Custer together for a Mexican hunting trip.**

Although the film was plainly a woebegone, foredoomed failure, the film makers still might have resuscitated their comic book character if they had analysed their problems in comparable fashion to the new Superman movies or to *Raiders of the Lost Ark*. Audiences are once again suckers for old-fashioned action and matinee heroics provided the context supplies a satisfactory contemporary attitude. Richard Lester places tongue in cheek only to validate the essential seriousness of Superman's dilemmas, while Spielberg dwarfs unwilling suspension of disbelief by sheer

scale and a fashionably shallow cynicism. Miscalculations dog every commercial decision behind *The Legend of the Lone Ranger*: all in all, it stands as an archetypal project for the disaster that was Lord Grade in theatrical film production. His men tried every formula imaginable to try to hit a blockbuster, only to prove, yet again, that no formula is worth its salt without the requisite secret ingredient: creative spark. Tender loving care at such cost generally looks ridiculous, like attention lavished on an imaginary infant.

The Lone Ranger film might have explored a connection between the hero and related Indian myths, delving deeper into Indian lore to connect the hero with atavistic power. Lenny Bruce played with some of the ambiguities attendant upon a man in a mask: there are certainly more sober possibilities here as well. *The Legend of the Lone Ranger* lacks soul, which is the only thing that can bestow conviction upon the legends of yesteryear.

There's still plenty of room for meaningful work in the Western genre, vide *The Outlaw Josey Wales*, *The Long Riders*, or even, for all its artistic shortcomings, *Heaven's Gate*. The problem remains one of commercial limitation — they cost too much relative to the size of the likely audience — and I fear it is insurmountable.

An entire generation has come of age without ever absorbing the panoply of conventions that are the lifeblood of any genre, but particularly of the Western. The entire lexicon of situations, confrontations, rituals and values mean nothing to them. A typical film-goer of median age in the US has never seen a Western in a theatre nor on prime-time television.

Yet put the same or similar conventions in outer space, and their verities may yet undergo artistic rejuvenation. It will take a while — until space operas have grown plentiful enough so that little in their stories can surprise. Then the shock of artistry may again be felt. For me, that will be the true race for space. MYRON MEISEL

BUTTERFLY

Her cheeks are curiously puffy, as if she wanted to understudy Marlon Brando in *The Godfather* or, like a hamster, she tucked away tomorrow's meal in them. Her hair is tousled blonde. Her eyes are blank blue and her mouth a pouting Bermuda triangle where men might lose themselves for ever.

Her legs are slim but short, even with a flimsy dress rucked up to her thighs. At first leer, she looks like a precocious little girl pretending to be an adult. Her full breasts seem to have been borrowed from a grown-up for the occasion.

Pia Zadora is an oddity, with an appearance calculated to appeal to Lolita-lovers — the humbug Humberts who have made respectable David Hamilton's misty-eyed view of adolescent girls — as well as to those who prefer more mature women. She is a nymphet offering pneumatic bliss.

She is also a naughty deed in a too serious world: the man-made star of the year's best bad film, *Butterfly*. What gives this movie the edge over much enjoyable hokum is the presence of Pia, the most ridiculous screen personality since Jayne Mansfield and Raquel Welch, in the days when she was a dedicated scientist aboard the *Fantastic Voyage*.

Preceded by much old-fashioned ballyhoo, financed by her rich, doting middle-aged husband, Pia Zadora was a star before *Butterfly* was released. After it reached the cinema, her lustre dimmed a little.

Sold on its sexual content, *Butterfly* was bound to disappoint. It nevertheless offers an hilarious attempt to sell a manufactured personality by means of a sleazy story that continually promises more than it is prepared to deliver.

Miss Zadora is surrounded by some excellent acting talent. The fine Stacy Keach, as her father Jess, walks through the film with the desperate look of a man who has taken the money and will run at any moment. Orson Welles lends his bulky authority to the role of a comic judge. And, in a barnstorming excess of melodrama, Lois Nettleton flares her nostrils and quivers her lip

as Jess's overdressed, consumptive wife.

Butterfly is based on a novel by James M. Cain, whose most famous book is *The Postman Always Rings Twice*. Cain is in the "tough-guy" tradition of American writing, always protesting too much at being compared to Hemingway.

There are many differences between the book and the film, all demonstrating the care with which Matt Cimber, producer, director and co-screenwriter, has packaged it to fit Miss Zadora. In outline, the stories are the same. It is a homely tale of incest and revenge, a hillbilly transformation of Jacobean tragedy.

Jess Tyler is a simple, honest man whose wife left him to run a boarding house-cum-brothel, taking her two young daughters with her. Suddenly, one of them, Kady, a sluttish 17 year-old, returns. She has run away from home and her new-born baby. She attracts and encourages Jess's sexual attentions. They make love, are seen and taken to court.

By this time, Jess knows that Kady is not his daughter but the child of his wife's lover. He is able to prove it — the butterfly of the title is a tell-tale birthmark — but then loses Kady to her young lover. In Cimber's version, Jess's

lust is stronger and his actions in trying to keep Kady for himself are less explicable.

However, there are other, greater differences. In Cain, Jess is a coal-miner and Kady a tough, practical girl who hates her baby. She is stronger than Jess, persuading him to set up an illicit still in the deserted mine so that they can sell corn liquor to the locals. In Cimber, Jess looks after a silver-mine, Kady loves her baby but would rather be rich. From the beginning she is a money-obsessed fantasy figure. Her boyfriend has moved up several social classes to become the weak son of a rich man, driving up to claim her in a huge white sports car.

If Kady dirties her hands in the movie, it is only to provide an excuse for that standby of Hollywood eroticism, the bathtub scene, made memorable in the past by such expert titillators as Jean Harlow, Joan Collins and Elke Sommer.

It is here that the film's dialogue, never less than funny, reaches heights of absurdity. Some of the slick *double entendres* of the father and daughter exchanges, which make the film almost a "Carry On At The Mine", derive from Cain, such as their opening remarks. "Something you want?" he asks. "How do I know

unless I know what you've got," she replies, doing her best to suggest Mae West.

Miss Zadora's wide-eyed mock-innocence is a constant source of pleasure. "I like doing things for a man," she lisps. And to Keach's question "What do you plan to do?", she answers sweetly "Keep you from being lonely." After a while every sentence is overloaded with suggestion, even Keach's line "I just don't want you pulling anything like you did yesterday".

It is perhaps matched by the dialogue between Keach and Lois Nettleton, coughing blood in bed. "I'm going to die." "I'm awful sorry." Or Miss Zadora's goodbye to Keach, as she leaves with her lover and not long after she has been making sweaty love with the man she thought was her father: "You're my daddy and you'll always be my daddy."

One of the great joys of the film is watching Miss Zadora deal with two problems. The first is suggesting a girl of 17, not always easy when you are 25. The images reinforce the notion of childhood. She goes barefoot, hangs on posts, sits on a trunk kicking her heels. The other is to be able to look her fellow actors in the eye. Miss Zadora is short and tends to stand on raised platforms whenever she can.

In the days of the studios, stars were never born, but made. Carefully photographed by consummate technicians of the camera, provided with new names and fictitious biographies, they were creatures removed from reality from the beginning. Pia Zadora, with her little girl poses and air of surprised sexuality, is a throwback to that tradition, except that she seems to have created herself, with a little help from the bulging wallet of her husband Meshulam Riklis.

To meet, she is as sharp as she is tiny, adept at manipulating journalists, aware of precisely what she is doing. She has said that she wants to play Lady Macbeth. If she ever does it on film, I will be the first in the cinema queue. Good laughs are hard to come by these days.
JOHN WALKER

TARZAN THE APE MAN

Individual tastes and standards of judgement being what they are, it's usually just about impossible to get a group of film critics to form a consensus of opinion. But when MGM's 1981 remake of *Tarzan the Ape Man* came along, the critical verdict was virtually unanimous. "A blinding bore," screamed the *Los Angeles Times*. "The dullest *Tarzan* movie ever made," echoed the *Hollywood Reporter*. "Lacking any focus, fun or excitement," the *Village Voice* exclaimed. "Lacerating ineptness," the *Los Angeles Herald-Examiner* declared.

How, a disinterested observer might wonder, could such a situation come about? Why was this particular film singled out for such severe lambasting? Wasn't it, after all, just another film version of Edgar Rice Burroughs' pop classic? Over 40 different *Tarzan* films had been produced prior to this one, none of them laying claim to anything in the way of emotional depth or artistic accomplishment. Weren't the members of the critical community overreacting just a bit? Using an elephant gun to quash a flea?

The simple answer to all these questions is that this *Tarzan* wasn't like any of the others, and critical reaction, though extreme, was understandable considering the overall circumstances. Instead of some mythical loinclothed Lord of the Jungle, the central point of focus for *Tarzan* 1981 was his mate Jane as embodied in the decidedly singular form of Bo Derek. Since the release of Blake Edwards' *'10'*, where she played the dream girl of a bemused Dudley Moore, the statuesque young starlet had become America's dream girl as well. Through the canny promotional efforts of her husband, former Hollywood leading man John Derek, the actress' image as seen in the Edwards film (cool reserved features, blonde hair in striking-looking cornrow braids) had come into the lives of millions via posters, calendars and picture books. An issue of *Playboy* magazine featuring a Bo layout (photographed, as are all Derek images, by John) became a top seller.

A pin-up however is one thing, an image on a movie screen is quite another. In *'10'*, under Edwards' expert direction, she was more than up to the decorative demands of the part. But could she carry a film all by herself? The Dereks thought so. Unperturbed at the prospect of transforming a poster icon into a celluloid one, the two were convinced that the *Tarzan* story was the best possible means for doing so. "I'll be wearing the Gibson Girl look," Bo declared prior to the film's production. "My clothes will be picked off piece by piece as I go through the jungle!"

While for Bo-lovers the prospect of such steamy shenanigans sounded alluring, to the executors of the Edgar Rice Burroughs estate, such a rumble in the jungle meant only one thing — the fair name of their grunting and groaning hero was about to be dragged through the metaphorical mud.

Bringing the Dereks into court over what they saw as the potential defamation of a pop icon's character, the Burroughs estate tried to stop the Dereks in their tracks. But the Dereks had a simple — and on paper rather convincing — response. According to them, their *Tarzan* was to be no different from any other. If the plot centred on Jane rather than the jungle lord, then so did the Thirties version of the story starring Johnny Weissmuller and Maureen O'Sullivan. If there were to be nudity in the film, it would proceed naturally from the dramatic situation; sex (the

Burroughs interest's main worry) would have its place in the film likewise.

In their own lovably cockeyed way, the Dereks were being quite honest about their aspirations for this *Tarzan*. But in the eyes of the Burroughs executors — and the general public — only one thing was involved: sex. Some six seconds of footage was removed from the film at the request of those who would guard the jungle lord's virtue. But in every way, shape and form, *Tarzan* proved to be exactly what John, Bo, and their panting followers had hoped for — a chance to display Bo in the altogether, at length. For close to two hours, *Tarzan the Ape Man* provides a veritable feast for Bo-worshippers. Photographed by John in a style somewhere between that of a Kodak commercial and Leni Riefenstahl's *Last of the Nuba*, Bo is seen clothed and (mostly) unclothed against stunning backdrops of rivers, mountains, forests and ocean shores. Were the film a 20 minute featurette with musical accompaniment, it might have achieved the status of a minor middle-brow softcore classic. Unfortunately, the Dereks saw fit to pad things out with characters and dialogue.

As written by Tom Rowe and Gary Goddard, the plot of this *Tarzan* is simply filler material for the moments when Bo isn't posing against some lush bit of scenery or other. The problem is that these moments give Richard Harris (playing Bo's father) the opportunity to run about shouting at the top of his lungs for extended periods of time. Bo, meanwhile, mumbles the inanities provided for her in a more quiet tone. Nevertheless, her basic performing style is no more suitable than Harris'. In the words of *Time* magazine, "She sucks in her stomach to look pretty, and chews her cuticles to suggest fear". As for the forgotten man in the midst of all of this, Tarzan, as played by newcomer Miles O'Keeffe, is merely a prop. He swells his pectorals, looks at Bo confusedly, and utters not a line. She looks up at him and coos appreciatively, but in the context of the action his position on

screen is about as important as that of a giant (and patently phoney) snake Bo tussles with at one point.

Still, complain as one might about the dialogue ("I'm still a virgin. I don't know whether that's good or bad," Bo mutters thoughtfully at one point), and the action ("The world's first all-moving picture calendar," proclaimed Vincent Canby in the *New York Times*) no moviegoer had any *real* cause for complaint. They had paid their money to see Bo Derek naked, and that's exactly what they got. As for the story, it was after all *Tarzan the Ape Man*, not *Hedda Gabler*.

For the record, the paying public was (in the short run at least) relatively satisfied. In a mere 17 days, Tarzan earned over 20 million dollars. In ordinary box office terms, that isn't so very remarkable these days. But considering the fact that the film was such a critical flop, such financial viability is noteworthy. Moreover, as the film cost somewhere in the neighbourhood of six to eight million dollars to produce (half the cost of most films from major studios these days) its chances of showing a profit would appear to be assured. In fact when put up against the string of costly flops MGM produced in 1981 *(Pennies from Heaven, Buddy Buddy, All the Marbles, Whose Life Is It Anyway?)* Tarzan was one of the few releases the company could point to with any sense of pride — on a financial level at least.

In the wake of *Tarzan*, the Dereks' equally low-budgeted *Pirate Annie* project (Bo as an Errol Flynn-style swashbuckler!) fell through. At present, plans for a Bo-starred version of *Adam and Eve* are in the works. "We're not very popular," Bo explained in an interview; "John and I like to do things our way". Whether the Dereks get their way in the future is open to question. But one thing is certain — Hollywood hasn't seen the last of slick producer-entrepreneurs constructing careers for their nubile young wives. There is, after all (just when you thought it was safe to go back to the movies)...Pia Zadora!

DAVID EHRENSTEIN.

DEATH WISH II

For some reason, people imagine that the film critic's life is one of boundless bliss. That we spend our lives spilling from taxicabs into air-conditioned viewing cinemas, being plied with martinis and canapés by watchful PR assistants, watching nothing but the movies of our choice, and then idly dictating a thousand or so carefully culled words to a lightly clad secretary. All of which is, of course, perfectly true. But there is a price to be paid.

Watching movies every day the critic soon comes to realise that for every good one there are (there must be) at least 15 which are stone cold dead in the market. This is not surprising, for if the pinnacle of the pyramid is to survive at its altitude then it needs the vast substructure to support it. The way that men and women of sane disposition cope with seeing so much dross is with humour and energy. But just occasionally there comes, squawking out of the chicken-run, a movie so vile that one's boy-scout ideals go out the window, a movie so devoid of any recognisable merit, reeking so strongly of that unmistakable tang of turkey, that whatever is said about it is done in a spirit of pure revenge. Life is after all short and two hours of it wasted on *Death Wish II* is best paid for in blood.

It may seem a little disingenuous, when dealing with a genre as blunt as the vigilante cycle of films, to complain of crudity, but even by the rebarbative standards of such humane gems as *Walking Tall*, *Magnum Force*, *Vigilante*, or even the more exalted *Taxi Driver*, *Death Wish II* is about as subtle as an ice-pick through the cerebellum. Charles Bronson is once more signalled as the decent voice of middle America, a man of no particular passions. (This in spite of already having led a one-man massacre on the low life of New York some five years earlier.)

Since Bronson has all the expressiveness of a stone Buddha, this is done largely by placing him in the context of a new family — a loving housekeeper (the minute you see such unquestioning devotion, you know that she is due for something nasty), a chic girlfriend (Jill Ireland giving a performance so wooden you can almost see the strings) and a catatonic daughter still recovering from *Death Wish I*, (aren't we all?). His well-heeled lifestyle is explained by having him wave around blueprints and murmur about facades at his architect's office.

The familiar muggings, now transferred to Los Angeles, very soon rear up again, in the shape of the usual posturing loons that directors, too long settled in the Babylonic retreats of the movie world, imagine constitute the threat of street crime. They steal Bronson's wallet, but not before Bronson has managed to beat one up in an alley-way (he can change from architect to vigilante faster than Superman, not even requiring a phone box and a clean pair of tights). Revenge comes shrieking back faster than Greek drama. Bronson's housekeeper is beaten, tied up, stripped and gang-raped with much lingering emphasis on the giggling bestiality of her attackers; then Bronson's daughter gets much the same treatment. Her flight from the gang is ended when she jumps through a window and is impaled on some railings below — a plagiarism so heavy-handed from so many better-made movies that the intended horror is lost.

Let there be no question about the portrayal of the violence in this movie. There is nothing, whether in the script, in the setting, in the direction or in the photography, to suggest anything other than that this is pure, leering voyeurism. Gratuitous? I doubt if the man could spell the word.

From here on, it is largely the mechanics of killing that propel the movie toward its wretched end. And even in this department, there is such a startling lack of invention that one can't help feeling Winner should be forcibly returned to directing the sort of amiable nudie flicks, set in naturist camps, with which he made his debut. "Do you believe in Jesus?" growls Bronson, spying a crucifix around the neck of one gulping mugger he has in his sights. "Yes I do," comes a strangled reply. "Well, you're going to meet him" is Bronson's final word before spreading the miscreant's brains across the wall. Such thoughtful dialogue managed to raise snorts of derision from an audience which looked dimly similar to the lot who stood and cheered when I saw *Death Wish I* in a shopping mall cinema in suburban New York in the early Seventies. Times change, tastes alter, only Winner's product gets irredeemably worse.

The above exchange is a model of economic wit, however, compared with later efforts at meaningful farewells. Despatching one more gibbering black psycho, who quite incidentally has been using a topless white girl as a shield, the best that Bronson can manage before the *coup de grace* is a gravelly "Goodbye", uttered with all the fake import of a Churchillian valedictory. (He has just previously shot a retreating mugger in the arse, the sort of misjudged piece of redneck bawdry with which this movie abounds.)

The film's main shootout in a deserted park between Bronson, aided by a New York cop who has been tailing him, and a squad of rippling bandits, armed to the teeth on account of having been surprised while doing a gun deal, results in noisy carnage, a burning Cadillac and a dying cop who manages to murmur "Get the motherfucker for me" before breaking out into the first few sentences of the Lord's Prayer as a final gesture. It's the sort of bad taste joke that one can imagine seeming rather funny on the set after a hard day's shooting, but it's exactly the kind of footage for which the cutting room floor was invented. Its inclusion suggests a film maker more short of material than anxious about creative decisions.

Faced with such a grade A, solid gold, surefire turkey, it is usually possible for even the meanest-minded reviewer to find some redeeming feature, some item of humour, some small gesture to which a brief allusion would establish at least the beginnings of fellow feeling, even compassion. After all such movies are often made by men of intelligence, of decent instinct, forced by hard times to pay for the mortgage with this kind of stuff. It would have been nice to find something, somewhere of that sort in *Death Wish II*, but it is impossible. To a movie shot with all the panache of an Indian restaurant commercial, there seems only one reasonable response; that of quietly ignoring it. CHRIS PEACHMENT

EVIL UNDER THE SUN

It is an opportunity, of course, to unleash rage. The screen has always swarmed with booby-films. Today especially it is rich in routine horrors: the haunted house, the unburied dead, the psychopath in the bedroom, the monster waiting in the basement for the unwary virgin. Most of them, though, aren't worth anger, they aren't worth even disgust. Somehow it is the movie which doesn't exploit sex, the harmless movie which draws the critic to attack. *Evil Under the Sun* is a harmless movie.

It is based on an Agatha Christie story; you can't get purer than that. It has all the advantages: a cast of famous and gifted players, a director skilled in the management of the thriller, a distinguished screenwriter, a cameraman with a long list of successes, costumes by a designer rightly a prize-winner, and a setting which any cruise-manager might envy. It was chosen for the 1982 Royal Film Performance. And it leaves one in a state of tepid indifference.

Like all Agatha Christie plots, it is about murder. Hitchcock once gave us a lesson (it was in *Torn Curtain*) about murder: killing a human being, he showed, is a hateful business. But the cinema has taken death to its heart: black comedy or thriller, mystery or morality, murder is the crux. Here it is treated as a puzzle. A number of characters are gathered in a luxury hotel on a Mediterranean island. The proprietress (Maggie Smith) has been an actress but not a successful one; her clients,

most of them, this hot bright summertime, have stage connections, in particular the former musical comedy star (Diana Rigg) who arrives with a trusting husband (Denis Quilley).

She, already hated by her stepdaughter and jealously disliked by the hotel proprietress, is tirelessly making enemies of the rest of the company — the biographer (Roddy McDowall) who can't secure her permission to publish his book with unwelcome revelations, the Broadway producers (James Mason and Sylvia Miles) trying to get her interested in a script, the millionaire (Colin Blakely) who can't detach her from the priceless jewel he has incautiously entrusted to her. Obviously she is the murder target. But then the puzzle: everybody had a reason to want her out of the way, everybody is under suspicion, but everybody has an alibi.

A typical Agatha Christie situation: little action, many questions. Hercule Poirot (Peter Ustinov, the best Poirot the cinema has so far found) happens to be taking a holiday, happens to be on the spot when the body is found on the beach. He is ready to observe, to interrogate, and to make inspired guesses. Somebody must have had the opportunity to alter somebody else's watch — and alter it back again; somebody must have needed, for reasons of camouflage or rather the removal of camouflage, to run the bathwater at an hour not normally spent taking a bath.

And the questions. Where was everybody when the midday gun went off? Why did the browbeaten wife (Jane Birkin) of the handsome young man flirting with the musical comedy star bother to tell that sullen stepdaughter to put her bathing cap on? And when the trivial incidents are given their place in the narrative — the bottle, for instance, thrown from the cliff and narrowly missing the biographer in his pedalo — everything has a reason, a motive, everything fits a treat.

But the reasons and motives are clear only in hindsight. And

murder, the ugly business of strangling a vain bitchy woman for her jewellery, has been reduced to a time-table.

Agatha Christie had a brilliantly ingenious mind. She could organise a crime for the printed page or the theatre. The cinema is another matter. In the cinema the minutiae of clues and clocks can lack the appearance of spontaneity. The precise machinery of retribution in *Murder on the Orient Express* worked, perhaps because the players had been less formally presented, perhaps because an imaginative writer had attended to the gathering speed of the story. Anthony Shaffer, the screenwriter here, is experienced in the translation of narrative to the screen. Nevertheless *Evil Under the Sun* comes out forced, calculated, an enclosed entertainment in spite of all the cliffs and sunsets over the sea.

For one needs to be persuaded. There is a theory that the cinema won't accommodate long speeches. It is a fallacy. A player relaxed in the conviction that what he is saying has significance for his hearers can hold a cinema audience for long minutes — Spencer Tracy could do it, Charles Laughton could do it. But when Ustinov, examining alibis, recapitulates the events of the past hours one is surprised by his control over the hotel guests. It is not his fault; the analysis is delivered with what

would be called command, but one divines behind him the lines on the printed page when the traditional detective traditionally unmasks the villain.

Throughout the conversations, especially the exchange of jibes between actress and hotel proprietress, one hears the staccato of the stage. These are the ripostes of third-rate theatre, with none of the glitter of wit. The smart, bitter society which the film attempts to evoke is a fake. The figures have no roots in the kind of life which is supposed to have produced them. Heretically one begins to wonder whether Agatha Christie's mild, amiable picture of the world is beginning to fade.

Possibly that suspicion is at the back of my hostility towards this harmless movie. You may say one should not treat a simple thriller, a pocket mystery, with the severity elicited by a serious film. But a mystery should stir curiosity, a thriller should excite. *Evil Under the Sun* has the endowments which ought to stir and excite. But the cast is trapped in unreality. All a good joke? A joke should have edge, murder should cut, and the edge here is blunted and softened. One longs to believe. But in this artificial sketch of a manufactured society there is nothing to believe in. There is no reality. Even the body on the beach is a lie. DILYS POWELL

AMERICAN POP

In 1981 two animated turkeys came squawking out of the coop. *American Pop* and *Heavy Metal* are intelligent beasts, with fine plumage:mutant turkeys, in fact, almost ready to turn into swans and fly for the sun.

American Pop comes from Ralph Bakshi, whose previous films establish its promising pedigree. *Fritz the Cat* (1972) brought cartoon animals out of the Walt Disney era into the R. Crumb one. *Heavy Traffic* (1973) mixed animation and live action to depict New York low life — and low as in *Last Exit to Brooklyn*, and much lower than in *Guys and Dolls. Coonskin* (1973) switched the Uncle Remus theme to Harlem — and was shelved after protests. *Hey Good Lookin'* (1975) was virtually *The Warriors* before its time. Shelved. *Lord of the Rings* (1978) blazed the sword and sorcery trail and turned the financial wolf away from Bakshi's studio door.

American Pop follows four generations of an American family, all caught up in music. 1905: Little Zalmie's family flee from Ukraine pogroms. His lifeline leads him through tenement fires, Bowery burlesque, Minsky's, World War I, and the gangster underworld, until around 1950 he "sings" to the Chicago Crime Commission. His son Benny crosses race lines to play with blacks, but turns to tunesmithing for cocktail piano, marries a Mafioso's daughter, and in World War II loses the spirit, and his life. His son Tony is reared in a Long Island suburb, hits the Kerouac trail, marries a waitress in Iowa, meets the San Francisco flower-people, and gurgles down the dope plughole himself. His son Pete learns the streetsmarts early, trades dope for his big break, and gets to lord it as a stadium-cramming rock superstar.

It's a Jewish answer to *Roots*, with music. It's also sleazy, mean and sad, which is the *Heavy Traffic* wavelength; that was semi-autobiographical, and maybe Bakshi will take it with him wherever he goes. The fourth generation success story is no less disquieting for being so long delayed.

The film's moral downbeat is unexpected and brave. It intensifies the thrust of Fosse's *All That Jazz*, which substitutes, for musical comedy, musical tragedy, showbiz obsession as spectacular suicide.
A succession of beautiful images — a jacuzzi for the optic nerve. The main style looks like rotoscoping but is subtler. Bakshi made a first, photographic, film, with actors against a bare wall, and based his drawings on it. It fits that modern fascination with images that get the best of both worlds, the photographic one and the painterly one.

With so much going for it, how come *American Pop* belongs down on the turkey farm? The American film critic Jonathan Rosenbaum told me that his Alabama schools spent more time teaching Alabama history than American history and more time on American history than on the rest of the world. When you allow for how schoolmarms spin out the grey flannel about Presidents and patriotism, the Constitution and progress, elections and World Wars, while hardly touching the social history of ordinary people, you can see why Bakshi turns to an alternative view of the American way.

But it's a superficial one. It's a media history book: sensationalism masquerading as nostalgia. The Ukraine scenes gripped me, as less familiar (though the source is *Fiddler on the Roof*), and so did the sweatshop scenes (*Hester Street*), and the recap of the zootsuit riots.

But this history book is a pageant of déjà vu. Its pages torn from *Life* magazine. Nothing connects. For example, war twice intervenes, putting paid to Zalmie's pure tenor as to Benny's songwriting. And what's wrong with that is our commonsense feeling that the changing key signatures of American pop were set not by bestial Huns but by change at home, and not by gangsters or bannerline stuff, but by the little things of which memories are made. Strafers' bullets didn't stop those full-throated tenors. Rather, the microphones let the crooners in, jazz syncopation caught the new industrial rhythms, and parlour and peasant music and Ruritanian operettas lost their relevance to the melting pot. Nor did World War II kill the old songwriting tradition. Sinatra, Bennett, Streisand and all those guys still flourish on it.

Though *American Pop* hints at a social history of pop music, it has to be *Hamlet* without the Prince. It misses out on Tin Pan Alley, market forces, and public demand. Instead it wheels out corny heavies like Mafiosi, LSD, War or (at that rate) Nameless Evil. Yet American pop is also about a fusion of positive things; barbershop quartets, Jewish cantors, Irish tenors, *The Birth of the Blues*, *American Graffiti*, gospel and good times.

Maybe Bakshi's really talking about something that's true and cynical and born from suffering but never quite gets to speak out. German bullets, dope, gangsters, are just shorthand for it. But because the film's theme isn't clear, a Will to Evil seems to imbue it.

Conversely, the personal story is so criss-crossed by public events that it too becomes thin, arbitrary, non-intimate. The multiplicity of characters, epochs and situations oversimplifies each one to the same sad QED. Finally it's as boring as your average Brecht play.

Moreover, there are subtle differences between comic strips and movies. Comics are read quickly (or at the reader's own pace) and taken (in a certain sense) lightly. Whereas the movie spectator has nothing but movie. That or darkness. He needs a thick, intimate, human interest to grip him. The secret of Hollywood movies is tight plotting and dramatic ambivalence. Which painterly-minded people often find very tricky to learn.

Similarly the vistas that look so mind-expanding in page panels easily become remote up there on the movie screen. And its single image loses that serial repetition which adds such graphic-dramatic interest to the page.

The one graphic flaw of *American Pop* hits it right here. The faces flicker so much I soon learned not to watch them closely. Surprisingly maybe, that hardly spoiled the overall pictures. But it further weakened our communion with the characters.

Both *American Pop* and *Heavy Metal* are dedicated to the notion that evil calls most of history's tunes. Which may appeal to their target audience, today's teenagers, whose cynicism intensifies their natural appetite for violence. *Mad Max* is a *Heavy Metal*-type story that works on the big screen (and how).

American Pop operates near the territory of Scorsese movies like *New York, New York* and *Raging Bull*. Both directors favour strong tableaux in a loose, "epic" form; slugging matches between personal energy and social pressures, lurking evil and self-destruction. Scorsese took great risks, Bakshi took greater ones.

I single out *American Pop* because it's a failed creative movie, a brave try at new developments. Like *Dom* and *Yellow Submarine*, it diversifies animation's visual repertoire, and borrows creatively from the whole gamut of modern illustration. It may seem conservative, insofar as its style is based on live-action continuities, which have tended to straitjacket cartoon action. Nonetheless, within that convention it's inventive, juggling haunting skyscraper-scapes, echoes of *Saturday Evening Post* covers and Edward Hopper paintings, and paradoxes like drawing the Western on the TV set.

It's still a turkey. But I'd rather hear it talking than all those middle-of-the-road birds.
RAYMOND DURGNAT

MOMMIE DEAREST

Biopics used to be laudatory, however cannibalistic, fictionalised, bathetic and, where possible, safely musical. *The Jolson Story*, Glenn Miller's, Benny Goodman's, *The Five Pennies, Night and Day* (Cole Porter had only joked about Cary Grant playing him), and Mickey Rooney whitewashing Lorenz Hart's life in *Words and Music*. Once the new industry of cinema books probed the dross beneath the filmland floss, films turned somewhat saltier to examine Jeanne Eagles, Buster Keaton, Lillian Roth, Joe E. Lewis, Ruth Etting. Minus song-and-dance, the genre backfired in the mid-Seventies. Few cared about James Brolin being Gable and Lombard being Jill Clayburgh (an absurd thought), much less for Rod Steiger's spirited W.C. Fields.

That's why Martin Sheen refused James Dean's story; Stephen McHattie made a passable stab at it. He was better than Nureyev's *Valentino* (but then, what isn't?). Cheryl Ladd still aims to bounce Jean Seberg's battered bones, having been warned off the Grace Kelly saga by Monaco. Michelle Phillips and Jaclyn Smith (the screen's newest Jackie Kennedy) battle on for the right to smite Gene Tierney. For the genre never dies. The moving finger having re-writ moved on to TV. Musicals still worked best. Kurt Russell as *Elvis*, Gary Busey, superb, as Buddy Holly. Kevin O'Connor and Kathryn Harrold became Bogie and Bacall which soon had John Wayne's producer sons stifling Dukepics by announcing their own, then cancelling it, all within a few months of the funeral. Swifter still, Anita Loos' niece fanfared an auntyopic plan a week after the obituaries.

On either screen, Garson Kanin's *Moviola* holds the clones' record: 20 or more, from Tony Curtis' bravura Selznick and Kristina Wayborn's Garbo to Clive Revill's Chaplin (due soon for both Broadway and Hollywood treatment), and a striking brunette named Barrie Longfellow as Joan Crawford. A flash of a TV commercial-length cameo, yet good, honest and

true. If only they'd left it there...

But no, we had *Mommie Dearest*. Or Crawford did. With both barrels. Her biopic, or more (im)precisely her stepdaughter's, became hailed, or to be wholly accurate, hyped (in a flop-saving exercise) as camp. Crap! Camp is a respectable enough handle for anything over the top. But, surely, with some style and panache to it. Like, say, Dietrich or Liberace. Beyond some 54 costume changes, there is no style in this filmic fertiliser. It is low camp. The lowest. A new nadir in Hollywood's often tasteless habit of feeding off its own, hitting a dame when she is not merely down, but dead, buried and unable to sue. The book was written after her death for much the same reason. Not so, says Christina Crawford. "The story wasn't yet finished." The will hadn't been read either... "Not since Lizzie Borden gave her mother 40 whacks has a daughter wreaked such vengeance on her mother," said *Time*. About the book. The film left most sane observers speechless. Anne Bancroft quit it because the script was a hatchet job. Faye Dunaway felt the same (exit: Christina as a $200,000 scenarist) and wanted a more balanced view. If *Mommie Dearest* is balanced, Faye's previously well tuned judgement had been Dunaway with due to too much TV. Since winning her *Network* Oscar (for a fair, 1977 version of a Crawford hustler), the actress fell into doing tele-biopics: Aimee Semple McPherson, Arthur Miller's Marilyn, Wallis Simpson, Eva Peron. She obviously figured Crawford was

meaty enough to force a big screen comeback.

Instead, it was a cheap shot winning a cult of insomniacs with nothing better to do once the gay bars closed than latch on to crummily made Z-movies on the midnight circuit, screaming out favourite dialogue in unison with the star turn. Altogether now: "Tina! Bring...me...the axe!" And one more time (pass the cold cream first): "How many times have I told you! No. Wire. Hangers. Ever!"

The late night crowd adored that. It would. It's a mindless pursuit. Like painting with numbers. And *Mommie Dearest* is a paint job. Powder 'n' paint. Dunaway looks uncannily like Crawford was the force-fed hype. It wasn't uncanny at all. Just a canny make-up job. The same could be done for Roger Moore. Or Miss Piggy. For photos... Once the face behind the adhesive had to smile, wince, glower, rant, rave, scream, holler, talk, it moved on its own jawline. Crawford went. Dunaway was back. Finding it impossible (or unnecessary) to act with her usual finesse inside the Tussaud *maquillage*.

The film was sold on the make-up. The face was the motif for the posters: a torn photo on the first US ads (before cashing in on wire hangers and The Biggest Mother of Them All line) and a hung painting dominating little Christina at table in the Euro-art. They matched the embarrassing performance.

So much emphasis was placed on this cloning, we have Dunaway playing Crawford in a

Crawford movie of the Crawford life. An infantile move, as if Errol Flynn's story could be told only in a porno flick, or Wayne's as a Western. Okay for a send-up sketch, not 129 minutes of unrelenting Metrocolor angst. Besides, Crawford never played Crawford 24 hours a day. Even Christina thought this performance was ludicrous.

Ronnie Barker could have done it. Stanley Baxter probably will. Charles Pierce has for years in America. Given the direction of Frank Perry (unbelievably the man who once made *Diary of a Mad Housewife*), what *Mommie Dearest* was aiming at was Tim Curry directed by John Waters. Which might have been acceptable if the scenario had the odd tincture of realism, credibility — let alone some truth.

Crawford adopted not two but four children: Christina, Christopher, and twins Cathy and Cindy. (She had a thing about C, and better luck, no doubt, with her poodles, Cliquot, Camille, Chiffon.) The twins aren't mentioned in the film. Nor are the poodles. Nor any explanation for the S&M looking harness Christopher wears in bed. It's a "sleep-safe" to stop kids falling out, although Crawford kept him in one until the age of 12 (which can't have solved bed-wetting problems). Apart from Howard Da Silva's Louis B. Mayer (Da Silva once played Krushchev!) and Mara Hobel's kiddy Christina, the casting is sufficiently out to allow the elder Christina a Southern accent for no reason other than Diana Scarwid being born in Savannah, Georgia.

And of Crawford's four husbands (Douglas Fairbanks Jr., Franchot Tone, Philip Terry) only the Pepsi boss, Alfred Steele, is depicted (safely dead, as well) cueing another risible Crawford movie scene of her dominating the Pepsi board. My favourite anecdote of Crawford is of those final Pepsi years. She drank it instead of tea or coffee. Every time she burped, she said "Thank you, Pepsi!" That doesn't sound much like *Mommie Dearest*. TONY CRAWLEY

RICH AND FAMOUS

One of the many ways a movie can achieve true badness is to succeed in pleasing the audience it was aimed at. Exploitation movies like *Swamp Thing* and *An Unsuitable Job for a Woman* are bad not because they pander, respectively, to American morons and foreign critics. They are bad because they sincerely and honestly want to give pleasure to their audience — and to no-one else at all.

In the majoritarian cinema practised in those Los Angeles municipalities (Culver City, Beverly Hills, Hollywood, Burbank, Universal City) collectively known as Hollywood, true badness has proven elusive of late. Technical advances and the professionalisation of screen actors have provided even horrors like *Rocky II* and *Any Which Way You Can* with flashes of watchability. Today, it takes a veritable master of the cinema to make a truly bad movie at a Hollywood studio. This, then, is the unique accomplishment of George Cukor in *Rich and Famous*.

Cukor, 83, has been making "women's pictures" practically since Eve (*The Philadelphia Story, Camille, Gaslight, Born Yesterday, A Star Is Born*). If anyone knows what women want to see on the silver screen, it is Cukor. In a season when most other MGM movies were cut off at the knees within yards of the starting gate, *Rich and Famous* drew enough female patronage to appease the studio's accountants.

The movie is a re-make, up-date and down-grade of *Old Acquaintance* (1943). Jacqueline Bisset, who designed the project as a Bisset vehicle, plays the long-suffering Bette Davis part. Candice Bergen impersonates bitchy Miriam Hopkins.

Good buddies in college, Bisset and Bergen grow apart thereafter. Bisset becomes famous as a novelist and Bergen becomes rich as a wife. Each envies the other, so Bergen becomes famous as a novelist and Bisset becomes... well, not rich: it's hard to say what does happen to her, but there are some sex scenes in which she achieves orgasm, which to a modern woman is like money in the bank. Can she, will she, dare she hold her lover, half her age and twice as bright?

Manipulative as the plot is, the movie's true badness lies elsewhere. Just as the wart on the end of the nose of the otherwise unexceptionally plain woman turns her into a witch, the decor of *Rich and Famous* makes it ugly. Bergen clomps through the picture in a wardrobe that she must have burned with loathing after the production wrapped. Frocks shaped like jack-o'-lanterns dyed arc-welder's blue are used to suggest her character's crassness, but the effect is so overly garish that a giggle is the only sane response.

If Bergen is sadistically overdressed, Bisset is masochistically underdressed. I'm not referring to the bed scenes, which offer their very own pinpricks of badness. Bisset's devotion to her craft is suggested by slobbing her down

into saggy pants and sloppy sweaters. Her hair is cropped and her face made up to look un-made-up. No wonder she can't hold her man.

The man in question, played by Hart Bochner, is a reporter from *Rolling Stone* who comes to interview Bisset. He is so good a reporter that he doesn't need to ask questions, take notes, or ever actually write anything. It's enough for him to be cleverer than his interviewee. He is so obnoxious and so opinionated, in fact, that Bisset immediately falls in love with him. Both Karen Black and Gregory Peck fell in love with and married people sent to interview them, and it is my hope that one day Dolly Parton will fall in love with me when I am sent to interview her, but I am fairly sure that interviewers do not as a rule obnox their subjects into bed.

Is this the end for Cukor? His last job before *Rich and Famous* was *The Corn Is Green* with Katharine Hepburn for American TV in 1979. His most recent work for the cinema was the unfortunate *The Blue Bird* in 1976. Cukor was actually the second director of *Rich and Famous*. Robert Mulligan began shooting the movie, but the 1980 American actors' strike forced the production to shut down. By the time the strike was settled, Mulligan was contracted to another project and a new director was needed instantly.

Cukor's first move was to scrap the week's worth of footage Mulligan had shot in New York's Central Park and build a fake Central Park in

California. The Algonquin Hotel was also mocked up on an MGM sound stage. In Cukor's MGM heyday you could set a film in New York without ever going there, but not today. Scene after chatter-heavy scene simply sinks lumpishly through the stagey artificiality of the settings.

During production of the movie, Cukor was lavish in his praise of the script's "wit and style". Here is a line Bergen has to huff at Bisset: "It is the habit of this community to be suspicious when a married man goes off with a married woman — especially when the woman happens to be the man's wife's best friend".

Maybe it isn't the script that makes the movie so bad. Maybe the script actually did have both wit and style. A less one-note actress than Bergen might somehow have turned that line into a good joke. In fact, if the whole piece had been played for the broadest laughs instead of for portentous solemnity, it might have been bearable to the non-swooning segment of the audience. But that would be like asking Barbara Cartland to be Mel Brooks.

Bisset plays the whole movie with a wistful expression, as if her character's predicament were not that of a low-rent sitcom. Hitherto best known for the "wet T-shirt look" she pioneered in *The Deep*, Bisset probably thought that *Rich and Famous* would become a feminist talking point and that she would become the new Jane Fonda. Sorry — it's back to the briny for Bisset. BART MILLS

PORKY'S

Porky's is the worst movie I have ever seen to gross more than a hundred million dollars, which is an incredible sum for an avowedly stupid comedy with no "names" and no discernible virtues. The film's success is due more to marketing methods than to any sociological substratum in its scenario. It does indulge a preppy-like bigotry and snobbery of the kind popularised in *Animal House*. Only this time the film's victims are not blacks but Florida rednecks in "gator" country where writer-director Bob Clark seems to have some adolescent experiences to exorcise. Actually, the movie is composed of half prurience on the high school level, and half vengeance on the louts in a poorer county that gives the movie both its title and its villains. Why this formula has succeeded so spectacularly baffles me. It is the most depressing phenomenon of mass culture I have witnessed in years, and I hate it. As it happens, I cannot improve on Dave Kehr's brilliant thumbnail capsule in *Film Comment*: "*Porky's* is *Death Wish* with pimples." Ugh!
ANDREW SARRIS

SO FINE

When the name of the Hollywood game is "packaging", critics' metaphors regularly tend to the culinary (Ingredients; The Recipe) or the scientific (Elements; Chemistry). Both glib parallels carry at least an appropriate whiff of the experimental — with the taste or volatility of the "product" merely a chance matter of the reaction of known constituents in one melting pot or another. A related combinant vocabulary might, with no less aptness, be employed in discussing *So Fine*, one of the year's most gaudily packaged of Hollywood artefacts — the terminology of the fashion world that is in large part the film's milieu; a world in which notions of inspired mix 'n' match also currently hold sway.

At any rate, it's not really the sort of movie to attract undue attention in the terms of the culture it comically opposes to that of the rag trade — the academic world. Semiologists and structuralists rarely concern themselves with flops, anyway. (While the rest of us, in the near-instant judgement business, generally just shrug our shoulders and pass gratefully on to the next hit or pet lost cause.)

Yet, in prospect at least, the components assembled for the appearance of *So Fine* in the winter collections (with that mixture of optimism, shrewdness and innate conservatism that characterises the Hollywood currency of The Deal) had a sort of respectable coherence. Indeed, involved in the ensemble were three much lauded, modish constructs: Author, Genre and Star. Specifically: Andrew Bergman, the screwball comedy, and Ryan O'Neal; each, in various two-piece combinations at least, having previously been brand leaders of Dollar Chic.

Writer/director Bergman was hitherto best known in the film business for dreaming up the idea of *Blazing Saddles* (genre parody par excellence), and he'd also written the screenplay for that knowing odd couple (Peter Falk/Alan Arkin) comedy of 1979, *The In-Laws*. To critics and the remainder-rack

enthusiast he had been the student author of a serious study of Hollywood strategies during the Depression era, *We're in the Money*. And to general readers he maintained a high profile with a couple of fine, funky, Chandleresque crime fiction novels set on the factoid fringe of vintage Tinseltown, *Hollywood and LeVine* and *The Big Kiss-Off of 1944*. On balance, good credentials for making commercial and critical capital out of the retrospective conjuncture of Hollywood and its (stylistic) history.

Considered as part of that history, the notion of screwball comedy occupies a fairly specific, timebound place, evoking infinite pleasurable memories of the likes of Howard Hawks, Billy Wilder, Cary Grant, Katharine Hepburn, Carole Lombard, scavenger hunts, pet leopards and dinosaur bones. Within the homage-strewn, Movie Brattish self-consciousness of recent years' retro stylings, its shade has been recalled only intermittently, but perhaps most tellingly in Peter Bogdanovich's jackdaw recreation of its crazy-quilt, cross-talk, cross-purpose slapstick, *What's Up, Doc?*, in which — and here the plot thickens — Ryan O'Neal took the honours as an ivory tower Bugs Bunny.

A (belated) overnight success in *Love Story*, O'Neal was still eminently bankable some dozen

years on, after three retro collaborations with Bogdanovich (the backward-looking *Doc?* followed by the in-period *Paper Moon* and *Nickelodeon*), odd sorties into spectacle with Kubrick (*Barry Lyndon*) and Attenborough (*A Bridge Too Far*), into abstract dramatics with Walter Hill (the remarkable *Driver*), and then a run for cover into pale mimicry (the *Love Story* sequel, *Oliver's Story*, and a repairing with Streisand in *The Main Event*).

So, even if all the separates were decidedly off the peg, the first guess predicted tailor-made teamwork. But, to run through the acute disappointment in terms of those opening metaphors, the menu turned out indigestible, the alchemy produced only dross, and the new clothes proved fit only for the emperor. Which is where the quality of the cloth — the script — comes in, with its jarring clashes of colour and texture between denim and tweed.

Uncomfortably straddling the worlds of "head-in-the-clouds" academia (he's a professor of literature angling for a university tenure against toadying rivals) and the "down-to-earth" rag trade (helping out in his father's harassed garment business), O'Neal's Bobby Fine actually splits his pants (a pair of too-tight jeans borrowed in haste from his mistress, married to the gangster squeezing his dad) and improvises a

promotional gimmick — bare-assed fashion — that serves as such both within the film (his dad's business booms) and outside it (as a convenient marketing image and hook). The wilder excesses of farcical plotting (eventually involving an incongruous collision of all the film's cultural archetypes on a grand opera stage) hold interest only inasmuch that, by and large, they don't really work. But what arises from that central image of torn fabric proves fascinatingly "cheeky" in more senses than one.

In following up his accidental trend-setting with an unexpected business flair, Fine gets into marketing his perspex-bottomed jeans in a big way — and the film virtually stops dead for a complete run-through of the choreographed production-number spectacle of his crass TV commercial. However, given the slant of the movie's own publicity and promotional campaign, what we really seem to be getting is the unique sight of a "trailer" for the film we're actually already watching — selling itself anew to an audience whose interest must be presumed (almost certainly correctly) to be flagging.

Throughout, Bergman pitches his screenplay alternately too high and too low — scoring easy points off the pretensions of the intellectuals while indulging in esoteric parallelisms of a text as highbrow as *Othello* — while his direction is never more than adequate in an anonymously frantic register. Jack Warden acts O'Neal off the screen with practised ease; art-movie import Mariangela Melato is suitably exotic as a second division Madeline Kahn; while the giant Richard Kiel carries an inevitable aura of comic-book cinema into whatever context he's placed in. On the whole, screwball comedy remains a matter of unassailable memories.

So Fine certainly wasn't the worst film of the year, or even perhaps the most disappointing given the promising elements of its "packaging", but it deserves at least bronze turkey status for the very *un*-natural commercial break at its heart. PAUL TAYLOR

FACES OF THE FUTURE
KRISTY McNICHOL

I am so high on Kristy McNichol after *Little Darlings, Only When I Laugh* (adding the prefix *It Hurts* in the UK) and *The Nights the Lights Went Out in Georgia* that I have faith she will survive even Christopher Atkins in *The Pirate Movie*. Of course, I have always been suspiciously susceptible to Nabokovian nymphets and perverse ingenues from the comparatively coy and innocent days of Gloria Jean to the steamy sagas of Jodie Foster. I had been watching Kristy McNichol more or less out of the corner of my eye as she grew up in a long-running classy television series called *Family*, and so I was not surprised by her polish and professionalism. But she has shown me considerably more in the past couple of years in the way she grabs the screen and holds it. These are hardly easy times for actresses of any age. On the one hand, most of the macho screenwriters and directors on the current scene barely know what a woman is, much less a woman's role, a woman's scene, or, God forbid, a woman's picture. Consequently, there are all sorts of talented females floating around as mere foils and mattress testers for the most idiotic of male fantasies.

Even McNichol has not had all that much to work with in her aforementioned screen appearances, but she has not seemed to notice the problem. She simply burst out of the screen with all her emotional barrels firing, and before you know it the screen is ablaze with the forgotten fireworks of being female. She can act, she can sing, and what is most important, she can simply be, and with a mysterious meld of insinuation made up of dramatically fierce eyes and sensually provocative lips cause somewhat limited movies to vibrate with feeling and humour.

ANDREW SARRIS

Kristy McNichol in 'It Hurts Only When I Laugh'

JEREMY IRONS

Jeremy Irons was propelled to public notice by the fortuitous coincidence of two glossy films based on novels best described as prestigious (where the quickness of the prose deceives the mind into believing, for a time, that it has experienced genuine magic): the TV serial *Brideshead Revisited* and the movie *The French Lieutenant's Woman.*

Fashion and glamour and luxury, mass appeal and respectability all met to make him a star. He gazed soulfully from the screens, big and little, quivering with repressed emotions at the sight of Catholic aristocracy and a hooded woman at a Dorset quayside. He became, as movie moguls say, "hot", although a cooler actor would be hard to find. Apart from revealing his genuine appeal and actorly skills, his arrival marked a swing away from the screen heroes of the 1960s and 1970s and a return to older values.

Forty years ago Irons would have been a rival to the most successful British film star, Leslie Howard. Like Howard, he combines a romantic appeal with an apparently aristocractic manner (as does his Brideshead co-star Anthony Andrews, who went on from that work to play the Scarlet Pimpernel, one of Howard's most famous roles). It matters not that Howard was the son of Hungarian immigrants or that Irons is the child of a chartered accountant and was born in the Isle of Wight.

Both suggest effortless good breeding. The film historian David Shipman wrote of Howard, "he seemed to have nostrils as sensitive as a thoroughbred's". Irons, too, acts with his nose. He is also aware that people tend to categorise him as an aristocratic actor, and he resents it. He met it first at drama college, where his tutor lamented that he had a face that would have launched a thousand films 30 years earlier. Then, of course, it was North Country actors like Albert Finney and Tom Courtenay, or Cockneys like Michael Caine who were successful.

Irons' abilities are wider than the well-bred stereotype might suggest. Karel Reisz chose him for *The French Lieutenant's Woman* after watching him play a Bavarian student in a TV play by Harold Pinter. Jerzy Skolimowski saw him as Charles Ryder in *Brideshead* and immediately decided that he was the perfect choice to play a Polish labourer in his post-Solidarity tragi-comedy *Moonlighting.* From working with Polish actors, Irons went straight to play a Scots Army officer in a BBC version of D.H. Lawrence's story *The Captain's Doll.*

After that, he was preparing to play Biggles, Capt. W.E. Johns' chauvinistic, Hun-hating pilot, hero of dozens of hearty adventures that once were schoolboy favourites. It is a role that could bring out a side of Irons that has been as repressed as Ryder: his comedy acting. Biggles is intended as a type of pre-war junior James Bond. Irons has the ability to add wit to the heroics. Indeed, like Leslie Howard, he is likely to be at his best in polished film comedies, the type of acting which requires great style and precision.

Irons' comic talents have been best displayed in a TV commercial (directed by Ridley Scott) for Croft's sherry, in which he played a monocled ass straight out of P.G. Wodehouse. It is that commercial which has made Irons an unusual actor in his attitudes and a film star who can reject, at least for the moment, commercial pressures. For it was so successful that he was asked to make two more. Rather than turn down the offer, he asked for a larger sum of money for a couple of days' work, enough to pay for 13 years' private education of his son.

His terms were accepted. It was only then he turned down the offer. Since then he has found it easier to refuse work that does not interest him and to accept roles that, in the thinking of Hollywood, do not advance his career. When Skolimowski wanted him for *Moonlighting*, he listened to an outline of the story and agreed to take the part the same day.

Irons' aim, he says, is a simple one: "to do good work". For that reason, for the next two years, he is more likely to be seen in the theatre than on the screen. He is joining the Royal Shakespeare Company where his wife Sinead Cusack is a leading actress. It is unlikely that we will see him in his favourite role, Richard II, as the RSC's Alan Howard has

Jeremy Irons in 'Moonlighting'

recently played the part. Nor does he wish to try Hamlet. But he does want to act in Shakespeare because he feels that is the best way for him to grow as an actor.

He believes that his future potential depends on what he does now, while he is in his thirties; he has to answer the challenge of playing the greatest roles in the British acting tradition. It is certainly true that many fine actors who abandoned theatre early and tried to return to it later have not fulfilled their potential. Richard Burton has only the ghost of the talent that electrified the Old Vic; Peter O'Toole was a tremendous Hamlet when young and a grotesque Macbeth when older; Albert Finney, a powerful and passionate stage actor in modern plays, was crude and clumsy in his classical stint at the National Theatre. And whatever happened to Anthony Hopkins?

The actors Irons admires are the undoubted stars who have nevertheless kept a distance from Hollywood, such as Sir Alec Guinness and Paul Scofield. "My father-in-law Cyril Cusack is what I mean by a star," says Irons. "People may not recognise him in the street, but on stage or film, he's magic." He is aware of how seductive cinema can be. "It's not just greed for money that drives actors on. The excitement and pressure of making a film are almost druglike, and you don't get that in the theatre."

Irons, then, is likely always to do the unexpected, to keep an audience guessing. In probably his best performance to date, as a Victorian officer and explorer stranded in Darkest Africa in Simon Gray's much underrated and commercially unsuccessful stage play *The Rear Column*, he did that perfectly. Once again, he was playing a member of the upper middle classes. But in the play's final, shocking moments it became clear that this epitome of duty and honour had turned cannibal.

It is the sort of role he delights in playing. And he acts them with an unmatched sensitivity. His future plans include possibly making a film with his friend David Essex. It is perhaps forgotten that Irons, like Essex, first made his mark in the Goon-like London production of the religious musical *Godspell* and once busked in Leicester Square.

He will try his best to be an unexpected actor, not easily categorised. I watched him on the set of *Moonlighting*, wearing clothes that a tramp would disdain to pick up between finger and thumb. He told me then "I'm fairly irresponsible and don't care that much if I fall flat on my face, so I hope I won't get frightened and play too safe.

"There's so much money involved in pictures. When a producer signs you for a part, he wants something specific from you and that's what you have to give him. In theatre, you can experiment. I don't want to surround myself with Hollywood mega-millionaire producers. If I play safe I will castrate myself as an actor."

And brushing a little dust off his sleeve, he exited left, pursued by fame. JOHN WALKER

KLAUS MARIA BRANDAUER

He arrives, so far as the screen in Britain is concerned, out of the blue; he disappears at the end of the film into a blinding dazzle of light. We have never seen him before; few of us had even heard of him. But once seen he is unforgettable, monumental in the mysterious business of acting.

His name is Klaus Maria Brandauer. He is Austrian, famous in the German-speaking theatre and particularly in Vienna. In England we know him now as the title-figure in the film *Mephisto*, a Hungarian-West German production shot in Budapest by the Hungarian director István Szabó. The Hungarian cinema has certainly moved in the last two or three decades. Twenty-seven years ago I was invited to spend a week in Budapest looking at new Hungarian films; I sat for hours in an empty cinema with an interpreter at my side, making the acquaintance of work by film makers who have since become internationally celebrated. István Szabó was among them: a young director still concerned with his own country and its problems. It is exciting to see him today, having broken the language-barrier and the national barrier, emerging as a significant name — and bringing to the world-screen a truly extraordinary player.

The film, based on a novel written in 1936 by Klaus Mann, son of Thomas Mann, is set in the early Thirties, terrifying age of the rise of the Nazis. Brandauer plays an actor (the character is said to be modelled on the German Gustav Gründgens) who uses the régime to further his career but is at the same time the tool of the dictators. We see him first as a young man practising in private, dancing with a black girl. He is agile, relaxed, excited. She laughs at him, but she recognises his basic seriousness about his work and his future: he is an actor, he will never be anything else, never care about anything else.

Catching at the fashion of the times — for one must remember that Germany in the Thirties was the home of

Klaus Maria Brandauer in 'Mephisto'

political cabaret and experimental theatre — he busies himself with left-wing drama: total theatre, he announces, theatre which must embrace everybody, the audience, the workers, the entire public. And in the company of liberal society he sees the chance to move from the position of a provincial actor to Berlin.

He will make a conquest of a girl with good connections (she is played by Krystyna Janda, often seen in Wajda's movies). One observes him carefully assuming the manner of a man deeply in love. He marries her; but when the Nazis seize power he refuses to exile himself with her and her family. Realising that as an actor he depends on language, his own language, he stays in Nazi Germany — still relying on the help of women, still sending flowers and flattery.

And he plays Mephistopheles in Goethe's *Faust*. Playing in chalk-white mask and naked skull he makes the role his own. He attracts the attention of the Nazi General (played with diabolical good humour by Rolf Hoppe); for the sake of his career he divorces his wife; and he is made director of the State Theatre. He is not quite indifferent to the fate of his former friends. He obtains a safe conduct out of Germany for the black girl, but when he intervenes in the case of opponents of the régime he is contemptuously threatened. He has the success he wanted, but he is trapped. He is the servant of a monstrous government, and knows it.

What is extraordinary is Brandauer's playing of a double part. Always the actor, he convinces — and yet one sees that nothing is true except his ambition. Watch him kneeling at the feet of the girl he is to marry: he is charming, he is seductive, but it is the charm and the seductiveness of a man playing a part. At the start, especially in scenes with the black girl (the only human

being with whom, perhaps because he is at ease and has no need to pose, he seems naturally happy), he has a kind of physical exuberance. He makes large gestures, moves excitedly. But when he is speaking of his "total theatre" his enthusiasm is carried along by its own impetus; as an advocate he is enjoying his own performance. With time the mood, or rather his presentation of the mood, changes. He is no longer the confident young player with left-wing political ideas; now ambition must subdue itself to its situation. No more fast, feverish gestures; he must be ingratiating, humble, gratefully eager to please.

And yet another change. In a position of authority at last, he must wear the mask of command while at the same time committing himself to obedience. With the air of a teacher, a philosopher, he interprets the works of Shakespeare, but interprets according to the tenets of his bosses. One looks at the face, grave behind its spectacles, controlled, certain of respect and admiration, even a little bland. It has put aside the past: the struggles, the enthusiasms so comfortably replaced, the ignominies, the friends dead and forgotten. But it is the same face, unmarked by the passage of time and history. For this is an actor performing strictly according to the demands of the immediate present.

He is young ambition dreaming of success, playing amorously with the beautiful black girl. He is the suitor, almost obsequious, of the daughter of a rich family. He is the professional taking a chance in a new political society, sacrificing his integrity rather than risk beginning again in a foreign country and a foreign tongue. At last he is the complete time-server in a murderous world. Most actors fight to present the truth of the character they are portraying. Brandauer in *Mephisto* fights to veil whatever truth may lie beneath that careful calm. For this is an actor playing an actor. An actor who never stops acting. DILYS POWELL

LAURENE LANDON

Whether or not you could deem an actress any kind of "overnight success" when her two films to date have pretty much sunk without commercial or orthodox critical trace, the notion has to be broad enough to admit anyone who's managed to make sufficient impression in such straitened surroundings as has Laurene Landon in a pair of this year's heavily flawed but nonetheless engaging near-miss oddities, *All the Marbles (The California Dolls* in the UK) and *I, the Jury.*

As the female wrestler Molly, half of a small halls-to-Reno tag-team managed and zealously hyped by Peter Falk in the Robert Aldrich movie, and as Velda, the resourceful gun-toting secretary to misogynist private eye Mike Hammer in the brash Mickey Spillane update, Laurene Landon hasn't exactly commanded top-billing yet, either. But her intriguing presence in each role — running in totally contradictory directions from the modish personae currently in Hollywood vogue, steering clear of either insecure feminism or "fatale" femininity — suggests she could easily inspire some maverick movie brat to some reckless casting very soon.

At the very least, and bearing in mind the fate of her vehicles to date, she could be set for canonisation as the latest "queen of the Bs", perhaps rivalling the comparatively veteran Mary Woronov for the mantle that hasn't really been picked up since the tragic death of Claudia Jennings.

Such speculative ruminations would normally now be backed up by a clutch of biographical determinants or previous filmographical trivia, setting out accidents of breeding or accretions of experience to account for suddenly apparent maturity as an actress. Unfortunately, you won't find either here. Neither would you find them at present in the places one normally looks for such data. Only one tantalising nugget of information stands out from a briefly dismissive review of

All the Marbles in an obscure imported journal — Landon, it confidently states, was a professional roller skater and basketball player.

So, one guesses hesitantly on the meagre evidence, the Aldrich film debut arose through the athletic, rather than the acting connection. Having dubiously grasped this as fact, however, what to make of it? As little as possible would seem the sensible course. Better to stick to on-screen testimony (and also to try to stop worrying about the voyeurist/sexist connotations of admitting taking pleasure in the spectacle of a woman and her representations in two films so evidently problematic in terms of their sexual politics).

In both *Marbles* (part self-reflexive auteurist stock-taking on Aldrich's behalf, part populist crowd-pleaser) and *Jury* (a fraught case of lowered horizons that presumably started as critique in the hands of Larry Cohen, and ended up a bundle of unresolved contradictions under journeyman director Richard Heffron), the temptation is present to define Landon's roles in terms of "honorary maleness". And when the contexts run exclusively to the macho worlds of the wrestling ring or the mean streets, and a degree of physicality is so definitely called for, it would have been understandable if Landon had succumbed. Yet in each case there is an unforced assertion

of being at ease with her own sexuality — even in such caricaturish aggressive depictions of "a man's world" — that "difference" isn't so much elided as made irrelevant.

Molly in *All the Marbles* has no need for agonising over her in-the-ring status as commodity spectacle, and Aldrich has no need to draw us a dividing line between the public Barbie-doll-with-bite and the private woman whose mildly aberrant pill-popping and only-half-convinced desire to quit are presented as responses to the economic circumscription of a small-time circuit of scratched livings. Her "professionalism" is merely the concomitant of an integrated personality: only when Falk arranges a demeaning mud-wrestling bout does the affront cut both the artist/athlete and the woman. As opposed to her partner Iris (Vicki Frederick), she has never needed or had a "relationship" with the Falk character, would not be tempted to use her body to buy a favour from a corrupt promoter, and offers no sign whatever of the lesbian traits Aldrich has in the past somewhat revelled in. To find such an adult, unneurotic female character at the end of a line largely composed of harridans, hookers and child-women (that is, the Aldrich filmography, which does have compensations) is remarkable in itself.

Landon's role in the

uneasily conventional, not to say anachronistic, remake of *I, the Jury* is itself more conventional. She sets up Velda as a wonderfully, coolly insolent sidekick/foil to Armand Assante's "Mr Unnecessary Violence" and is allowed a couple of moments of resourceful action in the comic-strip mayhem, but is then reduced by the demands of novel and script to the figure of imperilled victim, kidnapped by a sickie whose lack of sexual balance she has to try to fathom and self-preservingly assuage, with a spectacular rescue by Hammer ending/compounding the indignity. While on-screen, she mounts a considerable challenge to the dumb blonde stereotype, but is never given sufficient time in which to explode it. It's a mercy, though, that she's never quite cornered into the gross objectification of the movie's other female roles, a bevy of sex-clinic playmates and Barbara Carrera's stylised slinky seductress.

Of course the whole notion of the received image of an actress develops from a curious conjuncture of role, performance, persona and personality — elements it's probably futile to try to separate; and above all, elements whose successful combination may be inexplicable to, or unidentifiable to, the actress concerned. What alternatives are offered in terms of scripts and parts determine the direction of an acting career, and Hollywood is notorious for its profligacy in wasting its most individual female talent (cf. Tuesday Weld, Paula Prentiss, Susan Anspach, Candy Clark, and more).

But even if Laurene Landon fails or is prevented from consolidating her distinct promise, her contribution to this year's cinematic pleasure remains worthy of recognition and a degree of celebration. To pick up the punditry of the opening: if it's not stardom she's headed for, it'll be cult-dom for sure. And maybe when Hollywood gets around to a remake of *Dynamite Women . . .*

— PAUL TAYLOR

Laurene Landon in 'I, the Jury'

HOWARD E. ROLLINS JR.

Howard Rollins Jr. is the undoubted star of Milos Forman's *Ragtime*, the film taken from E.L.Doctorow's hit novel which mixes fiction and fact in what has been a great publishing success and a great movie failure. This strange circumstance is due to the powerful charm that Rollins exercises on both audience and director. Let me explain.

It is a part — pure fiction, of course — that destroys the chance of any other actor getting a look-in, an extraordinary piece of screen stealing due, no doubt, to the writing but also to Rollins' quite brilliant portrayal of a black man coolly irritated beyond all bounds by the white man's hypocrisy.

His role in the movie is the only one that tells a consistent story; it is as if he becomes for a while America's conscience, America's Christ. I'm sure it wasn't meant to be that way. After all, the other characters in the film have plenty of drama to keep them busy, lots of opportunities to impress.

For the record, the "factual" basis of the subject has to do with the murder of the architect Stanford White by the daft millionaire Harry Thaw who years later, when driving past the Albert Memorial said, not so daftly, "I shot the wrong architect.".

Other characters, quasi-fictional and pseudo-factual, are built into the plot of the book: Houdini and J.P.Morgan, Henry Ford and Pancho Villa. But all pale — if you'll excuse the expression — into insignificance, overshadowed by this handsome man and his inescapable charm.

The part of Coalhouse (*sic!*) Walker is simply told. He is a pianist in the tradition of Scott Joplin, who one day is insulted by an Irishman who puts shit in his brand new car. Since he cannot get the law — the white man's law — to force the culprit to clean up his car, he resolutely goes about terrifying the populace until he is killed. The inevitability of his death is recognised early on, the drama immaculately obeying the cathartic rules of Greek tragedy, a perfect hero with a fatal flaw, purging us with pity and terror until Nemesis brings the curtain down.

He suddenly appears some way into the film in a manner seemingly unrelated to the plot, a pianist wanting a job:

"If it's regular work, I'm interested," he says.

He plays. In the close-ups his fingers are long, tapering and sensitive — in reality, the fingers of one of my favourite supper club pianists, Russell Henderson — and he gets the job.

His child and the baby's mother have been taken in by a white family. He shows up at the house. His entrance is truly

Howard E. Rollins Jr. in 'Ragtime'

amazing. When you see his joy at seeing the child, you feel you are watching real life. When asked to sit down he doesn't. When asked what he plays he says, "Anything they want me to. And then I play ragtime."

He proposes to the baby's mother and invites the family to the wedding. He is confident, massively, delightfully confident. He has a car, impresses white folks.

They ask if he can read music. "I read so good, white folks think I'm fakin' it." Of course, this dialogue is not in the book. Howard Rollins has the scriptwriter and director in thrall. He meets up with the Irishmen who think he's a chauffeur. "It's my car," he tells them. "I own it." They prevent him proceeding without payment of a 25 dollar toll fee. He seeks out a policeman.

It is important to state that here we already see our hero has no chance of success. The audience, call it cynic or realist, knows full well that in 1906 the police are unlikely to side with a coloured man against someone of their own flesh tones. "Where is my car?" The car has been moved. "Officer! Could you please come here and look at this." There is shit, greenish and slimy, in the car. They tell him he shouldn't have stopped in front of a fire station. "I had no intention of stopping, but my way was blocked."

The policeman tries to make him move on. Politely.

"I'm not goin' nowhere until my car's cleaned."

The policeman gets ruffled.

"Why are you letting these men intimidate you?" asks Coalhouse. "I want the man who did it to clean it." He is uncompromising, heading for collision, Christ-like. Ostensibly, the voice of reason.

The cop says he's sorry and puts him under arrest. We understand why. The white father of the family pays his bail.

They visit the Model T. It is a wreck.

He goes to see a negro lawyer who tells him to be reasonable.

"Is that your advice? Learnin' how to be a nigger?"

He tries to bring a civil suit. The civil law is equally unhelpful and deliberately confusing.

The mother of his child dies on his account. It doesn't make much sense in the film. But, as a result, he blows up the fire station we saw earlier, killing some firemen. The young brother of the white family comes to join him. He is a firework manufacturer. "Fireworks. Bombs. It's the same thing," the young man says.

Ridiculous, I thought. In the novel it made slightly more sense. The girl had seemed to threaten the President's life, the young brother had already been heavily politicised. Not in the movie.

Eventually, Coalhouse and his gang break into New York's J.P.Morgan library, threatening to blow it up unless the Irish fireman is turned over to them and made to clean the car. At this point James Cagney is brought in on the other side of a situation he has been in many times. But Coalhouse doesn't say, "Come an' get me, copper."

They talk on the telephone. Booker T.Washington goes to see the revolutionary, talks of the "black" man. I ask you. In 1900. How did that get into the script?

The white father of the family is allowed to visit Coalhouse.

"It's your brother-in-law," Coalhouse tells the young explosives expert who is with his gang. Incredibly, the gang is allowed by the police to leave in the Model T. Ford, cleaned, natch. Coalhouse wants to die alone.

"How's my baby doin'?" he asks the white father of the family. Rollins, one notes, has a beautiful smile. The father is an optimist. Everything's going to be alright. "I'd like to believe you. I'd really like that." He makes Father leave the building. He suddenly gets in a temper. "Get the hell out o' here! Don't you understand anything, white man?" Alone, he prays.

He doesn't blow up the building. He comes out with his hands up. Cagney tells a sniper, "Fire." Rollins falls. In the book there had been a fusillade of bullets. The movie drifts into a patchy coda, a long shot of Houdini, a scene with Harry Thaw. But it is Coalhouse, as impersonated by Howard E.Rollins, whose smile, whose gestures are imprinted on memory. What's that word again? Charisma? Is that what they call it?

It's not Rollins' fault the movie wasn't a giant success. Nor, I suppose, the fault of the gifted director. Maybe, we can explain it by the perverse logic woven into the warp and woof of the enterprise. When you read a book, you sympathise with your hero in a quite imaginative fashion. But the film shows a black hero quite palpably getting away with murder. It must have been a real mind twister for all those chic American radicals and, apparently, they stayed away in droves. Howard Rollins is as good as he can possibly be. That seems to have been the trouble. MIKE SARNE

ABEL FERRARA/ZOE TAMERLIS

Art thrives on adversity, and poverty of means need not yield poverty of expression. Assiduous archeologists sifting through the dross of B-movies occasionally unearth and artifact of rare value, in which inspiration surmounts limitations, and a film achieves a peculiar beauty attendant on its aesthetic victory against formidable odds. The economics of the film industry have now banished the production of low-budget films to the underpopulated fringes of the business, and the joys of discovery amongst recent films have been rare. Still, no assessment of any year in cinema would be complete without some recognition of the signal achievement in the realm of what is now dubbed the "exploitation" film.

Made cheaply (for about $350,000) by some obviously hustling New Yorkers, *Angel of Vengeance* (released in the US under the title *Ms. 45*) applies a twist and variations to the familiar *Death Wish* formula of rampant vigilantism. Yet that vile Michael Winner opus otherwise bears little resemblance to this charged piece of film making. A deaf mute woman, lovely but almost pathologically shy, works in Manhattan's garment district. When she is raped twice in a single day, killing her second assailant, she is transformed into an obsessive murderer of men, until her rage is finally spent in an orgy of mayhem.

Director Abel Ferrara develops this rather tawdry tale with an astonishing plastic force, visual wit, strong control over emotional responses, expressionistic style and keen appreciation for the critical importance of establishing credible icons. As the hapless fury, Zoe Tamerlis makes one of the most exceptional debuts in recent film history, coming on like a rampaging Lillian Gish, equally startling and fascinating in mime and in repose. The film demands that her face carry an immense expressive burden, and the camera loves her.

Angel of Vengeance attracted a fair amount of

Zoe Tamerlis in 'Angel of Vengeance/Ms. 45'

favourable critical attention in the US where it was released theatrically almost two years after it was shot, winning the coveted Edgar G. Ulmer Award for 1981 and garnering a core of voting support for Zoe Tamerlis as best actress among the National Society of Film Critics. Even major newspaper critics in New York and Los Angeles praised the work, though the film attracted only modest business. According to Ferrara, the film's distribution in the UK has been stalled by withholding of censorship approval. Warner Brothers in London, however, say that after seeing the film — which had already acquired a British title *Angel of Vengeance* — they decided to "pass" on it.

Perhaps the most impressive aspect of Ferrara's direction is his brilliant measuring of technique. The exigencies of low budget film making often require unseemly haste, and Ferrara understandably throws away some minor scenes in single wide-angle shots, husbanding his resources so that when a shot or scene is essential, he can lavish on them the care necessary to make some brilliant choices register their fullest. Never has the rage and resentment of women at male harassment on the streets been

more forcefully conveyed, and the gender role reversal is not exploited in a manner that would negate the compelling underlying ideology of sexual politics.

Born in the Bronx in 1952, Abel Ferrara was entranced by movies since he saw his first film, Sirk's *Imitation of Life*. Together with the screenwriter of *Angel of Vengeance*, Nicholas St. John, and his future soundman, the teenage Ferrara made 8mm films. Reuniting a decade later, the same childhood group began making shorts and then feature films, adding the extraordinary talents of cinematographer James Momel. Their first generally-released film, *Driller Killer*, (1979), featured Ferrara as the eponymous assassin, a psychotic oil painter murdering derelicts with an electric drill plugged into a power belt worn around his waist. Today, Ferrara characterises that early work as being "like scratchings on a cave wall" in comparison with *Angel of Vengeance*, though the movie boasts William Friedkin among its adherents.

Ferrara tried to convey his affection for the often grim terrain of New York City by utilising locations throughout the City and seeing them, with Momel's aid, in a fresh, utterly

unsentimental manner. He likes the freedom to improvise production decisions, which he can only achieve by meticulous planning.

His next project will be another St. John screenplay, *Birds of Prey*, a "political war drama set in New York in 1994, when the whole City is an armed camp in the grip of a revolution, not unlike El Salvador today." Despite initial Hollywood interest in the wake of *Angel of Vengeance*, Ferrara remains determined to make the film in his own way and is prepared to shoot it once again on a low budget if that is necessary to preserve his artistic vision.

He had even been prepared to abandon production on *Angel of Vengeance* when an extensive search had failed to uncover the right actress for the lead. Then someone sent over Zoe Tamerlis, a 16 year-old student at Columbia. "As soon as I looked at her through the peephole in the door of my loft studio, I knew she was the one I wanted."

Tamerlis grew up in New York City but has been carefully cultivating an aura of mystery in Hollywood, appearing dressed in black and making sudden appointments in odd locations like a latter-day Harry Lime. Committed to expressing her radical politics on film, she has written a screenplay, an epic political drama called *Curfew: USA*, in which she is attempting to create a genuinely revolutionary cinema within the Hollywood tradition. Meanwhile, she has secured strong agency representation and has been vying for a number of roles.

According to Tamerlis, her performance in *Angel of Vengeance* provoked a sniper attack on her in New York, wounding her. Nevertheless, she makes an articulate case for her criticism of the American film industry even while she shrewdly exploits its appetite for the novel and the elusive. She has the talent to be an absorbing actress and the temperament to be a commanding personality, achievements of personal style that belie her 19 years.

MYRON MEISEL

WILLIAM HURT

"I'd seen his *Hamlet* in 1980. He's a heavyweight actor, there's no question about it." Arthur Penn on the unknown he selected to play primal scientist Eddie Jessup in *Altered States* before Penn argued with writer Paddy Chayefsky and Ken Russell made the film instead (wisely, for once, he retained Penn's cast) and Chayefsky took his name off it months before his death. Reeling or not from 18 months of flak on the set (he compared it to being mugged), the William Hurt bandwagon started rolling into high gear.

By the time he'd played Peter Yates' *Janitor* (US: *Eyewitness*) Darrly Deever, and then the reamed, steamed, dry-cleaned and bamboozled Ned Racine in Laurence Kasdan's *Body Heat*, Hurt had arrived as a powerhouse force; dramatic and erotic.

Hollywood and Hollywood fans weren't so sure who the hell he was. He's invariably stopped on the street, asked for his autograph and complimented on playing *The Elephant Man*.

Hurt has also been stung — heavily — by a plethora of WASP imagery, as if Hurt and Redford were the last remaining strains of pure Anglo-Saxon stock left among a Hollywood bursting at the seams with Jewish and Italian-American leading men. Hence *Rollisng Stone* covered Hurt as "The Great White Hope." Plus the sublime, "Say hello to one intense WASP."

He told them off, although *Time* and *Newsweek* had started it all. "I resist the notion of symbol. *I am not a symbol!*"

He *is* intense, though. The vocal delivery suits intellectual' debates. The shapeless duds and Lennon glasses endorse his seriousness. He talks the way people stuck too long in analysis do, droning on and on like their shrinks. He goes once a week. And it shows; without the humour of a Woody Allen.

"Sometimes," wrote his *Rolling Stone* chronicler Carole Caldwell, "he speaks as if he's smoked his first joint." Then she records him telling John Belushi, of all people, "I want to die by turbine, you know. Because you're sucked

into the turbine and whipped into instantaneous ether." Eddie Jessup lives! And there does seem more Jessup than, say Ned Racine, in his make-up, though such remarks set him off again, berating interviewers for putting *their* fantasies on him. That used to be what movies were all about. But he pleads, "We're not the characters we play." He's very serious about that. About everything. "What Bill was great about was reminding me . . . of the need of that seriousness," says Laurence Kasdan. "Usually on the set everything works against it. Bill is aggressive about staking out his right — and he was a wonderful influence on everyone."

A definite heavyweight, for all that. Economical on screen, he uses his eyes as much as the low, campus voice. He avoids hysterics, holds back, retains a certain mystery. He's more substantial, then, than being this year's Nick Nolte and has aspects of Gérard Depardieu about his big frame and range. His first two movie roles were well nigh interchangeable: obsessives, both. It took

William Hurt on the set of 'Body Heat'

Kasdan to groom Hurt. To alter his state physically, change the hairstyle (and colour) and add a tidy moustache to produce an Eighties' figure out of his previous hungover Sixties' appearance.

According to Arthur Penn, waiting his chance with him, Hurt knows what he's about and where he's headed. "He's a bright young theatre actor and

it was clear that he was going to have a great movie career. Just a question of when he chose to start. He didn't want to start with a part in a smallish picture. We hooked up and had a very good time together." They would. Both men are just as much at home on stage as the screen; maybe more so on stage. They don't enjoy Hollywood.

Hurt has been a member of the off-Broadway Circle Repertory Company since 1977. He won a Theatre World award first season out with it, for his work in Wedekind's *Lulu* and Alberto Unnaurato's *Ulysses in Traction* — plus an Obie trophy for *My Life*, by the scripter of his first TV work, *The Best of Families.* Christopher Reeve played the grandfather of Hurt's physicist in the Corinne Jacker play and later took the Hurt-created role of the paraplegic Vietnam vet in Lanford Wilson's *Fifth of July* to Broadway. Hurt, though, is touted to make the film version, which could make up for losing another part he created at the Circle. Stanley Kramer saw Hurt in Milan Stitt's *The Runner Stumbles*, bought it for Hollywood and gave the plum part of the priest accused of killing a nun he loved to. . . Dick Van Dyke!

Cagey about his goals ("I want to do it all") and indeed the seeds of his talent, Hurt says he may yet become a good actor — if he reaches 40. He wasn't concerned with acting early. In common with fellow WASP, Redford, he just kept moving around. Early childhood in Guam. Education in Boston, New York and London, including three years in theology college. Then, he bummed around Australian sheepfarms. He started acting with the Oregon Shakespeare Festival in O'Neill's *Long Day's Journey into Night*, switched to Joe Papp's New York Shakespeare Festival for *Henry V*, opposite Meryl Streep. His television work, far from the big three networks, involved two pieces for the PBS channel, including Paul Gallico's *Verna, USO Girl* with Sissy Spacek and Sally Kellerman.

It was in Papp's company

that he met and married Marybeth Hurt, the youngster of Woody Allen's *Interiors* family. Since their divorce, he's been living with New York ballerina Sandra Jennings.

Even with three films only, Hurt had made his mark enough for *Body Heat* to acknowledge the others. Kasdan shoots him upside down on a bed at one point, in a direct lift from the *Altered States* poster. Hurt's coming on to Kathleen Turner is reminiscent of his "Buff your floors, lady?" routine with Sigourney Weaver in *The Janitor*, just as his ferocious fight with Richard Crenna is an instant re-play of his tussle with the mad dog in the Yates film.

"His future is limited only by his ambition," notes Yates' scenarist, Steve Tesich, who, with Penn, was first alerted to Hurt's potential on the New York stage. Hurt's next three films are crucial, therefore (unless he *wants* to be Nick Nolte). They're due to be headed by Ivan Passer's *Eagle of Broadway*, simply because it offers the rare treat of working with Jimmy Cagney. The old-timer will play Bat Masterson . . . in his final years as a New York sports-writer!

Whatever the other films are, Hurt will continue flexing his stage muscles with the Circle Rep., where he recently played *Childe Byron* and *Richard II* for his mentor of the last five years, Marshall W. Mason, the off-Broadway Joe Papp. Mason lists Hurt's attributes as generosity, anger, sensitivity, a scathing sense of humour — that's a surprise — and, no surprise to Hurt's mounting legion of female fans, "lots of sexual heat".

This, then, is "the blond, hunky six-footer," who, according to *Time*, "will be the WASP movie idol of the Eighties." Through those three movies *Time* has not yet printed one disparaging word about Hurt. Then again, it has also refrained from pointing out that William McChord Hurt happens to be the stepson of Henry Luce III, son of *Time's* founder. No matter, this vibrant actor's fervid intellectuality overrides nepotism. TONY CRAWLEY

HARRISON FORD

"Then I'll see you in hell." The cry could have come from Errol Flynn, just before he swung down another rope, cutlass in teeth, boundless amusement on his face. In fact it was delivered by Harrison Ford in *The Empire Strikes Back* just as Han Solo's allies are attempting to dissuade him from what seems the sure death of going out into the snow to search for Luke Skywalker. The cry is a little muffled and, for all Ford's dynamism in these two latterday Flynn-like adventures, it doesn't quite ring true. One suspects he is a far more complex actor than the role of action man star might allow.

In fact, Ford is often disconcertingly anonymous. Who can remember his role in Francis Ford Coppola's *The Conversation*, as a corporation hatchet man, of which he says, rather gnomically, "There was no role there really, until I decided to make him homosexual." The tantalising clue still doesn't clear the memory.

It is also a mild surprise to learn that he was in *Apocalypse Now*, although the assurance that he played the Intelligence Colonel who briefed Martin Sheen about "terminating with extreme prejudice", before he disappeared into the heart of darkness, does bring a certain delayed shock of recognition. One need hardly be ashamed at the possible lack of attentiveness, since George Lucas, the director most responsible for turning Ford into a star, didn't recognise him either, until halfway through the sequence, in spite of Ford adopting the name Colonel Lucas prominently on his uniform name-tag. The evasiveness suggests a certain cautiousness, clearly visible in many of his roles, and a reticence about the full implications of being type-cast as the star of three out of the top four money-making films in history.

His career began falteringly in the mid-Sixties when he was signed to Columbia as part of their new talent deal. The movie in which he first appeared (as a bellboy delivering a message to James Coburn), *Dead Heat on a Merry-Go-Round* (1966), is unlikely to endure in the annals of cinema history. Nor will his small roles in *Luv*, *The Long Ride Home* and *Getting Straight*.

After that, he temporarily gave up acting and supported himself and his family doing carpentry, which included building a $100,000 studio for the musician Sergio Mendes. There seems something apt in the choice of profession, particularly when one thinks of Indiana Jones in *Raiders of the Lost Ark*, a man prepared

Harrison Ford in 'Raiders of the Lost Ark'

to go to the ends of the earth, but who seems rather more content to remain at home quietly devoting himself to his craft.

Ford's first useful break came when Coppola's casting director, Fred Roos, cast him in *American Graffiti*, the film which turned the tide in favour of the Seventies generation of Hollywood superbrats, and made George Lucas' name. Here the memory is not faulty. Throughout the film, drag-strip king Milner has had intimations that a stranger was in town, looking to take on his '32 Ford Deuce Coupe in a race. When the black '55 Chevrolet finally turns up, it has Harrison Ford in the driving seat, a braggart in a cowboy hat. After that came the usual rash of offers to play more people in cowboy hats, which Ford had the good sense to turn down. More carpentry was followed in 1974 by another offer from Fred Roos to play the role in *The Conversation* mentioned above. When Roos called him a third time it was about Han Solo.

There is a moment in *Star Wars* when all the messages coming in to a central control desk become just too much and Ford blasts the console with his space-gun. As an expression of long-sufferance pushed to the extreme, it never fails to win a murmur of audience appreciation, and is indicative of the minor felicities which Ford was able to wring from a role which looked largely secondary to a lot of machinery. His solo merchant-adventurer alone had the abrasiveness to take the edge off that unblinking spectacle of so many ingenious toys and so little human interest.

He followed *Star Wars* with a small role alongside Henry Winkler in *Heroes*, looked lost in the perplexity of a location far from home in *Force 10 from Navarone*; and then took the lead role of a US bomber pilot based in England for *Hanover Street*, which is memorable mainly for the fact that it was the first time that he got to kiss the girl. Strange, perhaps, that a young male lead's appeal should lie so far away from romance.

There is a telling moment in *Raiders of the Lost Ark* which has never failed to detonate an audience. Faced with a huge, unfriendly Arab in a soukh, barring the way with a fancy, sword-twirling display, the stage looks set for yet another five-minute set-piece fight. Instead, a look of weariness spreads across Ford's face, an expression of "Oh Christ, do I have to!", before he pulls a gun and despatches the problem in seconds. Ford is on record as having invented the scene and it chimes well with the kind of lackadaisical resignation which lies behind so much of his conventional heroics.

These heroics have led critics to all sorts of inapposite comparisons; Bogart, Gable, even John Wayne have been touted as his ancestors. But there is a much more thoughtful actor in whose footsteps Ford is treading, and that is Gary Cooper. Ford has never yet played a villain and it is hard to imagine him doing so with any conviction. Like Cooper, he lacks malice and the inclination to appear dishonest. His plainly-chiselled good looks are often fraught with internal musings, just as Cooper's were when wrestling with his pacifism in *Sergeant York*, and he has the very American virtues of simplicity and courage in the face of corruption which Cooper embodied in *High Noon*.

One longs to see Ford stretched in a role playing a Hemingway hero, just as Cooper best satisfied that author's requirements with his contribution to *A Farewell to Arms*. His role as Indiana Jones has already established him as the epitome of the unassuming, decent man who is quite prepared to be heroic when the occasion demands but is thoughtful enough not to be addicted to heroism for its own sake. It may be that the great days of action directors have passed, with no modern equivalent of a Hawks, Ford or Walsh to gain the best from Ford. What some future Peckinpah could do with a Harrison Ford, made anxious by middle-age, would be very interesting to see.
CHRIS PEACHMENT

NASTASSIA KINSKI

Nastassia Kinski's sudden rise to top-rank film stardom is an event fascinating both in itself, and in relation to the entire movie-making scene today. Hollywood history is filled with the names (and checkered careers) of pretty European starlets, but the stellar configuration formed by this German ex-model (and daughter of actor Klaus Kinski), at this particular time and place, is unique. Following her international success in Roman Polanski's *Tess*, no less than three major productions starring Kinski have been set in motion, one right after the other. While the third of this trio, James Toback's *Exposed*, awaits release at the time of writing, the other two, Francis Ford Coppola's *One from the Heart*, and Paul Schrader's *Cat People*, have already come and gone from American movie screens. Neither production met with either critical acclaim or popular success.

Ordinarily such a situation would spell disaster for anyone with hopes of becoming a major American film star. Yet Kinski's name and face continue to adorn countless magazine covers (from *Cinefantastique* to *Vogue*), and the atmosphere of excitement and expectancy that seems to surround her has actually increased rather than dwindled. Part of the reason for this unusual turn of events can, of course, be attributed to the fact that Kinski herself wasn't held responsible for the failure of the two films. General opinion was that she had simply done the best she could with material quite unworthy of her. However, even if it were possible to see Kinski sharing the blame along with Coppola and Schrader, this wouldn't necessarily work against her. Hollywood in the 1980s plainly and simply *needs* someone like Nastassia Kinski — for better or worse.

"She's got the Ingrid Bergman face, Bardot's lips, and Hepburn's personality — an audacious combination," crowed *Cat People* director Shrader in an interview in *American Film*. He might also have added that such a

Nastassia Kinski in 'Cat People'

combination hasn't been seen in Hollywood for some time, obsessed as it has been for the past few decades with such "real" and "everyday" types as Dustin Hoffman, Barbra Streisand, Al Pacino and Jill Clayburgh. At the same time, Kinski's youth and ripe sensuality came along at a moment when Hollywood had retreated from a brief embrace with (its watered-down version of) women's liberation (*Alice Doesn't Live Here Anymore*, *The Turning Point*, *An Unmarried Woman*). A return to the sex symbols of the past (Monroe, Novak, etc.) wouldn't really have been acceptable, although Kinski with her Jean Seberg hair and Leslie Caron fragility is another story. "(She is) the perfect blend of access and malleability," gushed super-critical critic John Simon in a *Rolling Stone* profile of unprecedented (for him) enthusiasm. "She brings out in every man the hunter or the preservationist," remarked the writer most noted for his hunting out of faults — physical as well as thespic — in the acting profession.

That Kinski is capable of setting such a hardened heart a-beating cannot of course be accounted for by powers solely Kinski's own. It takes more than simple physical beauty or even a suggestion of sexual availability to create an aura — especially one in which actual acting prowess has (so far) come only marginally into play. The setting created for her by Polanski in *Tess* is to a large degree responsible for the crystallization of a particular image of Kinski in the public mind. What has made that image viable, however, is another very different one manufactured by the great fashion photographer Richard Avedon, and successfully sold as a poster. Kinski is shown lying nude on her side, her body stretched out to its full length. Her face is turned towards the camera, plaintive yet impassive. An enormous snake is draped across her recumbent form, its tongue darting out to lick her ear. This image of a modern Eve, an enchantress who needs no apple to ensnare prospective Adams, meshes perfectly with

the ravishing (and ravished) innocent of Polanski's film.

As Kinski herself was the first to admit, her performance as Thomas Hardy's tragic heroine, Tess of the D'Urbervilles, was coaxed out and cared for by the great Polish director with the same sort of deliberate single-mindedness Josef Von Sternberg utilized to make Marlene Dietrich a star. But while in Sternberg's case the puppet came to overshadow the puppeteer, with Kinski and Polanski it was fully understood, by critics and public alike, that a skilful director had cleverly contrived to make an acting novice seem like a pro.

Hardy's story of a proud and beautiful innocent buffeted about by the cruel winds of fate fit perfectly into Polanski's plan of wresting from his lovely, but untrained, young star the sort of performance a more accomplished actress would not be capable of giving. At times, *Tess*'s Panavision cameras seem trained on a scene out of *cinema vérité*, as both character *and* performer struggle to find their way through the plot's thicket of emotional and psychological entanglements. The effect is unique. We feel for the actress and the character both at the same time, and in the same spirit. With Kinski's beauty emphasized over her acting ability, a note was struck — and through Avedon's photo underscored — that Kinski's successive films have continued to emphasize. Who better to play Coppola's Vegas circus star or Schrader's sexual-repressive-turned-panther? No questions about acting need be asked. Nastassia Kinski quite simple *is* — dreamy, exotic, not quite part of this world, yet at the same time not all that removed from it.

"I just want to be good at my job — be a good actress," Kinski has said. The question of whether such a transformation is possible, or in the present climate (as continued success in Hollywood means remaining essentially the same) is even feasible, remains to be answered. DAVID EHRENSTEIN

BERNADETTE PETERS

There's no shortage of great big brand-new eye-popping star actresses in America — television is bursting with them. American TV offers enormous power to anyone who commands high ratings. Accordingly all the Cheryls, Lindsays, Jaclyns and Lonis are busy using this power to shape vehicles for themselves as flattering as those that Thirties' film stars enjoyed.

For women who aspire to become Eighties' film stars, however, the rules are different. The parts are fewer and smaller, the chance to gain control of projects is minuscule, the odds against staying above the title are long. Julie Andrews, Marsha Mason and Bo Derek are married to the creative forces behind the films in which they star. Jane Fonda and Faye Dunaway are more concerned with television these days. Barbra Streisand and Bette Midler make a film every four years. Goldie Hawn, Jill Clayburgh and Meryl Streep are among the few who seem to be in control. But besides Nastassia Kinski, isn't there anyone new?

There is Bernadette Peters, who sprang full-grown on the American public this year in a parade of starring film roles, record albums, TV specials, magazine covers and of course newspaper interviews. Underneath all this uproar there was a rather retiring lady whose time for stardom seems to have arrived at the very moment that Hollywood's moguls realised she is more than just good friends with bankable comic Steve Martin.

Tulips, Heartbeeps, Pennies from Heaven and *Annie* were Peters' 1981-82 reward for her eight preceding years of journeyman bit-part work in the film industry. Once she was noticed, she proved to have the sort of kewpie-doll face and thrusting figure that led the studios to put her in period costume, whether past or future. In *Heartbeeps*, she and Andy Kaufman portrayed robots in 1995 who meet in a repair shop and decide to go on the razzle. In *Annie* Peters plays the supporting role of Lily St. Regis, who poses as Annie's rightful mum. In *Pennies from Heaven*, Peters played the Cheryl Campbell role of a schoolteacher drawn into sin by Steve Martin's deceits. Though the film gathered few pennies at the box office, the American critics thought it was splendid and daring and Peters was especially praised for projecting innocence and disillusionment equally well.

The moment was propitious for Peters to inform the world of her arrival as a star. "I should reinforce to myself that I'm doing well and earning money," she decided, hiring a press agent and giving momentary consideration to trading in her seven-year-old Japanese runabout.

At last, sitting in the press agent's office, wearing a ladder-backed peek-a-boo sweater which it would be unwise to wear backwards, Peters blows bubbles pleasantly, discussing her stardom campaign. She felt honoured to be asked to pose for the cover of last December's *Playboy* and for a spread inside which the press agent describes for those who missed it as "a history of women's lingerie from the 1850s to the 1940s. It's the first celebrity spread Playboy has ever run that has no nudity whatsoever." Pushing the *Playboy* connection, the press agent hired bunny-hutch cartoonist Vargas to execute diaphanous paintings of Peters for the cover of her recent album, *Now Playing*.

Peters herself is in two minds. In one breath, she says, "I have a period look, like a Vargas girl." In the next she says, "I feel like a very 'today' girl. I suppose today's look is a conglomeration of all the looks from the past..." Peters, 33, first experienced the past at a very early age. At 13, she toured America for the better part of a year in a road-show production of *Gypsy*. Peters' mother, who had found herself married to a bread salesman named Peter Lazzara, put her two daughters on the stage. "She gave me the 'Peters' name when I was nine," Peters says. "She told me my real name was too long for the marquees."

Peters would traipse into Manhattan from her home in an insalubrious outlying district called Ozone Park to take singing and tap-dancing lessons. "It was a hobby to me, to go in once a week. I didn't decide that I wanted to be in the business until I was seventeen. I used to play the piano. I was awful. My mother would say to my father, 'Listen, Peter! Isn't that wonderful!' She had high hopes for me. She'd wanted to be an actress herself, but it wasn't allowed. Now, she gets really upset when I forget to tell her when I'm going to be on TV."

From the age of five, Peters was appearing on New York TV shows like *The Horn and Hardart Children's Hour* and *Name That Tune*. She sang and danced in many Broadway musicals as a child, starting with *The Most Happy Fella* at age 11. In Hollywood from 1973, she got small parts in films like *The Longest Yard* and *W.C. Fields and Me*. In 1977 she was one of the leads in a series that ran on an American network for a season, *All's Fair*. Before *The Jerk* in 1979, her biggest film credit was playing a cabaret seductress in Mel Brooks' *Silent Movie* in 1976.

The Jerk, of course, starred Steve Martin, as did *Pennies from Heaven*. Are Martin and Peters a package? "Definitely not. I am a separate entity. Obviously, Peters doesn't want to boast about why she's suddenly the woman of the hour. "You make certain breakthroughs in the industry," she says vaguely. "Maybe it was being in *The Jerk*, I don't know." Nodding toward her press agent, she concludes, "I have a lot of people around who help me."
BART MILLS

Bernadette Peters in 'Pennies from Heaven'

QUOTES OF THE YEAR

"**T**HE WORST PART ABOUT BEING ME IS WHEN PEOPLE WANT ME TO MAKE THEM LAUGH."
Jack Lemmon

"I *do* work hard. I *do* yell. But all I demand is that people work as hard as I do. You know there were even stories going around about how I was supposed to have done things like...well, getting my secretary to peel grapes!"
Sylvester Stallone

"I don't like the fact, though, that I have to get older so fast, but I like the fact that I'm ageing so well. My friends tell me I keep getting handsomer the older I get. I have no doubt that's true. I had nowhere to go but up."
Dustin Hoffman

"My scenario for the future of New York is that in twenty five years it will be lived in only by working young gays and singles. For a weekend they'll all go out to the suburbs where they'll look at families behind Cyclone fences sort of like in safari country."
Candice Bergen

"Just because I'm showing somebody being disembowelled doesn't mean that I have to get heavy and put a message behind it."
George Romero

"I wasn't an ugly girl, but I wasn't queen of the prom either...I was always sort of the second-best friend to the most popular girl."
Bernadette Peters

"**I** LOVE COLLECTING AUTOGRAPHS! I THINK IT'S ENORMOUS FUN. I JUST MET RICH LITTLE AND HE GAVE ME *HIS*."
Brooke Shields

"When I was arrested in Helsinki for sitting with my feet up on a hotel table they stripped me naked and put me in a cornerless cell. All I could think of was that I was in 'The Trial'."
Bob Geldof

"I want everything. Not that I want everything right now; but I do want everything."
Nastassia Kinski

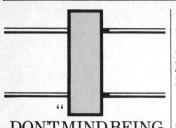

"DON'T MIND BEING NAKED BECAUSE I LIKE THE SENSUALITY OF A NICE BODY. THE TROUBLE IS, FOOD IS FUN, AND EXERCISING IS BORING."
Bo Derek

"I'd like to die by turbine. See, if you're sucked into a turbine, you get whipped into instantaneous ether."
William Hurt

"It used to be 'Five years in the making!! At a cost of ten million dollars!!' It used to be the thing to *sell* a picture on how much it cost, or how long it took to make. Now everybody is going, 'Oops, sorry!!'"
John Landis

"Passion is being able to express oneself totally in every circumstance."
Barbara Carrera

"Unless you provoke great pros and cons about your work you are really not a very important performer."
Bette Davis

"There is no such thing as a Jack Lemmon-type. That's why people don't imitate me."
Jack Lemmon

"They have on the street here in California in these big letters 'Right Lane Must Turn Right'. When first I see it, I say, 'Hey, what do you mean *must*?' I show you, I turn left and fuck you!"
Klaus Kinski

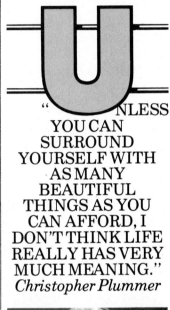

"UNLESS YOU CAN SURROUND YOURSELF WITH AS MANY BEAUTIFUL THINGS AS YOU CAN AFFORD, I DON'T THINK LIFE REALLY HAS VERY MUCH MEANING."
Christopher Plummer

"I haven't seen 'Commie Dearest' yet."
Paul Morrissey, on 'Reds'

"You've got to work in the media today because it's so dangerous. It's the only thing to do."
Julien Temple

"The confidence I now have is rooted in the discovery that who I am is okay."
Dudley Moore

"I don't use any particular method. I'm from the 'let's pretend' school of acting."
Harrison Ford

"I am really happy in an airplane, even though there is something so strange about being in the air and going somewhere else. I sometimes complain about it, but I complain about all the things I like."
Nastassia Kinski

"I've decided the ideal man doesn't exist. A husband is easier to find."
Britt Ekland

"I resent being written about like a playboy, and being described as Farrah's squeeze. Or Farrah's husband, or the father of Ryan's daughter, or anything but a private man and an actor. I'm as moody and complex and private as anyone I ever knew."
Ryan O'Neal

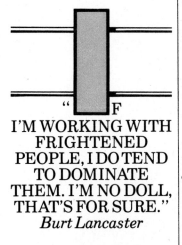

"**F**
I'M WORKING WITH FRIGHTENED PEOPLE, I DO TEND TO DOMINATE THEM. I'M NO DOLL, THAT'S FOR SURE."
Burt Lancaster

"I have a dread of being considered bland, but I've had to reconcile myself to the fact that's what I am."
George Segal

"I don't think I'd be good at directing. A good director needs to be a leader. I'm highly emotional. It's what fuels my acting."
Jane Fonda

"When I get a part and the days click up towards when I start working my face kinda changes and my voice will change. Even my hair will grow a different way."
Craig Wasson

"I rang my girlfriend last night from a massage parlour, a porno bookshop, a brothel and a sex cinema. That's where we were filming. It's that sort of a picture."
Michael Winner

"Journalists can't take your word for it that a single man's just bein' friendly with an attractive, independent gal. I don't blame 'em!"
Kris Kristofferson

"All I can say is, I'm sitting here because I believed it could happen. You know, I really am a manifestation of my own fantasy."
Sylvester Stallone

"Los Angeles is where you've got to be to be an actor. You have no choice. You go there or New York. I flipped a coin about it. It came up New York. So I flipped it again."
Harrison Ford

— 131 —

"I'M PRETTY INTROSPECTIVE. I'M NOT WHAT I'D CALL A HEDONIST: JUST IGNORE WHAT YOU READ — I DO."
Warren Beatty

"She's one of the funniest people I know. I called her once from Hollywood. 'I can't hear you too well,' she said. 'Hold on while I get my other glasses'."
Dudley Moore, about his mother

"I am in total awe of her. She's not only a fine human being with a big heart, and our best young actress in this country, but she's also just about the most energetic, imaginative person I have ever known."
Henry Fonda, about Jane Fonda

"I enjoyed the journey to the top but then I found myself disappointed."
Richard Dreyfuss

"LOVE JAMES M. CAIN'S WOMEN, THEY'RE ALL SO LUSTY AND STRONG. THEY'RE TEMPTRESSES."
Pia Zadora

"There is one thing I'm tired of, though, and that's folks coming up and shouting out, 'Hello, Dolly!' I wish they'd say, 'Dolly, hi, how are you?'"
Dolly Parton

"Milos Forman first mentioned it as a joke that I should come back, but it was the kind of remark my wife and doctor had been hoping to hear."
James Cagney

"We used to laugh so much then; now everybody is so solemn, so joyless. One must laugh. One cannot moan everlastingly."
Katharine Hepburn

"ALL MY LIFE I HAVE BEEN IMPASSIONED, DRIVEN BY MY INSTINCTS. I CAN NEVER BE SATISFIED BECAUSE MY DESIRE CONTINUES."
Klaus Kinski

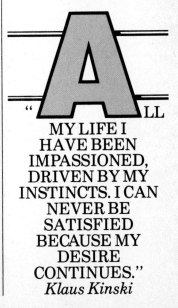

"I think the most underrated thing in the world is a good hot bath. With bubbles."
Burt Reynolds

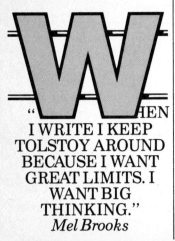

"WHEN I WRITE I KEEP TOLSTOY AROUND BECAUSE I WANT GREAT LIMITS. I WANT BIG THINKING."
Mel Brooks

"Faye Dunaway says she is being haunted by mother's ghost. After her performance in *Mommie Dearest*, I can understand why."
Christina Crawford

"We have no control over our conception, only over our creation."
Tony Curtis

"I never resented that dumb, fluffy blonde image — until I was confronted with it when I wasn't in a playful mood."
Goldie Hawn

"This is not an X-rated body. This is a PG body."
Mariel Hemingway

"Warren (Beatty) has an interesting psychology. He has always fallen in love with girls who have just won or been nominated for an Academy Award."
Leslie Caron

"I was born with success, with my parents. Lucky for me, I am able to handle it. Also, I damn well deserve it!"
Larry Hagman

"I'd love to work with Barbra Streisand again, in something appropriate. Perhaps *Macbeth*."
Walter Matthau

"I wish I looked like Raquel Welch, but I don't."
Liza Minnelli

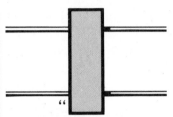

"I LOVED THE POWER, AND THE RESPONSIBILITY OF PORTRAYING SUCH A WOMAN, AND SHOWING — AND THIS IS *SO* SIGNIFICANT — THAT WOMEN ARE AS VARIED AS MEN."
Jill Clayburgh

"I love Barbra Streisand. She's such a brilliant talent. She's a very funny lady and I think she's also very sexy."
Goldie Hawn

"Glenda Jackson is an absolute dream boat, the epitome of professionalism, a splendid actress, and she has all the make-up of a fully rounded person."
Walter Matthau

YOU KNOW WHEN I KNEW I HAD SOME TALENT? I'LL TELL YOU THE DAY I KNEW, BECAUSE I REMEMBER IT. IT WAS RIGHT DAB SMACK IN THE MIDDLE OF THE SHOOTING OF *APOCALYPSE NOW*. I WAS IN THE MIDDLE OF THE PHILIPPINES, AND ONE DAY I KNEW I HAD TALENT."
Francis Coppola

"I enjoyed the dressing up, particularly after the war years. Now I have gone back to basics. I'm more confident in myself, so I can go about without looking like a Vogue ad."
Audrey Hepburn

"The trouble was that my offstage life coloured my career as an actor. The parts were always the same."
George Hamilton

"It would have been an insult if it had gone for only $20,000. Rosebud will go over my typewriter to remind me that quality in movies comes first."
Steven Spielberg, on paying $60,500 for a copy of the sled from 'Citizen Kane'

"I'm terribly complicted. I worry about everything — one of the reasons I can't read a newspaper in the morning. I'd spend all day thinking about the disasters, feeling sorry for victims. So I wait until my husband brings a paper home in the evening."
Jill Clayburgh

"Working with Dennis Hopper could easily put you off being exposed to foreigners."
John Hargreaves

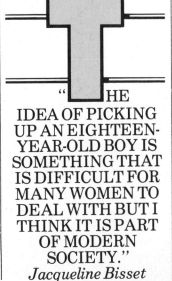

"**T**HE IDEA OF PICKING UP AN EIGHTEEN-YEAR-OLD BOY IS SOMETHING THAT IS DIFFICULT FOR MANY WOMEN TO DEAL WITH BUT I THINK IT IS PART OF MODERN SOCIETY."
Jacqueline Bisset

"You know I should be doing sophisticated comedies. Fate has led me to this sort of thing."
Michael Winner

"It's obvious that I've got big ones, and if people want to assume they're not mine, then let them."
Dolly Parton

"I've had a fascinating life. I don't think I'm the least bit peculiar, but people tell me that I am."
Katharine Hepburn

"N ENGLAND YOU WERE BOMBED AND ALL THAT, AND YOU'D THINK THAT ENGLAND WOULD BE MORE CONCERNED WITH NAZIS, BUT IN AMERICA PEOPLE THINK OF NOTHING ELSE. AN HOUR DOESN'T GO BY WHEN I'M NOT AWARE OF THAT PERIOD OF HISTORY."
Wallace Shawn

"There are moments when I perceive us as being on the brink of another Dark Age, a media blitzkrieg of mindlessness."
Candice Bergen

"Most of my close friends are actors or dancers. You can always tell a dancer because they move differently from other people."
Treat Williams

"They said I could keep the beard if they found one important American banker who wore one. They did, but he's been dead for a long time."
Kris Kristofferson, about his part in 'Rollover'

"Very handsome and very physical. The love scenes were like ballet."
Sylvia Kristel, about Nicholas Clay

"I'm fat, tall and ugly with a noisy voice."
John Rhys-Davies

"'M PROUD OF *LADY CHATTERLEY'S LOVER*. IT'S THE BEST FILM I'VE MADE SO FAR. MY MOTHER THINKS IT'S THE MOST BEAUTIFUL FILM SHE'S EVER SEEN."
Sylvia Kristel

"Look at all the film buyers and sellers in Cannes any year, and you're basically looking at a lot of shoe salesmen working out whether or not it should be sneakers or lace-ups next year."
David Hemmings

"Finally now I am the man I want to be. I don't drink. I don't smoke. I make love. You want to know the secret of life? The saliva of young girls."
Tony Curtis

SHOOTING HAS BEEN SUSPENDED

A survey of unfinished films by *David McGillivray*

For the past 90 years a major industry has flourished despite work methods which must horrify even the most broad-minded economist. Workers are hired even though they may be too old, too ill or temperamentally unsuited for the jobs; products are made for which there is no public demand and manufacture frequently commences before the management has acquired sufficient capital. Under normal circumstances such behaviour would be suicidal, but by sheer luck the film industry — for that, of course, is what I've described — has completed hundreds of thousands of movies and abandoned only a handful.

Most people would be hard-pressed to name more than one of these *films maudits*. Often enshrouded in mystery, they are the skeletons in their producers' cupboards. The rushes languish unseen on laboratory shelves, the titles are invariably left out of the filmographies of all concerned, and eventually the films pass out of history.

The unfinished film which springs most readily to mind is *I, Claudius*, which was left incomplete in 1937. This is remembered thanks to producer Bill Duncalf, who, in 1965, made *The Epic That Never Was*, a TV documentary which tried to account for the film's collapse. The findings were inconclusive, although the implication was that the official explanation (Merle Oberon's involvement in a car accident) was a cover-up for a kind of death wish developed from director Josef von Sternberg's incompatability with his star Charles Laughton. But however mismanaged the original production, *I, Claudius* is now firmly established as "one of the most intriguing legends in film history", an accolade awarded to only two unfinished films.

The other is Sergei Eisenstein's *Que Viva Mexico!*, a dramatised documentary which the Russian master began shooting in 1931. Here too "artistic differences"

Suspended: Eric Sykes in 'You'd Better Go in Disguise' (1973)

proved insurmountable. The novelist Upton Sinclair had given Eisenstein $25,000 to cover four months' shooting. At the end of 13 months, Eisenstein was still filming and the budget had escalated to $53,000. Not surprisingly Sinclair withdrew his backing, and such was his rancour that he refused even to let Eisenstein edit the material that existed. Over the years the film's reputation has grown from other people's attempts to salvage its remains. "I believe it would have been Eisenstein's greatest film", declared historian Jay Leyda.

The mismatching of creative talents has brought about the downfall of several lesser-known movies. In 1955, after years or pre-production, Bertolt Brecht set up a film of his play *Mother Courage*

starring his wife Helene Weigel (in the title role) and Simone Signoret. Constant disagreements between Brecht and his director Wolfgang Staudte shut down the film after ten days' shooting. To everyone's great remorse Brecht died suddenly a few months later. Weigel finally played *Mother Courage* on film in 1961, and in 1963 Staudte salved his conscience by directing a screen version of Brecht's *Die Dreigroschenoper*.

The arguments Jerry Lewis had with his producer during *Le Jour ou le Clown Pleura* not only wound up the film after eight weeks' shooting in 1972, but also put an end to Lewis' screen career for nearly a decade. Legally restrained from completing the film during that time, Lewis

eventually adapted its theme for his comeback picture *Hardly Working*. "Hardly funny", commented the trade paper *Variety*, reviewing the film in 1981, but its success in the USA and France restored faith in Lewis, who has since found the backing for two more films.

After only a few days' shooting in 1975, a Neil Simon comedy called *Bogart Slept Here* ground to a halt when Robert De Niro fell out with director Mike Nichols. The rift was irrevocable, but the property was far too valuable to sacrifice to star egos, and shooting began again with Herbert Ross replacing Nichols, and Richard Dreyfuss in De Niro's role. Released in 1977 under its new title *The Goodbye Girl*, it was an enormous hit. In a similar case, The Sex Pistols' film *Who Killed Bambi?* was abandoned in 1977 after three days, the amount of time it took Malcolm McLaren to realise that director Russ Meyer was never going to hit it off with Johnny Rotten and Sid Vicious. The Pistols finally made it to the screen in Julien Temple's *The Great Rock 'n' Roll Swindle* in 1980, and although this differed vastly from Meyer's concept, the influence of King Leer was detectable in the Brazilian sequences. Strangely *Who Killed Bambi?*'s title song turned up in Temple's film despite its complete irrelevance.

To date, alas, there has been no attempt to resuscitate *Trick Or Treat?*, the film of Ray Connolly's novel, which collapsed in 1976 after weeks of wrangling between director Michael Apted and his tempestuous leading ladies Bianca Jagger and Jan Smithers. Both Connolly and Kathleen Tynan, who was recruited to make script amendments, have written extraordinary accounts of this strife-torn production, about 20 minutes of which was completed.

But there is hardly any documentation at all concerning an ill-fated cartoon called *Destino*, which briefly united the talents of Salvador Dali and Walt Disney. Dali worked on this project at the Disney studio in 1946, but Disney pulled the plug on it after seeing a 15-second sequence showing two jewelled tortoises approaching each other across a typically Daliesque plane. There is no mention of *Destino* in either of Dali's autobiographies; one of Disney's biographers notes its existence, but only in passing. Could this momentous yet doomed collaboration have been deemed insignificant? Or did it stir up memories too painful to recall?

Abandoned movie projects certainly have caused great anguish to some. British actor John Hamill looks on his unfinished sex comedy *Doing the Best I Can* (1975) as "my failure" and refused to discuss it with me. Bill Whittaker, who produced Paul Watson's romantic drama *A Fine and Private Place* in 1970, was equally reluctant. "It's impossible to talk about this

sort of thing without personalities coming into it", he said, a confession which suggests that the film, begun during Bryan Forbes' controversial regime at Britain's Elstree studios, was aborted due to "artistic differences" and not, as the official press release maintained, "atrocious weather conditions".

Mother Nature is often used as a scapegoat when films fail to reach the screen in one piece. David Miller's offbeat comedy *The Bells of Hell Go Ting-a-ling-a-ling* (1967) had top-notch credentials (Gregory Peck and Ian McKellen; script by Roald Dahl; photography by Arthur Ibbetson) and finance from United Artists. Is it likely that such a film would have been scrapped after a couple of days because of unfavourable weather? That was the excuse that was given. The stoppage of Seth Holt's *Monsieur Lecoq* (1967), a comedy with Zero Mostel, was also attributed to the weather, although in this case seven

eighths of the picture was in the can. Editor Oswald Hafenrichter once told me that it would have been Holt's best film. This is improbable. Holt, who had a drink problem, already had one unfinished film (*Diabolique*, 1967) in his wake, and during production of *Lecoq* the word was out that it was not funny. Holt died in 1971 leaving a third film, *Blood from the Mummy's Tomb*, incomplete (the direction was taken over by Michael Carreras).

Strange as it may sound, sickness, injury and death are also poor grounds for abandoning a film, the reason being that doubles can usually be substituted for the missing, or indeed deceased, performers. Other actors stood in for James Dean during part of *Giant* (1955), Bela Lugosi in *Plan 9 from Outer Space* (1958), and Bert Lahr in *The Night They Raided Minsky's* (1968), and the most extreme example of this practice occurred when Bruce Lee died in 1973 after shooting only two

sequences of his last film *Game of Death*. Although it took Lee's studio five years to work out how to do it, the film was completed using a double for an astonishing 86 per cent of the running time.

Occasionally, however, doubling is out of the question. When Buster Keaton broke his leg during the filming of *The Electric House* in 1921, the footage was dumped. Marilyn Monroe's death put an end to *Something's Got to Give* in 1962. In 1964 Henri-Georges Clouzot's thriller *L'Enfer* failed to survive the illness of its star Serge Reggiani and then, a few weeks later, Clouzot himself. At the time of going to press, no decision has been made about *Brainstorm*, halted last year by the death of Natalie Wood. Director Douglas Trumbull maintains he can finish the film without her, but MGM/UA are said to be more interested in claiming the $15 million insurance.

To bring matters into perspective, however, it must be stated that death, disease

Suspended: Ronnie Corbett, Akim Tamiroff and Zero Mostel in 'Monsieur Lecoq' (1967)

and personal conflict assume little significance when measured against the commonest cause of movie breakdowns: money. Sometimes it runs out, sometimes the supply stops dead, and many is the poor fool who has set up a production on the strength of a promise only to discover that there was never any money in the first place. No wonder that in film circles the definition of a backer is someone who backs out at the last minute.

"Cash flow problems", to use the current euphemism, are nothing new. In 1922 Alfred Hitchcock's first film as a director, *Number Thirteen*, was suspended because the American finance dried up. But the bulk of the casualties have coincided with the growth of independent production since the end of World War II. The first major movie to collapse due to the hazards of alternative financing was Errol Flynn's production of *William Tell*, which shot for three weeks in 1954 in a purpose-built village in the Italian Alps. It was Jack Cardiff's first film as a director. Even Flynn's nosey biographer Charles Higham has been unable to explain why the film's leading financier suddenly decided to start writing rubber cheques. He may have been dissatisfied with the material that had been shot, or too embarassed to admit that he couldn't afford such folly, but either way his irresponsibility wrecked *William Tell* and left Flynn impecunious to his death.

Mysteries also surrounded the shaky deals that have driven a number of more recent productions on the rocks. One of them, ironically enough, was about the hard times of Errol Flynn. Called *The Greatest Mother of Them All*, it starred Peter Finch as Flynn and Alexandra Hay as his girlfriend Beverly Aadland, but only two reels were completed in the summer of 1969. "No-one was interested and we just couldn't get the financial backing to make the goddam thing", Finch told his biographer Trader Faulkner. Five days before the shooting of *The Play Room* was due to be completed in June, 1971, everything ground to a halt. Said producer-director Ken Annakin at the time: "The money just ran out". In 1975 *The New Spartans* managed to complete only nine days' filming before the axe fell. "It was crazy", said star Susan

George, "One minute we were working and the next minute we were told we needn't come in tomorrow". Many observers were gravely concerned by the collapse of this multi-million dollar spectacular, which, followed only weeks later by the *Trick Or Treat?* fiasco, **seemed to indicate the beginnings of the film industry's complete disintegration.**

In retrospect it can be seen that the films were not harbingers of a specific downward trend. Nevertheless the international recession of the Seventies did result in more films than ever before being suspended because of financial difficulties: *The Comforts of Home* (1974) with Stockard Channing; *Com-Tac 303* (1977) with Billy Dee Williams and Henry Fonda; *The Dream Time* (1973) with Mark Lester; *Morning Winter and Night* (1978) with Cliff Robertson and Brooke Shields; *The Micronauts* (1975-6) with Gregory Peck and Lee Remick; *Rider* (1975) with Oliver Reed and Orson Welles; *Sophie and the Captain* (1978) with Julie Christie; *A Voyage Round My Father* (1973) with Rex Harrison, Edward Fox, Wendy Hiller and Alastair Sim; and *Yockowald* (1976) with Tom Jones and Lee Strasberg.

The failure of many of these films may have been brought about by the kind of shyster backers mentioned earlier, but in at least two cases movies foundered due to bankruptcy. Eric Sykes had filmed 55 minutes of his comedy *You'd Better Go in Disguise* when his producer went broke in the summer of 1973. Three years later Sykes was still negotiating for a completion guarantee, but had given up hope when he had the good fortune to fall in with Thames TV, who gave him the go-ahead to re-make his film from scratch. Titled *If You Go Down in the Woods Today*, the new version was first aired in Britain last April. Poor Terence Young has not been so lucky. When his financiers were wound up in 1975, he had completed only 70 minutes of an action adventure called *Jackpot*. The stars were Richard Burton, James Coburn and Charlotte Rampling. "If only I could get those three together for one more week", moaned Young in 1978, "I could complete the picture". But this never happened; and the knife was twisted again when his latest film, *The Jigsaw Man*,

Suspended: Terence Young directing Sir Laurence Olivier in 'The Jigsaw Man' (1982)

starring Michael Caine and Laurence Olivier, was suspended in June of this year. **The producers admitted debts of over two million dollars.**

The processes involved in the suspension of a film are not pleasant. When the producer announces that there is not enough money to continue shooting, it is tantamount to declaring oneself unclean.

Nobody hangs around. The first to go are the crew. Unlike theatre folk, who magnanimously work for no money to help a show through a sticky patch, film technicians down tools like the proverbial shot. The artists will wait only until their next commitments arise. If, after a few weeks, alternative funding has not materialised, the sets will have to be dismantled because the studio space is needed. It is at this point that completion becomes economically impractical.

A couple of films have managed to overcome all the odds and resume shooting after long periods have elapsed, but the results have not justified the death-defying effort involved. The most pathetic instance was that of Peter Curran's comedy *The Cherry Picker*, which ran into cash flow problems in 1972 and was halted two thirds of the way through production. Curran won everyone's admiration by mortgaging his house in order to raise another £50,000; he even managed to write his leading lady out of the script when she refused to return. But when the film finally surfaced in 1974 it was revealed to be embarrassingly incoherent. It played for a few days on the south coast of England and was never seen again. *Winter Kills* suffered a

similar fate. With only one week's shooting to go, production was suspended in September 1977. To the astonishment of his associates, director William Richert succeeded in finally "wrapping" the film in March 1979. But although it was an **enjoyably zany thriller, with a particularly splendid performance from John Huston, the film was not able** to shake off the stigma of failure. It played to poor houses in America and was sold direct to TV in Britain.

Because history has shown that the unfinished film is with few exceptions designed to remain that way, one has to admire the example of *Don Quixote*, directed by the quixotic Orson Welles. Welles — who is responsible for at least four unfinished films, the first of which, *It's All True*, was scuppered as long ago as 1942 — began making his movie about Cervantes' hero in 1955. For reasons which vary depending on whose account one reads, the ending has never been shot. In order to complete *Don Quixote* Welles will require little short of a miracle. Both his stars — Francisco Reiguera and Akim Tamiroff — are dead, and his "child star", Patty McCormack, recently celebrated her 36th birthday. As if this wasn't daunting enough, Welles has admitted that he can't remember exactly whereabouts in the world he left the various pieces of the film. Yet in a TV documentary this year he seemed quite determined that the 30 year shooting schedule would be concluded. The title, however, is to be amended to *When Are You Going to Finish 'Don Quixote'?*

"TOGETHER AGAIN FOR THE FIRST TIME!"

So far this copyline has not been used in the advertising campaign for a film, or even for that of "a major motion picture". Many others, equally bizarre but not as nonsensical, have acquired varying degrees of immortality over the years. On the poster of *Niagara,* "A raging torrent of emotion that even nature couldn't control!" was the line accompanying the illustration of Marilyn Monroe lying across the Falls. "This Tartar woman is for me and my blood says *take her!*" was the deathless epigram uttered by John Wayne in the campaign for *The Conqueror.* Very little has changed. *Jon Stephen Fink* spreads the posters of the past year over his kitchen table and ruminates over which lines were used to sell what films

Around the time that *Legend of the Lone Ranger* was released last year, a radical new theory to explain why motion pictures are being made these days started to attract serious attention. The theory is this: *Motion pictures are made in order to justify the existence and rationalise the behaviour of the people who market them. A kinkier variation of this theory states that this has always been so, except in the case of films from Poland or Jamaica.*

Any intelligent mind, sensitive to the higher, purer aspirations of film making, might reject this theory as the cynical product of a crass, front-office, corporate mentality which can see no further than the LED figures flashing on a pocket calculator, or as the crackpot whining of, say, a very talented writer who through no fault of his own has been reduced to scribbling the odd piece of journalism now and then to keep body and soul together, maybe even directing too, if the so-called show business "community" hadn't slammed every door in his face, leaving him with a suit full of empty pockets and a heart full of broken dreams. But remember: they laughed at Erich von Daniken.

A short chat with anybody directly concerned with publicising or otherwise marketing movies will always come back to what they call the "bottom line". The "bottom line" that these people refer to is the value in local currency of the number of "admissions" sold to people who choose to spend a couple of hours in a

The film where you hiss the villain and cheer the hero.

THE LEGEND OF THE LONE RANGER

LEW GRADE and JACK WRATHER Present A MARTIN STARGER Production "THE LEGEND OF THE LONE RANGER" Starring KLINTON SPILSBURY · MICHAEL HORSE · CHRISTOPHER LLOYD and JASON ROBARDS as PRESIDENT ULYSSES S. GRANT Executive Producer MARTIN STARGER Screenplay by IVAN GOFF & BEN ROBERTS and MICHAEL KANE and WILLIAM ROBERTS Adaptation by JERRY DERLOSHON Based on stories and characters created by GEORGE W. TRENDLE and FRAN STRIKER Original Music by JOHN BARRY Director of Photography LASZLO KOVACS a.s.c. Produced by WALTER COBLENZ Directed by WILLIAM A. FRAKER Filmed in PANAVISION © 1981 ITC/Wrather Productions All Rights Reserved

'The Legend of the Lone Ranger': the picture nobody needed to make with the line nobody needed to use

cinema. The problem facing anybody directly concerned with this "bottom line" is plain to see: how to lure people off the streets and into that cinema for those two hours.

And this is how they do it:

In the first place, they know that we know what happens inside a cinema. Very large, attractive people loom in front of us, arrive and depart, enjoying as they go erotic, romantic, comic, and wholesome moments or

suffering tragic, violent, confusing and perverse ones. Whole decades pass in the space of as many minutes, or time stands still, even. These Big People journey to Jupiter and Beyond the Infinite, to Paris, Rio, Rome, New York, places where life as we know it *doesn't exist*, but they go to these fabulous places and what's more they take us with them! Big Men and Big Women who *don't really exist* outside of the Malibu Colony

are suddenly — our pals! They let us see them *do things* — commit murders, solve murders, start wars, end wars, make babies, raise babies, eat babies, involve us in problems we never knew concerned us and then solve those problems one way or another in just two hours! Seeing is believing.

We sit still and we watch events unfold and we refuse to disbelieve that those things *are happening*, right there inside that cinema. We suspend our disbelief with pleasure and with ease, and that's exactly what they bank on. Only they bank on us suspending our disbelief even before we pay the price of admission; they're counting on us to believe what they *tell* us. And why shouldn't we? Why shouldn't we have faith in their judgement, after all. They saw the movie already — at exclusive, private "screenings" where only their *friends* are invited, not piddling little journalists who have to depend on miniscule "research fees" just to scrape together the price of a few tickets to a provincial cinema where reels aren't always shown in the right order and the soundtrack barely squeezes through the secondhand Tannoy system. But yet again they've succeeded in getting somebody else inside.

How did they do it last year?

They did it by offering us the rare privilege of sharing The One Great Moment. The whole world held still when the tablets of *The French Lieutenant's Woman* were at last handed down the mountain, passed from John Fowles, who begat the novel, unto Harold Pinter, who begat the screenplay, unto Karel Reisz, who begat the film and finally unto us. All of this begetting was duly commemorated on programmes like *The South Bank Show*, while the restrained print ads hewed humbly to the storyline: "She was lost from the moment she saw him" — which isn't an unfair description of Sylvia Kristel as Lady Chatterley and Just Jaeckin as a director. "The classic of erotic literature," were the words writ, smallish, on the poster for *Lady Chatterley's Lover*, implying that if we went inside we'd see a classic of erotic film making. This promise was confused slightly by the appearance of ads for *Priest of Love*: "He was D.H. Lawrence. She was his Lady Chatterley. Their extraordinary romance was more tempestuous than any he wrote." The confusion was so great that a special press conference had to be arranged so that Janet Suzman and Sylvia Kristel could be photographed together to prove that they were not the same person. No such confusion attended the arrival of Michael Cimino's *Heaven's Gate*. Pre-empting obvious comment the banners read, "The most talked about film of the decade!" and, "As brutal, beautiful, vicious and vast as America itself". The ambiguity of that second line (did it refer to the film, the deal, the budget or Cimino's ego?) had a dual purpose. First, to raise that question in people's minds, along with the hint that the answer might be found inside; and second, to fragment actual responses to the movie. So many people

"An extraordinary film, a big romantic adventure." *Vincent Canby* NEW YORK TIMES

REDS AA

WARREN BEATTY · DIANE KEATON

'Reds': Warren Beatty hugging a bundle of period laundry

"It's not over... It's not over..."

endless love AA

PolyGram Pictures presents
A Keith Barish-Dyson Lovell Production
A film by Franco Zeffirelli · Brooke Shields · Martin Hewitt · Endless Love AA
Shirley Knight · Don Murray · Richard Kiley · Penelope Milford · Beatrice Straight · Based on the book by Scott Spencer
Screenplay by Judith Rascoe · Executive Producer Keith Barish
Produced by Dyson Lovell · Directed by Franco Zeffirelli
Released in the UK by Barber International Films Ltd.
PolyGram Pictures

Soundtrack album available on Mercury Records and Tapes

'Endless Love': a slogan which anticipates the exclamation of entire cinema audiences up and down the country

were seen leaving the cinema and immediately forming a new ticket queue that all the receipts for *Heaven's Gate* in Britain are believed to come from the same 350 people. Meanwhile, Enterprise with *Absolution* and 20th Century Fox with *The Final Conflict* aimed for the jugular, trading on religion and associated form's of paranoia. Above *Absolution*'s title appear the somehow familiar words, "Thou Shalt Not Kill..." and underneath the cryptic legend, "...a thriller mystery," a confuse-and-conquer tactic similar to that of *Heaven's Gate*. "The power of evil is no longer in the hands of a child," was Fox's warning not to the public, but to youthful directors of future *Omen* instalments. Another crypto-biblical slogan was affixed to ads for *Deadly Blessing* and lo, it read: "To the valley of beauty came the shadow of death." Deeply stirring, profoundly familiar and yet, somehow totally meaningless. Wiser heads agreed on the eternal verity expressed in *Tattoo*, that "Every great love leaves its mark," a fact attested to by Franco Zeffirelli, who ought to know since "Franco" is Italian for "Mark". The great love which got away from him last year was endless, *Endless Love*. "It's not over...It's not over..." says the speech bubble over poor prostrate Martin Hewitt's head, anticipating the exclamation of entire cinema audiences up and down the

country.

And they invited us to witness The Great Event, too. Paramount left us in the care of Warren Beatty who convinced the always quotable Vincent Canby of the *New York Times* that *Reds* was "An extraordinary film, a big romantic adventure". That fact didn't need to be inferred

from the poignant still used for the *Reds* poster, which showed Warren Beatty hugging a bundle of period laundry known by the *cognoscenti* to be Diane Keaton. Indeed, the saga of the film's production became a feature of its promotion through the usual channels of articles and interviews. The larger irony went mostly unnoticed and altogether untapped as a publicity resource after the Oscar awards, namely, the spectacle of the orchestra there serenading Mr. Beatty with a chorus of the Communist International. Truly, Hollywood is a magic place. But no more so than the African *veldt* circa 80,000 years BC. Covering all angles, the marketing genii in possession of *Quest for Fire* illustrated this seminal adventure with a comic book illustration depicting four hairy people with sticks standing underneath a sheep's

F ourteen years ago, "2001: A Space Odyssey" was the astounding epic that aroused a generation, telling them where they might be headed.

Now, 20th Century-Fox presents a science fantasy adventure that will arouse this generation, telling us where we might have begun.

QUEST FOR FIRE AA

A Science Fantasy Adventure

MICHAEL GRUSKOFF Presents an ICC INTERNATIONAL CINEMA CORPORATION Production
of a JEAN-JACQUES ANNAUD Film "QUEST FOR FIRE" AA
EVERETT McGILL · RAE DAWN CHONG · RON PERLMAN · NAMEER EL-KADI
Music by PHILIPPE SARDE · Special Languages Created by ANTHONY BURGESS · Body Language & Gestures by DESMOND MORRIS
Co-Producers JACQUES DORFMANN and VERA BELMONT · Based on the Novel by J.H. ROSNY, Sr.
Executive Producer MICHAEL GRUSKOFF · Produced by JOHN KEMENY and DENIS HEROUX · Directed by JEAN-JACQUES ANNAUD
Original Soundtrack Album available on RCA Records and Tapes · Available in Paperback from Penguin Books

'Quest for Fire': a comic book illustration depicting four hairy people standing underneath a sheep's bladder...

bladder which is somehow radiating cosmic energy in every direction. So the point wouldn't be lost, a text accompanied the picture explaining how 20th Century Fox might be in line to collect next year's Nobel Prize for Anthropology: "Fourteen years ago, '2001: A Space Odyssey' was the astounding epic that aroused a generation, telling them where they might be headed. Now, 20th Century Fox presents a science fantasy adventure that will arouse this generation, telling us where we might have begun". The "us" in this case being ad agency copywriters. A First Place Award ought to be handed to the designer(s) of the evocative ads for Peter Weir's *Gallipoli*, which pulled us into the film's very last moment, courageously, before any money changed hands. That subtlety was balanced by the bold panoramic illustration of the events in Moustapha Akkad's *Lion of the Desert*. This time the style eerily anticipated certain front pages of *The Daily Mail* in recent days, or harked back to illustrations familiar to readers of the *Illustrated London News* published during the Great War.

'Excalibur': a return to the days of ancient-speak advertising

Apposite, at least, unlike the feeble blurb announcing the long awaited *Ragtime*. (Cue Marvin Hamlisch playing score of *The Sting*, backwards...) "What a time it was, an incredible time, a bad time, a good time..." That could describe my cousin's *bar mitzvah*, although he would prefer to remember it the way *Excalibur* was heralded: "Forged by a god. Foretold by a wizard. Found by a King". A slightly telegrammatic style was favoured by the *Mad Max 2* folks, who fell back on the tried and true adjectives, "Ruthless ... Savage ... Spectacular!" The year's grace note was struck by *Shogun's* slogan, taken from the 17th Century Japanese poet Basho: "In the Kingdom of Death, love flowers, a single lily". It's just possible that Basho may

have penned the line for *Deadly Blessing*, too.

They challenged us and bribed us with secrets, too. "She'll never rest until her tale is told." This, from *Ghost Story*, a secret longing for the widest possible exposure. It was also hinted that, despite newsflashes from American space probes, "On Jupiter's moon, something deadly is happening", so Sean Connery took us there in *Outland* to find out what it was. Whispered, too, from the humid recesses of Florida's mean streets, "She taught him everything she knew — about passion and murder", she being Kathleen Turner and he being William Hurt, both gooey with each other's *Body Heat*. Another couple of stunning confidences offered to us were, "If you fool around with a cop like Sharky — you'd better be either very tough...or very beautiful", and about James Caan, "Tonight his take-home pay is $410,000...tax free. He's a thief". The fact that "take-home pay" *means* wages free of tax didn't occur to anybody, unless it was the intention to devise a line of copy as clumsy as the British title, *Violent Streets*. The original title was *Thief*. Another name switch muddied the promotional waters of *The Janitor* (original title, *Eyewitness*). The most cryptic print ad consisted of two stills from the film, one in which a pliant Sigourney Weaver gazes longingly over the rounded shoulders of William Hurt, still suffering, it seems, from a lingering dose of body heat. Inset is a second still — a figure of a man in an empty corridor. A secret *and* a challenge in that one. The unabashed dares came from *Wolfen*, whom, we were warned, "...can tear the scream from your throat", something like John Landis' *An American Werewolf in London*, which was also dubbed "A masterpiece of terror". The Critic's Circle Award for Most Ambitious Claim has to go to the paranoid fantasy *The Burning*. Clearly formulated by grown-up Sixties dropouts, the second string of the Secaucus Seven, echoing down the lanes of memory come the words, "Don't look he'll see you. Don't breathe he'll hear you. Don't move you're dead." That last line must have been used by good guy and bad guy alike in hundreds of Westerns and gangster pictures. In a mad flourish of self-reference, the publicity gremlins at

'The Burning': the paranoid fantasy that wins Critic's Circle Award for Most Ambitious Claim

Barber International (or Avco Embassy, as the case may be) emblazoned ads for *Escape from New York* with the motto of their own *metier*: "...Breaking out is impossible. Breaking in is insane."

The past year was not without its film ads of conscience and commitment. The question facing the boys and girls at UIP was how to convince the general public that a movie about a paralytic eloquently arguing for his own death really constituted a fun night out. Despite the memorable West End and Broadway success of *Whose*

'Whose Life is it Anyway?': Step aside, Vincent Canby etc!

Life is it Anyway?, a fresh approach was called for. Step aside, Vincent Canby! Make room, Pauline Kael! Move over, Dilys Powell! P. Waterhouse of Streatham, London SW16 makes it clear: "...It was a true life sort of situation...I was a bit scared actually..." and Chauvac, curiously also of Streatham goes on record with, "...I was very impressed...you really need to see it..." These quotes from Ordinary People stood alongside their photographs, the implication being that we could track them down and ask them what they said on either side of those tell-tale dots... Torn from the graffiti of modern-day office block walls came the rousing (if slightly diffident) feminist raspberry, "I have the right...Or I should...To give myself freely as I choose". In an attempt to out-Australia the Australians, Enterprise offered us *The End of August*, a title chosen over that of the novel on which it was based, *The Awakening*, and even over the one favoured in marketing research surveys, *I'm a Real Angry Woman*. Tony Richardson's *The Border* wasn't sold as a Tony Richardson film, but as a Jack Nicholson film, neatly avoiding the subject itself, i.e. the problem and plight of illegal Mexican immigrants into the US. Nevertheless, those in need could have their consciences massaged by attending any one of the dozen or so foreign films which cropped up in specialist houses dotted around the major population centres. The funny thing about foreign (i.e. non-English speaking) films is that they are all marketed in about the same way. Quotes. Quotes, quotes and more quotes and maybe a moody drawing. This isn't film fun, nope, it's Art. So, a movie about a tortured, driven, duped German actor

(*Mephisto*) is served up in exactly the same way as a passionate tour through the labyrinth of femininity (*City of Women*). Which, in turn, is quite the same approach taken with intrigue in Beirut (*Circle of Deceit*) and drug addiction in Berlin (*Christiane F.*). Here are a few quotes. See if you can tell which title they're tacked on to: "...a bold, disturbing picture...", "...brilliantly observed...I rate it a *must*...", "One of the best we'll see this year...", "Brilliant...A stunning film", "A moving and thought provoking picture", "Few other recent releases can approach the film for urgency, power and importance." Answers on page 289.

And they wore the boaters and striped jackets of carnival barkers, pulling us into the ten-cent tent. Basically, it was the same show inside, even if "juvenile" and "mature" programmes were promised. The jaded teenybopper set were advised to make a beeline

Goes Heavy Metal. Thinking back over the memorably unmemorable advertisements (not to say releases) of 1981-82, I retain the impression of there having been a small avalanche of bromide, anodyne, safe, tidy efforts aimed at an imaginary audience of stable, modish "professionals". Precisely, luke-warm comedies with "mature" subject matter. Recall *Loving Couples*? That was the update of *Bob and Carol and Ted and Alice* with the mix 'n' match torsoes and legs, and oh yes, the knowing little arrowhead popping out of the "o" in *Loving* and the delicate wee cross emerging from the "o" in *Couples*. Have to be an adult to understand that, pal! Ditto the *double entendre* which described the Dereks' *Tarzan the Apeman*, viz, "The most exciting pair in the jungle". If *Arthur* was this genre's mascot, ("I race cars, I play tennis, I fondle women, but I have weekends off and I am my own boss..."), then

serious issues which beset us all if we are *Rich and Famous* (not to mention Bisset and Bergen), "From the very beginning, they knew they'd be friends to the end. What they didn't count on was everything in between". But who does these days?

Recognition ought to be made of the least inspired idea of 1981 and I mean the picture nobody needed to make...but they made *Legend of the Lone Ranger* for no reason, apparently, other than as an excuse to invoke the words, "The film where you hiss the villain and cheer the hero". Additionally, or accidentally,

this was an answer to critics of the craft who accuse advertising copywriters of being remote from real life. Recognition ought also be given to the most inspired line of the year and I mean the one nobody needed to write to pull in the crowds awaiting a sequel to *The Rocky Horror Picture Show*. The sequel turned out to be *Shock Treatment*, and underneath the warmly grinning and weirdly forbidding face of Richard O'Brien appear the soothing words, "Trust me, I'm a doctor". Just the right attitude to the whole dirty business.

'Tarzan the Apeman': the double-entendre of the year, delivered with a simplicity, and simple-mindedness, befitting a 'Carry On' film

for *Heavy Metal*, which promised to take them, among other places, to "A universe of sexual fantasies". This particular universe exists, apparently, "beyond the future" cheek-by-jowl with that of "awesome good" and "terrifying evil". Anyhow, kids who arrived too late to get into *Heavy Metal* hustled over to make the last show of *Herbie Goes Bananas*. "Olé! It's south of the border disorder when..." etcetera, this, underneath a cartoon version of "The Rape of the Sabine Women", a subtle marketing ploy which combines an appreciation of highbrow classical art with the jolly, unpredictable antics of an unnaturally independent Volkswagen. The talk on the street, though, is that young audiences are waiting for somebody to produce *Herbie*

Alan Alda's *The Four Seasons* was its flagship. Cartoon portraits of Mr. Alda and Carol Burnett toasting each other — with *Martinis*, what else? — and the words "Here's to our friends...and the strength to put up with them." The happy, bobbing, friendly letters of the title were surmounted by another drawing, of a pondful of happy, bobbing, friendly, well, hey! Waitaminute! Those are our *neighbours*! And here come the rest of them, out of the time-warp opening on the late Fifties feature-length sitcoms — *So Fine*: "There's only one thing that could keep them apart...the seven-foot thing that she's married to," and *First Monday in October*: "In the Supreme Court, there are only eight of them against all of her," and for those given more to contemplating the

'Shock Treatment': just the right attitude

OF PUBS AND PIRACY

Colin Vaines outlines a new problem for the film industry

If there was one problem which plagued the film business more than any other in the last 12 months, it was video piracy. Piracy of feature films has proved to be *the* growth industry of the Eighties, with England regarded as the piracy centre of the world. Unless the problem is checked, it seems certain to result in many legitimate video companies going out of business, and, with revenue diverted from the film makers, a massive reduction in the number of feature films produced each year.

The extent of the problem can be gauged from figures released by the British Videogram Association, which represents major companies such as Thorn-EMI, Warner Brothers, MGM, and 20th Century Fox. These show that in 1981, 78 per cent of the pre-recorded video cassettes available in the UK were illegal copies, raking in an incredible £182 million for the pirates. In America, pirates earned nearly double that amount.

Over half the pirate tapes available in the UK were bogus copies of legitimate releases by major companies. Counterfeiting, an anonymous pirate stated in a video trade paper, has now become the biggest money-spinner for the pirates, as prices have dropped on obviously pirated products (that is, films which are unavailable legitimately).

The fantastically rapid growth of video piracy clearly has left the film industry reeling. Piracy of features has, of course, gone on for years — but before 1980, it mainly involved ardent film collectors who paid considerable sums for illegal 16mm copies. The advent of home video machines and the speed with which they became a commonplace item in affluent households caused the problem to explode. The film companies were hopelessly ill-prepared to fight piracy on the massive scale which developed within a few years. Things were not helped either by the tardiness

'Monty Python's Life of Brian':
banned in Irish cinemas, seen in Irish pubs

of the major companies in making their movies available on tape.

While there were perfectly understandable reasons for this delay in releasing films on tape — the distributors obviously hoping to make some money from a cinema release before launching the cassette of a film — the result was that the market was wide open for the pirates to step in. All a would-be pirate had to do was bribe a lab technician or cinema projectionist to let him have a print of a film for a few hours, video tape it, and then run off hundreds of copies from his master cassette.

The quality of the pirated tapes proved to be unimportant. No matter how bad the picture quality was (and on pirated cassettes it was and is truly abysmal), video machine owners leapt at the chance of seeing new films within days of their release in the cinema — and in many cases, long *before* their release in the cinema.

Several factors have aided the growth of piracy. In addition to the gap between theatrical and video release of a film, the spiralling cost of cinema-going is an important factor. For the price of one cinema ticket, it is possible to hire a tape — legal or illegal — for several days. More significantly, for the same price one can buy many pirated tapes.

But the biggest incentive to the pirates in the UK was, and still is, the woeful lack of legal deterrents in this country. Under the present law, pirates brought to court are dealt with under civil law and are liable to be fined just £2 per cassette, up to a maximum of £50. Damages sometimes can be obtained; and in certain cases, if conspiracy can be proved, the case can be dealt with more severely under criminal law. But quite clearly, while the penalties remain so light in the majority of cases, they simply are not effective enough. The result of this ludicrous situation is that England has become the international centre for video piracy, with both small-time and big-time operators at work.

As the British Videogram Association has pointed out: "Video piracy now involves both organised crime, which finds it as effective a way of raising funds as prostitution and drugs, and individuals, many of whom have never been involved in crime before. A husband and wife team, for instance, can churn out hundreds of copies from a pre-recorded cassette. There is quite a handsome business in duplicating that tape over and over again."

With an estimated 1½ million video recorders installed in private homes, it is easy to see the size of the market for major feature films

on cassette. But in addition to screenings of pirate tapes in private homes, there is the added headache for the film business of illegal screenings in pubs, with new films — in many cases pirated copies — being shown to attract custom. The problem is widespread in Britain, but to a large extent is controllable because most pubs belong to one of the major breweries. It is thus a relatively simple matter for a "cease and desist" letter from lawyers representing the Society of Film Distributors to be despatched to the appropriate brewery when these illegal screenings come to light.

In Ireland, however, the situation is far more serious, with the threat of closure hanging over many cinemas as a result of illegal screenings of pirated films. Earlier this year, pubs all over the country were showing tapes of films like *Death Wish II* and *Lady Chatterley's Lover*, months before they were released in cinemas — and in their original, uncensored versions, the Irish theatrical prints being heavily cut. Pubs also screened for their patrons films which had been banned outright by the Irish censor, such as *Monty Python's Life of Brian*. Said one leading Irish exhibitor: "It's catastrophic for cinemas. People are saying it's cheaper to go to the pub, have a drink, and watch the latest movie than it is to see that movie in the cinema. Unless something is done, in my opinion there will be no cinema business as we know it in Ireland within twelve months."

As in England, the fines for video piracy or for illegal screenings are ridiculously low. But the problem is made worse by the Irish courts' refusal to accept a copy of a film's copyright document — they will only accept the original document, which generally is held in America and is almost impossible to obtain — and by the fact that the majority of pubs in the Republic are independently owned. "So whereas in

England the SFD can write to the brewers, here they have to deal with each individual pub," said our embittered Irish exhibitor, who went on to raise a common complaint among exhibitors and film makers — that there are not enough people from the distribution companies monitoring piracy.

Stories are now commonplace in the film industry of producers and directors touring the world to promote their film, only to find in every country they visit that their film has been available for several weeks — or months — as a pirated cassette, with no indication that the film's distributor has taken, or is going to take, any action against the pirates — usually because the problem is too widespread and consequently out of control.

In Britain, the record of the film companies in fighting piracy is very good compared to much of the rest of the world. The Society of Film Distributors has been dealing with around 40 cases a month for the last two years. Some are dealt with by a simple "cease and desist" letter, others in the courts.

However, because of the poor legal deterrents and the continuing expansion of the problem, the trade decided early in 1982 to launch a major crackdown on piracy, with three major bodies — the SFD, the BVA, and the Motion Picture Export Association of America — joining forces to hit the pirates hard. The BVA set up a £¼ million fighting fund to tackle the problem, adopting a two-pronged approach: firstly, to persuade the Government to increase the penalties for piracy, and secondly to investigate alleged piracy and bring as many culprits to court as possible, with the hope of deterring by continual harassment as much as anything else.

Well-known counterfeit video cassettes. 'Chariots of Fire' was one...

To help in this work, the BVA called in the British Phonographic Industry's crack anti-piracy unit, which has done much in recent years to eliminate record and tape piracy in the UK. Within a few months a major victory was won in the High Court when three people alleged to have been involved in a large scale conspiracy to counterfeit video cassettes of films such as *Superman* and *Chariots of Fire* had to pay £750,000 in damages and costs to five leading film and video companies.

The size of the settlement, and the enormous amount of publicity engendered by the case, gave a terrific boost to the anti-piracy campaign. The BVA warned that it was the first of "many, many actions that would be brought in the months to come." And indeed action soon followed against many other individuals and groups from various parts of the country who were alleged to have been involved in either manufacturing or hiring out pirate tapes.

All the trade bodies fighting

the pirates have been involved in lobbying the Government in an attempt to tighten up the copyright laws and make the penalties for piracy more serious. The Government may introduce new legislation on copyright in 1983, but the BVA, the SFD and the MPEAA are pressing for immediate action. They want piracy to be dealt with under criminal law, with substantial fines and prison sentences as the penalties. It does seem unlikely that the Government will take any action before 1983; but Parliament *is* aware of the problem, through the action of the trade bodies involved in the anti-piracy campaign, and through a motion tabled by an all-party group of MPs.

The motion calls on the Government to stamp out pirate video cassettes as a matter of urgency, pointing out the gravely damaging effect they are having on both production and distribution in the UK. Shortly after it was tabled, a copy of the motion was sent out to 15,000 dealers by Thorn-EMI Video Programmes as part of the anti-piracy drive. The letter urged dealers to write to their local MPs and ask them to support the motion in Parliament.

The trade has also been investigating other ideas to combat piracy in the last twelve months. One company produced special reflective security labels for its cassette jackets, and another launched a security system involving coded information within the cassette which was alleged to be impossible to copy.

One independent distributor experimented with an almost

simultaneous cinema and video release of a film. Cinema owners claimed that it hurt their business, but the distributor argued that not only did this rapid video release beat the pirates into the marketplace, the publicity resulting from it probably boosted admissions at cinemas where the film was just opening. Whether exhibitors like it or not, simultaneous cinema and video release looks certain to be commonplace in the future, as one of the few effective ways of combating piracy. Another development which may affect piracy is the introduction of the video disc. Films on disc are relatively cheap, and in a form which is difficult to pirate.

It's hard to tell at this time what effect other anti-piracy measures will have. Opinions differ about the extent to which organised crime is involved in piracy, but if it is small — as has been claimed by several pirates — then the problem may be solved by the introduction of tougher penalties. One former pirate has gone on record as saying that virtually all the main suppliers of pirated material in the UK would pull out of the business if they faced prison sentences.

If, on the other hand, the involvement of organised crime is significant — as the BVA and SFD claim — then threats against the investigators and those who could give evidence will make the going hard. Clearly, though, changes in the law will be a step in the right direction. Otherwise irreparable damage may be done to the film and video business in the UK.

...'Superman' was another

THE MAKING OF 'HEAVEN'S GATE'
A CHRONOLOGICAL HISTORY

Out of a clear blue Montana sky, Michael Cimino descended by helicopter to inspect the Western town specially built for his third film. It was his town. And he didn't like it. "It's all wrong!" No, he was assured, it was exactly as per his approved blueprints. "I don't know from blueprints," said Cimino. "I do know it's wrong. Move it back ... three feet either side." The construction boss suggested it would be easier, quicker, cheaper too, to move one side back six feet ... "No," yelled Cimino. "Do as I say." Impossible. In Hollywood labour terms, it proved cheaper to raze it down and raise it all up again. Cost: one million dollars. This is the story of how the whole thing ended up costing 40 million.

By Tony Crawley

1971. Michael Winner offers Western script by contract-writer Gerald Wilson to United Artists, backers of his previous oaters. Despite low $4 million budget, UA passes. Winner puts scenario on his Piccadilly shelf. Title: *The Johnson County War.* Meanwhile ... Michael Cimino, ex-New York, Long Island, Yale graduate school and Green Beret, intense, private (keeps his age, now 39, secret) arrives in Hollywood, determined to direct. Rents small house, writes scripts including *Thunderbolt and Lightfoot* and... *The Johnson County War.* The first is sent to Clint Eastwood, the other to Steve McQueen. Nothing like starting at the top.
1972. Cimino makes his first sale to Universal. Douglas Trumbull directs Cimino's (and two others') *Silent Running.* Good; too early for the sf boom.
1973. Steve McQueen agrees to star in *The Johnson County War* — the Winner version. "He'd read Cimino's version and turned it down, then accepted mine. He rang Daily Variety to announce it as his next film. I said, 'Steve, don't rush. Let's make the picture, never mind the announcement.' Then McQueen's *Papillon* deal recovered and ... I never saw him again! I never got to make the picture, but it made a great announcement." Cimino wins Eastwood instead, directs his *Thunderbolt* script for Clint's Malpaso company.
1974. The film is released as the last of Eastwood's UA commitments, making about $18 million world-wide. Cimino's début, praised for "flamboyant energy", wins him offers. "I decided to gamble and get involved with projects I really want to do."

20th Century Fox had two: *Pearl*, the Janis Joplin story (later submerged into *The Rose*) and the Frank Costello biopic — on the assumption that "the new Coppola" was best for gangsters. Both projects lost in Fox management shuffle.
1975. Paramount calls. Another gangster idea. Three weeks into pre-production, another shuffle... "I had this terrible feeling I'd let everything slip by. People just forget who you are."
November 1976. Cimino outlines *The Deer Hunter* to EMI in Hollywood. It takes him two hours. "OK, do it — start by March 17." He has no script, locations or stars ready.
June 27, 1977. *The Deer Hunter* starts with Cimino shooting winter in summer among innumerable headaches.
November 1977. Cimino in London *en route* to Los Angeles, after completing film in Thailand. It takes him 14 hours a day for three months simply to view his footage. Rows aplenty about length of film (and of editing). Universal, the US distributors, want three-and-a-half hours slashed to two. EMI just want it finished for October opening and consider bouncing Cimino.
January 21, 1978. Kris Kristofferson, fed up with movies (or vice-versa?) after UA's *Vigilante Force*, walks out of Peter Hyams' *Hanover Street* in London.
November 1978. United Artists announce Cimino's third movie *The Johnson County War.* Star: Kristofferson.
December 5, 1978. One of UA's trade ads, refers to Cimino as a masterful story-teller, mentioning his new film, and his script for Norman

Jewison's *Dogs of War*, both due for UA release; like *Deer Hunter* in most of Europe, South America, Far East and ... Iran. UA calls itself 'traditionally the place for such talented independent film makers as Michael Cimino."
December 1978. Rapid demise of Travolta's *Moment By Moment* enables *Deer Hunter* to open, two months late, in time for Oscar consideration. Screening twice a day only, due to its inordinate length, at $4 a ticket, it takes $19,640 in a week *and* the New York Critics' best film honours. First of many.
February 2, 1979. Film re-opens in New York at $5 a seat. Still intact. "A film lives, becomes alive, because of its shadows, its spaces," says Cimino, "and that's what people wanted to cut."
February 20, 1979. Cimino signed to make more shadows and spaces in a drama "of epic proportions" for Warners. Untitled film to be made by his Partisan Productions, produced by *The Deer Hunter's* production consultant Joann Carelli. Just like *Johnson County War.*
March 10, 1979. Cimino wins directing award from American Directors' Guild. Since 1948, two winners only have not gone on to Oscar glory in same year.
April 9, 1979. And the winner is ... *The Deer Hunter.* Five times. Best film, director, supporting actor Christopher Walken, editing, sound. They know who Cimino is now ...
April 16, 1979. He begins *Johnson County War* — now *Heaven's Gate* — in Montana. Budget: $7.5million. Script *sans* prologue or epilogue, inserted later to suit his Oscar elevation to ... important film maker.

April 30, 1979. After two weeks of shooting, Cimino is two weeks behind schedule.
August, 1979. 16 weeks into 17-week schedule, UA take over fiscal control of *Heaven's Gate* and publicly reveal first concern about rising costs — $21 million now, $30 million when (if) filming finishes in October when John Hurt due in London for *The Elephant Man.*
August 6, 1979. *La femme flic* starts shooting in France minus its star. Miou-Miou replaces Isabelle Huppert, stuck at Cimino's *Gate* until November.
September 6, 1979. Cimino's champagne party celebrates shooting the millionth foot of film.
October 1, 1979. John Hurt begins *Elephant Man.*
October 1979. Montana locations end. But no wrap party. Shooting is hardly over. Two weeks of locations during post-production — in England says Cimino. No, in Massachusetts and Rhode Island, insists UA.
November 1979. Free at last! Isabelle Huppert starts jammed Euro-schedule with Godard's *Slow Motion* in Switzerland.
December 1979. Huppert begins Marta Meszaros' *Inheritance* in Hungary.
January 9, 1980. *The Deer Hunter* is tenth in Variety's 1979 box office champs with North American rentals of $26,927,000. Double that for the world business. No wonder UA left Cimino alone ..
February 24, 1980. Producer Joann Carelli tells Sunday Times *Heaven's Gate* will open in New York on Nov. 16, and London for Christmas with royal premiere. Running time will be 190 minutes, eight more than *The Deer Hunter.*
March 1980. Isabelle Huppert

starts *La dame aux Camelias* in Rome.

April 10, 1980. Huge relief at UA. Principal photography completed on *Heaven's Gate*. Cimino got his way about filming Harvard prologue at Oxford.

May 9-23, 1980. Huppert has three films, from three countries, in competition at the 23rd Cannes festival.

June 23, 1980. Hollywood's Western revival, sparked off by Cimino's *Gate*, fizzles. *Bronco Billy, Tom Horn, Urban Cowboy*. Only UA's *Long Riders*, fresh from Cannes, doing well.

July 23, 1980. Whoops! Kodak's centenary series of trade ads feature Cimino's first US *Gate* interview: "If you don't get it right, what's the point?" Hollywood directors being sacked like ninepins. Richard Fleischer makes a new career out of picking up other people's movies.

October 1, 1980. UA fretting over *Gate's* 210 minutes, with final reels still being cut. It means less screenings per day and forever to get the money back. Film due to open, in time for an Oscar nod, by December 17.

October 22, 1980. Cancel last telex! New York premiere now November 19, with LA on 21st. Final (?) Budget: $32 million.

October 29, 1980. UA switches mass-release dates for 100 screens, from December 19 to February 20, due to remixing soundtracks of 35mm prints. Gossip has UA execs saying the film is too long, incoherent, unwieldy and must be removed from Cimino's grasp and cut afresh. One exec says it'll be lucky to earn $20

million. Not good news for UA with business already 32 per cent down.

November 11, 1980. *Gate* gloom continues at UA, but production chief Steven Bach announces new $303 million programme — $168 million for 1981 projects, including *Rocky III* and Altman's *Lone Star*. "Starting now, you'll see a different kind of picture coming out of United Artists ... larger, more commercial movies." The little films are not dead, though, they're part of UA's "responsibility to train people who will be the Francis Coppolas and Michael Ciminos of 10 years from now."

November 15, 1980. Well, maybe not the Ciminos ... *Heaven's Gate* budget now tallied as $34 million.

November 17, 1980. The MPAA awards *Gate* an R rating — usually an X, or debatable AA in Britain. The US Catholic Conference dub it B — "morally objectionable in part for all." All UA Investors?

November 18, 1980. *Heaven's Gate* unwrapped for New York press, with hopes of *Deer Hunter* lightning striking twice. It doesn't. New York Times' Vincent Canby:

unmitigated disaster; Daily News' Kathleen Carroll: could be mistaken for a Russian anti-capitalist epic; Time's Richard Corliss: random sequences from some lost eight-hour masterwork, with a grandeur in the *folie*, but not in its repetitions and ellipses. As for Cimino, Corliss sums up the reaction: "From nearly every movie man came the cackle of contumely; the arrogant director had committed career hara-kari."

November 19, 1980. *Gate* opens and closes — withdrawn by UA after one day in New York and Toronto at Joann Carelli's request. Cimino agreed. New Yorkers had spent $100,000 in advance sales. A year before they'd paid $308,000 for *Apocalypse* reservations.

November 20, 1980. Los Angeles opening cancelled. No chance of Oscar nominations, as films have to play one full LA week before December 31. New York's Cinema 1 given the option to pull now or wait out the week. Or longer. It waits the week out only. *Gate's* opening is a complete *débâcle*. Cimino pleads in an open letter to UA to "finish" the film, so "prematurely rushed for

opening deadline." He can re-cut (from 219 to about 130 minutes, it's suggested) and show it to UA in a month. Transamerica Corporation, the UA owners, write off a secret amount of the $35 million. Or: "We have made a prudent conservative accounting judgment that in all likelihood the amount of recoupment will not be substantial enough to justify carrying the film on our books at the full investment cost." If only we could all do that ... Re-editing will cost yet another million, matching the amount spent and lost on the premiere advertising. The soundtrack LP goes out as planned. Composer David Mansfield deserves the break — has best stuff in film: written independently of finished scenes and supervised by Joann Carelli.

November 25, 1980. Film pulled from Cinema 1, where it's recognised as an endangered species and earns $39,000 in a week. Reasonable enough. *The Deer Hunter's* first week hit only $19,640, and replacement, *Apocalypse Now*, doesn't top *Gate's* take after a full month ($26,305).

November 26, 1980. Variety runs a rare editorial: "A Bad Week For Show Business" — the MGM Grand Hotel fire in Las Vegas, the deaths of Mae West and George Raft, and *Gate*. Uninspired Variety headline for the affair: "UA, director's paradise under loss cloud," recovers on turn-page heading: "UA's Paradise Loss." Not as neat as the week before: "Reagan Sweeps As Carter Weeps."

December 17, 1980. First

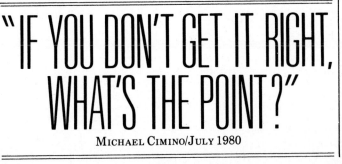

"IF YOU DON'T GET IT RIGHT, WHAT'S THE POINT?"

MICHAEL CIMINO/JULY 1980

Gate fall-out. Norbert T. Auerbach replaces Andy Albeck as UA president. Nothing to do with that film. Of course not! Albeck remains chief executive officer and becomes chairman, says changes first discussed in December, 1979. Auerbach talks of tighter discipline in future, with a production dept. rep. assigned to movies to alert studio of potential Cimino-ing. He promises to wield an axe; insists Steven Bach's production chief's job is safe. Albeck believes an excellent film is still in the *Gate* footage. Somewhere.

December 19, 1980. Cimino early for once. Shows off his new 165 minute cut. Told to shave another fifteen minutes from the pro and epilogues.

December 23, 1980. 20th Century Fox chairman Dennis C.Stanfill terrifies Hollywood by hinting *average* budgets will hit $25 million by 1985 — $14m. to produce and $11m. to market. (Stanfill is ousted by July, 1981).

January 1981. First issue of Cinema '81 in France runs Jean-Pierre Coursdon's passionate *Gate* defence: another masterpiece defiled by Americans because it hits too close to home about the real West, the roots of the American dream. (Cimino says he never reads reviews, but spouts much of this line at Cannes in May).

January 17, 1981. UA's Steven Bach in London says the new *Gate* is down to 148 minutes and will most likely be 135. "The movie was far too long and, rather than let it go down the drain, we pulled it in for repairs... Cimino was extraordinarily co-operative under extraordinary circumstances. I prefer Michael to stay on and finish the film. If he didn't, I'd be very sorry." He kills stories of re-cutting costing $10 million. "The lay press writes whatever it wants" and considers a bill of $600,000, moving the final budget to $36 million — "certainly in the price range of movies we've made before." He then equates *Gate*'s "triangular love story" with *Gone With the Wind*! Vincent Canby's review? "No film is an unqualified disaster. Period."

January 29, 1981. With Cimino, incognito, the "penultimate" *Gate* is sneaked in Calumet City, a working-class Chicago district. Customers thought they were attending Michael Mann's *Thief (Violent Streets)* — and *Gate* reels are literally sneaked into the theatre in *Streets* cans. Audience didn't have a clue what they were watching — the film had no titles — until a quiet announcement after lights dimmed. Further previews set for other blue-collar regions as the film is now biased towards its violence for *The Deer Hunter* crowd.

February 12, 1981. In first public appearance as UA president, Norbert Auerbach ("We face a crisis of control, and have to deal with it on all levels") screens an excerpt from the new version at the closing banquet of the Sho West '81 trade convention at the MGM Grand Hotel in Vegas. The Grand is back in business. People aren't so sure about UA.

February 20, 1981. UA's chief executive officer and chairman — remember Andy Albeck — goes. Early retirement, it says here. Auerbach more or less in full charge; untainted by *Gate*.

March 3, 1981. *Gate* chosen to close the tenth LA Filmex in April — the new 135 minute version, to begin US release next day. Steven Bach, among Filmex trustees, must have helped, although festival director Gary Essert says the original was unanimously liked by "our Swiss and French consultants, who thought it was one of the finest American films they'd seen." Film also rumoured for Cannes.

March 4, 1981. New version screened again in Chicago, touting for business this time. Exhibitors only invited. No wives. And no press.

March 10, 1981. Auerbach means business. UA ask for $35,000 in upfront guarantees from Chicago cinemas booking *Gate*. More quietly, UA agrees to renew terms if film doesn't perform.

March 17, 1981. First Cimino-ed victim among UA directors. Altman's *Lone Star* film among two cancelled by Steven Bach: "Not ready for March shooting." Altman says Auerbach didn't like script. Also the date of UA's revised *Gate* publicity kit. Film no longer described as "an intelligent, beautifully mounted story" and the "cattlemen" of the old synopsis are now "zealous landowners and stock growers" as per US history, Cimino-style. There's biographies of all cast and crew stars, but not of the director.

April 7, 1981. Fox takes over *Lone Star* — minus Altman. News to him. "I've never pulled out of the project." Altman's five-picture deal with Fox concluded with *Health* in 1979 — still sight unseen.

April 11, 1981. "Where I see budgets running away from us, I'll stop them. I'd rather take a $3-4 million loss than let a picture run away from us." Auerbach is in London, to view the new Bond, and announce new product including Barbra Streisand's directing bow, *Yentl* — a $13 million budget and if she goes over, she pays for it herself.

April 14, 1981. Still editing, *Gate* slated for 850 openings in North America on April 24. And Cannes.

April 23, 1981. D-Day, Mark II. New version officially unveiled at Filmex. UA keep critics out. Cimino and Carelli met by pickets from the American Humane Association, alleging cruelty to animals in the film — "the blowing up of a horse, maltreatment of pack mules, trip-wiring horses and illegal cockfighting." Across town, critic Prof. Arthur Knight runs the original *Gate* for his University of Southern California film class, suddenly tripled in size to 700 people. "News travels fast," says Knight. The assembly cheers all names in the credits — boo Cimino's. As at Filmex, people walk out.

April 24, 1981. Film re-opens nationwide. Reviews are no better. What's dead is dead. "The film's coda no longer baffles, it disappoints," writes *Time*'s Richard Corliss, mourning the original's "brazen visual virtuosity ... they can still be seen, in postcard glimpses ... but they are subordinated to a small story and to Cimino's notion of Hollywood Marxism: the poor are better than the rich because they are more photogenic." New running time: 153 minutes in 70mm and, minus certain titles and wrap music, 149 in 35mm.

April 27, 1981. Larry Cohen sacked from directing his script of Mickey Spillane's *I, The Jury*, after six days — one day and $1 million over schedule. "I could not indicate ... that I'd get back on budget." Replaced by Richard T. Heffron.

May 2, 1981. One week's *Gate* returns are in and couldn't be more damning. At some 810 (not 850) cinemas, it's earned as little as $1.3 million dollars an average of $1,600 per screen. At New York's Astor Plaza, which costs $17,500 a week to run, *Gate* made ... $10,000! Most of this income drops by half in second week, when *Heaven's Gate* is doubled up with *Fame* or *American Pop*.

May 5, 1981. Visibly stunned, Norbert Auerbach says, "We had repeatedly said we were guardedly optimistic, but let's face it, the picture has been totally rejected by the public, and by most of the press, even in its new version ... We don't have to pull it out ... They're doing it for us. We don't have to take any action at all." Except weep. Final budget count puts *Gate* at around $40 million, though Auerbach insists it's $36 million. He adds the *débâcle* will not affect Steven Bach's production job. "We have repeatedly said that we're not blaming Steve for *Heaven's Gate*." Who then?

May 19, 1981. Cimino touted for a Cannes prize — any prize (Francois Mitterrand Trophy for Socialist Westerns?) as festival authorities want to hit back at Hollywood for launching its own Film Market ... *and* re-discovering Abel Gance while the French remain uninterested in the

Napoleon Coppola is showing all over America. It's taking more money than *Gate,* for sure.

May 12, 1981. MGM reveals take-over bid for beleaguered UA.

May 14, 1981. So much for job safety. Steven Bach sacked by Auerbach. Bach may not be to blame, but like Albeck, he's the scapegoat. Replaced by Raphael Etkes, from the troubled Filmways.

May 17, 1981. Auerbach at Cannes, accompanied — not by Bach, but by a toy Leo the Lion, as the rumoured $400 million sale of UA to MGM draws nigh.

May 18, 1981. As well as MGM, he talks about *Gate.* "We're hoping that it will be perceived and received differently here. It's not unusual that a film shot down by US critics is received well here. I don't blame the press. Things that go with Michael Cimino's personality made for an unkind attitude. Also, the press having been so negative the first time couldn't very well turn around and say that the film was a masterpiece."

May 20, 1981. *Heaven's Gate,* unveiled at Cannes festival as *La Porte Du Paradis.* Cimino and Auerbach share Press conference table with Kristofferson, Huppert but not producer Carelli. No fireworks, except for Cimino stating, "When (historical) details no longer serve the function of the story — discard them"! Auerbach stoutly refuses to place blame for UA's demise on Cimino, but agrees that, "if *Heaven's Gate* had been a smashing success in the United States, it's quite possible that Transamerica would have been able to obtain a better price."

May 21, 1981. $380 million proves the aggregate price as the deal goes through and

MGM buys UA from Transamerica. Both companies to continue as separate entities. For how long?

May 22, 1981. French reviews are warmer, sacrilegiously comparing Cimino to Ford and Anthony Mann — his film to *Birth of a Nation.* His defence counsel, Jean-Pierre Coursdon, approves new cut, though preferring the artistic integrity of the original. Paris fans hardly agree. Another bad opening: $44,000 at five cinemas after one week.

May 26, 1981. Cimino's producer, Joann Carelli, talks. "(UA) may have seemed supportive in one sense, but actually did an injustice to the creative people involved by allowing them to go wild. We underwent at least four major management changes while the film was being made, so it's hard to point fingers at anyone in particular."

May 27, 1981. Cannes awards presented. Nothing for

Gate, Cimino, or anyone concerned with it. UA's Paris man, Andre Damon, is livid. "For the second year, no director's prize. I've never heard of a festival without a director's award. It's ridiculous!" No, just a problem for the jury believing it was not Cimino's wish to enter new version at Cannes, says president Jacques Deray. He'd have given the director's nod to Cimino — shared with John Boorman for *Excalibur.*

June 16, 1981. Transamerica announce that its *Gate* write-off amounts to $29 million. Or, again in conglomeratese, that UA has established an additional reserve fund amounting to about $29 million, before taxes, against its remaining investment in the fiasco. In Hollywoodese, MGM ain't paying for UA's turkey.

June 19, 1981. Martin Scorsese reopens *his* UA turkey, *New York, New York,* in his "originally intended" version at (where else?) Cinema 1 in New York. It goes so well in its 163-minute cut, it's held over.

June 23, 1981. Back in Hollywood, the bearded Norbert Auerbach promises UA's future budgets will be kept beneath MGM's $15 million ceiling. He thinks *Gate* is being turned into a TV mini-series. "Had I been in charge, the past overbudget problems wouldn't have happened." Steven Bach? Well, Auerbach had been sincere and true when saying Bach would never be the scapeGate, but well, he'd been used to operating in a different way under Andy Albeck. "Neither he nor I felt comfortable."

Bach, meantime, has himself a new job. At MGM.

July 1, 1981. *Heaven's Gate* has now been passed down the line to UA's television, video and specialised market entity, euphemistically called United Artists Classics. That's the branch which rescued Ivan Passer's *Cutter and Bone (Cutter's Way).* They're cutting *Gate* down to the bone, for re-release in a third version, or more likely a fast TV sale, with less triangular romance and more of Buddy Van Horn's action. And a new title. Well, not that new. *The Johnson County War.*

January 19, 1982. Forgotten in the high finances of *Reds,* *One From The Heart* and Lew Grade, Cimino comes back. The re-formed CBS (TV) Theatrical Films issue a 39 picture schedule including *Nitty Gritty* to be helmed by Cimino, exec produced by Carelli, but produced and scripted by others. Subject: Black comedies about the electronic news media. Cimino strikes back?

March 23, 1982. Not forgotten in France, the original 225 minute *Heaven's Gate* unveiled for Paris critics on the giant 240 square metre Kinepanorama screen on Avenue de la Motte-Picquet. Verdict: they liked it. It opened to the public in September — the only full release for the full-sized *Gate* in the world.

EPILOGUE. Michael Winner, who could have saved UA so much angst: "Gerald Wilson wrote a totally different version . . . nothing whatsoever to do with *Heaven's Gate.* My script still exists, but I don't think it's likely to be made, do you?"

CREDIT WHERE CREDIT IS (SOMETIMES) DUE

Associate producer. First assistant director. Focus puller. Best boy.
What do they all mean and, mainly, what do they all do? *Quentin Falk* de-mystifies the terms and defines the jobs

It is probably only since the advent of the big special effects movies that the cinema-going public has, so blatantly, been made to become aware of The Credits — that mine of information tacked on before and after a film. The film "buff" has, of course, always revelled in just such information — a pleasure now many times magnified as credits presently more resemble a novella than what was once a seemingly brief

of purposes. Firstly, it helps to fulfil certain contractual requirements. One hardly needs reminding that the creation of a movie is not just a period of shooting, followed by editing and scoring music. It is as likely as not to have been preceded by a frenzied period of wheeling and dealing, known euphemistically as "pre-production", in which a script has been commissioned and completed, a director signed, finance arranged and

why there are listed, often in almost tedious detail, every Tom, Dick or Harriet that functioned on the project.

Mind you, just as you should read between the lines of, say, a newspaper article, so you must be ready to read regularly between the credits of a feature film. It's often the information that credits purport to tell you, but due to a combination of circumstances, don't truly give you, that's often the most intriguing to unravel.

was generally known that a veritable horde of writers including, allegedly, Robert Towne and Elaine May, worked at various times during the development of *Reds*. And yet the final writing credit reads "by Warren Beatty and Trevor Griffiths." You can always tell when there have been a mass of hands in the writing pie — and hands that have gained due acknowledgement. Look at the *Superman* roll of honour which

ARREN BEATTY · DIANE KEATON · EDWARD HERRMANN · JERZY KOSIN
NICHOLSON · PAUL SORVINO · MAUREEN STAPLETON · Photography B'
STORARO · Edited by DEDE ALLEN · Original Music by STEPHEN SONDH
ONAL Music by DAVE GRUSIN · Production Design by RICHARD SYLBER
stume Design by SHIRLEY RUSSELL · Written by WARREN BEATTY and
TREVOR GRIFFITHS · Produced and Directed by WARREN BEATTY

acknowledgement of the numerous talents that comprised a movie.

It could be said that the growth of the Megadollar Movie has spawned Megacredits, which sort of makes sense. And yet, if you look closely, you'll probably find that the really giant pictures tend to offer you an absolute minimum of information at the kick-off, leaving the floodgates to open as the final scene fades from the screen. So just who is trying to impress whom, when it is likely that only the really committed (plus friends of the cast and crew) will stay in their seats as neat lists of personnel, under a multitude of sub-headings, unfold on the screen before the theatre lights finally come up.

It has to be said, before we examine particular credits in more detail, that the information serves a multitude

stars "packaged" — though not necessarily in that order.

Credits, then, act as a kind of contractual shorthand for how that final "deal" was struck with all the various elements. The more producers and executive producers listed, generally the more complicated the financial structure. The more prominent the stars' names, whether "above the title" (that is, ahead of the film's title), or "below the title", whether "single screen" (that is, flashed up alone on the screen), or in a clutch, will be a guide to the particular star's importance and/or price — or, perhaps to be more accurate, as to how successful the agent has been in tending to the peculiar needs of his client.

Secondly, credits serve as a genuine acknowledgement from the management, as it were, of the collaborative nature of the medium. Which is

Take, for instance, a film called *Continental Divide*, directed in the United States by a Briton Michael Apted (who made the hugely successful *Coalminer's Daughter*). On the film, fellow Britons, writer Jack Rosenthal and continuity lady Zelda Barron, get a joint associate producer credit which has really nothing to do with their normal functions.

The fact is, Rosenthal re-wrote Lawrence Kasdan's script and Barron worked closely on the film in her usual capacity. However, because these were British personnel working in a "foreign" location, local protocol (in other words, the heavy arm of indigenous union and guild) was such that neither could be acknowledged in those particular roles. The new credit was, therefore, devised as a kind of thank-you.

In much the same way, it

has "Story by ...", "Screenplay by ..." (and there are four names there which means there must have been a good deal of writing and re-writing), "Creative consultant ..." (which generally means an overall refining brief along the way) and the always curious "Additional script material by ...", as if a few gags had been added as an afterthought. *Superman* must hold the present record for credits with more than 400 names listed.

Thirdly, credits would appear simply to serve as ego-massage. Surely there can be no other explanation for the director who seeks such twee acknowledgements as " A film by ...", ".... film of..." or "A .... film", instead of good old plain "Directed by ..." just once off.

So then, who does what on a movie, and just what do such quaint terms as *best boy* and *key grip* actually mean? It is extraordinary how often one gets asked the question — what's the difference between the *producer* and the *director* — a confusion sometimes compounded when one person is credited with both roles?

In a nutshell, the *producer* organises the cash (the word "organises" is used advisedly since it seems generally to be held that a producer never uses his own money which a term like "provide" could perhaps indicate), while the *director* supervises the film's content.

It has often been said that the producer's role is to provide the enviroment in which the director can do his best work. Which is why, if the *producer* or *executive producer* on a film can be identified as the money man, then the *associate producer* plays such an important role in the day-to-day logistical organisation of a movie. Bearing in mind that the cost of shooting the average movie runs at around $300,000 a week (and that's discounting stars' and director's salaries), correct budgeting and scheduling is of paramount importance to prevent the *runaway* production, such as *Heaven's Gate*, where original estimates of cost and time go wildly out of control.

If the producer is often characterised as the cigar-smoking wheeler-dealer, then the most popular image of the director is that of the rampant megalomaniac, immortalised by Peter O'Toole in *The Stunt Man*. The late Peter Collinson, whose films included *A Long Day's Dying* and *The Italian Job*, was once heard to say that he was "strictly an 'action' and 'cut' director. All that (and here he would indicate the process of actors spouting dialogue) doesn't interest me!" That is one extreme. There are also directors who are pre-occupied with actors and dialogue perhaps to the detriment of actual camera movement. There appear to be no real norms. What is clear is that, however talented the directional fountainhead, the film making process does remain essentially a collaborative one — a fact freely, and regularly,

acknowledged by the director, even one as tempestuous as Alan Parker.

Assembling a crew must be rather like hand-picking a small army for a specialised campaign. Making a movie, even in the wild open spaces, is a claustrophobic, even incestuous, business. The outsider coming in "cold" on a film crew *in situ* will find pretty much a closed shop. Choosing the elements to make up the various departments that comprise the average 80-person shooting unit is therefore often crucial.

The producer and director will often seek out past collaborators, particularly in the areas of cinematography and editing. This provides, of course, a useful shorthand in a time-pressured business. The departments themselves — camera, sound, design, make-up, hair and wardrobe — will regularly contain small teams of people who have, as often as not, worked together on previous assignments. While the day-to-day administration is usually handled by the producer or associate producer, he, in turn, will probably be aided by a *production manager* as well as a *location manager*, the latter dealing with the particular logistics of a locale that the unit is visiting.

Walking in on a film set, the outsider could be forgiven for mistaking the *first assistant director* for the top man himself. The *first* is generally the noisiest man on a film set. As the director's right-hand man, he has to exhort the troops to a state of immediate preparedness for a "take". Some directors are so reticent that they'll even leave the first to utter the immortal "action" and "cut".

There is also the scurrilous tale of a fairly recent

megadollar war epic where the director was so pre-occupied entertaining press and visiting celebrities, that the first, with the help of the *camera operator*, virtually directed all the key sequences on the picture. Curiously, very few firsts have graduated to director successfully whereas cinematographers and editors seem to have made the transition with ease.

The first is, himself, supported by a *second assistant* and *third assistant*, responsible, in varying degrees, for comings and goings of cast, organisation of extras and prevention of unwanted personnel and transport in the immediate vicinity of the set. Hovering as close to the director as the first is the *continuity*, or script, *girl* who, as the job suggests, is keeping details of the shoot from take to take in order to keep the director minutely briefed during a process that has the added complication of generally being assembled out of chronological order.

The art department is probably earliest in on a film. Its head, the *production designer* (sometimes known as the *art director*, sometimes aided by one), is the architect of the piece, designing paraphernalia and sets which are then realised by the *construction manager* and his team. On American productions, this often includes a *key grip*, who is employed partly as a construction worker, partly as a back-up to the camera crew.

The camera department is usually a four-man team, topped by the *director of photography*, or *lighting cameraman*, with an *operator*, who physically wields the camera, a *focus puller* and *clapper/loader*, who

manoeuvres the clapper-board at the beginning of each take as well as loading film into the camera itself.

They, in turn, are supported by the electrical department, supervised by the *chief electrician*, or *gaffer* with a second-in-command known as *chargehand electrician*, or *best boy* (not, as some might have thought, a reference to the director's friend). Integral to all this is the sound department, featuring most prominently the *sound mixer*, who actually records the live sound on the set, and his *boom operator*, the gentleman who hovers with a giant sausage-shaped appliance in the vicinity of the required action.

Once principal photography (that period of actual shooting of a picture) is completed, it's back to the studio and cutting rooms for the phase known as post-production when all the elements — which may further comprise special effects, re-recording of sound, music composition and recording, dubbing and editing — finally are blended together, via *rough cut* and *fine cut*, to the final *answer print* — the finished film.

A complicated period of post-production will generally result in the credits list being at least trebled. One, however, could not really leave the subject finally without remarking on the splendidly bizarre nature of some of the credits that have rolled before our eyes in this past year. They surely reached their apotheosis in that quaint epic *Quest For Fire* with a fine double, "Special languages created by Anthony Burgess" and "Body language and gestures created by Desmond Morris."

Where credits are concerned, it could be said that *The End* is just merely the beginning.

THE SHOW GOES ON FOREVER

A view of Hollywood's 54th annual big night out by *Al Clark*

It was a cheeky question but it got the right answer. I was going to be in Los Angeles anyway, watching a lot of splatter-matter horror movies at the American Film Market in the company of varying combinations of anxious-looking people with casual jackets and congested schedules. I had always wanted to go to the Academy Awards, the consequence of a childhood spent mostly in cinemas. So when I met someone who was attending because a film she had produced had been nominated, I asked if I could accompany her. It was one of those moments when rejection seems a perfectly tolerable prospect and acceptance is a pleasurable bonus. The reply was yes.

It is difficult to convey adequately, and without too much star-struck awe, the degree of interest which surrounds the Academy Awards in America, particularly in Los Angeles itself. One might have thought, with some justification, that after 53 years of Oscar presentations the temperature would have cooled. After all, Hollywood is not supposed to be what it once was. There are still celebrities to ogle, and certainly many of them are very rich, but somewhere along the way the place seems to have lost...well, its *graciousness*. It is difficult to specify when the rot set in,

but it was probably in the late Sixties when a common interest in drugs and excess — certainly no strangers to the film world in the days when the studio police had hush-deals with the city cops — united it with the rock music low-life which was living out its glamorous degeneracy much more seriously. Suddenly all the movie stars under 50, and a few over, began turning up at parties in Indian shirts, Nehru jackets and medallions, and adopting the genial, egalitarian forever-young attitudes that went with them. This acted as a combination of red rag and white flag to the Sunset Strip freeloaders: the light show had moved to Bel Air.

Charles Manson put an end to all that, but once everybody had retreated back into their houses, brought in the security patrols and started sleeping with guns by their bedside, it was too late. They had lost their class. Too many drug dealers and opportunists knew their telephone numbers, proffered eagerly after a few joints under the fairy lights. In the old days, they would have just said "Call my agent" and still managed to make it sound charming.

The Academy Awards are now presented in this atmosphere of bodyguards, bullet-proof vests and guard dogs, and it seems to have got worse in recent years (the murder of John Lennon; Jodie

Foster obsessively worshipped by the man who tried to kill Reagan; Theresa Saldana attacked outside her house by some zealot who had travelled from Scotland). There is a new apartment block in the *Alphaville*-style suburb Century City which advertises itself as the safest building in America. Armed guards patrol the 21 floors, supplemented by the most complex closed-circuit television monitoring system outside nuclear missile bases. Warren Beatty, whose film *Reds* has been nominated more times than memory can recall, doesn't live there yet, but his home in Beverly Hills has been described as "an electronic castle" which includes a kidnap-proof vault.

So, impressed by a tradition so unyielding that it eclipses anything so trivial as personal paranoia, I go to the hire shop and assemble the mandatory components: tuxedo jacket, trousers, shirt, bow tie, cummerbund, shoes. I am informed that I must be "standard Hollywood size" since everything fits me first time. I am unaware of any further implications and would anyway choose to disregard them. The next step is to change into these clothes in a hotel room. It takes so long you can almost hear your beard growing, but there are compensations. It is remarkable the extent to which formal wear on the afternoon of the Academy Awards can only mean one thing. There is nothing obsequious about the response it elicits; it is simply a case of *you must be going*, with the recognition that it implies. Where have they seen you before? In my case, of course, they haven't.

The limousine driver arrives shortly after four. He would have arrived shortly before four, but it's raining and Los Angeles, not being a city equipped to deal with rain, has come to a relative standstill. This does not bode well for arriving at the ceremony on time, since we are in Hollywood and the event is taking place at the Dorothy Chandler Pavilion downtown.

Downtown is the centre of a city that is supposed to have no centre, and it is agreeable to observe that the organisers wear their city-pride sufficiently on their sleeve to make the participants travel outside their rarefied pedestrian-free suburbs to a location where they will be cheered by general humans who have little to do with the film industry. (It must be said, however, that it is difficult to find anyone in Los Angeles who has *nothing* to do with the film industry. On my first visit there, a taxi driver bringing

The big line-up. "The thing to remember about Hollywood is that it knows how to put on a show"

me in from the airport informed me that he had been served his breakfast that morning by a waitress who claimed to have given James Mason a blow-job at the Beverly Wilshire Hotel in 1953.)

Our driver is called John and he is the best driver you can imagine. Good humoured, engaging, obliging, years of experience have taught him everything about the people he points in the right direction: how much privacy they want, how much conversation. You can imagine him being a

friend forever, provided that somebody is paying the bill. If you wanted to elope, he would take you to Reno or Las Vegas in the middle of the night and still find time for a shave before his next assignment in the morning. Instinctively you know that he is on first-name terms with all the hotel receptionists in Southern California.

There are two carpeted approaches to the Dorothy Chandler Pavilion. If the television crew does not recognise you, you walk straight ahead. If they do, you

are escorted to a gazebo out of the rain near the crowd, which gathers outside making enough uncontrolled noise to suggest some grisly action replay of Nathanael West's *The Day of the Locust*. There the chosen are interviewed briefly. They are not expected to emit anything more than the customary platitudes. If they did, it would be considered a lapse of etiquette.

This is the first taste of the television cameras and it will not be the last. One of the details which becomes apparent about the Academy

Awards show is that it is a *show*: not so much an event which is covered by television as a television programme with very expensive live extras. In many respects, it belongs to ABC television and tonight's sponsors — Buick, Coca-Cola, General Electric, Polaroid, Revlon and some benefactor-come-lately called L'Eggs Products Inc.

On each side of the stage are screens which reveal to the audience what the television viewers are seeing, and every ten minutes or so, when the performance is punctuated by

— 153 —

Warren Beatty ... "applauds Paramount in particular and capitalism in general"

advertising, the whole thing literally stops. A giant corpulent longhair — with a brightly-coloured headband incongruously complementing his tuxed-up correctness, making him resemble some forgotten Quicksilver Messenger Service roadie who has strayed into the costume department — wanders across the stage with a broom. He can't be sweeping it, unless the presenters and prize-winners are surreptitiously eating peanuts and throwing away the shells, so one assumes that he is polishing it for the cameras in case it loses its lustre over the marathon running time. The idiot boards, positioned at the centre of the auditorium and employed by everyone who can legitimately prepare a speech (everyone, that is, apart from those winners who are supposed to convey some element of surprise and spontaneity), are hastily re-arranged by an energetic three-man team:one to hold the stand in place, another to change the cards, a third to pick them up from the floor.

The audience, far from being distracted by all these lapses of continuity, have been on enough film sets to relish the familiarity of the short takes and long breaks. They can talk to the person in the next seat,

look around them for people who are more famous than they are, or wander out and check their appearance in the lobby mirrors. They can even have a drink at the micro-bar (micro as in very small *and* poorly stocked) where they will be served by a harassed woman who does not care whether you are Charlton Heston or the air conditioning engineer's nephew. Or they can watch the consummate master of ceremonies Johnny Carson lining up his next cue.

Carson has been compering these shows for several years now and you can tell. He treads the tightrope perfectly: sufficiently showbiz for the audience to feel that he's a pal, and just acerbic enough for them to realise that if there's a good crack to be made nobody gets off the hook. In effect, he is a less ingratiating but equally accomplished successor to Bob Hope, whom he sportingly acknowledges from the stage. In addition to the four old lags (Hal Kanter, Melville Shavelson, Jack Rose and Melvin Frank) who script the show — although what scripting there may be in the weary banality of the introductions and prepared speeches is a tribute to the powers of job creation — Carson has six "special material" writers including,

rather coyly, himself. The jokes, it has to be said, aren't bad: industry jokes about third world countries adopting United Artists executives, Pia Zadora jokes ("Welcome to the Dorothy Chandler Pavilion. Next year it may be called the Pia Zadora Pavilion. We're waiting for the cheque to come through"), running jokes about the length of the ceremony ("In keeping with the trend towards nostalgia, try to cast your minds back to the beginning of the show"). His material, special and otherwise, varies but his timing is impeccable and he has the great asset of making all his stories sound like the kind he'd tell a few other people across a table.

The show begins. Maureen Stapleton, who has given many distinguished but unrewarded performances over the years, receives the Best Supporting Actress award. "I'm thrilled, happy — and sober," she observes before going on to thank everyone she has ever met in her entire life. Particular among these for some reason is Joel McCrea.

One advantage of being able to watch television monitors at a live event is that it provides an opportunity to observe the behaviour of people sitting in other parts of the auditorium. When Miss Stapleton mentions Joel McCrea, Jack Nicholson, who is in what appears to be a threesome with Diane Keaton and Warren Beatty, can be lip-read repeating increduously "*Joel McCrea?*"

Nicholson, one notices, is looking pretty rakish. As a nominee he does not have to accord with the etiquette incumbent on the numerous celebrity presenters (although Howard Rollins Jr. is a nominee and he *does* present an award, possibly to make up the racial balance figures). So, although superficially he appears as dandied-up as anybody else, he looks *different*. For a start he is wearing shades — not those tastefully tinted, beige, aviator-style, coked-up-executive shades; just shades, small dark ones which allow no access to the eyes they conceal. Also his suit doesn't fit properly — the trousers are too baggy, the jacket too tight. He looks like someone who has been involved in some other activity — gardening perhaps, or gambling, or presiding over a cockfight in Tijuana — when the call came through telling him to get into a tuxedo, *any* tuxedo and make his way

quickly to the Dorothy Chandler Pavilion. Accordingly, he looks as if he is enjoying the surrealism of it all, smiling that great smile that manages to be open and shifty at the same time, that both participates in an event and observes its absurdities.

For a while though, even a bedazzled outsider will find some difficulty in getting excited. The minor awards are handed out, punctuated by all the customary waffle about creativity and collaboration. Nobody wishes to appear self-glorifying, so they all recite these endless lists, apparently memorised, of people whose help made it all possible. Everybody applauds dutifully. Then there are the special awards. Cubby Broccoli, winner of the Irving Thalberg Award, has it presented to him by Roger Moore, with whom he spends months haggling over money before the announcement of each new James Bond film. Barbara Stanwyck, receiving an Honorary Award from John Travolta, is brief and touching. Danny Kaye, winner of the Jean Hersholt Humanitarian Award, is long-winded and mawkish. The nominated songs, which are staged throughout the show at points where it might be in danger of lapsing into torpor, are staged with varying degrees of ostentation, most notably by Sheena Easton who performs 'For Your Eyes Only' with enough dancers and outer-space hardware to suggest a takeover of Cape Canaveral by the cast of *Fame*. The budget for this three-minute interlude of risible excess would comfortably finance a week's shooting on a modest feature film, but nobody blinks an eyelid.

The thing to remember about Hollywood is that it knows how to put on a show. Even a dance tribute to some forgotten golden age, which takes a golden age to finish, makes up in flair for what it lacks in dignity. Bugger dignity! Istvan Szabo the director of *Mephisto*, voted Best Foreign Film, understands this. When he receives the award he is just beside himself and needs reinforcements. So he calls up a crony. The crony, who may well have been called Klaus — in which case he is none other than the leading actor in the film — leaps through the audience and the two of them bearhug each other to a standstill before getting down to some serious celebrating. It is a marvellous moment. During it, an Oscar winner has disregarded protocol and just gone apeshit.

Nobody else does. Warren Beatty, looking agreeably at ease considering the disappointments he will have to endure, does not resemble a man with a kidnap-proof vault at home. Accepting his director's award for *Reds*, he acknowledges his co-workers — some of them, like Robert Towne and Elaine May, unacknowledged on the film's credits — and applauds Paramount in particular and capitalism in general for allowing such a film to exist. Colin Welland, who wins the Best Original Screenplay award for *Chariots of Fire*, *tries* to be all overcome by emotion but conveys little more than empty jingoism. Only weeks after rising expectantly when the same award was announced at the Academy Awards' British counterpart BAFTA, only to fall back despondently into his chair when the name in the envelope turned out to be Bill Forsyth, he goes into overtime to rub in his accomplishment. "The British are coming!" he concludes triumphantly, bringing new dimensions to bad manners. One can only speculate about what the numerous unemployed Hollywood scriptwriters thought about it all.

When *Chariots of Fire* also receives the Best Film Award, it does not just mean the sound of cash registers, although it means that as well. It means a boost for the reputation of the British film industry, and for films which do not cost a mortgage on Universal Studios to produce. It also means an orgy of self-congratulation for those who backed it or voted for it. One of Ronald Reagan's favourite films of the past year, *Chariots of Fire* is the perfect Oscar winner for 1982: traditional, decent, professional and, above all, correct in the qualities it champions. The people who bet money on these things should have seen it coming. *Reds* is too inappropriate (even warm-hearted liberalism has its limits), *Raiders of the Lost Ark* too frivolous, *Atlantic City* too enigmatic, *On Golden Pond* — well, that has won enough.

Not only has its writer Ernest Thompson delivered a real raspberry of a speech to anyone who has failed to recognise his genius in the past, but neither Katharine Hepburn (on stage in New York) nor Henry Fonda (ill in Bel Air) are present to collect their acting awards. The latter's daughter Jane accepts for him, and she simply radiates caring awareness. He's watching the show at home on television, she announces; she and the grandchildren will be over with the award right away. And so on. Jane Fonda is a talented actress, and probably a very nice person, but she has no idea where the dividing line

Jane Fonda ... "flies the Fonda flag and doesn't care who knows it"

lies between sincerity and unctuousness. Of course, this is a sentimental occasion and Hollywood has always had a soft spot for its old, even if as in Fonda's case it never acknowledged them when they were young. Jane Fonda flies the Fonda flag and doesn't care who knows it. She talks to the audience as family. If there were time she would no doubt give us a progress report on her father's condition. As it is, she leaves the stage and, presumably, goes to visit him. The following morning a photograph in the paper shows Fonda, flanked by a smiling wife and daughter, looking sick and haunted.

Later, however, the talk is all about Bette Midler's racy presentation speech for Best Song and, inevitably, about *Chariots of Fire*, whose posters are no doubt being altered overnight to include the all-important new detail — "Best Picture". There is no talk in the car park opposite the Dorothy Chandler Pavilion where the astonishing spectacle of MacDonald Carey being mobbed by a group of autograph-hunting Chicano children is on view. Nor at the Formosa Café next to Goldwyn Studios on Santa Monica Boulevard where the barman, surrounded by autographed pictures of yesterday's hard-drinking heroes, is talking Academy Awards. "Hey, you're all prettied up!" he remarks winningly to us. But there is plenty of talk about *Chariots of Fire* at the Governors' Ball, held after the awards at the Beverly Hilton. On the way in, I cross eyes with Gregory Peck, on his way out. The crowd begins to shout his name. Looking around for somebody in a tuxedo with whom he might empathise, he gives the great Gregory Peck rueful look, the one that says "you and I, we understand the pressures of fame".

Inside, I try to understand them by spending a few minutes holding the Oscar awarded to Michael Kahn, the editor of *Raiders of the Lost Ark*, with whom we share a table. I am no wiser. A lot of famous people are dancing to a ballroom orchestra. Some go on to other parties. Things begin to fade around two. Half an hour later the place is deserted. There's obviously a lot of jogging to be done in the morning.

As we leave, I notice how quiet it all seems without the usual squadron of cars purring outside. I remember Carson's tart, if obvious, parting joke after the awards, when people were already filing out to their cars. "There's a car blocking the entrance," he announced solemnly. "Does anybody here have a Mercedes?"

David Puttnam and Hugh Hudson accept the 'Chariots of Fire' Best Picture award — "the British are coming!"

THE AWARDS

THE ACADEMY OF MOTION PICTURE ARTS AND SCIENCES 'OSCARS'

BEST PICTURE

Chariots of Fire

BEST DIRECTOR

Warren Beatty
Reds (US)

BEST ACTOR

Henry Fonda
On Golden Pond

BEST ACTRESS

Katharine Hepburn
On Golden Pond

BEST SUPPORTING ACTOR

John Gielgud
Arthur

BEST SUPPORTING ACTRESS

Maureen Stapleton
Reds

BEST ORIGINAL SCREENPLAY

Colin Welland
Chariots of Fire

BEST SCREENPLAY ADAPTATION

Ernest Thompson
On Golden Pond

BEST CINEMATOGRAPHY

Vittorio Storaro
Reds

BEST FOREIGN LANGUAGE FILM

Mephisto (Istvan Szabo, Hungary)

BEST ORIGINAL SCORE

Vangelis
Chariots of Fire

BEST ORIGINAL SONG

'Arthur's Theme (Best That You Can Do)'
Arthur

BEST COSTUME DESIGN

Milena Canonero
Chariots of Fire

BEST EDITING

Michael Kahn
Raiders of the Lost Ark

BEST MAKE-UP

Rick Baker
An American Werewolf in London

BEST ART DIRECTION

Norman Reynolds,
Leslie Dilley
Raiders of the Lost Ark

BEST SOUND

Bill Varney, Steve Maslow,
Gregg Landaker,
Roy Charman
Raiders of the Lost Ark

BEST VISUAL EFFECTS

Richard Edlund, Kit West,
Bruce Nicholson,
Joe Johnston
Raiders of the Lost Ark

THE BRITISH ACADEMY OF FILM AND TELEVISION ARTS FILM AWARDS

BEST FILM

Chariots of Fire

BEST DIRECTOR

Louis Malle
Atlantic City

BEST ACTOR

Burt Lancaster
Atlantic City

BEST ACTRESS

Meryl Streep
The French Lieutenant's Woman

BEST SUPPORTING ARTIST

Ian Holm
Chariots of Fire

BEST SCREENPLAY

Bill Forsyth
Gregory's Girl

'The French Lieutenant's Woman'

BEST ORIGINAL FILM MUSIC

Carl Davis
The French Lieutenant's Woman

THE MICHAEL BALCON AWARD

David Puttnam

THE FELLOWSHIP OF THE ACADEMY

Andrzej Wajda

BEST CINEMATOGRAPHY

Geoffrey Unsworth/
Ghislain Cloquet
Tess

BEST PRODUCTION DESIGN/ART DIRECTION

Norman Reynolds,
Leslie Dilley
Raiders of the Lost Ark

BEST EDITING

Thelma Schoonmaker
Raging Bull

BEST SOUND

The French Lieutenant's Woman

VARIETY CLUB OF GT. BRITAIN AWARDS

BEST ACTOR

Jeremy Irons
The French Lieutenant's Woman

BEST ACTRESS

Dee Hepburn
Gregory's Girl

MOST PROMISING ARTISTES

Ian Charleson and Ben Cross
Chariots of Fire

'Raiders of the Lost Ark'

'Ticket to Heaven'

'Moonlighting'

'Mad Max II'

'Possession'

'Arthur'

'Pennies from Heaven'

'Winter of our Dreams'

'Quest for Fire'

'An American Werewolf in London'

'Passione D'Amore'

'Gallipoli'

'Man of Iron'

'The German Sisters'

'Raiders of the Lost Ark'

'Ticket to Heaven'

'Moonlighting'

'Mad Max II'

'Possession'

'Arthur'

'Pennies from Heaven'

'Winter of our Dreams'

'Passione D'Amore'

'Gallipoli'

'Quest for Fire'

'Man of Iron'

'An American Werewolf in London'

'The German Sisters'

GOLDEN GLOBE AWARDS

BEST MOTION PICTURE DRAMA

On Golden Pond

BEST MOTION PICTURE COMEDY OR MUSICAL

Arthur

BEST FOREIGN FILM

Chariots of Fire

BEST MOTION PICTURE ACTRESS, DRAMA

Meryl Streep
The French Lieutenant's Woman

BEST MOTION PICTURE ACTOR, DRAMA

Henry Fonda
On Golden Pond

BEST MOTION PICTURE ACTRESS, COMEDY OR MUSICAL

Bernadette Peters
Pennies from Heaven

BEST MOTION PICTURE ACTOR, COMEDY OR MUSICAL

Dudley Moore
Arthur

BEST MOTION PICTURE ACTRESS, IN A SUPPORTING ROLE

Joan Hackett
Only When I Laugh

BEST MOTION PICTURE ACTOR, IN A SUPPORTING ROLE

John Gielgud
Arthur

NEW STAR OF THE YEAR IN A MOTION PICTURE

Pia Zadora
Butterfly

BEST DIRECTOR MOTION PICTURE

Warren Beatty
Reds

BEST SCREENPLAY MOTION PICTURE

Ernest Thompson
On Golden Pond

DAVID DI DONATELLO AWARDS

BEST FILM

Ricomincio Da Tre
(Massimo Troisi)

BEST DIRECTOR

Francesco Rosi
Tre Fratelli

BEST ACTOR

Massimo Troisi
Ricomincio Da Tre

BEST ACTRESS

Mariangela Melato
Aiutami A Sognare,
Valeria D'Obici
Passione D'Amore

BEST SCREENPLAY

Tonino Guerra and
Francesco Rosi
Tre Fratelli

BEST CINEMATOGRAPHY

Pasqualino De Santis
Tre Fratelli

BEST SUPPORTING ACTOR

Charles Vanel
Tre Fratelli

BEST SUPPORTING ACTRESS

Laura Antonelli
Passione D'Amore

BEST FOREIGN FILM

Kagemusha
(Akira Kurosawa, Japan)

BEST PRODUCERS (FOREIGN)

Francis Coppola
and George Lucas
Kagemusha
Studio Obiektiv Budapest
Angi Vera

BEST SCREENPLAY (FOREIGN)

Jean Grualt
Mon Oncle D'Amerique
(France)

BEST ACTRESS (FOREIGN)

Catherine Deneuve
The Last Metro (France)

BEST ACTOR (FOREIGN)

Burt Lancaster
Atlantic City (US)

FRENCH CESAR AWARDS

BEST FILM

Quest for Fire

BEST DIRECTOR

Jean-Jacques Annaud
Quest for Fire

BEST ACTOR

Michel Serrault
Garde A Vue

BEST ACTRESS

Isabelle Adjani
Possession

BEST FOREIGN FILM

The Elephant Man

BEST FIRST FILM

Diva

BEST SCREENPLAY

Garde A Vue

BEST EDITING

Garde A Vue

BEST SUPPORTING ACTOR

Guy Marchand
Garde A Vue

BEST SOUND

Diva

BEST MUSIC

Diva

BEST PHOTOGRAPHY

Diva

SPECIAL CESAR

Andrzej Wajda

STANDARD BRITISH FILM AWARDS

BEST FILM

The French Lieutenant's Woman (Karel Reisz)

BEST ACTOR

Bob Hoskins
The Long Good Friday

BEST ACTRESS

Maggie Smith
Quartet

BEST SCREENPLAY

Colin Welland
Chariots of Fire

PETER SELLERS AWARD FOR COMEDY

Bill Forsyth
Gregory's Girl

BEST PHOTOGRAPHY

John Alcott
The Shining

BEST ART DIRECTION

Roy Walker
The Shining

CRITIC'S CIRCLE AWARD

BEST ENGLISH LANGUAGE FILM

Chariots of Fire
(Hugh Hudson, UK)

BEST FOREIGN LANGUAGE FILM

Man of Iron
(Andrzej Wajda, Poland)

BEST DIRECTOR

Andrzej Wajda
Man of Iron

BEST SCREENPLAY

Colin Welland
Chariots of Fire

BEST PHOTOGRAPHY

Freddie Francis
The Elephant Man

MOST PROMISING DIRECTOR

Bill Forsyth

AUSTRALIAN FILM INSTITUTE AWARDS

BEST FILM

Gallipoli
(Peter Weir)

BEST DIRECTOR

Peter Weir
Gallipoli

BEST ACTOR

Mel Gibson
Gallipoli

BEST ACTRESS

Judy Davis
Winter of Our Dreams

BEST SUPPORTING ACTOR

Bill Hunter
Gallipoli

BEST SUPPORTING ACTRESS

Judy Davis
Hoodwink

BEST CINEMATOGRAPHY

Russell Boyd
Gallipoli

BEST SCREENPLAY

David Williamson
Gallipoli

BEST EDITING

William Anderson
Gallipoli

BEST ART DIRECTION

Gallipoli

BEST SOUND

Gallipoli

BEST ORIGINAL SCORE

Rory O'Donoghue and
Grahame Bond
Fatty Finn

BEST COSTUME DESIGN

Norma Morceau
Fatty Finn

CANNES FILM FESTIVAL

PALME D'OR

Missing (Costa Gavras, US)
Yol (Yilmaz Guney and
Serif Goren, Turkey)

JURY PRIZE

La Notte di San Lorenzo
(Paolo and Vittorio Taviani,
Italy)

BEST ACTOR

Jack Lemmon
Missing (US)

BEST ACTRESS

Jadwiga Jankowska Ciesla
Another Kind of Look
(Hungary)

CORK FILM FESTIVAL

BEST DOCUMENTARY

Tough, Pretty, and Smart (US)

BEST ANIMATED FILM

The Sweater (Canada)

BEST FILM ON ART

Eisenstaedt: Germany (US)

BEST FICTION FILM

All Brings Night (UK)

BEST STUDENT FILM

Madonna and Child (UK)

EUROPEAN COMMUNITY AWARD

To the Western World (UK)

FESTIVAL OF NATIONS TAORMINA

GOLD CHARYBDIS

Ticket to Heaven
(Ralph L. Thomas, Canada)

SILVER CHARYBDIS

Land and Sons
(August Gudmundsson,
Iceland)

BRONZE CHARYBDIS

Index (Janusz Kijowski,
Poland)

GOLD MASK (BEST PERFORMANCE)

Lila Kedrova
Tell Me a Riddle (US)

BEST DIRECTOR

Werner Herzog
Fitzcarraldo (W. Germany)

BEST SCREENPLAY

Jerzy Skolimowski
Moonlighting (UK)

BEST PHOTOGRAPHY

Bruno Nuytten
L'Invitation Au Voyage
(France)

SPECIAL 35TH CANNES ANNIVERSARY PRIZE

Identification of a Woman
(Michaelangelo Antonioni,
Italy)

VENICE FILM FESTIVAL

GOLDEN LION BEST FILM

The German Sisters
(Marguerite Von Trotta,
W. Germany)

GOLDEN LION BEST ARTISTIC/ PROFESSIONAL COLLABORATION

Sogni D'Ore
(Nanni Moretti, Italy)
They Don't Wear Black Ties
(Brazil)

BEST ACTORS

Robert De Niro,
Robert Duvall
True Confessions (US)

SILVER MASK

Nick Mancuso
Ticket To Heaven (Canada)

BRONZE MASK

Dennis Christopher
Fade To Black (US)
Mercedes Sampietro
Gary Cooper Who Art
In Heaven (Spain)

SAN SEBASTIAN FILM FESTIVAL

INTERNATIONAL CRITICS' PRIZE

Tales of Ordinary Madness
(Marco Ferreri, Italy)

AVORIAZ FESTIVAL OF FANTASTIC FILMS

GRAND PRIX

Mad Max II
(George Miller, Australia)

SPECIAL JURY AWARD

Wolfen
(Michael Wadleigh, US)

SPECIAL MENTION

Memiors of a Survivor
(David Gladwell, UK)

BERLIN FILM FESTIVAL

GOLDEN BEAR

Veronika Voss
(Rainer Werner Fassbinder,
W. Germany)

SILVER BEAR

Creeps (Wojciech
Marczewski, Poland)

BEST DIRECTOR

Mario Monicelli
The Marquess of Grillo
(Italy)

BEST ACTOR

Michel Piccoli
A Strange Affair (France)
Stellen Skargaard
The Simple-Minded Murderer
(Sweden)

BEST ACTRESS

Katrin Sass
On Probation (E. Germany)

SILVER BEAR FOR SINGLE OUTSTANDING ACHIEVEMENT

Zoltan Fabri for the script
of Requiem (Hungary)

CHICAGO FILM FESTIVAL

GOLDEN HUGO

The German Sisters
(Marguerite Von Trotta,
W. Germany)

SILVER HUGO

Passion D'Amore
(Ettore Scola, Italy)

BOOKS

ANATOMY OF THE MOVIES
ed. David Pirie
(Windward, £7.95)
Most people who are interested in films, I'd say, have little knowledge of the workings of the industry which produces them. Unless of course they happen to work in it or report on it, in which case they probably know too much for their own good. This book is the perfect primer: individuals contribute articles on the aspects of the business they know best, resulting in informed accounts of everything that happens before, during and after the making of a movie. As enjoyable and illuminating as the text are the statistical tables and explanatory illustrations, which attractively reinforce the general de-mystification of a business all too keen to obfuscate.

BARBRA
Donald Zec and Anthony Fowles
(New English Library, £7.95)
Pithily written (as one would expect from Zec, solo or in collaboration) and nicely presented, this is a cool appraisal rather than a hysterical demolition of the Streisand myth. Treading the tightrope between acknowledging her considerable assets and

confirming her to be the tiresome egotist most of her co-stars apparently think she is, it is more than merely readable, but less than completely engrossing.

BEFORE I FORGET
James Mason
(Hamish Hamilton, £9.95)
Light, enjoyable, anecdotal autobiography, with Mason's own drawings supplementing a text which is rarely exciting or revealing but at least conveys the impression of being all his own work. Apart from a brief epilogue, it finishes with his work on *Lolita* 20 years ago, so one assumes there is more to come.

BETTE
Charles Higham
(New English Library, £7.95)
Higham is not known for his kindness towards the subjects of his biographies, but with Davis his admiration clearly eclipses his inclination. The result is an enormously entertaining account of a successful career and a courageous life, in which determination challenges fragile health, bad luck and a succession of broken reed husbands — and wins.

BETTE DAVIS — MOTHER GODDAM
Whitney Stine
(Star, £1.95)
The sub-title doesn't really help distract one from making comparisons with the

similarly-named book about Davis's old sparring partner Joan Crawford. Davis wasn't such a nutter, so her story doesn't have the grisly compulsiveness of Crawford's. But Mr Stine has produced a thorough and readable biography, while Davis herself adds some of her own unique spice in the form of sporadic asides and interjections that make one wish she'd written the whole thing herself. Maybe she will; she's still very much alive and kicking.

BETTY GRABLE — THE RELUCTANT MOVIE QUEEN
Doug Warren
(Robson Books, £7.50)
The Forties' forces pin-up who specialised in musical comedy and, for a time, owned Hollywood's best insured — and most palpitated over — legs went down to the big C in July 1973; Mr Warren's ordinary biography of his rather ordinary star (multiple marriages, feuds with the studio, a fortune blown on nags) fails to bring her back to life. But then I never was a fan.

THE BIG BOOK OF B MOVIES
Robin Cross
(Muller, £4.95)
Affectionate, erudite (but not *too* erudite) survey of low-budget second features,

THE BIG BOOK OF B MOVIES *or* **HOW LOW WAS MY BUDGET**

ROBIN CROSS

over 350 stills

acknowledging their expertise under pressure, their pace and vulgarity, their occasional ineptitude. Following an introductory chapter dealing with what the B-movie units of each major studio produced, it is subdivided by genre and supplemented by wittily captioned stills. A pity, then, that the general air of thoroughness should be deflated by pointless errors like attributing *Touch of Evil* to MGM, when elementary research would have revealed the company to be Universal, and giving two different years of release to *The Locket* four pages apart.

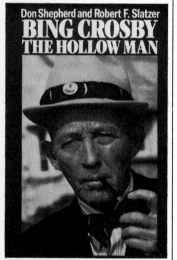

Don Shepherd and Robert F. Slatzer
BING CROSBY THE HOLLOW MAN

BING CROSBY: THE HOLLOW MAN
Don Shepherd and Robert F. Slatzer
(W.H. Allen, £7.95)
Much in the style of José Ferrer in *The Great Man*, the authors set out to chronicle the life of one of America's best loved entertainers and found themselves portraying a cruel, selfish boozer and philanderer who neglected his family. An

intriguing read which thankfully lacks the gloating quality of most hatchet jobs, it makes up for in efficiency what it lacks in style.

BOGART
Terence Pettigrew
(Proteus, £4.95)
Subtitled "a definitive study of his film career", this is little more than a weary succession of synopses and newspaper cuttings, linked by a few dutiful opinions. Some good stills though, which Bogart zealots might consider worth the purchase price.

CLUCK!

The
True Story of Chickens
in
The Cinema
Jon-Stephen Fink
with additional material by
Mieke van der Linden.

CLUCK!
Jon Stephen Fink
(Virgin, £3.95)
Drolly solemn amalgam of anthropological thesis and oblique conspiracy theory about chickens — their history, their relation to humans, their place in the cinema — supplemented by an exhaustive chronicle of chicken scenes in films, chicken-starred according to significance (four for "awesome consequence", one for "elementary incident"). Very funny once you accept the highly suspect basic premise, utterly debilitating in its erudition, full of trivial data for people, like this reader, who are interested.

COMBAT FILMS 1945-1970
Steven Jay Rubin
(McFarland/Bailey Bros. & Swinfen, £8.35)
With a cover resembling a do-it-yourself schoolbook doing its best to camouflage a well illustrated interior, Rubin's survey of war films (American, unless *The Longest Day* and *The Bridge on the River Kwai* count as British) is fine as far as it goes. Indeed, it's very good as far as it goes, concentrating on the eight

Combat Films 1945-1970

STEVEN JAY RUBIN

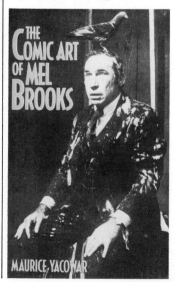

BOGART
A definitive study of his film career.
TERENCE PETTIGREW
Illustrated.

movies about World War Two he has selected as examples worthy of examination. It just doesn't go far enough, the numerous absences giving a rather pretentious air to the book's overly emphatic title.

THE COMIC ART OF MEL BROOKS
Maurice Yacowar
(W.H. Allen, £7.95)
Sound, sober appraisal of Brooks' career, which gets the biographical stuff out of the way briskly and concentrates on what he produced: the material for television, the records and the seven films. Extremely thorough if not especially revealing.

THE COMIC ART OF MEL BROOKS
MAURICE YACOWAR

COSTUME DESIGN IN THE MOVIES
Elizabeth Leese
(Ungar, £6.95)
If you're suddenly curious as to who dressed Elsa Lanchester for *The Bride of Frankenstein*, you won't, unfortunately, find the answer here. Rather this ambitious, sadly cramped book is a comprehensive encyclopaedia of fashion designers who were recruited to the cinema. Designers are listed alphabetically and there is an

index of film titles at the back. Several glorious pictures — sadly all in monochrome — catch the eye, but an overloaded lay-out will tax even 20/20 vision. Still a must, even if it's just a start at tackling a subject that could, doubtless eventually will, fill a score of volumes.

ELIZABETH TAYLOR — THE LAST STAR
Kitty Kelley
(Michael Joseph, £8.95)
Richard Burton, her fifth and sixth husband — for whom she had, and probably still has, an all-eclipsing passion — called her "Tubby". His successor John Warner referred to her as "my little heifer". Self-absorbed to the point of obsession, coarse, generous, highly-sexed, illness-prone, predatory, hilariously undiplomatic and behaving increasingly like the character she played in *Who's Afraid of Virginia Woolf?*, Taylor is the perfect subject for this kind of anecdotal biography as she sweeps through hotels with her monarchical entourage, her ostentation matched only by her disregard for house-training her beloved dogs, whose traces remain to this day on hotel carpets all over the world. The biography of the year, no question about it.

FILM REVIEW 1981-82
F. Maurice Speed
(W.H. Allen, £9.95)
The time-honoured movie annual covering the British releases of the year separately in words and pictures, and repeating much of the information in the process. Impeccably researched as ever, it is notable that this zeal for detail is not extended to the remainder of its contents: a nostalgic, repetitive history of Rank (desperately in need of cutting), a mysteriously dated 'Letter from Hollywood' (left over from the year before, surely) and an introduction which applauds the Rank circuit for not showing a film as brilliant as *Raging Bull*, which I saw in a Rank cinema, on the grounds of violence and bad language.

THE FILMS IN MY LIFE
Francois Truffaut
(Penguin, £3.50)
While acknowledging the great PR job they did for American cinema in elitist circles, I'm inclined to be suspicious of *Cahiers* critics, even if they subsequently became famous French film directors, because they tended to attribute all kinds of spurious (and invariably unintended) qualities to any old crap that smelt right. Truffaut does too occasionally (*Land of the Pharaohs, Destination Gobi*), but he has taste and knows how to justify it better than most. An entertaining and well translated series of articles.

FILM TRICKS: SPECIAL EFFECTS IN THE MOVIES
Harold Schechter and David Everitt
(Columbus, £7.95)
More lavishly illustrated and historically based than its rival publications, this study of special effects in the cinema covers everything from schlock to horror, disaster to big-screen spectacle. Particularly impressive are the uses made of film frames to illustrate certain subtle techniques from the gore of *Maniac* to Christopher Lee's icy death plunge as Count D.

THE FILMS OF BURT REYNOLDS
Nancy Streebeck
(Citadel/LSP, £12.50)
Standard film book format (biogs, credits and reviews of movies) lifted out of the doldrums by the eminently amiable Mr Reynolds' annotations to his own films: "I asked other directors for advice: Bob Aldrich told me

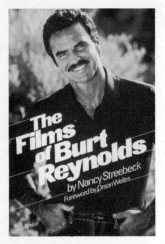

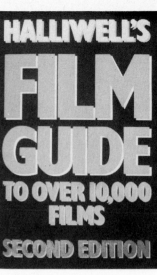

GREAT FILM EPICS
Mike Munn
(Illustrated Publications, £6.95)
Soundly researched and full of intriguing detail and great pictures, this still fails to satisfy, largely because of the writing, which is film-fan-cosy — chatty and lifeless, like a cross between a school essay and a press office puff. An appreciation of the epic requires, above all, a sense of ridicule (most epics are fun and nonsense in about equal measures) and a fondness for *The Egyptian*, in which Victor Mature utters the immortal line "More wine, you waddling toad!" Both are absent here.

always to listen to everybody and Mel Brooks told me to remember to fire someone the first day." The foreword is written by Orson Welles who must have been out at the time.

FOREVER EALING
George Perry
(Pavilion, £8.95)
An exemplary history of the film studio most closely associated with British cinema, and of Michael Balcon who steered it throughout the era by which it is identified. Affectionate, great looking, easy to read, one can work overtime to fault it and still find difficulty.

FROM SCARFACE TO SCARLETT
Roger Dooley
(Harcourt Brace Jovanovich/LSP, £11.95)
Very long (over 600 pages), exhaustively researched history of American cinema in the Thirties, subdivided by genre and examining the five thousand or so films released during the decade. Nicely written, persuasively erudite, it is probably the most thorough account of a single period of film-making to be found between two covers.

GOLDEN HILL TO GOLDEN SQUARE
W. 'Bill' Cartlidge
(New Horizon, £5.75)
Direly uncontroversial autobiography of and by the man who rose between 1920 and 1979 to be an executive director of the ABC leisure group (now EMI Film and Theatre Corporation). One for the Cartlidge family and hyper-British-film addicts only.

HALLIWELL'S FILM GUIDE
Leslie Halliwell
(Granada, £4.95)
The paperback version of the second edition, minus illustrations, covering films up to the autumn of 1978. Functional and apparently thorough, although the absence of the first film I looked up to check (Sidney Lumet's *Blood Kin* made in 1969) makes one wonder what other omissions there might be.

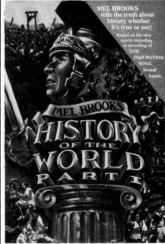

HISTORY OF THE WORLD — PART 1
Mel Brooks
(Virgin, £1.95)
What good jokes there are in Brooks's inflated *Carry On* of a film do not transfer well to what is — with its sequence of stills following the narrative line — little more than a very expensive cinema programme. The inserted flexi-disc of 'The Inquisition Song' provides further proof that if there's anything less funny than a comic sequence that fails to hit the mark, it's a record of it.

1,344 FILMS DESCRIBED AND ILLUSTRATED
THE HOLLYWOOD MUSICAL

EVERY HOLLYWOOD MUSICAL FROM 1927 TO THE PRESENT DAY

FOREWORD BY GENE KELLY

CLIVE HIRSCHHORN

THE HOLLYWOOD MUSICAL
Clive Hirschhorn
(Octopus, £10.95)
In the style of previous Octopus epics like the MGM and Warner Brothers histories (the latter authored by Hirschhorn), a splendidly documented, illustrated and indexed chronological account of 1,344 American song-and-dance movies, starting with the original version of *The Jazz Singer* in 1927 and — the pickings decreasing gradually along the way — finishing with the lamentable remake in 1980. Quite simply the last word on the subject.

THE HOLLYWOOD RELIABLES
James Robert Parish with Gregory W. Mank
(Arlington House/LSP, £14.95)
Six brief biographical studies — Dana Andrews, Wallace Beery, Pat O'Brien, Walter Pidgeon, Spencer Tracy and Robert Young — supplemented by detailed filmographies and well-chosen stills. What these actors have in common, it seems, is that they were solid, flexible, unflamboyant. "They could be counted on not to outshine the stars," say the authors, although what Tracy, a leading man who outshone everybody, is doing among that lot remains a mystery. In fact, the book itself is a bit of a mystery: efficiently assembled, soundly researched but lacking in liveliness and, ultimately, a bit pointless.

HOLLYWOOD'S VIETNAM
Gilbert Adair
(Proteus, £7.95)
Subtitled 'From *The Green Berets* to *Apocalypse Now*', this is an enjoyable and informative account of the film world's treatment of the Vietnam war. Well researched,

attractively presented, its only real liability is a scrappy chronological filmography which includes films not mentioned in the text for reasons the author should, but doesn't, explain.

THE HORROR FILM HANDBOOK
Alan Frank
(Batsford, £9.95)
Subdivided into films, people and themes, a useful, well-presented alphabetical chronicle of information about horror movies, although one would have liked a little more opinion and comment to liven up the inevitable cumulative blandness. And what are *Jaws* and *Jaws 2* doing here?

HUMPHREY JENNINGS: FILM-MAKER, PAINTER, POET
Mary-Lou Jennings
(BFI, £3.75)
Born in 1907, his life cut tragically short by a fall in 1950, Jennings' best-known

work is as a director of taut, lyrical documentaries about a most un-lyrical subject — Britain at war. Appreciations and essays from the likes of Lindsay Anderson, Kathleen Raine and others describe a far larger talent (Jennings had tried his hand at Surrealism, both pictorial and poetic, prior to the world going mad), one that, if his life hadn't been so tragically edited, would doubtless have gone on to produce even more resonant work. Thorough and scholarly, but poorly illustrated — the book started life as an exhibition guide for a show at London's Riverside in early 1982 — but still an eye-opening appetiser to a neglected and far from minor talent.

THE ILLUSTRATED DIRECTORY OF FILM STARS
David Quinlan
(Batsford, £14.95)
Not quite as exhaustive as Katz in the sheer number of people it packs in — wisely, it confines itself to film stars — but still a huge, quite superb book with complete filmographies of everyone one

can imagine, supplemented by pithy, perceptive descriptions and, most importantly, a photograph of everyone at the time of their most characteristic work. A commendable work of reference which will continue to gain in value.

— 165 —

THE ILLUSTRATED MOVIE QUIZ BOOK
Rob Burt
(Severn House, £2.95)
Heavily-illustrated movie quiz sampler with over one thousand Hollywood-related teasers in such categories as Players, Movie Makers (the two not clearly differentiated), the Big Picture (*Casablanca, A*

Hard Day's Night etc.), and Screen Test. Comes with a foreword by Croydon's Human Blob, Barry Norman, which chortles: "*Everybody* is an expert on the cinema". No, they're not, but what the hell, it's all money. Which motion picture did that one come from?

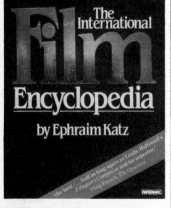

THE INTERNATIONAL FILM ENCYCLOPEDIA
Ephraim Katz
(Papermac, £7.95)
Finally, the affordable paperback edition. No illustrations nor entries on individual films, but detailed outlines on countries, technical terms and processes, plus biographies and filmographies of actors, directors, producers, writers and pretty much everyone connected with films who deserves attention. Quinlan is probably better on the actors themselves, particularly the minor ones,

but it is difficult to think of a more complete reference volume about cinema in general. It only goes up to 1979, so a sequel should be on the way.

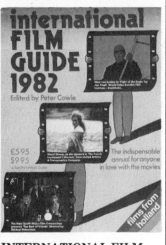

INTERNATIONAL FILM GUIDE 1982
ed. Peter Cowie
(Tantivy, £5.95)
More for students of the industry than people who confine themselves to enjoying films, this nevertheless continues to provide an invaluable source of information, particularly on countries about whose output we would hear little otherwise.

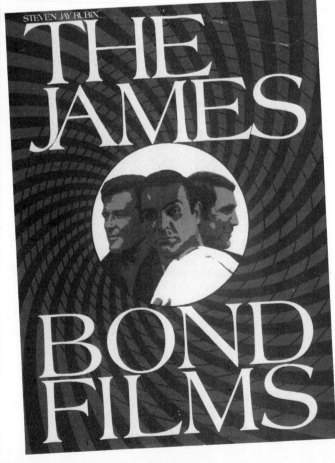

THE JAMES BOND FILMS
Steven Jay Rubin
(Talisman, £5.95)
A useful, unexciting, but thorough and anecdotal film-by-film account of the background to a dozen Bond movies. Great stills, immaculate research, rather dull presentation.

JAZZ IN THE MOVIES
David Meeker
(Talisman, £9.95)
Thorough, well-presented and illustrated reference guide to jazz on film. Entries are listed and numbered by name of film with an accompanying index of artists enabling one to check,

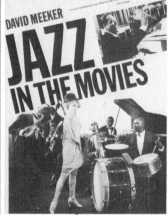

for instance, the credits of John Coltrane or Coleman Hawkins both legit and illegit, ghosted or credited, in the cinema and on TV. Over 3,700 entries. What's the difference between *Batman* the movie and *Batman* the TV series? Answer: Nelson Riddle. Find out this kind of thing before Riddle's estate suppresses the evidence . . .

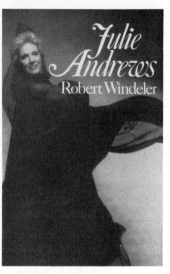

JULIE ANDREWS
Robert Windeler
(W.H. Allen, £8.95)
A slightly updated edition of the biography originally issued in 1973, when Andrews was in semi-retirement following the combined disasters of *Darling Lili* and a cancelled television series, and her husband Blake Edwards had more or less been shown to the door in Hollywood. The decade which included their triumphant return as a team with *10* and *Victor/Victoria* is all compressed into about eight pages of text. Capable stuff, but very thin all round.

LIMELIGHT AND AFTER
Claire Bloom
(Weidenfeld & Nicolson, £8.95)
The *Limelight* part — which occupies three-quarters of this soundly written though doggedly uncontroversial autobiography — is an engaging, familiar account of an English childhood interrupted by World War Two and an early visit to America. It also chronicles her beginnings in the theatre, an abortive film debut and, more significantly, the circumstances which led to becoming Chaplin's leading lady at the age of 20. As with most of her other achievements, she attributes this mainly to good fortune with a modesty which only occasionally borders on the

Claire Bloom
Limelight and After

The Education of an Actress

MAKING A MONSTER
Al Taylor and Sue Roy
(Crown, £8.95)
Much-illustrated and no-nonsense study of Hollywood's great sci-fi and horror movie make-up artists:

THE CREATION OF SCREEN CHARACTERS BY THE GREAT MAKEUP ARTISTS
Making a Monster
A behind-the-scenes look at the great film makeup artists, their careers and creations, from *Frankenstein* to *Star Wars*, with revealing information on how to make your own monsters
Al Taylor and Sue Roy
Introduction by Christopher Lee • Over 400 illustrations

The NEW GERMAN CINEMA
John Sandford

suffocating. The final quarter — observations on various subjects under a pretentious general title — reveals very little about a life which must surely have been more interesting than this.

MAGIC IN THE MOVIES
Jane O'Connor and Katy Hall
(Columbus, £5.95)
Did you know that the *Star Wars* robot R2D2 cost over a hundred thousand dollars to develop? What *you* get for *their* money is the mainspring of this study of movie special effects: *Jaws* which used three sharks, and not merely the one man-muncher; Boris Karloff's make-up (by the highly regarded Jack Pierce); miniaturisation (as in *It's a Mad Mad Mad Mad World*); optical illusion, and even miniature rear-screen projection; mastered by the inimitable Ray 'Sinbad' Harryhausen who merits three whole pages to himself in what is a competent but rather sketchy survey.

MAGIC IN THE MOVIES
THE STORY OF SPECIAL EFFECTS
JANE O'CONNOR & KATY HALL

Tom Burman of *Close Encounters* fame; Jack Dawn who created the beasties and nice ones of *The Wizard of Oz*, Rick Baker who was on the inside (in every sense) of Dino De Laurentiis' *King Kong* and many more. With over 400 pictures, and written in an easy, informative style, not just a book for the connoisseur of foam rubber and plaster.

Monty Python Complete and Utter Theory of the Grotesque
EDITED BY JOHN O. THOMPSON

MONTY PYTHON COMPLETE AND UTTER THEORY OF THE GROTESQUE
ed. John O. Thompson
(BFI, £2.50)
Priced like a book, though little more than an extended pamphlet with newspaper extracts punctuated by a lot of quasi-analytical piffle. Just to give you an idea: it includes passages from 'Nonsense: Aspects of Intersexuality in Folklore and Literature' and 'Rabelais and His World'.

THE MOVIES
Richard Griffith, Arthur Mayer and Eileen Bowser
(Columbus, £13.95)
The second updating (the first was in 1970) of the time-honoured colossus among film

THE MOVIES
REVISED & UPDATED EDITION OF THE CLASSIC HISTORY OF AMERICAN MOTION PICTURES
RICHARD GRIFFITH, ARTHUR MAYER & EILEEN BOWSER

illustrated history of this kind, but even allowing for that, this still seems flimsy. Handsomely produced, though.

THE MOVIE QUOTE BOOK
Harry Haun
(Omnibus, £4.95)
Immaculately researched, endlessly browsable, extremely funny 400-page compendium of quotes from films, arranged under subject headings. It doesn't include

picture books. Absolutely exhaustive on the early years of movie-making, it gets discernibly thinner as it goes along, to the point where the last couple of decades appear to be over in a blink, even if they aren't. One doesn't expect a lot of analysis in an

The Movie Quote Book.
Harry Haun.

every film by any means, and sometimes not even the best quotes from those present, but a great read under any circumstances and a tribute to the many screenwriters represented.

THE NEW GERMAN CINEMA
John Sandford
(Eyre Methuen, £4.95)
An intelligent, well-written and thorough appraisal of post-war German cinema from the time of direct intervention by Russian and American forces to the gradual establishment in the Sixties of the New Wave. Particularly strong on finance and on individual Krauteurs such as Kluge, Herzog, Wenders, Schlondorff and, most of all, Fassbinder whose death no doubt adds to the impact and point of this excellent study. Wide and well-reproduced illustrations.

THE NEW ITALIAN CINEMA
R.T. Witcombe
(Secker and Warburg, £6.95)
Thorough, unpartisan but often stodgy survey of Italian cinema in the Sixties and (primarily) the Seventies. Whitcomb's main thesis is that the country's cinema output after the golden age of Fellini, Pasolini, Antonioni and Visconti has long been undervalued and possesses a bleak thematic unity of its own. His method, to compare two directors (Bellochio and Cavani, Bolognini and Bertolucci, Rosi and Petrie etc.), has its advantages (the bringing out of the theme of fatherhood in directors as seemingly different as Bertolucci and Bolognini) but the book is beset by the usual problems of excessive film narrative and by the necessity of much prior knowledge of the subject on the part of the reader.

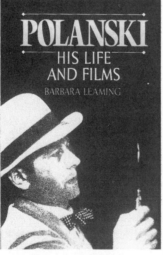

OF MUPPETS AND MEN
Christopher Finch
(Michael Joseph, £12.50)
For people with very large coffee tables who don't demand too much text, this good-looking volume, subtitled 'The Making of the Muppet Show', reveals many of the behind-the-scenes secrets (or at least the ones the creators choose to reveal) and illustrates them with numerous photographs. As an occasional admirer of the series, rather than a committed zealot, I could never understand why, a guaranteed audience apart, so many otherwise po-faced celebrities were quite happy to make fools of themselves on this particular programme — and, in some cases, come all the way to England to do so. This book makes the attractions evident.

POLANSKI: HIS LIFE AND FILMS
Barbara Leaming
(Hamish Hamilton, £5.95)
Despite the obvious lack of co-operation of her subject, Leaming's study is a healthy antidote to the more sensationalist Polanski literature, a work which manages to pull off the almost impossible, combining a thorough and frank biography with a sensitive evaluation of the director's work. Indeed Leaming shows the one inspiring and reinforcing the other. Polanski, child of the Polish ghettos, refugee, fated husband of murdered Sharon Tate, is a director obsessed not merely with violence but with our voyeuristic attitudes to it. A thorough, entertaining and anecdotal study of this fascinating, aggressive, surviving cinematic genius.

POPULAR TELEVISION AND FILM
ed. Tony Bennett, Susan Boyd-Bowman, Colin Mercer and Janet Woollacott.
(BFI/Open University, £6.25)
A series of essays on aspects of film and television from an avowedly semiological standpoint, much emphasis being placed on text, subject, structure, genre and "industry". Subject areas range from comedy, crime fiction and soccer reportage on TV to the ideology of *Jaws*. Though much of the writing is pompous and over-earnest, there are many intellectually nutritional passages, notably a critique of science programmes on television which seeks to expose their tendency towards mystification, and a punchy debate between Messrs Colin McArthur and MacCabe on the significance of Jim Allen's *Days of Hope.*

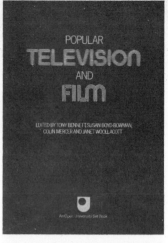

P.S. I LOVE YOU
Michael Sellers
(Collins, £7.95)
PETER SELLERS
Derek Sylvester
(Proteus, £4.95)
Soon after Alexander Walker's distinguished biography — issued before our year of coverage began — comes Michael Sellers' account of his father's life, portraying him as a gifted, funny, occasionally loveable man whose off-camera behaviour seemed governed entirely by whim and tantrum, with homes, lovers, wives and children shuffled around in accordance with whatever personal exorcism he was conducting. Surprisingly lacking in bitterness, and with considerable powers of recollection, Sellers is already more of an adult than his

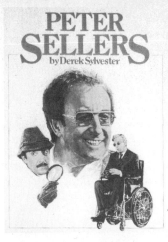

PETER SELLERS
by Derek Sylvester

father ever was although it remains to be seen whether he will ever be as talented. Sylvester's book is short, fast and has lots of pictures: a career history, efficiently written and perfectly serviceable.

PUNCH AT THE CINEMA
Foreword by Dilys Powell
(Robson Books, £7.50)
Whoever assembled this one knows the cartoons are the first things we turn to in Britain's oldest humour weekly — hence a last page index of artists; plus reviews, interviews by the score, real and parodied. Some of the best of the latter are, pleasant surprise, the work of Bryan Forbes, axeing the hacks with relish. Biggest oversight: lack of original dates of publication of material that spans a quarter century. Otherwise, several reliably "safe" laughs from a likeable battery of older mavericks — Benny Green, Barry Took, Alan Coren etc.

RAISING CAINE
William Hall
(Sidgwick & Jackson, £7.50)
Emphasised on the jackets of biographies as an indication of having successfully enlisted the co-operation of the subject,

the term "authorised" has always had an unattractive ring about it, suggesting in about equal measures toadying on one part and censorship on the other. There is little evidence of either in this agreeably candid, if rather unsensational, study of Maurice Micklewhite's patient but determined rise from an East End childhood to fame and, very clearly, fortune as Michael Caine. He is presented as — and probably is — an honest and engaging man who makes no attempt to disguise the fact that he became involved with acting to escape his background, and now enjoys the luxuries of stardom. He also admits to taking parts for money. Certainly he has made more cruddy films than most of his status, but I bet he doesn't cry about it.

THE REAL OSCAR
Peter H. Brown
(Arlington House/LSP, £9.95)
An entertaining and revealing behind-the-scenes account of

Oscar history, particularly good on the outrageous string-pulling and in-fighting which has always, it appears, underlined the craving for the coveted statuette. Soundly written, endlessly anecdotal, there must be another book this year as scurrilously enjoyable as this one. Right now, it is difficult to think of it.

SCREEN STARS OF THE SEVENTIES
David Castell
(LSP, £3.95)
Despite an intelligent introduction and a useful list of major film awards in the decade in question, really nothing more than a glorified puff list of anyone who made a commercially notable movie during the Seventies. As well as Stallone, De Niro, Spacek and Streep, there are entries on the likes of John Wayne, Peter Sellers and Charlton Heston which makes the whole idea of a specifically Seventies classification almost meaningless.

SCREEN WORLD
Ed. John Willis
(Muller, £10.95)
32nd volume of the hardy

evergreen, covering the American film year of 1980 with credits, stills and miscellaneous data. Attractively presented as ever, and always intriguing in its sheer exhaustiveness (including a colossal number of US films that never cross the ocean), it would benefit from an article or two of critical assessment to complement the customary avalanche of facts.

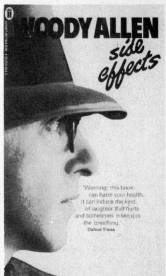

SIDE EFFECTS
Woody Allen
(New English Library, £1.50)
Seventeen more short pieces in which, as before, Allen delights — and is perhaps at his best — in parody, be it by aping scientific investigators, philosophers or UFO nuts. As always there's the feeling, after reading three or four items that one could write one just as easily. The delicious one-line throwaways are not so easy to concoct, however, and admiration seeps back, although one knows that more regular practitioners — Donald Barthelme, John Sladek — have taken the form far further. But they don't make movies, great or small, and Allen's peripheral activities remain wittily re-readable.

TELEVISION 1970-1980
Vincent Terrace
TV DETECTIVES
Richard Meyers
(both Tantivy/Barnes, £9.50)
Complementary to each other in some respects and highly recommended to anyone with the slightest interest in television. The first is an illustrated listing of all the

series (including imported ones), pilot films and variety specials shown on American television between the years stated, complete with synopses, credits, transmission dates, running times, and, best of all, bits of added trivia: the name of Lou Grant's publisher's dog (Barney, later Max), Police Woman's address (102 Crestview Drive, Los Angeles) etc. The second is obviously more specialised, a survey of the sleuths who made their mark on the box from the late Forties onwards. Presented chronologically, and supplemented by some nicely stagey pictures.

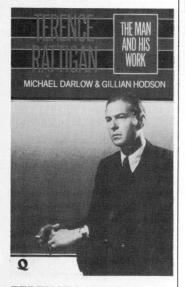

TERENCE RATTIGAN: THE MAN AND HIS WORK
Michael Darlow and Gillian Hodson
(Quartet, £6.95)
Acclaimed biography of playwright Rattigan, completed two years after his death in 1977 and written with the full co-operation and help of the man himself, whose

critical reappraisal in recent years this work has both aided and reflected. Though obviously primarily concerned with his work in the theatre, it provides illuminating insights into Rattigan's numerous film activities (notably his work with Graham Greene and Anatole de Grunwald) and his first job as a Warner Brothers scriptwriter at what was in 1936 the very princely sum of £15 a week. An exceptional piece of work.

THEY DIDN'T WIN THE OSCARS
Bill Libby
(Arlington House/LSP, £9.95)
Self-explanatory title: individual well-remembered performances that didn't win, particular actors and actresses who never won, and what the competition was like on the occasions they failed. Some familiar reiterated details (Richard Burton nominated seven times without winning), some unfamiliar (Deborah Kerr, a six-time loser), and some bordering on the remarkable (Edward G. Robinson never even *nominated*!) A bit waffly,

and reading too much like a continuous list, it nevertheless provides an instructive browse.

WOODY ALLEN
Myles Palmer
(Proteus, £6.50)
It's doubtful that Palmer has ever met the very private Mr Allen, but as a work of cobbling, this is rather better than average. The laughs come from Woody's records and films, but did you know that editor Ralph Rosenblum was largely responsible for making

a coherent movie from the mess that was *Take the Money and Run?* Only if, like Palmer, you've read the latter's memoir, *When the Shooting*

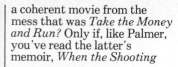

Stops ... the Cutting Begins. Hackwork, but fluently presented, and with the good grace to admit its sources straight off.

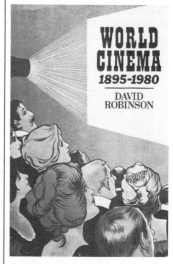

WORLD CINEMA 1895-1980
David Robinson
(Eyre Methuen, £5.95)
First published in 1973, now revised and updated, Robinson's history of the cinema is the most striking attempt anyone has made in recent years (the more recent the year, the more difficult the undertaking) to put *world* cinema, as opposed to merely English language, into some kind of context by which it may be studied. All the more remarkable, therefore, that it should be an entertaining and discursive read as well as a sound, academic thesis. Compressed enough for one to *want* to read it, it first engages the attention, then retains it.

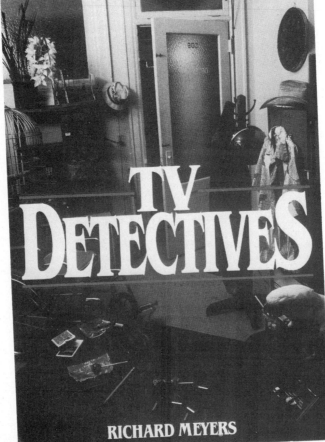

OBITUARIES

Compiled by *David McGillivray*

JACK ALBERTSON
Beginning as a Broadway chorus boy, Albertson then spent 30 years in vaudeville, burlesque, radio and television stooging for most of America's leading comedians. In films from 1947, latterly as lovable grandpas, he was usually in comedy although he won an Academy Award for a straight role in *The Subject Was Roses* (1967). Absent from the screen since 1972, he scored a big success in the TV series *Chico and the Man* (1974-8). He made a final film appearance in *Dead and Buried* (1981). Died in Hollywood, November 24, aged 74.

GLENN ANDERS
Primarily a stage actor — he made his Broadway debut in 1919 and was still active in the theatre in the Sixties — Anders made one memorable screen appearance as the sinister lawyer in *The Lady from Shanghai* (1948). His other films were *Laughter* (1930), *By Your Leave* (1935), *Nothing But the Truth* (1941), *Nancy Goes to Rio* (1950) and three in 1951: *Tarzan's Peril* (GB: *Tarzan and the Jungle Queen*), the re-make of *M*, and *Behave Yourself*. At some time in the Sixties he retired to Mexico and had been assumed dead for several years. Died in New Jersey, October 26, aged 92.

GREGOIRE ASLAN
Krikor Aslanian
Turkish by birth, Aslan moved in 1915 to Paris, where he

worked as a drummer for Ray Ventura and his Collegians, and later joined a theatre company. In films since 1938, he was in demand to play foreigners in British movies of the Fifties, but after his first American film, *The Devil at Four O'Clock* in 1961, he became an international actor appearing in *Cleopatra* (1962), *The High Bright Sun* (1965), *Our Man in Marrakesh* (1966), *You Can't Win 'em All* (1970), *The Golden Voyage of Sinbad* (1973) and finally *Meetings with Remarkable Men* (1978). He was a star in France, where he was known as "Coco", a nickname coined in the Twenties. Died in Cornwall, England, January 8, aged 73.

NILS ASTHER
Born in Denmark of Swedish parents, Asther has appeared in silent films in Germany, Denmark and Sweden before moving to Hollywood, where he was an exotic leading man for Garbo, in *The Single Standard* (1929) and *Wild Orchids* (1929), Crawford, in *Our Dancing Daughters* (1928) and *Letty Lynton* (1932), and Stanwyck, in *The Bitter Tea of General Yen* (1933). His talkies became increasingly routine and he moved to Britain for four years, but he made a star comeback in *The Man in Half Moon Street* in Hollywood in 1944. His last American film was *That Man from Tangier* (1950). Returning to Sweden in 1958, he worked mainly in the theatre, but made a few more films, the last of which was *Gudrun* (1963). Died in Stockholm, October 13, aged 84.

ALAN BADEL
This distinguished British actor made his film debut in 1941, but played leads for only a brief period in the Fifties, when he was John the Baptist in *Salome* (1953) and Wagner in *Magic Fire* (1956). He then returned to the theatre and was not seen again on screen until *This Sporting Life* in 1963, after which he played a number of fine supporting roles, usually as a suave villain. His last film was

Nijinsky (1980). Shortly after completing the BBC television serial *The Woman in White*, he died in Chichester, March 19, aged 58.

JOHN BELUSHI
After working with the improvisational Second City Troupe in Chicago, Belushi became America's most talked-about alternative comedian in the NBC TV show *Saturday Night Live* and made an even bigger impact in his second film *National Lampoon's Animal House* in 1978. He was subsequently teamed with his *Saturday*

Night Live partner Dan Aykroyd in *1941* (1979), *The Blues Brothers* (1980) and *Neighbors* (1981), and also appeared in *Old Boyfriends* (1979) and *Continental Divide* (1981). He overdosed himself with heroin and cocaine in Hollywood, March 5, aged 33.

TERRY BISHOP
Beginning as a sound technician in 1930, Bishop later became a scriptwriter and began directing documentaries in 1940. His highly acclaimed work culminated in *Daybreak in Udi*, which won an Academy Award in 1950. In 1952 he began directing unremarkable second-features, including *You're Only Young Twice* (1952), *Cover Girl Killer* (1959), *The Unstoppable Man* (1961) and his last, *Bomb in the High Street* (1963), but in the Fifties he was best known in the

business for churning out episodes of such TV series as *Robin Hood, Sword of Freedom* and *William Tell*. In 1964 he returned to documentaries and had just completed *Suddenly Among Strangers* when he died on October 30 aged 69.

STEPHEN BOSUSTOW
The Canadian-born former film extra who revolutionised the American cartoon film first worked as an animator for Ub Iwerks and Walter Lang. In 1934 he joined the Disney studio, where he contributed to *Snow White and the Seven Dwarfs, Pinocchio, Fantasia* and *Dumbo*. He produced his first independent cartoon in 1943, and in 1945 founded UPA, whose house style — simple drawings and blotches of colour — became instantly recognisable. Their most famous characters, the strange schoolboy Gerald McBoing-Boing and the myopic Mr Magoo, won three Academy Awards in the Fifties. Together with his son Nick, Bosustow later formed a company to make educational films. Their cartoon *Is It Always Right?* won an Oscar in 1970. Died in Los Angeles, July 4, aged 69.

KEEFE BRASSELLE
On the road as a band vocalist, drummer and comedian since his teens, Brasselle ended up in Hollywood, where he won a one-line part in *Janie* (1944). For the next ten years he was a lightweight young lead, notably in *A Place in the Sun* (1951) and *The Eddie Cantor Story* (1953), in which he played the title role. Disappearing in the mid-Fifties, he re-emerged in 1964 as the producer of *The Reporter, The Baileys of Balboa* and *The Cara Williams Show*, three flop series for CBS. He subsequently worked his experience as a TV producer into a novel, *The Cannibals*. In the Seventies Brasselle made the headlines by getting into trouble with the law. He also appeared in two more films, *Black Gunn* (1973) and *If You Don't Stop*

It...You'll Go Blind!!! (1974), which he also co-directed. An alcoholic, he died of cirrhosis of the liver in Downey, California, July 7, aged 58.

VIRGINIA BRUCE
Helen Briggs
Bruce was an ingenue who arrived with the birth of the talkies in 1929, but despite above average ability in both straight and musical roles, she was invariably overshadowed in vehicles for other performers. Exceptions included *Jane Eyre* (1934), in which she had the title role, *The Mighty Barnum* (1934) and *Times Square Lady* (1935). Her films in the Forties were mostly routine and she faded out in the Fifties, making her last appearance in *Strangers When We Meet* in 1960. Her first husband was John Gilbert. She died in California, February 24, aged 72.

VICTOR BUONO
A latter-day Laird Cregar, the heavyweight Buono drew excellent notices in his first film *Whatever Happened to Baby Jane?* in 1962, but was never able to top his performance as the unctuous English pianist. His only memorable lead was in the second feature *The Strangler* in 1964, and for the rest of the Sixties he was typecast as a comical bad man. More recently the majority of his performances were in independent productions which ended up on the shelf, although he was popular on TV in *Batman* and *The Man from Atlantis*. His last film was *Sam Marlowe, Private Eye* in 1980. Died in Apple Valley, California, January 1, aged 43.

HOAGY CARMICHAEL
Hoagland Carmichael
Carmichael wrote 'Stardust', probably the world's most recorded song. His other hits included 'Georgia on My Mind', 'Lazy River' and 'I Get Along Without You Very Well'. He began writing for the movies in the Thirties; his song 'In the Cool, Cool, Cool of the Evening', featured in *Here Comes the Groom*, won an Oscar in 1951. After taking a small role in *Topper* (1937), he went on to make a number of film appearances, usually as a laconic pianist. He is best remembered for *To Have and Have Not* (1944) and *The Best Years of Our Lives* (1946). His last film was *Timberjack* in 1955, but he continued to

Hoagy Carmichael

appear on TV until the Seventies. Died in Palm Springs, California, December 27, aged 82.

PADDY CHAYEFSKY
Sidney Stuchevsky
Chayefsky was the writer most associated with the new wave of socially-conscious TV drama in America in the Fifties. He adapted his most famous play, *Marty*, for the screen in 1954, and won his first Oscar. He then adapted three more of his teledramas, *The Catered Affair* (GB: *Wedding Breakfast*) in 1956, *The Bachelor Party* (1957) and *Middle of the Night* (1959). In the Sixties his infrequent scripts were more commercial, but still highly respected; he won two more Oscars for *The Hospital* (1971) and *Network* (1977). He used the pseudonym "Sidney Aaron" for his last picture, an adaptation of his novel *Altered States*. Died in New York, August 1, aged 58.

STANLEY CLEMENTS
Soon after coming to the screen in 1941, Clements became one of the semi-delinquent East Side Kids in *Smart Alecks* and *'Neath Brooklyn Bridge*. He was a tough kid in most of his other Forties films, notably *Going*

My Way (1944) and *Bad Boy* (1949). In the Fifties, when the East Side Kids had become the Bowery Boys, Clements rejoined them, appearing in their last seven second features as a replacement for Leo Gorcey. In the Sixties he was mainly on TV, but had character roles in *Tammy and the Doctor* (1963), *That Darn Cat!* (1965) and *Panic in the City* (1968). Died in California, October 16, aged 55.

GHISLAIN CLOQUET
Belgian-born, but based in France since the Thirties, Cloquet began work as a cameraman for Alain Resnais in 1953. He went on to photograph four features for Robert Bresson and four for the Belgian director André Delvaux. Although he also shot two American films — *Mickey One* (1965) and Woody Allen's *Love and Death* (1975) — his name remained almost unknown outside the Continent until he replaced the late Geoffrey Unsworth on Roman Polanski's *Tess* in 1979. The following year he accepted an Oscar for the film's magnificent lighting, but died in Paris, November 2, aged 57 before he was able to claim a British Academy Award for the same picture.

HANS CONRIED
Conried was a versatile character actor who perfected his talent for European accents on radio before making his screen debut in 1938. He was rarely off the screen during the Forties and Fifties, often in walk-ons although he had leads in *The Twonky* and *The Five Thousand Fingers of Dr T* in 1953. A favourite stooge of Jerry Lewis, he was also regularly employed by the Disney studio; his was the voice of Captain Hook in *Peter Pan* (1953) and his last films in the Seventies were for Disney. After playing in *Barefoot in the Park* in Seattle, he died in Burbank, California, January 5, aged 64.

DENYS COOP
In films since 1936, Coop became a camera operator in 1948 and photographed his first film, *Girl on the Boat*, in 1961. He was responsible for some of the finest black and white photography in Britain in the Sixties — *A Kind of Loving* (1962), *This Sporting Life* (1963), *Bunny Lake Is Missing* (1965) — but his career tailed off surprisingly quickly. As early as 1970 he had returned to second unit work (on *Ryan's Daughter*) and in recent years he had worked in horror and on the special effects for the first two *Superman* films. His last credit was for "additional photography" on *Venom* (1982). Died in London, August 16, aged 61.

MELVYN DOUGLAS
Melvyn Hesselberg
There were two quite separate phases to Douglas' career. In the Thirties and Forties he was Hollywood's most debonair romantic lead, unforgettable opposite Irene Dunne in *Theodora Goes Wild* (1936), Garbo in *Ninotchka* (1939) and Norma Shearer in *We Were Dancing* (1942). Tiring of being typecast, he left films in 1951 and spent the next ten years on stage and TV. He returned

to the screen as an old man, first in *Billy Budd* (1962) then in a succession of excellent character roles. He won Academy Awards for *Hud* (1963) and *Being There* (1979) and was also impressive in *I Never Sang For My Father* (1970), *The Seduction of Joe Tynan* (1979) and his last film *Ghost Story* (1981). Died in New York, August 4, aged 80.

PENELOPE DUDLEY WARD
On stage from 1933 and in films from 1935 Penelope Dudley Ward was a refined but enchanting English leading lady who, despite starring in some of the most famous British films of the Forties, was quickly forgotten after her marriage in 1948 to director Carol Reed, and subsequent retirement. She appeared in *The Citadel* (1939), *Major Barbara* (1941), *In Which We Serve* (1943), *The Demi-Paradise* (1943) and finally *English Without Tears* (1944). Died in London, January 21, aged 67.

ALLAN DWAN
Joseph Dwan
Canadian-born, but in the USA from 1893, Dwan was the veteran of an estimated 1,500 films, 400 of which he directed (between 1910 and 1958). He was also a major innovator, supervising the world's first crane shot and America's first dolly shot, both in 1915. His most successful period was from 1916 to 1929, when he directed Douglas Fairbanks (most notably in *Robin Hood*). In the Thirties he directed mainly B films, but his career revived somewhat in the Forties, when he made *Brewster's Millions* and *The Sands of Iwo Jima*. He retired in 1958 after *Enchanted Island*. Died in Woodland Hills, California, December 21, aged 96.

RAINER WERNER FASSBINDER
Fassbinder was a remarkably prolific producer, director writer and actor who worked in radio, television, cinema and theatre, but who will be remembered as the key figure in the new German cinema movement of the Seventies. He made his first film in 1965, but *Fear Eats the Soul* (1974) was the first to register with international audiences. His other films, often inspired by the Hollywood romances of the Forties, included *The Bitter Tears of Petra von Kant* (1972),

Effi Briest (1974), *Fox* (1975), his first English-speaking film *Despair* (1978) and *The Marriage of Maria Braun* (1978). Shortly after completing *Querelle* he committed suicide in Munich, June 10, aged 36.

ABEL GANCE
Far more famous in his nineties than he was at any other time in his career, Gance was originally an actor-writer, who made his first film in 1911. His technically innovative widescreen epic *Napoleon* (1927) was cold-shouldered with the arrival of sound and later released in a heavily-cut version. Gance continued making films until 1971, but with no great success. Then, in 1980, the original version of *Napoleon* was restored by Kevin Brownlow and has since played to packed houses around the world. Gance was planning a new film, *Christopher Columbus*, when he died in Paris, November 10, aged 92.

GLORIA GRAHAME
Gloria Hallward
Best known as a sulky bad girl, Grahame was at her best in the Forties and Fifties, when she played in melodramas like *Crossfire* (1947), *In a Lonely Place* (1950), *The Bad and the Beautiful* (1952), for which she won an Academy Award, and *The Big Heat* (1954). In an offbeat piece of casting she sang 'I Cain't Say No' in *Oklahoma!* (1955). Disappearing at the end of the Fifties, she returned to the screen in 1966 to play mothers and horror film queens, usually without much enthusiasm. In recent years she had worked on the stage in England, and was rehearsing *The Glass Menagerie* when she was taken ill. Died in New York, October 5, aged 55.

MARGOT GRAHAME
Beginning in the Thirties as a juvenile in Whitehall farces on stage and screen, Grahame was far too sexy an actress for Britain to handle and she went to Hollywood, where she was better employed in *The Informer* (1935), *The Three Musketeers* (1936), *The Soldier and the Lady* (GB: *Michael Strogoff*) (1937) and *The Buccaneer* (1938). She then returned home, but Britain had nothing to offer her until 1947, and thereafter she was more often on stage than screen. After *Saint Joan* (1957) little was heard of her, and when she died in London, January 1, aged 70, it was revealed that she had been living in some poverty.

SARA HADEN
The daughter of silent screen actress Charlotte Walker, Haden was on stage before making her screen debut in *Spitfire* in 1934. She played a variety of character parts in such films as *Magnificent Obsession* (1935), *Our Vines Have Tender Grapes* (1945) and *She-Wolf of London* (1946), but she is best remembered as Millie, the spinster aunt in the *Andy Hardy* films made between 1937 and 1947. She made a comeback in *Andy Hardy Comes Home*, the attempt to revive the series in 1958. Died in Woodland Hills, California, September 15, aged 82.

HOPE HAMPTON
After winning a beauty contest in 1917, Hampton became a film extra then graduated to leading roles in such silents as *The Bait* (1921), *The Gold Diggers* (1923), *The Truth About Women* (1924) and *The Unfair Sex* (1926). Despite a sideline as an opera singer, she did not succeed in talkies, but was celebrated in later life as a socialite. Married from 1923 to 1946 to a wealthy French financier, she was to be seen at every opening and first night in New York until quite recently. Died in New York, January 23, aged 84.

ANN HARDING
Dorothy Gatley
Harding was a classy romantic heroine, whose husky voice was an immediate attraction when she made her screen debut (after stage experience) in 1929. Her big success in the Thirties was *The Animal Kingdom* (1923), but after a number of flops in the mid-Thirties, she left films,

returning in 1942 to play character roles in programmers though sometimes in better films — *The Magnificent Yankee* (1950), *The Man in the Grey Flannel Suit* (1956). She was last seen on screen in 1956 and on TV in 1965, after which she retired. Died in Sherman Oaks, California, September 1, aged 79.

EDITH HEAD
The cinema's most famous costume designer for over 40 years, and the winner of an unprecedented eight Academy Awards, Edith Head was a fashion writer before joining Paramount in 1923. Her first solo credit was for *She Done Him Wrong* in 1936. She became head of design in 1938 and remained at Paramount until 1967. During this time some of her most outstanding designs were seen in *The Heiress* (1949), *All About Eve* (1950), *Samson and Delilah* (1950), *The Ten Commandments* (1955) and *Inside Daisy Clover* (1965). In 1967 she went to Universal, where she worked on *Sweet Charity* (1969), *The Sting* (1973), *Sextette* (1979) and *Dead Men Don't Wear Plaid* (1981), which she completed just before her death in Los Angeles on October 24. She was 82.

WILLIAM HOLDEN
William Beedle
An overnight star following his first major role in *Golden Boy* in 1939, Holden was typecast as a young rogue until Billy Wilder saw his potential and cast him as the opportunist screenwriter in *Sunset Boulevard* (1950). Three years later he won an Oscar for *Stalag 17*, also directed by Wilder. For the rest of the Fifties Holden was an international superstar; his many hits included *The Moon*

Is Blue (1953), *Love Is a Many-Splendored Thing* (1955), *Picnic* (1955) and *The Bridge on the River Kwai* (1957), the pinnacle of his career. As a mature actor his greatest success was *The Wild Bunch* (1969), but he continued playing leads up until his death from a fall in his Santa Monica apartment at some time before November 15. He was 63.

STANLEY HOLLOWAY
Beginning as a monologuist and revue artist before 1920, Holloway was 86 when he made his last film and over 90 when he talked about his career on the BBC programme *Human Brain*. In films since 1921 he was primarily a comic actor until the Forties, when he switched to straight parts in *Caesar and Cleopatra* (1945), *The Winslow Boy* (1948) and

Hamlet (1948). But it was his subsequent comedy roles in the Ealing films *Passport to Pimlico* (1949), *The Lavender Hill Mob* (1950) and *The Titfield Thunderbolt* (1953) which brought him his greatest success and led eventually to his immortal characterisation of Dolittle in the stage (1956) and film (1964) versions of *My Fair Lady*. Died in Littlehampton, Sussex, January 30, aged 91.

DAME CELIA JOHNSON
One of Britain's most distinguished dramatic actresses, Dame Celia made her stage debut in provincial rep in 1928 and remained in the theatre for most of her career. From 1942 to 1957, however, she was seen quite regularly in films as a refined heroine, and starred in the classic *Brief Encounter* (1946) as well as three other works by Coward, *In Which We Serve* (1942), *This Happy Breed* (1944) and *The Astonished Heart* (1949). When, after a 12-year absence, she returned to the screen in *The Prime of Miss Jean Brodie* (1969), she

Dame Celia Johnson

had become fascinatingly wrinkled, and spent her remaining years playing cultured elderly ladies. Died in Oxfordshire, April 25, aged 73, shortly after opening in a new play *The Understanding*.

VICTOR JORY
Almost always a villain when he wasn't playing Red Indians, Canadian-born Jory was on stage from 1917 and in films from 1932. Up until the Sixties the bulk of his appearances were in Westerns, but when he was able to break out of the rut he was memorable in *A Midsummer Night's Dream* (1935), *The Adventures of Tom Sawyer* (1938) and *Gone with the Wind* (1941). Later in his career he had strong character roles in *The Fugitive Kind* (1960) and *The Miracle Worker* (1963), and he was last seen as an ancient Indian in *The Mountain Men* (1980). Died in Santa Monica, California, February 11, aged 79.

CURT JURGENS
German-born, but an Austrian citizen since the Fifties, Jurgens made his film debut in 1935, although it was not until *The Devil's General* in 1955 that he began working

regularly outside Germany and Austria. For the rest of the Fifties he starred in major productions — *This Happy Feeling* (1957), *Me and the Colonel* (1958), *The Inn of the Sixth Happiness* (1958) and *The Blue Angel* (1959) — but from the Sixties onwards he seemed satisfied to travel to any country to appear in any film which required the added dignity his participation seemed to guarantee. His more distinguished appearances were in *Lord Jim* (1964), *The Battle of Britain* (1969), *Nicholas and Alexandra* (1971) and *The Spy Who Loved Me* (1977). Died in Vienna, June 18, aged 66.

PATSY KELLY
In vaudeville as a teenager and later in Earl Carroll's variety shows, Kelly was brought to Hollywood in the Thirties to appear (often opposite Thelma Todd) in 50 comedy shorts for Hal Roach. Her first feature was *Going Hollywood* (1933) after which she made a niche for herself playing nervous maids. She had only one star role (in *Kelly the Second* in 1936). Absent from the screen from 1944, she made a comeback in *Please Don't Eat The Daisies* in 1960. Her only important subsequent film part was in *Rosemary's Baby* (1968), but in 1973 she won a Tony award for her role — as a maid — in the stage revival of *No, No, Nanette*. Died in Woodland Hills, California, September 24, aged 71.

ROBERT KRASKER
A cameraman whose skill with black and white, colour and widescreen earned him the right to work on only the most prominent films from the beginning to the end of his

career, the Australian-born Krasker came to England in 1930 and worked as a camera operator for Korda before photographing his first feature in 1943. His best work was seen in *Henry V* (1945), *Brief Encounter* (1945), *Odd Man Out* (1947), *The Third Man* (1950), for which he won an Oscar, *El Cid* (1961), *The Fall of the Roman Empire* (1964) and *The Heroes of Telemark* (1965). He came out of retirement in 1980 to light the short *Cry Wolf*. Died in London, August 16, aged 68.

SAM KYDD
After working on the peripheries of show business and organising the entertainment in a prisoner of war camp, Kydd was given a couple of lines in *The Captive Heart* (1946), on which he was working as a military adviser. For the next 35 years he played over 150 bit parts in British films, usually as a serviceman or labourer. He played leads only on TV, notably in *Crane* and its spin-off *Orlando* in the Sixties. After his last film appearance ("Lock Keeper" in *Eye of the Needle*) he was working on the Granada TV soap opera *Coronation Street* when he was taken ill. Died in London, March 26, aged 67.

HARVEY LEMBECK
On stage from 1948 and in films from 1950, Lembeck was invariably cast as servicemen, and was therefore a natural choice for the TV series *Sergeant Bilko* in which he played his most well-known part, Corporal Rocco Barbella, from 1955 to 1959. Subsequently he played mostly in comedy and had a regular part (as Hell's Angels leader Eric von Zipper) in AIP's *Beach Party* series in the Sixties. Not often seen in recent years, he ran a school for comedians. He died in Beverly Hills, January 5, aged 58, while working on an episode of the TV series *Chips*.

LOTTE LENYA
Karoline Blamauer
The foremost interpreter of her composer husband Kurt Weill's work, Lenya appeared in the stage (1928) and film (1931) version of *Die Dreigroschenoper/The Threepenny Opera*, and after Weill's death in 1950, she was regularly involved in recordings and stage productions of his other operas. She dabbled in films,

most memorably in *From Russia with Love* (1963) as the spy with knives in her shoes. She also had a cameo as a heavy-handed masseuse in *Semi-Tough* (1977). Died in New York, November 27, aged 83.

RONALD LEWIS
First seen in the stage (1952) and film (1953) versions of *The Square Ring*, Lewis unwisely accepted studio contracts which constricted him to supporting roles throughout the Fifties. He graduated to leads in the Sixties, but only in minor comedies, thrillers and action pictures. After 1965 he was mainly on stage and TV, but returned to the screen to play the father of the hero in *Friends* (1971) and its sequel *Paul and Michelle* (1974). Bankrupted in 1980, he was found dead in London, January 11, aged 53.

ARTHUR LOWE
Lowe spent ten years in bit parts before he found fame in the Sixties as the officious Leonard Swindley in TV's *Coronation Street* and its spin-off series *Pardon the Expression* and *Turn Out the Lights*. Subsequently he became one of Britain's best-loved character comedians, a star in the TV (1967-77) and film (1971) versions of *Dad's Army*, and the player of juicy supporting roles in such films as *The Ruling Class* (1971), *The Lady Vanishes* (1979) and *Sweet William* (1979). He had completed his last film *A Woman for All Time*, and was appearing in the play *Home at Seven* in Birmingham when he died on April 15, aged 66.

PAUL LYNDE
First discovered in the stage revue *New Faces of 1952* (he was also in the 1953 film version), Lynde then marked time until being rediscovered in the 1960 Broadway musical *Bye Bye Birdie*. Subsequently TV occupied most of his time, and he was best known in America for his cynical wisecracks on the game show *Hollywood Squares*. His twitching mannerisms were in vogue in such Sixties films as *Bye Bye Birdie* (1963), *Send Me No Flowers* (1964) and *How Sweet It Is* (1968). He was then absent from the screen until *The Rabbit Test* (1977) and *The Villain* (GB: *Cactus Jack*) in 1979. Found dead in Beverly Hills, January 11, aged 55.

ROBERT LYNN
Son of the British comedian Ralph Lynn, this minor British director began as a camera assistant in 1936. His few films included *Postman's Knock* (1961), *Dr Crippen* (1962) and *Victim Five* (1965). Sporadic work during the Seventies included producing *The Railway Children* (1970), directing episodes of TV's *Space 1999* (1976), and co-directing the second unit on *Superman* (1978). He was subsequently inactive. Died in Great Missenden, Buckinghamshire, in January, aged 64.

HUGH MARLOWE
Hugh Hipple
After a variety of jobs Marlowe became a radio announcer in 1932 and then went on the stage before passing a screen test in 1937. A popular juvenile in the Forties, he worked his way up to good parts in *Twelve O'Clock High* and *All About Eve* in 1950. Then, after the TV series *Ellery Queen* in 1954, his career plummeted, but he kept going until the Sixties, when he had supporting roles in *Castle of Evil* (1966) and *The Last Shot You Hear* (1968). Died May 2, aged 71.

ROSS MARTIN
Martin Rosenblatt
Polish-born, but resident in the US since childhood, Martin was in public relations before becoming a radio actor. Moving to films in 1954, he played colourful character roles in *The Colossus of New York* (1958), *Experiment in Terror* (GB: *The Grip of Fear*) (1962), *The Ceremony* (1964) and *The Great Race* (1965), but he was best known for his role as Artemis Gordon, master of disguise, in the TV series *The Wild, Wild West* (1965-8). Died in Ramona, California, July 3, aged 61.

JESSIE MATTHEWS
On stage from 1917 and in films from 1923, Matthews became Britain's biggest musical star of the Thirties; her greatest success, *Evergreen* (1934), was the only British musical of the period to be enjoyed abroad. Her other hits in Britain included *The Good Companions* (1932) and *Gangway* (1937). Her film career stopped after *Forever and a Day* in 1943, and when she next appeared on screen, in *tom thumb* in 1958, she was in a homely character part. She made a major comeback in the Sixties in the radio soap opera *The Dales*, but her only other film appearances were cameos in *The Hound of the Baskervilles* (1978) and *Second Star on the Right* (1980). Died in London, August 20, aged 74.

FRANK McHUGH
On stage from the age of three, McHugh began in films in 1926 and was an invaluable supporting actor during the Thirties, when he was usually the comic sidekick or friend of the hero. He was in many classics, including *Little Caesar* (1930), *The Front Page* (1931), *42nd Street* (1933) and *Going My Way* (1944), and he was in 11 films with his real-life friend James Cagney. Not regularly seen on the big screen since the Fifties, he continued to work on TV. Died in Greenwich, Connecticut, September 11, aged 83.

ROBERT MONTGOMERY
Henry Montgomery Jnr.
Originally a juvenile lead on Broadway, Montgomery was signed to MGM in 1929 and remained with the studio until 1948. He usually played romantic heroes opposite the likes of Norma Shearer and Helen Hayes, but was successfully cast against type as the psychotic killer in *Night Must Fall* (1937). After directing part of *They Were Expendable* (1945), he was allowed to direct *The Lady in the Lake* (1946), but its first-person camera gimmick was unpopular. So were his remaining films as director-star, and he left the movies after *The Gallant Hours* (1960). Died in New York, September 27, aged 77.

DIANA NAPIER
Molly Ellis
A well-bred actress with an extremely brief career, Napier was put under contract to Korda and played supporting roles in *Wedding Rehearsal* (1933), *Catherine the Great* (1934) and *The Private Life of Don Juan* (1934), Douglas Fairbanks Snr's last film. In 1936 she married tenor Richard Tauber and appeared opposite him in *Land Without Music* (1936) and *Pagliacci* (1937). She was then off the screen until *I Was a Dancer* (1948), her last film. Died in Windlesham, Surrey, March 12, aged 76.

WARREN OATES
On TV since 1954, often in Western series, Oates came to films in 1958 and played supporting roles as cowboys, gangsters and other heavies until 1969 when *The Wild Bunch* turned him into an unconventional star. His films since then include *Two-Lane Blacktop* (1971), *Chandler* (1971), *Dillinger* (1973), *Badlands* (1973), *China 9 Liberty 37* (1978), *1941* (1979), *The Border* (1981) and his last, *Blue Thunder* (1981). Died in Los Angeles, April 3, aged 53.

NIGEL PATRICK
Nigel Wemyss
A versatile British actor, Patrick never quite made the first division and latterly worked mainly in the theatre. On stage from 1932 and in films from 1939, he was a success in his first leading screen role, as a spiv, in *Spring in Park Lane* (1947), and in the early Fifties he was one of Britain's top ten film stars. He made one Hollywood film, *Raintree County* in 1957, and on his return to Britain began

directing films and plays. His last film as an actor was *The Mackintosh Man* (1973), but he was seen, shortly before he died, in the LWT television play *Blunt Instrument*. Died in London, September 21, aged 68.

ELEANOR POWELL
Generally agreed to have been the cinema's greatest female tap dancer, Powell made her

Broadway debut in 1929. Her first screen appearance was a guest spot in the film version of *George White's Scandals* for Fox in 1935, but it was MGM who made her a star the following year in *Broadway Melody of 1936*. Although she made only nine more major movie appearances, most of them were tremendous successes. She retired in 1943 to marry Glenn Ford. Her last film was *Duchess of Idaho* in 1950, but she made a comeback in cabaret in 1961. Shortly before her death she paid a touching tribute to her former co-star Fred Astaire at an American Film Institute dinner. Died in Beverly Hills, California, February 11, aged 69.

ROMY SCHNEIDER
Rosemarie Albach-Retty
An elegantly beautiful Austrian star, Schneider made her screen debut in 1953 in a supporting role to her mother Magda Schneider in the German film *Wen der weisse Flieder blüht*. After several more German pictures, she moved to France in 1959. *Boccaccio 70* (1962) brought her international recognition and she appeared in *The Victors* (1963), *What's New, Pussycat?* (1965), *Otley* (1968), *The Assassination of Trotsky* (1971) and *Ludwig* (1972). She then spent the next ten years working almost entirely in France. Her last film was *La Passante du Sans Souci*. Died in Paris, May 29, aged 44.

RETA SHAW
This American supporting actress made her stage debut in 1947 and went on to appear in a number of musicals including the original production of *Gentlemen Prefer Blondes*. She went to Hollywood in 1956 to repeat her stage role in *Picnic*, and this was followed by *All Mine*

to Give (GB: *The Day They Gave Babies Away*) (1956), *Man Afraid* (1956), *The Pajama Game* (1957), *The Lady Takes a Flyer* (1957), *Pollyanna* (1960), *Bachelor in Paradise* (1961) and *Mary Poppins* (1964). From 1968-9 she played the housekeeper in the TV series *The Ghost and Mrs Muir*. She then made a brief comeback in *Escape to Witch Mountain* (1975). Died in Encino, California, January 8, aged 69.

LEE STRASBERG
Austrian by birth, but an American citizen since 1936, Strasberg, the founder in 1948 of New York's Actors' Studio, became the most famous acting teacher since Stanislavsky. Among his pupils were Brando, Steiger, Dean and Monroe. It was a more recent pupil, Al Pacino, who persuaded Strasberg to make his film debut, aged over 70, in *The Godfather Part II* (1974). He was later seen in *The Cassandra Crossing* (1977), *...And Justice For All* (with Pacino again) (1980) and *Going in Style* (1980) among others. Considering his reputation, his performances were disappointing. Died in New York, February 16, aged 81.

TOM TULLY
The veteran of over 5,000 radio performances, Tully moved first to Broadway then, in 1944, to Hollywood, where he became a useful supporting actor for authoritarian roles in films such as *Where the Sidewalk Ends* (1950), *The Caine Mutiny* (1954), *Ten North Frederick* (1957), *The Carpetbaggers* (1964), *Coogan's Bluff* (1968) and his last *Charley Varrick* (1973). From 1954-8 he was also in the TV series *The Lineup*. His last appearances were made after he had had a leg amputated. Died April 27, aged 85.

VERA-ELLEN
Vera-Ellen Westmehr-Rohe
Another American muscial star who retired surprisingly early, Vera-Ellen was a Radio City Music Hall Rockette before starring in her first movie *The Wonder Man* in 1945. She will be remembered for three classic musicals, *On the Town* (1949), *Call Me Madam* (1953) and *White Christmas* (1954). She also appeared in eight more musicals and in a straight role in *The Big Leaguer* (1953). She retired after making *Let's Be*

Happy in Britain in 1956. Died after a long illness in Los Angeles, August 30, aged 61.

GEORGE VOSKOVEC
Jiri Voskovec
Born in Czechoslovakia, Voskovec made his film debut there in 1930, and ran the anti-Fascist Liberated Theatre of Prague before the Nazi threat forced him to flee to the USA. Here he directed plays and from 1952 appeared on the screen in middle-European character parts. He was in *Twelve Angry Men* (1957), *Mister Buddwing* (GB: *Woman Without a Face*) (1966), *The Boston Strangler* (1968), *Somewhere in Time* (1980) and finally *Barbarosa* (1981). He also worked in Britain both on stage — *The Diary of Anne Frank* (1956) — and screen — *The Spy Who Came in From the Cold* (1965). Died in Pear Blossom, California, July 1, aged 76.

HARRY WARREN
Salvatore Guaragna
After working in many branches of show business, Warren settled down to become the cinema's most prolific songwriter, contributing to over 75 films. He was at Warner Brothers from 1932-9; Fox from 1940-4; MGM from 1944-52; and Paramount from 1952-61. He won Oscars in 1935 for 'Lullaby of Broadway' (featured in *Gold Diggers of 1935*); 1943 for 'You'll Never Know' (from *Hello 'Frisco Hello*); and 1946 for 'The Atchison, Topeka and the Santa Fe' (from *The Harvey Girls*); he also won a special Oscar in 1981. His other hits included the score of *42nd Street* (1933), 'September in the Rain', 'Jeepers Creepers', 'The More I See You' and 'You Must Have Been a Beautiful Baby'. Died in Los Angeles, September 22, aged 87.

RITA WEBB
Rita Webb's career began at 14 when she ran away from school to be a dancer at London's Metropolitan music hall. In films from 1949, she played only charwomen, nosey neighbours and "old bags", and became one of Britain's most easily recognisable small part players. Most of her work — particularly on TV — was in comedy, but she played the occasional straight role, for example in *Suddenly Last Summer* (1959) and her last film *Venom* (1981). Died in London, August 30, aged 77.

NATALIE WOOD
Natasha Gurdin
A child star who made the grade both as a teenager and a mature actress, Wood was four when she first appeared on screen in *Happy Land* (1943). After 20 more child roles, she came of age in *Rebel Without a Cause* (1955) and was thereafter groomed as a juvenile lead by Warner Brothers. Her most successful period was the first half of the Sixties, when she appeared in *Splendour in the Grass* (1961), *West Side Story* (1961), *Gypsy* (1962), *Love with the Proper Stranger* (1963), *Sex and the Single Girl* (1964) and *The Great Race* (1965). The unpopular *Inside Daisy Clover* (1965) began a decline for Wood which continued throughout the Seventies, and in recent years she had worked

mainly in television, notably in the re-make of *From Here to Eternity* (1979). While making *Brainstorm*, she drowned off Catalina Island on November 29. She was 43.

WILLIAM WYLER
One of the all-time great directors, German-born Wyler went to Hollywood in 1920, worked first as a publicist and then, in 1925, began directing two-reel Westerns. His first important film was *Dodsworth* (1936) and for the next 30 years Wyler directed a series of intelligent, though often sentimental, dramas renowned for their fine performances and photography (the latter often by Gregg Toland). Their titles are legendary: *Dead End* (1937), *Wuthering Heights* (1939), *The Little Foxes* (1941), *Mrs Miniver* (1942), *The Best Years of Our Lives* (1946), *The Big Country* (1958) and *Ben Hur* (1959). He retired after *The Liberation of L.B. Jones* (1970). He won three Academy Awards. Died in Beverly Hills, July 27, aged 79.

THE LONG GOODBYE

...or, in two out of three cases, a longer one. William Holden and Natalie Wood died within the *Film Yearbook*'s period of coverage and are already represented in the obituaries. In August, Henry Fonda finally surrendered to heart disease. When he went, one was reminded of Holden and Wood as well. Their passing somehow makes Hollywood a less enduring place of myth. All of them gave distinguished performances at different stages in their careers. More importantly, they were stars, viewed with affection by audiences throughout the world who, thanks to the wonder of dubbing, in many cases never even heard their proper voices. *John Walker* pays tribute to a trio without whom the old-style film world would have been poorer. And with whose deaths it may already be on its way out.

HENRY FONDA

He made a fine end. Henry Fonda's last role, a gift from his daughter Jane, was a good one. As an ageing professor, querulous and fearful but possessing inner strengths and finally allowing his emotions to flower, he gave a performance that won him the Oscar that had always eluded him.

On Golden Pond was, in truth, not a particularly good film. It was full of a too easy reassurance. But it did give Fonda a last chance to exhibit those skills that made him one of the best actors of his time. A year earlier, he had been awarded an Oscar for a lifetime's achievement, one of those gestures made when the Academy realise that, as usual, they have overlooked their most talented members until it is almost too late to recognise them.

Peter Ustinov once said of Fonda, "He has a sense of life being a marathon and of keeping something in reserve for the final stretches". And, indeed, he managed a last-minute sprint, a final burst of energy that carried him across the tape ahead of the field and gave his life the satisfying shape of one of his better movies.

Henry Fonda died on Thursday, August 12, after eight years of failing strength and heart trouble, painlessly and peacefully. His fifth wife Shirlee, to whom he had been happily married for 16 years, was by his bedside and his three children — Peter, Jane and Amy — were on their way to the hospital. There was no funeral. Fonda disliked ostentation and wasted words. He was always a private man.

He was also, of course, public property: an icon at which America could worship a dignified self-image. He represented all that was good, decent, honest, middle-class and Midwestern. As an actor he was never less than professional and even more at home on the stage than he was on the screen. He was one of the two actors that John Ford helped shape into all-American heroes; the other was John Wayne. But Fonda avoided the trap of the simple chauvinist bullies that Wayne sometimes portrayed. He could play outlaws too.

His association with Ford lasted from the grim social history of *The Grapes of Wrath* (1940) to the antic comedy of *Mr Roberts* (1955),

Fonda with Katharine Hepburn in his last film 'On Golden Pond' 1982

the postwar Broadway success in which he starred for 1,671 performances. Filming that, Fonda regarded himself as the guardian of the play's values and Ford broke his lifetime's habit of not getting drunk while working and punched him. They never worked together again.

It was Fonda's brilliant performance as the displaced Tom Joad in *The Grapes of Wrath* that made him a star. But before that, Ford had directed him in *Young Mr Lincoln* (1939), in which he played the future President as a struggling lawyer, and after it in *My Darling Clementine* (1946), in which he embodied all the pioneer virtues as Wyatt Earp, conveying a stubborn integrity and a commanding authority.

Fonda was born on May 16, 1905, the son of a printer, in

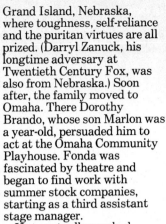

Grand Island, Nebraska, where toughness, self-reliance and the puritan virtues are all prized. (Darryl Zanuck, his longtime adversary at Twentieth Century Fox, was also from Nebraska.) Soon after, the family moved to Omaha. There Dorothy Brando, whose son Marlon was a year-old, persuaded him to act at the Omaha Community Playhouse. Fonda was fascinated by theatre and began to find work with summer stock companies, starting as a third assistant stage manager.

He eventually reached Broadway in a revue, New Faces, and signed to make two pictures a year in Hollywood before returning to New York to star in *The Farmer Takes a Wife*, which became his first film in 1935. Critics praised his "appearance of sincerity". It was after he made *Drums Along the Mohawk* (1939) for Ford that he was offered the role of Tom Joad by Zanuck. But the price exacted was a high one: a seven-year contract with Fox. Most of the films he made during that time were poor.

Fritz Lang's *The Return of Frank James* (1940) had its moments. He fought successfully to appear in Preston Sturges' *The Lady Eve* (1941), which gave him a chance to play comedy, as did *The Male Animal* (1942). And he was proud of *The Ox-Bow Incident* (1943), a commercial failure but one of the best westerns ever made. Its director, William Wellman, called him "Perhaps the best actor I ever directed and probably the most dedicated". The theme of an unjust lynching may have touched something deep inside Fonda, for as a child his father had taken him to see a black man snatched from prison and hanged from a post before being riddled with bullets.

When the war came Fonda enlisted in the Navy and, after some persuasion, managed to see action in the Pacific. His return to Fox was the triumphant *My Darling Clementine*, but his next collaboration with Ford was less successful. As the Catholic priest in *The Fugitive* (1947), based on a Graham Greene novel, he lacked the necessary existential despair; Ford, though, always regarded it as his favourite and most successful film.

Henry Fonda during his early years in Hollywood

Fonda went back to his first love, the stage, in *Mr Roberts*, a wartime tragi-comedy of a Naval officer, which occupied him for the next three years. He then appeared for another two years in John P. Marquand's *Point of No Return* and spent the best part of a year in Herman Wouk's *The Caine Mutiny Court-Martial*.

His film career never really recovered from the loss of momentum of that eight years' absence. He was fortunate enough to make his cinematic comeback in *Mr Roberts* (1955), although the part nearly went to Marlon Brando. And, because he could find no one to finance it, he turned producer of *Twelve Angry Men* (1957), Reginald Rose's drama about a jury in conflict which had been written for television. It provided him with a perfect part. Its director, Sidney Lumet, called Fonda "a barometer of truth".

As he grew older, he turned increasingly to the stage for sustenance. The 1960s were marked by a succession of indifferent movies. Exceptions were Don Siegel's *Madigan* (1968), although he disliked the film's political stance, and Sergio Leone's epic *Once Upon a Time in the West* (1969). This quintessential spaghetti western allowed him to massacre an entire family, including a nine-year-old boy. ("What'll we do with this one, Frank?" says his fellow gunman Jack Elam. "Well, now that you've called me by my name..." drawls Fonda, slowly drawing his gun and blasting the kid to kingdom come.)

In casting him as a blackhearted villain Leone was paying tribute to his identification with heroes. Fonda was never a heroic actor, in the way that Charlton Heston is, even when playing the good guy. There is an ordinariness about his heroism. His speech — slightly hesitant, often flat and uninflected — is not suited to rhetoric. His build — tall and rangy, growing to gauntness in his last years — never suggested physical strength. As a young man in Hollywood, he tried to build up his muscles and his weight without success.

It is significant that Leone's film was successful everywhere but in America. Even today, when it is shown on American TV, there is a commercial break as Fonda draws his gun on the child and

the film begins again after the killing. As Elia Kazan said to Joseph Mankiewicz when he cast Fonda as an evil warden in *There Was a Crooked Man* (1970), "Jesus Christ, you've picked the symbol of American middle-class morality. That's like spitting on the flag!"

Fonda carried his sense of morality over to his own life. He turned down the role of revenger in Michael Winner's *Death Wish*, finding the part "repulsive". He was married five times and told his biographer Howard Teichmann, "I'm goddammed ashamed of it". Emotionally, he was often rigid and unyielding. His relationship with his two children Jane and Peter was often stormy. They remembered him as a difficult and moody father, full of rage. It was not until his last years, after Peter had shown him the way, that he was able to tell his children that he loved them.

In his later years he lent his authority to many indifferent films. During the 1970s his great achievement was his one-man stage show *Clarence Darrow*, in which he played, with compelling power, the great American lawyer. But there was a succession of boring films: *Ash Wednesday* (1973) with Elizabeth Taylor, *Rollercoaster* (1977) which was a vehicle for the dreaded Sensurround, *Tentacles* (1977), an Italian-made rip-off of *Jaws*, starring a giant octopus, *The Swarm* (1978) about killer bees, and the disastrous *Meteor* (1978), in which he once again played a US President.

On Golden Pond (1981), which Jane Fonda financed, redeemed his reputation. Its theme of a man on the edge of death, its reconciliation scene between father and daughter (with Jane playing his daughter) mixed real life and fiction in a way which audiences found irresistible. And Fonda, summoning his last reserves of strength, used all his wiles to suggest both rigidity and vulnerability; he was, on film and in life, a man who had finally let down his defences and given expression to those feelings he had always kept locked away. He was a man confronting himself at last in his full knowledge, with shame but also with rightful pride. It was a fine end, linking up again with the honesty and courage of Tom Joad. And in Tom's farewell to his mother, Henry Fonda uttered his own memorial: "I'll be all around in the dark — I'll be everywhere".

WILLIAM HOLDEN

"He always wanted his own pool, but the price was a little high," was the epitaph delivered by William Holden at the beginning of *Sunset Boulevard*, as the body of Joe Gillis, the hack writer who had been drawn into the lurid melodrama of Hollywood, floated face down in death. In the space of that film Gillis followed a path it took Holden a lifetime to travel: from charming young man to someone who is caught in the trap of his own compassion and ends filled with self-disgust.

Gillis's epitaph might do for Holden himself. He was an increasingly reluctant actor who did his best to escape from the intense world of film into a wider and more active life and failed. His end was as unexpected as that of Gillis and no less melodramatic. He was found dead on November 16, 1981, having bled to death after falling and knocking himself unconscious. He had been drinking heavily, as he often did, and, life mirroring art, a visitor who might have found him in time to save his life was turned away from his apartment by a too-officious doorman.

Holden paid a price. His drinking began as a means of overcoming his inhibitions about acting and endured as a means of dealing with boredom. His acting continued, long after he had lost the desire for it, in order to finance his other interests: travel, wild-game conservation, his ranch in Africa. Occasionally in later life, a role would come along which matched his temperament and awakened some interest; the result would be a performance of often morose integrity, of a harshness where the pain of living became a fierce flame of joy.

If Holden had not existed, Billy Wilder would have invented him. It was Wilder who turned him from a pleasant young actor into a powerful and disturbing screen presence. And it was from the Austrian-born director that

William Holden in 'Wild Rovers' (1971), directed by Blake Edwards

the admiring Holden ("He has a brain full of razor blades," he once said of his mentor) learned that bitter-sweet world weariness, a cynicism cut by compassion, which marked his best performances. In turn, Wilder thought that Holden was an ideal film actor. "He is beyond acting. You never doubt or question what he is," he said.

It was a quality Holden shared with more immediately attractive screen personalities, such as James Stewart and Gary Cooper. He was a professional, able to turn a film star's mythic qualities (for a successful cinema actor becomes his own archetype) to good effect. In *The Wild Bunch*, he was perfect as an ageing outlaw who knows that he is on the way out and doesn't like it. In *Network*, he rose to the role of an honest man bewildered by the power of emotions he thought were under control. ("You can't blame the business. It's what

we do to ourselves," said *Network*'s author Paddy Chayefsky when he, Holden and other friends had dinner together on the evening of Peter Finch's funeral and began bitching at Hollywood.)

Holden began as a star in 1939 and managed to stay one for 42 years, an achievement in itself. After appearing as an extra in a couple of films, he emerged as the lead in *Golden Boy*, Clifford Odets' play about a violinist turned boxer. He and the play received the Hollywood treatment. In a publicity still taken before the film was made, Holden posed as a hairy-chested boxer. In the film itself, his chest was hairless. Holden never tried to fight the studio system.

John Garfield had been first choice for the role. Harry Cohn, the vulgarian who made Columbia a successful studio, tried 65 other actors before Holden was given the part. He was 21 and his inexperience came near to wrecking the

film, although his gaucheries merged with the character he played. Only Rouben Mamoulian's patient directing and the help of Barbara Stanwyck, who coached him in his role away from the studio, got him through.

He was then, if not quite the boy next door, a clean-cut young man from a conservative and puritanical middle-class family. He was born William Franklin Beedle in O'Fallon, a small Illinois town. His father, an industrial chemist, encouraged him to be athletic. His mother, a teacher, inculcated in him a simple, deeply-held morality.

Conservative in many ways he remained until the end of his life. Otherwise, his career is notable for his move away from the decencies of his upbringing — with its emphasis on order and family and children — to a more individual code. When, after many strains and some separations, his marriage to actress Brenda Marshall ended after 29 years, he said "Marriage was just a phase, and I grew out of it".

His discovery of his self was reflected in the role he played. If *Golden Boy* was the epitome of his clean-cut beginnings, then *Sunset Boulevard* (1950) marked the emergence of a more complex individual, one who stood outside the action and was at a remove from the rest of society. Holden had begun as part of Paramount's "Golden Circle" of young actors, which also included Susan Hayward and Robert Preston. Then, he wanted to be "the greatest screen actor in the world". He had been spotted acting in a college play and invited for a screen test, when he was put under contract. His name was changed because a studio executive thought it sounded too much like an insect.

The films he made were mostly forgettable exercises in the popular genres of the time: gangster movies, westerns, air force films and even a musical. In *Our Town* (1940) he was praised by the critic of the *New York Times* for his "clean

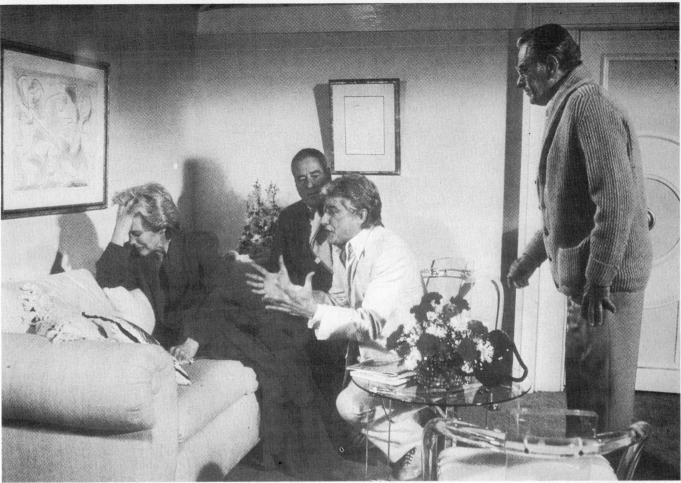

Edwards also directed Holden's last film 'S.O.B.' (1981), l. to r. Julie Andrews, Robert Webber, Richard Mulligan and Holden

and refreshing youthfulness''. Then came the war. ''I hope this makes a man of you,'' said Cohn when he went off to fight. He served for four years in the Army Air Force, returning to Hollywood as a maturer 28-year-old, with a wife and three children to support. There followed three years of indifferent films before Wilder turned him into a presence to be reckoned with.

After *Sunset Boulevard*, Holden seemed a tougher actor, showing signs of that disillusion that marks his finest performances. Wilder persuaded him to play the stooge to Judy Holliday in *Born Yesterday* (1951) and, as a reward, gave him another role, in *Stalag 17*, that took advantage of a personality increasingly at odds with his environment. As Sefton, a prisoner on the make and a man true to his own principles, Holden gave a dazzling, energetic performance that won him an Oscar. In Wilder's *Sabrina* (1954), however, he was out-acted by both Humphrey Bogart and Audrey Hepburn. The film was an unhappy experience, with Bogart endlessly baiting

Holden, calling him a mediocre actor at best.

While these films can still hold an audience, others that were much praised at the time, such as *Love Is a Many Splendoured Thing* (1955) and *Picnic* (1956), now seem grandiosely empty. And Holden's performance in *The Bridge Over the River Kwai* (1957), where Alec Guinness effortlessly steals every scene, was memorable to him only because he received a cut of the film's gross which, over the years, earned him more than three million dollars.

John Ford's *The Horse Soldiers* (1959) had him returning to earlier simplicities. It was a time when Holden no longer seemed interested in acting, an attitude no doubt helped by such films as *Satan Never Sleeps* (1962), in which he and the elegantly epicene Clifton Webb played a couple of Catholic priests in China, or *The Lion* (1962), in which he combined an off-screen interest in Africa and in his co-star Capucine. It was not until Sam Peckinpah cast him as the middle-aged outlaw in *The Wild Bunch* (1969) that he was

offered a role to fit his talents and character. Pike, the tired gang leader, fails to live up to his own conception of self and when he does re-assert his notion of honour, it kills him. Two years later, he played a depressed middle-aged cowboy in Blake Edwards' elegiac *Wild Rovers* (1971).

By then, Holden had lost his golden boy slimness and the athletic exuberance that led him, as a young man, to walk along the parapets of high bridges. Booze had raddled his face and added several inches to his waistline. On television in *The Blue Knight* (1973), he played a similar role, as a cop who was ''fifty lousy years old, far-sighted and just can't cut it anymore''. For that, he won an Emmy.

Network (1976) provided another juicy part, one that again reflected his own situation as an ageing star with marital problems. *Fedora* (1978) re-united him effectively with Billy Wilder in a bizarre swansong to the old Hollywood. *S.O.B.* (1981), an acid comedy with melodramatic overtones, almost a contemporary version of *Sunset Boulevard*, where

again he was an observer of Hollywood's mores, an outsider who joined in occasionally, for the fun of it, but withdrew when it became too painful. As he said in one of his last interviews, ''There is a point beyond acting, a point where living becomes important''.

Acting was a vocation, to be distinguished from his ''avocations'', such as his Mount Kenya Safari Club, with its game-ranch of 1,256 acres which now continues under Stephanie Powers, the actress who was his companion for the last nine years of his life. He quickly lost, as he acknowledged, his dedication to acting. When he appeared in films with great actors such as Alec Guinness or immensely skilled professionals such as Trevor Howard or Humphrey Bogart, his limitations were clear. But there was an admirable strength and stringency about Holden's best performances, qualities that enabled him to survive in Hollywood for more than 40 years before he made his fatal slip. He did get a pool of his own, but the price was still too high.

NATALIE WOOD

Did she fall or was she pushed to it? Prurient speculation over the death of Natalie Wood is likely to ensure for her a kind of immortality that neither her beauty nor her talent would have brought her. She was discovered drowned, floating in the water off Catalina Island, on November 29, 1981. She had been taking a weekend break from filming *Brainstorm* for MGM aboard her yacht with her husband Robert Wagner and her co-star Christopher Walken.

That much is certain. The rest, like the last moments of Marilyn Monroe, is noisy gossip. The official explanation was that she had drunk too much at dinner and had fallen while trying to get aboard a dinghy attached to the yacht. But there were those who whispered of suicide in a moment of desperation.

Natalie Wood was 43 when she died; yet she had been making films more-or-less nonstop for 38 years. Apart from her good looks, she was remarkable as one of the few child actresses to make the transition to adult success. But in all those years she appeared in only two movies that were significant at the time and which may last as long as the medium itself. In neither was her performance essential to the films' success. Her finest film, *The Searchers*, depended upon the combination of John Ford, John Wayne and scriptwriter Frank S. Nugent. And in *Rebel Without a Cause* it was the brooding presence of the definitive adolescent, James Dean, that gave the film its resonance.

Like her contemporary Tuesday Weld, Natalie Wood became the object of a small, curious cult. She was held in some esteem by her fellow professionals and was nominated for an Oscar three times: for her acting in *Rebel Without a Cause* (Sal Mineo was also nominated, but not Dean), *Splendour in the Grass* and *Love With the Proper Stranger*. But the humorous magazine *National Lampoon* also established a Natalie Wood Award for the year's worst performance.

There is an early publicity still which encapsulated her appeal. She leans winningly towards the camera as to a man offering candy. She is pig-tailed, wide-eyed and doll-like and smiling a dimpled smile that shows off her perfect teeth. She was five at the time. But her appeal never altered: it was always that of a pleasingly acquiescent little girl who needed protecting from the roughness of everyday living.

The image was often close to reality. Until she was 21 she had never written a cheque, travelled on a bus, bought a train ticket or hailed a taxi. Wherever she went, she took with her her Teddy bear. She never quite lost her apparent vulnerability and seeming innocence, and could occasionally turn them to effective use on film. Like many of her contemporaries, she studied at the Actors' Studio in New York, after coming under the influence of Elia Kazan, but her acting rarely seemed to connect with her own emotional life.

Her beauty was remarkable; there was a fragility about it, as well as a suggestion of passivity and docility, too. Over the years she learned her craft well. But not once did she do more than provide an audience with what pleased it. Her audience offered her love and she returned it. She never attempted to try for the danger and excitement inherent in great acting. She stayed within her limitations. Pauline Kael, film critic of the *New Yorker*, once complained of her "wind-up emotions" and there was often something mechanical about her performances, as of an eager student who has learned by rote.

That blandest of actors, Robert Wagner (who makes Roger Moore seem rough and rugged by comparison), seemed the ideal husband for her. She married him when she was 19 and divorced him six years later after a frantic affair with Warren Beatty, who made his screen debut with her in *Splendour in the Grass*. After Beatty left to pursue other women she married again, then eventually returned to Wagner, remarrying him in 1972.

Natalie Wood was born Natasha Gurdin in San Francisco on July 20, 1938. Her parents were of immigrant stock. Her father, whose family had come from Russia, trained as an architect and also worked as a set decorator. Her mother, who was of French descent, had been a ballet dancer and began taking her to dancing lessons as soon as she could walk.

Her first appearance — in *Happy Land* (1943) a sentimental and patriotic ghost story — resulted from a film being made in her neighbourhood. But the film's director Irving Pichel remembered her when he needed a child to appear with Orson Welles and Claudette Colbert in *Tomorrow Is Forever* (1946), another sentimental war movie. Pichel put her into his next film and then came a box office success: *Miracle on 34th Street* (1947), a piece of whimsy about Father Christmas. Suddenly, she was a child star to be reckoned with. In the next two years she made eight films.

Her transition to teenaged stardom came with Nicholas Ray's *Rebel Without a Cause* (1955), in which she played,

Wood's last completed film was 'The Last Married Couple in America' (1979) with George Segal

with touching success, James Dean's girlfriend. A year later John Ford put her into *The Searchers* as a young girl abducted by Indians. (Her little sister Lana played her younger self in the film.) It was a performance in which she was no more than a foil for the complexities of John Wayne's vengeful Ethan, hunting down the savages who have slaughtered his family. The film, probably Ford and Wayne's best and one that has influenced many younger directors and writers, will ensure that she will be remembered as a young and beautiful actress.

But that year she also went on to appear in two films with Tab Hunter — *The Burning Hills* and *The Girl He Left Behind* — and her career rarely rose above the mundane. Her freshness began to be replaced by a certain prissiness and her features acquired a tensed appearance, as though she were afraid they might crumble if she relaxed. Even in one of her better moments, in *West Side Story* (1961), in which Marni Nixon dubbed her singing voice, she paled before the hard, bright vitality of Rita Moreno.

Her triumph of that time, *Splendour in the Grass* (1961), directed by Kazan and scripted by the suicidal William Inge, now seems a romantically overblown melodrama. Her other success, *Love With the Proper Stranger* (1963), directed by Robert Mulligan, was an old-fashioned movie set among New York's Italian population (all sounding as if they'd stepped off the boats the day before, rather than three generations ago). She was a pregnant girl pursuing her casual lover until she could persuade him to chase her, whereupon she lets him catch her. It was a slightly dirtier, ethnic version of the Doris Day/Rock Hudson sex comedies of the period.

What it did reveal was that she had a talent for comedy. Blake Edwards was able to exploit it in *The Great Race* (1964), one of those hectic chase films which were a favourite of the time. Robert Mulligan's *Inside Daisy Clover* (1966), based on Gavin Lambert's novel, should have been her masterpiece. Its story of a teenaged waif who becomes a neurotic film star was close enough to her own life for her to find an emotional depth in the role. But, at 28, she found it difficult to play a young girl and the film

Natalie Wood in 1956

floundered.

Her light style added some attraction to *Bob and Carol and Ted and Alice* (1969), Paul Mazursky's comedy that teetered on the edge of sexual permissiveness without taking the plunge. Her style of glamorous acting was no longer what the public wanted, at least in the cinema, and she turned more to television which thrives on the kind of high-gloss soap opera which she could so effortlessly purvey. She starred in *The Affair* (1973), a sloppy love-story, with Wagner, in *Cat on a Hot Tin Roof* (1976), although she seemed out of touch with Tennessee Williams' steamier passions, and in *From Here to Eternity* (1979).

Her films of the 1970s — the private eye spoof *Peeper* (1976), the disaster movie *Meteor* (1978) and the comedy *The Last Married Couple in America* (1979) — were unremarkable. It is difficult to know how her career would have developed had she lived. Ageing movie actresses whose appeal has depended greatly on looks have always been very expendable. Her freshness and beauty had solidified, acquiring that preserved-in-aspic gloss, and her acting relied on long-acquired mannerisms, professionally deployed. She had been planning her stage debut in Los Angeles, in a revival of that romantic and melodramatic reversal of Cinderella, *Anastasia*. It was

an escape route other screen actresses have tried, with varying success. But there was little evidence from her movie performances that she would be able to cope with the less intimate demands of a large auditorium.

Her final film, *Brainstorm*, was nearly finished when she died. Its director, Douglas Trumbull felt that it would have been possible to release it with a little rejigging. But the movie's insurers seem to have felt otherwise.

Natalie Wood will live on, seen at her best in her two teenaged performances in *The Searchers* and *Rebel Without a Cause*: young, heartbreakingly beautiful and vulnerable, and promising a fulfilment that was never quite to come.

REFERENCE

PRODUCTION COMPANIES US

The Aldrich Company
606 North Larchmont Blvd.,
Los Angeles, CA 90004.
Tel: (213) 426 6511

Avco Embassy Pictures Corp.
956 Seward St., Los Angeles,
CA 90038.
Tel: (213) 460 7200

Batjac Productions, Inc.
Suite 400, 9570 Wilshire Blvd.,
Beverly Hills, CA 90212.
Tel: (213) 278 9870

Warren Beatty Productions
5451 Marathon St., Los Angeles,
CA 90038.
Tel: (213) 468 5000

Brut Productions, Inc.,
1345 Sixth Ave., New York,
NY 10019.
Tel: (212) 581 3114

Cannon Films, Inc.
6464 Sunset Blvd., Suite 1150,
Hollywood, CA 90028.
Tel: (213) 469 8124

CBS Theatrical Films
4024 Radford Ave., Studio City,
CA 91604.
Tel: (213) 760 6134

Chartoff-Winkler Productions
10125 West Washington Blvd.,
Culver City, CA 90230.
Tel: (213) 836 3000

Cinerama, Inc.
120 North Robertson Blvd.,
Los Angeles, CA 90048.
Tel: (213) 657 8420

Columbia Pictures
Columbia Plaza, Burbank,
CA 91505.
Tel: (213) 954 6000

Dino De Laurentiis Corporation
1 Gulf & Western Plaza,
New York, NY 10023.
Tel: (212) 399 0101

Walt Disney Productions
500 South Buena Vista St.,
Burbank, CA 91521.
Tel: (213) 840 1000

'An Eye for an Eye' from Avco Embassy

Faces International Films, Inc.
650 North Bronson Ave.,
Los Angeles, CA 90004.
Tel: (213) 840 0465

Filmways, Inc.
2049 Century Park East,
Suite 3500, Los Angeles,
CA 90067.
Tel: (213) 557 8700
540 Madison Ave., New York,
NY 10022.
Tel: (212) 758 5100

**First Artists Production
Company, Ltd.**
14651 Ventura Blvd., Ste. 210,
Sherman Oaks, CA 91403.
Tel: (213) 995 4121

**Samuel Goldwyn
Productions, Inc.**
1041 North Formosa Ave.,
Los Angeles, CA 90046.
Tel: (213) 650 2407

Hanna-Barbera Productions, Inc.
3400 Cahuenga Blvd.,
Hollywood, CA 90068.
Tel: (213) 851 5000

Hemdale Leisure Corporation
375 Park Ave., New York,
NY 10022.
Tel: (212) 421 9022

Horizon Pictures, Inc.
711 Fifth Ave., New York,
NY 10022.
Tel: (212) 421 6810

IPC Films, Inc.
10201 West Pico Blvd.,
Los Angeles, CA 90035.
Tel: (213) 277 2211

Jalem Productions, Inc.
141 El Camino, Suite 201,
Beverly Hills, CA 90212.
Tel: (213) 278 7750

Stanley Kramer Productions, Ltd.
Studio Center, 4024 Radford Ave.,
Studio City, CA 91604.

The Ladd Co.
4000 Warner Blvd., Burbank,
CA 91522.
Tel: (213) 954 6000

Edie and Ely Landau, Inc.
2029 Century Park East,
Los Angeles, CA 90067.
Tel: (213) 553 5010

Joseph E. Levine Presents, Inc.
277 Park Ave., New York,
NY 10017.
Tel: (212) 826 0370

Lion's Gate Films, Inc.
1861 South Bundy Drive,
Los Angeles, CA 90025.
Tel: (213) 820 7751

Lorimar Productions, Inc.
3970 Overland Ave., Culver City,
CA 90230.
Tel: (213) 202 2000

Lucasfilm, Ltd.
P.O. Box 2009, San Rafael,
CA 94912.
Tel: (415) 457 5282

MCA, Inc.
100 Universal City Plaza,
Universal City, CA 91608.
Tel:(213)985 4321
445 Park Ave.,
New York, NY 10022.
Tel: (212) 759 7500

The Malpaso Co.
4000 Warner Blvd., Burbank,
CA 91522.
Tel: (213) 954 6000

Manson International
9145 Sunset Blvd., Los Angeles,
CA 90069.
Tel: (213) 273 8640

Marble Arch Productions
12711 Ventura Blvd., Studio City,
CA 91604.
Tel: (213) 760 2110

Metro-Goldwyn-Mayer Film Company
10202 West Washington Blvd., Culver City, CA 90230.
Tel: (213) 558 5000

The Mirisch Corporation of California
3966 Overland Ave., Culver City, CA 90230.
Tel: (213) 202 0202

New World Pictures
11600 San Vincente Blvd., Los Angeles, CA 90069.
Tel: (213) 820 6733

Orion Pictures
75 Rockefeller Plaza, New York, NY 10019.
Tel: (212) 484 7000
4000 Warner Blvd., Burbank, CA 91522.
Tel: (213) 954 6000

Paramount Pictures Corporation
1 Gulf & Western Plaza, New York, NY 10023.
Tel: (212) 333 7000

Polygram Pictures
8255 Sunset Blvd., Los Angeles, CA 90046.
Tel: (213) 650 8300
810 Seventh Ave., New York, NY 10019.
Tel: (212) 399 4011

Rastar Films, Inc.
c/o Columbia Pictures Industries, Inc., Colgems Sq., Burbank, CA 91505.
Tel: (213) 843 6000

The Walter Reade Organization, Inc.
241 East 34th St., New York, NY 10016.
Tel: (212) 683 6300

RKO Pictures, Inc.
1440 Broadway, New York, NY 10018.
Tel: (212) 764 7000

RSO Films, Inc.
8335 Sunset Blvd., Los Angeles, CA 90069.
Tel: (213) 650 1234

Samarkand Motion Picture Productions, Inc.
598 Madison Ave., New York, NY 10022.
Tel: (212) 832 4913

Melvin Simon Productions, Inc.
260 South Beverly Drive, Beverly Hills, CA 90212.
Tel: (213) 273 5450

Aaron Spelling Productions, Inc.
132 South Rodeo Drive, Beverly Hills, CA 90212.
Tel: (213) 858 2000

The Taft Entertainment Company
10100 Santa Monica Blvd., Suite 2440, Los Angeles, CA 90067.
Tel: (213) 557 0388

Twentieth Century-Fox Film Corporation
Box 900, Beverly Hills, CA 90213.
Tel: (213) 277 2211
40 West 57th St., New York, NY 10019.
Tel: (212) 977 5500

United Artists Corporation
729 Seventh Ave., New York, NY 10019.
Tel: (212) 575 3000

Universal Pictures
445 Park Ave., New York, NY 10022.
Tel: (212) 759 7500

Warner Brothers, Inc.
75 Rockefeller Plaza, New York, NY 10019.
Tel: (212) 484 8000
4000 Warner Blvd., Burbank, CA 91522.
Tel: (213) 843 6000

Zanuck/Brown Company
20th Century-Fox Studio, Box 900, Beverly Hills, CA 90213.
Tel: (213) 203 3215

Zoetrope Studios
529 Pacific Ave., San Francisco, CA 94133.
Tel: (415) 788 7500

PRODUCTION COMPANIES UK

ABKCO Films Ltd.
2 Chandos St., London W1M 9DG.
Tel: (01) 580 4571

AZ Productions Ltd.
Lorrimer House, 47 Dean St., London W1.
Tel: (01) 734 4568

Boyd's Co. Film Productions Ltd.
8 Berwick St., London W1V 3RG.
Tel: (01) 734 1888/6571

Brent Walker Film Productions Ltd.
9 Chesterfield St., London W1.
Tel: (01) 491 4430

British Film Institute Production Board
27 Whitfield St., London W1.
Tel: (01) 580 2773

Burrill Productions Ltd.
51 Lansdowne Rd., London W11 2LG.
Tel: (01) 727 1442

Charter Film Productions Ltd.
8a Glebe Place, London SW3.
Tel: (01) 352 6838

Children's Film Foundation
EMI Elstree Studios Ltd., Boreham Wood, Herts.
Tel: (01) 953 1600

Columbia (British) Productions
St. Margaret's House, 19/23 Wells St., London W1.
Tel: (01) 580 2090

Walt Disney Productions Ltd.
68 Pall Mall, London SW1Y 5EX.
Tel: (01) 839 8010

EMI Films Ltd.
142 Wardour St., London W1A 3BY.
Tel: (01) 437 0444

English Film Co. Ltd.
Suite 4, 60/62 Old Compton St., London W1.
Tel: (01) 734 6197

Enigma Productions Ltd.
15 Queensgate Place Mews, London SW7.
Tel: (01) 581 0238

Eon Productions Ltd.
2 South Audley St., London W1Y 5DQ.
Tel: (01) 493 7953

Euston Films Ltd.
365 Euston Rd., London NW1.
Tel: (01) 387 0911

Falcon International Productions
Twickenham Film Studios, St. Margaret's, Twickenham, Middx.
Tel: (01) 892 4477

'Countryman' from Island Pictures

S. Benjamin Fisz Productions Ltd.
51 South Audley St., London W1.
Tel: (01) 493 7428

Mark Forstater Productions Ltd.
19 Courthope Rd., London NW3.
Tel: (01) 267 6178

Goldcrest Films and Television Ltd.
131 Holland Park Avenue, London W11.
Tel: (01) 602 6626

Grand Slamm Animation
100 St. Martins Lane, London WC2N 4AZ.
Tel: (01) 240 2017

Halas & Batchelor Animation Ltd.
3-7 Kean St., London WC2.
Tel: (01) 240 3888

Hammer Film Productions
EMI Elstree Studios, Boreham Wood, Herts WD6 1JG.
Tel: (01) 953 1600

Handmade Films Ltd.
26 Cadogan Square,
London SW1
Tel: (01) 584 8345

Hawk Films Ltd.
c/o Bromhead Foster,
9 Clifford St.,
London W1.

Island Pictures
8-10 Basing St., London W11.
Tel: (01) 727 7500/7600

ITC Entertainment Ltd.
ACC House, 17 Great Cumberland
Place, London W1A 1AG.
Tel: (01) 262 8040

Ladd Company (GB) Ltd.
44 Earlham St., London WC2.
Tel: (01) 836 7673

**Limelight Film & Video
Production Ltd.**
16 Ingestre Place,
London W1R 3LP.
Tel: (01) 734 2228

London Film Productions Ltd.
37 Bedford St.,
London WC2E 9EN.
Tel: (01) 379 3366

Lorimar Services Ltd.
16 Berkeley St., London W1.
Tel: (01) 493 1564

Lucasfilm (UK) Ltd.
5/6 Yarmouth Place, London W1.
Tel: (01) 409 2200

Memorial Films Ltd.
Lee International Studios,
128 Wembley Park Drive,
Wembley, Middx.
Tel: (01) 902 1262

Metro-Goldwyn-Mayer
11 Hamilton Place, London W1.
Tel: (01) 493 5994

Metropolis Pictures Ltd.
8-10 Neals Yard, London WC2.
Tel: (01) 836 1056

Midnight Films Ltd.
1/2 Slingsby Place,
London WC2E 9AB.
Tel: (01) 240 5667

Milesian Film Productions Ltd.
49 Berkeley Square,
London W1X 5DB.
Tel: (01) 491 2625

**Norfolk International
Pictures Ltd.**
107/115 Long Acre,
London WC2E 9NT.
Tel: (01) 240 0863

Open Road Films Ltd.
25 Jermyn St., London SW1.
Tel: (01) 437 4534

Orion Pictures Company
135 Wardour St.,
London W1V 4AP.
Tel: (01) 434 3830/3893

Pacesetter Productions Ltd.
82 Wardour St.,
London W1V 3LF.
Tel: (01) 437 3907

David Paradine Productions Ltd.
Suite 1, Audley House,
9 Audley St., London W1Y 1WF.
Tel: (01) 629 3793

Paramount Pictures (UK) Ltd.
162/170 Wardour St.,
London W1V 4AB.
Tel: (01) 437 7700

Picture Palace Productions Ltd.
71 Beak St., London W1.
Tel: (01) 439 9882

Polygram Leisure Ltd.
15 Saint George St.,
London W1R 9DE.
Tel: (01) 499 0422

Polytel Films Ltd.
1 Rockley Rd.,
London W14 0DE.
Tel: (01) 743 3474

Poseidon Films Ltd.
52 Shaftesbury Ave.,
London W1.
Tel: (01) 734 4441

Romulus Films Ltd.
113 Park Lane,
London W1Y 3LE.
Tel: (01) 493 7741

Sydney Rose Productions Ltd.
9 Clifford St., London W1.
Tel: (01) 439 7321

Rosemont Productions
Pinewood Studios, Iver Heath,
Bucks.
Tel: Iver (0753) 651700

Salon Productions Ltd.
13/14 Archer St., London W1.
Tel: (01) 437 0516/734 9472

Sawbuck Productions Ltd.
28a Dawson Place,
London W2.
Tel: (01) 221 5159

Scimitar Films Ltd.
6-8 Sackville St.,
London W1X 1DD.
Tel: (01) 734 8385

Screenpro Films Ltd.
5 Meard St., London W1.
Tel: (01) 439 7691

Silverwold Film Productions
Pinewood Studios,
Iver Heath, Bucks.
Tel: Iver (0753) 651700

**Southbrook International
Films Ltd.**
55 South Audley St.,
London W1Y 5DR.
Tel: (01) 491 7024

Southern Pictures
58 Frith St., London W1V 5TA.
Tel: (01) 439 2367

Robert Stigwood Group
67 Brook St.,
London W1Y 1YE.
Tel: (01) 629 9121

**Sunn Classic Productions
(GB) Ltd.**
37-39 Great Marlborough St.,
London W1.
Tel: (01) 437 9556

Sword and Sorcery Productions
20 Stradella Rd.,
London SE24 9HA.
Tel: (01) 274 3205

Trident Films Ltd.
Trident House, Brook Mews,
London W1Y 2PN.
Tel: (01) 493 1237

**Twentieth Century-Fox
Film Co. Ltd.**
31 Soho Sq., London W1V 6AP.
Tel: (01) 437 7766

Universal Pictures Ltd.
170 Piccadilly, London W1V 9FH.
Tel: (01) 629 7211

Virgin Films
95-99 Ladbroke Grove,
London W11.
Tel: (01) 229 1282

Warner Brothers Productions Ltd.
Warner House, Pinewood Studios,
Iver Heath, Bucks.
Tel: Iver (0753) 654545

Michael White
13 Duke St., St. James's,
London SW1 6DB.
Tel: (01) 839 3971

The Who Films
112 Wardour St., London W1.

Richard Williams Animation Ltd.
13 Soho Sq., London W1V 5FB.
Tel: (01) 437 4455

Winkast Programming Ltd.
Pinewood Studios, Iver Heath,
Bucks.
Tel: Iver (0573) 651700

'Time Bandits' from Handmade

FILM STUDIOS US

ABC Television Center
4151 Prospect Ave., Los Angeles,
CA 90027.
Tel: (213) 663 3311

Beckett Stages
1224 North Vine St., Los Angeles,
CA 90038.
Tel: (213) 465 7141

The Burbank Studios
4000 Warner Blvd., Burbank,
CA 91522.
Tel: (213) 954 6000

CBS Studios
6309 Eleanor Ave., Los Angeles,
CA 90038.
Tel: (213) 464 9118

Cine-Video
948 N. Cahuenga Blvd.,
Hollywood, CA 90038.
Tel: (213) 464 6200

Columbia Pictures
Colgems Sq., Burbank, CA 91505.
Tel: (213) 954 6000

Walt Disney Productions
500 South Buena Vista St.,
Burbank, CA 91503.
Tel: (213) 845 3141

Jerry Fairbanks Productions
826 North Cole, Los Angeles,
CA 90038.
Tel: (213) 462 1101

Falcon Studios
5526 Hollywood Blvd.,
Los Angeles, CA 90028.
Tel: (213) 462 9356

An aerial view of 20th Century Fox Studios

Samuel Goldwyn Studios
1041 North Formosa Ave.,
Los Angeles, CA 90046.
Tel: (213) 650 2500

Hollywood General Studios, Inc.
1040 North Las Palmas Ave.,
Hollywood, CA 90038.
Tel: (213) 469 9011

International Studios
846 Cahuenga Blvd.,
Los Angeles, CA 90038.
Tel: (213) 466 3534

**Major Independent Film
Studios, Inc.**
1207 North Western Ave.,
Los Angeles, CA 90029.
Tel: (213) 461 2721

Metro-Goldwyn-Mayer, Inc.
10202 West Washington Blvd.,
Culver City, CA 90230.
Tel: (213) 836 3000

NBC Television
3000 West Alameda Ave.,
Burbank, CA 91503.
Tel: (213) 845 7000

Paramount Studios
5451 Marathon St.,
Los Angeles, CA 90038.
Tel: (213) 468 5000

Producers Studio, Inc.
650 North Bronson Ave.,
Los Angeles, CA 90004.
Tel: (213) 466 3111

Rampart Studios
2625 Temple St., Los Angeles,
CA 90026.
Tel: (213) 385 3911

**Twentieth Century-Fox Film
Corporation**
10201 West Pico Blvd.,
Los Angeles, CA 90035.
Tel: (213) 277 2211

U.P.A. Pictures, Inc.
4440 Lakeside Drive,
Burbank, CA 90621.
Tel: (213) 842 7171

Universal City Studios
Universal City Plaza,
Universal City, CA 91608.
Tel: (213) 985 4321

Warner Brothers, Inc.
4000 Warner Blvd.,
Burbank, CA 91522.
Tel: (213) 843 6000

Zoetrope Studios
529 Pacific Avenue,
San Francisco, CA 94133.
Tel: (415) 788 7500

FILM STUDIOS UK

Bray Studios
Down Place, Windsor Rd.,
Water Oakley, Windsor, Berks.
Tel: (0628) 22111

Bushey Film Studios
Melbourne Rd., Bushey, Herts.
Tel: (01) 950 1621

Edinburgh Film & TV Studios
Nine Mile Burn, Penicuik,
Midlothian, EH26 9LT.
Tel: Penicuik (0968) 72131

EMI Elstree Studios
Boreham Wood, Herts.
Tel: (01) 953 1600

Isleworth Studios
Studio Parade, 484 London Rd.,
Isleworth, Middx.
Tel: (01) 568 3511

Lee International Film Studios
Wembley Park Drive,
Wembley, Middx.
Tel: (01) 902 1262

National Film Studios of Ireland
Ardmore, Bray, Co. Wicklow.
Tel: Bray 862971

Pinewood Studios
Iver Heath, Bucks.
Tel: Iver (0753) 651700

The Production Village
100 Cricklewood Lane,
London NW2.
Tel: (01) 450 8969

St. John's Wood Studios Ltd.
87a St. John's Wood Terrace,
London NW8 6PY.
Tel: (01) 722 9255

Shepperton Studio Centre
Studios Rd., Shepperton,
Middx TW17 OQD.
Tel: Chertsey (09328) 62611

Twickenham Film Studios
The Barons, St. Margarets,
Twickenham, Middx.
Tel: (01) 892 4477

Shepperton Studios from the air

FILM DISTRIBUTORS UK

Alpha Films Ltd.
13/14 Archer St., London W1.
Tel: (01) 437 0516/439 4451

Amanda Films Ltd.
303 Finchley Rd.,
London NW3 6DT.
Tel: (01) 435 6001

Artificial Eye Film Co. Ltd.
211 Camden High St.,
London NW1 7BT.
Tel: (01) 267 6036

'Celeste' from Artificial Eye

Barber International Films Ltd.
113-117 Wardour St.,
London W1V 3TD.
Tel: (01) 437 0068

**Blue Dolphin Film
Distributors Ltd.**
84 Wardour St.,
London W1V 3LF.
Tel: (01) 437 1435/1517

**Bordeaux Films
International Ltd.**
92 Wardour St., London W1.
Tel: (01) 434 4359

**Brent Walker Film
Distributors Ltd.**
147-149 Wardour St., London W1.
Tel: (01) 434 1961

**British Film Institute Film and
Video Library**
81 Dean St., London W1V 6AA.
Tel: (01) 734 6451

Cannon Distributors (UK) Ltd.
111 Wardour St., London W1.
Tel: (01) 439 0111

Cinegate Ltd.
Gate Cinema, 87 Notting Hill
Gate, London W11.
Tel: (01) 727 2651

**Columbia-EMI-Warner
Distributors Ltd.**
135 Wardour St.,
London W1V 4AP.
Tel: (01) 734 6352

Connoisseur Films Ltd.
167 Oxford St.,
London W1R 2DX.
Tel: (01) 734 6555

Contemporary Films Ltd.
55 Greek St., London W1V 6DB.
Tel: (01) 734 4801

Curzon Film Distributors Ltd.
38 Curzon St., London W1Y 8EY.
Tel: (01) 629 8961

Walt Disney Productions Ltd.
68 Pall Mall, London SW1.
Tel: (01) 839 8010

Eagle Films Ltd.
Gala House, 15-17 Old Compton
St., London W1V 6JR.
Tel: (01) 437 9541

Enterprise Pictures Ltd.
27 Soho Sq., London W1Y 6BH.
Tel: (01) 734 3372

**Entertainment Film
Distributors Ltd.**
60-66 Wardour St., London W1.
Tel: (01) 734 4678/9

Essential Cinema Ltd.
122 Wardour St., London W1.
Tel: (01) 437 8127

Facelift Film Distributors
Suite 4, 60-62 Old Compton St.,
London W1.
Tel: (01) 439 2047

Gala Film Distributors Ltd.
Gala House, 15/17 Old Compton
St., London W1V 6JR.
Tel: (01) 734 3701

Golden Era Film Distributors
138 Wardour St.,
London W1V 4JP.
Tel: (01) 437 1407/6628

**Grand National Film
Distributors Ltd.**
13-14 Dean St.,
London W1V 6AH.
Tel: (01) 437 5792/6

**GTO Films and Video
International**
115-123 Bayham St., Camden
Town, London NW1 0AL.
Tel: (01) 485 5622

**Handmade Films
(Distributors) Ltd.**
26 Cadogan Square,
London SW1X OJP.
Tel: (01) 581 1265

Hemdale Leisure
37 Duke St., London W1.
Tel: (01) 486 8591

ITC Film Distributors Ltd.
14-15 Carlisle St.,
London W1V 5RE.
Tel: (01) 439 6611/4

Jay Jay Film Distributors Ltd.
32a Clarendon Way, Marlings
Park, Chislehurst, Kent BR7 6RF.
Tel: Orpington 21143/20870/39925

**Lagoon Associates
Productions Ltd.**
6 Penzance Place,
London W11 4AP.
Tel: (01) 221 6149

London Film Ltd.
37 Bedford St.,
London WC2E 9EN.
Tel: (01) 379 3366

Mainline Pictures
1 Prince of Wales Passage,
117 Hampstead Rd.,
London NW1.
Tel: (01) 388 4527/4761/3993

'The Proud Ones' from Gala

Miracle International Films Ltd.
92/94 Wardour St.,
London W1V 4JH.
Tel: (01) 437 0507

New Realm Distributors
22-25 Dean St., London W1.
Tel: (01) 437 9243

Oppidan Entertainments Ltd.
28 Berkeley St.,
London W1X 5HA.
Tel: (01) 437 6537/499 5945

Rank Film Distributors Ltd.
127 Wardour St., London W1.
Tel: (01) 437 9020

**Sunn Classic Productions
(GB) Ltd.**
37-39 Great Marlborough St.,
London W1.
Tel: (01) 437 9556

'The Conductor' from Cinegate

Supreme Film Distributors Ltd.
Suite 6, 60-62 Old Compton St.,
London W1.
Tel: (01) 437 4415

Target International Pictures Ltd.
60-66 Wardour St., London W1.
Tel: (01) 439 4451

Tigon Film Distributors Ltd.
14-15 Carlisle St.,
London W1V 5RE.
Tel: (01) 439 6611

**Twentieth Century-Fox
Film Co. Ltd.,**
31 Soho Sq., London W1V 6AP.
Tel: (01) 437 7766

United International Pictures Ltd.
Mortimer House, 37-41 Mortimer
St., London W1A 2JL.
Tel: (01) 636 1655

Watchgrove Distributors Ltd.
47 Greek St., London W1.
Tel: (01) 437 3945.

FILM MAGAZINES

American Cinematographer
(monthly) ASC Holding Corp.,
P.O. Box 2230, Hollywood,
California 90028, USA.

American Film
(10 p.a.) American Film Institute,
John F. Kennedy Center for the
Performing Arts,
Washington DC 20566, USA.

L'Avant-Scene (Cinema)
(monthly) 27 rue Saint-André des
Arts, 75006 Paris, France.

Bianco E Nero
(quarterly) via Tuscolana 1524,
00173 Rome, Italy.

Cahiers Du Cinema
(monthly) 9 Passage de la Boule-
Blanche, 75012 Paris, France.

Chaplin
(bi-monthly) Filmhuset,
Box 27 126, 102 52 Stockholm,
Sweden.

Cineaste
(quarterly) 419 Park Avenue
South, New York, NY 10016, USA

Cinefantastique
(quarterly) P.O. Box 270,
Oak Park, Illinois 60303, USA.

Cinema 81...82
(monthly) 6 rue Ordener,
75018 Paris, France.

Cinema Canada
(bi-monthly) Box 398, Outremont
Station, Montreal H2V 4N3,
Canada.

Cinema Papers
(quarterly) Main Office,
644 Victoria Street,
North Melbourne 3051, Australia.

Cinema Sessanta
(bi-monthly) Piazza dei Caprettari
70, 00186 Rome, Italy.

Cine-revue
(weekly) Rue de Danemark 5,
1060 Brussels, Belgium.

Dirigido Por
(monthly) Tenor Vinas, 8, 1°.1ª,
Barcelona 21, Spain.

Film
(monthly) British Federation of
Film Societies, 81 Dean Street,
London W1V 6AA.

Film Bulletin
(bi-monthly) Wax Publications
Inc., Publications/Editorial
Offices, 1239 Vine Street,
Philadelphia 19107, USA.

Film Comment
(bi-monthly) 140 West 65th Street,
New York, NY 10023, USA.

Film Dope
(irregular) 40 Willifield Way,
London NW11 7XT.

Film Quarterly
(quarterly) University of
California, Berkeley,
California 94720, USA.

Film Reader
(irregular) Film Division,
Northwestern University,
Evanston, Illinois 60201, USA.

Film Review
(monthly) Old Court Place,
42-70 Kensington High Street,
London W8 4PL.

Films and Filming
(monthly) Brevet Publishing Ltd.,
445 Brighton Road,
South Croydon, Surrey CR2 6EU.

Films on Screen and Video
(monthly) Thelmill Ltd.,
34 Buckingham Palace Road,
London SW1.

Films In Review
(10 p.a.) P.O. Box 589, Lennox Hill
Sta, New York, NY 10021, USA.

Image et Son/Ecran
(monthly) 3 rue Récamier,
75341 Paris 07, France.

Interview
(monthly) 860 Broadway,
New York, NY 10003, USA.

Jump Cut
(quarterly) P.O. Box 865,
Berkeley, California 94701, USA.

M/F Journal
(irregular), 22 Chepstow Crescent,
London W11 3EB.

Monthly Film Bulletin
(monthly) British Film Institute,
81 Dean Street, London W1V 6AA.

Movie
(irregular) 25 Lloyd Baker Street,
London WC1X 9AT.

Photoplay
(monthly) Subscription
Department, MAP Ltd.,
13-35 Bridge Street,
Hemel Hempstead, Herts.

Positif
(monthly) Nouvelles Editions
Opta, 30 boulevard de Sebastopol,
75004 Paris, France.

Screen
(quarterly) S.E.F.T.,
29 Old Compton Street,
London W1V 5PL.

Screen International
(weekly) 6-7 Great Chapel Street,
London W1.

Sight and Sound
(quarterly) British Film Institute,
81 Dean Street,
London W1V 6AA.

Variety (weekly)
49 St James Street, London SW1.

Velvet Light Trap
(irregular) P.O. Box 3355,
Madison, Wisconsin 53704, USA.

FILM ARCHIVES

AUSTRALIA

Australian Film Institute
PO Box 165, Carlton South,
Victoria.
Tel: (613) 347 6888

National Film Archive
National Library of Australia,
Parkes Place, Canberra 2600.
Tel: (61 62) 621111

AUSTRIA

Österreichisches Filmarchiv
Rauhensteingasse 5,
A-1010 Vienna 1.
Tel: (43 222) 529936

Österreichisches Filmmuseum
Augustinerstrasse 1,
1010 Vienna 1.
Tel: (43 222) 523426/526206

BELGIUM

Cinémathèque Royale de Belgique
Ravenstein 23, 1000 Brussels.
Tel: (32 2) 513 41 55

CANADA

Cinémathèque Québécoise
335 boul. de Maisonneuve est,
Montreal, H2X 1K1.
Tel: (1 514) 845 8118

**National Film, Television
and Sound Archives**
395 Wellington St., Ottawa,
Ontario, K1A ON3.
Tel: (1 613) 995 1311

Ontario Film Institute
770 Don Mill Rd., Don Mills,
Ontario, M3C IT3.
Tel: (1 416) 429 4100

CZECHOSLOVAKIA

Czechoslovak Film Institute
(Ceskoslovensky filmovy ustav)
Narodni trida 40,
110 00 Prague 1.
Tel: (42 2) 260087

DENMARK

Det danske filmmuseum
St. Søndervoldstraede,
1419 København K.
Tel: (45 1) 576500

FRANCE

**Centre National de la
Cinématographie Service des
Archive du Film**
Rue Alexandre Turpault,
78390 Bois D'Arcy, Paris.
Tel: (33 1) 460 2050/2879

Cinémathèque de Toulouse
3 rue Roquelaine, 3100 Toulouse.
Tel: (33 61) 489075

Cinémathèque Francaise
Palais de Chaillot,
pl. du Trocadero, Paris 75116.
Tel: (33 1) 5532186

GERMAN DEMOCRATIC REPUBLIC

Staatliches Filmarchiv der D.D.R.
Hausvogteiplatz 3-4, 108 Berlin.
Tel: (37 2) 2124324

GERMAN FEDERAL REPUBLIC

Bundesarchiv-Filmarchiv
Am Wöllershof 12,
D 5400 Koblenz.
Tel: (49 261) 3991

Deutsches Filmmuseum
P.B. 3882, 6000 Frankfurt am Main.
Tel: (49 611) 2123369/2124274

Deutsches Institut für Filmkunde
Schloss, 6200 Wiesbaden-Biebrich.

Stiftung Deutsche Kinemathek
1000 Berlin 19, Pommernalle 1.
Tel: (49 30) 3036234

GREAT BRITAIN

Barnes Museum of Cinematography
Fore St., St. Ives, Cornwall.

British Film Institute: Library Services
127 Charing Cross Rd.,
London WC2H 0EA.
Tel: (01) 437 4355

British Film Institute: National Film Archive
81 Dean St., London W1V 6AA.
Tel: (01) 437 4355

Imperial War Museum
Lambeth Rd., London SE1 6HZ.
Tel: (01) 735 8922

The John Grierson Archive
University of Stirling,
Stirling FK9 4LA, Scotland.
Tel: (0786) 3171

Scottish Film Archive
74 Victoria Crescent Rd.,
Glasgow G12 9JN.
Tel: (041) 334 9314

GREECE

Tainiothiki tis Ellados
1 Kanari St., Athens 138.

HUNGARY

Hungarian Institute of Film Science and Archives
Nepstadion ut. 97, 1143 Budapest.
Tel: (36 1) 429599

"Secrets of the Film Archives"

INDIA

National Film Archive of India
Ministry of Information and
Broadcasting, Law College Rd.,
Poona 411 004.
Tel: 58516

IRELAND

Liam O'Leary Film Archives
Garden Flat, 74 Ranelagh Rd.,
Dublin 6.

ISRAEL

Archion Israeli Leseratim
43 Jabotinsky St., Jerusalem.
Tel: (972 2) 60872/67131

ITALY

Cineteca Italiana
Via Palestro 16, 20121 Milan.
Tel: (39 2) 799224

Cineteca Nazionale
Via Tuscolana 1524, 00173 Rome.
Tel: (39 6) 7490046

Museo Nazionale del Cinema
Piazza San Giovanni 2,
10122 Turin.
Tel: (39 11) 510370

JAPAN

Japan Film Library Council
Ginza-Hata Building 4-5, 4-chome,
Ginza, Chuo-ku, Tokyo.
Tel: (81 3) 561 6719

NETHERLANDS

Stichting Nederlands Filmmuseum
Vondelpark 3, 1071 AA,
Amsterdam.
Tel: (31 20) 831646

NEW ZEALAND

National Film Library
Cubewell House, Kent Terrace,
Box 9583, Wellington.

New Zealand Film Archive
P.O. Box 9544, 15 Courtenay
Place, Wellington.
Tel: (64 4) 850 162

NORWAY

Norsk Filminstitutt
Postboks 5, Røa, Oslo 7.
Tel: (47 2) 242994

POLAND

Filmoteka Polska
ul. Pulawska 61, 00-975 Warsaw.
Tel: 455074/455404

PORTUGAL

Cinemateca Portuguesa
Rua de S. Pedro de Alcântara 45,
1200 Portugal, Lisbon.
Tel: (351 19) 367481

SPAIN

Filmoteca Nacional de Espana
Carretera Dehesa de la Villa s/n,
Madrid 35.
Tel: (34 1) 2434795

SWEDEN

Cinemateket
Box 27126, S-102 52
Stockholm 27.
Tel: (46 8) 630510

SWITZERLAND

Cinémathèque Suisse
Casino de Montbenon, Esplanade
de Montbenon, 1000 Lausanne.
Tel: (41 21) 237406

USA

Academy of Motion Picture Arts and Sciences
Margaret Herrick Library,
8949 Wilshire Blvd., Beverly Hills,
CA 90211.
Tel: (213) 278 8990

American Film Institute
John F. Kennedy Center for the
Performing Arts,
Washington DC 20566.
Tel: (202) 828 4000

**American Film Institute:
Louis B. Mayer Library**
2021 North Western Ave.,
Los Angeles, CA 90027.
Tel: (213) 2788777

George Eastman House
Department of Film,
900 East Ave., Rochester,
NY 14607.
Tel: (716) 271 3361, ex 213

Library of Congress
Motion Picture, Broadcasting
and Recorded Sound Division,
Washington DC 20540.
Tel: (202) 287 5840

*Henri Langlois, founder and head
of Cinémathèque Francaise*

Museum of Modern Art
Department of Film,
11 West 53 St., New York,
NY 10019.
Tel: (212) 956 4212 (Study
Center)/956 4209 (Stills)

Pacific Film Archive
University Art Museum,
2621 Durant Ave., Berkeley,
CA 94720.
Tel: (415) 642 1413

USSR

Gosfilmogond
Belye Stolby, Moskovskaja
oblast.
Tel: (7 095) 1360516

FILM FESTIVALS

BERLIN

International Film Festival
Budapester Strasse 50,
D-1000 Berlin 30, W. Germany.
Tel: (49 30) 263461.
Held: February

BRUSSELS

International Film Festival
32 Avenue de l'Astronomie,
1030 Brussels, Belgium.
Tel: (32 2) 218 1267.
Held: January-February

CAMBRIDGE

Cambridge Film Festival
10 City Road, Cambridge.
Tel: (0223) 311639.
Held: July

CANNES

Cannes International Film Festival
71 rue du Faubourg St Honoré,
75008 Paris, France.
Tel: (331) 266 9220.
Held: May

CHICAGO

Chicago International Film Festival
415 North Dearborn St., Chicago,
Illinois 60610, USA.
Tel: (312) 644 3400.
Held: November

CORK

International Film Festival
38 MacCurtain St., Cork, Ireland.
Tel: (0002) 502221.
Held: October

EDINBURGH

International Film Festival
Film House, 88 Lothian Rd.,
Edinburgh EH3 9BZ, Scotland.
Tel: (031) 228 6382.
Held: August

FLORENCE

Festival dei Popoli
via del Proconsolo 10,
50122 Firenze, Italy.
Tel: (39 55) 294353.
Held: December

Berlin Film Festival poster

HONG KONG

Hong Kong International Film Festival
City Hall, Edinburgh Place,
Hong Kong.
Tel: 5-261528/5-264482.
Held: April

KARLOVY VARY

International Film Festival
c/o Ceskovensky Filmexport,
28 Vaclavske nam, Prague 1,
Czechoslovakia.
Tel: (422) 263766.
Held: July

LOCARNO

Locarno Film Festival
PO Box 186, CH-6600 Locarno,
Switzerland.
Tel: (41 93) 31 11 88.
Held: August

LONDON

London Film Festival
National Film Theatre,
South Bank, London SE1 8XT.
Tel: (01) 928 3842.
Held: November

LOS ANGELES

Los Angeles International Film Exposition (Filmex)
6230 Sunset Blvd., Hollywood,
CA 90028, USA.
Tel: (213) 469 9400.
Held: March

MANILA

Manila International Film Festival
Cultural Centre of the Philippines,
Roxas Blvd., Manila,
The Philippines.
Tel: (632) 57 39 61.
Held: January

MELBOURNE

Melbourne Film Festival
PO Box 357, Carlton South,
Victoria 3053, Australia.
Tel: (613) 347 4828.
Held: June.

MILAN

M.I.F.E.D. — International Film, TV Film & Documentary Market
Largo Domodossola 1,
20145 Milan, Italy.
Telex: 331360 EAFM.
Held: April/October

MONTREAL

World Film Festival
1455 Ouest Blvd. de Maisonneuve,
Montreal, Quebec H3G IM8,
Canada.
Tel: (514) 879 4057.
Held: August-September

NEW DELHI

International Film Festival
Directorate of Film Festivals,
Lok Nayak Bhavan, 4th Floor,
Khan Market, New Delhi 110 003,
India.
Tel: (91 22) 615953/622033.
Held: January

NEW YORK

New York Film Festival
The Film Society of the Lincoln
Centre, 140 West 65th St.,
New York, NY 10023, USA.
Tel: (212) 765 5100.
Held: September-October

OBERHAUSEN

Westdeutsche Kurzfilm Tage
Grillostrasse 34, 4200 Oberhausen
1, German Federal Republic.
Tel: (49 208) 825 2652.
Held: April

ROTTERDAM

Film International
Westersingel 20,
3014 GP Rotterdam, Holland.
Tel: (31 10) 363111.
Held: January

SAN SEBASTIAN

San Sebastian International Film Festival
Apartado Correos 397, Reina
Regente s/n, San Sebastian, Spain.
Tel: (34 43) 424106/424108.
Held: September

SYDNEY

Sydney Film Festival
Box 4934 GPO, Sydney 2001,
Australia.
Tel: (612) 660 3909.
Held: June

THESSALONIKI

Thessaloniki International Film Festival
Thessaloniki 36, Greece.
Tel: (30 31) 220 440.
Held: September

TORONTO

Toronto International Film Festival
Suite 206, 69 Yorkville Ave.,
Toronto, Ontario M5R 1B7,
Canada.
Tel: (416) 967 7371.
Held: September

VENICE

La Biennale de Venezia
Ca' Giustinian, San Marco,
301 Venice, Italy.
Tel: (39 41) 700311.
Held: September

Edinburgh Film Festival poster

VIENNA

Viennale
Künstlerhaus, Karlsplatz 5,
1010 Vienna, Austria.
Tel: (43 222) 659833.
Held: November

ZAGREB

World Festival of Animated Films
c/o Zagreb Film, Nova Ves 18,
41000 Zagreb, Yugoslavia.
Tel: (38 41) 276 580.
Held: June

GOVERNMENT DEPARTMENTS AND ORGANISATIONS CONNECTED WITH FILM

AUSTRALIA

Australian Film Commission
8 West St., North Sydney,
N.S.W. 2060.
Tel: (61 2) 922 6855
(Each of the states has its own
Film Corporation)

AUSTRIA

Bundesministerium für Handel
Gewerbe und Industrie, Sektion 1,
Abt. Filmwirtschaft,
Stubenring 1, 1010 Vienna.
Tel: (43 222) 7500

**Bundesminsterium für Unterricht
und Kunst**
Sektion IV, Film und
Lichtbildwesen, Strozzigasse 2,
1080 Vienna.
Tel: (43 222) 425618

BELGIUM

**Ministry of Education and Culture
(Cinema Dept.)**
7 quai du Commerce,
1000 Brussels.
Tel: (32 2) 217 4190

CANADA

**Canadian Film
Development Corp.**
Suite 2220, Tour de la Bourse, C.P.
71, Montreal, Quebec H4Z 1A8.
Tel: (514) 283 6363
Suite 602, 111 Avenue Rd.,
Toronto, Ontario M5R 3J8.
Tel: (416) 966 6436

CZECHOSLOVAKIA

**Central Management of the
Czechoslovak Film**
Jindrisska 34, 112 06 Prague 1.
Tel: (422) 223751

DENMARK

Danish Government Film Office
Vestergade-27,
1456 Copenhagen K.
Tel: (45) 123686

FRANCE

**Centre National de la
Cinématographie**
12 rue de Lubeck, 75016 Paris.
Tel: (33 1) 553 9340

GERMAN DEMOCRATIC
REPUBLIC

DEFA
c/o DEFA Aussenhandel,
Milastra. 2, Berlin 1058

GERMAN FEDERAL
REPUBLIC

Bundesminsterium für Wirtschaft
Villemombler Str. 76,
Bonn-Duisdorf.
Tel: (49 2221) 761

**Filmförderungsanstalt des
Öffentlichenrechts (FFA)**
Budapester Str. 41, PO Box
301/87, 1000 Berlin 31.
Tel: (49 30) 261 6006

GREAT BRITAIN

British Film Fund Agency
7 Portland Place,
London W1N 4HS.
Tel: (01) 323 2741

**Department of Education
and Science**
Office of Arts and Libraries,
Elizabeth House, York Rd.,
London SE1 7PH.
Tel: (01) 928 9222

Department of Trade
Films Branch, 16-20 Great Smith
St., London SW1P 3DB.
Tel: (01) 215 7877

**National Film Finance
Corporation (incorporating the
National Film Development Fund)**
22 Southampton Place,
London WC1 2BP.
Tel: (01) 831 7561

HUNGARY

**Central Board of Hungarian
Cinematography**
Szalai u. 10, 1054 Budapest.
Tel: (36 1) 126417

Mafilm
Lumumba u. 174, 1145 Budapest.
Tel: (36 1) 631473

INDIA

Film Finance Corporation Ltd.
1st Floor, 13-16 Regent Chambers,
Nariman Point, Bombay 40021.
Tel: (91 22) 231861

**National Film Development
Corporation**
Shiv Sagar Estate, "D" Block,
5th Floor, Dr. Annie Besant Rd.,
Worli, Bombay 400018.
Tel: (91 22) 372393

IRELAND

**Department of Industry
Commerce & Tourism**
Kildare St., Dublin 2.
Tel: (0001) 789411

ITALY

**Ministry of Tourism
and Entertainment**
Via della Ferratella 51, Rome.
Tel: (39 6) 7732

JAPAN

Agency for Cultural Affairs
2-2 Kasumigaeseki, Chiyoda-ku,
Tokyo 100.
Tel: (81 3) 581 4211

NETHERLANDS

**Ministry of Cultural Affairs,
Recreation & Social Welfare**
Steenvoordelaan 370,
Rijswijk (Z.H.)
Tel: (31 3452) 949233

**Netherlands Information Service,
Communication Techniques Dept.**
Anna Paulownastraat 76,
2518 BJ The Hague.
Tel: (31 70) 614181

NEW ZEALAND

Film Industry Board
Department of Internal Affairs,
Private Bag, Wellington.
Tel: (64 4) 738699

New Zealand Film Commission
PO Box 11-546, Wellington.
Tel: (64 4) 722360

POLAND

Ministry of Culture and Art
Central Board of Cinematography,
Warsaw.
Tel: 26789

SPAIN

**Direccion General del Libro y de la
Cinematografia**
Ministerio de Cultura, Paseo de la
Castellana 109, Madrid 16.
Tel: (34 1) 455 5000

SWEDEN

Svenska Filminstitutet
Filmhuset, Borgvagen, Box
27126, S-102 52 Stockholm 27.
Tel: (46 8) 630510

SWITZERLAND

Federal Office of Cultural Affairs
Film Section, Postfach 3000
Bern 6.
Tel: (41 31) 619271

USA

**International Communications
Agency**
1776 Pennsylvania Avenue NW,
Washington, DC 20546.
Tel: (202) 376 7806

US Department of Commerce
Bureau of Domestic Commerce,
Consumer Goods & Services
Division, Washington, DC 20230.
Tel: (202) 967 3793

USSR

**State Committee of
Cinematography of the USSR
Council of Ministers**
7 Maly Gnesdnikovsky Pereulok,
Moscow.
Tel: (7 095) 229 9912

*'An Unsuitable Job for a Woman':
part-financed by the National Film Finance Corporation*